THIRD EDITION

An Introduction to
Theories
of Personality

B. R. HERGENHAHN

Hamline University

PRENTICE HALL, Englewood Cliffs, New Jersey 07632

Library of Congress Cataloging-in-Publication Data
HERGENHAHN, B. R. (DATE)
    An introduction to theories of personality / B.R. Hergenhahn.—3rd ed.
    p.   cm.
    Includes bibliographical references.
    1. Personality.   I. Title.
BF698.H45   1990
155.2—dc20   89-39436
                                                           CIP

Dedicated to those who spent their lives
studying personality so that we might better
understand ourselves and others.

Editorial/production supervision: Mary Anne Shahidi
Cover and interior design: Lee Cohen
Manufacturing buyer: Ray Keating/Bob Anderson
Photo editor: Page Poore

© 1990, 1984, 1980 by Prentice-Hall, Inc.
A Division of Simon & Schuster
Englewood Cliffs, New Jersey 07632

Printed in the United States of America
10 9 8 7 6 5 4 3 2 1

ISBN 0-13-474362-8

Prentice-Hall International (UK) Limited, *London*
Prentice-Hall of Australia Pty. Limited, *Sydney*
Prentice-Hall Canada Inc., *Toronto*
Prentice-Hall Hispanoamericana, S.A., *Mexico*
Prentice-Hall of India Private Limited, *New Delhi*
Prentice-Hall of Japan, Inc., *Tokyo*
Simon & Schuster Asia Pte. Ltd., *Singapore*
Editora Prentice-Hall do Brasil, Ltda., *Rio de Janeiro*

Contents

3 ■ Carl Jung   57

4 ■ Alfred Adler   89

5 ◼ Karen Horney   118

6 ■ Erik H. Erikson   143

7 ■ Gordon Allport   174

8

Raymond B. Cattell   205

9

Burrhus F. Skinner   232

10 ■ John Dollard/Neal Miller   270

11 ■ Albert Bandura/Walter Mischel   309

12 ■ Edward O. Wilson/David P. Barash 341

13 ■ George Kelly   395

14 ■ Carl Rogers   431

15 ■ Abraham Maslow   465

Preface

A number of substantial changes were made in the third edition of this text. The topics and pedagogical devices that were added include:

Popper's philosophy of science

Ellenberger's and Sulloway's efforts to demythologize the Freudian legend

Jung's childhood dreams, visions, and fantasies

Ellenberger's notion of creative illness

Adler's concept of safeguarding strategies

Horney's work on feminine psychology

Erikson's concepts of ritualizations and ritualisms

Allport's distinction between extrinsic and intrinsic religion

Allport's distinction between must and ought conscience

Token economies

An entirely new chapter on sociobiology, featuring the work of Edward O. Wilson and David P. Barash

Rogers's thoughts on modern marriage

Maslow's thoughts on transpersonal or fourth force psychology

Discussion of the relationship between the biographies of the personality theorists and the theories that they developed

Experiential exercises

Suggested readings

Evaluation sections were expanded to include empirical research, criticisms, and contributions

In preparing the third edition of this text I find that it is still my contention that it is in an Introduction to Theories of Personality course that the student experiences the full richness of psychology. It is in such a course that the student experiences everything from psychology's most rigorous scientists to its most mystical nonscientific thinkers. It is in such a course that the student reviews answers to questions such as: "What, if anything, do all human beings have in common?" "What accounts for individual differences among people?" "How are the mind and the body related?" "How much of what we call personality is inherited and how much results from experience?" and "How much of human behavior is determined and how much of it is a function of free will?" It is in such a course that the major theories of human motivation are reviewed and the major schools, paradigms, or "isms" within psychology are sampled; for example, psychoanalysis, behaviorism, humanism, and existentialism. It is in such a course that the student is exposed to the history of psychology, from Freud to the modern theorists, including Rogers, Skinner, May, Bandura, Mischel, Wilson, and Barash. It is also in such a course that students encounter information that helps them to make sense out of their own lives and their relationships with other people. What other psychology course covers as much territory? My answer is none, and therefore it is my belief that if a student were to take only one psychology course beyond the introductory course, it should be an Introduction to Theories of Personality course.

Although this text covers all of the topics already mentioned, its main purpose is to summarize the major theories of personality. The text is built around the belief that it is misleading to search for *the* correct theory of personality. Rather, it is assumed that the best understanding of personality comes from looking at it from a variety of viewpoints. Thus, theories representing the psychoanalytic, sociocultural, trait, learning, sociobiologic, and existential-humanistic paradigms are offered as different, yet equally valid, ways of approaching the study of personality.

As with the two previous editions of this text, it was a pleasure to work with the people at Prentice Hall. Susan Finnemore, the psychology editor, was supportive and informative. Mary Anne Shahidi, the production editor, coordinated such activities as copyediting, permissions, proofreading, and indexing. Mary Anne was efficient, effective, and understanding, and a pleasure to work with. Lee Cohen, the designer, created attractive cover and interior designs.

I would like to express my appreciation to the following individuals who reviewed the second edition of this text and made many valuable suggestions for the improvement of this edition: Wayne Moellenberg, University of New Mexico; Robert A. Neimeyer, Memphis State University; Elaine Nocks, Furman University; and Vivian Travis, Winthrop College. I would like to express my special appreciation to David Barash, University of Washington, who reviewed the chapter on sociobiology and made several recommendations that greatly strengthened the chapter. I would also like to thank John Brennan, Hamline University, who also read the chapter on sociobiology and made a number of suggestions that improved the chapter. Although all of the reviewers were helpful, they are not responsible for any discrepancies that remain in the book; I alone am to blame for the final product.

As one writes a book, other responsibilities usually suffer. I would like to thank the members of Hamline's Psychology Department for covering for me as this text was being revised: Jerry Greiner, Kim Guenther, Chuck LaBounty, and Matt Olson.

Lastly, I would like to give special thanks to Linda Samson who not only typed the several drafts of the revised manuscript but also proofread them and made a number of improvements in grammar, spelling, and content. Linda also did a great deal of detective work involved in preparing a manuscript such as tracking down elusive references. Linda's contributions to this project were monumental.

B. R. HERGENHAHN
Hamline University
Saint Paul, MN

1

What Is Personality?

The term *personality* comes from the Latin word **persona,** which means mask. Those defining personality as a mask look on personality as one's public self. It is that aspect of ourselves that we select to display to the world. This definition of personality implies that important aspects of a person remain concealed for some reason. Other definitions of personality range all the way from the popular notion that personality allows a person to be socially effective (a person may be viewed as having a wonderful personality, a terrible personality, or no personality at all), to highly technical definitions involving mathematical formulations. Many answers exist to the question of personality. In fact, every theory of personality can be viewed as an attempt to define personality and these definitions differ markedly from one another.

Three Concerns of Personality Theory.   Kluckhohn and Murray (1953, 53) observe that every human being is: (1) like every other human being; (2) like some other human beings; and (3) like no other human being. We are like all other human beings insofar as there is a **human nature** that describes "humanness." One task of the personality theorist, then, is to describe what all human beings have in common, what we come equipped with at birth—that is, to describe human nature. Next we are like *some* other human beings insofar as we share a common culture. For example, it may be part of human nature to adorn one's body, to attempt to make sense of the universe and one's place in it, to seek a mate and produce offspring, to care for one's offspring, and to live cooperatively with one's fellow humans. It is culture, however, that determines how these needs are satisfied. In our culture, for example, if one wants to marry, he or she must have only one wife or husband at a time. Lastly, each human is unique because no other human being has neither his or her particular cluster of genes nor his or her particular cluster of personal experiences.

In describing personality, then, the personality theorist attempts to show how we are the same as other humans, and how we are different from them. The former concern is with the nature of human nature, and the latter concern is with **individual differences.** It is one achievement to *describe* the components of human nature and the characteristics on which humans differ; it is another to *explain* their origins, how they interact, how they change over time, and their functional significance. It is the job of personality theory to both describe what humans are like and to explain why we are like that—to describe and explain both human nature and individual differences. This is a large order and no single theory has been successful at completely doing both. Rather, different theories emphasize different aspects of human nature and individual differences, and offer different descriptions and explanations of them. For this reason, the best understanding of personality, at the present time, is provided by the composite of many theories of personality instead of by any single theory.

Proposed Determinants of Personality

In this section we will review some of the factors that have been stressed by various personality theorists in their attempt to explain personality. We shall see that one theorist may emphasize one or more of the following factors, whereas other theorists will minimize them or ignore them altogether.

Genetics.   What is probably the most common lay explanation of personality is based on genetics. If asked, people on the street would tend to express the belief that personality characteristics are present for the same reasons that eye color, hair color, or physique are present. To ask why a person is shy is basically the same as asking why he or she is tall. Both characteristics, according to this viewpoint, are genetically determined. Common statements such as "He has an Irish temper," "She takes after her father," or "He has his uncle's artistic tendencies," all imply a genetic explanation of personality, because they all have an "It's in the blood" tone to them.

The reader should not be left with the impression that only nonprofessionals look on personality characteristics as being inherited. Recently some important research has suggested that heredity plays a far greater role in determining personality than was previously suspected. Mischel (1981) states the view held by most personality theorists concerning the relative contributions of genetics and environment (for example, family, society, and culture) to personality:

> Imagine the enormous differences that would be found in the personalities of twins with identical genetic endowments if they were raised apart in two different families—or, even more striking, in two totally different cultures. Through social learning, vast differences develop among people in their reactions to most of the stimuli they face in daily life. As a result of social processes, stimuli that terrify one person may delight the next and leave a third indifferent. (311)

For the past several years, however, Thomas J. Bouchard, Jr., has been studying identical twins separated at birth and reared apart, and his results contradict Mischel's conclusions. Bouchard consistently finds great similarity in the personalities of identical twins even when they had no contact with each other and were reared by different families. Bouchard (1984) concludes, "Both the twin studies and adoption studies . . . converge on the surprising finding that common family environmental influences play only a minor role in the determination of personality" (174–75). In other words, if children reared in the same family have similar personality characteristics, that fact seems to be explained more by their common genes than by their common family experiences. After reviewing the work of Bouchard and others, Holden (1987) concludes:

> Although behavioral geneticists quibble about each others' methodologies, most appear to be in accord with the conclusion that the common environment seems to have a negligible role in creating personality similarities among family members. From the standpoint of the organism, it seems, there may be no such thing as a common environment for two given individuals unless those individuals also have all their genes in common. (600)

The recently developed field of sociobiology (chapter 12) also stresses the role of genetics in its explanation of personality. In fact, all theories of personality are built on an inherited quality, whether it be physiological needs, described, for example, by Freud (chapter 2), Skinner (chapter 9), Dollard and Miller (chapter 10), and Maslow (chapter 15); the tendency toward self-actualization, described, for example, by Jung (chapter 3), Horney (chapter 5), Rogers (chapter 14), and Maslow (chapter 15); or social interest, as discussed by Adler (chapter 4). Thus, the question is not whether or not genes influence personality, but rather, to what degree and in what manner.

The question of how much of personality is influenced by inheritance is as old as psychology itself. The **nativism-empiricism controversy** (also called the nature-nurture controversy) can be seen in every major category within the field of psychology, and personality theory is no exception. In general, the nativist claims that an important attribute, such as intelligence, is genetically determined. The nativist would say, for example, that the maximum level of intelligence that a person can attain is determined at conception, and life's circumstances, at best, can help the person to realize this genetically determined intellectual potential. The empiricist, conversely, believes that a person's major attributes are created by experience. Intelligence, to the empiricist, is determined by a person's experiences rather than by his or her genetic endowment. To the empiricist, the upper limit of a person's intelligence is found in the environment, not in the genes.

The nativism-empiricism controversy manifests itself in many ways in personality theory. Therefore, we will confront it several times in this text.

Traits.   Several personality theorists believe that what distinguishes one person from another is the traits that they possess. Some traits, it is assumed, are learned (for example, food preferences), and others are genetically determined (for example, one's emotional makeup); some exert a powerful influence in one's life (for example, one's intelligence), and others have only a minor influence (for example, fashion preferences). Trait theorists tend to believe that the traits that one possesses remain relatively constant throughout one's life and, therefore, they believe one's behavior will remain consistent across time and similar situations. The theories of Allport (chapter 7) and Cattell (chapter 8) stress the importance of traits in their explanations of personality.

Sociocultural Determinants.   To a large extent one's culture determines what are considered proper dating practices, marital arrangements, child-rearing practices, political and religious institutions, education, justice, and ways people of other cultures are viewed. These, and other cultural variables, have a significant impact on one's personality. It is cultural variables that explain many important individual differences among humans, that is, differences among people of different cultures.

More specifically, some theorists say that one's personality can be viewed as a combination of the many roles he or she plays. If you were asked to start a blank sheet of paper with the words "I am" and then to list all of your qualities, you would have a rather extensive list. For example, you may be female, 20 years old, a college student, a Methodist, from the Midwest, 5 feet 4 inches, a member of several organizations, a Democrat, attractive, a Virgo, a psychology major, and so on. Each entry on your list has a prescribed role associated with it, and for each role, society has defined what is an acceptable range of behavior (norms). If one deviates from that range, he or she will confront social pressure of some kind. Indeed, what is considered normal behavior and what is considered abnormal is, to a large extent, determined by how one behaves relative to societal expectations.

Other sociocultural determinants of personality would include the socioeconomic level of one's family, one's family size, birth order, race, religion, the region of the country in which one was raised, the educational level attained by one's parents, and the like. One simply does not have the same experiences in a financially rich home as one would have in a financially poor home. These fortuitous circumstances into which a person is born (for example, culture, society, and family) certainly have a major impact on personality. Again, this point is one that each personality theorist accepts; it is just a matter of how much they emphasize it. The theories of Adler (chapter 4), Horney (chapter 5), Erikson (chapter 6), and Rogers (chapter 14) stress the importance of sociocultural determinants of personality.

Learning. Those accepting a genetic explanation of personality represent the nativism side of the nativism-empiricism controversy. Those emphasizing the learning process in their explanations of personality represent the empiricism side. An example is the learning theorist's contention that we are what we have been rewarded for being; therefore, if our history of reward had been different, our personality would be quite different. The difference between a successful person and an unsuccessful one, according to some learning theorists, is to be found in patterns of reward, not in the genes.

A powerful implication of this theoretical position is that one can control personality development by controlling the circumstances under which rewards are dispensed or withheld. Theoretically, it is possible to create any kind of personality by systematically manipulating reward. Those emphasizing the genetic basis of personality would deny that personality is as pliable as the learning theorist suggests. The theories of Skinner (chapter 9), and Dollard and Miller (chapter 10) emphasize the importance of reward in the learning process. Bandura and Mischel (chapter 11) also stress the learning process but deny the importance of reward in that process.

Considerable compatibility exists between those stressing sociocultural determinants in their explanation of personality and those stressing the learning process. Both accept **environmentalism.** That is, they both believe that personality results from one's life experiences. One's personality is shaped either by cultural expectations or by patterns of reward in the environment.

Existential-Humanistic Considerations. Theories emphasizing existential-humanistic principles ask such questions as the following. What does it mean to be aware of the fact that ultimately you must die? How do the human needs for predictability and security relate to the human needs for adventure and freedom?

Such theories stress the importance of free will. Humans may be "thrown" by circumstances beyond their control into certain conditions of life, but how they value, interpret, and respond to those conditions is a matter of personal choice. For example, you may be born a male, a female, rich, or poor; or during peace, war, famine, or bountiful times. You may have been abused as a child or you may have been raised under loving conditions. No matter what conditions you find yourself in or what experiences you have had, it is you that gives those conditions or experiences whatever meaning they have for you. It is you who is in charge of your life; therefore, you alone are responsible for the kind of person you become. The theories of Kelly (chapter 13), Rogers (chapter 14), Maslow (chapter 15), and May (chapter 16) fall into this category.

Unconscious Mechanisms. In many important respects, theories that emphasize unconscious mechanisms are the opposite of existential-humanistic theories. The primary concern of these so-called depth theories is to discover the underlying causes of behavior. According to this viewpoint, because the ultimate causes of behavior are unconscious and typically have their origins in childhood, the search for them is extremely complicated. Complex tools are needed in the search, tools such as dream and symbol analysis, free association, hypnosis, and the analysis of lapses of memory. According to this theory, because that which characterizes the unconscious mind can manifest itself in consciousness in any number of ways, one cannot really understand much about a person by studying his or her conscious experience. To understand personality, one must somehow get beneath the arbitrary manifestations of the unconscious mind to the unconscious mind itself. In other words one must get beneath a person's mask. A personality theorist holding this position would not ask a person why he or she acts in a particular way, because the real causes of the behavior are typically not known to that person. The theories of Freud (chapter 2), Jung (chapter 3), and Horney (chapter 5) stress unconscious mechanisms in their analysis of personality.

Cognitive Processes.   Currently great interest exists in cognitive processes in personality theory. Such processes determine how information from the environment is perceived, retained, transformed, and acted on by a person. Those theories stressing cognitive processes are typically interested in self-regulated behavior and focus on the importance of self-reward, which comes from goal attainment, rather than on rewards that come from sources outside the person. Cognitively oriented theories also tend to emphasize the importance of present experience and future goals in determining behavior and de-emphasize the importance of the past. Theories featuring cognitive processes include those of Bandura and Mischel (chapter 11) and Kelly (chapter 13).

Personality as a Composite of Factors.   Because almost every theory of personality contains elements of all of the explanations just reviewed, perhaps it is safe to say that personality is a function of all of them. The elements emphasized will depend on which specific theory of personality one considers. Assuming that, the situation can be summarized as follows:

Genetics
Learning
Culture-society
Self-awareness   } Personality
Traits
Unconscious mechanisms
Cognitive processes

Issues Confronting the Personality Theorist

Personality theorists are in the unique position in psychology of studying the entire person. Most other psychologists are concerned with only one aspect of humans such as child development, old age, perception, intelligence, learning, motivation, or memory. It is only the personality theorist who tries to present a complete picture of the human being.

The task is monumental and is obviously related to developments in all other aspects of psychology. The personality theorists attempt to synthesize the best information from diverse portions of psychology into a coherent, holistic configuration. As personality theories have attempted this synthesis through the years, they have tended to address several questions related to human nature and individual differences. These are questions for which extremely different answers exist; no matter what the answer, however, each personality theory discusses each of the following issues directly or indirectly.

What Is the Relative Importance of the Past, the Present, and the Future? One question here is how childhood experiences are related to adult personality characteristics. A related question is: Are there critical, irreversible stages of personality development? Freud, for example, said that personality was essentially fully developed by the end of the fifth year of life. Other theorists stress the importance of future goals for human behavior. Goal-directed or future-oriented behavior is also called **teleological behavior,** and it plays a prominent role in the theories of Jung (chapter 3), Allport (chapter 7), and Bandura and Mischel (chapter 11). Both the learning theorists, for example, Skinner (chapter 9) and the existential-humanists, for example, May (chapter 16) tend to stress the importance of the present in their explanations of personality.

What Motivates Human Behavior?   Almost every theory of personality postulates a "master" motive for human behavior. That is, they specify what they feel is the major driving force behind most of what humans do. Freud, Skinner, and Dollard and Miller postulate **hedonism,** or the tendency to seek pleasure and avoid pain. Jung, Horney, Maslow, and Rogers postulate **self-actualization,** or the impulse to realize one's full potential. Adler postulates a striving for superiority. May and Kelly postulate a search for meaning or the reduction of uncertainty. Wilson and Barash postulate the desire to create and maintain a compatibility between our biologic nature and culture. Bandura and Mischel postulate the need to develop cognitive processes that are effective in dealing with the world.

How Important Is the Concept of Self?   Those theories that view human behavior as smooth running, consistent, and well organized need somehow to account for these characteristics of behavior. Several theories postulate the **self** as the organizing agent of personality. Also, it is often the self that is postulated as the mechanism providing individual consistency over time and across situations. The theories of Horney (chapter 5), Allport (chapter 7), and Rogers (chapter 14), rely heavily on the concept of self. Other theorists claim that employing the concept of self simply switches all of the questions we have about the person to questions about the self. In other words, the self is viewed as a homunculus (that is, little person) inside the person who causes one's actions. According to the opponents of the self concept, exactly how the self causes a person's actions remains a mystery. The concept of ego is often used in the same way as the concept of self and is criticized for the same reason. Skinner (chapter 9) is a theorist who is highly critical of self theories.

How Important Are Unconscious Mechanisms?   The depth theories, such as those of Freud and Jung, focus on the unconscious mind. Theories that emphasize unconscious mechanisms confront questions such as: What is the relationship between the conscious and unconscious minds? How can the unconscious be investigated? Can persons ever become aware of their own motives and, if so, how?

Unconscious mechanisms are also important to many theorists stressing sociocultural determinants of personality (for example, Adler, Horney, and Erikson) and to the sociobiologists (for example, Wilson and Barash). Conversely, trait theorists (such as Allport and Cattell), learning theorists (including Skinner, Dollard and Miller, and Bandura and Mischel), and existential-humanistic theorists (for example, Kelly, Rogers, Maslow, and May), all either deny or minimize the importance of unconscious determinants of personality.

Is Human Behavior Freely Chosen or Is It Determined?   If all the influences acting on a person at any given time were known, would it be possible to predict that person's behavior with complete accuracy? If your answer is yes, you are a determinist. If your answer is no, you hold out for at least a little free will. Notice that this question assumes that we could know all the factors influencing a person's behavior, and that is impossible. For this reason, even strict determinists realize their predictions about behavior must be probabilistic. Most personality theorists are determinists, but, as we have seen, they stress different determinants of behavior.

The only theorists who reject the doctrine of **determinism** are the existential-humanists who believe that human behavior is freely chosen. For them, we are masters of our own destiny. We are not victims of our biography, our culture, our genes, our traits, our patterns of reward, or any other factors.

What Can Be Learned by Asking People about Themselves?   Examining the contents of one's own mind is called introspection, so this question concerns the extent to which introspective reports can be trusted. Answers to this question are provided by existentialists, who claim that introspection is the most valuable tool available for studying personality, to some learning theorists, who claim that introspection is not only invalid but unnecessary. In between the two extremes are the theories of Freud and Jung according to which introspective reports are useful if they are interpreted by a trained analyst.

Uniqueness versus Commonality.   We saw earlier that each person is unique, because no cluster of genes or environmental experiences will be the same for any two persons. It is also true that all human beings have a great deal in common. The fact that we share similar brains and sensory apparatuses and a culture with other humans means that we respond as others do to many situations. To a large extent, what we find aesthetically pleasing, what makes us laugh or cry, and our beliefs concerning the supernatural are culturally determined. Thus, it is possible to emphasize either the fact that each human being is unique, or the fact that each human has much in common with other humans. Both emphases are found in personality theories. The intense study of the unique individual is called **idiographic research,** and the study of groups of individuals is called **nomothetic research.** Theorists such as Allport (chapter 7) and Skinner (chapter 9) use the idiographic approach because they emphasize the uniqueness of each individual. Theorists such as Cattell (chapter 8) emphasize the nomothetic approach because they stress traits that many individuals have in common.

Are People Controlled Internally or Externally?   Where is the locus of control for human behavior? Some theorists stress internal mechanisms such as traits and self-regulatory systems, for example, Allport (chapter 7), Cattell (chapter 8), Horney (chapter 5), Rogers (chapter 14), and Maslow (chapter 15); others stress external factors such as environmental stimuli and patterns of reward, for example, Skinner (chapter 9) and Dollard and Miller (chapter 10); still others emphasize the importance of both internal and external controls, for example, Bandura and Mischel (chapter 11). Variables controlling a person's behavior from the inside are called **person variables,** those controlling from the outside are called **situation variables.** The determination of the relative importance of person and situation variables for human behavior is one of the primary concerns of current personality theorists.

How Are the Mind and the Body Related?   The question here is how can something purely mental (such as the mind, thoughts, consciousness, or subjective reality) influence something purely physical (such as the brain, the body, or behavior)? The question is as old as psychology itself and is still very much alive. One proposed answer is that no problem really exists because no mind exists; what we refer to as mental states are nothing more than subtle bodily responses. This position is called **physical monism.** Another answer is that mental events are merely the byproducts of bodily responses and, therefore, can be ignored in the analysis of human behavior. This position is called **epiphenomenalism.** Another proposed solution claims that an external event causes both bodily and mental events at the same time, but the two kinds of events are independent of each other. This position is called **parallelism.** Finally, some maintain that the mind influences the body and that the body influences the mind (such as when Freud maintains that pathogenic ideas can cause bodily ailments). This position is called **interactionism.** We will see that virtually all positions on the mind-body question are represented by the various personality theorists.

What Is the Nature of Human Nature?   How a theorist answers this question determines the major thrust of his or her theory. Some answers include the following. The **empirical theory** states that people become what they experience, and the **rational theory** states that human behavior is, or can be, under the control of thoughtful, logical, rational thought processes. The **animalistic theory** states that humans are nothing but animals. The **sociobiological theory** claims that humans inherit behavioral tendencies from our evolutionary past, but that these tendencies can be modified by rational thought or by cultural influence. The **existential theory** states that the most important point about humans is our ability to choose courses of action and to assign meaning to the events in our lives. The **humanistic theory** claims humans are born basically good; if we engage in undesirable behavior it is because culture, societal, or family conditions have forced us to do so. The **mechanistic theory** states that humans are automatons that respond automatically to environmental events. The automatic response can be a simple response to an environmental stimulus or can be a response given after information from the environment has been processed through several information-processing systems. In either situation the response is automatic and machine like. In the latter case, the mechanistic theory of human nature likens humans to computers. Again, virtually all assumptions about human nature are found in the various theories of personality.

How Consistent Is Human Behavior?   Those theorists who stress traits, habits, genetics, or unconscious mechanisms in their explanations of personality assume that a person's behavior should be consistent in similar situations and over time. For example, it is assumed that a person who possesses the trait of honesty should be honest in most situations in which honesty or dishonesty is possible. Likewise, an aggressive person should be aggressive in a wide variety of situations. Most personality theorists assume that a person's behavior is consistent, and they see their job as accounting for that consistency. Recently, however, it has been discovered that human behavior may not be as consistent as has been traditionally assumed. For example, after a careful review of studies investigating the consistency of behavior across time and across similar situations, Mischel (1968) concluded that human behavior is too inconsistent to be explained in terms of traits. More recent evidence suggests that some persons are consistent in some ways but not in others; these areas of consistency vary from person to person. The questions that personality theorists must confront are: How consistent is human behavior? What constitutes consistency? What accounts for individual differences in consistency? What variables account for consistency and for inconsistency?

How Do We Find the Answers?

Epistemology.   **Epistemology** is the study of knowledge. It tries to answer such questions as: What does it mean to know? What are the limits of knowledge? Because science, at least in part, is a method of gaining knowledge, it can be considered an epistemological pursuit.

Science.   **Science** combines two ancient philosophical positions on the origins of knowledge. One of these positions, called **rationalism,** contends that one gains knowledge by exercising the mind; in other words, by thinking, reasoning, and using logic. According to the rationalist, information must be sorted out by the mind before reasonable conclusions can be drawn. The other philosophical position, called **empiricism,** contends that sensory experience is the basis of all knowledge. In its extreme form, empiricism states that we know only what we experience. Thus, the rationalist emphasizes mental operations, whereas the empiricist equates knowledge with experience. Science combined the two positions, thereby creating an extremely powerful epistemological tool.

Scientific Theory.   In the realm of science, rationalism and empiricism meet in **scientific theory.** This marriage of philosophical schools is seen in the following quotation by S. S. Stevens: "Science seeks to generate confirmable propositions by fitting a formal system of symbols (language, mathematics, logic) to empirical observations" (1951, 22).

The first step in utilizing scientific theory involves making a number of observations concerning some problem or phenomenon of interest. Next, one attempts to make sense out of these observations by thinking about, grouping, and synthesizing them. This attempt at making observations more constructive by thinking about them in various ways is a rational endeavor.

Thus, in science, observations are made (empiricism) and then they are organized in some meaningful way (rationalism). Next, the scientist has to check to see if the groupings are, in fact, meaningful. If they are, they should indicate where to look for additional information. In other words, if the concepts used to organize the original observations are to be truly useful, they must do two things: (1) synthesize observations and (2) generate new research. This process can be represented schematically as follows:

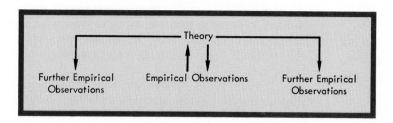

We see that a scientific theory comes into existence to explain several observations (its **synthesizing function**), and when it exists, it must be able to suggest other places where the researcher could look for additional information. A theory's ability to generate new research is called its **heuristic function.**

An example of the foregoing would be as follows. Let us say young Freud is talking with a friend when it is discovered that he (the friend) had missed an appointment at the dentist. This observation registers in Freud's sensitive mind. Later, Freud observes other lapses of memory and notes that they all have something in common. They all seem to involve painful or anxiety-related experiences. Freud speculates that many disturbing thoughts are repressed; that is, they are held in the unconscious mind, thereby preventing the discomfort that would be caused by their conscious recognition.

The theoretical notion of the repression of disturbing thoughts serves two purposes. It helps to make sense out of previously disjointed observations, and it aids in discovering other truths. For example, if disturbing thoughts are repressed, the unconscious mind will be a veritable storehouse of such thoughts, which could be released under the appropriate circumstances. In other words, if one could tap the contents of the unconscious mind with such devices as hypnotism, dream analysis, or free associations, one should find an abundance of repressed memories. Thus, we have the rudiments of one of history's great theoretical developments.

Science and Personality Theory

Scientific theories differ in their rigor. In such sciences as physics or chemistry, theories are highly developed. The terms used in them are precisely defined, and a high correspondence exists among the words, signs, and symbols in the theory and the empirical events it purports to explain. The use of complex mathematics is quite common in such theories.

In psychology, theories exist for almost all stages of development. In areas such as psychophysics and learning theory, psychology has theories that rival those in the physical sciences in terms of rigor. Many theories in psychology are in their infant stages, however, containing terms that are not precisely defined; the relationship between their terms and empirical events is not a tight one. Most personality theories are in the latter category. In fact, some theories of personality make no claim to being scientific in the sense that they can be tested under highly controlled conditions. Such theories claim that their verification comes either from everyday experience or from clinical practice.

To say that most personality theories lack rigor is not to apologize for them, nor is it to conclude that they are not useful. Each personality theory can be seen as a way of viewing personality; therefore, each theory provides us with a different viewpoint. In the final analysis, we probably learn more about some issue by viewing it from a variety of angles than we would by burrowing in deeply from one angle.

Imagine yourself in a dark room in which you cannot touch a complex object directly. As long as the room remains dark, you will know nothing about the object except that it is there. Now suppose that a faint light illuminates part of the object, thus allowing you to see part of it. You now know more about the object than you did before, but much remains unknown. Now another beam of light falls on the object, then another and another. You walk around the object noting what has been illuminated by the various beams of light. Because the beams are coming from different directions, many beams allow you to learn more about the object. Some beams are narrow and bright, concentrating on a small area but exposing greater detail. Other beams are broader but dimmer, allowing you to learn about a larger area but in less detail. Some beams may overlap others, but all are useful. In fact, the greater the number of beams and angles, the more information you will have because each beam illuminates a part of the object of interest that previously was dark.

Kuhn's View of Science.   The preceding analogy is a rough description of what occurs during a scientific investigation, only with slight changes in terminology. For example, Thomas Kuhn (1973) indicates that most scientists accept a "point of view" concerning their subject matter as they carry out their research. This viewpoint guides their research activities and to a large extent determines what is studied and how it is studied. Kuhn calls a viewpoint shared by many scientists a **paradigm.** For example, years ago most physicists accepted a Newtonian viewpoint in doing their work, but now most follow an Einsteinian viewpoint. The dominant paradigm in physics shifted from Newton's theory to Einstein's theory.

In psychology, no one paradigm ever guided all psychological research. Rather, several paradigms have always existed simultaneously. In addition, the term paradigm, as it applies to psychology, corresponds to groups of interrelated theories commonly called a "school of thought" or an "ism" instead of to a single theory, as is the case of physics. In either case, a paradigm can be considered a way of looking at and investigating a certain subject. Therefore, different scientists exploring the same subject matter will go about their work differently, depending on which paradigm is guiding their research activities.

The most important point regarding paradigms is that it is not necessary to consider one correct and the others incorrect; they all simply generate different research methodologies. This point brings us back to our beam-of-light analogy. One can think of paradigms as beams of light; some paradigms are highly developed and concentrate on a small area, providing great detail but within a limited domain, whereas other paradigms cover an extremely large domain but do so at the expense of detail. As with our beams of light, both kinds of paradigms are useful in that they furnish information that would otherwise remain obscure.

So how do these ideas relate to personality theory? Personality is a complex topic, and many approaches to its study exist. In fact, these approaches are paradigms, and everything that has been said applies to them. In the remainder of this text, we will sample paradigms that guide research in the area of personality. These six paradigms are listed along with the theories that have been chosen to represent them.

PSYCHOANALYTIC PARADIGM
Sigmund Freud
Carl Jung

SOCIOCULTURAL PARADIGM
Alfred Adler
Karen Horney
Erik Erikson

TRAIT PARADIGM
Gordon Allport
Raymond B. Cattell

LEARNING PARADIGM
B. F. Skinner
John Dollard and Neal Miller
Albert Bandura and Walter Mischel

SOCIOBIOLOGIC PARADIGM
Edward Wilson and David Barash

EXISTENTIAL-HUMANISTIC PARADIGM
George Kelly
Carl Rogers
Abraham Maslow
Rollo May

Notice that each paradigm is named for its central theme. The psychoanalytic paradigm focuses on the analysis of the psyche, and the sociocultural paradigm focuses on the study of societal-cultural factors influencing personality. The trait paradigm emphasizes the importance of the various traits that persons possess, and the learning paradigm focuses on the importance of learning for personality development. The sociobiologic paradigm emphasizes the inherited tendency to engage in certain social behaviors, and the existential-humanistic paradigm focuses on free choice and personal responsibility.

Again, the reader need not bother to attempt to find the paradigm that is most correct. All paradigms provide useful information about personality; the information generated by one paradigm is just different from that generated by others. To attempt to build a house with only one tool, such as a hammer, or a saw, or a screwdriver, would be ineffective. Likewise, attempting to understand personality using only one theoretical orientation would leave huge gaps in one's understanding. This text will offer a variety of theories, which collectively will provide a much greater understanding of personality than any one of them taken alone could do.

Popper's View of Science.   We have just reviewed Kuhn's view of science with his emphasis on the concept of paradigm. It is also important to review Karl Popper's view of science because it has special relevance to personality theory. According to Popper, if a theory can account for everything that could possibly happen, the theory cannot be considered scientific. Such a theory explains everything and, therefore, it explains nothing. To be scientific, a theory must make **risky predictions.** That is, it must make predictions that have a chance of being incorrect. If a theory does generate predictions (hypotheses) that are not confirmed, the theory is considered to be invalid and should be revised or abandoned. So, to be scientific, a theory must generate hypotheses that could invalidate the theory if they are not confirmed; this is what is meant by making risky predictions. If, conversely, a theory makes predictions so general that anything that happens can be considered to be in accordance with the theory, no conceivable observation could be made that would falsify or refute the theory. Thus, according to Popper and his **principle of falsifiability** (also called the principle of refutability), all scientific theories must be falsifiable. Astrology, for example, cannot be considered scientific because each horoscope is so general as to apply to almost anyone. If astrology made highly specific, verifiable, and potentially false predictions about the major events in the lives of individuals, then the predictions could be objectively evaluated, but it does not do so.

Popper's principle of falsification is especially important in the realm of personality theory. Many theories of personality are extremely difficult, if not impossible, to falsify. Hergenhahn (1986) gives the following example:

> Freud's theory . . . makes no risky predictions. Everything that a person does can be "explained" by Freud's theory. If, for example, Freud's theory predicts that on the basis of early experience a man should hate women, but is found to love them, the Freudian can say that he is displaying a "reaction formation." That is, he really does hate women on the unconscious level, and he is simply going overboard in the opposite direction in order to reduce the anxiety that his recognition of his true hatred of women would cause. Astrology suffers the same fate, since there is no conceivable observation that could be made that would refute its claims. Contrary to common belief, if every conceivable observation agrees with a theory, the theory is weak, not strong. (27)

Many theories of personality cannot pass the test of falsifiability and, therefore, according to Popper, cannot be considered to be scientific. It must be remembered, however, that personality is enormously complex and has many subjective components that cannot be observed directly. Also, the systematic, objective study of personality is relatively new compared to the subject matters of the older, more established sciences. Finally, to say that a theory is not scientific is not to say that it is useless. Popper (1963) makes the following observation:

> Historically speaking all—or nearly all—scientific theories originate from myths, and . . . a myth may contain important anticipations of scientific theories. . . . I

thus [feel] that if a theory is found to be non-scientific, or "metaphysical" . . . it is not thereby found to be unimportant, or insignificant, or "meaningless," or "non-sensical." (38)

We believe that although the theories that follow vary in terms of their scientific rigor, all of them contribute significantly to our understanding of personality.

EXPERIENTIAL EXERCISES

1. Place the words "I am" at the top of a blank sheet of paper and proceed to list the characteristics that are true about you at the moment. Briefly describe the culturally prescribed role associated with each item on your list. Do you believe that a person who either refuses to play a socially prescribed role, or is incapable of doing so, will experience social pressure of some kind? Explain.

2. Formulate your own theory of personality. Indicate what your theory stresses. For example, what assumption about human nature does it make? Does it stress the importance of the past, present, or the future? Unconscious mechanisms? Would you place it within the existential-humanistic paradigm? If not, which one? Is your theory falsifiable? Save your theory and compare it to the one that you will be asked to formulate at the end of this book.

3. List several of your most important personality characteristics and also those of someone with whom you are very familiar. Note that the adjectives that you use in this exercise will suggest the kinds of personality characteristics that you think are most important and, therefore, might suggest which of the theories covered in this text will appeal to you the most.

4. How does the consistency-inconsistency controversy apply to your own personality? Are there some aspects of your personality that you consider to be consistent over time and across situations and some that you consider to be inconsistent? Give examples of each. Attempt to account for both the consistent and inconsistent aspects of your personality.

5. We typically identify a person as a specific individual when he or she is born, and claim that he or she remains the same individual until he or she dies. Specify what you believe makes a person the same person throughout his or her lifetime. What, for example, justifies punishing a person for a crime that he or she committed twenty or more years ago? On what basis is it concluded that, at that later time, we are punishing the same person who committed the crime? Another way to approach this problem is to specify what would need to change about a person before you would be willing to conclude that he or she is no longer the same person. His or her physical appearance? Beliefs? Memories? Gender? A combination of these characteristics? Something else?

DISCUSSION QUESTIONS

1. What three points, which are true about humans, do personality theories attempt to explain?

2. Give an example of how each of the following might influence a person's personality: genetics, traits, sociocultural determinants, learning, existential-humanistic considerations, unconscious mechanisms, and cognitive processes.

3. Which of the factors listed in the previous question does the author of your text accept as a contributor to personality? Explain.

4. Discuss the nature-nurture controversy.

5. What is determinism? Give examples of the

kinds of determinism that are represented among the personality theories. What is the alternative to believing that human behavior is determined?

6. Describe the following proposed answers to the mind-body question: physical monism, epiphenomenalism, parallelism, and interactionism.

7. Briefly discuss each of the following theories of human nature: empirical, rational, animalistic, sociobiologic existential, humanistic, and machine.

8. What is a scientific theory, and what are its functions?

9. Summarize Kuhn's view of science. Be sure to include in your answer a definition of the term *paradigm*.

10. Describe Popper's principle of falsifiability and explain why, in terms of this principle, astrology and Freud's theory of personality cannot be considered scientific.

11. Does it make sense to search for *the* correct theory of personality? Explain your position on the matter.

12. Which kinds of personality theories would expect considerable consistency in human behavior and which would not? Explain.

SUGGESTIONS FOR FURTHER READING

COAN, R. W. (1977). *Hero, Artist, Sage, or Saint? A Survey of Views on What Is Variously Called Mental Health, Normality, Maturity, Self-Actualization, and Human Fulfillment.* New York: Columbia University Press.

A creative and readable survey of definitions of normality, mental health, and morality throughout history and across cultures.

EVANS, R. I. (1976). *The Making of Psychology: Discussions With Creative Contributors.* New York: Alfred A. Knopf.

Provocative interviews with many of psychology's most important contributors including many covered in this textbook. See, for example, Skinner, Miller, Allport, Rogers, Bandura, Jung, and Erikson.

KUHN, T. S. (1973). *The Structure of Scientific Revolutions* (2d ed.). Chicago: University of Chicago Press.

Kuhn's classic work showing that scientific activity is not nearly as objective as has been traditionally believed. Rather, scientists become emotionally involved in the paradigm that guides their research and are thus blinded to other, perhaps better, explanations of the phenomena they are investigating. This book shows that science typically progresses by revolution (the overthrow of a paradigm) rather than by evolution (the slow, ever closer approximation to truth).

PERVIN, L. A. (1984). *Current Controversies and Issues in Personality.* New York: John Wiley and Sons.

An excellent review of the major controversies in contemporary personality theory.

Topics covered include person versus situation variables; nature-nurture interaction; reasons why people tend not to help each other; relationships among thoughts, emotions, and overt behavior; gender differences in personality; the usefulness of the concept of self; and ethics in personality research.

RUBINSTEIN, J., and B. SLIFE (1988). *Taking Sides: Clashing Views on Controversial Psychological Issues* (5th ed.). Guilfort, CT: The Dushkin Publishing Group.

An excellent presentation of both sides of the debates concerning important current psychological issues. The issues debated include: Can deception in research be justified? Is our behavior primarily determined by biologic processes? Do attitudes affect cancer? Has science discredited extrasensory perception? Can computers think? Can intelligence be increased? Can suicide be rational? Is psychotherapy effective? Is pornography harmful? Should insanity be considered a legal defense for criminals?

STANOVICH, K. E. (1986). *How to Think Straight about Psychology.* Glenview, IL: Scott, Foresman.

An extremely readable, humorous, and informative account of science in general and psychology's status as a science in particular.

STEVENSON, L. (1987). *Seven Theories of Human Nature.* (2d ed.). New York: Oxford University Press.

An excellent, concise, and readable discussion of the theories of human nature postulated by Christianity, Freud, Lorenz, Marx, Sartre, Skinner, and Plato.

GLOSSARY

Animalistic theory of human nature. The contention that humans are animals, and, perhaps except for complexity, we are the same as other primates. That is, we share drives, motives, and instincts with other primates.

Determinism. The belief that all behavior is caused and is therefore not free. According to the determinist, the accuracy with which behavior can be predicted is directly proportional to the knowledge of the causes of that behavior. That is, if all the causes were known (an impossible situation), behavior could be predicted with complete accuracy.

Empirical theory of human nature. The contention that those qualities that characterize persons come from experience. Those personality theories that stress the importance of learning or sociocultural experiences accept the empirical theory of human nature.

Empiricism. The contention that an attribute is determined by experience rather than by genetics. Within epistemology, it is the belief that all knowledge is derived from sensory experience.

Environmentalism. The belief that the determinants of behavior are found in the environment instead of in the person.

Epiphenomenalism. The contention that mental events are the byproducts of bodily events. Bodily events cause mental events but mental events cannot cause bodily events. Mental events, therefore, can be ignored in the analysis of human behavior.

Epistemology. The study of the nature of knowledge.

Existential theory of human nature. The contention that the most important point about humans is their ability to choose. According to this theory of human nature humans are what they choose to be.

Hedonism. The contention that the major motive in life is to seek pleasure and avoid pain.

Heuristic function of a theory. A theory's ability to generate new information.

Human nature. Those qualities that characterize all humans. One job of the personality theorist is to specify the nature of human nature.

Humanistic theory of human nature. The contention that humans are born basically good. If humans do bad things it is because a sick culture, society, or family causes them to do so. Unless their natural inclinations are interfered with, people will live in peace and harmony with each other.

Idiographic research. The intense study of a single person.

Individual differences. The important ways in which humans differ from one another. One of the jobs of the personality theorist is to describe and explain individual differences.

Interactionism. The contention that the mind influences the body and that the body influences the mind. That is, that the mind and the body are causally related.

Introspection. Self-examination. The directing of one's thoughts inward to discover truths about one's self.

Mechanistic theory of human nature. The contention that humans respond in an automatic, machinelike manner to environmental circumstances. The machine envisioned can be simple as in the stimulus-response theories, or it can be complex as in the theories emphasizing information-processing mechanisms. In the latter theories the human is often likened to a computer.

Mind-body problem. The problem of specifying how something mental (cognitive) can influence something physical, such as the body.

Nativism. The contention that an attribute is determined by genetics rather than by experience.

Nativism-empiricism controversy (also called the nature-nurture controversy). The argument concerning the extent to which an attribute, such as intelligence, is influenced by inheritance as opposed to experience.

Nomothetic research. The study of groups of individuals.

Paradigm. A term used by Kuhn to describe a theoretical viewpoint shared by many researchers.

Parallelism. The contention that an environmental event causes both mental and bodily reactions at the same time. According to this proposed answer to the mind-body question, bodily and mental phenomena run parallel to each other and are, therefore, not causally related.

Person variables. Those important variables contained within persons thought to be responsible for their behavior. Traits, habits, memories, information-processing mechanisms, and repressed early experiences exemplify person variables. Personality theories emphasizing person variables predict considerable consistency in behavior across time and similar situations.

Persona. A Latin word meaning mask.

Physical monism. The contention that no mind-body problem exists because no mind exists. No mental events occur, only physical ones.

Principle of falsifiability (also called the principle of refutability). Popper's contention that a scientific theory must make risky predictions, that is, it must make predictions that could conceivably be false and, if so, would refute the theory.

Rational theory of human nature. The contention that what distinguishes humans from other animals is the human ability to engage in rational thought. Humans are viewed as rational animals.

Rationalism. The belief that knowledge can be gained only by exercising the mind; for example, by thinking, deducing, or inferring.

Risky predictions. Predictions that run the risk of being incorrect. According to Popper, for a theory to be considered scientific it must make risky predictions.

Science. The epistemological pursuit that combines the philosophical schools of empiricism and rationalism.

Scientific theory. Combination of the philosophical schools of rationalism and empiricism, with two major functions: (1) it synthesizes (explains) many observations, and (2) it generates new information.

Self. A concept employed by several personality theorists to account for the facts that human behavior is smooth running, consistent, and well organized. The concept of self has also been used to explain why we are aware of ourselves as individuals.

Self-actualization. The situation that exists when a person is acting in accordance with his or her full potential.

Situation variables. Those variables found in the environment thought to be responsible for behavior. Stimulus-response theories and those stressing the importance of patterns of reward exemplify theories emphasizing situation variables. Theories emphasizing situation variables expect behavior to be less consistent than those theories emphasizing person variables.

Sociobiological theory of human nature. The contention that we inherit behavioral dispositions from our evolutionary past, but that those dispositions can be modified by rationality or by cultural influence.

Synthesizing function of a theory. A theory's ability to organize and explain several otherwise disjointed observations.

Teleological behavior. Purposive behavior. Behavior that is motivated by the future rather than by the past or the present. Teleological behavior is said to be goal directed.

2

Sigmund Freud

Freud (1917/1966, 284–85) observed that humans have had three major blows to their self-esteem. The first came from Copernicus, who demonstrated that the earth was not the center of the universe, as humans had so egotistically believed. In fact, Copernicus showed that the earth was not even the center of our solar system, a fact that was not easily digested.

The second blow came from the work of Charles Darwin, who demonstrated that humans were not the product of "special creation," but were descended from and continuous with the so-called lower animals.

As the dust caused by Darwin's revelations was settling, our self-esteem was salvaged by the belief that humans were *rational* animals. Although we descended from lower animals, somewhere in the process of evolution we became qualitatively different from them by becoming dependent on our intellect. Animals were driven by instinct; only human behavior was rationally determined.

It was Freud who dealt the third blow to human self-esteem by demonstrating that human behavior is primarily instinctive and motivated mainly by unconscious mechanisms. In other words, according to Freud, humans are anything but rational animals. Whether one agrees with Freud's theory or not, Freudian concepts have completely revised the way we look at human nature. In fact, it is probably accurate to say that no single person has so revolutionized the way we view ourselves as Freud did.

Sigmund Freud

Biographical Sketch

Sigmund Freud was born on 6 May 1856 in Freiberg, Austria (now Pribor, Czechoslovakia). As we shall see shortly, however, it is possible that Freud was born on 6 March instead of 6 May. When Freud was four years old, he and his family moved to Vienna, where he continued to live for nearly eighty years. His father (Jakob) was a not-too-successful wool merchant and a strict authoritarian as a father. At the time of Freud's birth, his father was forty years old, and his mother, who was his father's third wife, was a youthful twenty. Freud was the first of seven children born to his mother, Amalie Nathansohn Freud, in the course of ten years. It is interesting to note that Amalie was Jakob Freud's third wife, not his second as has been commonly believed. Examination of the town records of Freiberg in 1968 revealed that Jakob's second wife had been a woman named Rebecca, about whom practically nothing is known. Years earlier it was also discovered by examining the birth register of Freiberg that Sigmund Freud's official birthday was 6 March 1856, not 6 May as is commonly reported. Ernest Jones, Freud's official biographer, suggests that the discrepancy reflects only a clerical error, but others see it as more significant. For example, Balmary (1979) believes that Freud's parents reported the birth date of 6 May to conceal the fact that Freud's mother (Amalie) was pregnant with Sigmund when she married Jakob. In her book, *Psychoanalyzing Psychoanalysis: Freud and the Hidden Fault of the Father* (1979), Balmary speculates that both "family secrets" (the fact that Amalie was Jakob's third, not his second, wife, and that Freud's mother was pregnant when she married) had a profound influence on Freud and his sub-

Sigmund Freud, Age Sixteen, with His Mother, Amalie Nathansohn Freud, in 1872.

sequent theorizing. Jakob had two sons by his first wife (Sally Kanner) and was a grandfather when Sigmund was born. It is interesting to note that Jakob Freud's second son by his first marriage was about the same age as Sigmund's mother. It is also interesting to note that Sigmund and his mother had a strong, powerful relationship, the effects of which Freud felt throughout his life. In fact, Freud attributed much of his success to his mother's faith in him. Freud's mother died on 12 September 1930 at the age of ninety-five.

Freud was always an outstanding student and graduated at the head of his high school class. At home, his brothers and sisters were not allowed to study musical instruments because doing so might disturb Sigmund's studies. He entered medical school at the University of Vienna when he was seventeen years old, but it took him almost eight years to finish a four-year medical course, mainly because he pursued many interests outside of medicine. Freud went to medical school because medicine was one of the few careers open to a Jew in Austria at that time. He was never really interested in becoming a medical physician but saw the study of medicine as a way of engaging in scientific research.

Freud hoped to become a professor of neurology and published several highly regarded articles on that topic. He soon discovered, however, that advancement within the academic ranks would be extremely slow for a Jew, and this realization, along with the fact that he needed money, prompted him to enter private practice as a clinical neurologist in 1886.

In 1886, he was finally able to marry Martha Bernays, to whom he had been engaged since 1882. During their five-year engagement, Freud wrote more than 400 letters to his fiancée. They remained married until Freud's death. They had six children, three daughters and three sons. One daughter, Anna, became a famous child psychiatrist in London.

The Cocaine Incident. In 1884, Freud began experimenting with cocaine after hearing from a German army physician that the drug enhanced the endurance of soldiers. Taking the drug himself, Freud found that it relieved depression and increased his ability to concentrate; furthermore, it appeared to have no negative side effects. Eventually Freud published six articles on cocaine, recommending it as a stimulant, local anesthetic, cure for indigestion, and harmless substitute for morphine. One of Freud's friends, Carl Koller, learned from Freud that cocaine could be used as an anesthetic during eye operations, and Koller presented a paper describing an experiment in which it was successfully used as such. Koller's paper caused a sensation and brought him worldwide fame almost overnight. Freud deeply regretted just having missed receiving this professional recognition himself.

Although cocaine was of value in eye surgery, many of Freud's other beliefs concerning the "magical substance" were soon proved false. Freud treated one of his close friends with cocaine to terminate his addiction to morphine, and the friend became addicted to cocaine instead of morphine. Reports of cocaine addiction were beginning to pour in from all over the world, and cocaine came under heavy attack from the medical community. Because Freud was closely associated with the drug that proved to be so harmful, his medical reputaion suffered considerably. To a large extent it was this cocaine episode that created the skepticism with which Freud's later ideas were met by his medical colleagues.

Early Influences on Freud's Theory

Freud's Visit with Charcot.   In 1885, Freud received a small grant that allowed him to study with the famous French neurologist **Jean-Martin Charcot** (1825–93) who was experimenting with hypnotism. At the time, Charcot was at the peak of his career and in the history of French medicine was considered second in prominence to only Louis Pasteur. By endorsing the use of hypnotism, Charcot dramatically reversed the negative attitude toward the phenomenon held by members of the medical community since, in the 1770s, Franz Anton Mesmer (1734–1815) claimed that it resulted from the rearrangement of animal spirits within the body. After hypnotizing a patient, Charcot demonstrated that various kinds of paralyses could be created and removed artificially through the inducement of the hypnotist. Thus, it was demonstrated that physical symptoms could have a *psychological* origin as well as a physical or organic origin. Charcot was so impressed by the mind's ability to create and remove physical symptoms that he wondered if his discovery could eventually explain faith healing (Sulloway 1979, 30).

Jean-Martin Charcot Demonstrating Hypnotism.

(Culver Pictures, Inc.)

Charcot's observations had clear implications for the treatment of **hysteria.** Hysteria is a term used to describe a wide variety of symptoms such as paralysis, loss of sensation, and disturbances of sight and speech. Originally, it was assumed that hysteria was exclusively a female disorder (*hystera* is the Greek word for uterus). Because it was often impossible to find anything organically wrong with hysteric patients, the medical community tended to view them as malingerers, and the physicians who agreed to treat them were typically discredited. Charcot's research indicated that the physical symptoms of hysteric patients could be psychogenic, and therefore the disease must be taken seriously even if symptoms cannot be explained in terms of organic dysfunction. Thus, Charcot did much to make the treatment of hysteria respectable. Charcot also convincingly demonstrated that, contrary to what most physicians had believed, hysteria was not an exclusively female disorder. By showing the psychogenic nature of bodily symptoms, Charcot had provided a new approach to studying hysteria, an ailment that had puzzled the medical community for centuries. Freud was soon to explore the implications of this approach.

Freud's Visit with Bernheim. After Freud returned from his visit with Charcot, he attempted to use hypnotism in his private practice but was only partially successful. In an effort to improve his skills as a hypnotist, Freud traveled back to France in 1889. This time, however, he visited **Hippolyte Bernheim** (1840–1919) in Nancy, France. Like Charcot and his colleagues, members of the "Nancy School" were experimenting with hypnosis as a means of treating hysteria. Freud learned information from this visit that would profoundly influence both his later theorizing and his therapeutic method. Bernheim would hypnotize persons, and while they were under hypnosis he had them perform various acts. While still under hypnosis, he would instruct them not to remember what they had done while under hypnosis when they awoke. This created **posthypnotic amnesia,** that is, the person was unable to recall what he or she had done while hypnotized. Bernheim went on to prove that the amnesia was not complete, however. He showed that if the hypnotist insisted strongly and convincingly that the memory would return, it would do so. To facilitate this recall Bernheim would place his hand on the forehead of the awake person as he insisted that the events that occurred during the hypnotic session be remembered. Freud learned from Bernheim that persons can have memories that they are not aware of; however, under pressure these memories can be retrieved.

A second important lesson that Freud learned from Bernheim involved **posthypnotic suggestion.** To exemplify this phenomenon Bernheim hypnotized a woman and told her that after waking and after a specified period of time had expired, she would walk over to the corner of the room, pick up the umbrella that was found there, and open it. After being aroused from the hypnotic trance and after the designated period of time had expired, she did exactly that. When questioned as to why she had opened the umbrella, the woman said that she wanted to see if it belonged to her. Freud learned from this that behavior can be caused by ideas of which a person is totally unaware. Thus, Freud learned from his visit with Bernheim that behavior can be caused by unconscious ideas, and that these ideas can be brought into consciousness under the right circumstances.

Freud got many of the ideas that were to characterize psychoanalysis ultimately from Charcot and Bernheim; many others he got from Josef Breuer.

Josef Breuer and the Case of Anna O.   Freud first met **Josef Breuer** (1842–1925) when both men were engaged in neurological research in the late 1870s. Breuer was fourteen years older than Freud and, like Charcot, was a highly regarded physician and researcher. Breuer gave Freud advice, friendship, and loaned him money. Most important for the development of psychoanalysis, however, was Breuer's treatment of a young woman anonymously referred to as Fräulein Anna O.

Anna O. was twenty-one years old when Breuer began treating her in December 1880 and her treatment continued until June 1882. Anna O.'s symptoms included paralysis of various parts of her body, problems with vision, periodic deafness, a nervous cough, periodic aversion to nourishment and liquids, suicidal impulses, an occasional inability to speak in her native German language while retaining an ability to speak in English, and various kinds of hallucinations. Anna O.'s condition was diagnosed as hysteria.

Much to his amazement, Breuer found that if Anna O. traced a symptom back to its original occurrence it would disappear either temporarily or permanently. Breuer found that Anna O. was able to discuss the origins of her various symptoms while she was either hypnotized or when she was very relaxed. Working several hours each day for more than a year, Breuer systematically removed each of Anna O.'s symptoms in this manner. Anna O. herself called this laborious procedure the "talking cure" or "chimney sweeping"; Breuer called it the method of **catharsis.** Aristotle had originally used this term to describe the emotional release and feeling of purification that an audience experienced while viewing a drama. It turned out that most of Anna O.'s symptoms originated from a series of traumatic experiences she had as she was nursing her dying father.

Several important facts were learned from Breuer's treatment of Anna O. Perhaps most important was the fact that her condition improved when she openly expressed her feelings. Breuer also observed that as treatment continued, Anna O. began transferring to him the feelings that she had toward her father. This phenomenon, in which a patient responds to the analyst as if he or she were an important person in the patient's life is called **transference.** Freud was later to consider transference to be a vital part of effective psychoanalysis. Likewise, Breuer was becoming emotionally involved with Anna O. The phenomenon of an analyst forming an emotional attachment to a patient is called **countertransference.** Because of the considerable amount of time Breuer was spending with Anna O. and the deep feelings they were developing toward each other, Breuer's marriage began to suffer; as a result, he decided to stop seeing his patient. Anna O. was so disturbed by this that she was thrust into hysterical (that is, imaginary) childbirth. Jones (1953) describes what happened next:

> Though profoundly shocked, he [Breuer] managed to calm her down by hypnotizing her, and then fled the house in a cold sweat. The next day he and his wife left for Venice to spend a second honeymoon, which resulted in the conception of a daughter. (225)

In *Studies on Hysteria* (1895), which Breuer coauthored with Freud, Breuer concluded that his treatment of Anna O. was successful. It turns out, however, that this was not the case.

Jones (1953, 223) identified Anna O. as Bertha Pappenheim (1859–1936) and we will review some of the details of her life next.

The Fate of Bertha Pappenheim.   Through some clever detective work Ellenberger (1972) was able to discover what happened to Bertha Pappenheim after Breuer had terminated her treatment. Documents uncovered by Ellenberger indicate that she was admitted into a sanatorium in 1882, still suffering many of the same ailments described earlier by Breuer. While at the sanatorium she was treated with substantial amounts of morphine, and the record shows that she continued to receive injections of morphine after her release from the sanatorium several months later. Little is known about the next few years of her life but she eventually emerged as a social worker in the late 1880s. Her accomplishments thereafter were truly impressive: She was the director of an orphanage in Frankfurt for 12 years (1895–1907); she founded a league of Jewish women (1904); she founded a home for unwed mothers (1907); she traveled to the Near East, Poland, Russia, and Rumania to help orphaned children and to help solve the problems of prostitution and white slavery; she became a leader in the European feminist movement; and she became a playwright and an author of children's stories. In addition she was an outspoken opponent of abortion.

Throughout her professional life Bertha Pappenheim maintained a negative attitude toward psychoanalysis and never allowed any of the girls under her care to by psychoanalyzed. A hint of her feminism is seen in the following statement made by her in 1922 (quoted by Jones 1953, 224) "If there is any justice in the next life women will make the laws there and men will bear the children." By the time she died in March 1936, she had become an almost legendary figure and tributes to her came from prominent persons throughout Europe. In 1954 the German government issued a stamp bearing her picture in her honor as part of a series of stamps paying tribute to "helpers of humanity." Interest in "Anna O." remains high and fourteen interpretations of her case can be found in Rosenbaum and Muroff (1984).

The Development of Free Association.   After spending about six months studying with Charcot in Paris, Freud returned to Vienna and his association with Breuer. Freud tried hypnosis for awhile but was not impressed with the results. Freud eventually gave up hypnosis because he found that not all his patients could be hypnotized. One of his patients, Frau Emmy Von N., became furious with him over his constant interruptions while trying to hypnotize her. She expressed the desire simply to be allowed to speak her mind without being interrupted.

Next, Freud tried hand pressure, a technique that he had learned from Bernheim, instead of hypnosis. He would place his hand on his patients' foreheads and instruct them to begin talking when he released the pressure. Although this technique was somewhat successful, he eventually abandoned it and settled on **free association,** which he called "the fundamental rule of psychoanalysis."

All of Freud's experiences with hypnosis and hand pressure and his recollection of an essay by Ludwig Borne, which had been given to him when he was fourteen, gradually evolved into the technique of free association. The following quotation from Borne's essay entitled, "The Art of Becoming an Original Writer in Three Days," contains the seeds of what later became the technique of free association.

Take a few sheets of paper and for three days on end write down, without fabrication or hypocrisy, everything that comes into your head. Write down what you think of yourself, of your wife, of the Turkish War, of Goethe, of Fonk's trial, of the Last Judgment, of your superiors—and when three days have passed you will be quite out of your sense with astonishment at the new and unheard-of thoughts you have had. (Freud 1920b/1955, 265)

Breuer and Freud worked on several cases of hysteria and in 1895 published the book *Studies on Hysteria,* which is usually considered the beginning of the psychoanalytic movement. Although their book is now regarded as having monumental significance, it then was met with negative reviews, and it took thirteen years to sell 626 copies. Breuer and Freud, who had been extremely close friends, soon parted company because of Freud's insistence that sexual conflicts were the cause of hysteria.

Freud began his highly influential self-analysis in 1897. He began this self-analysis for both theoretical and personal reasons; for example, he had a dread of railroad travel and was preoccupied by thoughts of his own death. The main vehicle in his self-analysis was the interpretation of his own dreams. This analysis finally resulted in what many consider Freud's greatest work, *The Interpretation of Dreams,* published in 1900. As with his earlier book, written with Breuer, this one also met with considerable criticism, and it was eight years before 600 copies were sold, for which Freud received the equivalent of $209. Eventually, however, the importance of the book was realized, and it was translated and published throughout the world.

It was after the publication of *The Interpretation of Dreams* that the psychoanalytic movement began to gain momentum. International recognition finally came when Freud and a few of his close followers were invited by G. Stanley Hall to give a series of lectures in America at Clark University in 1909. Although Freud did not care much for America and never returned, he looked on his visit to Clark University as highly significant in the development of the psychoanalytic movement.

In 1923, it was discovered that Freud had cancer of the mouth, which has been linked to his smoking twenty cigars a day, a habit that he did not abandon even after his cancer was detected. From 1923 to his death in 1939, he underwent thirty-three operations. Although in constant pain because of his refusal to accept pain-reducing drugs, his mind remained alert, and he worked on his theory until the end of his life.

When the Nazis came to power in 1933, they publicly burned Freud's books in Berlin as a Nazi spokesman shouted, "Against the soul-destroying overestimation of the sex life—and on behalf of the nobility of the human soul—I offer to the flames the writings of one Sigmund Freud!" (Schur 1972, 446). Freud resisted leaving Vienna even after it was invaded in 1938. Finally, after his daughter Anna had been arrested and her house repeatedly overrun by gangs of Nazis, he agreed to go to London. Four of his sisters were later killed by the Nazis in Austria. Freud died in London, on 23 September 1939.

The Instincts and Their Characteristics

For Freud, all aspects of the human personality are derived from biologic instincts. This point cannot be stressed too much. No matter how lofty the thought or the accomplishment, it ultimately relates to the satisfaction of a physiological need.

Freud's theory is a hedonistic one, in that it assumes that humans, like other animals, continually seek pleasure and avoid pain. When all the bodily needs are satisfied, one experiences pleasure; when one or more needs are not satisfied, one experiences discomfort. The main motive for humans, then, is to obtain the steady state that one experiences when all of one's biologic needs are satisfied.

An **instinct** has four characteristics: (1) a *source*, which is a bodily deficiency of some kind; (2) an *aim*, which is to remove the bodily deficiency, thereby re-establishing an internal balance; (3) an *object*, which is those experiences or objects that reduce or remove the bodily deficiency; and (4) an *impetus*, which is determined by the magnitude of the bodily deficiency. For example, a person experiencing the hunger instinct will need food (source), will want to eliminate the need for food (aim), and will seek and ingest food (object). The intensity with which these activities occur will depend on how long the person has gone without food (impetus).

Life and Death Instincts. All the instincts associated with the preservation of life are called the *life instincts*, and the psychic energy associated with them collectively is called the **libido.** In Freud's earlier writings, he equated libido with sexual energy but in light of increased evidence to the contrary and because of severe criticism from even his closest colleagues, he expanded the notion to include the energy associated with all of the life instincts including sex, hunger, and thirst. Freud's final position was that libidinal energy is expended to prolong life. Freud also referred to the life instincts collectively as **eros.**

The death instinct, named **thanatos,** stimulates a person to return to the inorganic state that preceded life. Death is the ultimate steady state, because there is no longer the struggle to satisfy biologic needs. Quoting Schopenhauer, Freud claimed that "the aim of all life is death" (1920a/1955, 38). The most important derivative of the death instinct, or the death wish as it is sometimes called, is aggression, which, according to Freud, is the need for self-destruction turned outward to objects other than the self. Cruelty, suicide, murder, as well as aggression, were thought by Freud to derive from the death instinct. Even though Freud never developed thanatos as fully as eros, it was nonetheless an important part of his theory.

Divisions of the Mind

The Id

The mature adult mind has three divisions: an **id,** an **ego,** and a **superego.** At birth, however, the entire mind consists of only the id (from the German *das es,* meaning "the it"). The id consists of pure, unadulterated, instinctual energy and exists completely on the unconscious level. The id cannot tolerate the tension associated with a bodily need and therefore demands the immediate removal of that tension. In other words, the id demands immediate gratification of bodily needs and is said to be governed by the **pleasure principle.**

The id has two means of satisfying bodily needs, **reflex action** and **wish fulfillment.** Reflex action is responding automatically to a source of irritation. For example, an infant may sneeze in response to an irritant in the nose or reflexively move a confined limb, thereby freeing it. In both cases, reflex action is effective in reducing tension. Coughing and blinking would also be examples of reflex action.

Wish fulfillment is more complicated. In addition to the characteristics of instincts described earlier, instincts can be considered mental representations of physiological needs. It is within the id and via the concept of instinct that Freud comes to grips with the mind-body question. The mind-body question asks how physiological events and psychological events are related to each other. It is a question to which every theory with a cognitive component eventually must address itself.

Freud's answer to the mind-body question was as follows. A biologic deficiency (a need) triggers in the id an attempt to reduce the tension associated with that need by imagining an object or event that will satisfy the need. For example, the need for food will automatically trigger in the id a food-related image, which has the effect of temporarily reducing the tension associated with the need for food; this is called wish fulfillment. At this point, Freud appears to become quite mystical. Because the id is entirely unconscious, what images does it conjure up in response to the various needs? Certainly, it cannot conjure up a hamburger in response to the hunger drive, because it never experienced a hamburger or anything else that is directly related to the reduction of the hunger drive. The alternative seems to be that the id has available to it the inherited residuals of experience from preceding generations. If so, it has available to it the images of things that consistently satisfied the needs of humans through many past generations. It is the latter view that Freud accepted and in so doing he embraced Lamarck's notion of the **inheritance of acquired characteristics** about which we will say more later. Hall describes Freud's belief as follows.

> Freud speaks of the id as being the true psychic reality. By this he means the id is the primary subjective reality, the inner world that exists before the individual has had experience of the external world. Not only are the instincts and reflexes inborn, but the images that are produced by tension states may also be innate. This means that a hungry baby can have an image of food without having to learn to associate food with hunger. Freud believed that experiences that are repeated with great frequency and intensity in many individuals of successive generations become permanent deposits in the id. (1954, 26–27)

In any case, wish fulfillment can never really satisfy a bodily need except on a temporary basis. Another component of the personality must develop to make real satisfaction possible and that component is the ego. As we have seen, the id attempts to reduce needs through hallucinations (mental pictures of objects that could satisfy a need). These are called the **primary processes.** The primary process of the id, however, is ineffective in ultimately alleviating the need. The id cannot distinguish between its images and external reality. In fact, for the id, its images are the only reality.

The Ego

Eventually, the ego (from the German *das ich*, meaning "the I") develops and attempts to match the images of the id with objects and events in the real world. This matching process was called **identification** by Freud. The ego is governed by the **reality principle** and operates in the service of the id. In other words, the ego comes into existence to bring the person into contact with experiences that will truly satisfy his or her needs. When the person is hungry, the ego finds food; when the person is sexually aroused, the ego finds appropriate sexual objects; and when the person is thirsty, the ego finds liquid. The ego goes through the process of **reality testing** to find appropriate objects. Because the ego is aware of both the images of the id and external reality, it operates on both the conscious and unconscious level. The realistic efforts of the ego that bring about true biologic satisfaction are called **secondary processes,** which are contrasted with the ineffective primary processes of the id. The relationship between the id and the ego is summarized in the following diagram:

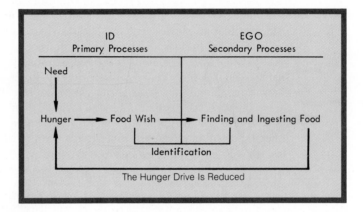

The Superego

If the only two components of the personality were the id and the ego, we would have a hedonistic animalistic person who, when in a need state, would seek immediate gratification of needs (id) from appropriate environmental objects (ego). The superego, a third component of the personality, makes this process much more complicated, however. The superego (from the German *das überich*, meaning "the over I") is the moral arm of the personality. It develops from the internalized patterns of reward and punishment that the young child experiences. That is, depending on the values of the parents, certain things the child does or says are rewarded and thereby encouraged; other things the child does or says will be punished and thereby discouraged. Those experiences that bring reward and punishment are gradually internalized, and the superego is said to be fully developed when self-control replaces environmental or parental control.

The fully developed superego has two subdivisions. The **conscience** is the internalized experiences for which the child had been consistently punished. Engaging in these behaviors now, or even thinking about engaging in them, makes the child feel guilty or "naughty." The second subdivision of the superego is the **ego ideal,** which is the internalized experiences for which the child had been consistently rewarded. Engaging in these behaviors now, or even thinking about engaging in them, makes the child feel successful or proud.

The superego constantly strives for perfection and is, therefore, as unrealistic as the id. Any experience that violates the internalized values of the child is not tolerated by the superego. So now, the job of the ego becomes much more complicated. Not only must the ego find objects and events that satisfy the needs of the id, but it also must find objects and events that do not violate the values of the superego. If, for example, the need to urinate arises while one is on a city bus, the id would demand immediate gratification through urination. The ego would allow this to happen by causing, in the case of a boy, the pants to be unzipped and so on. Urinating on a city bus, however, would in all likelihood violate an internalized value of the superego and considerable guilt or anxiety would be experienced as the result of this behavior. The ego, aware of both the needs of the id and of the superego, would probably, in this case, cause the person to get off the bus at the next stop and enter a service station washroom in which urination would satisfy all the components of the personality. It is no wonder the ego is called the executive of the personality.

Cathexis and Anticathexis

Freud's most influential teacher was the renowned physiologist Ernst Brücke (1819–92) who along with Hermann Von Helmholtz (1821–94) and a few other physiologists had succeeded in revolutionizing the field of physiology. The revolution consisted of purging physiology of all subjective, nonscientific concepts and terminology. Their goal was to explain all physiological events in terms of known, measurable, verifiable physical events. That is, living systems were viewed as dynamic energy systems that obey the laws of the physical universe. It was in this "Helmholtz school of medicine" that Freud received his early training; this training had a strong and lasting influence on him.

One Helmholtzian concept that Freud adopted was the **principle of conservation of energy.** This principle states that within a system energy is never created or lost but only rearranged or transformed from one place or form to another. The principle did not originate with Helmholtz, but he was the first to apply it to living organisms. For example, Helmholtz demonstrated that the total energy expended by an organism equalled the amount of energy associated with the food and oxygen it consumed.

Freud took the principle of conservation of energy and applied it to the human mind. According to Freud, each person is born with more or less the same amount of **psychic energy** and that amount remains more or less the same from birth to death. This energy, however, can be transformed and rearranged, and it is how the energy is distributed at any given time that determines a person's personality characteristics.

Freud used the term **cathexis** (from the Greek *kathexo*, meaning to occupy) to describe the investment of psychic energy in the thoughts of objects or processes that will satisfy a need. The energy itself never leaves the body, but if considerable energy is invested in the image of an object, an intense longing occurs for it in the form of thoughts, images, and fantasies. These thoughts and feelings continue until the need is satisfied at which point the energy dissipates and is available for other cathexes. Again, if only the id and the ego existed, humans would be animalistic. That is, needs would arise, an image (wish) of an object that would satisfy that need would be formed, and that wish would be endowed with energy, thereby creating a tension that continues until the need is satisfied. There would be no regard for other people and no differentiation between acceptable and unacceptable objects with which to satisfy needs. As we have seen, however, with the development of the superego comes the need to inhibit certain primitive desires. This requires the expenditure of energy to prevent unacceptable cathexes. Freud called the energy expended to prevent undesirable cathexes an **anticathexis.** Because the emergence of an unacceptable cathexis would cause anxiety, the ego and the superego often team up to create an anticathexis powerful enough to inhibit the strong primitive cathexes of the id. In such cases, the original need does not disappear. Instead, the original cathexis is displaced to other, safer objects. Cathexis, anticathexis, and **displacement** can be exemplified as follows.

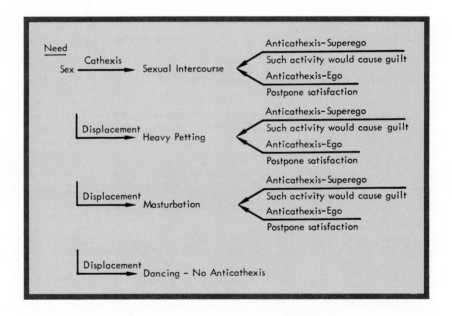

Notice that through the series of displacements, the source, aim, and impetus of the instinct remained the same; only the object changed. It should also be realized that anticathexes require the expenditure of some of the finite amount of psychic energy that one has available. This means that if one's superego is overly restrictive it may require too much of the psychic energy available, and normal cognitive functioning may be impaired.

Anxiety

According to Freud, the most overwhelming experience of anxiety humans have is when we are separated from our mother at birth. Freud called this experience the *birth trauma,* because we suddenly go from an environment of complete security and satisfaction to one in which the satisfaction of our needs is far less predictable. The feeling of helplessness following birth is, according to Freud, the basis of all subsequent feelings of anxiety.

The function of anxiety is to warn us that if we continue thinking or behaving in a certain way, we will be in danger. Because anxiety is not pleasant, we will do what is necessary to reduce it. That is, we will tend to terminate those thoughts or actions that cause anxiety. Freud distinguished three kinds of anxiety: **Reality anxiety,** which is caused by real, objective sources of danger in the environment and is the easiest kind of anxiety to reduce, because doing so solves problems objectively, such as leaving a building that is on fire. **Neurotic anxiety** is the fear that the impulses of the id will overwhelm the ego and cause the person to do something for which he or she will be punished. Examples would include becoming overly aggressive or giving in to one's sexual desires. Generally, this fear is one of becoming animal-like. **Moral anxiety** is fear that the person will do something contrary to the superego and thus experience guilt. For example, if one has learned that being honest is good, then even thinking of being dishonest would cause moral anxiety. Thus, anxiety controls our behavior by causing us to avoid threatening experiences in the environment, to inhibit the impulses of the id, and to act in accordance with our internalized values.

One of the biggest jobs the ego has is to avoid or reduce anxiety. In addition to anticathexis, the ego has several other processes available to it for use in its battle against anxiety; these processes are referred to collectively as the ego-defense mechanisms.

Ego-Defense Mechanisms

If normal, rational approaches of the ego to the reduction or removal of anxiety are ineffective, the ego may revert to irrational methods called **ego-defense mechanisms.** All ego-defense mechanisms have two things in common: (1) They are unconscious; that is, the person is always unaware that he or she is using them, and (2) they falsify or distort reality. Freud's daughter Anna (1936) was mainly responsible for elaborating the ego's mechanisms of defense, and we will consider several of them.

Repression.   This is the most basic defense mechanism because for any of the other defense mechanisms to occur, **repression** must occur first. Repression is the mechanism by which the ego prevents anxiety-provoking thoughts from being entertained on the conscious level. These thoughts can be either those innately part of the id, in which case their repression is referred to as **primal repression,** or they can be memories of painful experiences from one's lifetime, in which case their repression is referred to as **repression proper.** In either case, the ego keeps the potentially anxiety-producing thought in the unconscious with an anticathexis whenever it threatens to reach consciousness. It is important to realize what Freud considered to be innately part of the id. The primary drives that we share with other animals are inherited as part of the id, but, according to Freud, much more is contained in the id than physiological needs. As was mentioned earlier, Freud was an ardent Lamarckian. That is, he believed that we inherit memories of what our ancestors had learned from their experiences. Freud believed that our id comes well stocked with inherited prohibitions because of the punishment our ancestors received for engaging in certain behaviors. Many of the events that cause anxiety in our lifetimes do so because of the experiences of our ancestors. Thus, we can fear castration, believe we have been attacked as children by an adult, and avoid incest, not necessarily because we have learned to do so in our lifetimes, but because these thoughts are part of our **phylogenetically inherited endowment.**

Consider the following quotation.

> The experiences of the ego seem at first to be lost for inheritance; but when they have been repeated often enough and with sufficient strength in many individuals in successive generations, they transform themselves, so to say, into experiences of the id, the impressions of which are preserved by heredity. Thus in the id, which is capable of being inherited, are harboured residues of the existence of countless egos. (Freud 1923/1961, 38)

Thus, if our ancestors were consistently punished for certain activities, we are born with the tendency to inhibit those activities. The impulse to engage in those tendencies (for example, incest or violence) continues to exist in the id, however, and energy must be expended to inhibit them and related impulses. Another way to state Freud's position is to say that he believed at least part of human morality is inherited. In *Totem and Taboo* (1913/1958) Freud said, "I have supposed that the sense of guilt for an action has persisted for many thousands of years and has remained operative in generations which can have no knowledge of that action" (157–58). Freud's firm belief in Lamarck's concept of the inheritance of acquired characteristics is stated in his last book, *Moses and Monotheism* (1939/1964):

> We become aware of the probability that what may be operative in an individual's psychical life may include not only what he has experienced himself but also things that were innately present in him at his birth, elements with a phylogenetic origin—an *archaic heritage.* (98)

For Freud, the mechanism of repression was of vital importance, because repressed thoughts do not stop having an influence on our personality; they simply are not readily available in consciousness. The whole purpose of procedures such as dream analysis, free association, hypnosis, and the analysis of slips of the tongue or memory lapses (which we will discuss later) is to attempt to discover repressed thoughts so that their effects on one's personality can be determined. Not all material in the unconscious mind is repressed, however. An abundance of information exists that is simply not relevant to a person at any given moment, such as names, telephone numbers, or dates. Although the person is not momentarily aware of this kind of information, he or she can easily become aware of it when it is needed. Such information is said to exist in the **preconscious.**

Displacement.   As we have seen earlier, **displacement** is the substitution of one need satisfier for another. For example, the ego may substitute an available object for one that is not available, or it may substitute a nonanxiety-provoking object or activity for one that does cause anxiety, as in the chart in which dancing was finally substituted for other sexual activities. With displacement, what a person truly desires is repressed and is replaced by something safer.

In his book *Civilization and Its Discontents* (1930/1961), Freud indicated that civilization itself depends on the displacement of libidinal energy from one object to another. When a displacement results in something advantageous to civilization, it is called **sublimation,** such as when sexual impulses are displaced into such activities as painting, writing, building, or just plain hard work. "Sublimation of instinct," wrote Freud, "is an especially conspicuous feature of cultural development; it is what makes it possible for higher psychical activities, scientific, artistic or ideological, to play such an important part in civilized life" (1930/1961, 63).

All impulses can be displaced, even those associated with the death instinct. For example, the impulse toward self-destruction can be displaced to the destruction of others, and an aggressive impulse directed toward a threatening person like a boss or a parent can be displaced to less threatening objects such as other cars on the street while driving home, children, household pets or, quite commonly, to athletic teams opposing the home town team. These are examples of **displaced aggression,** one of Freud's most popular concepts.

Identification.   Freud used the term **identification** in two ways. The one that we have already covered is the process by which the ego attempts to match objects and events in the environment to the subjective wishes of the id. The term identification is also used to describe the tendency to increase personal feelings of worth by taking on characteristics of someone viewed as successful. A statement like "our team won" would be an example. Other examples would include a young woman having her hair styled in a way similar to a respected national leader's or a young man acting suspiciously like Robert Redford after just seeing a movie in which Mr. Redford made love to several beautiful women.

The child also identifies with his or her parents (accepts their values), thereby eliminating the punishment that comes from having contrary values. This is how the superego develops.

Projection.   This mechanism is the one by which something that is true of the person and would cause anxiety if it were recognized is repressed and seen in someone else instead. For example, the statement "I want to go to bed with him" may be true, but because it causes anxiety, it is converted into "He wants to go to bed with me." Also, the statement "I failed the test because I'm stupid," although perhaps true, is converted into statements such as "Our textbook is terrible," "She's the worst teacher I've ever had," or "The test had a number of trick items."

In general, **projection** is repressing anxiety-provoking truths about oneself and seeing them in others instead, or by excusing one's shortcomings by blaming them on environmental or life's circumstances.

Reaction Formation.   This mechanism is the one by which objectionable thoughts are repressed and their opposites expressed. For example, the person who is most attracted to sexual materials may become the town censor or the mother who really does not care much for her child may become overprotective. Freud believed that the clue in determining the difference between a **reaction formation** and true feelings is the degree to which the feelings are emphasized. People displaying a reaction formation tend to be more intense and extravagant in their emotions, as when a boyfriend insists, "I love you, I love you, I love you more than anything in the world," or when someone says, "You should meet my mother. She is absolutely wonderful beyond belief." In Shakespeare's *Hamlet*, "The lady doth protest too much," and in so doing reveals her guilt.

The following is a letter written to Masserman, a famous psychologist who was doing work in alcoholism in cats. The letter was written by an antivivisectionist who claimed to be terribly concerned with what Masserman was doing to his research animals. See if you can find evidence in the letter that its author was basically a violent person, and that his or her affiliation with the antivivisectionists was, therefore, a reaction formation.

> I read [a magazine article . . . on your work on alcoholism]. . . . I am surprised that anyone who is as well educated as you must be to hold the position that you do would stoop to such a depth as to torture helpless little cats in the pursuit of a cure for alcoholics. . . . A drunkard does not want to be cured—a drunkard is just a weak minded idiot who belongs in the gutter and should be left there. Instead of torturing helpless little cats why not torture drunks or better still exert your would-be noble effort toward getting a bill passed to *exterminate* the drunks. They are not any good to anyone or themselves and are just a drain on the public, having to pull them off the street, jail them, then they have to be fed while there and it's against the law to feed them arsenic so there they are. . . . If people are such weaklings the world is better off without them. . . .
>
> My greatest wish is that you have brought home to you a torture that will be a thousand fold greater than what you have, and are doing to the little animals. . . . If you are an example of what a noted psychiatrist should be I'm glad I am just an ordinary human being without letters after my name. I'd rather be myself with a clear conscience, *knowing that I have not hurt any living creature*, and can sleep without seeing frightened, terrified dying cats—because I know they must die after you have finished with them. No punishment is too great for you and I hope I live to read about your mangled body and long suffering before you finally die—and I'll laugh long and loud. (Masserman 1961, 35)

Rationalization. Through this mechanism, the person rationally justifies behavior or thoughts that may otherwise be anxiety provoking. The ego excuses through logic (although faulty) outcomes that would be disturbing if they were not explained in some way. The "sour grapes" **rationalization** is quite common. Aesop in 500 B.C. told of a fox who saw clusters of grapes hanging from a trellised vine. It tried everything in its power to reach them, but nothing worked. Finally, it turned away saying, "The grapes were probably sour anyhow." Minimizing something to which one has aspired but failed to obtain is a common form of rationalization. Likewise, something that at first was not overly attractive may be glorified after it is obtained. This has been called a "sweet lemon" rationalization.

Regression. With this mechanism, the person returns to an earlier stage of development when he or she experiences stress. For example, a child may revert to bed wetting or thumb sucking when a new sibling is born. We will have more to say about **regression** in our discussion of the psychosexual stages of development, to which we turn next.

The Psychosexual Stages of Development

Freud believed that every child goes through a sequence of developmental stages, and that the child's experiences during these stages determine adult personality characteristics. In fact, Freud believed that for all practical purposes, the adult personality is formed by the end of the fifth year of life.

Each stage has an **erogenous zone** associated with it, which is the greatest source of stimulation and pleasure during that particular stage of development.

To make a smooth transition from one psychosexual stage to the next, the child must be neither undergratified nor overgratified, both of which cause the child to be fixated at that stage. A **fixation** occurs when a substantial amount of psychic energy remains cathected in images of objects that can satisfy the needs corresponding to a particular stage of development. Again, a fixation can occur either because the needs corresponding to a stage are consistently frustrated (undergratified) or are satisfied too often and too easily (overgratified). An example of the latter would be an infant being breast-fed whenever it showed the least sign of hunger or discomfort. Fixation and regression go hand in hand, because, when a person regresses, he or she tends to go back to the stage at which that person had been fixated. In addition, persons who are fixated at a certain stage will as an adult, display personality characteristics corresponding to that stage. We will see examples of this next.

Oral Stage.   The **oral stage** occurs during the first year of life, and the erogenous zone during this stage is the mouth. During the early oral stage (less than eight months old) pleasure comes mainly from the mouth, lips, and tongue, through the activities of sucking and swallowing. According to Freud, an adult who is fixated at the early oral stage will engage in an abundance of oral activities such as eating, drinking, smoking, and kissing. This person also will engage in activities that are symbolically equivalent to those oral activities, such as collecting things, being a good listener (taking in knowledge), or being what is labeled a gullible person, that is, a person who "swallows" anything he or she hears. Such a person is called an **oral-incorporative character.**

In the later oral stage (from eight months to about a year), experience is concentrated on the teeth, gums, and jaws and pleasure comes from activities such as biting and devouring. An adult fixated at the late oral stage could be a fingernail biter and also would like eating. This person also would engage in activities symbolically equivalent to biting, such as sarcasm, cynicism, and ridicule. Such a person is called an **oral-sadistic character.**

Anal Stage.   The **anal stage** occurs during the second year of life, and the erogenous zone is the anus-buttocks region. It is during this stage that the child must learn to control his or her physiological processes so that they function in accordance with the demands of society. That is, the child must be toilet trained.

In the first part of the anal stage, pleasure derives from feces expulsion. Fixation at this level could result in an adult having physical problems such as a lack of sphincter control or enuresis. Symbolically, the person would be overly generous, wanting to give away everything he or she owns and would also tend to be creative. Such a person is called an **anal-expulsive character.**

In the later anal stage, pleasure comes from feces possession. Fixation here could manifest itself physically, in a problem with constipation, or, symbolically, in stinginess, parsimony, orderliness, and a tendency toward perfectionism. Such a person is called an **anal-retentive character.**

Phallic Stage. This stage occurs from about the third year of life to about the fifth year, and the erogenous zone is the genital area. This is one of the most complicated and controversial of Freud's stages. It is during this stage when our subsequent adjustments to members of the opposite sex are determined. The **phallic stage** is the scene of the Oedipus and Electra conflicts, the resolutions of which have profound influences on adult life.

The male child experiences the **Oedipus complex,** which is named after an ancient play by Sophocles entitled *Oedipus Tyrannus,* in which King Oedipus killed his father and married his mother. According to Freud, both male and female children develop strong, positive feelings toward the mother because she satisfies their needs. Likewise, both male and female children resent the father, because he is regarded as a rival for the mother's attention and affection. These feelings persist in the boy but change in the girl.

The boy begins to fear the father as the dominant rival and this fear becomes **castration anxiety.** That is, the boy develops the fear of losing his sex organs, because they are assumed to be responsible for the conflict between him and his father. According to Freud, it is not necessary for a male child to be overtly threatened with castration to develop castration anxiety. Boys may have the opportunity to observe that girls do not possess penises and assume that they once did. That is, boys may believe that girls lost their penises because their penises, like their own, were the source of trouble with their father. Also, castration anxiety could result from the phylogenetic memory of actual castrations that occurred in the distant past. In other words, according to Freud, male children could inherit castration anxiety.

> It is not a question of whether castration is really carried out; what is decisive is that the danger is one that threatens from outside and that the child believes in it. He has some ground for this, for people threaten him often enough with cutting off his penis during the phallic phase, at the time of his early masturbation, and hints at the punishment must regularly find a phylogenetic reinforcement in him. (Freud 1933/1964, 86)

No matter what its source, castration anxiety causes a repression of the sexual desire for the mother and hostility toward the father. Next, the boy identifies with his father, thereby gaining vicarious satisfaction of his sexual impulses toward his mother. In a sense, the boy becomes the father and thereby shares the mother. By identifying with his father the male child not only shares the mother, he also accepts his father's notions of right and wrong as his own, thereby completing the development of his superego. That is, his father's morality becomes his morality. This describes what was for Freud the healthy resolution of the Oedipus complex.

For the female child, the situation is more complex and more pessimistic. The female counterpart of the Oedipus complex is the **Electra complex,** named after another play by Sophocles entitled *Electra,* in which Electra causes her brother to kill her mother, who had killed Electra's father.

As we have seen, female children also start life with a strong attraction to the mother. This attraction is reduced, however, when the girl discovers that she does not possess a penis. Whereas a male child assumes that female children once had penises and had lost them, the female child assumes that all other children possess penises, but that for some reason she was deprived of one. The female child holds the mother responsible for purposely depriving her of this valued organ. The rejection of the mother is coupled with an attraction to the father, whom she knows possesses the valued organ, which she wants to share. Her positive feelings toward the father, however, are mixed with envy because he has something that she does not. She is said to have **penis envy.** Freud leaves the girl suspended between the mother and father with positive and negative feelings toward both. She is said to be sexually ambivalent. The female child leaves the phallic stage with a double approach-avoidance conflict, which can be diagrammed as follows:

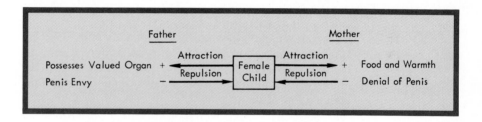

Unlike castration anxiety in boys, which is quickly repressed, Freud believed that penis envy, in one form or another, could last for years. According to Freud, the only hope for girls is eventually to have a male baby, thereby finally obtaining a penis, although only symbolically (Freud 1933/1964, 128).

Homosexuality is thought to occur if the normal identifications are reversed— for example, if the boy identifies strongly with the mother or if the girl identifies strongly with the father.

Regression to the phallic stage for the male would include displaying many of the father's characteristics and, also typically, brashness and an overconcern with masculinity and virility. Regression to the phallic stage for the girl would exemplify penis-envy-related activities. These activities could include seeking to share a penis—for example, promiscuity or seductiveness, or activities that symbolically castrate men, such as embarrassing, deceiving, or hurting them.

The first three psychosexual stages, called the *pregenital stages,* are by far the most important to personality development. As we mentioned earlier, Freud believed that the basic ingredients of the adult personality are formulated by the end of the phallic stage.

Latency Stage. The **latency stage** lasts from about the sixth year to about the twelfth year. This is a time when sexual interests are repressed and displaced to substitute activities such as learning, athletics, and peer group activities. That is, during this stage libidinal energy is sublimated.

Genital Stage. This is the final stage of development and begins at puberty. It is the time at which the person emerges from the pregenital stages as the adult he or she is destined to become. The child is sometimes transformed from a selfish, pleasure-seeking child to a realistic socialized adult with heterosexual interests leading to marriage and perhaps child rearing. If, however, the experiences during the pregenital stages cause fixations, they will manifest themselves throughout one's adult life. Only psychoanalysis could dredge up the remnants of these early experiences, which otherwise would remain repressed into the unconscious, and cause the individual to face them, thereby reducing their influence on his or her life.

In fact, the process of psychoanalysis can be viewed as a means of discovering repressed thoughts that are having a negative influence on one's life. The question is, how does one gain access to thoughts that have been actively held in the unconscious mind all one's life? It is to this question that we turn next.

Tapping the Unconscious Mind

If repressed anxiety-provoking thoughts are effectively anticathected by the ego or superego, how can we come to know what they are? To say the least, it is not easy, but it is the business of psychoanalysis to attempt to do so. Freud employed several methods of determining the contents of the unconscious mind, and we will examine a few of them.

Free Association.   Earlier in this chapter we showed how the technique of free association gradually evolved. To stimulate free association (the "Fundamental Rule of Psychoanalysis"), Freud instructed his patients as follows:

> You will notice that as you relate things various thoughts will occur to you which you would like to put aside on the ground of certain criticisms and objections. You will be tempted to say to yourself that this or that is irrelevant here, or is quite unimportant, or nonsensical, so that there is no need to say it. You must never give in to these criticisms, but must say it in spite of them—indeed, you must say it precisely *because* you feel an aversion to doing so. . . . Finally, never forget that you have promised to be absolutely honest, and never leave anything out because, for some reason or other, it is unpleasant to tell it. (1913/1958, 134–35)

The idea was that even in conscious expressions, there are hints as to the contents of the unconscious mind that the trained observer could detect. What is not said is as important as, if not more important than, what is said. Topics to which patients offer strong **resistance** provide the analyst with useful hints to problem areas in the unconscious mind. One reason that Freud abandoned hypnosis is because a hypnotized patient does not display revealing resistances. During the course of free association resistance can take the form of telling carefully structured stories, long periods of silence, refusing to say something considered (by the patient) silly or embarrassing, avoiding certain topics, the tendency to report events in a highly intellectual, unemotional manner, "forgetting" important insights that had been gained from previous therapeutic sessions, and hiding important thoughts behind excessive emotion. In addition, if the therapeutic process appears dangerously close to revealing anxiety-provoking material, the patient may be late for an appointment or not show up at all.

Revealing the contents of the unconscious mind is difficult and requires a great deal of time. Typically a patient undergoing psychoanalysis is in therapy for four to six fifty-minute sessions per week for several years. To facilitate the flow of ideas Freud had his patients lie on a couch in a dim room while he sat in back out of the patient's view. Freud remained out of sight for two reasons: (1) he did not want his gestures and expressions to influence the patient's thoughts, and (2) he could not stand being stared at for hours on end.

It should be realized that although Freud referred to his major therapeutic technique as "free association," he believed the reported associations to be anything but "free" in the sense of being random or accidental. Rather the patient's associations reflect the complex ways that unacceptable impulses are repressed, displaced, and in other ways disguised. Thus, a patient's associations may seem free but to the trained analyst, they reflect the complex interactions between the conscious and unconscious levels of the mind.

Dream Analysis. Freud considered his book, *The Interpretation of Dreams* (1900/1953) to be his most important contribution and it was this book that finally brought Freud the professional recognition that he had been seeking. Freud believed that it was in dreams that the contents of the unconscious were most available, still hidden, or distorted but available. Indeed, Freud thought that "The interpretation of dreams is the royal road to knowledge of the unconscious activities of the mind" (1900/1953, 608).

It is interesting to note that the notion of the Oedipal complex was arrived at when Freud began his own dream analysis. Freud became extremely depressed when his father died, although his father had been ill, and his death was imminent. Freud was confused by his depression until the explanation came to him in a dream. After carefully analyzing the symbols contained in one of his dreams, Freud concluded that his extreme reaction to his father's death was explained by the fact that unconsciously he wanted his father to die, and therefore he felt guilty. Further analysis showed that Freud had sexual desires for his mother and viewed his father as a competitor for his mother's affection. Freud felt that such impulses (lust for the mother and wanting the father dead) were universal among boys—thus the birth of the Oedipal conflict.

According to Freud, a dream is caused when the events of the day activate unacceptable impulses in the unconscious mind, causing them to seek conscious expression. At night, as the person sleeps, these impulses continue to seek conscious expression, but the ego realizes that if the contents of a dream are too threatening, they will cause the dreamer to awake prematurely. The ego, therefore, censors the impulses by driving them back into the unconscious. If these unacceptable impulses are ever to be consciously recognized they must be at least partially camouflaged. Freud referred to the various mechanisms that make impulses more acceptable by distorting their true meaning collectively as **dream work.** The two most important kinds of dream work are condensation and displacement.

Condensation occurs when a dream element represents several ideas at the same time. For example, one person in a dream can represent several people in the dreamer's waking life. **Displacement** occurs when an unacceptable dream-thought is replaced by a thought that is symbolically equivalent but is acceptable, such as when penises become objects such as baseball bats or flagpoles; breasts become mountains, balloons, or cantaloupes; and sexual intercourse becomes dancing or horseback riding, to give but a few examples. Freud believed that most of the symbols that occur in a particular person's dream are derived from the events in that person's life. Freud did believe, however, that some dream symbols were universal. For example, kings and queens symbolize mothers and fathers; boxes, chests, and cupboards symbolize the womb; walking up or down staircases, ladders, or steps symbolize sexual intercourse; haircutting, baldness, and decapitation symbolize castration; small animals symbolize children; and long, stiff objects symbolize the penis. The symbols that occur in a person's dream can come from events in the person's waking life, from his or her childhood, or from the phylogenetic heritage of the human species (again we see Freud embracing Lamarck's notion of the inheritance of acquired characteristics).

The dream work creates several disjointed symbols that have little meaning to the dreamer, and thus they are allowed past the censor and enter consciousness. The dream symbols no longer cause anxiety because they represent unacceptable wishes, but they do cause anxiety for another reason. Because the rational (secondary) processes of the ego seek to interact with the physical world in a logical, intelligible manner, the meaningless symbols attempting to enter consciousness after being acted on by the dream work cannot be tolerated. To make the material acceptable, the ego engages in what Freud called **secondary revision** (sometimes called secondary elaboration). That is, the ego synthesizes the symbols in some coherent fashion. It is this secondary revision that we recall as a dream. When we recall a dream, we describe its **manifest content** or about what it appeared to be. More important is the dream's **latent content,** which consists of the repressed thoughts that were seeking expression.

Dream work and secondary revision act on a dream to make its content more acceptable but still the latent meaning is always there for the trained observer to discover. Because dreams always contain at least some threatening material, the patient and therapist must work quickly before their contents are repressed again. The nature of dreams and the process of repression explain why the memory of dreams is so short-lived.

Everyday Life. In 1901, Freud wrote a book entitled *The Psychopathology of Everyday Life,* in which he gave numerous examples of how repressed thoughts manifest themselves in the course of everyday living. Being a determinist, Freud believed that all human behavior had a cause, that nothing happened simply by chance—not even "accidents." Freud believed that little "mistakes" such as temporary lapses of memory provided information about the unconscious mind. For example, one may forget a potentially painful visit to the dentist or psychoanalyst. One may forget a date altogether or show up on Saturday instead of on Friday, when the date actually was. One may stop at a green light on the way to his or her mother-in-law's house.

Slips of the tongue, which have come to be known as **Freudian slips,** are also thought to reveal unconscious motives. Legend has it that once Freud was introduced as Dr. Sigmund Fraud. Zimbardo and Ruch (1977, 416) report that a radio announcer who was reading a commercial for Barbara Ann Bread instead of saying "Barbara Ann for the best bread" read "Barbara Ann for the breast in bed."

Even actual accidents were thought by Freud to have meaning. After all, an automobile accident is a socially acceptable way of not getting somewhere. The main point here is that just because a thought is repressed does not mean that it goes away; it is always there striving for expression, and these manifestations in everyday life are another way of getting a glimpse into the unconscious.

Humor.   According to Freud, **humor** allows the expression of repressed thoughts in a socially approved manner. In his book *Jokes and Their Relation to the Unconscious* (1905), Freud indicated that through humor a person can express aggressiveness (for example, practical jokes) or sexual desires without the fear of retaliation by either the ego or the superego. Jokes, then, are very much like dreams in that both allow the compromise expression of unacceptable impulses, and both employ condensation, displacement, and symbolization. The purpose of both jokes and dreams is to satisfy unacceptable impulses indirectly that would be shocking if expressed directly. A joke that is too blatant fails to be humorous just as a nightmare fails to preserve the sleep of the dreamer. In both cases the impulses involved were not disguised enough. Also jokes, like dreams, are usually forgotten quickly, for they too deal with "dangerous" material. In fact, for a joke to be "funny," it *must* contain anxiety-provoking material. According to Freud, we laugh only at jokes that bother us. An examination of American humor shows sex, elimination, and death to be favorite topics and this would indicate to a Freudian that they contain an abundance of repressed thoughts. In fact, say the Freudians, one way to discover what has been repressed in a person's unconscious mind is to examine what he or she finds humorous.

Freud's View of Religion

When our ancestors were children they turned to their fathers for protection and guidance. Fathers tended to be revered, feared, and relied on. According to Freud, it is understandable that our ancestors would have created a God with the same characteristics as real fathers. According to Freud, these infantile conceptions of the father were generalized to an image of a deity who had to be blindly obeyed, just like a real father. This God protects his children from natural disasters such as earthquakes, storms, floods, volcanic eruptions, and disease. God, and the religions based on his existence, protect humans from feeling helpless and from feeling confused in light of the many apparent contradictions in life. Typically, religions teach that life continues after death; life after death can be perfect even if life on earth was not; good persons will eventually be rewarded and bad ones punished; the difficulties one may experience in his or her life serve a higher purpose, and therefore no need for despair exists; and, in general, the world is being governed by a providence of superior wisdom and infinite goodness who relates to humans with the intimacy of a loving father. Religions also teach that it is God's will that humans inhibit their sexual and aggressive tendencies to live in harmony with their fellow humans. About the role that religion has played, and is playing, in the lives of so many humans, Freud says: "The whole thing is so patently infantile, so foreign to reality, that to anyone with a friendly attitude to humanity it is painful to think that the great majority of mortals will never be able to rise above this view of life" (1930/1961, 21).

Perhaps, according to Freud, the uneducated masses will always need the illusions of religion to cause them to restrain their passions, but educated, intelligent persons should live their lives according to scientific facts, not illusions. It is time, says Freud, to admit that our ancestors were wrong about religion; miracles never existed; natural disasters kill both believers and nonbelievers; no life after death occurs; and the course of human history is explained by evolutionary principles rather than the unfolding of a divine plan. Furthermore, although civilization does require rules, regulations, and inhibitions these should be justified on rational grounds rather than claiming that they are the will of a deity. In other words, humans should be shown how various sanctions ultimately work to their own self-interests and, for that reason, should strive to preserve them.

Freud hoped that religion would eventually be replaced by rational, scientific principles. Just as Freud took no pain-killing drugs during his sixteen-year bout with cancer, he believed that humans could and should confront reality without the aid of illusions. In his book *The Future of an Illusion* (1927/1961) Freud places his faith in science:

> No belittlement of science can in any way alter the fact that it is attempting to take account of our dependence on the real external world, while religion is an illusion and it derives its strength from its readiness to fit in with our instinctual wishful impulses. . . . Our science is no illusion. But an illusion it would be to suppose that what science cannot give us we can get elsewhere. (56)

Freud's View of Human Nature

To Freud, humans were mainly biologic organisms whose master motive was the satisfaction of bodily needs. Cultural achievements in the sciences, arts, and religion were regarded mainly as displacements away from the more direct (and natural) ways of satisfying our biologic needs in general and our sexual needs in particular. Freud looked at humans as hedonistic creatures driven by the same impulses that drive "lower" animals. Religion and civilization developed either because of our fear of the unknown, or because we needed protection against our own inborn aggressive tendencies.

Freud seemed to grow more pessimistic with age, a fact that many attribute to his worsening cancer of the mouth and throat. In 1930, in his book *Civilization and Its Discontents* (1930), he reacted to the statement "Thou shalt love thy neighbor as thyself," as follows:

> What is the point of a precept enunciated with so much solemnity if its fulfillment cannot be recommended as reasonable? . . . Not merely is this stranger in general unworthy of my love; I must honestly confess that he has more claim to my hostility and even my hatred. He seems not to have the least trace of love for me and shows me not the slightest consideration. If it will do him any good he has no hesitation in injuring me, nor does he ask himself whether the amount of advantage he gains bears any proportion to the extent of the harm he does to me. Indeed, he need not even obtain an advantage; if he can satisfy any sort of desire by it, he thinks nothing of jeering at me, insulting me, slandering me and showing his superior power; and the more secure he feels and the more helpless I am, the more certainly I can expect him to behave like this to me. . . . Indeed, if this grandiose

commandment had run "Love thy neighbour as thy neighbour loves thee," I should not take exception to it. . . .

The element of truth behind all this, which people are so ready to disavow, is that men are not gentle creatures who want to be loved, and who at the most can defend themselves if they are attacked; they are, on the contrary, creatures among whose instinctual endowments is to be reckoned a powerful share of aggressiveness. As a result, their neighbour is for them not only a potential helper or sexual object, but also someone who tempts them to satisfy their aggressiveness on him, to exploit his capacity for work without compensation, to use him sexually without his consent, to seize his possessions, to humiliate him, to cause him pain, to torture and to kill him. *Homo homini lupus* [Man is a wolf to man]. (1930/1961, 110–11).

Although pessimistic, Freud believed that humans could, and should, live more rational lives, and the information that his theory provided could help them do so. To live rationally one must come to understand the workings of his or her own mind. Freud (1917/1955) said:

The news that reaches your consciousness is incomplete and often not to be relied on. . . . Even if you are not ill, who can tell all that is stirring in your mind of which you know nothing or are falsely informed? You behave like an absolute ruler who is content with the information supplied him by his highest officials and never goes among the people to hear their voice. Turn your eyes inward, look into your own depths, learn first to know yourself! (143)

Recent Modifications of the Freudian Legend

Few would doubt that Freud was one of the most influential figures in human history. Recently, however, several researchers have provided information that requires rather substantial changes in the traditional view of Freud and his ideas.

Freud's Revision of His Seduction Theory. In April 1896, Freud delivered a paper entitled "The Aetiology of Hysteria" in which he declared that his observations led him to conclude that hysteria is caused by a sexual seduction that had been experienced by the patient in childhood, and that the seducer was an adult, typically a parent. Freud's address to his colleagues was met with total silence and he was urged not to publish his findings, because doing so would damage his professional reputation beyond repair. Despite the warnings, however, Freud published his article (1896), and he continued to experience professional, emotional, and intellectual isolation. Even Wilheim Fliess (1858–1928), Freud's closest friend at the time, was not supportive of Freud's seduction theory. In September 1897, Freud abandoned his seduction theory for reasons that are still not entirely clear. Freud's seduction theory was never scientifically refuted nor was there much discussion about its merits; it was met mainly with disgust and general disapproval. In any case, Freud acknowledged that he had made a mistake in believing his patients that a *real* seduction had occurred in their childhoods. His revised position was that the seductions were most often imaginary. Freud later claimed that this change from real to imagined seductions marked the real beginning of psychoanalysis as a science, therapy, and profession.

Jeffrey Masson in his book *The Assault on Truth: Freud's Suppression of the Seduction Theory* (1984) explores the many reasons that Freud revised his theory and concludes he did so mainly because he lacked personal courage, not for any clinical or theoretical reasons. Masson, the former projects director of the Sigmund Freud Archives, bases his conclusion on several previously unpublished or newly discovered letters and other documents. Masson, himself a psychoanalyst, also concludes that psychoanalysis would be better off today had Freud not revised his seduction theory.

> By shifting the emphasis from an actual world of sadness, misery, and cruelty to an internal stage on which actors performed invented dramas for an invisible audience of their own creation, Freud began a trend away from the real world that, it seems to me, is at the root of the present day sterility of psychoanalysis and psychiatry throughout the world. (144)

After Fliess, *Sandor Ferenczi* (1873–1933) was Freud's closest analytic friend. At first, Ferenczi accepted the validity of Freud's revised seduction theory, but his clinical practice caused Ferenczi to go back to the original seduction theory. That is, the seductions reported by patients are more often real than fantasized. In 1932 Ferenczi said:

> Above all, my previously communicated assumption, that trauma, specifically sexual trauma, cannot be stressed enough as a pathogenic agent, was confirmed anew. Even children of respected, high-minded puritanical families fall victim to real rape much more frequently than one had dared to suspect. Either the parents themselves seek substitution for their lack of [sexual] satisfaction in this pathological manner, or else trusted persons such as relatives (uncles, aunts, grandparents), tutors, servants, abuse the ignorance and innocence of children. The obvious objection that we are dealing with sexual fantasies of the child himself, that is, with hysterical lies, unfortunately is weakened by the multitude of confessions of this kind, on the part of patients in analysis, to assaults on children. (Quoted in Masson 1984, 148)

In essence, Ferenczi was repeating what Freud had said in 1896 when he proposed his seduction theory. Masson (1984) concludes "It is as if Ferenczi were demonstrating to the analytic world how psychoanalysis could have developed had Freud not abandoned the seduction hypothesis" (150).

Correcting the Freudian Myths. Freud and his followers have tended to paint Freud as a lonely, heroic figure who suffered discrimination because he was a Jew and because of the difficulty others had in accepting his bold, creative, original ideas. Henri Ellenberger has done much to demythologize the Freudian legend. According to Ellenberger (1970) the Freudian legend has two main features.

> The first is the theme of the solitary hero struggling against a host of enemies, suffering "the slings and arrows of outrageous fortune" but triumphing in the end. The legend considerably exaggerates the extent and role of anti-Semitism, of the hostility of the academic world, and of alleged Victorian prejudices. The second

feature of the Freudian legend is the blotting out of the greatest part of the scientific and cultural context in which psychoanalysis developed, hence the theme of the absolute originality of the achievements, in which the hero is credited with the achievements of his predecessors, associates, disciples, rivals, and contemporaries. (547)

According to Ellenberger a careful reading of the facts indicates that Freud's career was only slightly hampered by anti-Semitism; that Freud experienced no more than the normal amount of hostility from his fellow physicians and not nearly as much as several more prominent physicians did; and that most of Freud's ideas concerning dreams, the unconscious mind, and sexual pathology were not original. Ellenberger (1970) says "Much of what is credited to Freud was diffuse current lore, and his role was to crystallize these ideas and give them an original shape" (548).

Freud and his early followers had a low tolerance for criticism and usually attributed it to a lack of understanding, resistance, or bigotry. Frank Sulloway in his book *Freud, Biologist of the Mind: Beyond the Psychoanalytic Legend* (1979), however, concludes that most of the criticisms directed at psychoanalysis as it began to become popular were rational and justified. Sulloway (1979) summarizes those criticisms:

> In addition to the criticisms that had already been raised before Freud acquired a substantial following, common objections against psychoanalysis now began to include: (1) that psychoanalysts were continually introducing their assertions with the statement, "We know from psychoanalytic experience that . . . ," and then leaving the burden of proof to others; (2) that Freud's disciples refused to listen to opinions that did not coincide with their own; (3) that they never published statistics on the success of their method; (4) that they persisted in claiming that only those who had used the psychoanalytic method had the right to challenge Freud; (5) that they saw all criticism as a form of "neurotic resistance"; (6) that psychoanalysts tended to ignore all work that had been done before them and then proceeded to make unwarranted claims about their own originality; (7) that they frequently addressed themselves to the wider lay audience as if their theories were already a proven fact, thus making their opponents seem narrow-minded and ignorant; (8) that so-called wild analysts, or individuals without proper training, were analyzing patients in irresponsible ways; and (9) that Freud's followers were becoming a sect, with all of the prominent features of one, including a fanatical degree of faith, a special jargon, a sense of moral superiority, and a predilection for marked intolerance of opponents. In their contemporary context, such criticisms were considerably more rational and had far more merit than traditional psychoanalytic historians have been willing to admit. (460)

Evaluation

Empirical Research. The many attempts to validate Freudian ideas experimentally have produced mixed results. In his review of numerous studies, J. McVicker Hunt (1979) found support for Freud's contention that early experience is important in molding adult personality but little support for the influence of specific psychosexual stages as Freud described them. In his review, Maddi (1972) found considerable support for the various mechanisms of defense postulated by Freud, especially repression. Maddi (1972) also found evidence that boys experience more castration anxiety than do girls. Silverman (1976), Blum (1962), and Hall and Van de Castle (1965) also found more castration anxiety in boys relative to girls and the reverse for penis envy. Kline (1972) reviewed more than seven hundred studies designed to test Freudian notions and concluded that Freudian theory could not be rejected on the basis of the research designed to test it because "Too much that is distinctively Freudian has been verified [and] there are few good experiments which actually refute the theory" (350). Fisher and Greenberg (1977) reach a similar conclusion: "Scanning the spectrum of tests we have applied to Freud's theories, we are generally impressed with how often the results have borne out his expectations" (393). Also, responding to the frequently made assertion that Freudian notions are too nebulous to be tested, Fisher and Greenberg (1977) say "We have actually not been able to find a single systematic psychological theory that has been as frequently evaluated scientifically as have Freud's concepts!" (396). Masling (1983) also reports numerous experiments that verify several Freudian notions.

Criticisms. Earlier we reviewed several criticisms of psychoanalytic theory that were made in Freud's day just as his theory was gaining widespread recognition. Many current critics of Freudian theory believe that those early criticisms are still valid. In addition, say the critics, Freudian theory can be criticized for being internally inconsistent; demonstrating male chauvinism (for example, girls long to have a penis); overemphasizing sexual motivation; overemphasizing unconscious motivation, being too pessimistic about human nature (for example, humans are basically aggressive and irrational); and equating the ultimate state of happiness with the tension-free state that results when all of one's biologic needs are satisfied.

Critics also claim that, although a few Freudian concepts have been supported by empirical research, most of his more important notions remain untestable. For example, how would one design an experiment to verify whether or not the mind is a closed energy system or whether the death instinct exists? Many important aspects of Freud's theory are not formulated precisely enough to generate risky predictions. As we saw in the last chapter, if a theory does not generate risky predictions it cannot be falsified, and, therefore, according to Popper, it is not scientific. From what has preceded, then, we can conclude that a few aspects of Freud's theory are scientific (testable), but many others are not.

Contributions. Despite the many criticisms of Freud's theory, most would agree that its overall value is positive and monumental. Freud contributed to our understanding of personality by demonstrating the importance of anxiety as a determinant of human behavior; showing that physical and physiological disorders can have psychological as well as physiological origins; showing that conflicts that originate in childhood have lifelong consequences, showing the importance of childhood sexuality in personality development; showing the many ways that persons defend themselves against unbearable anxiety; showing that much "normal" behavior is determined by the same processes that determine "abnormal" behavior; showing that many human problems result from the clash between the selfish, biologic nature of humans and our need to live harmoniously with other humans in society; and developing a technique for treating persons experiencing unbearable anxiety. Freud has provided us with a general framework with which to study personality. Even though portions of Freud's theory may be incorrect or vague and difficult to test, it has raised questions that researchers have been busy attempting to answer ever since.

As we pointed out at the beginning of this chapter, few people in history have had the impact on human thought that Freud has had. No major category of human existence has been untouched by his ideas. For example, he has had a profound influence on such areas as religion, philosophy, education, literature, art, and all of the social sciences. It is true that Freud had an exciting style of writing, and that sex is an interesting topic about which to write; however, many other reasons exist for the popularity of his ideas. Hall and Lindzey summarize the reasons for Freud's influence:

> A fine literary style and an exciting subject matter are not the main reasons for the great esteem in which Freud is held. Rather it is because his ideas are challenging, because his conception of man is both broad and deep, and because his theory has relevance for our times. Freud may not have been a rigorous scientist nor a first-rate theoretician, but he was a patient, meticulous, penetrating observer and a tenacious, disciplined, courageous, original thinker. Over and above all of the other virtues of his theory stands this one—it tries to envisage a full-bodied individual living partly in a world of reality and partly in a world of make-believe, beset by conflicts and inner contradiction, yet capable of rational thought and action, moved by forces of which he has little knowledge and by aspirations which are beyond his reach, by turn confused and clearheaded, frustrated and satisfied, hopeful and despairing, selfish and altruistic, in short, a complex human being. For many people, this picture of man has an essential validity. (1978, 70)

What follows in this text can be understood mainly as a reaction to Freud. Some theories support and extend his thoughts, and others refute them, but it was Freud who was first, and that is always the most difficult to be.

Summary

Freud shocked the world by demonstrating the importance of unconscious motivation in human behavior. Although originally intending to become a professor of neurology, Freud became increasingly interested in mental problems. Freud first believed cocaine to be a "magical substance" and prescribed it freely; when it was found to be addictive, however, Freud's medical reputation suffered considerably. From his visit with Charcot, Freud learned that physical disorders could have psychological as well as organic origins, and therefore hysteria should be viewed as a serious, treatable disorder. From Bernheim, Freud learned that behavior can be caused by ideas of which individuals are unaware. He also learned from Bernheim that unconscious ideas can be made conscious if certain procedures are followed. Freud learned from Breuer that when a patient openly discusses his or her problems, a release of tension called catharsis often occurs. Sometimes a patient responds to a therapist as if he or she were an important person in the patient's life, and this process is called transference. Also, the therapist sometimes becomes emotionally involved with the patient and this occurrence is called countertransference. After experimenting with several therapeutic techniques, Freud arrived at free association as a major means of studying the unconscious.

According to Freud, instincts constitute the driving force behind personality. Instincts have a source, an aim, an object, and an impetus. Freud referred to the life instincts collectively as eros and to the energy associated with life instincts as libido or libidinal energy. A death instinct, sometimes called thanatos, is responsible for aggression, which Freud believed was the tendency toward self-destruction turned outward.

The adult mind is divided into the id, the ego, and the superego. The id is the part of our mind that we share with lower animals and is governed by the pleasure principle. The ego is the executive of the personality and is governed by the reality principle. The superego is the moral component of the personality and consists of the conscience and the ego ideal. When a physiological need arises, the id creates a mental image of an object that will satisfy the need. This is called wish fulfillment, which is, along with reflex action, a primary process. Because wishes cannot satisfy needs, the ego must seek out real objects in the environment that will actually satisfy the need. These problem-solving skills of the ego are called secondary processes.

The investment of psychic energy in the image of an object that will satisfy a need is called cathexis. If a desired object conflicts with the values of the superego, anxiety will be experienced, the ego will resist the id's attempt to invest energy in its image, and an anticathexis will be said to have occurred. When an anticathexis occurs, the person will typically displace his or her desire to a substitute goal that does not cause anxiety. Freud discussed three kinds of anxiety: Reality anxiety, which is the fear of actual dangers in the environment; neurotic anxiety, which is the fear of being overwhelmed by one's id; and moral anxiety, which is experienced when a value internalized into the superego has been violated.

The ego-defense mechanisms are unconscious processes that reduce anxiety by distorting or falsifying reality. Repression is the most basic ego-defense mechanism because all the other ego-defense mechanisms first employ repression. Repression keeps anxiety-provoking thoughts in the unconscious mind and thus out of a person's awareness. Displacement is substituting a nonanxiety-provoking goal for one that does cause anxiety. If the displacement contributes positively to society, it is called sublimation. If aggression is displaced from its primary goal to a safer one or one that is socially approved, it is called displaced aggression. Identification is affiliating oneself with someone or something that will enhance one's feelings of worth. Projection involves seeing in others qualities that are true about oneself but would cause anxiety if recognized. Reaction formation is repressing anxiety-provoking impulses and exaggerating opposite impulses. Rationalization is giving "logical" explanations for behavior that would cause anxiety if it were not "explained away." Regression is returning to a stage of development where fixation had occurred when stress is encountered.

Freud believed that each child goes through certain psychosexual stages of development, and that the child's experiences during these stages determine what kind of personality he or she will possess as an adult. During each psychosexual stage an area of the body that is associated with maximum pleasure is called an erogenous zone. If, during any stage either too much or too little gratification occurs, fixation results, which means as an adult the person will possess traits characteristic of that stage. The first psychosexual stage is the oral stage. Fixation at the oral stage results in either an oral-incorporative character or an oral-sadistic character. The second psychosexual stage is the anal stage. Fixation at the anal stage results in either an anal-expulsive character or an anal-retentive character. The third psychosexual stage is the phallic stage, which is the scene of the Oedipus and Electra complexes. Typically during this stage, boys experience castration anxiety and girls experience penis envy. It is the phallic stage, according to the Freudians, that largely determines adult sexual preferences. The fourth psychosexual stage is the latency stage, during which time sexual interests are repressed and displaced to other activities such as learning and peer group activities. The final psychosexual stage is the genital stage, from which the individual emerges as the adult he or she is destined to become after various experiences during the preceding psychosexual stages.

Freud's major tools for investigating the unconscious mind were free association, dream analysis, everyday life, and humor. During free association Freud noted that patients would often resist pondering certain ideas, and Freud assumed that those ideas were especially anxiety provoking to the patient. While analyzing dreams, he differentiated between a dream's manifest content or its apparent meaning, and its latent content or its true meaning. The mechanisms that distort dreams were called collectively dream work, and included condensation and displacement. In everyday life Freud noted that people tended to forget anxiety-provoking experiences, sometimes had "accidents" on purpose, and sometimes exhibited "slips of the tongue" that revealed their true (unconscious) feelings. Freud also noted that jokes were like dreams because both allow the indirect expression of thoughts that, if expressed directly, would cause unbearable anxiety.

Freud believed that the helplessness that our ancestors felt when confronting the power of nature and the uncertainties of life caused them to create a God that had the characteristics of a powerful, all-knowing, and benevolent father. Freud believed that it is dangerous for contemporary humans to go on basing their lives on the irrational, wish fulfillments that constitute religion. It is better, according to Freud, to live in accordance with the objective facts provided by science. Freud was quite pessimistic about human nature. He believed that humans were animals frustrated by the demands of civilization. According to Freud, humans are aggressive and selfish by nature.

Recently the Freudian legend has been modified in several important ways. The reasons for Freud's abandonment of his seduction theory have been questioned. It has been suggested that the theory was correct and never should have been abandoned. It has also been discovered that Freud did not experience as much anti-Semitism nor rejection from the medical community as has been claimed. Finally, many of the ideas that were attributed to Freud were not original. The many attempts to empirically validate Freud's ideas have produced equivocal results. Critics say that many of Freud's most basic notions are incapable of falsification. Other criticisms include internal inconsistency, male chauvinism, overemphasis on sexual and unconscious motivation, being too pessimistic about the human condition, and equating true happiness with the tension-free condition that occurs when all of one's biologic needs are satisfied. Despite their possible shortcomings, Freud's ideas have influenced our understanding of every area of human existence. He has had a major influence on art, literature, philosophy, and science. His was the first comprehensive theory of personality, and, all theories of personality since can be considered reactions to Freud's theory.

1. Keep track of any dreams that you may have for a period of about a week. As soon as possible following each dream write down as much of it as you can remember. Look at the dreams as Freud would have. In other words, look at the manifest content of each dream, assuming that more basic latent content exists. Also, free associate to your dreams, again assuming that the associations triggered by the dream's manifest content will reveal something about the dream's latent content. Summarize what you feel your dreams reveal about the content of your unconscious mind.

2. Although, according to Freud, the ego-defense mechanisms function on the unconscious level, it is sometimes possible to detect one's own use of them by carefully observing one's own behavior. Make a list of your ego-defense mechanisms and give an example of your use of each of them.

3. Observe your own behavior for about a week and note the following: appointments for which you were late or missed altogether, slips of the tongue, memory lapses, any "accidents" that

you had, and any jokes you heard and found amusing. Analyze these everyday experiences with the idea that they may reflect the contents of your unconscious mind. Summarize your conclusions.

4. Freud believed that to a large extent anatomy is destiny. That is, whether one is born a boy or a girl will determine many of the personality characteristics that one will possess as an adult. Drawing on your own life's experiences give the reasons why you either accept or reject Freud's assertion.

5. Try your hand at free association. Using a tape recorder, speak your mind freely for fifteen or twenty minutes without concern for logic, meaning, or inhibitions. Now play the role of a psychoanalyst. Listen to the tape with the intent of discovering any deep, underlying memories that may be present but cannot be expressed openly. Be especially attentive to any signs of resistance. Describe what you think a psychoanalyst would conclude about your free associations.

1. Describe three major historical blows to the self-esteem of humans.
2. Describe what Freud learned from Charcot and Bernheim that was important in the evolution of his thinking.
3. Discuss what Freud learned from Breuer's treatment of Anna O.
4. What was the fate of Bertha Pappenheim?
5. Elaborate on the importance of the concept of instinct to Freud's theory.
6. Name the major divisions of the mind and describe their functions.
7. Differentiate between primary and secondary processes.
8. Discuss the relationships among the terms cathexis, anticathexis, and displacement.

9. Elaborate on the importance of the concept of anxiety to Freud's theory. Include the different kinds of anxiety in your answer.
10. Discuss the ego-defense mechanism of repression and tell why it is so important to Freud's theory.
11. Discuss the relationship between displacement and civilization.
12. Delineate the two meanings of the term identification in Freud's theory.
13. Define and give an example of the following ego-defense mechanisms: projection, reaction formation, and rationalization.
14. Describe the relationship between regression and fixation.
15. Discuss the psychosexual stages of develop-

ment. Include in your answer the major experiences that occur within each stage and their possible influences on adult behavior.

16. Discuss how dream work and secondary elaboration modified dreams to make them acceptable to the dreamer.

17. Discuss everyday life situations as a source of information about the unconscious mind.

18. Discuss humor as a source of information about the unconscious mind.

19. What conclusion can be reached about the efforts to empirically validate Freudian ideas?

20. Summarize the corrections that have been recently made in the Freudian legend.

21. Describe the influence Freud has had on various fields of human endeavor.

22. Summarize Freud's views on religion.

23. Summarize Freud's conception of human nature.

24. Give evidence that Freud accepted Lamarck's theory of evolution.

SUGGESTIONS FOR FURTHER READING

FREUD, ANNA. (1936/1966). *The Ego and the Mechanisms of Defense* (rev. ed.). New York: International Universities Press.

    In this classic book, Freud's daughter, Anna, elaborates on her father's notion of the ego-defense mechanisms.

FREUD, S. (1900/1965). *The Interpretation of Dreams*. New York: Norton.

    Freud himself considered this to be his most important work, and many agree with him. The major tool used by Freud in his self-analysis was the analysis of his own dreams. Freud's own dreams, along with the dreams of others, are presented, and the significance of their symbols is discussed in great detail.

FREUD, S. (1901/1965). *The Psychopathology of Everyday Life*. New York: Norton.

    The book in which Freud discusses the many ways in which the contents of the unconscious mind reveal themselves in everyday life. For example, through slips of the tongue, lapses of memory, incorrect memories, and "accidents."

FREUD, S. (1927/1961). *The Future of an Illusion*. New York: Norton.

    In this book Freud argues that religion operates to keep humans childlike and therefore religion must be discarded if humans are to live rational lives.

FREUD, S. (1930/1961). *Civilization and Its Discontents*. New York: Norton.

    In this book Freud discusses the many sacrifices and compromises that individual humans make when they live with fellow humans in civilized societies. Also, Freud continues his discussion of religion as "mass-delusion."

GAY, P. (1988). *Freud: A Life for Our Time*. New York: Norton.

    Peter Gay combines his considerable skills as both a historian and a psychoanalyst with the availability of previously unknown or inaccessible letters to create a fresh and illuminating perspective on Freud as a student, physician, father, psychologist, lover, victim, and victor. Although somewhat difficult, the book is well worth reading.

GILMAN, S. L. (ed.) (1982). *Introducing Psychoanalytic Theory*. New York: Brunner/Mazel Publishers.

    This book begins by reviewing the basic concepts of psychoanalysis and then presents a collection of essays written by prominent psychologists and psychiatrists specifically to introduce undergraduate students to Freud's most important concepts, for example, dream theory, transference, narcissism, psychopathology, and psychological development.

JONES, E. (1953, 1955, 1957). *The Life and Work of Sigmund Freud*. New York: Basic Books.

    This three-volume work presents the basic facts of Freud's life and describes how Freud's theory evolved throughout Freud's life. Interesting and very readable, but a growing number of scholars of Freud believe that the picture that Jones paints of Freud and his theory is more favorable than what the facts warrant.

SULLOWAY, F. J. (1979). *Freud: Biologist of the Mind*. New York: Basic Books.

    A challenging biography of Freud that has as one of its major goals the demythologizing of Freudian legend.

Anal-expulsive character. A character type that results from a fixation at the early anal stage. Such a person may have trouble controlling his or her bowels and may be overly generous.

Anal-retentive character. A character type that results from a fixation at the late anal stage. Such a person may suffer from constipation and may be stingy.

Anal stage. The second psychosexual stage and the one that occurs during the second year of life, during which time the anal area is the primary erogenous zone.

Anticathexis. The expenditure of energy to prevent a cathexis that would cause anxiety. For example, when sexually aroused the id will instinctively conjure up images of sexual intercourse. This natural cathexis may be too anxiety provoking, however, so the ego and the superego expend energy to inhibit it, forcing a displacement to less anxiety-provoking cathexes.

Anxiety. The general feeling of uneasiness that is experienced when one engages in, or thinks of engaging in, activities that violate the internalized values of the superego. Freud distinguished between three kinds of anxiety: reality, neurotic, and moral.

Bernheim, Hippolyte (1840–1919). The famous French neurologist from whom Freud learned that one's behavior can be determined by ideas of which he or she is unaware. He also learned from Bernheim that persons could become aware of unconscious ideas if pressured to do so.

Breuer, Josef (1842–1925). A famous physician who became Freud's close friend and with whom Freud coauthored *Studies on Hysteria* (1895). Breuer was the first to use the "talking cure" while treating hysteria, which later evolved into Freud's technique of free association.

Castration anxiety. A boy's fear that he is going to lose his sex organs, because they are regarded as the source of difficulty between the boy and his father.

Catharsis. The emotional relief that results when a person is able to ponder pathogenic ideas consciously. Physical disorders are often relieved following catharsis.

Cathexis. The investment of energy in the image of an object that will satisfy a need.

Charcot, Jean-Martin (1825–93). The famous French neurologist from whom Freud learned that physical disorders could have a psychological origin and that hysteria must, therefore, be taken seriously as a disease.

Condensation. A form of dream distortion in which one dream element represents several ideas at the same time. For example, one person in a dream may be a composite of several people in the dreamer's life.

Conscience. That part of the superego that results from the internalized experiences for which a child had been punished. This component of the personality is responsible for the experience of guilt.

Countertransference. The phenomenon that sometimes occurs during therapy, in which the therapist becomes emotionally involved with a patient.

Displaced aggression. Aggression directed toward a person or object less threatening than the one causing the aggressive impulse.

Displacement. The substitution of one cathexis that is anxiety provoking with one that is not. Also a form of dream distortion in which an acceptable image is substituted for an unacceptable one—for example, when one dreams of mountains instead of breasts.

Dream work. The various mechanisms that distort a dream's true meaning.

Ego. The executive of the personality whose job it is to satisfy the needs of both the id and the superego by engaging in appropriate environmental activities. The ego is governed by the reality principle.

Ego-defense mechanisms. Unconscious processes that falsify or distort reality to reduce or prevent anxiety.

Ego ideal. That part of the superego that results from the internalized experiences for which a child had been rewarded. This component of the personality is responsible for the experience of success and pride.

Electra complex. The situation that arises during the phallic stage during which a girl is attracted to her father and becomes hostile toward her mother.

Erogenous zone. An area of the body that is a source of pleasure.

Eros. All the life instincts taken collectively.

Fixation. Arrested development at one of the psychosexual stages because of the undergratification or overgratification of a need. Fixation determines the point to which an adult regresses under stress.

Free association. Called by Freud "The Fundamental Rule of Psychoanalysis," it entails instructing the patient to say whatever comes to his or her mind no matter how irrelevant, unimportant, or nonsensical it may seem.

Freudian slip. A verbal "accident" that is thought to reveal the speaker's true feelings, such as when Dr. Freud was introduced as Dr. Fraud.

Genital stage. The final psychosexual stage and the one that follows puberty. It is a time when the full adult personality emerges and when the experiences that occurred during the other psychosexual stages manifest themselves.

Humor. According to Freud, humor is a socially acceptable way of expressing repressed, anxiety-provoking thoughts—for example, thoughts involving sex or aggression.

Hysteria. A general term describing disorders such as paralysis of the arms or legs, loss of sensation, disturbances of sight and speech, nausea, and general confusion. Because hysteria has no organic cause, its root is assumed to be psychological. Until Charcot, hysteria was assumed to be exclusively a female disease. *Hystera* is the Greek word for uterus.

Id. The component of the personality that is completely unconscious and contains all the instincts. It is the animalistic portion of the personality, which is governed by the pleasure principle.

Identification. This term was used in two ways by Freud: (1) the matching of an idinal image with its physical counterpart, and (2) the incorporation of another person's values or characteristics either to enhance one's self-esteem or to minimize that person as a threat.

Inheritance of acquired characteristics. Lamarck's contention that the information learned during the lifetime of an organism can be passed on to the offspring of that organism.

Instinct. For Freud, instincts were the stuff from which personality is shaped. An instinct is the cognitive reflection of a biologic deficiency. Instincts have four characteristics—a source, an aim, an object, and an impetus—and can be divided into two categories—life and death.

Latency stage. The psychosexual stage that lasts from about the sixth year to about the twelfth year of life. It is a time when sexual activity is repressed and an abundance of substitute activities are engaged in, such as learning and athletics.

Latent content of a dream. The dream's true meaning, which is disguised or distorted by dream work.

Libido. In Freud's earlier writings, libido was the psychic energy associated with the sexual instinct, but later he expanded the concept of libido to include the energy associated with all the life instincts—for instance, hunger and thirst in addition to sex.

Manifest content of a dream. What a dream appears to be about to the dreamer.

Moral anxiety. Fear that one will do something contrary to the values of the superego and thus experience guilt.

Neurotic anxiety. Caused by the fear that the impulses of the id will overwhelm the ego, thereby causing the person to do something for which he or she will be punished.

Oedipus complex. The situation that arises during the phallic stage, in which a boy is attracted to his mother and hostile toward his father.

Oral-incorporative character. A character type that results from a fixation at the early oral stage. Such a person spends considerable time engaged in activities such as eating, kissing, smoking, and listening.

Oral-sadistic character. A character type that results from a fixation at the late oral stage. Such a person is orally aggressive and may be a fingernail biter and sarcastic.

Oral stage. The first psychosexual stage and the one that occurs during the first year of life, at which time the mouth is the primary erogenous zone.

Penis envy. The jealousy the girl experiences because males have a penis and she does not.

Phallic stage. The third psychosexual stage and the one that occurs from about the third to the fifth year of life, during which time the genitals are the primary erogenous zone.

Phylogenetically inherited endowment. The images that we inherit that reflect the consistent experiences of our ancestors. With his acceptance of such images Freud demonstrated his acceptance of Lamarck's theory of the inheritance of acquired characteristics.

Pleasure principle. The hedonistic principle governing the id that demands the immediate reduction of any tension associated with an unsatisfied biologic need.

Posthypnotic amnesia. An inability to remember what one has done while hypnotized.

Posthypnotic suggestion. The phenomenon whereby a person performs an act while awake that he or she was instructed to perform while under hypnosis. Typically, the person is unaware of the reason for performing such an act.

Preconscious. The state of information that is in the unconscious mind but has not been repressed. Such information enters consciousness easily when it is needed.

Primal repression. Repression of those anxiety-provoking thoughts that are innately part of the id and therefore independent of personal experience.

Primary processes. The processes available to the id for satisfaction of needs. Those processes are reflex action and wish fulfillment (hallucinations).

Principle of conservation of energy. The principle that states that the amount of energy within a system remains constant. Although the amount of energy in a system cannot be increased or decreased, it can be rearranged and transformed freely within the system. Freud viewed the mind as a closed energy system.

Projection. The ego-defense mechanism by which an anxiety-provoking thought is attributed to someone or something else instead of recognizing it as one's own.

Psychic energy. The more or less fixed amount of energy that Freud believed was available to drive the entire personality. According to Freud, psychic energy obeyed the principle of conservation of energy.

Rationalization. Giving a rational, logical (but incorrect) excuse for behavior or thoughts that cause anxiety. For example, one concludes that a test on which one performed poorly was ambiguous, rather than concluding that one was not properly prepared or perhaps stupid.

Reaction formation. The inhibition of an anxiety-provoking thought by exaggerating its opposite. For example, a person inclined toward pornography may become a censor.

Reality anxiety. Caused by real, objective sources of danger in the environment. It is the easiest kind of anxiety to reduce or prevent.

Reality principle. The principle governing the ego that causes it to do commerce with the environment in a way that satisfies both the id and the superego.

Reality testing. The process by which the ego finds environmental experiences capable of satisfying the needs of the id or superego.

Reflex action. The automatic reflexive response aimed at the removal of a source of irritation. Blinking to remove something from the eye would be an example.

Regression. Returning to an earlier stage of development when stress is encountered. For example, a person with a fixation on the oral stage may eat, drink, and smoke to an excess after encountering difficulties in a relationship.

Repression. The ego-defense mechanism by which anxiety-provoking thoughts are held in the unconscious mind, thereby preventing a conscious awareness of them.

Repression proper. Repression of those anxiety-provoking thoughts that result from painful experiences in one's lifetime.

Resistance. A patient's unwillingness to ponder and report anxiety-provoking thoughts during the therapeutic process. Freud believed that resistances were highly informative because they suggested what were troublesome topics for the patient.

Secondary processes. The realistic processes by which the ego operates to bring about true need reduction as opposed to the temporary need reduction that results from the wish fulfillments of the id.

Secondary revision. (also called secondary elaboration.) The resynthesizing of dream elements after they have been distorted by dreamwork. This resynthesizing gives the distorted dream elements enough meaning to be accepted into consciousness.

Seduction theory. Freud's early contention that hysteria results from an actual sexual seduction experienced during childhood. For reasons that are not entirely clear, Freud revised his theory to state that most seductions were imagined rather than real.

Sublimation. A displacement that results in a higher cultural achievement, such as when an artistic or scientific activity is substituted for sexual activity.

Superego. The moral component of the personality that has two parts; the conscience and the ego ideal.

Thanatos. The name given to the death instinct. The source of aggression that Freud felt was self-destruction turned outward.

Transference. The phenomenon that sometimes occurs during therapy in which a patient begins to respond to the therapist as if he or she were an important person in the patient's life, such as the patient's mother or father.

Wish fulfillment. The conjuring up of an image of an object or event that is capable of satisfying a biologic need. For example, a hungry person thinks of food-related objects.

3

Carl Jung

■ **CHAPTER OUTLINE**

A s we shall see in this chapter, Jung's is a complex theory of personality. In fact, the picture of human nature that he portrays is probably the most complicated developed by any personality theorist. As might be expected, Jung himself was a complicated person. Many of the details of his life are only recently coming to light, and they often are contradictory. For example, Stern (1976) portrays Jung as a prepsychotic (if not psychotic), opportunistic person with anti-Semitic and pro-Nazi leanings. On the other hand, Hannah (1976), a Jungian herself and a close friend of Jung's, portrays him as a brilliant, sensitive humanitarian who was anything but an anti-Semite or pro-Nazi. The Jung whom Hannah describes is indeed an uncommon, sometimes troubled, person with many idiosyncracies, but these, in her opinion, are attributes of a genius, not of a madman. Jung's own autobiography (1961) does not help much, because it is, Jung confessed, a combination of myth and fact.

It appears that many truths about Jung's personal life, if they are ever to be known at all, will need to unfold in the future. What follows is a summary of those facts about Jung over which little or no disagreement exists. As far as Jung's theoretical notions are concerned, as with any other personality theorists, either his ideas are valid and useful, or they are not. The personal experiences that gave rise to those ideas may be interesting in themselves, but they are scientifically irrelevant.

Biographical Sketch

Carl Gustav Jung was born on 26 July 1875 in the Swiss village of Kesswyl but grew up in the university town of Basel. Religion was a strong theme running through Jung's early years. There were nine clergymen in his family, including eight uncles and his father, who was a pastor of the Swiss Reformed Church. Jung's father viewed himself as a failure, and his religion was little comfort to him. As a child Jung often asked his father penetrating questions concerning religion and life but was unable to obtain satisfactory answers. It became clear to Jung that his father accepted church dogma completely on faith and was never really personally touched by real religious experience. According to Jung, these fruitless theological discussions alienated him from his father. Later in Jung's life religion became a vital part of his theory, but it was the kind of religion that touched individuals emotionally, and had little to do with specific churches or religious dogma.

Jung considered his mother to be the dominant member of the family, although he saw her as terribly inconsistent, which caused him to suspect that she was really two persons in one body. One person was kindly, extremely hospitable with a great sense of humor; the other was uncanny, archaic, and ruthless. Jung described how he reacted when his mother's second personality emerged, "I was usually struck to the core of my being, so that I was stunned into silence"(1961, 49). It is interesting that the young Jung thought that he, like his mother, was really two different people. One person he labeled number one (the schoolboy), the other number two (the wise old man). The wise old man was about 100 years older than the schoolboy who was apparently the "real" Jung. So strongly did Jung believe in this dual aspect of himself that he would often make a mistake of 100 years while dating his schoolwork; for example, he would write 1786 instead of 1886.

Perhaps because of the constant bickering of his parents, Jung began to isolate

Carl Jung

himself from his family in particular and the world in general. Increasingly his dreams, visions, and fantasies became his primary reality, and he developed the belief that this inner reality was furnishing him with secret knowledge that only a select few persons were given, and therefore it could not easily be shared with others. Jung was a lonely child, and he became a lonely adult.

> As a child I felt myself to be alone, and I am still, because I know things and must hint at things which others apparently know nothing of, and for the most part do not want to know. Loneliness does not come from having no people about one, but from being unable to communicate the things that seem important to oneself, or from holding certain views which others find inadmissible. . . . If a man knows more than others, he becomes lonely. (Jung 1961, 356)

Jung's Early Dreams, Visions, and Fantasies

Manikin.　When Jung was ten years old, he carved a wooden figure of a man from a ruler and kept it in a little wooden case. Jung dressed the figure in a coat, black boots, and a top hat and gave it a little stone of its own.

> This was *his* stone. All this was a great secret. Secretly I took the case to . . . the attic at the top of the house . . . and hid it with great satisfaction on one of the beams under the roof—for no one must ever see it! . . . I felt safe, and the torment-ing sense of being at odds with myself was gone. (Jung 1961, 21)

This figure became a refuge for Jung and whenever he was troubled he would visit his secret friend. At school Jung would write in a secret language on little scrolls of paper, which he would later place in the pencil case containing the manikin. The addition of each scroll required a solemn ceremonial act. Jung never worried about explaining these actions because they provided him with a sense of security. "It was an inviolable secret which must never be betrayed, for the safety of my life depended on it. Why that was so I did not ask myself. It simply was so" (Jung 1961, 22). Jung's "relationship" with his manikin lasted for about a year.

Stone.   When Jung was about seven years old, he discovered a large stone with which he began to play an imaginary game. First he would perceive himself as sitting on the stone, which he was. Then, however, he would assume the perspective of the stone. Jung imagined himself to be the stone being sat on by a boy. Jung found that he could switch perspectives with ease. In fact, it was difficult for Jung to tell if he was sitting on the stone or if he was the stone being sat on. "The answer remained totally unclear, and my uncertainty was accompanied by a feeling of curious and fascinating darkness. But there was no doubt whatsoever that this stone stood in some secret relationship to me. I could sit on it for hours, fascinated by the puzzle it set me" (1961, 20).

When Jung returned to this stone thirty years later, as a married, professionally successful man, the magic of the stone returned immediately: "The pull of that other world was so strong that I had to tear myself violently from the spot in order not to lose hold of my future" (1961, 20).

Phallus Dream.   Although strange, the manikin and stone experiences were not frightening to Jung. In fact, the manikin provided him with an element of peace and security. Other mystical experiences that the young Jung had were not as tranquil, however. A dream that Jung had when he was about four years old was terrifying to him. In this dream Jung discovered a stone-lined hole in the ground, peered down, and saw a stone stairway leading downward. Jung descended and at the bottom found a round arch closed off by a lush, green curtain. Pushing the curtain aside, Jung observed a rectangular chamber about thirty feet long. In the chamber was a platform on which was a rich, magnificent, king's golden throne. Standing on the throne was an object 12 to 15 feet high and about 2 feet thick. The object consisted of skin and naked flesh, and on the top was a rounded head with no face or hair. On the top of the object was a single eye staring upward. This was obviously a giant phallus. Although the object did not move it gave the appearance of being able to. Within his dream Jung was paralyzed with terror and he dreamed he heard his mother saying "Yes, just look at him. That is the man-eater!" (1961, 12) Jung's fear intensified, and he awoke sweating and frightened to death. For many nights following, Jung could not go to sleep for fear of having that or a similar dream again.

The phallus dream haunted Jung for years and it influenced the view of Christianity that he was to have for many years. From his dream Jung concluded that the giant phallus was the underground counterpart of the Lord Jesus.

> At all events, the phallus of this dream seems to be a subterranean God "not to be named," and such it remained throughout my youth, reappearing whenever anyone spoke too emphatically about Lord Jesus. Lord Jesus never became quite real for me, never quite acceptable, never quite lovable, for again and again I would

think of his underground counterpart, a frightful revelation which had been accorded me without my seeking it. (1961, 13)

Jung was so shaken by the phallus dream that he did not mention it to anyone until he was sixty-five years old.

Throne Vision.   When Jung was about twelve years old he left school on a warm, summer day. The new, brightly glazed tiles on the roof of a nearby cathedral sparkled in the radiant sunshine. Jung was struck with the notion that God made that beautiful day and that beautiful church, and was viewing his creations from his golden throne high above in the blue sky. Suddenly Jung was struck with the idea that if he did not stop thinking, a terrible thought would enter his mind. He was convinced that if he continued thinking he would commit the most terrible sin, and his soul would be damned for all eternity. The next few days were torture for Jung as he tried desperately to fend off the forbidden thought. Jung described the events of the third night:

On the third night . . . the torment became so unbearable that I no longer knew what to do. I awoke from a restless sleep just in time to catch myself thinking again about the cathedral and God. I had almost continued the thought! I felt my resistance weakening. Sweating with fear, I sat up in bed to shake off sleep. "Now it is coming, now it's serious! I *must think*. It must be thought out beforehand. *Why* should I think something I do not know? I don't want to, by God, that's sure. But *who* wants me to? Who wants to force me to think something I don't know and don't want to know? Where does this terrible will come from? And why should I be the one to be subjected to it? I was thinking praises of the Creator of this beautiful world, I was grateful to him for this immeasurable gift, so why should I have to think something inconceivably wicked? (1961, 37)

Finally, Jung allowed himself to experience the forbidden thought:

I saw before me the cathedral, the blue sky. God sits on His golden throne, high above the world—and from under the throne an enormous turd falls upon the sparkling new roof, shatters it, and breaks the walls of the cathedral asunder.
    So that was it! I felt an enormous, an indescribable relief. Instead of the expected damnation, grace had come upon me, and with it an unutterable bliss such as I had never known. I wept for happiness and gratitude. (1961, 39–40)

This vision had a profound effect on Jung. He now believed that he knew what his father had not known about God. By taking the Bible's commandments as his guide, Jung's father had never directly experienced the will of God.

[Jung's father] believed in God as the Bible prescribed and as his forefathers had taught him. But he did not know the immediate living God who stands, omnipotent and free, above His Bible and His Church, who calls upon man to partake of His freedom, and can force him to renounce his own views and convictions in order to fulfill without reserve the command of God. In His trial of human courage God refuses to abide by traditions, no matter how sacred. In His omnipotence He will see to it that nothing really evil comes of such tests of courage. If one fulfills the will of God one can be sure of going the right way. (1961, 40)

Profound personal experiences, such as those just described, convinced Jung that there are aspects of the human psyche that are independent of any individual's personal experience. Jung (1961) summarized what he had learned from his fantasies:

> My fantasies brought home to me the crucial insight that there are things in the psyche which I do not produce, but which produce themselves and have their own life. . . . I understood that there is something in me which can say things that I do not know and do not intend, things which may even be directed against me. (183)

Jung eventually donated his professional life to understanding the nature and the origins of the many extraordinary psychological experiences that he had as a child.

Jung's Early Professional Life

Jung first wanted to study archaeology, but a dream convinced him to follow in his paternal grandfather's footsteps and become a medical physician. Jung became aware of the new field of psychiatry during his medical studies at the University of Basel, where he attained his medical degree in 1900. In psychiatry, Jung believed that he found his true calling. Jung's interest in unusual psychic phenomena never wavered and his dissertation for his medical degree was entitled "On the Psychopathology of So-Called Occult Phenomena" published in 1902. At this time Jung was almost totally absorbed with the study of the occult. He attended séances, participated in experiments with mediums, and devoured books on parapsychology. In addition to his visions and his readings in parapsychology, personal experience also seemed to confirm the existence of the supernatural. For example, as Jung was at home studying in his room, he and his mother heard a loud noise and observed that a solid table had split from the rim to the center and not along the joints as would be expected. Two weeks later, after another loud blast, it was discovered that the blade of a butter knife shattered into pieces. Examination by a cutler revealed no fault in the steel that would explain the explosion. Also Jung was entertaining a group by telling an imaginary story about a person he did not know, only to learn that he was clairvoyantly revealing true facts about the man. Lastly, Jung awoke one night with an extremely painful headache only to learn that one of his patients had shot himself in the head that very night.

Jung's first professional appointment was at the noted Burghölzli psychiatric hospital in Zurich where he worked under the supervision of Eugen Bleuler, who coined the term *schizophrenia*. Bleuler was interested in psychological tests and he encouraged Jung to experiment with the word-association test that had been used previously by Francis Galton (Darwin's cousin) and Wilhelm Wundt (the founder of the school of structuralism). We will have more to say about Jung's extensive use of the word-association test when we discuss complexes later in this chapter. In 1905, Jung was given a lectureship at the University of Zurich, where he lectured on psychopathology, psychoanalysis, and hypnosis. Also, Jung became clinical director of Burghölzli Hospital and head of the outpatient clinic. In 1909, Jung resigned his positions at the Burghölzli and his lectureship in 1914 to devote his time to his growing private practice, research, and writing.

On 14 February 1903, Jung married Emma Rauschenbach, the daughter of a rich industrialist, and they raised four daughters and a son. Emma herself became a practitioner of her husband's theory. During middle age Jung began a lengthy affair with a woman thirteen years his junior. Her name was Toni Wolfe, and she was an attractive, well-educated, former patient of Jung's. At first Jung's wife Emma was deeply upset, but their situation eventually worked out. Stern (1976) describes the situation:

> Jung's affair with Toni might have been less troublesome if he had not insisted on drawing his mistress into his family life and on having her as a regular guest for Sunday dinner. . . . Jung managed to maintain this asymmetrical triangle for several decades, drafting both women to serve his cause. Thus, Emma Jung was the first president of the Jungian "Psychological Club"; a few years after she resigned, Toni assumed the presidency. Both women published papers about Jungian psychology. (138–39)

Jung's Relationship with Freud

Jung first became interested in Freud after reading *The Interpretation of Dreams*. Jung began to apply Freud's ideas to his own practice and eventually wrote a monograph entitled *The Psychology of Dementia Praecox* (1907), summarizing their effectiveness. Jung had found considerable support for Freud's notion of repression in his own word-association studies, and he reported this fact in his book and in several articles. In 1906, Jung initiated correspondence with Freud, and in February of the following year, the two met in Freud's home in Vienna. Their first face-to-face meeting was intense and lasted thirteen hours. The two became extremely close friends, and when Jung returned to Zurich, a correspondence began that lasted about seven years. On the basis of the kind words that Jung was publishing about Freud's theory and because of the impression Freud had of Jung following their meeting, Freud decided that Jung would become his successor. On 7 April 1907, Freud wrote Jung:

> Your visit was most delightful and gratifying . . . you have inspired me with confidence for the future, [and] I now realize that I am as replaceable as everyone else and that I could hope for no one better than yourself . . . to continue and complete my work. I am sure you will not abandon the work, you have gone into it too deeply and seen for yourself how exciting, how far-reaching, and how beautiful our subject is. (McGuire 1974, 27)

In 1911 Freud did nominate Jung as the first president of the International Psychoanalytic Association and despite considerable opposition from the members, Jung was elected.

Jung traveled with Freud to America in 1909 to give a series of lectures at Clark University. Jung was invited primarily because of his experimentation with the word-association test. It was during this trip to the United States that Jung first

Photograph Taken During the Visit of Freud and Jung to Clark University, 1909. Top Row, from Left to Right: A. A. Brill, Ernest Jones (Freud's Biographer), and Sandor Ferenczi. *Bottom Row, from Left to Right:* Sigmund Freud, G. Stanley Hall (Then President of Clark University), and Carl Jung.

began to entertain doubts about the emphasis on sexual motivation in Freud's theory. His opposition to Freud was not expressed strongly, however, and the two remained close friends. Jung simply suggested to Freud that his theory might be more palatable to American audiences if he played down the role of sex. Freud viewed this suggestion as a departure from scientific ethics.

It was not until about the time that Jung was elected president of the International Psychoanalytic Association in 1911 that Jung openly expressed doubts about Freud's interpretation of libidinal energy as primarily sexual. Jung's book *The Psychology of the Unconscious* (1912), and a series of lectures he gave at Fordham University entitled *The Theory of Psychoanalysis* (1913a) amplified the differences between Jung's conception of the libido and Freud's. The following exchange of letters exemplifies the early disagreement between Freud and Jung over the nature of the libido. First Jung wrote:

Is it not conceivable, in view of the limited conception of sexuality that prevails nowadays, that the sexual terminology should be reserved only for the most extreme forms of your "libido," and that a less offensive collective term should be established for *all* the libidinal manifestations? (McGuire 1974, 25)

Freud responded to Jung as follows:

I appreciate your motives in trying to sweeten the sour apple, but I do not think you will be successful. Even if we call the unconscious "psychoid," it will still be the unconscious, and even if we do not call the driving force in the broadened conception of sexuality "libido," it will still be libido. . . . We cannot avoid resistances, why not face up to them from the start? (McGuire 1974, 28)

The relationship between Jung and Freud became so strained that they agreed to stop their personal correspondence in 1912, and in 1914 Jung completely terminated the relationship when he resigned his presidency of the International Psychoanalytic Association and also withdrew as a member. The break was especially disturbing to Jung, who was then almost forty years old. The separation from Freud caused Jung to enter what he called the "dark years," a period of four years during which he explored in depth his own dreams and fantasies, an activity that brought him, in the opinion of many, to the brink of madness.

Jung's Creative Illness.   Jung said, "After the parting of the ways with Freud, a period of inner uncertainty began for me. It would be no exaggeration to call it a state of disorientation. I felt totally suspended in mid-air, for I had not yet found my own footing" (1961, 170). According to Ellenberger (1970), what Jung experienced during the "dark years" following the collapse of his relationship with Freud was a **creative illness** which Ellenberger defines as:

A period of intense preoccupation with an idea and search for a certain truth. It is a polymorphous condition that can take the shape of depression, neurosis, psychosomatic ailments, or even psychosis. . . . Through out the illness the subject never loses the thread of his dominating preoccupation. It is often compatible with normal, professional activity and family life. But even if he keeps to his social activities, he is almost entirely absorbed with himself. . . . The subject emerges from his ordeal with a permanent transformation in his personality and the conviction that he has discovered a great truth or a new spiritual world. (447–48)

Disagreement exists concerning whether Jung went on a voluntary voyage of self-exploration during his creative illness (see, for example, Van der Post 1975) or if his journey represented a series of full-fledged psychotic episodes (see, for example, Stern, 1976). In any case, Jung continued to maintain his psychiatric practice and his home life during his illness. In fact, according to Jung, it was his family and his patients that kept him sane during his illness.

How strange it must have been for Jung to be engaged in this intense self-exploration at a time when he was treating psychotic patients. Strange or not, however, Jung seems to have learned a great deal about human psyche from both sources:

It is of course ironical that I, a psychiatrist, should at almost every step of my experiment have run into the same psychic material which is the stuff of psychosis and is found in the insane. This is the fund of unconscious images which fatally confuse the mental patient. But it is also the matrix of a mythopoeic imagination which has vanished from our rational age. Though such imagination is present everywhere, it is both tabooed and dreaded, so that it even appears to be a risky experiment or a questionable adventure to entrust oneself to the uncertain path that leads into the depths of the unconscious. . . . Unpopular, ambiguous, and dangerous, it is a voyage of discovery to the other pole of the world. (1961, 188–89)

Jung emerged from his creative illness with his own theory of personality, a theory that bore only a remote resemblance to that of his mentor, Freud. The results of his long, agonizing search of his own psyche are to be found everywhere in his theory.

Jung continued to develop his theory up to the time of his death, at the age of eighty-six, on 6 June 1961, at his tower home in Bollingen, Switzerland.

Libido, Equivalence, Entropy, and Opposites

Libido.   Freud and Jung disagreed about the nature of the **libido.** Freud saw libido mainly as sexual energy. Jung felt that this view was too narrow and instead defined the libido as general biologic life energy that is concentrated on different problems as they arise. For Jung, libido was a creative life force that could be applied to the continuous psychological growth of the person. In the early years of life, according to Jung, libidinal energy is expended mainly on eating, elimination, and sex, but as the person becomes more proficient at satisfying these needs, or as they become less important, libidinal energy is applied to the solution of more philosophical and spiritual needs. Thus for Jung, libido is the driving force behind the **psyche** (Jung's term for personality), which is focused on various needs as they arise, whether those needs are biologic or spiritual. Those components of the personality in which considerable libidinal energy is invested are said to be valued more than others. Thus, according to Jung, the **value** of something is determined by how much libidinal energy is invested in it.

Principle of Equivalence.   Jung drew heavily on the physics of his day for his theory of personality. His use of the principles of equivalence, entropy, and opposites demonstrates this orientation. The **principle of equivalence** is the first law of thermodynamics, which states that the amount of energy in a system is essentially fixed (conservation of energy), and if it is removed from one part of a system, it will show up in another. Applied to the psyche, this means that only so much psychic energy (libido) is available, and if one component of the psyche is overvalued, it is at the expense of the other components. If, for example, psychic energy is concentrated on conscious activities, then unconscious activities will suffer and vice versa. We will have more to say about this concept later.

Principle of Entropy.   The **principle of entropy** is the second law of thermodynamics, which states that a constant tendency exists toward the equalization of energy within a system. If, for example, a hot object and a cold one are placed side by side, heat will flow from the hot object to the cold one until their temperatures are equalized. Likewise, according to Jung, a tendency exists for all components of the psyche to have equal energy. For example, the conscious and unconscious aspects of the psyche would have equal energy and thus equal representation in one's life. The psychic balance, however, is extremely hard to achieve and must be actively sought. If the balance is not sought, the person's psychic energy will not be balanced and thus personality development will be uneven. That is, certain aspects of the psyche will be more highly valued than others.

Principle of Opposites.   The **principle of opposites** is found almost everywhere in Jung's writings. This principle is close to Newton's contention that "for every action there is an equal and opposite reaction" or Hegel's statement that "everything carries within itself its own negation." Every concept in Jung's theory had its polar opposite. The unconscious is contrasted with the conscious, the rational with the irrational, feminine with masculine, the animal with the spiritual, causality with teleology, progression with regression, introversion with extroversion, thinking with feelings, and sensing with intuiting. When one aspect of the personality is developed, it is usually at the expense of its polar opposite; for instance, as one becomes more masculine, one necessarily becomes less feminine. For Jung the goal of life, in accordance with the principle of entropy, is to seek a balance between these polar opposites, thereby giving both expression in one's life, which is more easily said than done. Such a synthesis is constantly aspired to but seldom accomplished. About the importance of these opposites and the conflicts between them, Jung said:

> The sad truth is that man's real life consists of a complex of inexorable opposites—day and night, birth and death, happiness and misery, good and evil. We are not even sure that one will prevail against the other, that good will overcome evil, or joy defeat pain. Life is a battleground. It always has been, and always will be; and if it were not so, existence would come to an end. (1964, 85)

Components of the Personality

Ego.   According to Jung, the **ego** is everything of which we are conscious. It is concerned with thinking, feeling, remembering, and perceiving. It is responsible for seeing that the functions of everyday life are carried out. It is also responsible for our sense of identity and our sense of continuity in time. Considerable similarity exists between Jung's concept of ego and Freud's.

Personal Unconscious.   The **personal unconscious** consists of material that was once conscious but was repressed or forgotten, or was not vivid enough to make a conscious impression at first. As in Freud's earlier concept of the preconscious, some material in the personal unconscious is readily available to the person, and a great deal of interaction occurs between it and the ego.

The personal unconscious contains clusters of emotionally loaded (highly valued) thoughts, which Jung called complexes. More specifically, a **complex** is a personally disturbing constellation of ideas connected together by common feeling tone (Jung 1913b/1973, 599). A complex has a disproportionate influence on one's behavior, in the sense that the theme around which the complex is organized keeps recurring over and over again in one's life. A person with a mother complex will spend a considerable amount of time on activities that are either directly or symbolically related to the idea of mother. The same would be true of a person with a father, sex, power, money, or any other kind of complex.

Jung's early claim to fame was a technique he used to study complexes. He took the **word-association test** developed much earlier by Francis Galton and Wilhelm Wundt, and redesigned it as a tool to tap the personal unconscious in search of complexes. It was this research on which he lectured at Clark University when he went there with Freud in 1909. Jung's technique consisted of reading to a patient a list of 100 words one at a time and instructing the patient to respond as quickly as possible with the first word that came to mind. Words such as child, green, water, sing, death, long, and stupid were used. How long it took the patient to respond to each word was measured with a stopwatch. Breathing rate also was measured, as was the electroconductivity of the patient's skin, which was measured with a galvanometer.

The following were used by Jung as "complex indicators," that is, factors that indicated the presence of a complex:

1. displaying longer-than-average reaction time to a stimulus word
2. repeating the stimulus word back as a response
3. failing to respond at all
4. using expressive bodily reactions, such as laughing, increased breathing rate, or increased conductivity of the skin
5. stammering
6. continuing to respond to a previously used stimulus word
7. reacting meaninglessly with made-up words, for example
8. reacting superficially with a word that sounds like the stimulus word (die-lie), for example
9. responding with more than one word
10. misunderstanding the stimulus word as some other word

Jung used his word-association test in many ways. For example, he found that male subjects tended to respond faster to stimulus words than female subjects did, and that educated people tended to respond faster than uneducated people. In addition, he found that members of the same family had remarkably similar reactions to stimulus words. The following shows the reaction of a mother and her daughter to several stimulus words (Jung 1909/1973, 469):

STIMULUS WORD	MOTHER	DAUGHTER
law	God's commandment	Moses
potato	tuber	tuber
stranger	traveler	travelers
brother	dear to me	dear
to kiss	mother	mother
merry	happy child	little children

For Jung, it was important to discover and deal with complexes, because they require the expenditure of so much psychic energy and therefore inhibit balanced psychological growth.

With his use of the word-association test, Jung demonstrated that it was possible to investigate the unconscious mind systematically. This accomplishment alone would have given Jung a prominent place in psychology's history.

Collective Unconscious.   This was Jung's boldest, most mystical, and most controversial concept. To understand the **collective unconscious** is to understand the heart of Jung's theory. The collective unconscious reflects the collective experiences that humans have had in their evolutionary past, or in Jung's own words, it is the "deposit of ancestral experience from untold millions of years, the echo of prehistoric world events to which each century adds an infinitesimally small amount of variation and differentiation" (Jung 1928, 162). Not only are fragments of all human history found in the collective unconscious but traces of our prehuman or animal ancestry are found there as well. Because the collective unconscious results from *common* experiences that all humans have, or have had, the contents of the collective unconscious are essentially the same for all humans. Jung says it is "detached from anything personal and is common to all men, since its contents can be found everywhere" (Jung 1917/1966, 66).

These ancestral experiences that are registered in the brain have been called at various times "racial memories," "primordial images," or more commonly, archetypes. An **archetype** can be defined as an inherited predisposition to respond to certain aspects of the world. Just as the eye and the ear have evolved to be maximally responsive to certain aspects of the environment, so has the brain evolved to cause the person to be maximally responsive to certain categories of experience that humans have encountered over and over again through countless generations. An archetype exists for whatever experiences are universal, those that each member of each generation must experience.

You can generate a list of archetypes yourself by simply answering the question: What must every human experience in his or her lifetime? One's answer must include such experiences as birth, death, the sun, darkness, power, women, men, sex, water, magic, mother, heroes, and pain. Humans have an inherited predisposition to react to instances of these and other categories of experience. Specific responses and ideas are not inherited; all that is inherited is a tendency to deal with universal experiences in some way.

According to Jung, what is carried from generation to generation are the emotional reactions to common human experiences. For example, when our ancestors experienced a bolt of lightening or a clap of thunder, it stimulated in them emotional responses that immediately took the form of myths. Jung (1917/1966) explained:

> One of the commonest and at the same time most impressive experiences is the apparent movement of the sun every day. We certainly cannot discover anything of the kind in the unconscious, so far as the known physical process is concerned. What we do find, on the other hand, is the myth of the sun-hero in all its countless variations. It is this myth, and not the physical process, that forms the sun archetype. The same can be said of the phases of the moon. The archetype is a kind of readiness to produce over and over again the same or similar mythical ideas.

Hence it seems as though what is impressed upon the unconscious were exclusively the subjective fantasy-ideas aroused by the physical process. We may therefore assume that the archetypes are recurrent impressions made by subjective reactions. (69)

Primitive humans responded to all of their emotional experiences in terms of myths, and it is myths that are registered in the collective unconscious and passed on to future generations. Jung (1931/1969) explained that for early humans what was imagined to be true was more important than what was objectively true:

His emotions are more important to him than physics; therefore what he registers is his emotional fantasies. . . . It is not thunder and lightning, not rain and cloud that remain images in the psyche, but the fantasies caused by the affects they arouse. (154–55)

What we inherit, then, is the tendency to re-experience some manifestation of these primordial myths as we encounter events that have been associated with those myths for eons. Each archetype can be viewed as an inherited tendency to respond emotionally and mythologically to certain kinds of experience—for example, when a child, a mother, a lover, a nightmare, a death, a birth, an earthquake, or a stranger is encountered.

The collective unconscious is by far the most important and influential part of the psyche and everything in it seeks outward manifestation. When the contents of the collective unconscious are not recognized in consciousness, they are manifested in dreams, fantasies, images, and symbols. Because few people fully recognize the contents of their collective unconscious, most can learn about themselves by studying the contents of their dreams and fantasies. In fact, according to Jung, humans can learn a great deal about their future by studying these dreams, because they symbolize basic human nature, as it someday is hoped to be understood. In that sense, the collective unconscious knows more than any single generation of humans knows. Jung gathered information about the archetypes from a wide variety of sources, including his own dreams and fantasies, primitive tribes, art, language, and the hallucinations of psychotic patients.

Although Jung recognized the existence of many archetypes, he wrote extensively on only a few. These were the persona, the anima, the animus, the shadow, and the self. We will consider each of these next.

Persona. **Persona** is the Latin word for mask, and Jung used this term to describe one's public self. The persona archetype develops because of humans' need to play a role in society. This is the part of the psyche by which we are known by other people. Jung points out that some people equate their persona with their entire psyche and that this is a mistake. In a sense, the persona is supposed to deceive other people, because it presents to them only a small part of one's psyche, but if people believe that they are what they pretend to be, they are deceiving themselves, and that is dangerous. Jung says that "Whoever builds up too good a persona for himself naturally has to pay for it with irritability" (Jung 1917/1966, 193). Jung describes the situation in which the persona is valued too highly as **inflation of the persona.** As with all components of the psyche, if the persona is valued too highly, it develops at the expense of other components.

Anima. The **anima** is the female component of the male psyche, which results from the experiences men have had with women through the eons. This archetype serves two purposes. First, it causes men to have feminine traits; second, it provides a framework within which men interact with women. Because men's relationship with women has included being nurtured (mother), being sexually involved (lover), and just being a friend, all of these are contained in the anima, and elements of each are projected on the women in one's lifetime. Because an archetype can be viewed as an ideal, real women may not correspond to it exactly. To make an adequate adjustment, there often must be a compromise between the ideal and the real. If a man insists that a particular woman corresponds to his innate image of women, the relationship may be doomed.

Animus. The **animus** is the masculine component of the female psyche. It furnishes the woman with masculine traits and also with a framework that guides her relationship with men. As the anima furnishes men with an ideal of the woman, the animus furnishes women with an ideal of the man; the insistence that a particular man lives up to that ideal may lead to conflict and disillusionment.

Thus, the male psyche has a strong female component, and the female psyche has a strong male component. The proper adjustment to this situation, according to Jung, is for both sexes to recognize that they possess traits of the opposite sex. Such a realization results in a more well-rounded, creative person. Again, a balance should be sought. For a man to deny his female tendencies is to deny an important part of his psyche; according to Jung, this outcome is unfortunate. Conversely, for a man to overemphasize his feminine traits is equally unfortunate.

If conscious recognition is not given to any component of the psyche, it will not disappear; it is forced to manifest itself on the unconscious level, where its effect is uncontrolled and irrational. Thus, if a women denies her masculine traits, they will continue to influence her life, but they will do so in indirect ways, such as through dreams and fantasies.

Shadow. The **shadow** is the darkest, deepest part of the psyche. It is the part of the collective unconscious that we inherit from our prehuman ancestors and contains all of the animal instincts. Because of the shadow, we have a strong tendency to be immoral, aggressive, and passionate.

As with all of the archetypes, the shadow seeks outward manifestation and is projected onto the world symbolically as devils, monsters, or evil spirits. It can even be projected onto a person, as Jung found out when he asked one of his young patients the following question:

> "How do I seem to you when you are not with me?" . . . She said, "Sometimes you seem rather dangerous, sinister, like an evil magician or a demon. I don't know how I ever got such ideas—you are not a bit like that." (1956, 91–92)

Jung suggested that she was projecting her shadow onto him and she then replied:

> "What, so I am a man, and a sinister, fascinating man at that, a wicked magician or a demon? . . . I cannot accept that, it's all nonsense. I'd sooner believe this of you!" . . . Her eyes flashed, an evil expression creeps into her face, the gleam of an unknown resistance never seen before. . . . In her glance there lurks something of

the beast of prey, something really demoniacal. . . . What have I touched? What new chord is vibrating? Yet it is only a passing moment. The expression on the patient's face clears, and she says, as though relieved, "It is queer, but just now I had a horrible feeling you had touched the point I could never get over . . . it's a horrible feeling, something inhuman, evil, cruel. I simply cannot describe how queer this feeling is." (1956, 92)

Not only does the preceding quotation describe the projection of the shadow; it also exemplifies Jung's approach to psychoanalysis. Jung's goal was to introduce his patient to the various components of his or her psyche, and when the components were known, to synthesize them into an interrelated configuration resulting in a deeper, more creative person. Unlike Freud, who thought the unconscious, irrational mind had to be made increasingly conscious and rational if humans were to become truly civilized, Jung believed the shadow should be recognized and then used rather than overcome. The animal nature of the shadow was, to Jung, a source of vitality, spontaneity, and creativity. The person who does not use his or her shadow, according to Jung, tends to be dull and lifeless.

Self.   The **self** is the component of the psyche that attempts to harmonize all the other components. It represents the human striving for unity, wholeness, and integration of the total personality. When this integration has been achieved, the person is said to be self-actualized. We will have more to say about the self when we consider "life's goal" later in this chapter.

Psychological Types

Introversion and Extroversion.   Jung thought that there were two general orientations the psyche could take in relating to the world. One was inward, toward the subjective world of the individual; and the other was outward, toward the external environment. Jung called these orientations **attitudes;** the former he labeled **introversion,** and the latter he labeled **extroversion.** The introvert tends to be quiet, imaginative, and more interested in ideas than in other people. The extrovert tends to be sociable, outgoing, and interested in people and environmental events.

The first attitude [introversion] is normally characterized by a hesitant, reflective, retiring nature that keeps itself to itself, shrinks from objects, is always slightly on the defensive and prefers to hide behind mistrustful scrutiny. The second [extroversion] is normally characterized by an outgoing, candid, and accommodating nature that adapts easily to a given situation, quickly forms attachments, and, setting aside any possible misgivings, will often venture forth with careless confidence into unknown situations. (Jung 1917/1966, 44)

The attitudes of introversion and extroversion were first presented by Jung at the International Psychoanalytic Congress at Munich in 1913. They were later elaborated in his book *Psychological Types* (1921). Jung used the notions of introversion and extroversion to explain why different persons develop different kinds of theories of personality. For example, Freud was an extrovert and thus developed a theory that stressed the importance of external events; for example, sex objects. Adler's theory (as we will see in the next chapter) stressed the importance of internal feelings, because Adler was an introvert (Jung 1917/1966, 41–43). Jung could easily have given his own theory as an example of a personality theory created by an introvert, instead of Adler's.

Functions of Thought.   In addition to the attitudes or general orientations, the **functions of thought** pertain to how a person perceives the world and deals with information and experience. The four functions follow:

> **Sensing**   Detects the presence of things. It indicates that something is there but does not indicate what it is.
>
> **Thinking**   Tells what an object is. It gives names to objects that are sensed.
>
> **Feeling**   Determines what an object is worth to the person. Pertains to liking and disliking.
>
> **Intuiting**   Provides hunches when factual information is not available. Jung says, "Whenever you have to deal with strange conditions where you have no established values or established concepts, you will depend upon the faculty of intuition" (1968, 14).

Examples of the functions of thought would be detecting the presence of an object in the environment (sensing), noting that the object is a stranger who is a member of the opposite sex (thinking), experiencing an attraction toward the person (feeling), and believing that the possibility of a long-term relationship with the person exists (intuiting).

Thinking and feeling are called **rational functions,** because they make judgments and evaluations about experiences. In addition, thinking and feeling are considered polar opposites, because, as Jung says, "When you think you must exclude feeling, just as when you feel you must exclude thinking" (1968, 16). Likewise, sensing and intuiting, the **irrational functions,** are thought to be polar opposites. Sensing and intuiting are considered irrational because they both occur independently of logical thought processes. Sensing occurs automatically because of the sensory mechanisms of the body, and intuiting involves a prediction made in the absence of factual information.

Ideally, the attitudes and functions would be equally developed and all would work in harmony; this situation, however, is seldom the case. Usually, one attitude and one function become dominant, and the other attitude and the other three functions remain undeveloped and unconscious. For the functions, the one opposite the dominant conscious one is the least developed, but the other two functions are subservient to the dominant function and in that way may become somewhat developed. For example, in a person whose thinking function is highly developed, the other three functions, especially feeling (the opposite of thinking), will be relatively undeveloped on the unconscious level and may be expressed in dreams, fantasies, or in odd and disturbing ways.

Eight Personality Types.   By combining the two attitudes and the four functions, Jung described eight different types of people. It should be noted, however, that these eight types probably never exist in pure form because each person possesses both attitudes and all four functions, and which is conscious and which is unconscious is a matter of personal development. The eight pure types are listed below, with a brief description of what the person would tend to be like.

Thinking Extrovert. Lives according to fixed rules. Objective and cold. Positive and dogmatic in his or her thinking. Feeling is repressed.

Feeling Extrovert. Very emotional and respectful of authority and tradition. Sociable person who seeks harmony with the world. Thinking is repressed.

Sensing Extrovert. Pleasure seeking, jolly, and socially adaptive. Constantly seeking new sensory experiences. Probably interested in such things as good food and art. Very realistic. Intuiting is repressed.

Intuiting Extrovert. Decisions guided by hunches rather than by facts. Very changeable and creative. Has trouble staying with one idea very long, rather moves from one idea to another very rapidly. Knows much about one's own unconscious. Sensing is repressed.

Thinking Introvert. Intense desire for privacy. Socially inhibited with poor practical judgment. Very intellectual person who ignores the practicalities of everyday living. Feeling is repressed.

Feeling Introvert. Quiet, thoughtful, and hypersensitive. Childish, enigmatic, and indifferent to the feelings and opinions of others. Very little expression of emotion. Thinking is repressed.

Sensing Introvert. Life guided by just what happens. Artistic, passive, and calm. Detached from human affairs because his or her main concern is about what happens. Intuiting is repressed.

Intuiting Introvert. The odd, eccentric daydreamer who creates new but "strange" ideas. Seldom understood by other people, but this is not a source of concern. Life guided by inner experiences rather than outer ones. Sensing is repressed. Jung would be an example.

Here we see Jung's principles of equivalence, opposites, and entropy in operation. Because only so much libidinal energy is available to a person, little will be left for the other components (principle of equivalence) if an abundance of this energy is invested in a particular component of the psyche. When something is conscious, its opposite is unconscious and vice versa (principle of opposites). A constant tendency exists for the libidinal energy to equalize itself across all components and levels of the psyche (principle of entropy). The components of the psyche that we have discussed in this section can be summarized as follows:

Attitudes	Functions of Thought		Levels
	Rational	*Irrational*	
Introversion Extroversion	Thinking Feeling	Sensing Intuiting	Conscious Unconscious

Stages of Development

Stages of development were not as important to Jung as they were to Freud, but he did talk about them in general terms. Jung's stages were defined in terms of the focus of libidinal energy. We saw earlier that Jung disagreed with Freud about the nature of the libido. Freud believed that the libido was mainly sexual in nature and how it was invested within the first five years of life determined, to a large extent, what a person's adult personality would be like. Jung, conversely, thought that libidinal energy was directed simply toward whatever was important to the person at the time and what was important changed as a function of maturation. Jung's stages of development can be summarized as follows.

Childhood (from birth to adolescence). During the early portion of this period, libidinal energy is expended on learning how to walk, talk, and other skills necessary for survival. After the fifth year, more and more libidinal energy is directed toward sexual activities and this focus of libidinal energy reaches its peak during adolescence.

Young Adulthood (from adolescence to about age forty). During this stage, libidinal energy is directed toward learning a vocation, getting married, raising children, and relating in some way to community life. During this stage the individual tends to be outgoing, energetic, impulsive, and passionate.

Middle Age (from about age forty to the later years of life). This stage of development was the most important for Jung. The person is transformed from an energetic, extroverted, and biologically oriented person to one with more cultural, philosophical, and spiritual values. The person is now much more concerned with wisdom and with life's meaning. The needs that must be satisfied during this stage are just as important as those of the preceding stages, but they are different kinds of needs.

It is a great mistake to suppose that the meaning of life is exhausted with the period of youth and expansion . . . the afternoon of life is just as full of meaning as the morning; only its meaning and purpose are different. . . . We are here outside the range of Freudian and Adlerian reductions; we are no longer concerned with how to remove the obstacles to a man's profession, or to his marriage, or to do anything that means a widening of his life, but are confronted with the task of finding a meaning that will enable him to continue living at all. (Jung 1956, 74)

Because it is during middle age that a person first begins to determine the meaning of life, it is a time when religion becomes important. Jung believed that every person possesses a spiritual need, which must be satisfied, just as the need for food must be satisfied. Jung's definition of religion, however, included any systematic attempt to deal with God, spirits, demons, laws, or ideals. We saw earlier that Jung did not have much patience with the kind of religion that involved religious denominations and dogma that was to be taken on faith.

The steady evolution of the psyche toward understanding, harmony, and wisdom is called **progression.** Progression occurs when libidinal energy causes growth. **Regression** occurs when libidinal energy "flows backward" away from the external environment and inward toward the unconscious. Jung thought that regression was not necessarily bad. For example, if one confronts a barrier in life and is, therefore, frustrated, one may regress and sample information in the unconscious that will solve the problem. This concept can be diagrammed as follows.

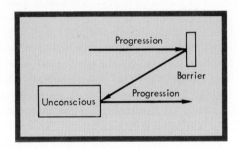

Time and time again Jung suggested that the proper use of the unconscious mind can be beneficial; ignoring it can be dangerous.

Life's Goal

According to Jung, life's goal is to attain the self-development that results when the many opposing forces in the psyche are known and unified. Jung called the innate tendency to seek a harmonious blending of various psychic forces **individuation.** Individuation is a complex, difficult journey of self-discovery. The process of individuation involves becoming aware of the anima or animus, the shadow, the persona, the attitudes, the functions of thought, and all other components of the psyche and giving them expression. Again, the goal is a harmonious blending of all components of the psyche; none of them is undervalued or overvalued. Achieving this difficult harmony results in what Jung called **self-actualization.** Self-actualization involves a blending of both the personal and the collective aspects of personality. If this blending is achieved the person not only becomes whole and unique but also revives his or her connection to all humankind. Jung (1966) said:

> The more we become conscious of ourselves, through self-knowledge, and act accordingly, the more the layer of the personal unconscious that is superimposed on the collective unconscious will be diminished. In this way there arises a consciousness which is no longer imprisoned in the petty, oversensitive, personal world of ego, but participates freely in the wider world of objective interests. The complications . . . are no longer egotistic wish-conflicts, but difficulties that concern others as much as oneself. . . . We can now see that the unconscious produces contents which are valid not only for the person concerned, but for others as well, in fact for a great many people and possibly for all. (178)

Elsewhere, Jung (1931/1966) elaborated on the concept of individuation:

This process is, in fact, the spontaneous realization of the whole man.... The more he is merely "I," the more he splits himself off from the collective man, of whom he is also a part, and may even find himself in opposition to him. But since everything living strives for wholeness, the inevitable one-sidedness of our conscious life is continually being corrected and compensated by the universal human being in us, whose goal is the ultimate integration of conscious and unconscious, or better, the assimilation of the ego to a wider personality. (292)

If the individuation process is successful the self emerges, or, as we have said, the person becomes self-actualized. The self becomes the new center of the personality and is experienced at being suspended between the opposing forces of the psyche. Jung thought that the self was symbolized by a **mandala,** which is the Sanskrit word meaning circle. The self is thought to be at the center of the circle, or midway between the many polarities that make up the psyche. Jung found variations of the mandala in different cultures all over the world, indicating to him its universality. As with all archetypes, the self creates a sensitivity to certain experiences, which in this particular case, is a sensitivity to symbols of balance, perfection, and harmony like the circle. An example of a mandala appears below.

Where does that leave all of us who are not self-actualized? According to Jung, we are in various degrees of trouble. The degree of our problem depends on how lopsided our development has been.

Modern man does not understand how much his "rationalism" (which has destroyed his capacity to respond to numinous symbols and ideas) has put him at the mercy of the psychic "underworld." He has freed himself from "superstition" (or so he believes), but in the process he has lost his spiritual values to a positively dangerous degree. His moral and spiritual tradition has disintegrated, and he is now paying the price for this break-up in world-wide disorientation and dissociation.... As scientific understanding has grown, so our world has become dehumanized. Man feels himself isolated in the cosmos, because he is no longer involved in nature and has lost his emotional "unconscious identity" with natural phenomena. These have slowly lost their symbolic implications. Thunder is no longer the voice of an angry god, nor is lightning his avenging missile. No river contains a spirit, no tree is the life principle of a man, no snake the embodiment of wisdom, no mountain cave the home of a great demon. No voices now speak to man from stones, plants, and animals, nor does he speak to them believing they can hear. His contact with nature has gone, and with it has gone the profound emotional energy that this symbolic connection supplied. (Jung 1964, 94–95)

Jung believed more to life existed than merely being rational. In fact, he believed that ignoring the irrational part of the psyche has caused many of our current problems.

[Contemporary man] is blind to the fact that, with all his rationality and efficiency, he is possessed by "powers" that are beyond his control. His gods and demons have not disappeared at all; they have merely got new names. They keep him on the run with restlessness, vague apprehensions, psychological complications, an insatiable need for pills, alcohol, tobacco, food—and, above all, a large array of neuroses. (Jung 1964, 82)

Again, the goal of Jungian therapy is to help the person on the way to self-hood.

Causality, Teleology, and Synchronicity

Causality.   Freud explained adult personality strictly in terms of prior experiences or **causality.** According to Jung, not only is such a belief incomplete, but it also gives one a feeling of despair and hopelessness. This theory maintains that what a person will become is a function of what one already has been.

Teleology.   Although Jung did not discount causality altogether, he thought **teleology** must be added to it to have a complete picture of human motivation. Teleology means that human behavior has a purpose; that is, our behavior is drawn by the future as much as it is pushed by the past. In other words, to understand a person truly, one must understand his or her goals and aspirations for future attainment on a personal level. On a more general level, all humanity is being drawn into the future by its collective unconscious. The sensitivities to certain experiences caused by the archetypes, in a sense, guide human behavior in the direction of further understanding and ultimately acting on the contents of the collective unconscious. On the individual level, one's life is greatly influenced by personal goals and aspirations, but all humans are driven by the self archetype toward greater understanding of their personalities and toward the harmonious blending of all its components. Jung's general view of human motivation can be represented schematically as follows.

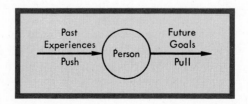

Synchronicity.   Jung referred to **synchronicity** as meaningful coincidence, as when one dreams of a person and shortly thereafter the person appears, or when one fantasizes about an event and the event occurs. According to Jung, such events are of such great importance to one's life that they must be more clearly understood. Synchronicity is one of Jung's more complex concepts, and we will discuss it only briefly here. For synchronicity to take place, two events need to occur independently of each other. That is, the two events have their own causality, but they are not causally related to each other. Then, at some point, an individual experiences them together, and in combination they have meaning to that person, whereas if they were experienced separately, they would not. It is this coming together in a meaningful way of two otherwise meaningless events that defines synchronicity. Progoff (1973) gives the following example of synchronicity from the life of Abraham Lincoln.

> There is a synchronistic event that occurred in the life of Abraham Lincoln that may say a great deal to us about the nature of Synchronicity and its future. During his early years, as we know, Lincoln found himself in a very difficult and conflicting situation. He had intimations of the fact that there was a meaningful work for him to do in the world. He realized, however, that work would require him to develop his intellect and to acquire professional skills. In conflict with these subjective feelings was the fact that, in Lincoln's frontier environment, intellectual tools for professional study were very difficult to find. He had reason to believe that his hopes would never be fulfilled.
>
> One day a stranger came to Lincoln with a barrel full of odds and ends. He said that he was in need of money and that he would be much obliged if Lincoln would help him out by giving him a dollar for the barrel. The contents, he said, were not of much value; they were some old newspapers and things of that sort. But the stranger needed the dollar very badly. The story tells us that Lincoln, with his characteristic kindness, gave the man a dollar for the barrel even though he could not imagine any use that he would have for its contents. Some time later, when he went to clear out the barrel, he found that it contained almost a complete edition of Blackstone's *Commentaries*. It was the chance, or synchronistic, acquisition of these books that enabled Lincoln to become a lawyer and eventually to embark on his career in politics. (170–71)

Note that the two events that came together were not causally related to each other but had their own lines of causality. On the one hand, we had an ambitious Lincoln, who was frustrated because of the lack of needed materials; conversely, we had a stranger with odds and ends who needed a dollar. Only when the two came together at a particular moment in Lincoln's life did they take on meaning. We might say that both Lincoln and the stranger were "lucky" to run into each other.

In a more complex way the concept of synchronicity can be applied to the relationship between the collective unconscious and various experiences we have. As we have seen, each archetype can be regarded as a predisposition to respond emotionally to a certain class of environmental events. In fact, an archetype can be considered a *need* to have certain kinds of experiences. Under these circumstances, when we have an experience that gives symbolic expression to an archetype, the experience is as satisfying as finding food is to a hungry person. This would explain why humans react emotionally to certain music, art forms, and various symbols in their lives. According to Jung, we all have archetypes and when our experiences give them expression, the result is emotionally satisfying. Because the archetypes have one causal heritage and the environmental events that give them symbolic expression have another, their coming together is coincidental and thus an example of synchronicity.

Examples of synchronicity can be found easily in everyone's life, but Jung is the only theorist who has explored the phenomenon.

Research Techniques

We have already viewed Jung's research using his word-association test; this research was his most scientifically orthodox. The other sources of evidence he used to support his theory were more controversial. For example, he studied in depth his own dreams and visions. He studied the contents of the hallucinations of psychotic patients. He studied the religions, rituals, myths, and symbols of various cultures from various eras. He traveled to such places as Arizona, New Mexico, Tunis, Uganda, India, and Kenya to do so. He studied theology, philosophy, mythology, literature, and poetry. He studied all forms of art and language. In short, he studied every major category of human existence, and everywhere he found support for his contention that humans are born with predispositions to respond to the world in certain ways. He believed that he found symbols corresponding to the content of the collective unconscious everywhere; symbols with powerful influences, yet not completely understood by those responding to them.

Psychotic Patients.   It was during his years at Burghölzli that Jung realized that much could be learned about the psyche by studying psychotic patients. Jung (1961) reflects:

> Through my work with the patients I realized that paranoid ideas and hallucina-
> tions contain a germ of meaning. A personality, a life history, a pattern of hopes
> and desires lie behind the psychosis. The fault is ours if we do not understand
> them. It dawned upon me then for the first time that a general psychology of the
> personality lies concealed within psychosis, and that even here we come upon the
> old human conflicts. Although patients may appear dull and apathetic, or totally
> imbecilic, there is more going on in their minds, and more that is meaningful, than
> there seems to be. At the bottom we discover nothing new and unknown in the
> mentally ill; rather, we encounter the substratum of our own natures. (127)

An encounter with a psychotic patient in 1906 exemplifies how we can learn about the psyche from mentally ill persons. Looking out the window, a patient called Jung over and told him that if he half closed his eyes and looked at the sun, Jung would be able to see a phallus hanging from it. Furthermore, the patient told Jung that if he moved his head, from side to side, the sun's phallus would swing back and forth. Finally, the patient asserted that it was the swinging of the sun's phallus that causes the wind (Jung 1931, 151–52). It was not until four years later that Jung would discover that the patient's hallucination may have reflected the contents of the unconscious mind. In 1910, Jung was reading a book about the rituals and visions of an ancient Greek religious cult. One of the visions described was that of the sun with a tube hanging from it, and the direction of the bending tube was determined by the direction of the wind. Because the patient could not have been aware of the ancient vision, Jung was startled by the similarity between the two visions. In subsequent years Jung learned that the sun-phallus or the divine phallus was a common theme in many primitive cultures. Because the many cultures displaying such a myth could not have communicated with each other it must be, concluded Jung, a manifestation of the collective unconscious.

Jung's Analysis of Dreams.   Like Freud, Jung viewed dreams as one of the most important sources of information about the unconscious mind. Although both men regarded dreams as important sources of information, Jung interpreted dreams differently from Freud. First, Jung disagreed with Freud's distinction between manifest and latent contents of a dream. To Jung, the content of a dream is just what it appears to be.

> I have long maintained that we have no right to accuse the dream of, so to speak, a deliberate [maneuver] calculated to deceive. Nature is often obscure or impenetrable, but she is not, like man, deceitful. We must therefore take it that the dream is just what it pretends to be, neither more nor less. (Jung 1917/1966, 100)

Later Jung stated:

> The dream comes in as the expression of an involuntary, unconscious psychic process beyond the control of the conscious mind. It shows the inner truth and reality of the patient as it really is: Not as I conjecture it to be, and not as he would like it to be, but *as it is.* (1931/1969, 139)

Jung's statements are a bit misleading, however, because the contents of dreams can include fragments of ancient symbols and myths and may require considerable knowledge of history, religion, and anthropology to comprehend them.

One of the most important functions of the dream, according to Jung, is to compensate for neglected parts of the psyche. For example, if the shadow is not given an opportunity to express itself consciously, it will manifest itself in dream content and one's dreams will be characterized by demons, devils, monsters, and passionate, immoral impulses. In other words, the person will have an abundance of nightmares. One way, therefore, to detect undeveloped portions of the psyche is to analyze the contents of dreams.

Jung was not restricted by ordinary methods of science, and he felt no need to apologize because he believed that traditional methods of science could not be applied to the richness of the human psyche. He thought that one's methods had to be as complex and flexible as what was being studied, and to be sure, the methods of laboratory science did not qualify. According to Jung, the arena of human experience, not the laboratory, is the proper place to study the human psyche. Jung gave the student of the psyche the following advice.

> Anyone who wants to know the human psyche will learn next to nothing from experimental psychology. He would be better advised to abandon exact science, put away his scholar's gown, bid farewell to his study, and wander with human

heart through the world. There in the horrors of prisons, lunatic asylums and hospitals, in drab suburban pubs, in brothels and gambling-hells, in the salons of the elegant, the Stock Exchanges, socialist meetings, churches, revivalist gatherings and ecstatic sects, through love and hate, through the experience of passion in every form in his own body, he would reap richer stores of knowledge than text-books a foot thick could give him, and he will know how to doctor the sick with real knowledge of the human soul. (Jung 1917/1966, 246–47)

Jung's View of Human Nature

Certainly Jung's view of human nature is among the most complex ever described. The human psyche is embedded in the past, present, and future; it consists of conscious and unconscious elements, masculine and feminine traits, rational and irrational impulses, spiritualistic and animalistic tendencies, and a tendency to bring all these contradictory tendencies and impulses into harmony with each other. Self-actualization is achieved when such harmony exists but self-actualization must be sought; it does not occur automatically. The Jungian analyst helps the person to differentiate and recognize the components of the psyche, which is a prerequisite to harmonizing them.

To Jung, the spiritual need must be satisfied, which usually happens during middle age, when many of the components of the psyche have been discovered. Religion, broadly defined, was to Jung a major vehicle in the journey toward self-actualization. If Freud was pessimistic about human destiny, Jung was optimistic. Jung's optimism, however, was contingent on humans coming to grips with their unconscious mind; if this is not accomplished, the projections of the unconscious mind will continue to cause gross irrationality in our lives and perhaps even a third world war. Jung's theory matches the complexity of our times; it is no wonder that its popularity is growing.

Evaluation

Empirical Research.   Empirical research designed to test Jung's theory has been relatively sparse, but there has been some. Research usually focuses on Jung's typology. For example, the Myers-Briggs Type Indicator Test (Myers 1962) is a standardized pencil-and-paper test designed to measure where individuals fall along four of Jung's bipolar dimensions: being introverted versus extroverted, thinking versus feeling, sensing versus intuiting, and sensing versus judging. Using the Myers-Briggs test, Kilmann and Taylor (1974) and Carlson and Levy (1973) confirmed several Jungian predictions about how various types should differ in the areas of memory and judgment. Also, Carlson (1980) found that introverts and extroverts differ in their memories, the way they describe the world, and the way they describe themselves. Several other personality theorists have found Jung's concept of introversion-extroversion useful (for example, Eysenck and Eysenck, 1985), and that concept is among the major personality dimensions measured by the popular Minnesota Multiphasic Personality Inventory.

Criticisms. Jung's theory, like all the theories covered in this text, has not gone uncriticized. He has been accused of being friendly toward occultism, spirituality, mysticism, and religion, all areas thought by many to emphasize the irrational. Jung believed that he was vastly misunderstood on this issue, however, and insisted that studying these topics in no way implied a belief in them. Rather, he studied them to gain information about the collective unconscious. He, like many contemporary personality theorists, believed that if the scientific method could not be applied to the study of a complex topic, the method should be discarded, not the topic. He thought that personality was an example of such a topic.

Jung's theory also has been attacked for being incomprehensible, unclear, inconsistent, and even contradictory. Also, his concept of self-actualization has been labeled elitist, because it is possible for only highly intelligent, well-educated persons with an abundance of leisure time to arrive at the degree of individuation necessary for self-actualization. This restriction omits most people.

Finally, Jung's theory, like Freud's, has been attacked as nonfalsifiable and therefore unscientific. Except for some research on psychological types and the functions of thought, little empirical research has been performed in an effort to validate the major components of Jung's theory. Jungian concepts such as the principles of equivalence, entropy, and opposites, as well as his notions of the collective unconscious and self-actualization go untested. Because Jung's theory makes few risky predictions it runs little risk of being proved incorrect. Jung would not be distressed by this observation, however. Except for his research using the word-association test, Jung sought validation for his theory not within controlled laboratory conditions but rather in the vast arena of human experience and within human intuition.

Contributions. On the positive side, Jung's theory can be credited with many original concepts in personality theory. His was the first theory to discuss the process of self-actualization, which is currently so popular among personality theorists. His was the first theory to emphasize the importance of the future in determining human behavior. Related to this idea was his stress on the importance of purpose and meaning in one's life. This theme is now emphasized in the existential-humanistic theories of personality. Jung's theory was optimistic about human destiny rather than pessimistic, as Freud's theory was. Jung's theory stressed the attainment of selfhood as a master motive in human behavior, rather than the sexual impulses and early experiences that Freud had stressed.

Somehow Jung's theory creates an image of the psyche that is believable in light of the times in which we live. He leaves us with an image of a psyche that is pushed by the past, pulled by the future, and is attempting to make sense of itself in the present. It is a complex psyche struggling to give expression to its various components. Such a psyche would cause a wide range of behaviors and interests, some of which might even be considered bizarre.

Summary

Biographical information portrays Jung as a complex person, who had a troubled childhood. He originally intended to study archaeology, but a dream caused him instead to study medicine. Although when they first met, Freud and Jung became close friends, theoretical differences between the two eventually caused them to terminate their association. A major disagreement between the two was about the nature of the libido. Freud saw it as mainly sexual energy, and Jung saw it as general energy that could be directed at various problems as they arose, whether they be biologic or spiritual.

Jung accepted the principle of equivalence, which states that the psyche consists of a finite amount of energy; the principle of entropy, which states that a constant tendency exists toward equalization of psychic energy among the various components of the psyche; and the principle of opposites, which states that for every mental process that exists, its opposite also exists. According to Jung, the psyche contains an ego (similar to Freud's concept of ego), a personal unconscious consisting mainly of repressed experiences from one's life, and the collective unconscious, which is a racial memory. The personal unconscious contains clusters of interrelated thoughts called complexes, which Jung studied using his word-association test. The collective unconscious is made up of archetypes, which are inherited predispositions to respond emotionally to certain categories of experiences. Archetypes result from common human experiences through the eons. The more highly developed archetypes include the persona, which is the tendency to select only a part of ourselves to offer to the public; the anima, which is the female component of the male psyche; the animus, which is the male component of the female psyche; the shadow, which is the part of our psyche that we share with lower animals; and the self, which is each person's goal of psychic wholeness and harmony.

Jung postulated two major attitudes or orientations that a psyche could possess: introversion and extroversion. The introvert tends to be inwardly oriented, whereas the extrovert tends to be externally oriented. In addition to the attitudes, Jung discussed four functions of thought: sensing, which detects the presence of objects; thinking, which tells us what an object is; feeling, which tells us whether an object is acceptable or unacceptable; and intuiting, which allows us to make guesses about objects or events in the absence of factual information. The thinking and feeling functions are rational, and the sensing and intuiting functions are irrational. By combining the two attitudes and the four functions, a description of eight different types of people is possible: a thinking extrovert, a feeling extrovert, a sensing extrovert, an intuiting extrovert, a thinking introvert, a feeling introvert, a sensing introvert, and an intuiting introvert.

Three stages of development were discussed: childhood (from birth to adolescence), during which time the skills necessary for survival are learned; young adulthood (adolescence to about forty years old), when a person typically learns a vocation, gets married, and raises children; and middle age (from about forty years of age to the later years), which was considered by Jung the most important time of life because philosophical and spiritual values are stressed, and the meaning of life is sought.

The investment of energy toward a greater understanding of one's psyche is called progression; the flow of energy inward to the unconscious is called regression. Jung used the term individuation to describe the tendency to learn about and harmonize the various components of the psyche. The self refers to a fully integrated psyche and is symbolized by mandalas.

Jung accepted both causality, which states that what we do is determined by our past, and teleology, which states that what we do is determined by our interpretation of the future. In addition, he accepted synchronicity, or meaningful coincidence, as a major influence in a person's life. The main function of dreams, according to Jung, was to compensate for an unevenly developed psyche by giving expression to those portions of the psyche that are unable to manifest themselves more directly.

Empirical research has verified Jungian predictions concerning psychological types and the functions of thought but most of Jung's major concepts have not been empirically tested. In addition to being criticized for being, to a large extent, nonfalsifiable, Jung's theory has been criticized for being mystical, inconsistent, unclear, and contradictory. Conversely, Jung's theory has been praised for accounting for the multitude of human attributes, emphasizing the importance of the future for human behavior, describing the self-actualization process, being optimistic about humans rather than pessimistic, and recognizing the importance of meaning for human existence.

EXPERIENTIAL EXERCISES

1. The following twenty items are from Jung's word-association test.

death	pity	unjust	anxiety
to sin	stupid	family	to abuse
money	book	friend	ridicule
pride	sad	happiness	pure
journey	to marry	lie	to beat

Respond to each word as quickly as you can. Using the criteria specified in the chapter, do you find any indication of a complex? If so, how would you describe that complex? Next, give the test to a close relative and see if you can detect a similar pattern of responding. Finally, give the test to a close friend and compare his or her reactions to your own and those of your relative. How do you explain the individual differences in responses to these words? Do you agree with Jung that a test such as this one can supply information concerning an individual's unconscious mind? Explain why you do or do not agree.

2. Describe how synchronicity has played a role in your life.

3. Assuming that Jung was correct in believing that dreams are compensatory, what do your dreams tell you about what aspects of personality are undeveloped? Jung thought that reoccurring dreams were of special relevance, so you may want to be especially attentive to such dreams in doing this exercise.

4. According to Jung, for humans to live together in social groups they must be willing to play social roles and conform to social mores. Jung refers to the innate tendency to have a public self as the persona. Assuming that Jung is correct in distinguishing between a superficial, public self and a more basic underlying, private self, describe the difference between the two as it applies to you. Give a few examples of how the public image that you project is different from your more private self.

5. According to Jung, primitive humans responded to their world in terms of myths and it is these myth-making tendencies that we inherit as archetypes. Explain the role that myth plays in your life. If, in your opinion, myth plays no role in your life, what would Jung say about you?

6. Ponder the eight pure personality types postulated by Jung. Which type best describes your personality? Which type best describes the person you are emotionally closest to? Without sharing your conclusion with that person, have him or her choose the type that he or she believes best describes himself or herself, and which type best describes your personality. Compare your choices. Discuss what you have learned.

DISCUSSION QUESTIONS

1. Describe the rise and fall of the relationship between Jung and Freud.
2. How did Freud and Jung differ in their definition of libido?
3. Explain the principles of equivalence, entropy, and opposites.
4. Describe Jung's use of the word-association test.
5. Describe Jung's concept of the collective unconscious. Be sure to include in your answer a description of the most fully developed archetypes.
6. List the opposites in Jung's theory.
7. What does it mean to say that a person can be deceived by his or her own persona?
8. In what way can the anima or the animus disrupt relationships with members of the opposite sex? In what way can they facilitate relationships?
9. Differentiate between introversion and extroversion.
10. Describe the four functions of thought.
11. Summarize the stages of human development as seen by Jung.
12. Differentiate between Jung's concepts of progression and regression.
13. Describe "life's goal" as Jung saw it.
14. Differentiate between causality and teleology.
15. Describe Jung's concept of synchronicity.
16. Summarize the kinds of evidence used by Jung to validate his theory.
17. Contrast Jung's method of dream analysis with Freud's.
18. Summarize Jung's view of human nature.
19. Compare and contrast Freud and Jung on each of the following: methodology, the nature of the unconscious mind, motivation, and religion.
20. Using Jung's concept of the collective unconscious, explain the widespread appeal of music and competitive sports.

SUGGESTIONS FOR FURTHER READING

HALL, C. S., and J. NORDLY, (1973). *A Primer of Jungian Psychology.* New York: New American Library.
    A short, readable introduction to basic Jungian theory.

HANNAH, B. (1976). *Jung: The Man and His Work.* New York: G. P. Putnam's Sons.
    A sympathetic biography of Jung written by one of his former students.

JUNG, C. G. (1961). *Memories, Dreams, Reflections.* New York: Random House
    Jung's autobiography. Provides a strikingly personal glimpse at the evolution of Jung's thinking, including a detailed description of the relationships, dreams, visions, and fantasies that shaped his theory.

MCGUIRE, W. (ed.). (1974). *The Freud/Jung Letters.* Princeton, NJ: Princeton University Press.
    The correspondence between Freud and Jung. The letters trace the development, course, and, finally, the collapse of the Freud-Jung relationship.

PROGOFF, I. (1973). *Jung, Synchronicity, and Human Destiny: Noncausal Dimensions of Human Experience.* New York: Dell Publishing.
    An in-depth, somewhat difficult, exploration of Jung's concept of synchronicity.

STERN, P. J. (1976). *C. G. Jung: The Haunted Prophet.* New York: Dell Publishing.
    A sharply critical biography of Jung.

GLOSSARY

Anima. The female component of the male psyche.

Animus. The male component of the female psyche.

Archetype. An inherited predisposition to respond emotionally to certain aspects of the world. All the archetypes taken together make up the collective unconscious.

Attitude. The general orientation the psyche takes when relating to the world. The two basic attitudes are introversion and extroversion.

Causality. The belief that a person's personality can be explained in terms of past experiences.

Childhood. The stage of development that lasts from birth to adolescence, during which time libidinal energy is invested in learning the basic skills necessary for survival and sex.

Collective unconscious. The collection of inherited predispositions that humans have to respond to certain events. These predispositions come from the universal experiences humans have had throughout their evolutionary past. For example, because all humans have had mothers, we are born with the tendency to respond emotionally to the general concept of mother. What is inherited is a sensitivity to certain categories of experience rather than specific ideas about or responses to those categories.

Complex. A set of interrelated ideas that are highly valued and that exist in the personal unconscious. A person with a power complex would spend a disproportionate amount of time and energy accumulating personal power.

Creative illness. According to Ellenberger, a period of intense preoccupation with a search for a particular truth. This search is usually accompanied by depression, psychosomatic ailments, neuroses, and perhaps psychotic episodes.

Ego. For Jung, the ego is everything of which we are conscious and entails performing the functions related to everyday life.

Extroversion. The tendency to be externally oriented, confident, outgoing, and gregarious.

Feeling. The function of thought that determines whether an object or event is valued positively or negatively.

Functions of thought. Determines how a person perceives the world and deals with information and experience. The four functions of thought are sensing, thinking, feeling, and intuiting.

Individuation. The process of coming to know, giving expression to, and harmonizing the various components of the psyche.

Inflation of the persona. A condition that exists when one's persona is too highly valued.

Introversion. The tendency to be internally oriented, quiet, subjective, and nonsocial.

Intuiting. The function of thought that makes hunches about objects or events when factual information is not available.

Irrational functions. Jung referred to sensing and intuiting as rational functions because they do not involve logical thought processes.

Libido. According to Jung, the general life energy that can be directed to any problem that arises, be it biologic or spiritual.

Mandala. The Sanskrit word for circle. For Jung the mandala was a symbol of wholeness, completeness, and perfection; that is, it symbolized the self.

Middle age. The stage of development that lasts from about forty years of age to the later years of life, during which time libidinal energy is invested in philosophical and spiritual pursuits. According to Jung, this stage of development is the most important.

Persona. The superficial aspect of the psyche that a person displays publicly. It includes the various roles one must play to survive in a society.

Personal unconscious. Consists of material that was once conscious and then repressed or material that was not vivid enough to make a conscious impression at first.

Principle of entropy. The second law of thermodynamics, which states that a constant tendency exists toward the equalization of energy within a system.

Principle of equivalence. The first law of thermodynamics, which states that the amount of energy in a system is fixed and, therefore, if some of it is removed from one part of the system, it must show up in another part.

Principle of opposites. The contention that each component of the psyche has an opposite. For example, the rational is the opposite of the irrational; the conscious is the opposite of the unconscious; and introversion is the opposite of extroversion.

Progression. The steady evolution of the psyche toward understanding and harmony.

Psyche. A term that Jung equated with personality.

Rational functions. Jung referred to thinking and feeling as rational functions because they involve making judgments and evaluations about experiences.

Regression. The opposite of progression. Occurs when psychic energy is directed inward, to the unconscious.

Self. The state of the psyche if the individuation process has been completely successful. When the various components of the psyche are harmonized, the self becomes the center of all of the various opposing psychic forces. The emergence of the self, coming into selfhood, and self-actualization were used synonymously by Jung.

Self-actualization. A state of balance and harmony that is reached when the various components of the psyche are recognized and given expression.

Sensing. The function of thought that detects the presence of objects.

Shadow. The deepest part of the collective unconscious, which contains all the animalistic urges that characterized our prehuman existence.

Synchronicity. Meaningful coincidence. When two independent events come together in a meaningful way.

Teleology. The belief that one's personality can be best understood in terms of one's future goals.

Thinking. The function of thought that tells what an object is.

Value. Varies as the amount of libidinal energy invested varies. Those components of the personality that have an abundance of libidinal energy invested in them are valued more than components with less energy invested in them.

Word-association test. A research technique that Jung used to explore the complexes within the personal unconscious. It consisted of reading one hundred words one at a time and having a person respond as quickly as possible with a word of his or her own.

Young adulthood. The stage of development that lasts from adolescence to about forty years of age. During this time libidinal energy is invested in learning a vocation, getting married, raising children, and participating in community life.

4

Alfred Adler

A

lfred Adler was born in a suburb of Vienna, Austria on 7 February, 1870. His father, Leopold, was a moderately successful grain merchant. Adler grew up under comfortable physical circumstances and was able to enjoy the open spaces, relative freedom from want, and a city (Vienna) that was one of the great cultural centers of Europe. In addition, he was able to share his love of music with his entire family.

Despite its apparent physical comfort, however, Adler looked on his childhood as miserable. He thought of himself as undersized and ugly. He was the third of seven children and had a severe rivalry with his older brother, who apparently was very athletic and a model child. Adler's mother seemed to prefer his older brother to him, but Adler got along very well with his father.

Adler's views of himself were not without foundation. He was a sickly child who was unable to walk until he was four years old. He suffered from rickets, which prevented him from engaging in any strenuous physical activity. Bottome relates one of Adler's early memories:

> One of my earliest recollections is of sitting on a bench bandaged up on account of rickets, with my healthy elder brother sitting opposite me. He could run, jump, and move about quite effortlessly, while for me, movement of any sort was a strain and an effort. Everyone went to great pains to help me and my mother and father did all that was in their power to do. (1957, 30–31)

When Adler was five, he caught pneumonia and almost died. In fact, he heard the doctor say to his parents, "Your boy is lost" (Orgler 1963). This illness, the death of a younger brother in a bed next to his when he was three, and being run over twice himself, convinced him that he should become a medical physician when he grew up.

Contrary to what one may think, Adler remained a friendly, sociable child with a genuine love for people (traits that he retained all his life). His unhappiness continued in school, where he began as a poor student (especially in mathematics). One of his teachers counseled his parents to train him as a shoemaker, because he apparently was not qualified for anything else. Eventually, however, Adler became one of the best students in his class.

Adler's childhood ambition was realized when he obtained his medical degree from the University of Vienna (Freud's alma mater) in 1895. He first specialized in ophthalmology (diseases of the eye) and later changed to general practice and finally to psychiatry. Two years after his graduation from medical school, he married Raissa Epstein, a rich Russian girl who came to Vienna to study. Raissa was a particularly liberated, domineering woman who was a militant socialist. It is interesting to note that, perhaps under his wife's influence, Adler's first publication came the year after he married Raissa, and it concerned the terrible working conditions of independent tailors and the need for socialized medicine for the poor. The Adlers had four children. One daughter (Alexandra) and his only son (Kurt) became psychiatrists and continued their father's work in individual psychology (individual psychology will be discussed shortly).

Alfred Adler

Adler read Freud's book *The Interpretation of Dreams* and wrote an article defending Freud's theoretical position. On the basis of this defense, Adler was invited by Freud to join the Vienna Psychoanalytic Society in 1902. Adler accepted Freud's invitation, thereby becoming one of Freud's earliest colleagues. Adler became president of the Society in 1910, just one year before his official break from the Freudian group. It appears now that joining the group may have been a mistake to begin with, because Adler had little in common with Freud. This incompatibility became increasingly obvious, and in 1911, while he was still president of the Vienna Psychoanalytic Society and after a nine-year association with Freud, he resigned from the society. The two men never met again. The differences between Adler and Freud that caused this separation were numerous and will be reviewed at the end of this chapter, but the following quotation from Ernest Jones lists a few of Adler's beliefs that were contrary to Freud's:

> Sexual factors, particularly those of childhood, were reduced to a minimum: a boy's incestuous desire for intimacy with his mother was interpreted as the male wish to conquer a female masquerading as sexual desire. The concepts of repression, infantile sexuality, and even that of the unconscious itself were discarded so little was left of psychoanalysis. (1955, 131)

Freud characteristically had a low tolerance for "defectors," and he remained hostile to Adler all his life. Adler was the pigmy in Freud's statement, "I made a pigmy great.'' Adler said of Freud's theory that it was founded on the mythology of sex and that psychoanalysis was stimulated by the selfishness of a pampered child. Freud, who could not understand the grief a friend was suffering over the death of Adler, said: "I don't understand your sympathy for Adler. For a Jewish boy out of a Viennese suburb a death in Aberdeen is an unheard of career in itself and a proof of how far he had got on. The world really rewarded him richly for his service in having contradicted psychoanalysis'' (Scarf 1971, 47).

After breaking with the Freudians, Adler and his followers formed a group that they first called the Society of Free Psychoanalytic Research, but they settled on the term **individual psychology** to describe their work. Unfortunately, individual psychology can be easily misunderstood, and the next section in this chapter attempts to clarify its meaning.

Adler served as a physician in the Austrian Army during World War I and, following his release, he was asked by the government to open a number of child-guidance clinics in Vienna. This was one of Adler's early efforts to apply his theory to the problems of child rearing, education, and other everyday problems. Many of his books, articles, and lectures (of which there were hundreds) were directed either toward teachers or toward the general public. Adler's fame quickly spread, and, in Vienna, he was surrounded by many students, friends, and admirers. Freud, disturbed by all this, proclaimed (incorrectly) that Adler's theory was actually nothing but psychoanalytic knowledge, which Adler had labeled his own by changing its terminology.

In 1926, Adler first visited the United States and was warmly received by educators. In 1927, he was appointed lecturer at Columbia University, and in 1932 he became a professor of medical psychology at the Long Island College of Medicine in New York. In 1935, partially because of the Nazi take-over in Europe, Adler made the United States his permanent home. He died of a heart attack on 28 May, 1937, in Aberdeen, Scotland, while on a lecture tour there.

There was one peak of popularity for Adlerian psychology in 1930 at the fifth International Congress of Individual Psychology in Berlin, which had over 2,000 participants (Ansbacher 1983). Another peak seems either to be here or on the way. According to Ansbacher:

> The Adlerian movement today numbers several thousand members in the United States, Canada, and European countries, especially Germany. It is composed of psychiatrists, psychologists, social workers, counselors, and educators, as well as lay people who accept the theory and apply the method of Adlerian psychology to family life and personal development. (1983, 76)

Adler's theory continues to be promoted today by the *American Journal of Individual Psychology* and by the American Society of Individual Psychology. Heinz and Rowena Ansbacher have summarized many of Adler's ideas in two volumes (1956, 1979). Adler's daughter Alexandra and his son Kurt are practicing Adlerian psychiatrists in New York. Adler was a strong believer in bringing his ideas to nonprofessionals, a task that is currently being perpetuated by Rudolf Dreikurs (1957, 1964).

Individual Psychology

In many ways, Adler's theory of personality is the opposite of Freud's. Freud saw individuals constantly in conflict with one another and with society, whereas Adler saw them seeking companionship and harmony. Freud ignored questions concerning life's meaning and the effects of future aspirations on one's life, whereas Adler made these questions a central part of his theory. Freud saw the mind as consisting of different components often in conflict with one another, whereas Adler viewed the mind as an integrated whole working to help attain the future goals of the person. So by choosing the term individual psychology for his theory, Adler by no means intended to imply that people are selfishly motivated to satisfy their own biologic drives. Rather, he meant that although individuals are unique, they are characterized by inner harmony and a striving to cooperate with fellow humans.

Adler's theory is related to humanism because of its concern with the positive relationships among humans. His theory is related to existentialism because of its concern with questions concerning the meaning of human existence. Adler, like the modern existentialists, believed that humans are future oriented (a belief shared by Jung), at least partially free to determine their own fate, and concerned with the meaning of life.

Adler's theory is related to Gestalt psychology because it emphasizes wholes and not parts. Such statements as "The whole is more than the sum of its parts," and "To dissect is to distort" characterize the beliefs of the Gestalt psychologist; they are statements with which Adler would agree. As already mentioned, Adler did not believe the mind to be divided into various components that were constantly warring with each other. Rather, he believed all aspects of the individual to be organized around a common purpose, a purpose that existed in the future and that had to be attained while working harmoniously with others and with society. Clearly, little similarity exists between Adler's individual psychology and Freud's psychoanalysis.

Organ Inferiority and Compensation

In 1907, Adler published his now famous essay entitled, "Organ Inferiority and Its Physical Compensation." In this essay, Adler put forth the idea that people are especially vulnerable to disease in organs that are less developed or "inferior" to other organs. For example, some persons are born with weak eyes, others with weak stomachs, others with weak hearts, and still others with damaged limbs. These biologic deficiencies cause problems in the person's life because of the stresses put on them by the environment. These organic weaknesses inhibit the person from functioning normally and, therefore, must be dealt with in some way.

Because the body acts as an integrated unit, a person can **compensate** for a weakness either by concentrating on its development or by emphasizing other functions that make up for the weakness. For example, someone with a frail body may work hard to overcome this frailty. Likewise, a blind person may concentrate on developing auditory skills. In both cases, a biologic weakness is compensated.

In some cases, a person may **overcompensate** by converting a biologic weakness into a strong point. That was the case when Teddy Roosevelt, who was an extremely frail child, became a hardy outdoorsman, and when Demosthenes overcame a speech impediment to become a great orator. At this early stage in the development of his theory, Adler emphasized biologic inferiority, compensation, and overcompensation.

Feelings of Inferiority

In 1910 Adler shifted his emphasis from actual **organ inferiority** to "subjective inferiority," or **feelings of inferiority.** Now compensation or overcompensation was directed toward either real or imagined inferiorities. At this point in his theorizing, Adler left the biologic sciences and entered psychology. Anything that caused inferiority feelings was a worthwhile topic to study.

Adler pointed out that all humans start life with feelings of inferiority, because we all are completely dependent on adults for our survival. Children feel completely helpless compared to the powerful adults on whom they depend. This feeling of being weak, impotent, and inferior stimulates in the child an intense desire to seek power, thereby overcoming feelings of inferiority. At this point in the evolution of Adler's theory, he stressed aggression and power as a means of overcoming feelings of inferiority.

Unfortunately, but mainly because of cultural conditions at the time that Adler was writing, he equated power and strength with masculinity and inferiority with femininity.

> Any form of uninhibited aggression, activity, potency, power, and the traits of being brave, free, rich, aggressive or sadistic can be considered masculine. All inhibitions and deficiencies, as well as cowardliness, obedience, poverty, and similar traits, can be considered as feminine. (Adler 1910/1956, 47)

At this point in the evolution of Adler's theory, to become more powerful meant to become more masculine and, consequently, less feminine. He referred to this striving to become more masculine as the **masculine protest.** Because both men and women seek to become powerful to overcome inferiority feelings, they both attempt to approximate the cultural ideal of masculinity. In other words, both men and women engage in the masculine protest. Adler believed, however, that the cultural overvaluation of masculinity over femininity was not positive for either men or women.

> What I have said concerning the hatreds and jealousies between nations and groups also holds good of the bitter struggle between the sexes, a struggle that is poisoning love and marriage and is ever born anew out of the inferior valuation of woman. The idealized picture of overestimated masculinity imposes both on the boy and the grown-up man the obligation of appearing, if not being, superior to woman. This causes him to distrust himself, to exaggerate his demands on life and his expectations from it, and increases his sense of insecurity. On the other hand,

a girl feels that she is valued less than a boy, and this may stimulate her either to exaggerated efforts to make up for her inadequacy and to fight real or apparent depreciation on all sides, or else may cause her to resign herself to her supposed inferiority. (Adler 1956, 452)

Are feelings of inferiority bad? No, said Adler. In fact, to be a human being means to feel inferior. It is a condition common to all humans and, therefore, is not a sign of weakness or abnormality. In fact, such feelings are the primary motivating force behind all personal accomplishments. One feels inferior and is therefore driven to accomplish something. A short-lived feeling of success exists after such an accomplishment, but in light of the accomplishments of others, one again feels inferior and again is motivated to accomplish more, and on it goes without end.

Even though feelings of inferiority act as a stimulus for all positive growth, however, they also can create neurosis. A person can become overwhelmed by feelings of inferiority, at which point he or she is prevented from accomplishing anything. Under these circumstances, feelings of inferiority act as a barrier rather than as a stimulus for positive accomplishment. Such a person is said to have an **inferiority complex.** According to Adler, all humans experience the feeling of being inferior, but in some it stimulates neurosis and in others it creates a need to succeed. We will have something to say about what makes the difference later in this chapter.

Striving for Superiority

Adler modified his theoretical position to state that it is not more aggression, power, or masculinity that we constantly seek, but superiority or perfection. Adler now referred to the striving for superiority as the **fundamental fact of life.** Adler's theory had evolved from the point at which it emphasized compensation for organ inferiority, to that at which subjective inferiority was compensated through aggression and power, to that at which the fundamental fact of life is that all humans strive for superiority-perfection. What is the origin of this striving for perfection? According to Adler, it is innate; it is "built in" all humans at birth.

> It runs parallel to physical growth. It is an intrinsic necessity of life itself. . . . All our functions follow its direction; rightly or wrongly they strive for conquest, surety, increase. The impetus from minus to plus is never-ending. The urge from "below" to "above" never ceases. Whatever premises all our philosophers and psychologists dream of—self-preservation, pleasure principle, equalization—all these are but vague representations, attempts to express the great upward drive . . . a fundamental category of thought, the structure of our reason . . . *the fundamental fact of our life.* (Adler 1930b, 398–99)

In his final theoretical position Adler retained striving for superiority as the master motive in his theory, but he changed from striving for individual superiority to striving for a superior or perfect society. As we have seen, Adler believed that feelings of inferiority could result in positive growth or in an inferiority complex. Adler also believed that striving for superiority could be beneficial or harmful. If a person concentrates exclusively on his or her own superiority while ignoring the needs of others and of society, he or she may develop a **superiority complex.** A person with a superiority complex tends to be domineering, vain, boastful, arrogant, and depreciative of others. According to Adler, such a person lacks social interest and is, indeed, undesirable.

Life-Style

All humans have the same ultimate goal, to strive for superiority, but how superiority is sought depends on a person's unique circumstances. The means by which a particular individual attempts to gain superiority is called the **life-style.**

A person's life-style determines which aspects of life are focused on and how; it gives an individual an identity; it determines how problems are solved; it determines what is perceived and what is ignored; and it specifies how future goals are to be attained. A healthy life-style will allow a person to approximate perfection and to get along harmoniously with others, and will contribute to the advancement of society's goals. A "mistaken" life-style is based on selfishness and is contrary to the aims of society.

When is one's life-style formulated? Here there is some agreement between Adler and Freud. Adler said that one's life-style was fairly well crystallized by the age of four or five. Although the young child has countless experiences, some of those experiences are perceived by the child as much more important than others. In Adler's youth, experience related to illness and death took on special significance. It is from the experiences that for some reason stand out as being extremely important that the young child forms his or her perception of himself or herself, the world, and the people in the world. It is important to remember, however, that for Adler subjective reality was more important than physical reality. That is, it is the child's *perception* of the major events in his or her life that determines his or her views, not actual reality. If the child perceives the world to be a harsh, unpredictable place, he or she will adjust by creating life's goals that incorporate those facts. If the child perceives the world as a warm, loving, predictable place, then those perceptions will be important in his or her adjustments to life. Because the important early experiences that mold a child's personality are those most vividly remembered through the years, they are the ones most likely to be reported as one's earliest recollections. It was for this reason that Adler believed that one's earliest memories provide important information about one's life goals and one's life-style. We will have more to say about the importance of first memories later in this chapter.

Again, what life-style a child develops depends on his or her personal circumstances. If a child has a particular reason (real or imagined) for feelings of inferiority, the life-style could be aimed at compensating or overcompensating for that inferiority. Or a life-style could develop when a child models himself or herself after someone perceived to be highly influential and effective.

Children look for the strongest person in their environment and make him their model or their goal. It may be the father, or perhaps the mother, for we find that even a boy may be influenced to imitate his mother if she seems the strongest person. . . . Later on, the ideal may become the doctor or the teacher. For the teacher can punish the child and thus he arouses his respect as a strong person. (Adler 1929/1969, 54)

Fictional Finalism

In 1911, Hans Vaihinger wrote a book entitled *The Philosophy of "As If."* Vaihinger's contention was that the lives of persons are guided by fictions made up by them to make life significant and organized. Although these subjective beliefs have no counterpart in reality, they are useful to the person attempting to grapple with the problems of existence. The person who believes a God exists acts "as if" there really is one and lives as if the soul will be judged on the basis of that behavior. Other fictions by which humans live would include "When I have enough money I will be happy," "To have a good wife and to raise children gives life its meaning," "If only I can get my Ph.D., everything will fall into place," "If I could only write a book, my financial problems would be over."

Adler embraced Vaihinger's thesis enthusiastically and made it an important part of his theory. He made **fictional finalism** the unifying principle of personality. Everything a person does, said Adler, is related to a final fictional goal. For Adler the future became much more important than the past to understanding human behavior. Adler believed that the idea of a fictional goal guiding behavior freed his theory from the determinism that characterized Freud's theory.

The concept of fictional finalism, which Adler later called "a guiding self-ideal," gave Adler's theory a strong teleological (future-oriented) component, but it did not ignore the past altogether. Now we can view the person as pushed by feelings of inferiority or imperfection toward perfection using his or her unique life-style as a means of attaining some future goal.

Adler emphasized that these future goals or ideals were convenient fictions invented to make life more significant than it otherwise would be. Healthy people, according to Adler, change fictions when circumstances warrant it. Neurotic persons, conversely, cling to their fictions at all costs. In other words, according to Adler, healthy individuals use fictional goals or ideals as tools in dealing with life. Life is unbearable without meaning, so they invent meaning. Life is chaotic without a plan for living, so healthy persons invent such a plan. For healthy persons, such goals, ideas, or plans are means of living a more effective, constructive life. For the neurotic, the idea that these plans are only tools is lost. The goals, ideals, or plans become ends in themselves, rather than means to an end. As such, they are retained even when they have become ineffective in dealing with reality. Thus, for Adler, an important difference between the healthy person and the neurotic is the ease with which a fictional life plan can be dispensed with if circumstances warrant it. The healthy or normal person never loses sight of reality, whereas for neurotic persons the fictional life plan becomes reality.

Adler (1912/1956) explained:

More firmly than the normal individual does the neurotic fixate his God, his idol, his personality ideal, and cling to his guiding line, and with deeper purpose he loses sight of reality. The normal person, on the other hand, is always ready to dispense with this aid, this crutch. In this instance, the neurotic resembles a person who looks up to God, commends himself to the Lord, and then waits credulously for His guidance; the neurotic is nailed to the cross of his fiction. The normal individual, too, can and will create his deity, will feel drawn upward. But he will never lose sight of reality, and always takes it into account as soon as action and work are demanded. The neurotic is under the hypnotic spell of a fictional life plan. (246–47)

We are reminded once again why Adler's theory is called individual psychology. The individual invents an ultimate goal and then invents a life-style as a means of achieving that goal. All of this invention implies a great deal of personal freedom, an implication that we will explore further when we discuss "the creative self" later in this chapter.

Social Interest

Adler's earlier theory had been criticized because it portrayed humans as selfishly motivated to strive for personal superiority. With his concept of **social interest,** Adler put such criticism to rest. Social interest was, according to Adler, an innate need of all humans to live in harmony and friendship with others and to aspire toward the development of the perfect society. The attainment of the perfect society replaced perfection of the individual as the primary motivation. A well-developed social interest relates to almost all aspects of one's life.

> It is almost impossible to exaggerate the value of an increase in social feeling. The mind improves, for intelligence is a communal function. The feeling of worth and value is heightened, giving courage and an optimistic view, and there is a sense of acquiescence in the common advantages and drawbacks of our lot. The individual feels at home in life and feels his existence to be worthwhile just as far as he is useful to others and is overcoming common, instead of private, feelings of inferiority. Not only the ethical nature, but the right attitude in aesthetics, the best understanding of the beautiful and the ugly, will always be founded upon the truest social feeling. (Adler 1956b, 155)

However, what we inherit, according to Adler, is the *potential* for social interest. If that potential is not realized, the person will live a most unfortunate life. Simply put, those without well-developed social interest are neurotic or even worse than neurotic. "In all human failure, in the waywardness of children, in neurosis and neuropsychosis, in crime, suicide, alcoholism, morphinism, cocainism, in sexual perversion, in fact in all nervous symptoms, we may read lack of proper degree of *social feeling.*" (Adler 1930b, 401)

According to Adler, each individual must solve three major problems in life, all of which require a well developed social interest: (1) *occupational tasks—* through constructive work the person helps to advance society; (2) *societal tasks—* this requires cooperation with fellow humans. Adler said: "It was only because man learned to cooperate that the great discovery of the division of labor was made, a discovery which is the chief security for the welfare of mankind" (1933, 132); (3) *love and marriage tasks*—the relationship between this task and the continuance of society is clear. Adler said: "On his approach to the other sex and on the fulfillment of his sexual role depends his part in the continuance of mankind" (1956, 132).

What determines whether a person will have a well-developed social interest or not? Primarily the mother. According to Adler, the first major social situation that the child encounters is in relation to the mother. The mother-child relationship acts as a model for subsequent social relationships with others. If the mother maintains a positive, cooperative atmosphere, the child will tend to develop social interest. If, however, the mother binds the child exclusively to herself, the child will learn to exclude other people from his or her life and will develop a low social interest. For Adler, it is the nature of the mother's early interactions with her child that primarily determine whether or not the child will have a healthy, open attitude toward other people.

In fact, in the following quotation we see that Adler believed the mother's job was monumental.

A mother is related not only with her children, but also with her husband and with the whole social life around her. These three ties must be given equal attention; all three must be faced calmly and with common sense. If a mother considers only her tie with her children, she will be unable to avoid pampering and spoiling them. She will make it hard for them to develop independence and the ability to cooperate with others. After she has succeeded in connecting the child with herself, her next task is to spread his interest towards his father; and this task will prove almost impossible if she herself is not interested in the father. She must turn the child's interest also to the social life around him, to the other children of the family, to friends, relatives, and fellow human beings in general. Her task is thus twofold. She must give the child his first experience of a trustworthy fellow being; and she must then be prepared to spread this trust and friendship until it includes the whole of our human society.

The task of the mother is to turn the child as early as possible into a co-worker, a fellow man who helps gladly and gladly lets himself be helped insofar as his own strength is not adequate. (Adler 1956, 373)

In the final version of Adler's theory, a person's life-style and fictional goal must take the improvement of society into consideration. If they do not, the person will be neurotic.

Mistaken Life-Styles

Any life-style that is not aimed at socially useful goals is a **mistaken life-style.** We already have encountered two examples, the person who seeks personal superiority (superiority complex) and the person who is so overwhelmed by feelings of inferiority so as to accomplish nothing (inferiority complex). Both individuals lack social interest and, therefore, their life-styles are mistaken or incorrect.

Adler delineated four types of people, who were labeled according to their degree of social interest. The four types of people are: (1) the **ruling-dominant type,**

(2) the **getting-leaning type,** (3) the **avoiding type,** and (4) the **socially useful type.** The first type attempts to dominate or rule people. The second type expects everything from others and gets everything he or she can from them. The third type "succeeds" in life by avoiding problems; such a person avoids failure by never attempting anything. The fourth type confronts problems and attempts to solve them in a socially useful way. The first three types have faulty life-styles because they lack proper social interest. Only "the socially useful type" can hope to live a rich, purposeful life.

Where do faulty life-styles originate? Adler said they begin in childhood, at the same time that a healthy life-style originates. Adler described three childhood conditions that tend to create a faulty life-style: The first is **physical inferiority,** which can stimulate compensation or overcompensation, which is healthy, or can result in an inferiority complex, which is unhealthy. The second is **spoiling** or **pampering,** which makes a child believe it is up to others to satisfy his or her every need. Such a child is the center of attention and grows up to be selfish, with little, if any, social interest. **Neglecting,** the third condition, causes the child to feel worthless and angry and to look on everyone with distrust. Adler considered pampering as the most serious of parental errors.

> The most frequent difficulty is that the mother excuses the child from giving her any help or cooperation; heaps caresses and affection on him; and constantly acts, thinks and speaks for him, curtailing every possibility of development. Thus she pampers the child and accustoms him to an imaginary world which is not ours and in which everything is done for the child by others. (Adler 1956, 373–74)

Adler elaborates on how pampered children (and adults) view the world.

> The pampered child is trained to expect that his wishes will be treated as laws. . . . When he comes into circumstances where he is not the center of attention and where other people do not make it their chief aim to consider his feelings, he will be very much at a loss: he will feel that his world has failed him. He has been trained to expect and not to give. . . . When he has difficulties before him, he has only one method of meeting them—to make demands on other people. . . . Grown-up pampered children are perhaps the most dangerous class in our community. (1931/1958, 16)

According to Adler, it is also pampering that creates the Oedipus complex, "We could probably induce an [Oedipus] complex in any child. All we would need is for its mother to spoil it, and refuse to spread its interest to other people, and for its father to be comparatively indifferent or cold" (1931/1958, 54). Adler viewed Freud's theory as the creation of a pampered child.

> And, indeed, if we look closely we shall find that the Freudian theory is the consistent psychology of the pampered child, who feels that his instincts must never be denied, who looks on it as unfair that other people should exist, who asks always, "Why should I love my neighbor? Does my neighbor love me?" (Adler 1931/1958, 97)

The opposite of pampering is neglect, and it too gives the child an erroneous impression of what the world is like. In the case of neglect the child develops the impression that the world is a cold and unsympathetic place, and it is on this impression that the child formulates his or her life's goal and life-style. According to Adler (1931/1958) the neglected child:

> Has never known what love and cooperation can be: he makes up an interpretation of life which does not include these friendly forces. . . . He will overrate [the difficulties of life] and will underrate his own capacity to meet them . . . [and] will not see that he can *win* affection and esteem by actions which are useful to others. (17)

Family experiences other than pampering and neglect can lead children to have a distorted view of the world and, therefore, faulty life-styles. According to Adler, other negative family experiences include failure to express a normal amount of tenderness or to consider sentimentality as ridiculous; excessive use of punishment, especially corporal punishment; establishment of standards of goals that are unattainable; excessive criticism of other people; and consideration of one parent as superior to the other.

It is important to remember when considering the factors that may lead to a mistaken life-style that it is the child's perceptions that are the determinants of his or her personality, *not* reality. A pampered child who feels neglected will develop the world view of a neglected child and vice versa. Adler said "It is not the child's experiences which dictate his actions; it is the conclusions which he draws from his experiences" (1931/1958, 123).

Safeguarding Strategies

According to Adler, neurotics know (or feel) that their goal of *personal* perfection is a mistaken one and may be exposed. Such public exposure would heighten the neurotic's already intense feelings of inferiority. Adler believed that neurotics use **safeguarding strategies** to protect what little self-esteem and illusions of superiority a mistaken life-style can generate. The feelings of self-esteem and superiority experienced by healthy persons are real because they are based on social interest and, therefore, they do not need to be supported by deceptive strategies. Adler's safeguarding strategies are similar to Freud's ego-defense mechanisms except, unlike ego-defense mechanisms, safeguarding strategies are used only by neurotics, can operate either on the conscious or unconscious levels, and protect persons from outside threats and the problems of life. Adler discussed three categories of safeguarding strategies: excuses, aggression, and distancing.

Excuses. The neurotic develops symptoms and uses them as **excuses** for his or her shortcomings.

> The patient . . . selects certain symptoms and develops them until they impress him . . . as real obstacles. Behind his barricade of symptoms the patient feels hidden and secure. To the question, "What use are you making of your talents?" he answers, "This thing stops me; I cannot go ahead," and points to his self-erected barricade. We must never neglect the patient's own use of his symptoms. To be overworked by grappling with his own neurotic difficulties in only an

extenuating circumstance, it is also the patient's inner relief from his striving for superiority. . . . The patient declares that he is unable to solve his task "on account of the symptoms, and only on account of these." He expects from the others the solution of his problems, or the excuse from all demands, or, at least, the granting of "extenuating circumstances." (Adler 1956, 265–66)

This safeguarding strategy consists of the "yes, but . . ." and "if only" excuses that protect a weak sense of worth and deceive neurotics, and those around them, into believing they are more worthy than they really are.

Aggression.   According to Adler, neurotics may also use **aggression** to protect their exaggerated sense of superiority and self-esteem. Neurotic aggression can take three forms: depreciation, accusation, and self-accusation. **Depreciation** is the tendency to overvalue one's own accomplishments and to undervalue the accomplishments of others. There are two common kinds of depreciation. The first is *idealization* or the use of standards so high in judging people that no real person could possibly live up to those standards; thus real people will be depreciated. Adler (1956) gives the following examples of idealization.

A short girl prefers tall men; or a girl falls in love only when the parents have forbidden it, while treating the attainable [partner] with open disdain and hostility. In the conversation and thoughts of such girls the limiting word "only" always crops up. They want only an educated man, only a rich man, only a real he-man, only platonic love, only a childless marriage, only a man who will grant his wife complete freedom. Here one sees the depreciation tendency so strongly at work that, in the end, hardly a man is left who would satisfy their requirements. Usually they have a ready-made, often unconscious, ideal to which traits of the father, a brother, a fairy-tale hero, a literary or historical character are admired. The more we become familiar with these ideals, the greater becomes our conviction that they have been posited as a fictional measure by which to depreciate reality. (268)

A second kind of depreciation is *solicitude,* which is exemplified when neurotics act as if other people are incapable of caring for themselves. Using this strategy, neurotics constantly offer advice, demonstrate concern, and generally treat other people as children. Neurotics thereby safeguard their vulnerable feelings of self-esteem by convincing themselves that other people could not get along without them.

The second kind of neurotic aggression discussed by Adler was **accusation** or the neurotic's tendency to blame others for his or her shortcomings and to seek revenge against them. Adler believed that an element of revenge exists in all neuroses and that neurotic symptoms are often designed to make others suffer. Adler (1956) said:

In the investigation of a neurotic style of life we must always suspect an opponent, and note who suffers most because of the patient's condition. Usually this is a member of the family. There is always this element of concealed accusation in neurosis, the patient feeling as though he were deprived of his right—that is, of the center of attention—and wanting to fix the responsibility and blame upon someone. (270)

Thus, according to Adler, neurotics have as a major goal to make those thought to be responsible for their misfortunes, suffer more than they do.

The third kind of neurotic aggression discussed by Adler is **self-accusation,** which involves:

> Cursing oneself, reproaching oneself, self-torture, and suicide. This may seem strange, until we realize that the whole arrangement of the neurosis follows the trait of self-torture, that the neurosis is a self-torturing device for the purpose of enhancing the self and depreciating the immediate environment. And indeed the first stirrings of the aggression drive directed against one's own person originate from a situation in which the child wants to hurt the parents or wants to attract their attention more effectively. (Adler 1956, 271)

Thus, in injuring themselves, neurotics are really attempting to hurt or at least get the attention of other people. Also, guilt-inspired confessions are often used to inflict misery on other people. Adler gives the example of a domineering woman who confessed to her husband that she had deceived him with another man twenty-five years before. She accused herself of being unworthy and attributed the confession to guilt. Adler asks "Who is so simple as to think that [this] is a case of the majesty of the truth vindicating itself after a quarter of a century?" (1956, 272). According to Adler, the facts of the case show that the woman was attempting to hurt her husband by her confession and self-accusation because he was no longer obedient to her.

Distancing. According to Adler, neurotics escape from life's problems by creating a distance between themselves and their problems. Adler discusses several ways in which neurotics distance themselves from the problems of life: moving backward, standing still, hesitation, constructing obstacles, experiencing anxiety, and using the exclusion tendency. *Moving backward* involves safeguarding a faulty life-style by reverting to a more secure, less complicated time of life. This form of distancing often involves the use of disorders such as attempted suicide, fainting, migraines, refusal to take food, alcoholism, and crime to obtain the attention of others, to gain some control over them, and to avoid social responsibility.

About *standing still* Adler (1956) said "It is as if a witches' circle had been drawn around the patient, which prevents him from moving closer toward the reality of life, from facing the truth, from taking a stand, from permitting a test or a decision regarding his value" (274). The disorders that Adler thought facilitate standing still include insomnia (with subsequent incapacity for work), a weak memory, masturbation, and impotence. *Hesitating* involves vacillation when faced with difficult problems. Adler believed that most compulsions serve the purpose of occupying the neurotic long enough so that he or she is finally able to say "It's too late now." Adler (1956) gives the following examples: "Washing compulsion, . . . coming too late, retracing one's steps, destroying work begun . . . or always leaving something unfinished are found very often. Equally often one sees that the patient, under an "irresistible" compulsion toward some unimportant activity or amusement, delays a piece of work or a decision until it is too late" (275).

Constructing obstacles creates distance so that it can be overcome, whereas other forms of distancing remove the neurotic from the problems of life. According to Adler, neurotics can create minor obstacles in their lives (distance) through such things as mild anxiety, certain compulsions, fatigue, sleeplessness, constipation, stomach and intestinal disorders, and headaches. These and other kinds of obstacles create a no-lose situation for the neurotic: "The patient's self-esteem is protected in his own judgment, and usually also his prestige in the estimation of others. If [he is unsuccessful] he can refer to his difficulties and to the proof of his illness which he has himself constructed. If he [is] victorious, what could he not have done if he were well, when, as a sick man, he achieved so much—one-handed, so to speak!" (1956, 276).

Experiencing anxiety amplifies all of the distancing strategies. Neurotics are often fearful of undertakings such as leaving home, separating from a friend, applying for a job, or developing opportunities for relationships with members of the opposite sex. Insofar as these and other experiences cause anxiety, neurotics will attempt to distance themselves from them. The greater the amount of anxiety, the greater the distance that is sought. Using the *exclusion tendency* to avoid life's problems, the neurotic lives within narrow limits. "He tries to keep at a distance the real confronting problems of life and confines himself to circumstances in which he feels able to dominate. In this way he builds for himself a narrow stable, closes the door, and spends his life away from the wind, the sunlight, and the fresh air" (Adler 1956, 278). Living in a "narrow stable" would include being habitually unemployed as an adult, indefinitely postponing marriage, doing poorly in school, and maintaining close social ties only with one's family members.

The various types of safeguarding strategies are summarized in Figure 4–1.

Creative Self

Hall and Lindzey call Adler's concept of the **creative self** his "crowning achievement as a personality theorist." They go on to say: "Here at last was the prime mover, the philosopher's stone, the elixir of life, the first cause of everything human for which Adler had been searching" (1978, 165–66).

With his concept of the creative self, Adler was saying that humans are not simply passive recipients of environmental or genetic influences. Rather, each person is free to act on these influences and combine them as he or she sees fit. Thus, no two people are ever the same even if the ingredients of their personalities are similar. We saw earlier that some persons with physical inferiorities compensate and become socially useful. Others develop an inferiority complex and accomplish

Figure 4–1.
A summary of the various strategies used by neurotics to protect their fragile and false sense of superiority and self-esteem.

SAFEGUARDING STRATEGIES

Excuses	Distancing
Aggression	Moving backward
Depreciation	Standing still
Idealization	Hesitating
Solicitude	Constructing obstacles
Accusation	Experiencing anxiety
Self-accusation	Using the exclusion tendency

nothing. To Adler, the difference is largely a matter of choice. Thus, heredity and environment provide the raw materials from which personality is formed by the creative self. According to Adler, heredity and environment provide only the "bricks which he uses in his own 'creative' way in building up his attitude toward life. It is his individual way of using these bricks—or in other words, it is his attitude toward life—which determines his relationship to the outside world" (1935/1956, 206).

The idea of choosing one's destiny is very compatible with the philosophy of existentialism. With this new component of Adler's theory, we have the healthy person *choosing* an ultimate goal and a life-style that agrees with the ideas of society. We see here another basic disagreement with Freud, who believed that human behavior was completely determined by biologic and environmental influences and was in no way free.

Adler was the first personality theorist to suggest that human behavior was not completely determined. He insisted that each person is free to determine his or her life. In other words, life, according to Adler, is open to many possible interpretations, and it is up to the person to choose the most effective and the most comfortable one. Any given person will have a certain biologic heritage and a certain array of past experiences, but it is the creative self acting on these variables and interpreting them that will determine the person's personality.

> We concede that every child is born with potentialities different from those of any other child. Our objection to the teachings of the hereditarians and every other tendency to overstress the significance of constitutional disposition, is that the important thing is not what one is born with, but what use one makes of that equipment. . . . As to the influence of the environment, who can say that the same environmental influences are apprehended, worked over, digested, and responded to by any two individuals in the same way? To understand this fact we find it necessary to assume the existence of still another force: the creative power of the individual. (Adler 1932/1979, 86–87)

Adler's concept of the creative self has turned out to be prophetic, because it is a dominant theme among many modern personality theories.

Methods of Research

Adler referred to birth order, first memories, and dreams as the three "entrance gates" to mental life, and he studied them extensively to discover the origins of a person's life goal and life-style.

Birth Order. It was Adler's contention that each child is treated differently within a family depending on its order of birth and this differential treatment influences the child's view of the world and thus its choice of a life's goal and life-style. "Above all," said Adler, "we must rid ourselves of the superstition that the situation within the family is the same for each individual child" (Adler 1933/ 1964, 229).

Adler concentrated his research on the first-born, second-born, youngest, and the only child. The **first-born child** is the focus of attention until the next child is born, at which time he or she is "dethroned." According to Adler, the loss caused by the birth of a sibling is deeply felt by the first born, because now the attention of the mother and father must be shared with a rival. The age of the first born when the second child is born can make a substantial difference, however. If the first born is old enough to have already developed a life-style and if that life-style is a cooperative one, then the first born may develop a cooperative attitude toward the new sibling. If not, the resentment toward the new sibling may last a lifetime.

The **second-born child** has to be extremely ambitious, because he or she is constantly attempting to catch up and surpass the older sibling. Of all the birth orders, Adler thought the second born was the most fortunate. According to Adler, the second-born child behaves as if in a race, as if someone were a step or two in front, and he or she had to rush to get ahead.

The **youngest child** is, according to Adler, in the second worst position after the first-born. Adler stated that the reason for this:

> Generally lies in the way in which all the family spoils them. A spoiled child can never be independent. He loses courage to succeed by his own effort. Youngest children are always ambitious; but the most ambitious children of all are the lazy children. Laziness is a sign of ambition joined with discouragement; ambition so high that the individual sees no hope of realizing it. (1931/1958, 151)

The youngest child, according to Adler, is the one most likely to seek a unique identity within a family such as becoming a musician in a family of scientists or vice versa.

The **only child** is like a first-born child who is never dethroned, at least by a sibling. The shock for the only child usually comes later (for example, in school) on learning that he or she cannot remain the center of attention. The only child often develops an exaggerated sense of superiority and a sense that the world is a dangerous place. The latter results if the parents are overly concerned with the child's health. The only child is likely to lack well-developed social interest and display a parasitic attitude expecting others to offer pampering and protection.

> Only children are often very sweet and affectionate, and later in life they may develop charming manners in order to appeal to others, as they train themselves in this way, both in early life and later. . . . We do not regard the only child's situation as dangerous, but we find that, in the absence of the best educational methods, very bad results occur which would have been avoided if there had been brothers and sisters. (Adler 1929/1964, 168–69)

Many factors can interact with the effects of birth order, bringing about results contrary to those generally expected. Such factors include the sex of older or younger siblings; the number of years that separate them; and, most important, the way the child views his or her relations with other members of the family. For many reasons, then, all of Adler's remarks concerning the effects of birth order must be interpreted as describing only general tendencies; Adler intended them to be viewed this way.

We will review the outcome of various attempts to empirically validate Adler's predictions concerning the effects of birth order on personality when we evaluate Adler's theory shortly.

First Memories.   For Adler, the best way to identify a person's life-style is to obtain the person's earliest recollections of infancy or childhood. These memories represent one's subjective starting point in life. It is irrelevant whether these memories are accurate or not. In either case they reflect the person's interpretation of early experiences, and it is this interpretation of experience that shapes the child's world view, life goal, and life-style. It is these *interpretations* of experience that are recalled as **first memories.** It follows that a close relationship among one's first memories, life's goal, and life-style must always exist. Adler (1956) explained.

> A depressed individual could not remain depressed if he remembered his good moments and his successes. He must say to himself, "All my life I was unfortunate," and select only those events which he can interpret as instances of his unhappy fate. Memories can never run counter to the style of life. If an individual's goal of superiority demands that he should feel, "Other people always humiliate me," he will choose for remembrance incidents which he can interpret as humiliations. Insofar as his style of life alters, his memories also will alter; he will remember different incidents, or he will put a different interpretation on the incidents he remembers.
>
> Most illuminating of all is the way the individual begins his story, the earliest incident he can recall. The first memory will show his fundamental view of life, his first satisfactory crystallization of his attitude. It offers us an opportunity to see at one glance what he has taken as the starting point for his development. (351)

As we have seen, Adler's own first memories were of illness and death, and it was his concern about these matters that steered him in the direction of a medical career. Hertha Orgler (1963), Adler's friend and biographer, reports that Adler gave up his general medical practice after the death of several of his diabetic patients (before the discovery of insulin). Apparently his old feelings of helplessness in the face of death were rekindled. Adler then turned to psychiatry, in which psychological death (of a mistaken life-style) and rebirth (the attaining of a new life-style with a healthy amount of social interest) were possible. Adler asked more than one hundred medical physicians for their earliest memories, and most of them were of either serious illness or a death in the family.

Dream Analysis.   Adler agreed with Freud on the importance of dreams but disagreed with Freud's approach to interpreting them. According to Freud, a dream allowed for the partial satisfaction of a wish that would be impossible to satisfy directly in a waking state. For Adler, dreams are another expression of one's life-style. To Adler, however, the occurrence of dreams almost always suggests that the dreamer has a mistaken life-style. Dreams, according to Adler, offer emotional support for mistaken life-styles. "Dreaming is the adversary of common sense. We shall probably find that people who do not like to be deluded by their feelings, who prefer to proceed in a scientific way, do not dream often or do not dream at all. Others, who are further away from common sense . . . have very frequent dreams" (Adler 1931/1958, 101). Typically, dreams support a faulty life-style by creating an emotional state that will carry over into waking life and will justify actions that are compatible with the dreamer's faulty life-style. For example, if a student unconsciously wants to create a distance between himself and an important examination, he may dream of being chased by criminals, fighting a losing war, or of being forced to attempt to solve insoluble problems. The student awakens from his dream experiencing such emotions as fear, discouragement, or helplessness; the very emotions that will support a decision to delay or avoid the forthcoming examination.

Adler (1931/1958) said:

> The purpose of dreams must be in the feelings they arouse. The dream is only the means, the instrument, to stir up feelings. The goal of the dream is the feeling it leaves behind. . . . The style of life is the master of dreams. It will always arouse the feelings that the individual needs. We can find nothing in a dream that we shall not find in all the other symptoms and characteristics of the individual. We would approach problems in the same way whether we dreamed or not; but the dream offers a support and justification for the style of life. (98, 101)

Adler emphasized the self-deceptive and therefore the unhealthy nature of dreams. "In dreams we are fooling ourselves. Every dream is an auto-intoxication, a self-hypnosis. Its whole purpose is to excite the mood in which we are prepared to meet the situation" (Adler 1931/1958, 101).

In summary, Adler believed that essentially every dream provides the self-deception necessary to maintain a mistaken life-style, and therefore people with healthy personalities dream little or not at all. That is, healthy persons require no self-deception and therefore do not require the irrational emotional support provided by dreams. Because modern research on dreaming indicates that all adult humans dream, such research either indicates that Adler was wrong in his analysis or that all adult humans have mistaken life-styles.

Behavioral Mannerisms.   In addition to analyzing birth order, first memories, and dreams Adler also observed a client's characteristic ways of behaving in order to gain an understanding of his or her style of life. He observed such things as how a client walked, spoke, dressed, and where and how he or she sat. He also observed if a client was constantly leaning on something, the distance maintained between the client and other people, and eye contact or the lack of it. The goal was always to understand how the client viewed the world and himself or herself. Information gained from observing mannerisms was added to information gained from other sources in hopes of developing a more accurate view of the person.

Goal of Psychotherapy

Healthy persons have well-developed social interest; unhealthy persons do not. Those with faulty life-styles, however, are likely to continue having them, because life-styles tend to be self-perpetuating. As we saw earlier, a life-style focuses a person on one way of looking at things, and this mode of perception persists unless the person runs into major problems or is made to understand his or her life-style through education or psychotherapy.

These foundations of every individual development do not alter, unless perchance some harmful errors of construction are recognized by the subject and corrected. Whoever has not acquired in childhood the necessary degree of social sense, will not have it later in life, except under the above-mentioned special conditions. No amount of bitter experience can change his style of life, *as long as he has not gained understanding.* The whole work of education, cure, and human progress can be furthered only along lines of better comprehension. . . .

Individual psychology considers the essence of therapy to lie in making the patient aware of his lack of cooperative power, and to convince him of the origin of this lack in early childhood maladjustments. What passes during this process is no small matter; his power of cooperation is enhanced by collaboration with the doctor. His "inferiority complex" is revealed as erroneous. Courage and optimism are awakened. And the "meaning of life" dawns upon him as the fact that proper meaning must be given to life. (Adler 1930b, 403–4)

By using an analysis of birth order, first memories, dreams, and mannerisms, Adlerians trace the development and manifestation of a mistaken life-style, one that necessitates therapy because it is ineffective in dealing with life's problems. The therapist, along with the patient, seeks a new life-style that contains social interest and therefore will be more functional.

The Adlerian approach to therapy avoided criticism, blame, punishment and an authoritarian atmosphere, because these things would amplify the patient's already strong feelings of inferiority. Rather, the therapist sits face to face with the patient and is informal and good humored. Patients are not allowed to use their neuroses, however, to gain the sympathy of the therapist as they once may have done with their parents or other persons. Although the therapist avoids pampering, he or she also avoids the opposite error of neglect. The Adlerian therapist believes that any insights gained should be explained with such clarity that they will be understood and accepted by the patient both intellectually and emotionally. The Adlerian therapist expects to see some improvement in the patient in about three months (with sessions once or twice a week), and considers it rare if the entire therapeutic process takes more than a year.

Adler was always very interested in common people and a high percentage of his clientele were from the lower and middle classes, a rarity among psychiatrists of his time. Also extremely unusual was the fact that Adler worked directly with children. Adler typically treated children in the natural setting of their homes and insisted that their parents were part of the therapeutic process. As a result of his approach to treating children, Adler is considered one of the founders of group and family psychotherapy. Also, Adler insisted on treating problem children in front of a public audience in mental health clinics to help the child realize that his or her difficulty is a community problem.

As innovative and effective as Adlerian psychotherapy is, Adler always insisted that the *prevention* of disorders through proper child rearing and education was far easier and less costly than treating disorders later with psychotherapy.

Summary of the Differences Between Adler and Freud

The major differences between Adler and Freud can be summarized as follows:

ADLER	FREUD
Mind viewed as an integrated whole	Mind viewed as consisting of warring factions
Emphasized conscious mind	Emphasized unconscious mind
Future goals important source of motivation	Future goals unimportant
Social motives primary	Biologic motives primary
Optimistic about human existence	Pessimistic about human existence
Dreams analyzed to learn about life-styles	Dreams analyzed to detect contents of unconscious mind
Humans at least partially free to determine their own personality	Personality completely determined by heredity and environmental factors
Minimized importance of sex	Maximized importance of sex
Goal of therapy to encourage life-style incorporating social interest	Goal of therapy to discover repressed early memories

Evaluation

Empirical Research

Most of the research generated by Adler's theory has explored the relationship between birth order and various personality characteristics. Many studies have found that first-born and only children have higher levels of educational aspiration and achievement than later-born children and are also more intelligent (for example, Wagner and Schubert 1977; Belmont and Marolla 1973; Falbo 1981; and Breland 1974). The explanation for these results is that first-born and only children receive greater parental attention and are the objects of greater parental expectations. Falbo (1981) also found that last-born children typically have lower self-esteem than first-born children. This result was explained by the fact that last-born children typically have competent older siblings with which to compare themselves. Zajonc and Markus (1975) studied the relationships among birth order, family spacing, and family size and intellectual development. It was found that the fewer the number of children in a family and the greater the spacing between children, the smarter each child is likely to be. Also it was found within a family, older children tend to be more intelligent than younger ones.

Caution is necessary when interpreting birth order studies because results are often contradictory. For this reason some researchers are very negative about birth order research in general. For example, Ernst and Angst (1983) reviewed the studies on birth order between 1946 and 1980. The hundreds of studies reviewed investigated the relationship between birth order and such variables as intelligence, school and occupational achievement, aggressiveness, self-esteem, empathy, creativity, and various kinds of mental illness. Ernst and Angst (1983) conclude that research on birth order has been characterized by numerous methodological flaws and is, therefore, not very useful.

> Birth order research seems very simple, since position in a sibship and sibship size are easily defined. The computer is fed some ordinal numbers, and it is then easy to find a plausible post hoc explanation for any significant difference in the related variables. If, for example, lastborn children report more anxiety than other birth ranks, it is because for many years they were the weakest in the family. If firstborns are found to be the most timid, it is because of incoherent treatment by an inexperienced mother. If, on the other hand, middle children show the greatest anxiety, it is because they have been neglected by their parents, being neither the first- nor lastborn. With some imagination it is even possible to find explanations for greatest anxiety in a second girl of four, and so on, ad infinitum.
> *This kind of research is a sheer waste of time and money.* (xi)

Several attempts have been made to make Adlerian concepts more measurable and thus more useful in counseling and therapeutic situations. Crandall (1980, 1981, 1982) has devised and utilized a scale for measuring level of social interest and found that social interest indeed varies with one's level of social adjustment, among other things. Thorne (1975) has devised a 200-item questionnaire called The Life Style Analysis, which is designed to determine a person's life-style. Rule (1972) and Rule and Traver (1982) have devised and used an Early Recollection Questionnaire, and Altman (1973) has created the Early Recollection Ratings Scale of Social Interest. Olson (1979) presents a collection of papers showing how early memories are used in clinical diagnosis and psychotherapy. Hafner, Fakouri, and Labrentz (1982) found that more alcoholics than nonalcoholics described their earliest memories as threatening.

Criticisms

Difficult to falsify. Like the theories of Freud and Jung, many of the terms in Adler's theory are not defined precisely enough to validate. Because they lack clear definition it is difficult, if not impossible, to determine the impact of such things as inferiority, superiority, social interest and creative power on a person's personality. Adler's contention that "Everything can also be different" (1956, 194) makes it practically impossible to make a falsifiable prediction using his theory. As we have seen, Adler believed that it was subjective reality that determines behavior, not objective reality. Therefore, if a person develops a personality unlike the one that is supposed to characterize his or her birth order, it can always be attributed to the person's unique perceptions of the situation. Also, Adler claimed that heredity and experience provide only the raw material of personality and the creative self acts on those materials to mold a unique personality. The concept of creative self, then, makes it impossible to predict adult personality characteristics on the basis of either heredity or environmental experience.

Overly simplistic.   Adler claimed that it is often a few early experiences that determine adult personality, and that if a person's interpretations of the world based on those experiences could be changed, an unhealthy life-style could be changed into a healthy one. Also, Adler relies almost exclusively on social factors in explaining personality, essentially ignoring biologic, hereditary factors. Finally, Adler contends that, in the final analysis, personality is, or could be, freely chosen by each person. Many modern personality theorists consider all of the above Adlerian assumptions to be overly optimistic. Also, with his belief that all humans are born with the innate potential for social interest, Adler has trouble explaining the widespread occurrence of war, murder, rape, crime, and other human acts of violence. Many believe that the theories of Freud and Jung are far better able to explain the realities of the human situation.

Contributions

The importance of social variables.   Although, as we have seen, many consider Adler's emphasis on social variables a negative aspect of his theory, others consider that emphasis as Adler's most significant contribution. Adler vividly pointed out that the world each person lives in is a world of his or her own creation. Furthermore, the most important factor in formulating that world view is one's relationships with other people. For example, one's family constellation is one variable that can influence one's world view. The importance of social variables for personality development were largely ignored by Freud and Jung.

Widely influential.   Adler's terms *life-style* and *inferiority complex* have become part of everyday language. In the realms of personality theory and psychotherapy we see Adler's influence in the contemporary emphasis on self-selected goals as determinants of behavior; social determinants of personality; family therapy, group therapy, and community psychiatry; the importance of subjective reality as opposed to objective reality; and personal freedom and responsibility in living one's life.

Several influential persons regard Adler's contribution to psychology as even greater than Freud's. For example, Albert Ellis says:

> Alfred Adler, more even than Freud, is probably the true father of modern psychotherapy. Some of the reasons are: He founded ego psychology, which Freudians only recently rediscovered. He was one of the first humanistic psychologists. . . . He stressed holism, goal-seeking, and the enormous importance of values in human thinking, emoting, and acting. He correctly saw that sexual drives and behavior, while having great importance in human affairs, are largely the result rather than the cause of man's non-sexual philosophies. . . .
>
> It is difficult to find any leading therapist today who in some respect does not owe a great debt to the Individual Psychology of Alfred Adler. (1970, 11)

Viktor Frankl stated that Adler's opposition to Freud:

> was no less than a Copernican switch. No longer could man be considered as the product, pawn and victim of drives and instincts; on the contrary, drives and instincts form the material that serves man in expression and in action.

> Beyond this, Alfred Adler may well be regarded as an existential thinker and as a forerunner of the existential-psychiatric movement. (1970, 12)

Adler's theory is very much in tune with the spirit of the times and no doubt will remain a force in psychology for some time to come.

Summary

Adler spent much of his childhood suffering from several physical ailments, feelings of inferiority, and a losing competition with his older brother. He was one of Freud's earliest associates, but numerous differences caused them to terminate their relationship, which made Freud bitter toward Adler until Adler's death. Adler disputed Freud's notions of repression, infantile sexuality, and the importance of the unconscious. Adler's viewpoint, called individual psychology, stressed the wholeness and uniqueness of each person as he or she struggles to overcome feelings of inferiority by aspiring toward some future goal. Adler's theory is compatible with Gestalt psychology, which emphasizes wholeness and interrelatedness; with existentialism, which is concerned with the meaning of human existence; and with humanism, which stresses the goodness of humans.

In the earliest version of his theory, Adler believed that people were motivated to compensate for actual physical weaknesses by emphasizing those qualities that would make up for those weaknesses. In some cases, he thought that a person could overcompensate and convert a weakness into a strength. Later, Adler extended his theory to include not only real physical weaknesses but imagined ones as well. Now compensation or overcompensation was directed at the feelings of inferiority resulting from either real or imagined inferiorities. In his early writing, Adler equated inferiority with femininity and superiority with masculinity. The striving to become more masculine in order to become more powerful was called the masculine protest. According to Adler, feeling inferior is not necessarily bad; in fact, such feelings are the motivating force behind all personal accomplishments. Some individuals, however, are not stimulated to growth by their feelings of inferiority. Rather, they are overcome by them, and they become a barrier to personal growth; such individuals are said to have an inferiority complex.

Adler's final theoretical position was that humans are primarily motivated to seek superiority or perfection. The superiority sought is compatible with society, however, and not a selfish, individual superiority. A person who selfishly seeks personal superiority while ignoring the needs of other people and of society is said to have a superiority complex. The means by which an individual attempts to gain superiority is called his or her life-style.

Adler believed that persons must insert meaning into their lives by inventing ideals or fictional goals that give them something for which to live and around which to organize their lives. Such fictions are called fictional finalisms. Healthy persons use such fictions as tools for living a more significant, effective life. For healthy persons, these fictions can easily be discarded if circumstances call for it. For neurotics, however, these fictions are confused with reality and therefore are retained at all costs.

Adler theorized that all persons have an innate need to live in harmony with other people; he called this need social interest. Each person must solve three major problems in life, and each requires a strong social interest: (1) occupational tasks, (2) societal tasks, and (3) love and marriage tasks. Adler believed that the nature of a child's interaction with the mother determined to what extent the child developed social interest. Any life-style not characterized by a strong social interest was labeled a mistaken life-style. Three types of people with a mistaken life-style are the ruling-dominant type, the getting-leaning type, the avoiding type. The socially useful type has a strong social interest, and therefore his or her life-style is not mistaken. Three childhood conditions that can cause a mistaken life-style are physical inferiority, spoiling or pampering, and neglecting. Because the feelings of self-esteem and superiority that are generated by a mistaken life-style are basically deceptive, they must be safeguarded. As the safeguarding strategies used by neurotics Adler listed excuses; aggression consisting of accusation, depreciation, and self-accusation; and distancing consisting of moving backward, standing still, hesitating, constructing obstacles, experiencing anxiety, and using the exclusion tendency.

Adler did not believe that personality was completely determined by biologic inheritance, early experiences, or the environment. He felt that each person is free to interpret life in any number of ways. The creative self allows us to be what we choose to be. Adler's research methods included the influence of birth order, first memories, and dream analysis. The major goal of psychotherapy was to correct a faulty life-style and to encourage social interest in its place.

Some of the major premises that differentiated Adler's theory from Freud's were Adler's emphasis on the conscious integrated mind, social motives, one's future goals, personal freedom, dreams as supportive of faulty life-styles, and his de-emphasis on sexual motivation. In addition, Adler was optimistic about the human condition, whereas Freud was pessimistic.

Adler's theory has been criticized for containing terms too nebulous to measure, making them nonfalsifiable, and for being too simplistic in its characterization of personality. The theory seems to overlook the baser side of human beings. Adler's theory has been praised for noting the importance of social variables in personality development and for introducing several useful terms, concepts, and methodologies that are useful for understanding personality and in the therapeutic process. Although there has been considerable research on the effects of birth order on various personality characteristics, the results have been equivocal and of questionable value. Research on the topics of social interest and first memories appears more promising.

Adler's theory seems to be increasing in popularity and can be regarded as a forerunner of the modern humanistic-existential personality theories.

EXPERIENTIAL EXERCISES

1. According to Adler, your life-style determines how you embrace the world. It includes your basic attitudes, values, traits, and beliefs. It reflects the strategy that you formulated early in life to overcome feelings of inferiority and achieve superiority or perfection. First, describe your life-style and then list your earliest memories. Adler thought that a relationship between first memories and chosen life-style usually exists. Discuss this relationship as it applies to you.

2. Adler identified four basic types of people: the ruling type, the getting type, the avoiding type, and the socially useful type. Indicate which of the four types characterizes you best and give evidence supporting your conclusion.

3. According to Adler, a person's behavioral mannerisms provides evidence of his or her life-style. Observe your own behavior and ask a close relative and a friend to also observe your behavior. Is there consistency among the various observations? What conclusions about your life-style can be drawn from your mannerisms?

4. According to Adler, each child is treated differently within a family depending on the child's order of birth. Given your birth order, describe how your experiences may have been different than a child with a different birth order. Discuss how the experiences caused by your birth order may have influenced your adult

personality. By interviewing acquaintances termine whether or not persons with the same birth order have similar personality characteristics.

5. According to Adler, the main source of meaning in one's life is provided by one's fictional final goal. It is around this goal that one's psychic life is integrated and all more immediate, concrete goals are steps toward the attainment of the fictional final goal. A glimpse of your own fictional goal can be provided by responding to the following questions: What is it that you value most highly? What is it that you see yourself striving for? How would you describe a future for yourself that you would consider optimal? Answer these questions and based on your answers, describe what seems to be your fictional final goal. Discuss how this goal influences your beliefs, choices, and actions.

6. Discuss the safeguarding strategies as they apply to your life. If you think that you do not employ such strategies, discuss a person that you know who does employ them.

DISCUSSION QUESTIONS

1. List as many points as you can about Adler's early life that ultimately became part of his theory of personality.

2. Why did Adler call his theory individual psychology?

3. Trace the evolution of Adler's theory from its concern with organ inferiority to its concern with social interest.

4. Describe Adler's early concept of masculine protest.

5. Distinguish between feelings of inferiority and an inferiority complex.

6. Explain why a superiority complex exemplifies a mistaken life-style.

7. According to Adler, what is a life-style?

8. Discuss Adler's concept of fictional finalism.

9. Discuss Adler's concept of social interest. Give a few examples of how the concept is used by Adler in this theory.

10. What is a mistaken life-style? Give a few examples of how such a life-style can occur.

11. Give an example of each of the following safeguarding strategies: excuses, aggression, and distancing.

12. Discuss Adler's concept of the creative self.

13. Summarize Adler's views on the effects of birth order on personality.

14. According to Adler, what is the goal of psychotherapy?

15. List the major differences between Adler's theory of personality and Freud's theory.

The Education of Children.
: Gateway Editions, Ltd.

atively applies his theory in the realm of education. The reader will find many of Adler's thoughts on education still relevant today. Contains an interesting introduction written by Rudolph Dreikurs the director of the Alfred Adler Institute of Chicago.

ADLER, A. (1931/1958). *What Life Should Mean to You.* New York: Capricorn Books.

A very readable and entertaining introduction to many of Adler's basic concepts.

ANSBACHER, H. L., and R. R. ANSBACHER (eds.). (1956). *The Individual Psychology of Alfred Adler.* New York: Basic Books.

The single best source of Adler's ideas.

ANSBACHER, H. L., and R. R. ANSBACHER (eds.). (1979). *Superiority and Social Interest.* New York: Norton.

An excellent summary of Adler's later writings. Also contains a previously unpublished biographical essay on Adler by his friend and co-worker Carl Furtmuller.

BOTTOME, P. (1957). *Alfred Adler: A Portrait From Life.* New York: Vanguard.

The most comprehensive biography of Adler available.

DREIKURS, R., and L. GREY. (1968). *A New Approach to Discipline: Logical Consequences.* New York: Hawthorne.

The authors apply Adler's notions to the areas of child rearing and education.

MOSAK, H. (1973). (ed.). *Alfred Adler: His Influence on Psychology Today.* Park Ridge, IL: Noyes Press.

A prominent Adlerian therapist edits a collection of papers showing the influence of Adlerian concepts on the therapeutic process.

ORGLER, H. (1963). *Alfred Adler: The Man and His Work.* New York: Putnam.

A good introduction to basic Adlerian concepts along with interesting biographical information.

GLOSSARY

Accusation. The form of neurotic aggression that involves the neurotic's blaming of other people for his or her shortcomings and seeking revenge against those people.

Aggression. As a safeguarding strategy aggression can take three forms: depreciation, accusation, and self-accusation. See also accusation, depreciation, and self-accusation.

Avoiding type person. A person exhibiting the mistaken life-style of avoiding the attempt to solve life's problems, thereby escaping possible defeat. Such a person lacks social interest.

Birth order. One of the areas that Adler studied in order to understand personality. He believed that different birth orders created different situations to which children must adjust and that this adjustment has a profound influence on personality development.

Compensation. Making up for a weakness, such as organ inferiority, either by overcoming it through concentrated effort or by emphasizing functions that substitute for the weakness.

Creative self. The free element of the personality that allows the person to choose between alternative life-styles and between fictional goals. It is the differential exercise of this creative power that is mainly responsible for individual differences.

Depreciation. The neurotic safeguarding strategy whereby one's own accomplishments are overvalued and the accomplishments of others are undervalued. Depreciation can take the form of *idealization* whereby standards used to judge people are so high that no real person could live up to them and is thus depreciated. Another form of depreciation is *solicitude* whereby neurotics act as if other people could not get along without them.

Distancing. The safeguarding strategy used by neurotics, which involves creating barriers between themselves and their problems in life. According to Adler, distancing can take the forms of *moving backward* or the use of childlike behavior in order to gain attention and control; *standing still* or the avoidance of failure by not attempting to do anything; *hesitating* or becoming involved in diversions until it is too late to confront a problem; *constructing obstacles* or the creation of minor obstacles so that they can be overcome thereby increasing the neurotic's false feeling of worth; experiencing *anxiety* is caused by the neurotic's inability to solve life's problems; the greater the ineptitude, the greater the anxiety and therefore, the greater the need for distancing; and using the *exclusion tendency* or the neurotic's tendency to confine their lives to the few areas in which they can dominate.

Dream analysis. Adler believed that the primary purpose of dreams was to create emotions that could be used by dreamers to support their mistaken life-styles. Dreams, then, were analyzed to learn about the life-styles of the dreamers.

Excuses. A safeguarding strategy whereby neurotics use their symptoms as excuses for their shortcomings.

Feelings of inferiority. The feelings that one has of being inferior, whether or not these feelings are justified by real circumstances. Such feelings, according to Adler, can lead either to positive accomplishments or to an inferiority complex.

Fictional finalism. The fictional future goal to which a person aspires. This goal is the end to which the person is aspiring, and his or her life-style is the means to that end.

First-born child. This child is the focus of attention until the birth of a sibling "dethrones" him or her. The loss felt by the first-born child when the second child is born often creates bitterness that causes problems later in life. Adler considered this to be the most troublesome birth position.

First memories. Adler's research technique of asking a person to describe earliest recollections. Adler thought that such recollections gave evidence of the origins of one's life-style.

Fundamental fact of life. Adler replaced his earlier contention that people seek power to overcome feelings of inferiority with the contention that they aspire to become superior or perfect. Adler referred to the latter contention as the fundamental fact of life. Adler's final position was that healthy persons aspire toward social rather than individual perfection. See also striving for superiority.

Getting-leaning type person. A person exhibiting the mistaken style of life that expects everything to be given to him or her by others. Such a person lacks social interest.

Individual psychology. Adler's term to describe his theory. The term "individual" was used to stress his belief that each person is an integrated whole striving to attain future goals and attempting to find meaning in life while working harmoniously with others.

Inferiority complex. The psychological condition that exists when a person is overwhelmed by feelings of inferiority to the point at which nothing can be accomplished.

Life-style. The means by which a person seeks to gain superiority. The person's life-style is the main theme running through his or her life and thus influences almost everything that person does. Life-style can be equated roughly with the term *identity*.

Masculine protest. Attempting to become more powerful by being more masculine, and thereby less feminine. According to Adler's earlier theorizing, both men and women attempt to gain power by becoming more like the cultural ideal of the man.

Mistaken life-style. Any life-style that is not aimed at socially useful goals. In other words, any life-style not including social interest.

Neglecting. A procedure that causes the child to feel worthless and angry and to look upon everyone with distrust.

Only child. This child is like a first-born child who was never dethroned. Only children, according to Adler, are often sweet, affectionate, and charming in order to appeal to others. Adler did not consider this birth position nearly as dangerous as the first-born's position.

Organ inferiority. The condition that exists when some organ of the body does not develop normally. Such a condition can stimulate compensation or overcompensation, which is healthy, or can result in an inferiority complex, which is unhealthy.

Overcompensation. The process by which, through considerable effort, a previous weakness is converted into a strong point. An example would be when a frail child works hard to become an athlete.

Physical inferiority. An actual physical weakness. See also organ inferiority.

Ruling-dominant type person. A person exhibiting the mistaken life-style that dominates and rules people. Such a person lacks social interest.

Safeguarding strategies. "Tricks" that neurotics use to preserve what little self-esteem and illusions of superiority that can be generated by a mistaken life-style. See also aggression, excuses, and distancing.

Second-born child. This child is very ambitious because he or she is constantly attempting to catch up and surpass the older sibling. Of all the birth orders, Adler felt that the second-born was the best.

Self-accusation. The form of neurotic aggression that involves the wallowing in self-torture, and guilt, the ultimate purpose of which is to hurt other people.

Social interest. The innate potential to live in harmony and friendship with others and to aspire to the development of a perfect society.

Socially useful type person. A person exhibiting a life-style containing a healthy amount of social interest. Such a life-style is not "mistaken."

Spoiling or pampering. Procedures that create a child who believes it is up to others to satisfy his or her needs.

Striving for superiority. What Adler called "the fundamental fact of life." According to Adler's final theoretical position, it is not the search for the power necessary to overcome feelings of inferiority that motivates humans; rather, it is the constant search for perfection or superiority. However, it was the perfection of society that Adler stressed, rather than individual perfection. See also fundamental fact of life.

Superiority complex. The psychological condition that exists when a person concentrates too much on his or her own need to succeed while ignoring the needs of others. Such a person tends to be vain, domineering, and arrogant.

Youngest child. According to Adler, the second-worst birth position after the first born. This child is often spoiled and therefore loses courage to succeed by his or her own efforts.

5

Karen Horney

Karen Horney (pronounced "Horn-eye"), was born Karen Danielson in a small village near Hamburg, Germany, on 16 September 1885 (the year that Freud was studying hypnotism with Jean Charcot in Paris). Her father (Berndt Henrik Wackles Danielson) was a Norwegian sea captain, and her mother (Clotilde Marie van Ronzelen) was a member of a prominent Dutch-German family. Karen's mother was eighteen years younger than the captain and was his second wife. The family consisted of four children from the captain's previous marriage and Karen's older brother, Berndt, who was considered the darling of the family. Karen's father was a tall, dashing, stern, God-fearing, religious fundamentalist who strongly believed that women were inferior to men and were the source of evil in the world. He often clashed with Karen's mother who was proud, beautiful, intelligent, and free thinking. Karen had mixed feelings about her father. On the one hand, she felt intimidated by his stern, self-righteous manner and by his derogatory statements about her appearance and intelligence. Conversely, he added adventure to her life by taking her along on at least three lengthy sea voyages and by bringing her exotic gifts from around the world. Perhaps it was because of these fond memories that Karen began wearing a captain's cap when she was in her thirties. As an example of her father's negative side, Karen recalled that after reading the Bible at length, he would sometimes explode in a fit of anger and throw the Bible at his wife. The children referred to him as the "Bible thrower" (Rubins 1978, 11). It is little wonder that Karen developed a negative attitude toward religion and a skepticism toward authority figures. After she was treated by a medical physician when she was twelve, Karen decided to become a medical physician herself—a decision that was strongly supported by her mother and opposed by her father.

In 1906, when Karen was twenty-one, she entered medical school at Freiberg, Germany, one of the few medical schools allowing women at the time. Shortly afterward she met Oskar Horney, an economics major on vacation from another institution, and was attracted to him because he was stern, intelligent, independent, and physically and emotionally strong. Karen married Oskar on 31 October, 1909 (the year that Freud and Jung gave a series of lectures at Clark University in the United States), and the union produced three daughters. By the time they married, Oskar had become a lawyer (as Karen's brother had also done). By 1910 Karen was pregnant with Brigitte, the first of their three daughters. Shortly before the birth of Brigitte, Karen's mother died of a stroke. It was also about this time that Karen was undergoing her own psychoanalysis in preparation for a career as a psychoanalyst. Needless to say, these were tense times in Karen's life. Within the space of just a few years she experienced marriage, the death of her mother, childbirth, and psychoanalysis.

It is interesting to note that although Karen felt essentially unwanted and unloved as a child, she was viewed by her own children as having a laissez-faire attitude toward them. Rubins (1978, 51) reports that during a Christmas dinner, the middle daughter, Marianne, leaned back too far in her chair. In an attempt to catch herself from falling she grabbed the table cloth and took to the floor with her the entire Christmas dinner. Oskar beat Marianne with a dog whip while the two other daughters cried, and Karen looked on without displaying any emotion.

The Horney marriage began to disintegrate in 1923, about the time that Karen's brother died of pneumonia at the age of forty. Shortly after her brother's death the Horney family went on vacation. Karen went swimming by herself and when she did not return for more than an hour, family members went looking for her. She was found clinging to a piling pondering whether to continue living or to take her own life. After much pleading she agreed to swim back to shore. This bout was but one of the many with deep depression that Karen experienced throughout her life. Also, about this time Oskar's life was becoming extremely difficult. The firm that he worked for went bankrupt, his investments failed, and he borrowed heavily to survive financially. After a near-fatal attack of meningitis, the formerly successful Oskar was himself bankrupt, morose, and withdrawn. He became increasingly difficult to live with, and in 1926 Karen and the three girls moved into a small apartment. It was not until 1936 that Karen officially filed for a divorce, and the divorce did not become final until 1939.

Horney completed her medical studies in 1913 at the University of Berlin. She was an excellent student throughout her academic career and was often first in her class. From 1914 to 1918, she received psychoanalytic training at the Berlin Psychoanalytic Institute. In 1919, at the age of thirty-three, she became a practicing

Karen Horney

psychoanalyst. From 1918 to 1932, she taught at the Berlin Psychoanalytic Institute, besides having a private practice.

In 1932, she accepted an invitation from Franz Alexander to come to the United States and become an associate director of the Chicago Institute of Psychoanalysis. Two years later, she moved to New York where she established a private practice and trained analysts at the New York Psychoanalytic Institute. At the New York Psychoanalytic Institute major differences between Horney and the traditional Freudians became apparent. Eventually the theses submitted by her students were routinely rejected because they reflected ideas contrary to traditional Freudian doctrine. Opposition to her ideas became strong enough to cause a restriction of her teaching duties and to bar her as a training analyst. Under such pressure Horney resigned from the New York Psychoanalytic Institute in 1941 and soon thereafter she founded her own organization called the American Institute for Psychoanalysis, where she continued to develop her own ideas and which she headed until her death on 4 December, 1952.

Basic Disagreements with Freudian Theory.   Horney was trained in the Freudian tradition, and all her work was influenced by that training. In fact, while at the Berlin Psychoanalytic Institute, she was psychoanalyzed by Karl Abraham and Hans Sachs, two of the most prominent Freudian analysts at that time. As time went on, however, Horney found it more and more difficult to apply Freudian notions to her work. She completely disagreed with Freud's notions of the Oedipal complex and his division of the mind into the id, ego, and superego. She thought that Freud's theory reflected a different country and a different time. To state it simply, Horney found that Freud's theory did not fit the problems that people were having during the Depression years in the United States. Sexual problems were secondary to several other problems that those special environmental conditions had created. Instead of sexual problems, people were worried about losing their jobs and not having enough money to pay the rent, buy food, or provide their children with needed medical care.

Horney reasoned that because such major differences exist in the kinds of problems that people experience from one country to another or from one time in history to another, they must be culturally rather than biologically determined, as Freud had assumed. So, although Horney was trained in the Freudian tradition and although she was deeply influenced by that training, her theory ended up being quite different from Freud's. To Horney, what a person experiences socially determines whether or not he or she will have psychological problems and, if so, what kind they will be. The conflict is caused by environmental conditions, not by opposing components of the mind (id, ego, and superego) as Freud had believed.

As we shall see, Horney did not abandon Freud's theory completely, but her viewpoint is much more compatible with Adler's than with Freud's.

Basic Hostility and Anxiety

In her book *The Neurotic Personality of Our Time* (1937), Horney elaborated her contention that neuroses are caused by disturbed human relationships. More specifically, she maintained that the rudiments of neurotic behavior are found in the relationship between parent and child. This point agrees with Freud's theory, because Horney also stressed the importance of early childhood experience in personality development. Horney, however, did not accept Freud's notion of the psychosexual stages of development. Like Adler, Horney believed that the child started life with a feeling of helplessness relative to the powerful parents. She believed that the two basic needs in childhood were **safety** and **satisfaction,** and that the child was completely dependent on the parents for their satisfaction. The need for satisfaction refers to the child's needs for food, water, and sleep. At least minimal satisfaction of such physiological needs is necessary for the child's survival. According to Horney, however, the satisfaction of physiological needs was less important for personality development than was the satisfaction of the need for safety. By the need for safety, Horney meant the need for security and freedom from fear.

Although each child is in fact helpless and dependent on the parents during the early years, this need not necessarily create a psychological problem. Horney did not agree with Adler's earlier view that each child feels helpless and inferior and spends the rest of his or her life compensating or overcompensating for this feeling. She felt that the condition of helplessness was a necessary but not a sufficient condition for the development of neurosis. Two possibilities exist: (1) The parents can demonstrate genuine affection and warmth toward the child, thereby satisfying the need for safety; or (2) the parents can demonstrate indifference, hostility, or even hatred toward the child, thereby frustrating the child's need for safety. The former condition leads to normal development, and the latter condition leads to neurotic development.

Horney called the behavior of parents that undermines a child's security the **basic evil.** A sample of such behavior is:

Indifference toward the child
Rejection of the child
Hostility toward the child
Obvious preference for a sibling
Unfair punishment
Ridicule
Humiliation
Erratic behavior
Unkept promises
Isolation of the child from others

A child who is abused by the parents in one or more of the preceding ways experiences **basic hostility** toward his or her parents. The child is now caught between dependence on the parents and hostility toward them, a most unfortunate situation. Because the child is in no position to change the situation, he or she must repress the hostile feelings toward the parents to survive. This repression of the child's basic hostility is motivated by feelings of helplessness, fear, love, or guilt (Horney 1937, 85). The child who represses basic hostility because of feelings of helplessness seems to be saying: "I have to repress my hostility because I need you'' (Horney 1937, 86). The child who represses basic hostility because of fear seems to be saying: "I have to repress my hostility because I am afraid of you" (Horney 1937, 86).

In some homes, real love for a child may be lacking, but at least there is some effort to make the child seem wanted. For example, verbal expressions of love and affection may be substituted for real love and affection. The child, according to Horney, has little trouble telling the difference but clings to the "substitute" love because that is all there is. This child says: "I have to repress my hostility for fear of losing love" (Horney 1937, 86). In our culture, the child may also repress basic hostility because of having been made to feel guilty about having any negative feelings about his or her parents. Such a child feels sinful or unworthy in feeling hostile toward the parents and therefore represses such feelings.

Unfortunately the feeling of hostility caused by the parents does not remain isolated; instead, it generalizes to the entire world and all the people in it. The child is now convinced that everything and everyone is potentially dangerous. At this point, the child is said to be experiencing **basic anxiety,** one of Horney's most important concepts. Horney described basic anxiety and its relationship to basic hostility as follows:

> The condition that is fostered or brought about by the factors I have mentioned . . . is an insidiously increasing, all-pervading feeling of being lonely and helpless in a hostile world. . . . This attitude as such does not constitute a neurosis but it is the nutritive soil out of which a definite neurosis may develop at any time. Because of the fundamental role this attitude plays in neuroses I have given it a special designation: the basic anxiety; it is inseparably interwoven with a basic hostility. (1937, 89)

About basic anxiety and the conditions that cause it, Horney stated that it is:

> The feeling a child has of being isolated and helpless in a potentially hostile world. A wide range of adverse factors in the environment can produce this insecurity in a child: direct or indirect domination, indifference, erratic behavior, lack of respect for the child's individual needs, lack of real guidance, disparaging attitudes, too much admiration or the absence of it, lack of reliable warmth, having to take sides in parental disagreements, too much or too little responsibility, overprotection, isolation from other children, injustice, discrimination, unkept promises, hostile atmosphere, and so on and so on. (1945, 41)

According to Horney, the origins of neurotic behavior are to be found in parent-child relationships. If the child experiences love and warmth, he or she will feel secure and probably develop normally. In fact, Horney thought that if a child were truly loved, he or she could survive a variety of abuses, such as periodic beatings and premature sexual experiences, without ill effects. If, however, the child did not feel loved, there would be hostility toward the parents, and this hostility would eventually be projected onto everything and everyone and become basic anxiety. According to Horney, a child with basic anxiety is well on the way to becoming a neurotic adult.

Adjustments to Basic Anxiety

Because basic anxiety causes the feelings of helplessness and fear, the person experiencing it must find ways to keep it to a minimum. Originally, Horney (1942) described ten strategies for minimizing basic anxiety, which she called **neurotic trends** or neurotic needs. As you read through these neurotic needs, you will note that they are needs that almost everyone has, and that is an important point. The normal person, in fact, has many or all of these needs and pursues their satisfaction freely. In other words, when the need for affection arises, one attempts to satisfy it. When the need for personal admiration arises, one attempts to satisfy that need, and so forth. The neurotic person, however, does not pass easily from one need to another as conditions change. Rather, the neurotic person focuses on one of the needs to the exclusion of all the others. The neurotic person makes one of these needs the focal point of life. Unlike the normal person, the neurotic person's approach to satisfying one of these needs is all out of proportion to reality, disproportionate in intensity, and indiscriminate in application, and when the need goes unsatisfied, it stimulates intense anxiety. "If it is affection that a person must have, he must receive it from friend and enemy, from employer and bootblack" (Horney 1942, 39).

The ten neurotic trends or needs follow (Horney 1942, 54–60).

1. Need for Affection and Approval.

A person emphasizing this need lives to be loved and admired by others. "Center of gravity in others and not in self, with their wishes and opinions the only thing that counts; dread of self-assertion; dread of hostility on the part of others or of hostile feelings within self" (1942, 51).

2. Need for a Partner Who Will Run One's Life.

A person emphasizing this need must be affiliated with someone who will protect him or her from all danger and fulfill all his or her needs. "Overevaluation of 'love' because 'love' is supposed to solve all problems; dread of desertion; dread of being alone" (1942, 52).

3. Need to Live One's Life within Narrow Limits.

A person emphasizing this need is very conservative, avoiding defeat by attempting very little. "Necessity to be undemanding and contented with little, and to restrict ambitions and wishes for material things; necessity to remain inconspicuous and to take second place; belittling of existing faculties and potentialities, with modesty the supreme value" (1942, 52).

4. Need for Power.

A person emphasizing this need glorifies strength and despises weakness. "Domination over others craved for its own sake; . . . essential disrespect for others, their individuality, their dignity, their feelings, the only concern being their subordination; . . . indiscriminate adoration of strength and contempt for weakness; dread of uncontrollable situations; dread of helplessness" (1942, 52–53).

5. Need to Exploit Others.

A person emphasizing this need dreads being taken advantage of by others but thinks nothing of taking advantage of them. "Others evaluated primarily according to whether or not they can be exploited or made use of; . . . pride in exploitative skill; dread of being exploited and thus of being 'stupid' " (1942, 54).

6. Need for Social Recognition and Prestige.

A person emphasizing this need lives to be recognized—for example, to have his or her name in the newspaper. The highest goal is to gain prestige. "All things—inanimate objects, money, persons, one's own qualities, activities, and feelings—evaluated only according to their prestige value" (1942, 54).

7. Need for Personal Admiration.

A person emphasizing this need lives to be flattered and complimented. This person wants others to see him or her in accordance with the idealized image he or she has of himself or herself. "Need to be admired not for what one possesses or presents in the public eye but for the imagined self; self-evaluation dependent on living up to this image and on admiration of it by others" (1942, 54).

8. Need for Ambition and Personal Achievement.

A person emphasizing this need has an intense interest in becoming famous, rich, or important, regardless of the costs. "Need to surpass others not through what one presents or is but through one's activities; self-evaluation dependent on being the very best—lover, sportsman, writer, worker—particularly in one's own mind, recognition by others being vital too, however, and its absence resented" (1942, 55).

9. Need for Self-Sufficiency and Independence.

A person emphasizing this need goes to great extremes to avoid being obligated to anyone and does not want to be tied down to anything or anyone. Enslavement is to be avoided at all costs. "Necessity never to need anybody, or to yield to any influence, or to be tied down to anything, any closeness involving the danger of enslavement; distance and separateness the only source of security; dread of needing others, of ties, of closeness, of love" (1942, 55).

10. Need for Perfection and Unassailability.

A person emphasizing this need attempts to be flawless because of hypersensitivity to criticism. "Relentless driving for perfection; . . . feelings of superiority over others because of being perfect; dread of finding flaws within self or of making mistakes; dread of criticism or reproaches" (1942, 55–56).

Again, normal people experience most, if not all, of the ten needs, and, when they do, put them in proper perspective. For example, normal people's need for power is not intense enough to cause a conflict with other needs, such as the need for affection. Normal people are in a position of satisfying all their needs, because they do not have an intense emotional investment in any one of them. The neurotic, conversely, has made one of the needs a way of life. The neurotic's whole life is spent attempting to satisfy just one of the needs at the expense of all the others. Because it is important that many of the other needs be satisfied, the neurotic is locked into a vicious circle. The more one neurotic need is emphasized as a means of coping with basic anxiety, the more other important needs go unsatisfied. The more these other needs go unsatisfied, the more basic anxiety the neurotic feels, and the more anxious this person feels, the deeper he or she burrows into the single strategy to cope with the anxiety. And on it goes.

Moving Toward, Against, or Away from People

In her book *Our Inner Conflicts* (1945), Horney summarized her list of ten neurotic needs into three general categories. Each of the three categories described the neurotic's adjustment to other people. These three categories of adjustment are considered by many to be Horney's most significant contribution to personality theory.

Moving Toward People

This adjustment pattern includes the neurotic needs for affection and approval, for a dominant partner to control one's life, and to live one's life within narrow limits. This person, whom Horney called the **compliant type,** seems to say, "If I give in, I shall not be hurt" (Horney 1937, 97).

> In sum, this type needs to be liked, wanted, desired, loved; to feel accepted, welcomed, approved of, appreciated; to be needed, to be of importance to others, especially to one particular person; to be helped, protected, taken care of, guided. (Horney 1945, 51)

It should be noted that, like the ten neurotic needs, these adjustments to other people also are based on basic anxiety, which is based on basic hostility. So, although a person may adjust to basic anxiety by **moving toward people** and by apparently seeking love and affection, the person still is basically hostile. Thus, the compliant person's friendliness is superficial and is based on repressed aggressiveness.

Moving Against People

In most ways, this person is the opposite of the compliant type. This adjustment pattern combines the neurotic needs for power, for exploitation of others, for prestige, and for personal achievement. This person, whom Horney called the **hostile type,** seems to say, "If I have power, no one can hurt me" (Horney 1937, 98).

> Any situation or relationship is looked at from the standpoint of "What can I get out of it?"—whether it has to do with money, prestige, contacts, or ideas. The person himself is consciously or semiconsciously convinced that everyone acts this way, and so what counts is to do it more efficiently than the rest. (Horney 1945, 65)

The hostile type is capable of acting polite and friendly, but it is always a means to an end. The origin of this adjustment technique is the same as for the compliant type, basic anxiety, which was originally based on feelings of insecurity.

Moving Away from People

This adjustment pattern includes the neurotic needs for self-sufficiency, independence, perfection, and unassailability. This person, whom Horney called the

detached type, seems to be saying, "If I withdraw, nothing can hurt me" (Horney 1937, 99).

> What is crucial is their inner need to put emotional distance between themselves and others. More accurately, it is their conscious and unconscious determination not to get emotionally involved with others in any way, whether in love, fight, co-operation, or competition. They draw around themselves a kind of magic circle which no one may penetrate. (Horney 1945, 75)

The relationship between the ten neurotic needs and the three major adjustment patterns to other people is summarized in Table 5–1. As with the ten neurotic needs, the normal person uses all three adjustments to other people, depending on which one is appropriate at the time. Neurotic persons cannot. They emphasize one of the three adjustments at the expense of the other two. This causes further anxiety, because all humans at various times need to be aggressive, to be compliant, and to be detached or withdrawn. The lopsided development of the neurotic causes further anxiety, which causes further lopsided development. Thus we have the vicious circle again.

It should be noted that the three adjustment patterns are basically incompatible. For example, one cannot move toward people and away from people at the same time. For both the neurotic and the normal person, the three adjustment patterns are in conflict with each other. For the normal person, however, the conflict is not as emotionally charged as it is for the neurotic one. Therefore, the normal person has much greater flexibility, being able to move from one adjustment mode to another as conditions change. The neurotic person must meet all of life's problems using only one of the three adjustment patterns whether that pattern is appropriate or not. It follows that the neurotic person is far less flexible and is therefore less effective in dealing with life's problems than the normal person is.

Table 5–1
"Solutions" to Neurotic Conflict

SELF-EFFACING SOLUTION: LOVE— "MOVING TOWARD" (COMPLIANCE)	EXPANSIVE SOLUTION: MASTERY— "MOVING AGAINST" (AGGRESSION)	RESIGNATION SOLUTION: FREEDOM— "MOVING AWAY" (DETACHMENT)
Need for: 1. Affection and approval 2. Partner to take control 3. Restriction of life to narrow borders "If you love me, you will not hurt me."	Need for: 4. Power and omnipotence and perfection 5. Exploitation of others 6. Social recognition and prestige 7. Personal admiration 8. Personal achievement "If I have power, no one can hurt me."	Need for: 3. Restriction of life to narrow borders 9. Self-sufficiency 10. Perfection and unassailability "If I withdraw, nothing can hurt me."
Identification with the despised real self	Identification with the ideal self	Vacillation between despised real self and ideal self

The relationship between the three major adjustment techniques and the ten neurotic needs.

(From Monte 1987, 426). Based on Horney, 1945, chaps. 3, 4, 5; 1942, chap. 2; and 1950, chap. 3.

Real and Idealized Self

According to Horney, each human is born with a healthy, **real self** that is conducive to normal personality growth. If people live in accordance with their real selves, they are on the road to **self-realization** which means they will approximate their full potential and live in harmony with their fellow humans. Unfortunately, the real self can be, and often is, distorted by the basic evil. Because of harsh treatment some children begin to view themselves as lowly and despicable; why else would they have suffered the abuse that they did? With the real self viewed incorrectly as negative, the person can no longer live in accordance with it. Instead, such a person creates an **idealized self** that has little relationship to reality. According to Horney, when a person's life is lived in accordance with an illusionary, idealized self instead of the real self, he or she is neurotic. The neurotic uses his or her idealized self as an escape from his or her real self, which is viewed negatively. Unlike the real self, the idealized self is an unrealistic, immutable dream.

When one's life is directed by an unrealistic self-image, one is driven by what *should be*, rather than what is. Horney refers to this as the **tyranny of the should:**

> Forget about the disgraceful creature you actually are; this is how you should be; and to be this idealized self is all that matters. You should be able to endure everything, to understand everything, to like everybody, to be always productive— to mention only a few of these inner dictates. Since they are inexorable, I call them "the tyranny of the should." (1950, 64–65)

Horney goes on to specify several "shoulds" governing the life of the person whose real self has been displaced by an unrealistic idealized self:

> He should be the utmost of honesty, generosity, considerateness, justice, dignity, courage, unselfishness. He should be the perfect lover, husband, teacher. He should be able to endure everything, should like everybody, should love his parents, his wife, his country; or, he should not be attached to anything or anybody, nothing should matter to him, he should never feel hurt, and he should always be serene and unruffled. He should always enjoy life; or, he should be above pleasure and enjoyment. He should be spontaneous; he should always control his feelings. He should know, understand, and foresee everything. He should be able to solve every problem of his own, or of others, in no time. He should be able to overcome every difficulty of his as soon as he sees it. He should never be tired or fall ill. He should always be able to find a job. He should be able to do things in one hour which can only be done in two or three hours. (1950, 65)

The neurotic is locked into the illusion of the ideal self, an illusion that does not reflect reality and one that tends to be unchanging. The more intensely the neurotic chases this ideal, the further the person is driven from the real self and the more intense the neurosis becomes. Horney (1945) explained:

> A person builds up an idealized image of himself because he cannot tolerate himself as he actually is. The image apparently counteracts this calamity; but having placed himself on a pedestal, he can tolerate his real self still less and starts

to rage against it, to despise himself and to chafe under the yoke of his own unattainable demands upon himself. He wavers then between self-adoration and self-contempt, between his idealized image and his despised image, with no solid middle ground to fall back on. (112)

For such a person, the only hope is a well-trained analyst.

Normal people, conversely, have dreams, but they are realistic and changeable. Normal people experience both success and failure, and both influence changes in their aspirations. Neurotic people experience mainly failure, because their ideals tend to be incompatible with their real selves.

Externalization

According to Horney (1945):

When discrepancies between the actual self and the idealized one reach a point where tensions become unbearable, [the person] can no longer resort to anything within himself. The only thing left then is to run away from himself entirely and see everything as if it lay outside. (115–16)

Horney refers to this tendency to see everything of importance occurring outside of oneself as **externalization,** which she defines as "the tendency to experience internal processes as if they occurred outside oneself and, as a rule, to hold these external factors responsible for one's difficulties. It has in common with idealization the purpose of getting away from the real self" (1945, 115).

Some similarity exists between externalization and the Freudian mechanism of projection, but, according to Horney:

Externalization . . . is a more comprehensive phenomenon; the shifting of responsibility is only a part of it. Not only one's faults are experienced in others but to a greater or lesser degree all feelings. A person who tends to externalize may be profoundly disturbed by the oppression of small countries, while unaware of how much he himself feels oppressed. He may not feel his own despair but will emotionally experience it in others. What is particularly important in this connection, he is unaware of his own attitudes toward himself; he will, for example, feel that someone else is angry with him when he actually is angry with himself. Or he will be conscious of anger at others that in reality he directs at himself. Further, he will ascribe not only his disturbances but also his good moods or achievements to external factors. While his failures will be seen as the decree of fate, his successes will be laid to fortuitous circumstances, his high spirits to the weather, and so on. (1945, 116)

Because the neurotic removes himself or herself as a determinant of anything significant, it is only natural that experiences external to one's self will be overvalued, especially other people. If any major change is going to occur in the neurotic's life, so reasons the neurotic, it must result from changing other people. "When a person feels that his life for good or ill is determined by others, it is only logical that he should be preoccupied with changing them, reforming them, punishing them, protecting himself from their interference, or impressing them" (Horney 1945, 116–17).

The neurotic becomes completely dependent on external factors in maintaining his or her idealized image. When these external factors do not support the neurotic's illusions that they actually are their idealized images, they feel a sense of rage but that too must be externalized. According to Horney (1945, 120–22) rage can be externalized in three ways: (1) If there are no inhibitions against hostility, anger is turned against others as either general irritability or as specific irritation concerning the faults in others that the neurotic really hates in himself or herself; (2) an incessant fear that the faults that one cannot tolerate in oneself will infuriate others; (3) the creation of bodily disorders such as intestinal maladies, headaches, fatigue, and so on.

Externalization does not help the neurotic's situation any; in fact, externalization makes the situation worse.

> Externalization is thus essentially an active process of self-elimination. The reason for its being feasible at all lies in the estrangement from the self that is inherent in the neurotic process anyhow. With the self eliminated, it is only natural that the inner conflicts, too, should be removed from awareness. But by making the person more reproachful, vindictive, and fearful in respect to others, externalization replaces the inner conflicts with external ones. More specifically, it greatly aggravates the conflict that originally set in motion the whole neurotic process: the conflict between the individual and the outer world. (Horney 1945, 130)

Because the attempt at self-obliteration through externalization is destined to fail, the neurotic is forced to resort to what Horney called "auxiliary approaches to artificial harmony."

Auxiliary Approaches to Artificial Harmony

According to Horney, neurotic persons lie to themselves when they attempt to live their lives according to their idealized self images and all of the "shoulds" associated with those images. To support that lie they need to externalize whatever real feelings they may have, another lie. To support those lies, or to control the damage done by them, neurotics need to employ other lies, and on it goes. Horney (1945) explained:

> It is a commonplace that one lie usually leads to another, the second takes a third to bolster it, and so on till one is caught in a tangled web. Something of the sort is bound to happen in any situation in the life of an individual or group where a determination to go to the root of the matter is lacking. The patchwork may be of some help, but it will generate new problems which in turn require a new makeshift. So it is with neurotic attempts to solve the basic conflict; and here as elsewhere, nothing is of any real avail but a radical change in the conditions out of which the original difficulty arose. What the neurotic does instead—and cannot help doing—is to pile one pseudo solution upon another. (131)

Horney described seven unconscious devices that neurotics use to deal with the inevitable conflicts that arise when one displaces one's real self with an idealized self. Horney viewed these devices as additional lies that neurotics use in attempting to live an illusionary life.

Blind Spots

This problem involves denying or ignoring certain aspects of experience, because they are not in accordance with one's idealized self-image. For example, if one views oneself as extremely intelligent, one will tend to overlook experiences that suggest one is stupid. Also, people who view themselves as Christ-like will remain oblivious to any blatant acts of aggression they engage in; those who view themselves as basically hostile will overlook any of their Christ-like attributes.

Compartmentalization

This concept involves dividing one's life up into various components with different rules applying to them. For example, one set of rules applies to one's family life and another set to one's business life. Thus, one can act in accordance with Christian principles at home and be ruthless in one's business dealings. The neurotic sees no conflict here, because "the situations are different." Horney (1945) elaborated on **compartmentalization.**

> There is a section for friends and one for enemies, one for the family and one for outsiders, one for professional and one for personal life, one for social equals and one for inferiors. Hence what happens in one compartment does not appear to the neurotic to contradict what happens in another. It is possible for a person to live that way only when, by reason of his conflicts, he has lost his sense of unity. (133–34)

Rationalization

According to Horney, **rationalization** is the kind of self-deception that involves giving logical, plausible, but inaccurate excuses to justify one's perceived weaknesses, failures, or inconsistencies. Compliant types must offer such excuses for acts of aggression, and hostile types must offer them for acts of kindness.

Excessive Self-Control

This is guarding against anxiety by controlling any expression of emotion. The goal here is to maintain rigid self-control at all costs. Horney (1945) elaborated:

> Persons who exert such control will not allow themselves to be carried away, whether by enthusiasm, sexual excitement, self-pity, or rage. In analysis they have the greatest difficulty in associating freely; they will not permit alcohol to lift their

spirits and frequently prefer to endure pain rather than undergo anesthesia. In short, they seek to check all spontaneity. (136)

Arbitrary Rightness

Often the life of a neurotic is characterized by indecision, ambiguity, and doubt but the feelings generated by these characteristics are intolerable. By using **arbitrary rightness** as a protective device in ambiguous situations the neurotic chooses one solution, one answer, one position and dogmatically declares that the problem is solved and the debate is over. The position taken by the neurotic becomes the "truth" and therefore cannot be challenged. The neurotic no longer needs to worry about what is right and wrong, or what is certain and uncertain.

Elusiveness

This technique is the opposite of arbitrary rightness. The elusive neurotic never makes a decision about anything. If one is never committed to anything, one can never be wrong, and if one is never wrong, one can never be criticized.

Cynicism

The elusive neurotic postpones making decisions, whereas the cynic does not believe in anything. Cynics take pleasure in pointing out the meaninglessness of the beliefs of others. Horney believed that this technique probably grew out of repeated failures with previous beliefs. By not believing anything, cynics are immune to the disappointment that comes from being committed to something that is shown to be false. Also, they are spared the difficult task of arriving at their own system of beliefs. They simply say *nothing* is worth believing. Also, by not accepting any moral values these neurotics justify their Machiavellian approach to interpersonal relationships.

Again, the difference between normal people and neurotics is one of degree. Normal people will undoubtedly use each of these secondary adjustment techniques at one time or another. Neurotics, however, will *overuse* one or more of them, thus reducing their flexibility and efficiency in solving life's inevitable problems.

Feminine Psychology

Horney strongly disagreed with Freud that women were destined to possess certain personality traits, such as sexual ambivalence, simply because they had a female anatomy. Horney believed that cultural factors were much more important in explaining the personality characteristics of both men and women than were biologic factors. Horney began writing articles on how culture influences female personality development in 1923 and continued to do so until 1937; these articles have been compiled in her book *Feminine Psychology* (1967).

Horney's Explanation of Penis Envy. According to Freud, one of the most traumatic experiences in the development of girls is their discovery that they do not possess penises, although boys do. They react to this discovery by wishing to have a penis and being envious of more fortunate males. In this biologic area females must settle only for symbols, thus they wish to have male children who will finally furnish them (symbolically) with their own penises. According to Freud, **anatomy is destiny** and women are destined to be inferior to men (or at least *feel* inferior) and have a contempt for their own sex because they lack penises.

Horney rejected the Freudian notion of penis envy and said instead that women often feel inferior to men because they are, indeed, *culturally* inferior to men. Because men control the power in culture, women may appear to wish to be masculine (to have a penis), whereas all they are attempting to do is participate in those desirable experiences that men have control over. Horney said, "Our whole civilization is a masculine civilization. The State, the laws, morality, religion, and the sciences are the creation of men" (1926/1967, 55). Horney (1939) continued:

> The wish to be a man . . . may be the expression of a wish for all those qualities or privileges which in our culture are regarded as masculine, such as strength, courage, independence, success, sexual freedom, right to choose a partner. (108)

Thus, it is not penises that women envy and desire, but the ability to influence and to participate in their culture freely.

Furthermore, Horney found that in her treatment of male patients, they often displayed an envy of motherhood at least as strong as the supposed penis envy displayed by women.

> From the biological point of view woman has in motherhood, or in the capacity for motherhood, a quite indisputable and by no means negligible physiological superiority. This is most clearly reflected in the unconscious of the male psyche in the boy's intense envy of motherhood. . . . When one begins, as I did, to analyze men only after a fairly long experience of analyzing women, one receives a most surprising impression of the intensity of this envy of pregnancy, childbirth, and motherhood, as well as of the breasts and of the act of suckling. (Horney, 1926/1967, 60–61)

Why does psychoanalysis seem to understand men better than women and to paint a more favorable picture of men than women? Horney answered "The reason for this is obvious. Psychoanalysis is the creation of a male genius, and almost all those who have developed his ideas have been men. It is only right and reasonable that they should evolve more easily a masculine psychology and understand more of the development of men than of women" (1926/1967, 54). Horney (1926/1967) continued:

> Like all sciences and all valuations, the psychology of women has hitherto been considered only from the point of view of men. It is inevitable that the man's position of advantage should cause objective validity to be attributed to his sub-

jective, affective relations to the woman ... the psychology of women hitherto actually represents a deposit of the desires and disappointments of men. (56)

Psychotherapy

As far as psychotherapeutic techniques are concerned, Horney borrowed much from Freud. She commonly used dream analysis and free association. Both were used, however, to discover which major adjustment technique a patient was using. She also believed strongly in Freud's concept of transference. "Were someone to ask me," she said, "which of Freud's discoveries I value most highly, I should say without any hesitation: it is his finding that one can utilize for therapy the patient's emotional reactions to the analyst and to the analytical situation" (1939, 154). For Horney, what was revealed through transference was, once again, the patient's major adjustment technique. Thus, hostile types attempted to dominate the therapist; the detached type waited like a bystander while the therapist provided a miraculous cure; and the compliant type attempted to use his or her pain and suffering to gain sympathy and help from the therapist.

The tendency for neurotics to externalize is a major obstacle in psychotherapy. Horney (1945) explained:

> A patient with a general tendency to externalize offers peculiar difficulties in analysis. He comes to it as he would go to a dentist, expecting the analyst to perform a job that does not really concern him. He is interested in the neurosis of his wife, friend, brother, but not in his own. He talks about the difficult circumstances under which he lives and is reluctant to examine his share in them. If his wife were not so neurotic or his work so upsetting, he would be quite all right. For a considerable period he has no realization whatever that any emotional forces could possibly be operating within himself; he is afraid of ghosts, burglars, thunderstorms, of vindictive persons around him, of the political situation, but never of himself. He is at best interested in his problems for the intellectual or artistic pleasure they afford him. But as long as he is, so to speak, psychically nonexistent, he cannot possibly apply any insight he may gain to his actual living, and therefore in spite of his greater knowledge about himself can change very little. (129–30)

Goal of Psychotherapy.   Like Adler, Horney believed that humans are born with a tendency toward positive growth but that this tendency could be interfered with by social forces. According to Horney, we strive toward *self-realization*, which involves being productive, truthful, and relating to fellow humans with a spirit of mutuality. If nothing interferes with this innate tendency, humans develop as normal, healthy persons. Horney (1945) compared her optimistic view of humans with Freud's pessimistic view.

> Freud's pessimism as regards neuroses and their treatment arose from the depths of his disbelief in human goodness and human growth. Man, he postulated, is doomed to suffer or to destroy. The instincts which drive him can only be controlled, or at best "sublimated." My own belief is that man has the capacity as well as the desire to develop his potentialities and become a decent human being, and

that these deteriorate if his relationship to others and hence to himself is, and continues to be, disturbed. I believe that man can change and go on changing as long as he lives. (19)

The goal of psychotherapy, then, is to bring the patient back in touch with his or her capacity for positive growth and for warm, productive relationships with his or her fellow humans. The patient must first be convinced that he or she has been living in accordance with an illusion (idealized self) and doing so made life much more frustrating than it needed to be. Gradually patients must be steered in the direction of self-realization by showing them their capacity for cooperative human relations, their true talents and creative powers, and their responsibilities. It is not enough that patients come to understand these qualities intellectually, they must understand them *emotionally* as well. The insights gained must become a living truth within the patient.

Horney describes the characteristics she hoped would emerge in patients if psychotherapy were effective (1945, 241–42). *Responsibility,* making decisions in one's life and accepting the consequences of those decisions and recognizing obligations to other people; *inner independence,* living in accordance with one's own values and respecting the right for others to do the same thing; *spontaneity of feeling,* to be able to honestly experience one's own love, hate, happiness, sadness, fear or desire; and *wholeheartedness* "To be without pretense, to be emotionally sincere, to be able to put the whole of oneself into one's feelings, one's work, one's beliefs" (Horney 1945, 242). When one displays these characteristics, he or she is on the road to self-realization.

The goal of psychotherapy is not to create perfect human beings, rather, it is to help persons that have been diverted from their self-realization process to become "real" people again instead of fictitious ones. Real people have real problems, real anxiety, real failures, and real successes. Horney (1939) said: "The aim of analysis is not to render life devoid of risks and conflicts, but to enable an individual eventually to solve his problems himself" (305).

In her book *Self-Analysis* (1942), Horney expressed the belief that people can go a long way in solving their own problems. After all, she asked, "How did humans ever solve their emotional problems before psychotherapy was available?" Her point is that obviously many people do not have severe emotional problems. Somehow, they have learned to solve problems, to minimize conflict, and to embrace life with spontaneity. The role of the therapist is to help the neurotic learn to respond in these ways and to go on acting in these ways after therapy is terminated. By **self-analysis,** Horney meant the analysis of one's own life; she did not mean that all people are equipped to solve deep emotional problems in either themselves or in others. For example, severely neurotic people are not in a position to solve their own problems and attempts to do so may do more harm than good.

Comparison of Horney and Freud

Early Childhood Experience

Both Freud and Horney thought that early childhood experiences were extremely important. The reasons that these experiences were important were different for the two, however. Freud believed that there were universal stages of development, and fixation at any particular stage strongly influenced one's adult personality. For Horney, it was the child's relationship to the parents that was important, because it was this relationship that determined whether or not the child would develop basic anxiety.

Unconscious Motivation

Both Horney and Freud emphasized the importance of unconscious motivation. For Horney, it was repressed hostility that led to basic anxiety, which led to neurosis. Thus, the basis of all neurotic behavior is repressed basic hostility, which, of course, is unconscious.

Biologic Motivation

Freud emphasized biologic motivation. To him, all conflicts are derived from attempts to satisfy biologic drives—especially the sex drive. Horney de-emphasized biologic motivation by stressing the importance of the child's need for a feeling of security. Thus, we say that Freud's is a biologic theory and Horney's is a social theory. For example, here is Horney's explanation of the Oedipus complex:

> If a child, in addition to being dependent on his parents, is grossly or subtly intimidated by them and hence feels that any expression of hostile impulses against them endangers his security, then the existence of such hostile impulses is bound to create anxiety.... The resulting picture may look exactly like what Freud describes as the Oedipus Complex: passionate clinging to one parent and jealousy toward the other or toward anyone interfering with the claim of exclusive possession.... But the dynamic structure of these attachments is entirely different from what Freud conceives as the Oedipus complex. They are an early manifestation of neurotic conflicts rather than a primarily sexual phenomenon. (1939, 83–84)

Psychotherapy

Horney used Freud's methods of free association and dream analysis, and agreed with Freud on the importance of transference. Freud, however, used all of these concepts to uncover repressed traumatic memories, whereas Horney used them to discover a neurotic's major adjustment technique.

Is Anatomy Destiny?

Yes for Freud, no for Horney.

Prognosis for Personality Change

Freud believed that personality was formulated early in life, and major changes thereafter were extremely difficult to make. Horney agreed that personality is strongly influenced by early experiences but that it remained changeable throughout life. Thus, she was much more optimistic than Freud. "Our daring to name such high goals rests upon the belief that the human personality can change. It is not only the young child who is pliable. All of us retain the capacity to change, even to change in fundamental ways, as long as we live" (Horney 1945, 242).

Evaluation

Empirical Research

Most of the research supporting Horney's theory is indirect. Horney believed that behavior disorders result when people attempt to live their lives in accordance with their idealized selves. Such people believe that they are brilliant, great lovers, paragons of virtue, unselfish, or courageous. They also see the source of everything important in their lives as external to themselves (externalization). In other words, Horney believed that a correlation existed between the irrational beliefs people had about themselves and psychopathology. Horney's suspicion has been confirmed in several areas. For example, people with several irrational beliefs about themselves are more likely to be depressed (see, for example, Dobson and Breiter 1983); to be socially ineffective (see, for example, Hayden and Nasby 1977); to have unhappy marriages (see, for example, Eidelson and Epstein 1982); and to be ineffective problem solvers (see, for example, Schill, Monroe, Evans, and Ramanaiah 1978).

Also, the rational-emotive therapy developed by Albert Ellis is based on the assumption that psychopathology results from the irrational beliefs held by patients. The rational-emotive therapist actively challenges the patient's erroneous beliefs and replaces them with more realistic thoughts and feelings. Considerable evidence exists that such therapy is effective (see, for example, Ellis and Greiger 1977; Smith 1983).

Criticisms

Unoriginal Contributions. Like Freud, Horney emphasized the importance of early childhood experience, unconscious motivation, and defense mechanisms. Also like Freud she used free association, dream analysis, and the analysis of transference in her approach to psychoanalysis. Like Adler, Horney de-emphasized the biologic origins of behavior disorders and instead emphasized their social origins. Adler's notion of safeguarding strategies is similar to Horney's neurotic solutions; both masked the person's real self. Both Horney and Adler believed that when a culture is male dominated, women will often attempt to become more masculine in order to gain power. Finally, both Jung and Horney employed the concept of self-realization (self-actualization for Jung), which in both cases meant the natural impulse toward healthy personality development. One way to view Horney's theory, then, is as a blending of the theories of Freud, Adler, and Jung.

Stimulation of Little Empirical Research.   Often a personality theory contains language and concepts that are too nebulous to verify empirically. Furthermore, those personality theorists who were also clinicians claim that the true value of their theories is determined by whether or not they enhance the therapeutic process. For them empirical verification using controlled experimental procedures is irrelevant. Both of the preceding statements are true for Horney's theory, although, as we have seen, some indirect empirical verification of the theory has occurred.

Disregard of Healthy Persons.   Although Horney did discuss the natural tendency toward self-realization, she concentrated almost exclusively on understanding persons who had their tendency toward self-realization disrupted, that is, neurotics.

Contributions

Original Ideas.   Although, as we have seen, some have criticized Horney for borrowing too heavily from Freud, Adler, and Jung, others see her blending of these (and other) theories as a highly original and important contribution to the understanding of personality. For example, her notions of the tyranny of the should and the major neurotic adjustment techniques, as well as her discussion of what happens when one becomes alienated from his or her real self, have had a significant influence on modern personality theory and therapeutic techniques (see, for example, Carl Rogers).

Self-Analysis.   Directly contrary to Freud and the other psychoanalysts at the time, Horney believed that many persons could and should analyze themselves, and she hoped her writings would help them to do so. Horney's book *Self-Analysis* (1942) was one of the first self-help books in psychology, and it created quite a controversy. Now it is generally believed that many troubled persons can improve their situations if given the proper information. However, most therapists believe, as Horney did, that severely disturbed persons must receive professional treatment.

Feminine Psychology.   Horney's thoughts on feminine psychology were among the first in an area that is so popular today. Although Horney was strongly influenced by Freudian theory and agreed with much of it, she disagreed with almost every conclusion that Freud reached about women. It must be realized that departing from Freudian dogma at the time was no easy matter. In fact, those who did so were excommunicated just as if they had violated religious dogma. Horney was excommunicated because she dared to contradict the master. As the reader may remember, Horney learned from observing her father as a child how devastating blind belief in religious dogma could be; perhaps that was one reason she decided not to let Freud go unchallenged.

Summary

Although Karen Horney was trained in the Freudian tradition, she departed from that tradition in several important ways. She stressed the importance of early parent-child relationships in her theory of personality development. If these relationships are positive, warm, and based on genuine love, the child will tend to develop normally. Normal people are flexible and spontaneous, and their goals are tied realistically to their abilities. That is, they live in accordance with their innate tendency toward self-realization. If, however, parents react to a child with indifference, superficiality, or aggression, the child will feel basic hostility toward the parents, which must be repressed because of the child's feelings of helplessness, fear, or guilt. The repressed hostility that the child feels for the parent is projected on the world in general, becoming basic anxiety. Basic anxiety is the feeling of being alone and helpless in a hostile world.

In order to combat basic anxiety, persons adopt one of three adjustments relative to other people. They move toward, against, or away from them. Normal persons display all three adjustments toward people depending on the circumstances. The neurotic's life, however, is dominated by one of the adjustments, and therefore, the other two go unsatisfied, causing greater conflict and anxiety. For neurotics, the real self is displaced by the idealized self, and their lives are governed by a list of unrealistic "shoulds" instead of goals based on their own experiences. Neurotics engage heavily in externalization. That is, they see the source of all important events in their lives as external to themselves.

Besides the major adjustment techniques of moving toward, against, or away from people, Horney also postulated the following secondary adjustment techniques: blind spots, in which inconsistencies in one's life are ignored; compartmentalization, in which one applies different values to different situations; rationalization, in which one gives logical but erroneous explanations for wrongdoings or shortcomings; excessive self-control, in which one minimizes failure by living within a narrow, predictable range of events; arbitrary rightness, in which one takes a stand that becomes equated with truth and therefore cannot be challenged; elusiveness, in which one avoids failure by postponing decisions; and cynicism, in which one believes nothing is worth commitment.

Horney wrote many articles showing that much that had been written about the female personality reflected male biases and misunderstandings. Horney believed, for example, that women often do aspire to be more masculine, but it is not because they have penis envy. Rather, being masculine in a male-dominated society is the only way to gain power. Just as many psychological problems are caused by culture, so are many of the differences between men and women. Horney thought that many female characteristics that Freud attributed to anatomy should be regarded as culturally determined.

For Horney, the goal of psychotherapy was to confront the patient with the fact that he or she is attempting to live an illusion (the idealized self). When this goal is accomplished, the therapist can help the patient to discover his or her real self and to start on the road to self-realization.

Horney agreed with Freud that much behavior is unconsciously motivated but disagreed with him on the importance of biologic motivation. Horney believed the social need for security was much more important than the need for biologic satisfaction.

Horney's theory is supported by the finding that as the number of irrational beliefs that people have about themselves increases so does the tendency to be depressed, to be socially ineffective, to have unhappy marriages, and to be poor problem solvers. Also, the rational-emotive therapy of Albert Ellis has shown that patients show improvement when their irrational beliefs are actively challenged and replaced by more realistic beliefs and feelings.

Horney's theory has been criticized for not being original, for not stimulating much empirical research, and for ignoring the personality development of healthy persons. Among the contributions made by Horney's theory are listed its creative blending of Freudian, Adlerian, and Jungian theory, its encouragement of self-analysis, and its elaboration of feminine psychology.

EXPERIENTIAL EXERCISES

1. Describe your own personality in terms of Horney's major adjustment techniques. Do you move toward, against, or away from people with about equal frequency? If not, which of the three do you emphasize? Using Horney's theory, attempt to explain why you use the major adjustment techniques the way that you do.

2. Horney said that each person is born with a tendency toward self-realization, that is, toward normal, healthy growth. The tendency toward self-realization, however, can be disrupted by "basic evil," in which case the real self is displaced by an idealized self. The person living in accordance with an idealized self is, according to Horney, living an illusion. Are you living in accordance with your tendency toward self-realization or is your life governed by an idealized self? Explain.

3. Give an example of your use of externalization. Also, give examples of how you have used blind spots, compartmentalization, rationalization, excessive self-control, arbitrary rightness, elusiveness, and cynicism.

4. Respond to Freud's contention that "anatomy is destiny" from Horney's viewpoint and then from your own.

DISCUSSION QUESTIONS

1. Explain why Freud's theory of personality is called a biologic theory and why Horney's is called a social theory.

2. Differentiate between those childhood experiences that Horney thought conducive to normal development and those she thought conducive to neurotic development.

3. Describe "basic hostility" and "basic anxiety" and explain how the two are related.

4. List a few examples of what Horney called the neurotic needs or trends, and describe the difference between the normal person's adjustment to these needs and that of the neurotic individual.

5. Summarize the three major adjustment patterns relative to other people.

6. Describe the difference between the real and the idealized self. Explain the difference in the relationship between the real and the idealized selves for the normal person versus the neurotic person.

7. List the major differences that exist between neurotic and normal people according to Horney.

8. Discuss Horney's concept of externalization.

9. Give a brief definition and an example of each of the following secondary adjustment techniques: blind spots, compartmentalization, rationalization, excessive self-control, externalization, arbitrary rightness, elusiveness, and cynicism.

10. Summarize Horney's reaction to the Freudian contention that women experience penis envy.

11. Describe the process and goals of psychotherapy as Horney viewed them.

12. Compare Horney's theory of personality with Freud's theory.

SUGGESTIONS FOR FURTHER READING

HORNEY, K. (1937). *The Neurotic Personality of Our Time.* New York: Norton.

> Horney's first book. Describes the cultural origins of psychological disturbances and the many ways in which neurotics attempt to cope with their anxiety.

HORNEY, K. (1939). *New Ways in Psychoanalysis.* New York: Norton.

> Horney elaborates the differences between her approach to psychoanalysis and Freud's, and also criticizes many of the basic tenets of Freudian psychoanalysis.

HORNEY, K. (1942). *Self-Analysis.* New York: Norton.

> Horney presents her basic ideas so that nonprofessionals can use them to solve many of their emotional problems.

HORNEY, K. (1945). *Our Inner Conflicts.* New York: Norton.

> Horney summarizes what had previously been her ten neurotic needs into the three major adjustment techniques of moving toward, against, and away from people.

HORNEY, K. (1950). *Neurosis and Human Growth: The Struggle Toward Self-Realization.* New York: Norton.

> This work, Horney's last book, ties together the many strands of her theory that were presented in her earlier works.

HORNEY, K. (1923–1937/1967). *Feminine Psychology.* New York: Norton.

> Topics covered include the following. On the genesis of the castration complex in women, the flight from womanhood, inhibited femininity, premenstrual tension, the distrust between the sexes, problems of marriage, the overvaluation of love, and the neurotic need for love.

HORNEY, K. (1980). *The Adolescent Diaries of Karen Horney.* New York: Basic Books.

> A glimpse of Horney's personal experiences as she was growing up.

INGRAM, D. H. (1987) (ed.). *Karen Horney: Final Lectures.* New York: Norton.

> Edited transcriptions of the tape recording of the last five lectures that Horney gave before she died. Also includes a personal reminiscence of Horney as a teacher by one of her ex-students.

RUBINS, J. L. (1978). *Karen Horney: Gentle Rebel of Psychoanalysis.* New York: Dial.

> An extremely interesting, readable biography of Karen Horney.

GLOSSARY

Anatomy is destiny. The contention of some personality theorists, Freud for example, that one's gender determines, to a large extent, one's personality characteristics.

Arbitrary rightness. Exemplified when issues arise that have no clear solution one way or the other, and a person arbitrarily chooses one solution, thereby ending debate.

Basic anxiety. The psychological state that exists when basic hostility is repressed. It is the general feeling that everything and everyone in the world are potentially dangerous.

Basic evil. Anything that parents do that undermines a child's security.

Basic hostility. The feeling that is generated in a child if needs for safety and satisfaction are not consistently and lovingly satisfied by the parents.

Blind spots. Denying or ignoring certain aspects of experience because they are not in accordance with one's idealized self-image.

Compartmentalization. Dividing one's life up into various components with different rules applying to the different components.

Compliant type person. A person who uses "moving toward people" as the major means of reducing basic anxiety.

Cynicism. The strategy in which a person believes in nothing and is therefore immune to the disappointment that comes from being committed to something that is shown to be false.

Detached type person. A person who uses "moving away from people" as the major means of reducing basic anxiety.

Elusiveness. Opposite to arbitrary rightness. The elusive person never makes decisions about anything. Without a commitment to anything this person can never be wrong.

Excessive self-control. Guarding against anxiety by denying oneself emotional involvement in anything.

Externalization. Similar to Freud's ego-defense mechanism of projection. The belief that all the major influences in one's life are external to oneself.

Hostile type person. A person who uses "moving against people" as the major means of reducing basic anxiety.

Idealized self. The fictitious view of oneself, with its list of "shoulds" that displaces the real self in the neurotic personality.

Moving against people. A major adjustment to basic anxiety that uses the tendency to exploit other people and to gain power over them. Horney referred to the person using this adjustment technique as the hostile type.

Moving away from people. A major adjustment to basic anxiety that uses the need to be self-sufficient. Horney referred to the person using this adjustment technique as the detached type.

Moving toward people. A major adjustment to basic anxiety that uses the need to be wanted, loved, and protected by other people. Horney referred to the person using this adjustment technique as the compliant type.

Neurotic need for a partner who will run one's life. The attempt to escape basic anxiety by affiliating oneself with a partner who will run one's life.

Neurotic need for affection and approval. The attempt to escape basic anxiety by making love and affection the central theme in one's life.

Neurotic need for ambition and personal achievement. The attempt to escape basic anxiety by becoming famous, rich, or important.

Neurotic need for perfection and unassailability. The attempt to escape basic anxiety by striving to become flawless.

Neurotic need for personal admiration. The attempt to escape basic anxiety by continuously seeking compliments.

Neurotic need for power. The attempt to escape basic anxiety by gaining power over the environment and over other people.

Neurotic need for self-sufficiency and independence. The attempt to escape basic anxiety by avoiding all obligations.

Neurotic need for social recognition and prestige. The attempt to escape basic anxiety by gaining social prestige.

Neurotic need to exploit others. The attempt to escape basic anxiety by taking advantage of other people.

Neurotic need to live within narrow limits. The attempt to escape basic anxiety by living a very restricted life.

Neurotic trends. Ten strategies for minimizing basic anxiety.

Rationalization. Giving "good" but erroneous reasons to excuse conduct that would otherwise be anxiety provoking. Horney used this term in much the same way that Freud did.

Real self. The self that is healthy and conducive to positive growth. Although each person is born with a healthy real self, the view of this real self can be distorted by the "basic evil." The basic evil causes a person to view his or her real self negatively and then attempt to escape from it. Even though the neurotic views his or her real self negatively it remains a source of potential health and positive growth.

Safety. The child's need for security and freedom from fear that Horney believed must be satisfied before normal psychological development could occur.

Satisfaction. The meeting of such psychological needs as those for water, food, and sleep required for a child's biologic survival.

Self-analysis. The process of self-help that Horney believed people could apply to themselves to solve life's many problems, to maintain a reasonable relationship between the real self and the idealized self, and to minimize conflict. She did feel, however, that severe emotional problems needed to be treated by a professional analyst.

Self-realization. The innate tendency to strive for truthfulness, productivity, and harmonious relationships with fellow humans.

Tyranny of the should. Refers to the fact that when one's idealized self is substituted for the real self, one's behavior is governed by several unrealistic "shoulds."

6

Erik H. Erikson

E rik Erikson was born of Danish parents in Frankfurt, Germany, on 15 June, 1902. His father abandoned the home before Erikson was born, and three years later his mother married Erikson's pediatrician, Dr. Theodore Homberger. The fact that Dr. Homberger was not Erik's real father was kept a secret throughout his childhood, but he still developed the feeling that somehow he did not belong to his parents and fantasized about being the son of "much better parents." Erikson used his stepfather's surname for many years and even wrote his first articles using the name Erik Homberger. It was only when he became a United States citizen in 1939 that he changed his last name to Erikson.

Erikson's feeling of not belonging to his family was amplified by the fact that both his mother and stepfather were Jewish, and he was, because of his Scandinavian heritage, tall, with blue eyes and blond hair. In school he was referred to as a Jew, whereas at his stepfather's temple, he was called a "goy" (the Yiddish word for gentile). Is it any wonder why the concept of "identity crisis" was later to become one of Erikson's most important theoretical concerns?

After graduating from a gymnasium, roughly equivalent to an American high school, he rebelled against his stepfather's desire for him to become a physician by studying art and roaming freely around Europe. Generally, Erikson was not a good student in school but did have artistic ability.

The year 1927 was a turning point in Erikson's life. In that year, he was invited by an old school friend, Peter Blos, to come to Vienna to work at a small school attended by the children of Freud's patients and friends. He was hired first as an artist, then as a tutor, and, finally, he was asked by Anna Freud if he would like to be trained as a child analyst. Erikson accepted the offer and received his psychoanalytic training under Anna Freud, for which she charged him seven dollars per month. Anna Freud's particular brand of psychoanalytic theory, which differed in several ways from her father's, had a profound influence on Erikson, and in 1964 he showed his appreciation by dedicating his book *Insight and Responsibility* to her.

The situation was perfectly suited to Erikson. He was asked to join a group of people who were considered at that time to be outside the medical establishment. By joining this group of "outcasts," he could maintain his identity as the "outsider." Conversely, because it was the function of the group to help disturbed people, he could at least indirectly satisfy his stepfather's desire for him to become a physician.

His graduation from the gymnasium, a Montessori diploma, and his training as a child analyst by Anna Freud are the only formal training Erikson ever had. Because Erikson earned no advanced degrees, he is a clear example of Freud's contention that one need not be trained as a physician to become a psychoanalyst.

In 1929, Erikson married Joan Serson, a Canadian woman who was also a teacher at the school at which Erikson worked. In 1933, in response to the increasing Nazi threat, the Eriksons (now with two sons) moved first to Denmark and then to Boston, Massachusetts, where he entered private practice as a child analyst.

Besides his private practice, Erikson was a research fellow under the supervision of Henry Murray in the Department of Neuropsychiatry at the Harvard Medical School. Erikson enrolled at Harvard as a Ph.D. candidate in psychology but dropped out of the program within a few months. Perhaps, because he had already been voted a full member of the Vienna Psychoanalytic Society, he considered further formal education unnecessary.

Between 1936 and 1939, Erikson held a position in the Department of Psychiatry at the Yale University Medical School, where he worked with both normal and emotionally disturbed children. It was also about this time when Erikson came in contact with the anthropologists Ruth Benedict and Margaret Mead, and in 1938 he went on a field trip to the Pine Ridge Reservation in South Dakota to observe the child-rearing practices of the Sioux Indians. Anthropological studies such as this one increased Erikson's awareness of the importance of social and cultural variables to personality development, an awareness that ultimately was to permeate his entire theory of personality.

In 1939 Erikson moved to California, where he became a research associate at the Institute of Child Welfare at the University of California. By 1942 he was a professor of psychology but lost his professorship in 1950, when he refused to sign a loyalty oath. Later, when the University of California found him "politically reliable," he was offered his job back but refused to accept it, because other professors had been dismissed for the same "crime."

In 1950, the same year he left the University of California, Erikson published his now-famous book, *Childhood and Society*, which strongly emphasized the importance of social and cultural factors to human development. This book also greatly elaborated the functions of the ego, which launched what is now called "ego psychology." We will have more to say about ego psychology later in this chapter.

Eric Erikson

Between 1951 and 1960, Erikson lived in Stockbridge, Massachusetts, where he was both a senior staff consultant at the Austin-Riggs Center (a treatment center for disturbed adolescents) and a professor in the Department of Psychiatry at the University of Pittsburgh Medical School.

In 1960, Erikson returned to the Harvard Medical School, where he was a professor of human development and taught "The Human Life Cycle," an extremely popular undergraduate course. According to Erikson, his students renamed this course "from womb to tomb." At Harvard, Erikson also led a seminar in which the lives of great or historical persons were analyzed. By now colleges and universities throughout the world invited him to lecture. In 1962 he traveled to India to conduct a seminar on the life cycle. While there he became intensely interested in Mahatma Gandhi, whose nonviolent protest against British imperialism dramatically changed the British Empire.

As we shall see in this chapter, Erikson has made several contributions to psychology. One is the application of his theory of development to the study of major historical figures. Such an endeavor has been labeled **psychohistory.** Erikson has analyzed such historical figures as Adolf Hitler, Maxim Gorky, Martin Luther, and Mahatma Gandhi. Erikson's book *Gandhi's Truth* (1969) was awarded both a Pulitzer Prize and a National Book Award in philosophy and religion.

Throughout most of his writings, Erikson insists that a strong relationship existed between his theory and Freud's, but one gets the impression that this is mostly a tribute to Freud. Although it is true that some similarities between the theories of Erikson and Freud exist, the differences between the two are more important. Erikson's theory, for example, is much more optimistic about the human capacity for positive growth. We will compare Erikson's theory to Freud's throughout this chapter, but for now we will point out one common feature of the theories. Both have transcended the bounds of psychology and have influenced a variety of other fields, such as religion, philosophy, sociology, anthropology, and history.

Although Erikson retired from Harvard in 1970, he continued to develop his theory until his death in 1982.

Anatomy and Destiny

The closest that Erikson comes to traditional Freudian theory is in the chapter "The Theory of Infantile Sexuality" in his book *Childhood and Society* (1963). In this chapter, Erikson summarizes his research on ten-, eleven-, and twelve-year-old boys and girls in California. The children were instructed by Erikson to "construct on the table an exciting scene out of an imaginary moving picture" (98). The children were to use toy figures and various-shaped blocks. Much to Erikson's surprise, in over a year and a half, about 150 children constructed about 450 scenes, and not more than about six were scenes from a movie. For example, only a few of the toy figures were given names of actors or actresses. But if the children were not following Erikson's suggestion in creating their scenes, what was guiding their activities? The answer to this question came when Erikson noted that the common themes or elements in the scenes created by boys were quite different from those created by girls.

Erikson observed, for example, that the scenes created by girls typically included an enclosure that sometimes had an elaborate entrance and contained such elements as people and animals. The scenes created by girls tended to be static and peaceful, although often their scenes were interrupted by animals or dangerous men. The scenes created by boys often had high walls around them and had many objects such as high towers or cannons protruding from them. The scenes created by boys also had relatively more people and animals outside the enclosure. The boys' scenes were dynamic and included fantasies about the collapse or downfall of their creation.

Examples of scenes created by boys and girls are shown in Figure 6–1. Erikson concluded that the scenes created by the children were outward manifestations of their genital apparatus. This tendency was so reliable that Erikson was surprised and uneasy when a departure from it occurred. For example, Erikson stated:

> One day, a boy arranged . . . a "feminine" scene, with wild animals as intruders, and I felt that uneasiness which I assume often betrays to an experimenter what his innermost expectations are. And, indeed, on departure and already at the door, the boy exclaimed, "There is something wrong here," came back, and with an air of relief arranged the animals along a tangent to the circle of furniture. Only one boy built and left such a configuration, and this twice. He was of obese and effeminate build. As thyroid treatment began to take effect, he built, in his third construction (a year and a half after the first) the highest and most slender of all towers—as was to be expected of a boy. (1963, 101)

It should be emphasized, however, that Erikson never said that biology was the *only* factor that determined how a person perceives and acts on the world. Social factors are also important. We are told by our culture how boys and girls are supposed to act and think, and these cultural dictates will obviously influence our outlook.

> Am I saying, then, that "anatomy is destiny"? Yes, it is destiny, insofar as it determines not only the range and configuration of physiological functioning and its limitations but also, to an extent, personality configurations. The basic modalities of woman's commitment and involvement naturally also reflect the ground plan of her body. . . . [But] a human being, in addition to having a body, is *somebody*, which means an indivisible personality and a defined member of a group. . . . In other words, anatomy, history, and personality are our combined destiny. (Erikson 1968a, 285)

Needless to say, Erikson's views of male-female differences have not gone uncriticized. One reaction came from Naomi Weisstein (1971), in her article, "Psychology Constructs the Female, or the Fantasy Life of the Male Psychologist (with Some Attention to the Fantasies of His Friends, the Male Biologist and the Male Anthropologist)." Weisstein argues that psychology does not know what either men or women are really like, because it deals with only the cultural stereotypes of both. She insists that what have been called biologically determined differences in behavior between the sexes are really better explained as the result of social expectations. She concludes that insofar as there are differences between the sexes, they are the result of cultural expectations and the prejudices of male social scientists.

Figure 6–1.
*A and B exemplify
scenes created by
girls, and C and D
exemplify scenes
created by boys.*

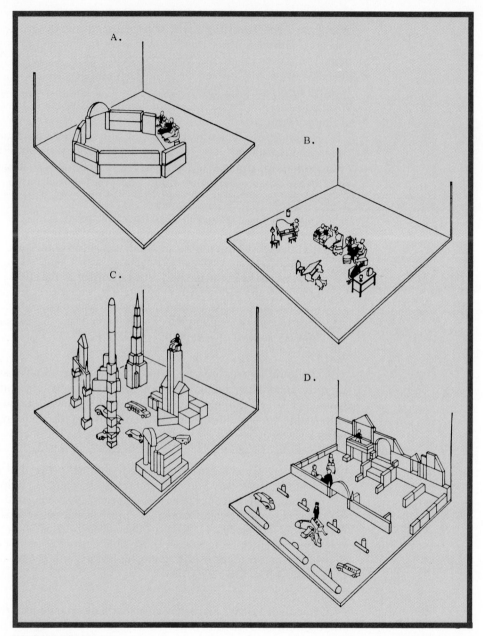

(from Erikson 1963, 100–105.)

Paula Caplan (1979) also criticizes Erikson's contention that the kind of sex organs that one possesses influences how one interacts with the world. She is especially critical of Erikson's assertion that a woman's kinesthetic experience of her own "inner space," that is, of her own uterus, determines *even partially,* her personality characteristics. It was Erikson's belief that it was the female child's experience of this "inner space" that influenced the configurations she produced during his play experiments. Caplan (1979) points out that Erikson's claim is impossible.

> The most important physiological factor to take into account is that there is no inner space. The walls of the uterus touch each other, as do the walls of the vagina. They are open only when separated by and filled with substances, as in intercourse or pregnancy. If girls' play constructions were to represent their uteri, they should look more like folded flapjacks than enclosures. Further, although the penis is external and erectable, so is the clitoris, although to a lesser degree. The movement of the ovum is as important for fertilization as that of the sperm, and although not as highly mobile as the sperm, both ovum and uterus move (the uterus contracts often in orgasm and delivery and certainly expands in pregnancy). So differences in play constructions should, if biologically based, be different in degree rather than in kind. (101–2)

Caplan repeated much of Erikson's research on play constructions only she used preschool children as her subjects. She justified using children who were younger than those used by Erikson because of Erikson's claim that gender differences in personality manifest themselves throughout the life span. Caplan (1979) summarizes her results: "No sex differences were found in the frequency of constructions of simple enclosures, enclosures only in conjunction with elaborate structures or traffic lanes, height of structures, construction of a tower, or construction of a structure, building, tower, or street—all categories in which Erikson had reported sex differences" (105). Caplan interprets her results as indicating that there are no sex-determined personality characteristics. If these characteristics existed, they would have been evident in her young subjects. Rather, she says, the personality differences between men and women that emerge later are due exclusively to differential socialization practices. Therefore, anatomy is definitely *not* destiny.

Erikson reacted to criticisms such as those above in his essay entitled, "Once More the Inner Space" (1975). Essentially he said that (1) psychoanalytic truths are often disturbing and he can understand people's being upset by them, and (2) biology is only one strong determinant of personality; culture is another.

Another important point should be made about Erikson's view of sexual differences. He never says that males are better than females or vice versa. Rather, he says that there are important differences between males and females and that male traits and female traits complement each other. In some cultures, such as ours, the male role has been glorified relative to the female role, but Erikson finds this unfortunate. He feels that both men and women are hurt by current cultural stereotypes. Erikson stated that "only a renewal of social creativity can liberate both men and women from reciprocal roles which, in fact, have exploited both" (1975a, 237).

Ego Psychology

Erikson's view of the relationship between biology and personality exemplifies a point on which he was in close agreement with Freud. In this section, we will review the part of Erikson's theory that most disagrees with Freud.

According to Freud, the job of the ego was to find realistic ways of satisfying the impulses of the id while not offending the moral demands of the superego. Freud viewed the ego as operating "in the service of the id" and as the "helpless rider of the id horse." The ego, according to this view, has no needs of its own. The id was the energizer of the entire personality, and everything a person did was ultimately reduced to its demands. As we saw in chapter 2, Freud viewed enterprises such as art, science, and religion as mere displacements or sublimations of basic idinal desires.

The first shift away from Freud's position came from his daughter Anna in her book *The Ego and the Mechanisms of Defense* (1936). Anna Freud suggested that instead of emphasizing the importance of the id, psychoanalysis should "acquire the fullest possible knowledge of all the three institutions [that is, id, ego, and superego] of which we believe the psychic personality to be constituted and to learn what are their relations to one another and to the outside world" (1936, 4–5). Erikson was obviously influenced by his teacher, Anna Freud, but he felt that she did not go far enough. Roazen stated:

> Erikson respects Anna Freud's *The Ego and the Mechanisms of Defense* for having conclusively organized the nature of the defensive ego. The problem for Erikson was that Anna Freud had described the ego's functions in terms of warding off quantities of drives, whereas Erikson wanted to go further and extend his reach beyond mere defensiveness to adaptation. (1976, 22)

Erikson gave the ego properties and needs of its own. The ego, according to Erikson, may have started out in the service of the id but, in the process of serving it, developed its own functions. For example, it was the ego's job to organize one's life and to assure continuous harmony with one's physical and social environment. This conception emphasizes the influence of the ego on healthy growth and adjustment and also as the source of the person's self-awareness and identity. This contrasts sharply with the earlier Freudian view that the ego's sole job was to minimize the id's discomfort. Because Erikson stresses the autonomy of the ego, his theory exemplifies what has come to be called **ego psychology.** Although, as we saw in chapter 4, there are those who credit Alfred Adler with the founding of ego psychology, it is an honor generally given to Erikson, because he actually emphasized the term *ego* in his theory. Adler indeed described behaviors and adjustment patterns that were independent of biologic drives (for example, striving for superiority, creative self, and social interest), but he did not stress the difference between idinal functions and ego functions.

Indeed, Erikson's entire theory can be viewed as a description of how the ego gains or loses strength as a function of developmental experiences.

Epigenetic Principle, Crises, Ritualizations, and Ritualisms

Epigenetic Principle.   Erikson sees life as consisting of eight stages, which stretch from birth to death. According to Erikson, the *sequence* of the eight stages is genetically determined and thus is unalterable. Such a genetically determined sequence of development is said to follow the **epigenetic principle,** a term that Erikson borrowed from biology. Erikson describes this principle as follows:

> Whenever we try to understand growth, it is well to remember the *epigenetic principle* which is derived from the growth of organisms *in utero.* Somewhat generalized, this principle states that anything that grows has a ground plan, and that out of this ground plan the parts arise, each part having its special ascendancy, until all parts have arisen to form a functioning whole. (1968a, 92)

Although, according to Erikson, personality unfolds across eight stages of development, all eight developmental stages are present in rudimentary form at birth. As each personality characteristic unfolds, it is incorporated into characteristics that developed during previous stages, thus creating a new configuration of personality characteristics. In other words, each stage, as it unfolds, builds on those that preceded it. Erikson (1963) said "The strength acquired at any stage is tested by the necessity to transcend it in such a way that the individual can take chances in the next stage with what was most vulnerably precious in the previous one" (263). According to the epigenetic principle, the personality characteristics that become salient during any particular stage of development exist before that stage and continues to exist after that stage. For social and biologic reasons, however, the development of a certain personality characteristic becomes the focus of one stage as opposed to other stages.

Crises.   Each stage of development is characterized by a **crisis.** The word "crisis" is used by Erikson as it is used by physicians, that is, to connote an important turning point. Thus, the crisis characterizing each stage of development has a possible positive resolution or a negative one. A positive resolution contributes to a strengthening of the ego and therefore to greater adaptation. A negative resolution weakens the ego and inhibits adaptation. Furthermore, a positive crisis resolution in one stage increases the likelihood that the crisis characterizing the next stage will be resolved positively. A negative resolution in one stage lowers the probability that the next crisis will be resolved effectively. Erikson does not believe that a solution to a crisis is either completely positive or completely negative. Rather, he says the resolution of a crisis has both positive and negative elements. It is when the *ratio* of positive to negative is higher in favor of the positive that the crisis is said to be resolved positively. We will say more about this in our discussion of the first stage of development, to which we will turn shortly.

Although biology determines when the stages will occur, because the maturational process determines when experiences become possible, it is the *social* environment that determines whether or not the crisis associated with any given stage is resolved positively. For this reason, the stages proposed by Erikson are called **psychosocial stages of development,** to contrast them with Freud's *psychosexual* stages.

Ritualizations and Ritualisms.   For Erikson, it is essential to realize that personality development occurs within a cultural setting. Rather than viewing humans as being at war with their culture, as Freud did, Erikson emphasizes the compatibility between individuals and their culture. In fact, to a large extent it is the job of culture to provide satisfactory ways of satisfying both biologic and psychological human needs. According to Erikson, a person's internal and external experiences must fit together, at least to some degree, if an individual is to develop and function normally in a particular culture. Erikson (1963) says "Each successive stage and crisis has a special relation to one of the basic elements of society, and this for the simple reason that the human life cycle and man's institutions have evolved together" (250). Elsewhere Erikson (1975b) says that there must be a:

> Mutual fit of individual and environment—that is, of the individual's capacity to relate to an ever expanding life space of people and institutions on the one hand, and, on the other, the readiness of these people and institutions to make him part of an ongoing cultural concern. (102)

The harmonious interplay between unfolding personality requirements and existing social and cultural conditions is made possible by **ritualizations.** According to Erikson (1977), ritualizations are recurring patterns of behavior that reflect those beliefs, values, customs, and behaviors that are sanctioned by a particular society or culture. Although it is ritualizations that make life meaningful within a particular society or culture, most individuals engage in them without knowing that they are doing so.

> [Each child must] be coaxed and induced to become "speciated" during a prolonged childhood by some form of family: he must be *familiarized by ritualization* with a particular version of human existence. He thus develops a distinct sense of corporate identity. . . . We must realize from the outset that ritualization is an aspect of everyday life which is more clearly seen in a different culture or class or even family than in our own, where, in fact, ritualization is more often than not experienced simply as the only proper way to do things; and the question is only why does not everybody do it our way. (79–80)

Ritualizations, then, are culturally approved patterns of everyday behavior that allow a person to become an acceptable member of the culture. They include characteristic ways in which we relate to each other such as shaking hands, kissing, and hugging. They provide guides that set the boundaries between acceptable and unacceptable behavior. For example, you may be permitted to make bodily contact with a stranger at a dance, but such behavior may not be tolerated under other circumstances. Likewise, it may be permissible for a woman to wear a bikini on a beach, whereas such attire may cause a stir at work or at school. Ritualizations guide almost every aspect of social behavior and are the mechanisms by which persons of a certain culture become "socialized."

Erikson referred to a culture as "a particular version of human existence," suggesting that many equally valid versions exist. Indeed, Erikson believed that except for the requirement that ritualizations satisfy basic human needs, they are arbitrary. For example, many cultural variations exist for courting, mating, and child-rearing practices, but these differences are less important than the fact that they all encourage reproduction and the perpetuation of the culture in which they occur. For some persons, the arbitrary nature of ritualizations is lost, and their functional value is overlooked. For these persons, ritualizations take on a significance far beyond what is necessary. Erikson referred to such exaggerated ritualizations as **ritualisms.** Ritualisms are inappropriate or false ritualizations, and they are the causes of much social and psychological pathology. For example, a ritualization within a culture might encourage addressing certain accomplished persons with titles and thus encourage a sense of respect for their status. To idolize or worship such persons, however, would be an inappropriate exaggeration of that ritualization and would thus be a ritualism. A ritualism then is a ritualization that has become mechanical and stereotyped. Such empty ceremonies lack the power to bond people of a culture together, thus subverting the original purpose of the ritualization.

We will discuss the ritualizations and the ritualisms associated with each stage of development in the next section.

Eight Stages of Personality Development

The most famous aspects of Erikson's work are his descriptions of the eight developmental stages through which he felt all humans pass and what happens to the ego during each of these stages. The first five stages of personality development proposed by Erikson closely parallel Freud's proposed psychosexual stages of development in the time at which they are supposed to occur. As to what is supposed to occur during these stages, however, little agreement exists between Erikson and Freud. The last three stages are Erikson's own and represent one of his major contributions to psychology. It should be noted that the epigenetic principle determines the exact order in which the stages must occur; however, when they occur cannot be specified exactly. Therefore, the ages associated with each of the following stages should be viewed only as approximations. We will label each stage according to the developmental level at which it occurs and according to the crisis it features.

1. Infancy: Basic Trust versus Basic Mistrust.   This stage lasts from birth through the first year and corresponds closely to Freud's oral stage of psychosexual development. This is the time when children are most helpless and thus most dependent on adults. If those caring for infants satisfy their needs in a loving and consistent way, they will develop a feeling of **basic trust.** If, however, their parents are rejecting and satisfy their needs in an inconsistent manner, they will develop a feeling of mistrust.

If care is loving and consistent, infants learn that they need not worry about a loving, reliable parent and therefore are not overly disturbed when that parent leaves their sight.

> The infant's first social achievement, then, is his willingness to let the mother out of sight without undue anxiety or rage, because she has become an inner certainty as well as an outer predictability. Such consistency, continuity, and sameness of experience provide a rudimentary sense of ego identity which depends, I think, on the cognition that there is an inner population of remembered and anticipated sensations and images which are firmly correlated with the outer population of familiar and predictable things and people. (Erikson 1963, 247)

The basic trust versus **basic mistrust** crisis is resolved when the child develops more trust than mistrust. Remember, it is the ratio of the two solutions that is important. A child who trusted everyone and everything would be in trouble. A certain amount of mistrust is healthy and conducive to survival. It is the child with a predominance of trust, however, who has the courage to take risks and who is not overwhelmed by disappointments and setbacks.

Erikson says that when the crisis characterizing a stage is positively resolved, a **virtue** emerges in one's personality. A virtue can be considered something that adds strength to one's ego. In this stage, when the child has more basic trust than basic mistrust, the virtue of **hope** emerges. Erikson defines hope as "the enduring belief in the attainability of fervent wishes, in spite of the dark urges and rages which mark the beginning of existence" (1964, 118).

We can say that trusting children dare to hope, a process that is future oriented, whereas children lacking enough trust cannot hope, because they must worry constantly about whether their needs will be satisfied and therefore are tied to the present.

Numinous versus Idolism.   The primary ritualization during this stage is the **numinous.** The numinous involves the various ways that mothers attend to their infants' needs in a particular culture. That is, the ways that she "recognizes" the infant: Her ways of touching, smiling, naming, feeding, and looking. Although personal, these mother-infant interactions also reflect culturally sanctioned child-rearing practices. As a result of these mother-infant interactions the child develops positive feelings toward his or her mother, and these feelings cause the infant to be socially responsive. Thus, the mother's warm, predictable caring for the child creates in the child a desire to seek interactions with persons other than the mother.

If the infant's normal reverence and respect for the mother become exaggerated, the ritualism of **idolism** results. Idolism occurs when normal respect and deep appreciation for a person becomes excessive admiration and idealization. Idolism steers the developing child in the direction of blind hero worship.

2. Early Childhood: Autonomy versus Shame and Doubt.   This stage occurs from about the end of the first year to about the end of the third year and corresponds to Freud's anal stage of psychosexual development.

During this stage, children rapidly develop a wide variety of skills. They learn to walk, climb, push, pull, and talk. More generally, they learn how to hold on and to let go. Not only does this apply to physical objects but to feces and urine as well. In other words, children now can "willfully" decide to do something or not to do it. Thus, children now are engaged in a battle of wills with their parents.

The parents must perform the delicate task of controlling the child's behavior in socially acceptable directions, without injuring the child's sense of self-control or autonomy. In other words, the parents must be reasonably tolerant but still be firm enough to assure behavior that is socially approved. If the parents are overly protective or unjust in their use of punishment, the child will be doubtful and experience shame. "From a sense of self-control without loss of self-esteem comes a lasting sense of good will and pride; from a sense of loss of self-control and of foreign overcontrol comes a lasting propensity for doubt and shame" (Erikson 1963, 254).

About shame Erikson said: "Shame supposes that one is completely exposed and conscious of being looked at: in one word, self-conscious. One is visible and not ready to be visible" (1963, 252).

If the child develops more autonomy than **shame and doubt** during this stage, the virtue of **will** emerges. Erikson defined will as "the unbroken determination to exercise free choice as well as self-restraint, in spite of the unavoidable experience of shame and doubt in infancy'' (1964, 119).

Notice that the virtues emerging as the result of positive crises resolutions are *ego* functions. For example, the virtues of hope and will have some influence on the quality of one's life but little on survival. Persons without much hope or will, will survive; that is, they will be able to satisfy their biologic (idinal) needs, but they probably would not be flexible, optimistic, or generally as happy as those with more hope and will.

Judiciousness versus Legalism.   Autonomy is best served when one's will is freely exercised. Because each culture restricts some behaviors and allows others, however, the child must learn to discriminate between right and wrong, between what is acceptable and what is unacceptable. Erikson called **judiciousness** the ritualization by which the child learns what is culturally sanctioned and what is not. Through judiciousness the child learns the laws, rules, honored practices, and regulations that characterize its culture. Before this stage it was the responsibility of the parents to guide the child's behavior properly. Now, however, as the rules and regulations of a culture are internalized, the child begins to judge his or her own behavior as well as that of others. Children must learn to judge themselves as others judge them. As the superego develops, it is used by the child in making these moral evaluations.

The perversion of the ritualization of judiciousness is the ritualism of **legalism,** which Erikson defines as, ''The victory of the letter over the spirit of the word and the law. It is expressed in the vain display of righteousness or empty contrition, or in a moralistic insistence on exposing and isolating the culprit whether or not this will be good for him or anybody else'' (1977, 97). For the legalistic child or adult, the punishment and humiliation of transgressors is more important than the intent of the law that was transgressed.

3. Preschool Age: Initiative versus Guilt.   This stage occurs from about the fourth year to about the fifth year and corresponds to Freud's phallic stage of psychosexual development.

During this stage the child is capable of still more detailed motor activity, more refined use of language, and a more vivid use of imagination. These skills allow the child to *initiate* ideas, actions, and fantasies, and to *plan* future events. According to Erikson, the child during this stage ''is apt to develop an untiring curiosity about differences in sizes in general, and sexual differences in particular . . . his learning is now eminently intrusive and vigorous: it leads away from his own limitations and into future possibilities'' (1959, 76).

In the preceding stages children learned that they were people. Now they begin to explore what kind of person they can become. During this stage, limits are tested to find out what is permissible and what is not. If parents encourage children's self-initiated behaviors and fantasies, the children will leave this stage with a healthy sense of **initiative.** If, however, parents ridicule the children's self-initiated behavior and imagination, they will leave this stage lacking self-sufficiency. Instead of taking the initiative, they will tend to feel guilty when pondering such behavior and therefore will tend to live within the narrow limits that others set for them.

If children develop more initiative during this stage than **guilt,** the virtue of

purpose will emerge. Erikson defined purpose as "the courage to envisage and pursue valued goals uninhibited by the defeat of infantile fantasies, by guilt and by the foiling fear of punishment" (1964, 122). Children who have met the crisis of the first three stages possess the positive virtues of hope, will, and purpose.

Authenticity versus Impersonation.   In addition to playing with toys, children at this stage typically engage in a great deal of playacting, imitating, wearing costumes, and even pretending to be various kinds of animals. Such play provides them with a kind of intermediate reality where they can explore the relationship between their inner and outer worlds. Both positive and negative roles are played to reconfirm the limits on behavior. Through the process of "trying on" various roles and reconfirming what is possible and what is not, children discover the "mix" of roles that is just right for him or her. Erikson refers to those activities as the ritualization of **authenticity.**

Exaggeration of the ritualization of authenticity results in the ritualism of **impersonation,** which occurs when one confuses one's true self with one or more of the roles that one plays. Rather than a role becoming just a part of the true self or furnishing information about it, the child becomes the role he or she plays. What is lost in such a case is the rich blending of personality characteristics that have developed during previous stages, into a unique, authentic person.

4. School Age: Industry versus Inferiority.   This stage lasts from about the sixth year to about the eleventh year and corresponds to Freud's latency stage of psychosexual development. Most children attend school throughout this stage.

It is during this stage that children learn the skills necessary for economic survival, the technological skills that will allow them to become productive members of their culture.

> The inner stage seems all set for "entrance into life," except that life must first be school life, whether school is field or jungle or classroom. The child must forget past hopes and wishes, while his exuberant imagination is tamed and harnessed to the laws of impersonal things—even the three R's. For before the child, psychologically already a rudimentary parent, can become a biological parent, he must begin to be a worker and potential provider. (Erikson 1963, 258–59)

School is the place where children are trained for future employment in and adjustment to their culture. Because in most cultures, including our own, surviving requires the ability to work cooperatively with others, social skills are among the important lessons taught by the schools.

The most important lesson that children learn during this stage is "the pleasure of work completion by steady attention and persevering diligence" (Erikson 1963, 259). From this lesson comes a sense of **industry,** which prepares children to look confidently for productive places in society among other people.

If children do not develop a sense of industry, they will develop a sense of **inferiority,** which causes them to lose confidence in their ability to become contributing members of society. Such children are more likely to develop a "negative identity," a concept that will be explained in our discussion of the next stage.

Another danger associated with this stage is that children will later overvalue their places in the work place. For such people, work is equated with life, and they thus are blinded to the many other important aspects of human existence. "If he accepts work as his only obligation, and 'what works' as his only criterion of worthwhileness, he may become the conformist and thoughtless slave of his technology and of those who are in a position to exploit it" (Erikson 1963, 261). According to Erikson, the skills necessary for future employment must be encouraged during this stage but not at the expense of several other important human attributes.

If children's sense of industry is greater than their sense of inferiority, they will leave this stage with the virtue of **competence.** "Competence . . . is the free exercise of dexterity and intelligence in the completion of tasks, unimpaired by infantile inferiority" (Erikson 1964, 124). Like the other virtues discussed earlier, competence comes from loving attention and encouragement. A sense of inferiority comes from ridicule or lack of concern by those persons most important to the children.

Formality versus Formalism.   During this stage children learn that to be a productive member of their community they must possess real (not imagined) skills and knowledge. Erikson calls the ritualization corresponding to this stage **formality** and it involves learning the appropriate ways of doing tasks. Whatever the child does, whether it be at school, at home, at work, or on the athletic field, he or she must learn to do it "properly."

The exaggeration of the ritualization of formality results in the ritualism of **formalism.** Formalism is demonstrated when an overconcern with technique, and a blindness to the purpose and meaning of a task occur. The student whose only concern is with high grades exemplifies formalism. Erikson (1977) says of formalism:

> Whatever the name, it must express the fact that human striving for method and logic can also lead to that self-enslavement which makes of each man what Marx called a "craft-idiot," that is, one who for the sake of a proficiency will forget and deny the human context within which it has a significant and maybe dangerous function. (106)

5. Adolescence: Identity versus Role Confusion.   This stage occurs between about twelve years and twenty years of age and corresponds roughly to Freud's genital stage of psychosexual development. Erikson is known best for his description of this psychosocial stage, for it contains his now-famous concept of **identity crisis.**

Erikson thought that this stage represented the transition period between childhood and adulthood. In the preceding stages, children were learning what they were and what it was possible for them to do, that is, the various roles that were available to them. During this stage children must ponder all this accumulated information about themselves and their society and ultimately commit themselves to some strategy for life. When they have done this, they have gained an identity and have become adults. Gaining a personal **identity** marks the satisfactory end of this stage of development. The stage itself, however, is seen as a time of searching for an identity but not of having one. Erikson called this period a **psychosocial moratorium,** by which he meant an interval between youth and adulthood. Erikson (1964) vividly describes what it is like to be in this period between childhood and adulthood.

> Like a trapeze artist, the young person in the middle of vigorous motion must let go of his safe hold on childhood and reach out for a firm grasp on adulthood,

depending for a breathless interval on a relatedness between the past and the future, and on the reliability of those he must let go of, and those who will "receive" him. (90)

Erikson has used the term identity (sometimes called ego identity) in a variety of ways. For example, it is "a feeling of being at home in one's body, a sense of 'knowing where one is going,' and an inner assuredness of anticipated recognition from those who count" (Erikson 1968a, 165). Erikson made no apology for using the term identity in a variety of ways. Because it is a complex concept, he thought it must be approached from many angles.

If young adults do not leave this stage with an identity, they leave it with **role confusion** or perhaps with a **negative identity.** Role confusion is characterized by the inability to choose a role in life, thus prolonging the psychological moratorium indefinitely, or to make superficial commitments that are soon abandoned. Negative identities are all those roles that children are warned not to assume. Erikson defined negative identity as "an identity perversely based on all those identifications and roles which, at critical stages of development, had been presented to the individual as most undesirable or dangerous, and yet also as most real" (1959, 131). Erikson gave an example:

> A mother who is filled with unconscious ambivalence toward a brother who disintegrated into alcoholism may again and again respond selectively only to those traits in her son which seem to point to a repetition of her brother's fate, in which case this "negative" identity may take on more reality for the son than all his natural attempts at being good: he may work hard on becoming a drunkard. (1959, 131)

For Erikson, the concepts of role confusion and negative identity explain much of the unrest and hostility expressed by adolescents in this country. For example, the adolescent may lash out at those identities that do not fit him.

> The loss of a sense of identity often is expressed in a scornful and snobbish hostility toward the roles offered as proper and desirable in one's family or immediate community. Any aspect of the required role, or all parts, be it masculinity or femininity, nationality or class membership, can become the main focus of the young person's acid disdain. (Erikson 1959, 129)

Why should an adolescent choose a negative identity if a positive one were not available? Erikson said because he would "rather be nobody or somebody bad, or indeed, dead—and this totally, and by free choice—than be not-quite somebody" (1959, 132).

If young adults emerge from this stage with a positive identity rather than with role confusion or a negative identity, they also will emerge with the virtue of **fidelity.** Erikson defines fidelity as "the ability to sustain loyalties freely pledged in spite of the inevitable contradictions of value systems" (1964, 125).

The stages preceding this provided the child with the qualities from which an identity could be derived. In this stage, the person has to assimilate this information. The development of an identity marks the end of childhood and the beginning of adulthood. From this point on, life is a matter of acting out one's identity. Now that the person "knows who he or she is," the task of life becomes one of carrying "that person" optimally through the remaining stages of life.

Ideology versus Totalism.   The ritualization corresponding to this stage is **ideology.** The adolescent searches for an ideology that synthesizes all of the ego developments from the previous stages. The ideology furnishes a "game plan" for life; it gives life meaning. An identity cannot emerge until all previous ego functions are integrated and commitment to an ideology allows such integration. A chosen ideology could be religious, political, or philosophical. The only stipulation is that acting in accordance with it furthers both individual and cultural goals.

The exaggeration of the ritualization of ideology results in the ritualism of **totalism.** Totalism involves the unquestioning commitment to overly simplistic ideologies. For example, adolescents may accept the values mouthed by various "heroes" in religious cults, musical groups, drug cultures, athletics, delinquent gangs, motion pictures, or political groups. According to Erikson, when adolescents overidentify with such groups or individuals, it is because they seem to provide answers to life's most difficult questions. The simplistic thinking involved in totalism, then, can make life easier for the troubled adolescent and, if it is temporary, it may not be harmful. It is when totalism lasts beyond the time when an identity should be achieved that it becomes a problem.

Erikson (1968b) gives examples of how confused adolescents may attempt to simplify their lives.

> To keep themselves together, they temporarily overidentify . . . with the heroes of cliques and crowds. On the other hand, they become remarkably clannish, intolerant, and cruel in their exclusion of others who are "different," in skin color, cultural background . . . and often in entirely petty aspects of dress and gesture arbitrarily selected as the sign of an in-grouper or out-grouper. It is important to understand . . . such intolerance as the necessary defense against a sense of identity diffusion, which is unavoidable at a time of life when the body changes its proportion radically . . . and when life lies before one with a variety of conflicting possibilities and choices. Adolescents temporarily help one another through such discomfort by forming cliques and by stereotyping themselves, their ideals, and their enemies. . . . It is difficult to be tolerant if deep down you are not quite sure that you are a man (or a woman), that you will ever grow together again and be attractive, that you will be able to master your drives, that you really know who you are, that you know what you want to be . . . and that you will know how to make the right decision without, once [and] for all committing yourself to the wrong friend, sexual partner, leaders, or career. (200)

6. Young Adulthood: Intimacy versus Isolation.   This stage lasts from about twenty years to about twenty-four years of age. For this and the remaining psychosocial stages, there is no corresponding Freudian psychosexual stage of development.

Freud once defined a healthy person as one who loves and works; Erikson agrees with this definition. Only the person who has a secure identity, however, can risk entering into a love relationship with another. The young adult with a strong identity eagerly seeks intimate relationships with others.

> The young adult, emerging from the search for and the insistence on identity, is eager and willing to fuse his identity with that of others. He is ready for intimacy,

that is, the capacity to commit himself to concrete affiliations and partnerships and to develop the ethical strength to abide by such commitments, even though they may call for significant sacrifices and compromises. (Erikson 1963, 263)

People who do not develop a capacity for productive work and **intimacy** withdraw into themselves, avoid close contacts, and thus develop a feeling of **isolation.**

Erikson lists what an intimate relationship should be for it to be beneficial to both the individual and society:

1. Mutuality of orgasm
2. With a loved partner
3. Of the other sex
4. With whom one is able and willing to share a mutual trust
5. And with whom one is able and willing to regulate the cycles of
   a. work
   b. procreation
   c. recreation
6. So as to secure to the offspring, too, all the stages of a satisfactory development (1963, 266).

If individuals develop a greater capacity for intimacy than for isolation during this stage, they also will emerge with the virtue of **love.** Erikson defines love as "the mutuality of devotion forever subduing the antagonisms inherent in divided function" (1964, 129).

Affiliation versus Elitism.   Once an identity has been achieved and an ideology has been chosen that allows for the productive manifestation of that identity, a person can affiliate productively with fellow humans in work, friendship, and love. The ritualization characterizing this stage is **affiliation,** which is the various ways that a culture sanctions caring, productive relationships between adults. The marriage ceremony and the subsequent honeymoon are two such sanctioning rituals. The wedding ceremony may involve the exchange of rings and a pledge of fidelity. We see in the wedding ceremony elements of the ritualizations from previous stages. For example, the ceremony casts a numinous (that is, a feeling of reverence) spell; it has a judicious element in that certain rights are bestowed; the ceremony and subsequent marital relationship may reflect earlier experimentation with role playing; formality is reflected in the fact that the ceremony includes elements that must be performed according to accepted practice; and the mutual pledges taken by the man and woman affirm their identities as husband and wife. Affiliation further prepares individuals to live harmoniously with fellow humans within a culture.

The exaggeration of the ritualization of affiliation results in the ritualism of **elitism.** Those individuals who experience a sense of isolation rather than intimacy, tend to surround themselves with small groups of like-minded individuals rather than forming deeply emotional relationships with healthy individuals. Their lives tend to be characterized by snobbery, status symbols, and membership in exclusive clubs; because such relationships are not truly intimate, they continue the person's sense of isolation within his or her culture.

7. Adulthood: Generativity versus Stagnation.   This stage occurs from about twenty-five to about sixty-four years of age and is called middle adulthood.

If one has been fortunate enough to develop a positive identity and to live a productive, happy life, one attempts to pass on the circumstances that caused these things to the next generation. This can be done either by interacting with children directly (they need not be one's own), or by producing or creating things that will enhance the lives of those in the next generation.

> Generativity, then, is primarily the concern in establishing and guiding the next generation, although there are individuals who, through misfortune or because of special and genuine gifts in other directions, do not apply this drive to their own offspring. And indeed, the concept generativity is meant to include such more popular synonyms as *productivity* and *creativity*, which, however, cannot replace it. (Erikson 1963, 267)

The person who does not develop a sense of **generativity** is characterized by "stagnation and interpersonal impoverishment" (Erikson 1963, 267).

If the ratio of generativity to **stagnation** is in favor of the former, one leaves this stage with the virtue of **care,** which Erikson defines as "the widening concern for what has been generated by love, necessity, or accident; it overcomes the ambivalence adhering to irreversible obligation" (1964, 131).

Generationalism versus Authoritism.   The ritualization characterizing this stage is **generationalism,** which involves the many ways in which older adults transmit cultural values to the next generation. Parents, teachers, physicians, and spiritual leaders are especially influential in conveying cultural values to children. All healthy adults, however, are concerned with providing children with the same kinds of experiences that they were fortunate enough to have. That is, with experiences that both facilitate personality growth and perpetuate cultural values.

The exaggeration of the ritualization of generationalism results in the ritualism of **authoritism.** Authoritism occurs when authority figures in a culture use their power not for the care and instruction of the young, but for their own selfish purposes.

8. Old Age: Ego Integrity versus Despair.   This stage occurs from about the age of sixty-five to death and is called late adulthood. Erikson defines **ego integrity** as follows.

> Only in him who in some way has taken care of things and people and who has adapted himself to the triumphs and disappointments adherent to being, the originator of others or the generator of products and ideas—only in him may gradually ripen the fruit of these seven stages—I know no better word for it than ego integrity. (1963, 268)

According to Erikson, it is only the person who can look back on a rich, constructive, happy life who does not fear death. Such a person has a feeling of completion and fulfillment. The person who looks back on life with frustration experiences **despair.** As strange as it may seem, the person experiencing despair is not as ready for death as the person with a sense of fulfillment, because the former has not yet achieved any major goals in life.

Not only are the eight stages progressively related to each other, but the eighth stage is directly related to the first. In other words, the eight stages are interrelated in a circular fashion. For example, the adult's attitude toward death will directly influence the young child's sense of trust. Erikson said "it seems possible to further paraphrase the relation of adult integrity and infantile trust by saying that healthy children will not fear life if their elders have integrity enough not to fear death" (1963, 269). If the person has more ego integrity than despair, his or her life will be characterized by the virtue of **wisdom,** which Erikson defines as "detached concern with life itself, in face of death itself" (1964, 133).

Integralism versus Sapientism.   If all has gone well in one's life, one realizes how instrumental he or she has been in perpetuating culture. That is, the person has a sense of immortality, knowing that the culture that he or she helped sustain will survive his or her own death. The ritualization of **integralism** involves the final unification of previous ritualizations. This last integration of the ritualizations puts life, and therefore death, into perspective.

> We can see now what rituals must accomplish: by combining and renewing the ritualizations of childhood and affirming generative sanction, they help to consolidate adult life once its commitments and investments have led to the creation of new persons and to the production of new things and ideas. And, of course, by tying life cycle and institutions into a meaningful whole, they create a sense of immortality not only for the leaders and the elite but also for every participant. And there can be little doubt that the ritualizations of everyday life permits, and even demands, that adults forget death as the inscrutable background of all life, and give priority to the absolute reality of world views shared with others of the same geography, history, and technology. By means of ritual, in fact, death becomes the meaningful boundary of such reality. (Erikson 1977, 112–13)

The exaggeration of the ritualization of integralism results in the ritualism of **sapientism,** which Erikson defines as, "The unwise pretense of being wise" (1977, 112). The older person experiencing despair instead of ego integrity may play the role of a person having all the answers, of being absolutely right; however, he or she is unable to place his or her life in the context of continuous cultural evolution. Such a life is seen as having little meaning.

The eight stages of development and their associated crises, virtues, ritualizations, and ritualisms are summarized in Table 6–1.

Goal of Psychotherapy

Erikson stresses that his psychotherapeutic practices differ from those of traditional psychoanalysis because modern times have created different kinds of disorders. For example, Erikson explained that "the patient of today suffers most under the prob-

Table 6–1
*The Eight Stages of
Development and
Their Associated
Crises, Virtues,
Ritualizations, and
Ritualisms*

STAGE	APPROXI-MATE AGE (YEARS)	CRISIS	VIRTUE	RITUAL-IZATION	RITUAL-ISM
Infancy	Birth–1	Basic trust versus basic mistrust	Hope	Numinous	Idolism
Early child-hood	1–3	Autonomy versus shame and doubt	Will	Judicious-ness	Legalism
Preschool age	4–5	Initiative versus guilt	Purpose	Authentic-ity	Imperson-ation
School age	6–11	Industry versus inferi-ority	Compe-tence	Formality	Formal-ism
Adolescence	12–20	Identity versus role confusion	Fidelity	Ideology	Totalism
Young adult-hood	20–24	Intimacy versus isola-tion	Love	Affiliation	Elitism
Adulthood	25–64	Generativity versus stagnation	Care	Genera-tionalism	Authorit-ism
Old age	65–Death	Ego integrity versus despair	Wisdom	Integral-ism	Sapient-ism

lem of what he should believe in and who he should—or, indeed, might—be or become; while the patient of early psychoanalysis suffered most under inhibitions which prevented him from being what and who he thought he knew he was" (1963, 279).

For Erikson, the main focus in the therapeutic process is the patient's ego, which must be strengthened to the point at which it can cope with life's problems. "Rehabilitation work can be made more effective and economical if the clinical investigation focuses on the patient's shattered life plan and if advice tends to strengthen the resynthesis of the elements on which the patient's ego identity was based" (1959, 43).

Erikson believed that the traditional technique of releasing the contents of the unconscious mind could do more harm than good. Erikson said that the psychoanalytic method "may make some people sicker than they ever were . . . especially if, in our zealous pursuit of our task of 'making conscious' in the psychotherapeutic situation, we push someone who is leaning out a little too far over the precipice of the unconscious" (1968a, 164).

Erikson had his patients sit across from him in an easy chair rather than lie down on a couch because the former creates a more equitable situation for the patient than the latter did.

Briefly stated, the healthy person is one whose ego is characterized by the eight virtues resulting from the positive solution of each crisis in the eight stages of development. The purpose of psychotherapy is to encourage the growth of whatever virtues are missing, even if it means going back and helping the person to develop a sense of basic trust. For Erikson, the outcome of every crisis resolution is *reversible*. For example, the person leaving the first stage of development without basic trust may later gain it, and the person having it may lose it.

Comparison of Erikson and Freud

The major areas in which Erikson and Freud differ are listed next.

Development

Freud concentrated his studies on the psychosexual stages of development coming before the age of six, because he thought that most of what is important to personality development occurs by then. Erikson studied development as it occurred throughout life. Although Jung, too, believed that important developments occurred throughout one's life, Erikson's description of the development process was much more detailed than Jung's.

Ego Psychology

Erikson shifted attention away from the id and toward the ego. Rather than seeing the individual as warring with society, Erikson saw society as a potential source of strength.

As we have seen, Erikson believed that culture must provide ritualizations that help persons positively resolve the crises characterizing the various stages of development. The individual serves culture and culture serves the individual.

Unconscious Mind

Although Erikson's theory emphasizes the conscious ego, he does not neglect unconscious mechanisms completely. In fact, although the ego gains strength from certain social experiences, the experiences themselves are largely unconscious.

Dream Analysis

Although Erikson minimized the use of dream analysis in his practice, he did agree with Freud's contention that dreams provide information about the unconscious and that dream work creates dream symbols with more than one meaning. Furthermore, Erikson believed that free association was an effective way of studying dreams. Most important to Erikson, however, was the ego's influence on dreams. Healthy egos remain powerful even during sleep and they make compromises with idinal impulses that produce dreams of success and achievement so that the dreamers can awake with a sense of competence and wholeness. Erikson also believed that dreams often suggest solutions to the dreamer's problems. In fact, during therapy a patient may dream dreams for the sole purpose of their being analyzed by the dreamer's analyst, "Once we set out to study our dreams . . . we may well dream them in order to study them" (Erikson 1977, 134). Furthermore, the patient may oblige the therapist by having just the kind of dream that the therapist is looking for:

Patients . . . know that they will or should report their dreams, and this in the context of a therapeutic style: wherefore Jungian or Freudian patients, for example, seem to differ radically in their manifest dream imagery. Their dreams, in fact, can be seen to reflect the vision of the respective "schools"—a therapeutic community, then, maybe seasoned with a bit of obliging "politic"? (Erikson 1977, 134)

Thus, although Erikson agreed with Freud that dreams may provide information about unconscious, idinal desires, he chose to concentrate on the aspects of dreams that were constructive and teleological and therefore useful and refreshing to the dreamer. If dream analysis was used at all by Erikson, it was used to determine the strength of the dreamer's ego, rather than as a way of discovering repressed, traumatic experiences.

Psychotherapy

We have seen that Erikson considered people healthy if they successfully traversed the eight stages of life, acquiring the virtues of hope, will, purpose, competence, fidelity, love, care, and wisdom. If people do not acquire these virtues, their egos will be weaker than they otherwise would be, and it is the job of the therapist to help provide the circumstances under which the virtues can develop. This is in marked contrast to Freud's belief that therapy facilitates the understanding of unconscious mechanisms, using techniques such as dream analysis and free association.

Religion

Freud took a dim view of religion, saying that it was merely a collective neurosis based on infantile fears and desires. Erikson totally disagreed. For him, religion was something that many people truly need. For centuries humans have used religion to make the events of their lives more understandable and therefore less threatening. Without it, according to Erikson, the lives of millions of persons would be filled with uncertainty. In this respect, Erikson agrees with Jung and Adler.

According to Erikson, a key function of religion is to provide a "Shared world image. For only a reasonably coherent world provides the faith which is transmitted by the mothers to the infants in a way conducive to the vital strength of *hope*" (Erikson 1968a, 106). In other words, for adults to instill hope in their children they must have faith in their world. Erikson did not believe, however, that religion was the only thing that could provide a world image conducive to trust, hope, and faith. Many people, he said, derive faith from such secular areas as science and social action (1963, 251).

We see that although Erikson calls himself a Freudian, his theory has little in common with Freud's. In addition, his conception of human nature is in marked contrast to Freud's. Perhaps, as we have already suggested, Erikson's insistence that his theory is closer to Freud's than it really is, reflects Erikson's deep appreciation that the Freudians took him into their camp, thus solving his own severe identity crisis.

Evaluation

Empirical Research

Like so many personality theories, Erikson's theory cannot be evaluated on only the basis of laboratory investigations, at least not yet. Erikson did not create his theory with the researcher in mind. He attempted to classify conceptually several items related to personality development, and one either believes that they are clarified or they are not; either his theory is a useful guide to understanding personality or it is not. "The proof lies in the way in which the communication between therapist and patient 'keeps moving,' leading to new and surprising insights and to the patient's greater assumption of responsibility for himself" (Erikson 1964, p. 75). The point is that Erikson felt that there are ways other than laboratory investigations to evaluate a personality theory. Despite Erikson's feelings about the need to verify his theory scientifically, others have taken it on themselves to do just that. For example, Ciaccio (1971) asked 120 male white children to make up stories about five pictures. The boys were equally divided into three groups consisting of five-, eight-, and eleven-year-old children. With the help of several judges, the stories the children told were categorized sentence by sentence according to which stage of development it best corresponded. The percentages of each child's sentences that expressed concern with the first five of Erikson's stages were recorded. The data tended to support Erikson's theory. The five-year-old children showed the greatest number of themes corresponding to stage 2 (46 percent); next was stage 3 (42 percent). The eight-year-old children showed the greatest number of themes corresponding to stage 3 (56 percent), with stage 2 second (20 percent). The eleven-year-old children showed the greatest number of themes corresponding to stage 4 (44 percent), with stage 3 second (26 percent).

By far most of the research generated by Erikson's theory has involved the concept of identity. Several researchers have devised methods of quantifying the concept of identity so that it can be investigated experimentally (see, for example, Marcia 1966; Bourne 1978; Rosenthal, Gurney, and Moore 1981). Research using one or more of these objective measures of identity has found that identity achievers choose more difficult academic majors (for example, chemistry, engineering, biology, mathematics) than those chosen by nonachievers (for example, anthropology, education, and physical education) (Marcia and Friedman 1970); identity achievers have higher grades than nonachievers (Cross and Allen 1970); identity achievers show greater tolerance for outgroups and higher levels of logical and moral reasoning than nonachievers (Cote and Levine 1983; Rowe and Marcia 1980; Waterman 1982); many students achieve both occupational and ideological identities sometime between their freshman and senior years, indicating that adolescence is a time of profound psychosocial growth, just as Erikson said that it was (Waterman, Geary, and Waterman 1974; Adams and Fitch 1982); attainment of identity is far more likely if a sense of trust, autonomy, initiative, and industry had been attained in the earlier stages of development (Waterman, Buebel, and Waterman 1970); the development of an identity greatly increases the probability of achieving an intimate relationship during middle age (Kahn, Zimmerman, Csikszentmihalyi, and Getzels

1985; Schiedel and Marcia 1985; Tesch and Whitbourne 1982); and persons experiencing role confusion are much more affected by peer pressure than are identity achievers (Adams, Ryan, Hoffman, Dobson, and Nielsen 1985).

Criticisms

Difficult to Test Empirically. We have seen that Erikson had little interest in empirically testing his own theory and what research he does report (for example his research on the play activities of boys and girls) lacks quantification and statistical analysis. Others, however, have had some success in verifying some Eriksonian concepts related to the stages of development and especially that of identity.

Overly Optimistic View of Humans. Although claiming a close affiliation with Freud's theory, Erikson painted a much rosier picture of humans than did Freud. Little in Erikson's theory described an intense struggle to keep our animalistic nature in check. By emphasizing and expanding the functioning of the ego, Erikson concentrated on problems of identity, problem solving, and interpersonal relationships rather than on the taming of powerful sexual and aggressive instincts. To some critics, Erikson's portrayal of humans is too optimistic, unrealistic, and simplistic. Roazen (1976) finds Erikson's description of the optimal adjustment to the final stage of life especially naive.

> This final stage of the life cycle, about which Erikson has written relatively little, seems least satisfactory of all. Why should wisdom be defined by the acquiescence in the inevitable? It can just as well be argued that wisdom should also lead to dissatisfaction, even rage, at past personal mistakes, unfortunate chance, or uncorrected social injustices. Any old person is likely to be emotionally less elastic than in younger years. Not all development results in gains. As a matter of fact, there would be something peculiar if aging did not involve depression—not only does an older person lose some of his powers, but loved ones die. Whatever satisfactions can be foreseen in what has been, in Erikson's terms, generated for the future, death is lonely and often painful. (116)

Support of Status Quo. Essentially Erikson defines a healthy person as one who adjusts to, accepts, and passes on to the next generation, the elements of his or her culture. To many critics, this definition sounds like Erikson is advocating conformity. Indeed, Erikson insists that ego development is enhanced by engaging in the cultural ritualizations that are available at various stages of development. In other words, Erikson insists that healthy egos require the support of culturally sanctioned roles, and this insistence is taken by many as endorsement of those roles. For those seeing gross injustices, dangerous values, shallowness, and even stupidity in their culture, it makes little sense to define mental health in terms of adjustment to such an abnormal situation.

Excessive Moralizing. Erikson's definition of the positive adjustments to crises at various stages of development are in accordance with Christian ethics and, as we have seen, with existing social institutions. The danger in this (as in all theories) is that Erikson may be describing what he hopes will be rather than what is. Roazen (1980) elaborates:

Confusing "ought" and "is" statements can lead to . . . undesirable consequences. . . . There is the danger of conservatism—throwing a mantle of morality over the preexisting world and endorsing everything that already "is" with an ethical sanction. Erikson's message communicates too much of what we want to hear. His hopefulness is too often allied to social conservatism. (1980, 339)

Roazen (1976) comments further on Erikson's moralizing:

As one reflects on the implications of Erikson's ego psychology, with its deferential attitude toward the benefits of pre-existing social institutions, a consistent ethical mood does emerge; marriage, heterosexuality, and the raising of children are unquestionably part of what he takes the good life to consist of. (171)

The criticism that Erikson's theory is too moralistic is closely related to the criticism that his theory supports the status quo.

Failure to Acknowledge Influences on His Theory Properly.   One criticism here concerns Erikson's insistence on being a "post-Freudian" when, in fact, little of substance is similar between his theory and Freud's. It has been suggested that Erikson continued to label himself a Freudian to avoid being "excommunicated" from psychoanalytic circles. In other words, it has been suggested that his motives were pragmatic and political. Conversely, Erikson, although giving perhaps too much credit to Freud, neglected to acknowledge properly theorists such as Adler and Horney who stressed the importance of social variables before Erikson.

Contributions

Vast Expansion of Psychology's Domain.   Despite Erikson's lack of scientific rigor, his theory is considered by many to be one of the most useful ever developed. Henceforth, when you encounter the terms *psychosocial development, ego strength, psychohistory, identity, identity crisis, and lifespan psychology,* keep in mind that they all are concepts that were first articulated by Erikson and have since become an important part of psychology.

Erikson's theory has been successfully used in such areas as child psychology and psychiatry, vocational counseling, marital counseling, education, social work, and business.

Development of Ego Psychology.   By developing and promoting ego psychology Erikson encouraged the study of healthy people in addition to neurotics and psychotics; encouraged the study of personality development across the entire lifespan; and painted a dignified picture of humans. Also, by rejecting Freud's contention that society is necessarily a source of conflict and frustration and by stressing the positive influences of society instead, Erikson promoted the integration of psychology with such disciplines as sociology and anthropology.

Summary

Though Erikson had only the equivalent of a high school diploma, he was invited to work in a small school established to care for children who either were receiving therapy from Anna Freud or who had parents who were receiving therapy from Sigmund Freud. Erikson worked as a tutor for awhile but eventually went into training to become a child analyst under the supervision of Anna Freud. Anna Freud's interest in the ego had a lasting effect on Erikson, who is usually credited with founding ego psychology. Ego psychology emphasizes the autonomous functions of the ego and de-emphasizes the importance of the id to personality development.

Erikson agrees with Freud that one's sex markedly influences one's personality, but does not believe that masculine traits are better or worse than feminine traits. Rather, he believes that masculine and feminine traits complement each other.

The most widely known aspect of Erikson's theory is his description of the eight stages of personality development. According to Erikson's epigenetic principle, the stages unfold in a sequence that is genetically determined. Each of the eight stages is characterized by a crisis, which can be resolved positively or negatively. The stages and the crises characterizing them are: (1) infancy—basic trust versus basic mistrust, (2) early childhood—autonomy versus shame and doubt, (3) preschool age—initiative versus guilt, (4) school age—industry versus inferiority, (5) adolescence—identity versus role confusion, (6) young adulthood—intimacy versus isolation, (7) adulthood—generativity versus stagnation, (8) old age—ego integrity versus despair.

Society provides experiences that are conducive to the positive resolutions of the various crises; such experiences are called ritualizations. Distortions or exaggerations of ritualizations are called ritualisms. The ritualization characterizing the first stage is the numinous, whereby the child's positive interactions with his or her mother make it generally socially responsive. When the numinous is exaggerated, it becomes the ritualism of idolism or the excessive admiration of people. The ritualization characterizing the second stage is judiciousness through which the child learns the cultural definition of right and wrong. The exaggeration of judiciousness results in the ritualism of legalism, which is a preoccupation with laws instead of what those laws are designed to accomplish. The ritualization corresponding to the third stage is authenticity, which involves playing several roles to examine possibilities for living one's life. The exaggeration of authenticity results in the ritualism of impersonation, whereby one confuses a role he or she is playing with his or her true personality. The ritualization characterizing the fourth stage is formality, which involves learning the correct way of acting in a culture. The exaggeration of formality results in the ritualism of formalism, which is an over-concern with how tasks are done instead of why they are done. The ritualization characterizing the fifth stage is ideology, which involves embracing a philosophy of life that synthesizes all previous ego developments. The exaggeration of ideology results in the ritualism of totalism, or the embracing of simplistic ideas because they seem to make life easier. The ritualization characterizing the sixth stage is affiliation, which involves the sharing of one's life in caring, productive ways with fellow humans. The exaggeration of affiliation results in the ritualism of elitism where one's life is shared superficially with small groups of individuals similar to oneself. The ritualization characterizing the seventh stage is generationalism, which involves all of the ways in which healthy adults help the younger generation adjust to their culture. The exaggeration of generationalism results in the ritualism of authoritism, which involves the use of one's authority for self-serving reasons. The ritualization characterizing the eighth stage is integralism, which involves a synthesizing of all the elements of one's life. The exaggeration of integralism results in the ritualism of sapientism, which is the pretense of being wise.

If a crisis is resolved positively, a virtue will be gained that strengthens the ego. If the crises characterizing the eight stages of development are resolved positively, the person will live later years with the virtues of hope, will, purpose, competence, fidelity, love, care, and wisdom. Such a person is called healthy by Erikson, because he or she looks back on life with positive feelings and does not fear death. Children familiar with older people with these attributes are more likely to develop basic trust than basic mistrust.

One of the most important stages of development is the fifth stage, because it is when the identity crisis occurs. It is during this stage that people attempt to find out who they are and where they are going in life. If people find answers to these questions, they will leave this stage with an identity; if not, they will leave this stage with role confusion. It is also possible for people to develop a negative identity, which is the antithesis of a role that society has deemed desirable.

For Erikson, the outcomes of the experiences during the stages of development are reversible; that is, a favorable outcome can become unfavorable, and an unfavorable outcome can become favorable. In fact, Erikson viewed the therapeutic process mainly as a means of reversing the outcomes of various stages of development. For Erikson, the goal of therapy was to strengthen the conscious ego, rather than to understand the contents of the unconscious mind, as was the case with Freud. Many other differences exist between Freud's theory and Erikson's. For example, Freud viewed religion as a collective neurosis based on infantile desires, fear, and ignorance. Erikson, conversely, saw religion as a necessity of life and conducive to healthy adjustment.

Although Erikson felt no need to test his theory empirically, others made attempts to do so. Most of the research generated by Erikson's theory has focused on the stages of development and on his concept of identity. These studies have tended to support predictions based on Erikson's theory. Erikson's theory has been criticized for being generally difficult to test empirically; portraying humans too simplistically or too optimistically; supporting the status quo; and for being too moralistic. Also Erikson had been criticized for not properly acknowledging those who influenced him. Contributions of Erikson's theory include the vast expansion of psychology's domain; its widespread usefulness; the development of ego psychology, which is as concerned with healthy people as with unhealthy people, studies personality development across the entire lifespan, and stresses the fact that societal forces are conducive to personality development and are therefore not necessarily a source of conflict and frustration.

EXPERIENTIAL EXERCISES

1. Probably the most significant event in a person's life occurs when he or she gains an identity. Erikson believed that this occurs toward the end of the fifth stage of development. The alternative to leaving this stage with an identity is to leave with role confusion. Drawing on the information in this chapter would you say that you have developed an identity or are you experiencing role confusion? Give evidence to support your answer.

2. Erikson asserted that one cannot experience true intimacy with another human until one has gained an identity. That is, two persons cannot share themselves in a deep, loving relationship unless they have both gained an identity. Respond to this assertion as it applies to your life and as it applies to the relationship of a close friend.

3. To minimize life's confusion, adolescents often will idolize and overidentify with a teacher, a television star, an athlete, or even a friend. Was there someone in your adolescent years whom you idolized? If so, was this overidentification helpful? Harmful? Explain.

4. What did Erikson say characterizes the relationships of persons experiencing either role confusion or negative identities? Respond to

Erikson's assertion in terms of those you know.

5. Analyze your own personality in terms of Erikson's theory. How have you resolved the crises that you have gone through? Which of the Eriksonian virtues do you possess? What stage are you now in? Does Erikson's description of that stage seem valid to you?

DISCUSSION QUESTIONS

1. Describe Erikson's early experiences that you think may have stimulated his later interest in the concept of identity crisis.

2. Describe the relationship between anatomy and destiny as viewed by Erikson.

3. Compare ego psychology with traditional psychoanalytic theory.

4. Why are Erikson's stages of development labeled psychosocial rather than psychosexual?

5. Summarize the eight stages of development suggested by Erikson. Include in your summary that crisis that characterizes each stage and the virtue that emerges if the crisis is resolved positively.

6. Define ritualization and ritualism. List the ritualizations and ritualisms for each stage of development and give an example of each.

7. In what ways are the psychosocial stages interrelated?

8. Summarize the major differences between the theories of Erikson and Freud.

9. Erikson has been accused of being unduly influenced by Christian ethics in his theorizing. Respond to this accusation.

10. Describe Erikson's contributions to psychology.

11. Discuss the criticisms of Erikson's theory.

SUGGESTIONS FOR FURTHER READING

COLES, R. (1970). *Erik Erikson: The Growth of His Work*. Boston: Little, Brown.

As a Harvard psychiatrist and an ex-student of Erikson, Coles provides an interesting and sympathetic account of the personal and historical influences that shaped Erikson's thinking.

ERIKSON, E. H. (1963). *Childhood and Society* (2d ed.). New York: Norton.

Erikson's first and most comprehensive book. In addition to introducing the eight stages of personality development, this book contains several case studies and describes his study of the Sioux and Yurok Indians.

ERIKSON, E. H. (1964). *Insight and Responsibility*. New York: Norton.

Focuses on the "virtues" that are added to one's ego if the crises associated with the various stages of development are resolved positively.

ERIKSON, E. H. (1968a). *Identity: Youth and Crisis*. New York: Norton.

Expands his notion of the interrelatedness of the stages of development by showing how aspects of the identity crisis occur before and after the fifth stage of development. Expands the notions of identity and negative identity and shows their relevance to various ethnic and social groups.

ERIKSON, E. H. (1975b). *Life History and the Historical Moment*. New York: Norton.

In a series of essays, Erikson discusses how the concept of "identity crisis" has been abused, his views on the women's movement, and the significance to his theory of his own adolescent identity crisis.

ERIKSON, E. H. (1977). *Toys and Reasons: Stages in the Ritualization of Experience.* New York: Norton.

Erikson expands his theory to include the concepts of ritualization and ritualism.

ROAZEN, P. (1976). *Erik H. Erikson: The Power and Limits of a Vision.* New York: Free Press.

An interesting and highly readable account of the growth of Erikson's ideas. Roazen is much more critical of Erikson than are other biographical accounts (see, for example, Coles 1970).

GLOSSARY

Adolescence. The fifth stage of development.

Adulthood. The seventh stage of development.

Affiliation. The ritualization characterizing the sixth stage of development. This involves sharing one's identity with fellow humans in a caring, productive way. For example, by entering into an intimate relationship with a member of the opposite sex who has also gained an identity.

Anatomy and destiny. Freud thought that many important personality traits were determined by one's sex. Erikson believed the same but thought that one's culture was another powerful influence on one's personality. Although Erikson believed men and women had different personality characteristics, he did not consider one set of characteristics better than the other.

Authenticity. The ritualization characterizing the third stage of development. This involves playful role playing to discover possible ways of living one's adult life.

Authoritism. The ritualism that can occur during the seventh stage of development. This involves using power for selfish gains instead of helping others.

Autonomy. The sense of being relatively independent of external control, which arises if the crisis characterizing the second stage of development is resolved positively.

Basic mistrust. The lack of trust of the world and the people in it, which arises if the crisis characterizing the first stage of development is resolved negatively.

Basic trust. The general feeling of trust of the world and the people in it, which arises if the crisis characterizing the first stage of development is resolved positively.

Care. The virtue that arises when a person leaves the seventh stage of development with a greater sense of generativity than of stagnation.

Competence. The virtue that arises if a child leaves the fourth stage of development with a greater sense of industry than of inferiority.

Crisis. A problem that characterizes a stage of development that can be resolved positively, thus strengthening the ego, or resolved negatively, thus weakening the ego. Each crisis, therefore, is a turning point in one's development.

Despair. The lack of satisfaction with life and the fear of death, which characterize the person who has negatively resolved the crisis that occurs during the eighth and final stage of development.

Early childhood. The second stage of development.

Ego integrity. The satisfaction with life and the lack of fear of death, which characterize the person who has positively resolved the crisis that occurs during the eighth and final stage of development.

Ego psychology. A theoretical system that stresses the importance of the ego as an autonomous part of the personality instead of looking at the ego as merely the servant of the id.

Elitism. The ritualism that can occur during the sixth stage of development. This involves the superficial relationships with groups of like-minded individuals that people without identities seek out.

Epigenetic principle. The principle that states that a sequence of growth is genetically determined and that each stage, once developed, gives rise to the next.

Fidelity. The virtue that arises at the end of the fifth stage of development if one has a sense of identity instead of role confusion.

Formalism. The ritualism that can occur during the fourth stage. This involves a preoccupation with how things work, or with one's work, and a disregard for the reason why things function as they do or why various kinds of jobs exist.

Formality. The ritualization corresponding to the fourth stage of development. This involves the learning of how various things work in one's culture.

Generationalism. The ritualization that characterizes the seventh stage of development. This involves the many ways in which healthy individuals help younger people to have experiences conducive to healthy personality growth.

Generativity. The impulse to help members of the next generation, which arises when the crisis characterizing the seventh stage of development is resolved positively.

Guilt. The general feeling that develops in a child if the crisis characterizing the third stage of development is resolved negatively.

Hope. The virtue that arises if a child leaves the first stage of development with more basic trust than basic mistrust.

Identity. The sense of knowing who you are and where you are going in life, which develops when the fifth stage of development is resolved positively. The emergence of an identity marks the end of childhood and the beginning of adulthood. Probably Erikson's most famous concept.

Identity crisis. The crisis that characterizes the fifth stage of development, which results either in the person's gaining an identity (positive resolution) or in role confusion (negative resolution).

Ideology. The ritualization characterizing the fifth stage of development. This involves the arrival at a philosophy of life that makes one's past, present, and future meaningful.

Idolism. The ritualism that can occur during the first stage of development, where instead of a child learning a warm, positive feeling toward others, he or she tends to worship them.

Impersonation. The ritualism that can occur during the third stage of development. This involves confusing playing a role with one's true personality.

Industry. The sense of enjoyment from work and from sustained attention, which arises if the crisis characterizing the fourth stage of development is resolved positively.

Infancy. The first stage of development.

Inferiority. The loss of confidence in one's ability to become a contributing member of one's society, which arises if the crisis characterizing the fourth stage of development is resolved negatively.

Initiative. The general ability to initiate ideas and actions and to plan future events, which arises if the crisis characterizing the third stage of development is resolved positively.

Integralism. The ritualization characterizing the eighth stage of development. This involves the wisdom to place one's own life in a larger perspective. That is, to see one's finite life as contributing to immortal culture.

Intimacy. The ability to merge one's identity with that of another person, which arises if the crisis characterizing the sixth stage of development is resolved positively.

Isolation. The inability to share one's identity with that of another person, which results if the crisis characterizing the sixth stage of development is resolved negatively.

Judiciousness. The ritualization characterizing the second stage of development. This involves the many ways that children learn right from wrong.

Legalism. The ritualism that can occur during the second stage of development. This involves a preoccupation with rules and regulations themselves instead of with what they were designed to accomplish.

Love. The virtue that arises if one leaves the sixth stage of development with a greater sense of intimacy than of isolation.

Negative identity. An identity that is contrary to the goals of society. Negative identities are all those roles that a child is warned *not* to assume.

Numinous. The ritualization characterizing the first stage of development. This involves the many culturally determined ways in which mother and infant interact.

Old age. The eighth stage of development.

Preschool age. The third stage of development.

Psychohistory. The term used to describe Erikson's use of his developmental theory of personality to analyze historical figures.

Psychosocial moratorium. The time during the fifth stage of development when the adolescent is searching for an identity.

Psychosocial stages of development. Erikson's eight stages of human development, so named to emphasize the importance of social experience to the resolution of the crises that characterize each stage.

Purpose. The virtue that arises if a child leaves the third stage of development with a greater sense of initiative than of guilt.

Ritualisms. Distorted or exaggerated ritualizations.

Ritualizations. Behaviors that reflect and thereby perpetuate the beliefs, customs, and values that are sanctioned by a particular culture.

Role confusion. The state produced by not acquiring an identity during the fifth stage of development. The state is characterized by an inability to choose a role in life and represents the negative resolution of the identity crisis.

Sapientism. The ritualism that can occur during the eighth stage of development. This involves the pretense of being wise.

School age. The fourth stage of development.

Shame and doubt. The feelings that develop instead of the feeling of autonomy when the crisis characterizing the second stage of development is resolved negatively.

Stagnation. The lack of concern about the next generation that characterizes the person whose crisis during the seventh stage of development was resolved negatively.

Totalism. The ritualism that can occur during the fifth stage of development. This involves the embracing of simplistic ideas mouthed by various "heroes" because those ideas may temporarily make life more tolerable.

Virtue. An ego strength that arises when the crisis characterizing a stage of development is resolved positively.

Will. The virtue that arises if the child leaves the second stage of development with a greater sense of autonomy than of shame and doubt.

Wisdom. The virtue that arises if a person has more ego integrity than despair during the eighth and final stage of development.

Young adulthood. The sixth stage of development.

7

Gordon Allport

Gordon Allport was born in Montezuma, Indiana, on 11 November, 1897, making him the first American-born personality theorist covered thus far in this text. Allport was the youngest of four sons. His father was a physician, his mother a schoolteacher, and both had a strong, positive influence on him. In his brief autobiography, he said:

> My mother had been a school teacher and brought to her sons an eager sense of philosophical questioning and the importance of searching for ultimate religious answers. Since my father lacked adequate hospital facilities for his patients, our household for several years included both patients and nurses. Tending office, washing bottles, and dealing with patients were important aspects of my early training. . . . Dad was no believer in vacations. He followed rather his own rule of life, which he expressed as follows: If every person worked as hard as he could and took only a minimum financial return required by his family's needs, then there would be just enough wealth to go around. Thus it was hard work tempered by trust and affection that marked the home environment. (1967, 4–5)

Allport credited his lifelong concern with human welfare and his strong humanistic psychology to experiences like those described above.

Although Allport was born in Indiana, he grew up in Cleveland, Ohio, where he attended public schools. At the urging of his older brother Floyd (who himself became a famous psychologist), who had graduated from Harvard two years earlier, Gordon Allport entered Harvard in 1915. He barely passed the entrance examination and his early grades were C's and D's. He worked hard, however, and finished the year with straight A's. He graduated from Harvard in 1919 with a major in economics and philosophy.

Apparently not sure of what to do next and still seeking his personal identity, he spent the next year teaching English and sociology at Robert College in Istanbul, Turkey. Allport enjoyed teaching so much that he decided to accept a fellowship offered to him by Harvard to do graduate work in psychology.

On his way back to the United States, Allport stopped in Vienna to visit one of his brothers. While there he had an experience that was to have a profound effect on his later theorizing. He wrote to Freud asking for permission to visit with him and permission was granted. Allport described his brief visit with Freud:

> Soon after I had entered the famous red burlap room with pictures of dreams on the wall, he summoned me to his inner office. He did not speak to me but sat in expectant silence for me to state my mission. I was not prepared for silence and had to think fast to find a suitable conversational gambit. I told him of an episode on the tram car on my way to his office. A small boy about four years of age had displayed a conspicuous dirt phobia. He kept saying to his mother, "I don't want to sit there . . . don't let that dirty man sit beside me." To him everything was *schmutzig* [filthy]. His mother was a well-starched *Hausfrau*, so dominant and purposive looking that I thought the cause and effect apparent.
>
> When I finished my story Freud fixed his kindly therapeutic eyes upon me

and said, "And was that little boy you?" Flabbergasted and feeling a bit guilty, I contrived to change the subject. While Freud's misunderstanding of my motivation was amusing, it also started a deep train of thought. I realized that he was accustomed to neurotic defenses and that my manifest motivation (a sort of rude curiosity and youthful ambition) escaped him. For therapeutic progress he would have to cut through my defenses, but it so happened that therapeutic progress was not here an issue. (1967, 7–8)

Allport learned from this experience that it is possible for "depth" psychology to dig so deeply that more important truths may be overlooked. Allport felt that he had perfectly valid, conscious reasons for visiting Freud and for telling him his little story, which were completely missed by Freud in his attempt to arrive at a "deeper" truth. As we shall see throughout this chapter, Allport believed the best way of discovering a person's true motives is to ask the person. Throughout his life, Allport displayed a dislike for psychoanalytic theory.

Allport returned to Harvard, where he earned his M.A. in 1921 and his Ph.D. in 1922, at the age of twenty-four. His early work was indeed indicative of what was to become Allport's own brand of personality theory. His first publication was coauthored with his brother Floyd and was entitled, "Personality Traits: Their Classification and Measurement" (Allport and Allport 1921). His Ph.D. dissertation was entitled, "An Experimental Study of the Traits of Personality."

Gordon Allport

Aided by a traveling fellowship, Allport spent the school year from 1922 to 1923 at the University of Berlin and the University of Hamburg, and the school year from 1923 to 1924 in England at Cambridge University. In 1924, he returned to Harvard, where he taught the first course on personality ever offered in the United States. The course was entitled, "Personality: Its Psychological and Social Aspects."

Allport married Ada Lufkin Gould on 30 June, 1925, and their one child, Robert Brandlee, now is a pediatrician. Except for a four-year appointment at Dartmouth College from 1926 to 1930, Allport was at Harvard for his entire professional career. Allport died of lung cancer on 9 October, 1967, one month before his seventieth birthday.

As we shall see, Allport was truly an eclectic theorist, taking the best from a wide variety of other theories of personality. Allport, however, was the first to criticize what he considered the worst in those theories. At one time or another, Allport took issue with psychoanalysis, behaviorism (stimulus-response [S-R] psychology), animal research designed to provide information about humans, and statistical methods of studying personality, such as factor analysis. For example, Allport said that psychologists such as Freud and Jung had created:

> A kind of contempt for the "psychic surface" of life. The individual's conscious report is rejected as untrustworthy, and the contemporary thrust of his motives is disregarded in favor of a backward tracing of his conduct to earlier formative stages. The individual loses his right to be believed. And while he is busy leading his life in the present with a forward thrust into the future, most psychologists have become busy tracing it backward into the past. (1960, 96)

Allport believed strongly that the principles governing the behavior of lower animals or neurotic humans are different from those governing the behavior of healthy adult humans; therefore, little can be learned about one by studying the other. "Some theories of becoming are based largely upon the behavior of sick and anxious people or upon the antics of captive and desperate rats. Fewer theories have derived from the study of healthy human beings, those who strive not so much to preserve life as to make it worth living" (Allport 1955, 18).

Indeed, Allport battled with any viewpoint in psychology that obscured human individuality or dignity. If one had to isolate the dominant theme running through all of Allport's works, it is *the importance of the individual*. This theme put Allport in a position contrary to "scientific" psychology, because it was considered the job of science to find the general laws governing all behavior. Science was interested in what is generally true, and Allport was interested in what is specifically true.

Allport believed that psychological research should have practical value, and in addition to his books on personality theory, which we will consider in this chapter, he wrote such books as:

The Individual and His Religion (1950)

The Nature of Prejudice (1954)

The Psychology of Rumor (1947), with L. Postman

Allport received many honors. In 1939, at the age of forty-one, he was elected president of the American Psychological Association, he received the Distinguished

Scientific Contribution Award from the American Psychological Association in 1964, and in 1966 he became the first Richard Clarke Cabat Professor of Social Ethics at Harvard. Allport's most prized honor, however, was two handsomely bound volumes of the publications of fifty-five of his former Ph.D. students, given to him in 1963 with the dedicatory inscription "From his students—in appreciation of his respect for their individuality" (Allport 1967, 24).

What Is Personality?

In his 1937 book *Personality: A Psychological Interpretation*, Allport introduced the study of **personality** to America. From the very beginning, Allport was opposed to the established viewpoints of psychoanalysis and behaviorism. Allport's early theorizing was influenced mainly by Gestalt psychology, which he encountered in Germany after his graduation from Harvard, and by his strong humanistic tendencies developed early in his life. As we saw in chapter 4, Gestalt psychology emphasized the wholeness and interrelatedness of conscious experience and was appalled by an attempt to subdivide it in order to study it more thoroughly. Gestalt psychology also ignored the unconscious mind almost completely. Allport said that Gestalt psychology was "the kind of psychology I had been longing for but did not know existed" (1967, 10). In fact, Allport distrusted science as a source of information about personality. He was more comfortable with the traditional descriptions of humans found in literature and philosophy. This is not to say that Allport ignored information provided by the scientific method; clearly he did not. He did not want to be restricted, however, to scientific method in his efforts to understand personality. He believed that much useful nonscientific information had accumulated through the years, and that it would be foolhardy not to make use of that information.

In 1937, Allport reviewed the history of the word personality, beginning with its ties to the Latin word *persona*, which means mask. He then reviewed fifty definitions of personality before arriving at his own, now-famous, definition: "Personality is the dynamic organization within the individual of those psychophysical systems that determine his unique adjustments to his environment" (1937, 48).

In 1961 Allport changed the phrase "unique adjustments to his environment" to "characteristic behavior and thought" (28). Because Allport's definition of personality acts as a summary of most of his major concepts, we shall examine its key components more carefully.

Dynamic Organization

This refers to the fact that personality, though always organized, is constantly changing. Personality, according to Allport, is never something that is; rather, it is something that is **becoming.** Although enough similarity exists within people to maintain their identity from one experience to another, in a sense they never are quite the same people they were before a particular experience. Allport borrowed this idea from the ancient Greek philosopher Heraclitus, who said, "Nothing is, everything is becoming," and "No man can step into the same river twice." It is the same with personality; it has organization and continuity within the person, but it is constantly changing or becoming something different.

Psychophysical Systems

According to Allport: "The term 'psychophysical' reminds us that personality is neither exclusively mental nor exclusively neural. The organization entails the operation of both body and mind, inextricably fused into a personal unit" (1937, 48).

Determine

According to Allport, personality was not an abstraction or a convenient fiction; it actually existed: "Personality *is* something and *does* something. . . . It is what lies *behind* specific acts and *within* the individual" (1937, 48). Allport believed that the person is by no means simply a passive reactor to the environment. Rather, a person's behavior is generated from within by the personality structure.

Characteristic Behavior and Thought

It has been mentioned that Allport revised his definition of personality in 1961 by deleting the phrase "unique adjustments to the environment" and replacing it with "characteristic behavior and thought." He did so because he believed the earlier statement placed too much emphasis on survival and thus on the satisfaction of biologic needs. His revised definition covered *all* behavior and thought, whether or not they were related to adaptation to the environment. One's dreams for the future, for example, are just as important as satisfying the hunger drive, but they have little or nothing to do with biologic survival.

Both versions of Allport's definition of personality stress the importance of individuality. In the 1937 definition, the word "unique" was used; in the 1961 definition, the word "characteristic" was used. Indeed, as we have seen, the emphasis on studying individual human beings rather than on the laws governing all human beings was a constant theme running through all of Allport's work. He repeatedly said that no two humans are alike, and therefore the only way to learn about a particular person is to study that particular person.

Allport distinguished among the terms personality, character, temperament, and type.

Character

Allport was bothered by the term **character,** because it implied the moral judgment of a person, such as when it is said that a person has "a good character." Allport preferred "to define *character* as *personality evaluated,* and *personality* . . . as *character devaluated*" (1961, 32).

Temperament

Allport referred to temperament, intelligence, and physique as the **raw materials of personality** and all three are genetically determined. **Temperament** is the emotional component of the personality, which Allport described as:

> The characteristic phenomena of an individual's emotional nature, including his susceptibility to emotional stimulation, his customary strength and speed of response, the quality of his prevailing mood, and all peculiarities of fluctuation and intensity in mood, these phenomena being regarded as dependent upon constitutional makeup, and therefore largely hereditary in origin. (1961, 34)

Type

A **type** is a category in which one person can be placed by another person. In other words, we use the word type when we are describing other people. Types, therefore, are ways of categorizing people. If a person continually acts aggressively, we may say he or she is the aggressive type, which is to say that his or her behavior fits into this category. Personality, conversely, is something that is within a person, causing him or her to behave in certain ways. We can say that personality generates behavior patterns that can be described as types.

Criteria for an Adequate Theory of Personality

In 1960, Allport described five characteristics that he believed any good theory of personality should possess.

1. Views personality as contained within the person   According to Allport, those theories that explain personality in terms of the various roles people play or in terms of behavior patterns elicited by environmental circumstances are inadequate. In other words, personality must be explained in terms of internal mechanisms, rather than of external mechanisms. Not surprisingly, Allport's theory meets this criterion.

2. Views person as filled with variables that contribute to his or her actions This statement, which is very much related to point 1, was made to show Allport's disdain of those behaviorists who assumed, for methodological reasons, that the human organism was empty. To these S-R psychologists (discussed in chapters 9 and 10), the proper way to study human behavior was to make a "functional analysis" of stimulating conditions (S) and responses to those conditions (R). Such psychologists prided themselves on studying the *empty organism* (B. F. Skinner led this group). Allport believed that this position was especially distasteful and dehumanizing: "Any theory of personality pretending adequacy must be dynamic and, to be dynamic, must assume a well-stocked organism" (Allport 1960, 26).

Again, Allport's theory of personality fulfills this requirement for an adequate theory of personality.

3. Seeks motives for behavior in present instead of past Here Allport is expressing his dissatisfaction with psychoanalytic theory, which traces adult motives to childhood experiences. According to Allport, neurotics may be prisoners of their past, and psychoanalytic methods may be useful in dealing with them, but the motives for healthy, mature adults are found in the present. Furthermore, healthy, normal adults are aware of their motives and can describe them accurately if asked to do so.

> When we set out to study a person's motives, we are seeking to find out what that person is trying to do in his life—including, of course, what he is trying to avoid and what he is trying to be. I see no reason why we should not start our investigation by asking him to tell us the answers as he sees them. (Allport 1960, 101)

We will see in our discussion of functional autonomy, later in this chapter, that Allport saw adult motivation as separate from earlier experiences. By emphasizing the importance of the present, Allport's theory has much in common with the social learning theory of Bandura and Mischel (chapter 11) and with the existential-humanistic theories of Kelly, Rogers, Maslow, and May (chapters 13–16).

4. Employs units of measure capable of "living synthesis" According to Allport, the integrity of the total personality must never be lost. People are more than a collection of test scores or conditioned reflexes. Whatever units of measure are used to describe a person, they must be capable of describing the whole, dynamic personality:

> To say that John Brown scores in the eightieth percentile of the "masculinity-femininity" variable, in the thirtieth percentile on "need for achievement" and at average on "introversion-extroversion" is only moderately enlightening. Even with a more numerous set of dimensions, with an avalanche of psychometric scores, patterned personality seems to elude the psychodiagnostician. (Allport 1960, 30)

Allport's theory never lost sight of the whole person. As we shall see, the unit of measure that he felt made this possible is the "trait."

5. Adequately accounts for self-awareness Humans are the only animals aware of their own awareness, and this fact, according to Allport, must be considered in any adequate account of personality. We shall explore Allport's attempt to deal with this difficult problem when we discuss the "proprium" later in this chapter.

We see that Allport's theory is five for five in terms of meeting his own criteria for an adequate theory of personality. Other theorists, of course, would have their own criteria, which Allport's theory would not fit.

Allport's Concept of Trait

We have seen that Allport felt an adequate theory of personality would employ units of measure capable of "living synthesis." For Allport, that unit was the **trait.** To help describe the various traits that people may possess, Allport and Odbert (1936) examined 17,953 adjectives that have been used to characterize people. Allport, however, certainly did not equate traits with names. Traits, for Allport, were real biophysical structures. In 1937, Allport said that he did not believe that:

> Every trait-name necessarily implies a trait; but rather that behind all confusion of terms, behind the disagreement of judges, and apart from errors and failures of empirical observation, there are none the less *bona fide* mental structures in each personality that account for the consistency of its behavior. (289)

Allport defined a trait as "a neuropsychic structure having the capacity to render many stimuli functionally equivalent, and to initiate and guide equivalent (meaningfully consistent) forms of adaptive and expressive behavior" (1961, 347).

Traits account for the consistency in human behavior. Because no two people possess exactly the same pattern of traits, each confronts environmental experiences differently. A person possessing a strong trait of friendliness will react differently to a stranger than a person possessing a strong trait of suspiciousness. In both cases the stimulus is the same but the reactions are different, because different traits are involved. Or, as Allport explained, "The same fire that melts the butter hardens the egg" (1961, 72).

People's traits organize experiences, because people confront the world in terms of their traits. For example, if people are basically aggressive, they will be aggressive in a wide range of situations. Traits will guide their behavior, because people can respond to the world only in terms of their traits. Traits, therefore, both initiate and guide behavior. How a trait influences the way one will react to various situations is shown in Figure 7–1.

Traits cannot be observed directly, and therefore their existence must be inferred. Allport suggested the following criteria for assuming the evidence of a trait:

> The *frequency* with which a person adopts a certain type of adjustment is one criterion of a trait. A second criterion is the *range of situations* in which he adopts this same mode of acting. A third criterion is the *intensity* of his reactions in keeping with this "preferred pattern" of behavior. (1961, 340)

> It is only the repeated occurrence of acts having the same significance (equivalence of response) following upon a definable range of stimuli having the same personal significance (equivalence of stimuli) that makes necessary the inference of traits and personal dispositions. These tendencies are not at all times active, but are persistent even when latent, and have relatively low thresholds of arousal. (1961, 374)

Allport's theory predicts a great deal of cross-situational consistency in a person's behavior. The kind of consistency displayed is assumed to be determined

Figure 7–1.
*How one might react
to various situations
if one had a strong
aggressiveness trait.*

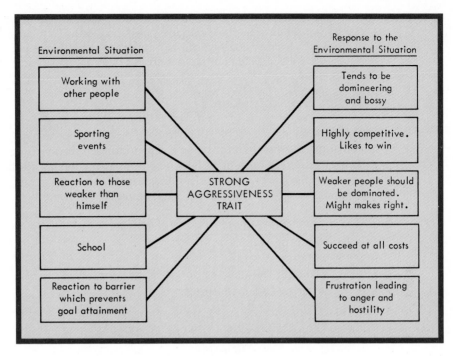

Figure 7–1.
How one might react to various situations if one had a strong aggressiveness trait.

by the traits that a person possesses. Although consistency of behavior is predicted or assumed by most personality theories, it has recently been found that a person's behavior is not nearly as consistent from one situation to another as it had been thought to be. We will examine this consistency-versus-inconsistency controversy in more detail when we review social learning theory in chapter 11.

Interaction of Traits and Situations.   To be fair to Allport, it must be noted that he never said that the possession of a trait or a pattern of traits necessarily caused a person to act the same in *all* similar situations. *Some* consistency in behavior must exist before a trait or pattern of traits is assumed to exist, but instances of inconsistency do not necessarily suggest that such traits do not exist. For Allport, a person's traits create a possible range of responses to a given situation but it is the nature of the situation itself that determines which of the potential behaviors actually occur.

Allport (1961) described how he felt traits and situations interacted:

We are forced . . . to the conclusion that while the situation may modify behavior greatly, it can do so only within the limits of the potential provided by the personality. At the same time, we are forced to concede that traits of personality must not be regarded as fixed and stable, operating mechanically to the same degree on all occasions. Rather we should think of traits as *ranges of possible behavior*, to be activated at varying points within this range according to the demands of the situation.

It is wrong to say that Jim has *y*-amount of anxiety, or of extraversion, or of aggressiveness. Rather we should say that he has *upper and lower limits* of these traits. This would mean that he never shows more than *x*-amount and never less than z-amount. His exact location within the range at any given time will depend on what the situational cues bring forth. To put the matter slightly differently, we may conceive of [the] situation as "pulling" a person higher or lower on his scale of potentialities, but always within his particular limits. (180–81)

Traits Are Not Habits

Habits are more specific than traits. For example, one may have the habits of brushing one's teeth, putting on clean clothing in the morning, brushing one's hair, washing one's hands, and cleaning one's nails. One has all these habits, however, because one has the trait of cleanliness. In other words, a trait synthesizes a number of specific habits. This can be diagrammed as follows:

SPECIFIC HABITS	*TRAIT*
Brushing Hair	
Brushing Teeth	
Washing Hands	Cleanliness
Wearing Clean Clothing	
Cleaning Nails	

Traits Are Not Attitudes

Attitudes, like habits, are more specific than traits. A person has an attitude toward something; for instance, a certain person, a brand of automobile, or travel. A trait, conversely, is much more general. For example, if a person is basically aggressive, he or she will tend to act aggressively toward strangers, acquaintances, animals, world affairs, and the like. A second distinction between attitudes and traits is that attitudes usually imply evaluation; that is attitudes are usually for or against something; they are either positive or negative; and they imply either acceptance or rejection of something. Traits, conversely, are responsible for all behavior and cognitions whether or not evaluation is involved.

Kinds of Traits

First, Allport distinguished between **individual traits** and **common traits.** As their names imply, individual traits are those possessed by a particular individual, and common traits are those shared by several individuals. The distinction between individual and common traits is determined mainly by what is being specified. Any group can be described by its traits. For example, a group can be described as friendly, aggressive, or intelligent. Likewise, any individual can be described by his or her traits; one can be described as friendly, aggressive, or intelligent. When traits are used to describe a group, they are called common traits; when they are used to describe an individual, they are called individual traits. Although recognizing the existence of both kinds of traits, Allport believed strongly that the personality theorist should focus on individual traits.

The distinction between individual and common traits is often confused by the assumption that an individual trait is one that only a single individual possesses. This assumption is not true. It is almost impossible to imagine any individual without some degree of friendliness, honesty, neatness, aggression, or any other trait. What Allport meant by individual uniqueness is the pattern of traits that an individual possesses. That is, one person may have a strong friendliness trait, a weak honesty trait, and a moderate aggressiveness trait. Another person may be moderate in friendliness, honesty, and aggressiveness. When the list of traits is extended and when it is realized that each trait can be possessed to almost any degree, the number of possible trait configurations is extremely large. What Allport meant by individual traits was really a unique *pattern* of traits possessed by a particular individual. Furthermore, it is important to remember that a trait specifies a possible range of behaviors. For example, many people are aggressive, but no two people are aggressive in exactly the same way and under exactly the same circumstances. Thus, individuals differ not only in the pattern of traits that they possess but also in how any particular trait manifests itself in their personalities. Common traits consist of that pattern of traits found to characterize a group of individuals. Using common traits, it can be said that a group was on the average very friendly, moderately aggressive, very intelligent, and so on. Thus, the same trait names are used to describe both individuals and groups.

Borrowing his terms from the philosopher W. Windelband, Allport insisted that the personality theorist use the **idiographic method** of research, which is the intense study of a single case, and avoid the **nomothetic method,** which studies groups of individuals and analyzes averages. Allport felt that averages were merely abstractions and really described no single individual accurately. In other words, Allport believed that the only way to learn about a particular person is to study that person, because no two people have exactly the same configuration of traits.

Later in the evolution of his theory, Allport came to believe that using the term "trait" to describe both group and individual characteristics was confusing. He therefore retained the term "common traits" to describe characteristics of groups but changed the term "individual trait" to **personal disposition,** which he defined as "a generalized neuropsychic structure (peculiar to the individual), with the capacity to render many stimuli functionally equivalent, and to initiate and guide consistent (equivalent) forms of adaptive and stylistic behavior" (1961, 373). Note that the definition of personal disposition is essentially the same as the earlier definition of trait.

Having decided on the study of personal dispositions, it was clear to Allport that not all the dispositions that a person possesses have the same impact on personality. He therefore distinguished among cardinal, central, and secondary dispositions.

Cardinal Dispositions

If one possesses a cardinal disposition, it influences almost everything one does. When one thinks of Don Juan, for example, one thinks of a man possessed by romance, and when one thinks of Florence Nightingale, one thinks of a person driven by human compassion. Both individuals exemplify **cardinal dispositions.** Cardinal dispositions are observable in only a small number of people.

Central Dispositions

Think of a person you know quite well. Now pretend you have been asked to write an honest letter of recommendation for that person. Jot down the person's characteristics that you would mention in such a letter. Those terms on your list describe that person's central dispositions and summarize the consistencies in the person's behavior. Examples might be punctuality, neatness, creativity, and persistence.

Allport believed that each person possesses surprisingly few central dispositions. "When psychology develops adequate diagnostic methods for discovering the major lines along which a particular personality is organized (personal dispositions), it may turn out that the number of such foci will normally vary between five and ten" (1961, 367).

Secondary Dispositions

Secondary dispositions apply to a much more specific range of behaviors than do either cardinal or central dispositions. Secondary dispositions are close to habits or attitudes but are still more general than either. These would include a person's idiosyncrasies, such as preferences for certain kinds of food or clothing.

Process of Becoming

Earlier we saw that Allport defined personality as a "dynamic organization." We also saw that Allport believed personality to consist of biologic as well as psychological structures, such as personal dispositions. The fact that all of the diverse aspects of personality are continuous and are organized, implies the existence of an organizing agent. In ancient times this agent was called the soul. Later it was called the self or ego. Allport believed that all of these terms were too nebulous, and renamed the organizer of the personality the **proprium.** The proprium includes all the facts about a person that makes him or her unique. Allport defined proprium as follows:

> Personality includes these habits and skills, frames of reference, matters of fact and cultural values, that seldom or never seem warm and important. But personality includes what is warm and important also—all the regions of our life that we regard as peculiarly ours, and which for the time being I suggest we call the *proprium.* The proprium includes all aspects of personality that make for inward unity. (1955, 40)

This inward organization and self-awareness are not present at birth, but, rather, evolve slowly over time. Allport believed that full propriate functioning characterizes only the final stage of an eight-stage developmental sequence that starts at birth and continues until adulthood.

1. Sense of bodily "me" (first year) Infants learn that their bodies exist because of the many sensations they experience. Although the sense of **bodily "me"**

is the first aspect of the proprium to evolve, it remains a lifelong anchor of our self-awareness. The sense of bodily "me" is used to distinguish what is part of oneself, and therefore, warm and intimate and what is foreign to oneself. Allport (1961) vividly demonstrates the difference between what is perceived as belonging to oneself and what is not:

> Think first of swallowing the saliva in your mouth, or do so. Then imagine spitting it into a tumbler and drinking it. What seemed natural and "mine" suddenly becomes disgusting and alien. Or, to continue this unpleasant line of thought for a moment, picture yourself sucking the blood from a prick in your finger; then imagine sucking blood from a bandage around your finger. What you perceive as belonging intimately to your body is warm and welcome; what you perceive as separate becomes instantly cold and foreign. (114)

2. Sense of self-identity (second year)   With this sense comes the realization that there is self-continuity over time. That is, children come to realize that they are the same people although there are changes in their size and experiences. The development of language is directly related to the development of **self-identity.** Specifically, children learn their name, which acts as an anchor for their identity, through a variety of experiences. "By hearing his name repeatedly the child gradually sees himself as a distinct and recurrent point of reference. The name acquires significance for him in the second year of life. With it comes awareness of independent status in the social group" (Allport 1961, 115).

3. Sense of self-esteem (third year)   This is the feeling of pride that emerges when children learn they can do things on their own. During this stage children often seek complete independence from adult supervision.

4. Sense of self-extension (fourth year)   During this stage children learn the meaning of the word "mine." Now they realize that not only do their bodies belong to them, but so do certain toys, games, parents, pets, sisters, and so on. At this time the sense of self is extended to external objects.

5. Emergence of self-image (fourth to sixth year)   During this stage children develop a conscience, which acts as a frame of reference for "the good me" and "the bad me." Now children can compare what they do with the expectations others have of them. It is also during this stage that children begin to formulate future goals for themselves.

6. Emergence of self as a rational coper (sixth to twelfth year)   At this stage children recognize "thinking" as a means of solving life's problems. In a sense children begin to think about thinking.

7. Emergence of propriate striving (twelfth year through adolescence)   At this stage of development, people become almost completely future oriented. Long-term goals are created that give organization and meaning to life. According to Allport, the primary objective in life is not **need reduction,** as so many theorists would have us believe. Rather, it is **need induction** that is important. In other words, healthy adults create problems by formulating future goals, which, in many cases, are unattainable.

> Propriate striving confers unity upon personality, but it is never the unity of fulfillment, of repose, or of reduced tension. The devoted parent never loses con-

cern for his child; the devotee of democracy adopts a lifelong assignment in his human relationships. The scientist, by the very nature of his commitment, creates more and more questions, never fewer. Indeed, the measure of our intellectual maturity, one philosopher suggests, is our capacity to feel less and less satisfied with our answers to better and better problems. (Allport 1955, 67)

> The possession of long-range goals, regarded as central to one's personal existence, distinguishes the human being from the animal, the adult from the child, and in many cases, the healthy personality from the sick. (Allport 1955, 51)

8. Emergence of self as knower (adulthood)   The final stage of development occurs when the self is aware of, unifies, and transcends the preceding seven aspects of the self. In other words, the **self as knower** synthesizes all of the propriate functions. In our daily experience it is most often the case that several, if not all, aspects of the proprium function simultaneously. Allport (1961) gave the following example:

> Suppose that you are facing a difficult and critical examination. No doubt you are aware of your high pulse rate and of the butterflies in your stomach (bodily self); also of the significance of the exam in terms of your past and future (self-identity); of your prideful involvement (self-esteem); of what success or failure may mean to your family (self-extension); of your hopes and aspirations (self-image); of your role as the solver of problems on the examination (rational agent); and of the relevance of the whole situation to your long-range goals (propriate striving). In actual life, then, a fusion of propriate states is the rule. And behind these experienced states of selfhood you catch indirect glimpses of yourself as "knower." (137)

The term *proprium* refers to all eight aspects of the self. The development of the proprium is summarized in Table 7–1.

Conscience.   According to Allport, the conscience emerges along with several aspects of the proprium; especially self-esteem, self-image, and propriate striv-

Table 7–1
Eight Stages of Development of Proprium and Functions Associated with Them

PERIOD OF DEVELOPMENT	PROPRIATE DEVELOPMENT
1. First year	Infant learns that he or she exists, through the many sensations experienced
2. Second year	Child learns that his or her identity remains intact although circumstances change
3. Third year	Feeling of pride results from individual accomplishments
4. Fourth year	Child extends his or her self-image by recognizing that certain objects belong to him or her
5. Fourth to sixth year	Child develops a conscience or a superego; now can deal with the concepts of right and wrong
6. Sixth to twelfth year	Child uses reason and logic to solve complex problems
7. Twelfth year through adolescence	Child formulates future goals and begins to organize his or her life around them
8. Adulthood	Individual who has synthesized the preceding stages of development emerges

ing. Allport sees normal conscience evolving in two stages. First a **must conscience** exists, which is the only kind of conscience a child has. The must conscience evolves out of parental restrictions and prohibitions, which, after becoming internalized, guide behavior even when the parents are not present. On this point, Allport was in agreement with Freud: "There seems to be no doubt that this early stage of conscience is, as Freud argued, due to the internalization of tribal and parental values. Violation causes anxiety and guilt even though immediate punishment does not threaten" (1961, 135).

Gradually must conscience is displaced by **ought conscience.** Must conscience is sustained by fear of punishment, whereas ought conscience is tied closely to the person's proprium. For example, the young adult realizes that if certain long-term goals are to be attained certain experiences ought to be sought out and others avoided. Allport (1961) summarized the distinction between must conscience and ought conscience:

> There remain many "musts" in adulthood, but they spring now from a rational recognition of consequences and are seldom felt any longer as matters of conscience: I *must* obey traffic regulations. I must have the electric wiring repaired. I must not show her my true feelings. But, on the other hand, I *ought* to vote. I ought to write that letter. I ought to study harder. I ought to pursue the good as I see it. These are propriate value-judgments. No one will punish me if I fail to live according to my own preferred style. . . . Mature conscience, then, is a sense of duty to keep one's self-image in an acceptable shape, to continue one's chosen lines of propriate striving—in short, to build (and not tear down) one's style of being. Conscience becomes a kind of generic self-guidance. Emphasis has shifted from tribal and parental control to individual control. (136)

Thus, Allport agreed with Freud concerning the development of must conscience but disagreed with Freud's contention that the internalized values of authority figures guide a person's moral behavior throughout his or her life. Allport did agree that the morality of *some* adults is governed by infantile prohibitions and restrictions, but these adults are unhealthy. Normal adult morality is of the ought variety and is therefore rational, future oriented, and personal.

Functional Autonomy

Allport had four requirements for an adequate theory of motivation.

1. It must recognize the contemporary nature of motives   As we have seen, Allport did not believe that the child is the father of the man, as the psychoanalysts believed. According to Allport, for a motive to be a motive, it must exist in the present. "Whatever moves us," Allport said, "must move us now" (1961, 220).

2. It must allow for the existence of several kinds of motives   Allport believed that to reduce all human motivation to one factor, such as drive reduction or aspiring for superiority, was foolhardy. "Motives are so diverse in type that we find it difficult to discover the common denominator" (1961, 221).

3. It must recognize the importance of cognitive processes   To Allport, it was impossible to truly understand a person's motives without knowing his or her plans, values, and intentions. He believed that perhaps the best way to understand a person's personality structure is to ask: What do you want to be doing five years from now? No other theorist covered thus far put nearly as much trust in a person's cognitive processes as Allport did.

4. It must recognize that each person's pattern of motivation is unique   Just as no two people have the same configuration of traits, neither do they have the same configuration of motives. Because Allport believed that traits initiated behavior, they can be equated with motives. Allport asked: "What is the relation between units of motivation and units of personality? I would suggest that all units of motivation are at the same time units of personality" (1960, 118).

Allport introduced a motivational concept that he felt satisfied the foregoing requirements. This was **functional autonomy,** which he defined as "any acquired system of motivation in which the tensions involved are not of the same kind as the antecedent tensions from which the acquired system developed" (1961, 229).

Functional autonomy, which is probably Allport's most famous concept, simply means that the reasons why an adult now engages in some form of behavior are not the same reasons that originally caused him or her to engage in that behavior. In other words, past motives are not functionally related to present motives. Allport offered the following example:

> A student who first undertakes a field of study in college because it is required, because it pleases the parents, or because it comes at a convenient hour may end by finding himself absorbed in the topic, perhaps for life. The original motives may be entirely lost. What was a means to an end becomes an end in itself. (1961, 235–36)

Allport believed that when motives became part of the proprium they were pursued for their own sake and not for external encouragement or reward. Such motives are self-sustaining because they have become part of the person. To say that healthy adults pursue goals because they are rewarded for doing so was, to Allport, ridiculous. For example, Allport commented:

> How hollow to think of Pasteur's concern for reward, or for health, food, sleep, or family, as the root of his devotion to his work. For long periods of time he was oblivious to them all, losing himself in the white heat of research. And the same passion is seen in the histories of geniuses who in their lifetimes received little or no reward for their work. (1961, 236)

Allport distinguished between two kinds of functional autonomy: (1) **Perseverative functional autonomy** refers to repetitious activities in which one blindly engages and that once served a purpose but no longer do so. These activities occur independently of reward and independently of the past but are low-level activities of little importance. An example would be when a man still rises at 7:30 each morning although he has been retired for some time. (2) **Propriate functional autonomy** refers to an individual's interests, values, goals, attitudes, and sentiments.

Allport suggested that propriate functional autonomy was governed by three principles.

1. Principle of organizing energy level   This principle states that when one needs no longer to be concerned with survival and early adjustments in life, a considerable amount of energy becomes available to that person. Because this energy is no longer needed for basic adaptation, it can be diverted into propriate striving—for instance, future goals.

2. Principle of mastery and competence   There is an innate need for healthy adults to increase their efficiency and effectiveness and to aspire to greater mastery. In other words, according to Allport, healthy humans have a need to become better and better at more and more tasks. This is another case of drive induction, instead of drive reduction.

3. Principle of propriate patterning   The person's proprium is the frame of reference, which determines what is pursued in life and what is rejected. This means that although motives become functionally independent of the past, they do not become independent of the proprium. In other words, all motives must be compatible with the total self (proprium). This assures the consistency and the integration of the personality.

Not all behavior is caused by functionally autonomous motives. Much human behavior is stimulated by biologic drives, reflex action, reinforcement, and habit. Allport recognized this but felt that behavior under the control of functionally autonomous motives was characteristically human and therefore should be the personality theorist's focus of study.

The Healthy, Mature Adult Personality

Allport's theory did not grow out of psychoanalysis. In fact, he was not a psychotherapist and was not interested in emotionally disturbed people. He felt strongly that the principles governing the healthy, adult personality could not be learned by studying animals, children, the past, or neurotics. According to Allport, the difference between a neurotic and a healthy person is that the former's motives lie in the past, whereas the latter's lie in the future.

The concern that Allport had for studying healthy humans instead of neurotics is remarkably close to the position taken more recently by Maslow (see chapter 15). Maslow believed that psychologists, by being overconcerned with emotionally disturbed persons, were incapable of understanding healthy, exceptional persons. Maslow attempted to correct the situation by exploring the lives of what he called self-actualizing people. The list of characteristics that Maslow found such persons to possess is similar to the following list of attributes that Allport believed characterized the normal, healthy adult.

1. Capacity for self-extension   Healthy adults participate in a wide range of events. They have many friends and hobbies and tend to be active politically or religiously.

2. Capacity for warm human interactions Healthy adults are capable of intimate relationships with others without being possessive or jealous. Such people are compassionate, as evidenced by their ability to tolerate major differences in values and beliefs between themselves and others.

3. Demonstration of emotional security and self-acceptance Healthy adults have the tolerance necessary to accept the conflicts and frustrations inevitable in life. They also have a positive image of themselves. This is contrasted with the immature person, who is filled with self-pity and who has a negative self-image.

4. Demonstration of realistic perceptions Healthy adults see events as they are, not as they hoped they would be. Such persons display good common sense when appraising a situation and in determining adjustments to it.

5. Demonstration of self-objectification Healthy adults have an accurate picture of their own assets and liabilities. They also have a good sense of humor. Humor necessitates the ability to laugh at what one cherishes, including oneself. Persons who are not sure of themselves see nothing funny about jokes directed at them or at what they believe.

6. Demonstration of unifying philosophy of life According to Allport, the lives of healthy adults are "ordered or steered toward some selected goal or goals. Each person has something quite special to live for, a major intention" (1961, 294–95).

Allport, like Jung and Erikson and to a somewhat lesser degree like Adler, placed great importance on religion; and like Jung, Allport believed that the importance of religion can be realized only in adulthood. Allport believed that all healthy adults have a need for some unifying orientation, and although this orientation is commonly religious in nature it does not need to be.

> Psychologically speaking we should point to the close analogy that exists between a religious orientation and all other high-level schemata that influence the course of becoming. Every man, whether he is religiously inclined or not, has his own ultimate presuppositions. He finds he cannot live his life without them, and for him they are true. Such presuppositions, whether they are called ideologies, philosophies, notions, or merely hunches about life, exert creative pressure upon all conduct that is subsidiary to them (which is to say, upon nearly *all* of a man's conduct). (Allport 1955, 95–96)

We will have more to say about Allport's views on religion below, but first we will say a few words about Allport's view of the unhealthy individual.

Unhealthy Persons. According to Allport, the healthy person is one who displays the six characteristics listed earlier and who is in a constant state of becoming. Such a person is future oriented. The unhealthy person is one whose growth has been stifled. The motives of unhealthy persons are often found in his or her past rather than in the present. In his explanation of why some children develop into unhealthy adults, Allport essentially accepted Horney's position.

> All in all a generous minimum of security seems required in early years for a start toward a productive life-style. Without it the individual develops a pathological craving for security, and is less able than others to tolerate setbacks in maturity. Through his insistent demanding, jealousy, depredations, and egoism he betrays

the craving that still haunts him. By contrast, the child who receives adequate gratification of his infant needs is more likely to be prepared to give up his habits of demanding, and to learn tolerance for his later frustrations. Having completed successfully one stage of development he is free to abandon the habits appropriate to this stage and to enter the mature reaches of becoming. Having known acceptance in an affectionate environment he learns more readily to accept himself, to tolerate the ways of the world, and to handle the conflicts of later life in a mature manner. (1955, 32)

To overcome his or her difficulties, the unhealthy person must experience the love that he or she missed early in life. This love can be provided by family, friends, or a therapist. In any case, "Love received and love given comprise the best form of therapy" (Allport 1955, 33).

It is important to note that, according to Allport, the unhealthy person becomes healthy when he or she begins living in accordance with his or her proprium—that is, in accordance with his or her own personal goals, values, and aspirations. Health, therefore, is not defined in terms of adjustment to societal standards. In fact, conformity to societal standards can cause otherwise healthy persons to become unhealthy or such conformity can make unhealthy persons even more unhealthy. Allport explained why:

Society itself is sick. Why then make a patient content with its injustices, hypocrisies, and wars? And to what society shall we adjust the patient? To his social class, thus making him provincial and depriving him of aspiration? To his nation, thus giving him no vision of mankind as a whole? It is doubtful that we can accept society (any society) as a standard for a healthy personality. A head-hunter society demands well-adjusted head-hunters as citizens, but is the deviant in this group who questions the value of decapitation necessarily an immature human being? (1961, 305)

Religion

Freud viewed the need for religion as a characteristic of the weak or the neurotic, whereas Allport believed that a religious orientation often characterizes the healthy adult personality. Allport believed, however, that embracing some forms of religion was beneficial and embracing other forms was harmful. In other words, for Allport, there was healthy religion and unhealthy religion.

Extrinsic Religion

Extrinsic religion is unhealthy religion. It is immature and is often a carryover from childhood. Such religion constructs a deity who favors the interests of those who believe in him, "like a Santa Claus or an overindulgent father. Or the sentiment may be of a tribal sort: 'My church is better than your church. God prefers my people to your people' " (Allport 1961, 300). Extrinsic religion is often embraced because it is superficially useful. For example, membership in a church can be used to make business contacts or to become a respected member of the community. Extrinsic religion tends to be a divisive factor in a person's life rather than a unifying theme. In fact, embracing extrinsic religion creates an individual who lacks most, if not all, of the criteria of a healthy, mature adult.

> Studies show that ethnic prejudice is more common among churchgoers than among nonchurchgoers. This fact alone shows that religion is often divisive rather than unifying. Extrinsic religion lends support to exclusions, prejudices, hatreds that negate all our criteria of maturity. The self is not extended; there is no warm relating of self to others, no emotional security, no realistic perception, no self-insight or humor. (Allport 1961, 300)

Insofar as Freud criticized extrinsic religion, Allport agreed with him.

Intrinsic Religion

Intrinsic religion is healthy religion. Intrinsic religion motivates a person to seek and follow the value underlying all reality for its own sake and as an end in itself; directs the course of a person's life and development; facilitates the realization that many important experiences transcend one's own existence; provides a possible explanation for the many mysteries that characterize human existence, such as the fact that human behavior appears to be both free and determined, the simultaneous existence of good and evil, and the fact that the innocent often suffer; and creates a perspective within which to evaluate one's self and organize one's life. Intrinsic religion encourages an identification with all of humanity, not just with those who share one's beliefs. By providing a means by which a person can relate meaningfully to the totality of existence, intrinsic religion provides the kind of unifying theme that characterizes the healthy, mature adult personality.

Letters from Jenny

Given Allport's emphasis on the individual, how does one go about attempting to understand a specific person's personality? Allport believed that one of the best ways was to use **personal documents,** such as diaries, autobiographies, letters, or interviews. Allport's most thorough use of personal documents to describe an individual's personality was a collection of 301 letters written by Jenny Grove Masterson (a pseudonym) during an eleven-year period. The final version of this study was published as *Letters from Jenny* in 1965, although Allport had worked on the case for a number of years prior to that time.

Jenny was born in Ireland in 1868 and moved to Canada when she was five. She had five younger sisters and one younger brother, all of whom were very dependent on her, since her father had died when she was eighteen. Jenny outraged her family when she married a railway inspector, who had been married previously. She and her husband moved to Chicago, where she described life as boring. Her husband died in 1897, when she was twenty-nine years old. Shortly after her husband's death, Jenny gave birth to her only child, whom she named Ross. She worked hard and devoted herself to Ross. Until Ross was seventeen, he and his mother were very close, but at that time he left to go to Princeton. In his sophomore year Ross enlisted in the army, in the Ambulance Corps. Before his going overseas to France, Jenny visited Ross at Princeton and met two of his friends, Glenn and Isabel. It was with Glenn and Isabel that Jenny was later to correspond.

When Ross returned home, he had changed completely, and, except for finishing his degree at Princeton, his life was characterized by a series of failures and quarrels with his mother. The most intense quarrel followed Jenny's discovery of Ross's secret marriage. On this Allport commented: "On his first visit to her following her discovery she drove him out of her room with violent denunciations and a threat to have him arrested if he ever tried to see her again" (1965, 6).

Following this encounter, Jenny contacted Ross's old friends, Glenn and Isabel, who were now married and teaching in an eastern college town. They offered "to keep in touch" with Jenny, and the result was 301 letters. The correspondence started in March 1926, when Jenny was fifty-eight, and continued until October 1937, when Jenny died, at the age of seventy. She outlived her son Ross by eight years.

The letters are intriguing, and the reader is urged to read all of them. Two samples are given below to indicate the tone of the correspondence. In a letter dated 5 January, 1927, Jenny described her childhood as follows:

> My father dropped dead one day, and had no provision made for his family—7 of them, all under 18. Not one in the house capable of earning a penny. It was my salary that kept the house going. . . . No one ever denied it, or pretended to think otherwise, and when I dared to marry the man I had been in love with for years, but dreaded to take my money out of their house . . . why, they said I was like the cow that gave the milk and then kicked the pail. (Allport 1965, 27)

Jenny displays pessimism in a letter she wrote in June 1928:

> Anyway I am firmly convinced that I am "through" and ought to step out. I have done all, of any use, that it is possible for me to do in this world. Whether it was for good or bad it is over and done and nothing can change it now, "The moving finger writes, and having writ moves on" and my days for possible usefulness are past. I should step out, but am a coward. To suppose that Ross needs me would be indeed a joke. (Allport 1965, 50)

Allport had thirty-six judges read the letters in sequence, and they, along with Allport, used 198 trait names to describe Jenny. But when synonymous traits were lumped together, it was observed that Jenny could be described accurately using eight trait names. They were:

1. Quarrelsome—suspicious
2. Self-centered
3. Independent
4. Dramatic
5. Artistic
6. Aggressive

7. Cynical
8. Sentimental

Using a computer, Paige (1966) made a complex statistical factor analysis of Jenny's letters and isolated eight "factors" characterizing them.

1. Aggression
2. Possessiveness
3. Need for Affiliation
4. Need for Autonomy
5. Need for Familial Acceptance
6. Sexuality
7. Sentience (love of art, literature, etc.)
8. Martyrdom

On reviewing Paige's study, Allport concluded that nothing had been gained by using a computer. In fact, he thought that the subjective impressions of the judges were more informative.

There is probably no better example of what Allport meant by idiographic research than his analysis of Jenny's letters. It is because of this type of research that Allport has been accused of being more of an artist than a scientist.

Besides his studies of religion, prejudice, rumor, and his extensive idiographic study of Jenny through her letters, Allport also investigated expressive behavior and values. His studies of both expressive behavior and values retained his emphasis on the importance of the individual. His research on expressive behavior, for example, investigated a person's unique facial expressions, style of walking, speech mannerisms, and handwriting (see Allport and Vernon 1933; Allport and Cantril 1934). His *Study of Values*, first published with Vernon in 1931, is now in its third edition. To study values, Allport and his collaborators (Allport, Vernon, and Lindzey 1960) devised a scale that attempted to determine the extent to which a person emphasized the following values in his or her life:

1. *Theoretical*. The person emphasizing this value is primarily concerned with the search for truth.
2. *Economic*. The person emphasizing this value is very pragmatic and interested in the relevance of knowledge.
3. *Aesthetic*. The person emphasizing this value is strongly inclined toward artistic experiences.
4. *Social*. The person emphasizing this value gives high priority to developing and maintaining warm human relationships.
5. *Political*. The person emphasizing this value is primarily interested in attaining power.
6. *Religious*. The person emphasizing this value gives great importance to seeking unity and harmony in the universe.

Allport, Vernon, and Lindzey (1960) report that the scale produced the expected results; for example, clergymen scored highest on the religious value, art students scored highest on the aesthetic value, and business students scored highest on the economic value.

Evaluation

Empirical Research

Allport was the first to describe the personality in terms of traits, and therefore, the thousands of studies done involving personality traits can be seen as deriving from his theory. Also, Allport and his colleagues did more research to test their theoretical notions than any other personality theorists covered thus far in this text. They did extensive research on expressive behavior and provided one of the few tools by which to study human values. Although Allport's scale of values is more than fifty years old this simple, straightforward instrument is still being used. For example, Huntley and Davis (1983) found that physicians scored high on theoretical and social values and business people scored high on political and economic values. It is interesting that the value measures were obtained when the physicians and business people were still undergraduate college students twenty-five years earlier. Allport's early interest in expressive behavior is now reflected in numerous experiments on nonverbal communication and body language. (See Harper, Wiens, and Matarazzo 1978 for a review of such studies.) The idiographic approach to studying personality is currently represented among respected personality theorists (see, for example, Bem and Allen 1974). Also Wrightman (1981) has urged that researchers return to the use of personal documents as an aid in understanding personality.

Criticisms

Lack of Scientific Rigor.   Allport's theory was consistently criticized for being unscientific. Because all sciences seek to discover general laws, usually by using nomothetic methods, Allport's emphasis on the idiographic method, in which the single case is studied intensively, seemed unscientific. Furthermore, the study and understanding of *unique* individuals does not produce principles by which human behavior can be understood in general. For many, Allport's insistence on studying unique individuals is more like art than science. For example, the study of Jenny's letters may be interesting and pleasing, but unless it is possible to generalize what is found to other people, such a study is scientifically useless.

Circularity.   In Allport's theory traits are inferred from behavior and then are used to explain the very behavior that they were inferred from. For example, if we say that Linda is aggressive because she hit Bud, we cannot then say that Linda hit Bud because she is aggressive. Such circular reasoning tells us nothing about the cause of aggressiveness. Likewise, if a person acts suspicious in a variety of situations, we conclude that he or she possesses the trait of suspiciousness. When then asked *why* she acts suspiciously we say it is *because* she possesses the trait of suspiciousness. In other words, it cannot be claimed that someone acts suspiciously because they are suspicious. For Allport traits were used to both describe and explain behavior and that is circular.

Absence of Theory.   Some claim that Allport did an admirable job of describing personality but failed to explain it. A person's personality is described in terms of traits or dispositions arranged in a hierarchy, but little is said about how specific traits or dispositions develop or change.

Denial of Important Facts about and Approaches to Study of Personality. Allport was criticized for assuming a discontinuity between animals and humans, between child and adult, and between normal and abnormal. He was criticized for placing too much emphasis on the conscious mind at the expense of the unconscious mind and for stressing internal causes of behavior at the expense of external causes. Probably Allport's most severely criticized concept was functional autonomy. When most, if not all, accepted viewpoints in psychology were attempting to determine the relationship between early experience and adult personality, Allport claimed that such a relationship did not exist.

On the matter of unconscious motivation, it is ironic that the very experience that Allport had with Freud that caused Allport to mistrust depth psychology may in fact have supported it. The reader may remember that during his visit with Freud, Allport attempted to disrupt the awkward silence by relating the story of the little boy that he observed on the way to Freud's office who apparently had a strong aversion to dirt. On completing his story Freud inquired, "And was that little boy you?" Allport was flabbergasted and concluded that Freud had misinterpreted the significance of the whole incident. Allport told this story many times throughout his lifetime to demonstrate the ineffectiveness of psychoanalytic procedures. Faber (1970), however, suggests that Allport chose that particular story (of many that were possible) because of his preconceptions that Freud liked to hear "dirty" stories. Allport felt "naughty" in presuming to call on Freud, and he manifested this naughtiness by "pulling a dirty trick" on Freud. According to Faber, Freud saw through the entire situation and with his question attempted to put the conversation on a more honest level. Furthermore, Elms (1972) points out that Allport himself was a neat, orderly, punctual, and meticulous person. In fact, Allport was preoccupied with cleanliness and was known as "Mr. Clean Personality." According to Elms, Freud immediately saw Allport's "pathological" concern with dirt, and therefore his question to Allport was not as far off the mark as Allport suggested. Elms claims that Allport tried to change the topic immediately after Freud's question because Allport knew unconsciously that Freud was correct. Such insights demonstrate either that Allport was wrong in rejecting the importance of unconscious motivation, or that nothing exists that psychoanalytic theory cannot explain after the fact.

Inconsistency of Behavior Precludes Description in Terms of Traits.   As we have seen, Allport deduced the existence of traits or personal dispositions from consistencies in behavior. Although Allport believed that traits or personal dispositions allow a range of behaviors that are situationally determined, he still assumed considerable consistency in behavior across time and similar situations. Mischel (1968) examined Allport's assumption and concluded, "With the possible exception of intelligence, highly generalized behavioral consistencies have not been demonstrated and the concept of personality traits as broad response predispositions is thus untenable" (146). We will say more about Mischel's conclusion and reactions to it in chapter 11.

Behavioristic Critique.   The behaviorists believe that behavior should be explained in terms of environmental stimuli. The postulating of inner mechanisms such as instincts, an unconscious mind, or traits just creates additional mysteries that need to be explained. Once it is known that certain environmental conditions tend to produce certain kinds of behavior, the explanation is complete. To say that traits (or anything else) intervene between the environment and behavior is, at best, irrelevant. We will say more about the behavioristic position when we review Skinner's position in chapter 9.

Contributions

Original Concepts and Methodologies.   Allport pioneered the social psychological studies of such complex topics as prejudice, religion, rumor, and values. Also, he did more than anyone to define and clarify the concept of trait. Furthermore, Allport showed that a great deal could be learned about a person by using the straightforward methods of self-reports, personal documents, and the observation of expressive behavior. "Too often," Allport said, "we fail to consult the richest of all sources of data, namely, the subject's own self-knowledge" (1962, 413). Allport was willing to use whatever method he believed contributed to an understanding of human behavior. "Whatever contributes to a knowledge of human nature," he said, "is an admissible method to science" (1942, 140). Allport then facilitated the spirit of eclecticism that characterizes contemporary psychology.

Refreshingly New Way of Viewing Personality.   Like Adler's, Allport's theory can be considered a forerunner of the existential-humanistic theories that we will review in chapters 13 to 16. All such theories have in common the emphasis on the uniqueness of the individual, the belief that human motives are not merely biologic in nature, that humans are future oriented, and that psychology should be socially relevant. Allport believed in all of these statements. In fact, Allport resisted many extremely powerful trends in psychology because he believed that they caused humans to lose their individuality. The healthy person that Allport envisioned creates tension in his or her life by creating future goals, is rational, possesses an "ought" rather than a "must" conscience and if he or she is religious, it is intrinsic rather than extrinsic religion that is embraced. Allport's major concern, however, was with the dignity and uniqueness of each human being. He concluded in his 1961 book with the following statement:

> Psychology is truly itself only when it can deal with individuality. . . . We study the human person most fully when we take him as an individual. He is more than a bundle of habits, more than a point of intersection of abstract dimensions. He is more than a representative of his species, more than a citizen of the State, more than an incident in the movements of mankind. He transcends them all. The individual, striving ever for integrity and fulfillment, has existed under all forms of social life—forms as varied as the nomadic and feudal, capitalistic and communistic. No society holds together for long without the respect man shows to man. The individual today struggles on even under oppression, always hoping and planning for a more perfect democracy where the dignity and growth of each personality will be prized above all else. (573)

Summary

Allport was America's first personality theorist. In his 1937 definition of personality, he emphasized that personality was dynamic, organized, and unique. He also said that personality was real in that it both initiates and guides behavior. He distinguished between personality and character, which implies evaluation; temperament, which with intelligence and physique are the innate "raw materials" from which personality is constructed; and type, which is a classification used by one person to categorize another person. Allport theorized that traits provided the structure, the uniqueness, and the motivation that characterize a person's personality. Individual traits refer to those patterns of traits that characterize individuals and also the way in which a particular trait, such as aggressiveness, manifests itself in a particular individual's personality. What Allport originally called individual traits he later renamed personality dispositions, to avoid their confusion with common traits. Common traits are those that characterize groups of individuals.

Nomothetic methods are used to examine what people have in common, and the idiographic method is used to discover what is true about the individual. Because not all personal dispositions have the same influence on one's behavior, Allport distinguished between cardinal dispositions, which influence just about everything a person does; central dispositions, of which everyone has five to ten; and secondary dispositions, which are only slightly more general than a complex habit.

Allport believed that the mature adult personality matured slowly, through eight stages. The major attributes that emerge during each stage are: (1) the bodily self, (2) self-identity, (3) self-esteem, (4) self-extension, (5) self-image, (6) self as rational coper, (7) propriate striving; and (8) self as knower.

Allport distinguished between must conscience, which exists when a child's or an unhealthy adult's moral behavior is guided by the internalized values of authority figures and ought conscience, which exists when a person's moral behavior is guided by personal values and propriate strivings. Allport's most controversial concept was functional autonomy, which stated that although one set of circumstances originally may have explained the existence of a motive, that motive can exist in an adult independently of those earlier circumstances. In other words, what was once a means to an end can become an end in itself.

Allport was not very interested in studying animals, children, or neurotics. He was mainly interested in healthy, adult humans whom he believed had the following characteristics: (1) self-extension, (2) warm human interactions, (3) emotional security and self-acceptance, (4) realistic perceptions, (5) self-objectification, and (6) a unifying philosophy of life.

Allport agreed with Horney that the unhealthy person is one whose positive growth has been stifled by a lack of childhood security. To overcome the damage done by the lack of security the person must feel loved by family, friends, or a therapist. In addition to becoming unhealthy because of a lack of security, persons can also become unhealthy by conforming too much to the mores of society. This is because societies themselves can be sick. Religion too can be either healthy or unhealthy. Extrinsic religion is superficial and not conducive to personal growth; untrinsic religion involves the honest quest for meaning and a higher purpose in life, and can provide the kind of unifying philosophy of life that characterizes the personalities of healthy persons.

Letters from Jenny (1965) summarized Allport's major idiographic research project, in which a woman's dispositions were studied through the 301 letters she had written during an eleven-year period. Allport and his colleagues also did extensive research on expressive behavior and created a scale by which human values could be measured. Allport's influence on current research on personality can be seen in the popularity of the concept of trait, a call for greater use of personal documents in assessing personality, a re-emergence of idiographic research, and the popularity of experiments on nonverbal communication and body language.

Allport's theory has been criticized for being unscientific; being circular; not being a true theory; ignoring important facts about personality such as unconscious motivation and early experience; predicting that human behavior is more consistent than it actually is; and for postulating inner mechanisms that confuse rather than clarify our understanding of personality. Allport's theory has been praised for being the first to study such important topics as rumor, prejudice, and values; showing the benefits of accepting at face value personal reports and documents; using expressive behaviors in assessing personality; and for doing much to promote what is now called existential-humanistic psychology.

EXPERIENTIAL EXERCISES

1. Apply Allport's criteria for a mature, healthy personality to yourself. First, list the criterion that characterizes you the most, then second most, and so on. Be sure to elaborate on your unifying philosophy of life, if such a philosophy characterizes your life. Using Allport's criteria, do you think that you are a mature, healthy person? What, if anything, still needs working on?

2. Allport distinguished between extrinsic religion and intrinsic religion. Review his distinction and then indicate whether or not religion plays an important role in your life. If so, is it extrinsic or intrinsic religion?

3. According to Allport, the motives of healthy adults are grounded in the present, not in the past. In other words, their motives have become functionally autonomous or independent from the motivational forces that originally created them. Give two examples of functionally autonomous motives in your life. Describe what originally supported these motives and what supports them now.

4. Describe your own personality in terms of cardinal, central, and secondary dispositions. Because having a cardinal disposition is rare, you may need to start your self-description with a list of your central dispositions. According to Allport, the average college student has about seven central dispositions.

5. Allport was interested in all forms of expressive behavior including handwriting, doodles, gestures, and gait (walking style). He believed that such behavior reflected a person's unique cluster of personal dispositions. Analyze your own body language and nonverbal behavior, and also have a close friend observe and record your mannerisms and then compare notes. What consistencies were observed in your expressive behavior? What do they say about your personality?

6. Allport asserted that a qualitative difference exists between healthy, mature adults and neurotics, psychotics, and children. Based on your personal experience, explain why you either agree or disagree with Allport's assertion.

DISCUSSION QUESTIONS

1. First state Allport's definition of personality and then discuss each of the definition's major components.
2. Distinguish among the terms personality, character, temperament, and type.
3. Outline Allport's criteria for an adequate personality theory.
4. Describe Allport's concepts of trait and personal disposition. In your answer describe the various kinds of personal dispositions.
5. Distinguish among personal dispositions, habits, and attitudes.
6. Distinguish between nomothetic and idiographic research techniques.
7. List and describe the stages in the development of the proprium.
8. Discuss Allport's concept of functional autonomy.
9. List and describe the six characteristics of a normal, healthy, mature adult.
10. Summarize Allport's idiographic study of Jenny.
11. Explain why Allport had the attitude he did toward the use of lower animals, children, and neurotics as sources of information about personality.
12. Differentiate between must conscience and ought conscience and give an example of each.
13. Differentiate between extrinsic religion and intrinsic religion, and give an example of each.
14. List the criticisms of Allport's theory.
15. List the contributions of Allport's theory.

SUGGESTIONS FOR FURTHER READING

ALLPORT, G. W. (1937). *Personality: A Psychological Interpretation.* New York: Henry Holt.

> This was Allport's first major contribution and continues to be valuable as an introduction to his early ideas. This book established Allport as a pioneer in the realm of personality theory.

ALLPORT, G. W., and LEO POSTMAN (1947). *The Psychology of Rumor.* New York: Holt, Rinehart and Winston.

> A summary of Allport's and Postman's research on rumor transmission.

ALLPORT, G. W. (1950). *The Individual and His Religion.* New York: Macmillan.

> Allport's views on the function of religion in the mature, healthy personality.

ALLPORT, G. W. (1955). *Becoming: Basic Considerations for a Psychology of Personality.* New Haven, CT: Yale University Press.

> Contains a historical-philosophical survey of the use of the concept of self. The book discusses the evolution of the self, the requirements for maturity, the social aspects of behavior, and the future orientation of the healthy individual.

ALLPORT, G. W. (1961). *Pattern and Growth in Personality.* New York: Holt, Rinehart and Winston.

> A revision of Allport's 1937 book, which reflects his changing conceptions of such important concepts as functional autonomy and individual traits. He introduces his concept of personal disposition in this book.

ALLPORT, G. W. (1965). *Letters From Jenny.* New York: Harcourt, Brace and World.

> Jenny Masterson's letters are presented and analyzed according to Allport's theory as well as several other personality theories.

ALLPORT, G. W. (1967). "Autobiography," in *A History of Psychology in Autobiography,* vol. 5, ed. E. G. Boring and G. Lindzey. New York: Appleton-Century-Crofts.

> A most interesting autobiography. Allport discusses the personal events in his life that shaped his theory of personality.

GLOSSARY

Attitude. Attitudes, like habits, are much more specific than traits. One can, for example, have a favorable attitude toward boxing, but this is only a single manifestation of the more general trait of aggressiveness.

Becoming. Allport's description of the process by which the proprium develops. According to Allport, personality is never static; rather, it is always becoming something else.

Bodily "me." The attribute that emerges during the first stage in the development of the proprium. At this stage, infants learn that their bodies exist because of their sensory experience.

Capacity for self-extension. The participation in a wide range of events that characterizes the healthy, mature adult.

Capacity for warm, human interactions. The ability to have intimate relationships with others without being possessive or jealous. Such an ability characterizes the healthy, mature adult.

Cardinal dispositions. A "ruling passion" that influences almost everything a person does. Only a few individuals possess a cardinal disposition.

Central dispositions. Those qualities about a person that you would mention in a letter of recommendation. The five to ten characteristics that summarize a particular person's personality.

Character. A description of a person that includes a value judgment. A person's character can be "good" or "bad," whereas a personality cannot be.

Common traits. Traits used to describe a group of individuals.

Emotional security and self-acceptance. Two of the characteristics of a healthy, mature adult.

Extrinsic religion. Superficial religion that is participated in for entirely selfish, pragmatic reasons. Allport considered such religion to be unhealthy.

Functional autonomy. A motive that existed once for some practical reason later exists for its own sake. In other words, a motive that was once a means to an end becomes an end in itself. Allport's most famous and controversial concept.

Habit. A specific mode of responding—for example, putting on clean clothing in the morning—that develops because a more general trait exists—for example, the trait of cleanliness.

Idiographic method. A research method that studies a single case in great detail and depth.

Individual traits. Either the unique pattern of traits possessed by an individual or the unique way that a particular trait manifests itself in the personality of a particular person. For example, a particular person's way of displaying aggressiveness. Later in the development of his theory, Allport changed the term individual trait to personal disposition.

Intrinsic religion. Religion that seeks a higher meaning and purpose in life and provides possible answers to the many mysteries that characterize human existence. Allport considered such religion to be healthy.

Must conscience. The moral guide used by children whereby their moral judgments are determined by the internalized values of authority figures such as the parents. The must conscience is very much like the superego postulated by Freud.

Need induction. The creation of needs rather than their reduction. Allport believed that the healthy human lives in accordance with long-term goals, which create more problems than they solve. Thus, his theory is said to emphasize need induction rather than need reduction.

Need reduction. The satisfaction of a basic need. To many theorists, the elimination or reduction of needs is the primary goal in life. Allport did not agree.

Nomothetic method. A research method that studies groups of individuals and therefore concentrates on average performance rather than on the performance of a single individual.

Ought conscience. The moral guide used by normal, healthy adults whereby their moral judgments are governed by their own personal values and propriate strivings.

Perseverative functional autonomy. Low-level habits retained even though they are no longer functional.

Personal disposition. Identical to an individual trait. The term individual trait was changed to personal disposition to avoid confusion with the term common trait.

Personal documents. To Allport, one of the best ways to study an individual's personality was to examine personal documents, such as diaries, autobiographies, and letters.

Personality. According to Allport, personality is the dynamic organization within the individual of those psychophysical systems that determine characteristic behavior and thought.

Principle of mastery and competence. The principle that states that an innate need exists for humans to aspire to greater mastery and competence.

Principle of organizing the energy level. The principle that states that energy that was once used for survival can be changed into concern for the future, when survival is no longer an issue.

Principle of propriate patterning. The principle that states that the proprium is the frame of reference that is used by a person in determining what is worth pursuing and what is not.

Propriate functional autonomy. The important motives around which one organizes one's life. Such motives are independent of the conditions that originally produced them.

Propriate striving. The attribute that emerges during the seventh stage in the development of the proprium. At this stage, the adolescent becomes almost completely future oriented.

Proprium. All the facts about a person that make him or her unique.

Raw materials of personality. Temperament, intelligence, and physique.

Realistic perceptions. Those accurate perceptions that characterize the healthy, mature adult.

Secondary dispositions. More specific than cardinal or central dispositions but still more general than habits and attitudes. A secondary disposition may be a person's preference for loud clothing or for sweet food.

Self as a rational coper. The attribute that emerges during the sixth stage in the development of the proprium. At this stage, the child begins to use complex mental operations (thinking) to solve problems.

Self as knower. The attribute that emerges during the eighth and final stage in the development of the proprium. At this stage, the proprium is aware of, unifies, and transcends the preceding seven aspects of the proprium.

Self-esteem. The attribute that emerges during the third stage in the development of the proprium. At this stage, the child develops a feeling of pride by doing things on his or her own.

Self-extension. The attribute that emerges during the fourth stage in the development of the proprium. At this stage, the child's self-identity generalizes to external objects.

Self-identity. The attribute that emerges during the second stage in the development of the proprium. At this stage, the child develops a self-identity; for example, realizing that he or she is the same person although conditions change.

Self-image. The attribute that emerges during the fifth stage in the development of the proprium. At this stage, the child develops a conscience and begins to formulate future goals.

Self-objectification. The honest appraisal of one's assets and liabilities that characterizes the healthy, mature adult. A person with self-objectification typically has a good sense of humor.

Temperament. One of the raw materials from which personality is shaped. Temperament is the emotional component of the personality.

Trait. A mental structure that initiates and guides reactions and thus accounts for the consistency in one's behavior.

Type. A category into which one person can be placed by another person. To label a person as "an aggressive type" is to place him or her in a descriptive category based on behavior.

Unifying philosophy of life. The unifying theme that holds together the life of a healthy, mature adult and gives it meaning. Such a theme is often religious in nature, but, according to Allport, it does not need to be.

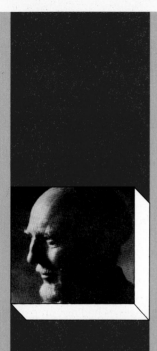

8

Raymond B. Cattell

Raymond B. Cattell was born in Staffordshire, England, on 20 March 1905. He remembers his childhood as a happy one, with an abundance of such activities as exploring caves, swimming, and sailing. He does report considerable competition with his brother, however, who was three years older. The fact that England entered World War I when Cattell was nine years old had a major effect on his life. Seeing hundreds of wounded soldiers treated in a nearby house that had been converted into a hospital taught him that life could be short and that one should accomplish as much as possible while one could. As we shall see, this sense of urgency about work has characterized Cattell throughout his academic life.

At sixteen Cattell entered the University of London, where he majored in physics and chemistry. He graduated at nineteen with high honors. Throughout his undergraduate years Cattell became increasingly concerned with social problems and increasingly aware that his background in the natural sciences had not prepared him to deal with those problems. These realizations prompted him to enter graduate school in psychology at the University of London, where he ultimately earned his M.A. and Ph.D. degrees. While in graduate school, he worked with the famous psychologist-statistician Charles E. Spearman, who invented the technique of factor analysis and applied it to the study of intelligence. As we shall see, Cattell used factor analysis extensively in his study of personality.

After receiving his Ph.D., Cattell had great difficulty finding work doing what he had been trained to do, so he accepted a number of what he called "fringe" jobs. He was a lecturer at the University of Exeter in England (1927 to 1932), and he was the founder and director of a psychology clinic in the school system in the city of Leicester, England (1932 to 1937). In 1937 he was invited by the prominent American psychologist Edward L. Thorndike to come to America to become his research associate at Columbia University. Cattell accepted Thorndike's invitation and remembers his first year in New York as depressing because he deeply missed England.

From 1938 to 1941, Cattell was the G. Stanley Hall Professor of Genetic Psychology at Clark University in Worcester, Massachusetts. In 1941 he moved to Harvard, where he was a lecturer until 1944.

In the years following graduate school, Cattell never lost interest in applying the statistical technique of factor analysis to the study of personality. Finally, at the age of forty, in 1945, Cattell was offered a position at the University of Illinois as research professor and director of the Laboratory of Personality and Group Analysis. Cattell's professional output while he was at the University of Illinois (1945 to 1973) was almost unbelievable. Without teaching responsibilities Cattell was finally able to pursue his ambition of scientifically determining the structure of personality. Cattell pursued his goal until at least 11:00 P.M. every night and observed that his car was easy for him to find in the parking lot because it was the only one left.

Cattell married Monica Rogers on 1 December, 1930, and had one son, who is now a surgeon. His wife left him a few years after their marriage, because of their poverty and because of his total dedication to his work. He was married again, on 2 April, 1946, to Alberta Karen Schuetter, a mathematician, with whom he eventually had three daughters and a son.

As already mentioned, early in life Cattell developed the belief that one should work hard and not waste time. Thus far, Cattell has published more than 350 professional articles and more than thirty books. Cattell's first article was published in 1928, when he was twenty-three years old. This means that he has published an average of a book or an article every other month for the last sixty years. It is not only the quantity of Cattell's work that is impressive, but its quality as well. His work at the Laboratory of Personality and Group Analysis has won him worldwide recognition as a personality theorist.

In 1953, Cattell wrote an essay on the psychology of the researcher, which won the Wenner-Gren prize, given by the New York Academy of Science, and he has held the Darwin Fellowship for Genetic Research. The scope of Cattell's research interests is evident when one considers that he has published articles in American, British, Australian, Japanese, Indian, and African journals.

In 1973 he established the Institute for Research on Morality and Self-Realization in Boulder, Colorado, where he pursued his lifelong interest in social problems. Since 1977 Cattell has been a visiting professor at the University of Hawaii at Monoa, as well as professor emeritus at the University of Illinois.

Factor Analysis

It seems fair to say that Cattell's theory of personality has not become overwhelmingly popular among those studying personality. His theory is indeed highly informative and in many ways unique among the personality theories, but its lack of wide acceptance can be explained by two facts. First, the sheer bulk of Cattell's

Raymond B. Cattell

work has made it impossible for the "outsider" to digest. For example, Wiggins said in the 1968 edition of the *Annual Review of Psychology:*

> Cattell occupies such a unique position in the field of personality structure that his work demands separate consideration. In the three years under review (May 1964–May 1967) Cattell has published four books, 12 chapters and 40 articles, a total of almost four thousand pages that must somehow be summarized. In addition, he has found time to launch a new journal (*Multivariate Behavioral Research*) and edit a massive handbook (*Handbook of Multivariate Experimental Psychology*). This alone would warrant separate consideration but there is more. The appearance of so many major works and especially the publication of his *Collected Papers (Personality and Social Psychology)* has once again forced an evaluation of a body of literature so vast, uneven, and demanding that many American workers have simply tended to ignore it. (313)

All that one could reasonably do with Cattell's theory would be to sample parts of it and hope that his most important concepts are included in that sample. Such a sample is offered in this chapter. Second, Cattell relies heavily on **factor analysis.** There is no doubt that the apparent complexities of this technique have caused many to overlook Cattell's theory. We contend, however, that factor analysis is only *apparently* complex, and that the logic behind it is simple and straightforward.

Because in most important ways, to understand factor analysis is to understand Cattell's theory of personality, we begin our discussion of his theory of personality with a rudimentary discussion of factor analysis.

The cornerstone of factor analysis is the concept of **correlation.** When two things vary together they are said to be correlated, that is, co-related. For example, a correlation exists between height and weight, because when one increases the other will also tend to increase. The stronger the tendency is for two variables to vary together, the stronger is the correlation between them. The strength of the relationship between two variables is expressed mathematically by a **correlation coefficient.** A correlation coefficient can vary in magnitude from + 1.00 to − 1.00. A coefficient of + 1.00 indicates a perfect **positive correlation** between two variables; that is, as measures on one variable increase, so will measures on the second variable. A coefficient of − 1.00 indicates a perfect **negative correlation** between two variables; that is, as measures on one variable increase, measures on the other variable will decrease. A correlation coefficient of + .80 indicates a strong positive correlation between two variables, but not a perfect one. That is, there is a tendency for the two variables to vary positively together. A coefficient of − .56 indicates a moderate negative correlation.

Cattell's procedure is to measure many persons in as many ways as possible. For example, he records the everyday behavior of various persons, such as how many accidents they had, the number of organizations to which they belonged, and the number of social contacts they had. He calls the information gathered by such observations **L-data,** the *L* for life record. He gives his subjects questionnaires on which they rate themselves on various characteristics. He calls the information gathered by such a technique **Q-data,** the *Q* for questionnaire. Q-data includes performance on standard self-report inventories and various scales that measure attitudes, opinions, and interests. Cattell realizes that Q-data has limitations. First, some persons may not know much about themselves and therefore their responses to questionnaires, inventories, and scales may not reflect their true personalities. Second, some subjects falsify or distort their responses to create a different image of themselves. For example, an aggressive person may believe his or her aggressiveness would be frowned on and may respond in ways that make him or her look passive. The possibility of falsification exists whenever it is clear to a person what personality attribute is being evaluated. To overcome the problems inherent in Q-data Cattell uses a third source of data that he calls **T-data,** the T for test. T-data is gathered in situations in which examinees cannot know what aspect of their behavior is being evaluated. Examples would include performance on word-association tests, the Rorschach ink-blot test, or the thematic apperception test. Cattell referred to such tests as *objective* because they were resistant to faking. Cattell and Warburton (1967) list more than 400 tests that appear to meet this criterion.

The next step is to intercorrelate all of the data, creating a **correlation matrix.** To simplify matters we will assume that the data we are analyzing consists of performance on five tests. A hypothetical outcome of such analysis is shown in Table 8–1.

Next the following assumptions are made:

1. Two tests that measure the same thing must give similar results. In other words, tests measuring the same ability will tend to be correlated.
2. The extent of agreement (correlation) between two tests will indicate the extent to which the two tests are measuring the same thing.

With these assumptions in mind, the correlation matrix is examined in order to find which tests are highly correlated with each other. In other words, clusters of correlations are sought. Such a search is called a **cluster analysis.** When a cluster of tests showing high correlation with one another is observed, the tests are considered to be measuring the same ability or characteristic. An ability discovered in such a way is called a **factor,** and in Cattell's theory the term factor can be equated with the term **trait.** For Cattell, factor analysis is a method used to discover traits, which he regarded as the building blocks of personality.

The procedures in Cattell's version of factor analysis can be summarized as follows:

1. Measure many people in a variety of ways (that is, gather L, Q, and T data).
2. Correlate performance on each measure with performance on every other measure. This creates a correlation matrix.

Table 8–1
Hypothetical Correlation Matrix Showing All of the Possible Intercorrelations among Five Tests

Tests	A	B	C	D	E
A	—	1.00	1.00	.00	.00
B	1.00	—	1.00	.00	.00
C	1.00	1.00	—	.00	.00
D	.00	.00	.00	—	1.00
E	.00	.00	.00	1.00	—

3. Determine how many factors (traits) need to be postulated in order to account for the various intercorrelations (clusters) found in the correlation matrix.

In the hypothetical correlation matrix depicted in Table 8–1, it is clear that Tests *A*, *B*, and *C*, have a great deal in common with one another, because they are perfectly correlated, but they have nothing in common with Tests *D* and *E*. Conversely, Tests *D* and *E* have a great deal in common, because they are perfectly correlated with each other, but they have nothing in common with Tests *A*, *B*, and *C*. Under these circumstances our correlation matrix has detected two separate factors or traits. One is measured by Tests *A*, *B*, and *C*, and the other is measured by Tests *D* and *E*.

A sample of the ways in which three tests could be related to each other is shown in Figure 8–1. The upper left corner of the picture shows what would happen if the three tests all measure separate factors. The upper right corner shows that Tests *A* and *B* tend to measure a common factor, but Test *C* measures a different factor. The lower left corner of the figure indicates that all three tests are measuring a common factor. The lower right corner of the figure shows Test *A* measuring one factor and Tests *B* and *C* measuring another factor.

Factor analysis, then, is a technique, based on the methods of correlation, that attempts to account for the interrelationships found among numerous measures. The technique is certainly not confined to the study of personality. As mentioned earlier, Cattell's mentor, Charles Spearman, used factor analysis to study intelligence; and Cattell, in addition to using it to study personality, used factor analysis to study the characteristics of groups, institutions, and even nations.

R- and P-Techniques.   During the early 1940s, when Cattell was a lecturer at Harvard, he often had lunch with Gordon Allport. At the time, Cattell's interest was primarily in discovering basic traits that constitute personality and then determining how persons differed in the degree to which they possessed those traits.

Figure 8–1

Examples of how three tests can be related to each other. See text for explanation.

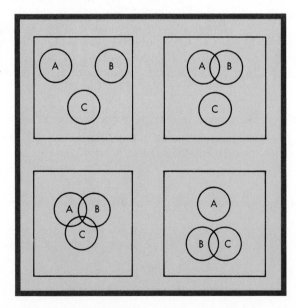

As we have seen, Cattell's approach to discovering traits was to measure many persons in many ways and to factor analyze the results. Allport expressed dismay that Cattell's approach stressed group performance (the nomothetic technique) and ignored the unique individual (the idiographic technique). As a result of Allport's influence, Cattell began to investigate how trait strengths differ in the *same* person from time to time. Cattell's early idiographic research was performed on his wife but was soon extended to other persons.

The kind of factor analysis that we described, in which many subjects are measured on many variables and the scores intercorrelated, is called the **R-technique.** The kind of factor analysis that traces the strength of several traits over a period of time for the *same person* is called the **P-technique.** Figure 8–2 shows the outcome of one P-technique study. This study measured the same individual eighty times on eight traits over a forty-four-day period. The person being studied kept a diary during the experiment, and several of his major experiences are indicated along the baseline of Figure 8–2. For example, he had to rehearse for a play in which he was to play the lead role, he had a cold, the play for which he rehearsed

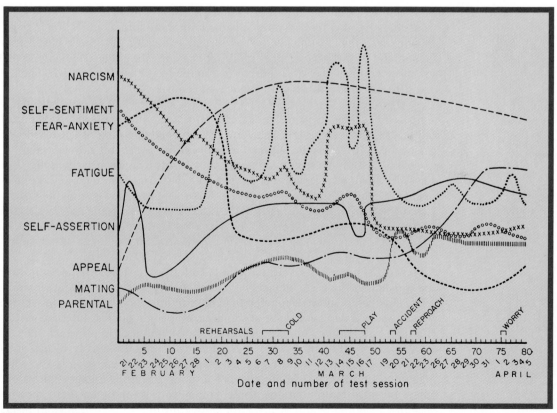

(From Cattell 1957, 553).

Figure 8–2 *An example of Cattell's P-technique in which certain traits that a person possesses are measured over time.*

was held, his father was in an accident, an aunt criticized him for not helping his family enough, and he was worried because his academic advisor was apparently hostile toward him. We can clearly see from Figure 8–2 that the various traits that one possesses will manifest themselves with varying strength as one's life circumstances change.

Categories of Traits

As already mentioned, Cattell considers traits as the building blocks of personality, and clearly the concept of trait is the most important concept in his theory. Most of his factor analytic research has been a search for personality traits, and that search has uncovered several categories of traits, which we will review next.

Surface and Source Traits

The difference between surface traits and source traits is probably the most important distinction made in Cattell's theory. **Surface traits** are groups of observations that are correlated. For example, people with more formal education may go to the movies less than people with less formal education do. Such observations are superficial in that they explain nothing. They are simply a statement of what kind of observed characteristics tend to be grouped together (correlated). Such characteristics can, and probably do, have many causes.

Source traits, conversely, are the causes of behavior. They constitute the most important part of a person's personality structure and are ultimately responsible for all of a person's consistent behavior. Thus, every surface trait is caused by one or more source traits, and a source trait can influence several surface traits.

For Cattell, the search for source traits starts by measuring everything one can measure about a large group of people. The measures are then intercorrelated, and a cluster analysis indicates which measures tend to be measuring the same things. Such a factor analysis yields surface traits. The surface traits are then analyzed to see which of them tend to be related to one another—in other words, stimulated by the same source. Such an analysis provides information about source traits.

Another way to describe the difference between source traits and surface traits is to say that the latter are always manifestations of the former. The source traits can be considered the basic elements of personality, in that everything we do is influenced by them. Cattell concluded that all individuals possess the same source traits but do so in varying degrees. For example, all people possess intelligence (a source trait), but all people do not possess the same amount of intelligence. The strength of this source trait in a given individual will influence many things about that person; for example, what the person reads, who his or her friends are, what he or she does for a living, and the person's attitude toward a college education. All of these outward manifestations of the source trait of intelligence are surface traits. Another example would be all of the outward things a person does in response to being hungry, such as going to the store, buying food, going home, preparing the food, and then eating. All of the observable behaviors related to eating exemplify surface traits, while the hunger drive that causes them exemplifies a source trait.

Our examples are somewhat misleading, however, because, as we have seen, hardly anything that a person does is caused by only one source trait.

After extensive research through the years, Cattell concluded that there are approximately sixteen source traits on which individuals or groups can be compared, and they are listed in Table 8–2.

Cattell (with Saunders and Stice) constructed his now-famous *Sixteen Personality Factor Questionnaire (16 PF)* (1950) around the sixteen source traits that his research had yielded. This test has been used to compare a wide variety of groups. The performance of several different groups on the 16 PF is shown in Figure 8–3.

Constitutional and Environmental-Mold Traits

Some source traits are genetically determined and are called **constitutional source traits,** and others result from experience and are called **environmental-mold traits.**

> If source traits found by factorizing are pure, independent influences, as present evidence suggests, a source trait could not be due both to heredity and environment but must spring from one or the other. . . . Patterns thus springing from *internal* conditions or influences we may call *constitutional source traits.* . . . On the other hand, a pattern might be imprinted on the personality by something external to it. . . . Such source traits, appearing as factors, we may call *environmental-mold traits,* because they spring from the molding effect of social institutions and physical realities which constitute the cultural pattern. (Cattell 1950, 33–34)

Thus, some of the sixteen source traits are determined genetically and some are culturally determined.

Ability Traits

Some source traits that a person possesses determine how effectively he or she works toward a desired goal; such traits are called **ability traits.** One of the most important ability traits is intelligence. Cattell has distinguished between two kinds of intelligence, *crystallized* and *fluid.* He defines **fluid intelligence** as "that form of general intelligence which is largely innate and which adapts itself to all kinds of material regardless of previous experience with it" (1965, 369). Cattell defines **crystallized intelligence** as "a general factor, largely in a type of abilities learned at school, representing the effect of past application of fluid intelligence, and amount and intensity of schooling; it appears in such tests as vocabulary and number ability measures" (1965, 369).

Cattell believes that too often a person's intelligence is equated with crystallized intelligence, which most traditional IQ tests attempt to measure. To help remedy the situation, Cattell developed the **Culture Fair Intelligence Test,** which was designed to measure fluid intelligence.

Cattell's most recent research has led him to conclude that both fluid intelligence and crystallized intelligence are strongly influenced by heredity. This research indicates that fluid intelligence is 65 percent inherited and crystallized intelligence is 60 percent inherited (Cattell 1979–80, 2:58). Thus according to Cat-

FACTOR	HIGH SCORE INDICATES A TENDENCY TOWARD	LOW SCORE INDICATES A TENDENCY TOWARD
A	*Affectia* Socially adjusted Easygoing Warmhearted Outgoing	*Sizia* Socially hostile Indifferent Reserved
B	*Intelligence* Alert Imaginative Thoughtful Wise	*Unintelligent* Dull Stupid Unimaginative
C	*Ego Strength* Unworried Mature Stoic Patient	*Ego Weakness* Anxious Infantile Worried Impatient
E	*Domination* Confident Boastful Competitive Assertive	*Subordination* Unsure Modest Accommodating Humble
F	*Surgency* Talkative Genial Cheerful Responsive Happy-go-lucky	*Desurgency* Silent Serious Depressed Seclusive
G	*Superego Strength* Conscientious Responsible Persevering Loyal	*Superego Weakness* Unscrupulous Frivolous Irresolute Undependable
H	*Parmia* Carefree Overtly interested in sex Venturesome	*Threctia* Careful Overtly disinterested in sex Shy
I	*Premisia* Introspective Sensitive Sentimental Intuitive	*Harria* Insensitive Practical Logical Self-sufficient
L	*Protension* Suspicious Jealous Skeptical Wary	*Alaxia* Credulous Trustful Unsuspecting Gullible
M	*Autia* Eccentric Imaginative Complacent Self-absorbed	*Praxernia* Practical Conventional Poised Earnest
N	*Shrewdness* Socially alert Insightful regarding others Expedient Calculating	*Artlessness* Socially clumsy Crude Indifferent Apathetic
O	*Guilt Proclivity* Timid Worrisome	*Guilt Rejection* Self-confident Cheerful

continued

	Depressed	Without fear
	Moody	Self-sufficient
Q(1)	*Radicalism*	*Conservatism*
	Encourages change	Rejects change
	Rejects convention	Disgusted by foul language
	Freethinking	Traditional
Q(2)	*Self-Sufficiency*	*Group-Adherence*
	Temperamentally independent	Seeks social approval
	Prefers working with a few assistants rather than a committee	Group dependent
	Prefers reading to classes	Prefers to travel with others
	Prefers textbooks to novels	Joiner
Q(3)	*High self-sentiment strength*	*Low self-sentiment strength*
	Controlled	Careless
	Sensitive to uncertainty	Rapidly changing interests
	Does not make promise he cannot keep	Tries several approaches to the same problem
	Does not say things he later regrets	Does not persevere in the face of obstacles
Q(4)	*High ergic tension*	*Low ergic tension*
	Tense	Relaxed
	Unexpected lapses of memory	Composed
	Suffers frustration because of unsatisfied physiological needs	Few periods of depression Disinclined to worry

* Note that each factor is bipolar. A high score on a particular factor indicates a tendency to possess the traits on the left of the diagram, and a low score indicates a tendency to possess the traits listed on the right side of the diagram.

tell, not only is one's general intelligence (fluid intelligence) strongly influenced by heredity but so is one's ability to benefit from experience and to use what one has learned (crystallized intelligence).

Temperament Traits

These are genetically determined characteristics which determine a person's general "style and tempo." **Temperament traits** determine the speed, energy, and emotion with which a person responds to a situation. They determine how mild-mannered, irritable, or persistent a person is. Temperament traits, therefore, are constitutional source traits that determine a person's emotionality.

Dynamic Traits

Other traits are the building blocks of personality, whereas dynamic traits set the personality in motion. **Dynamic traits** set the person in motion toward some goal;

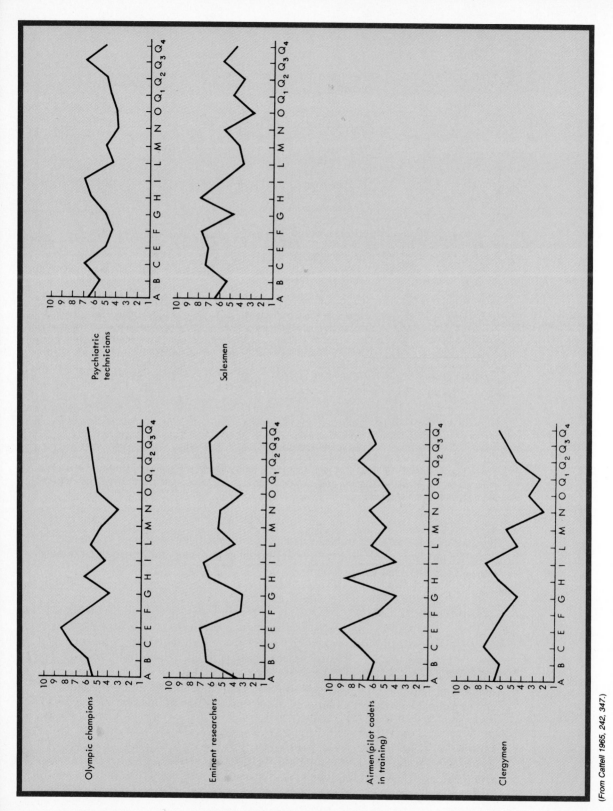

(From Cattell 1965, 242, 347.)

Figure 8–3 *A comparison of the performance of various groups on the Sixteen Personality Factor Questionnaire.*

they therefore are the motivational elements of personality. Cattell elaborated two different dynamic or motivational traits: ergs and metaergs. We will consider each.

Ergs and Metaergs

Ergs

An **erg** is a dynamic, constitutional source trait. An erg is similar to what other theorists have called drives, needs, or instincts. Cattell chose the term erg (from the Greek ergon, meaning energy), because he thought the other motivational terms were too ambiguous. The ergs provide the energy for all behavior. Cattell defines erg as:

> An innate psycho-physical disposition which permits its possessor to acquire reactivity (attention, recognition) to certain classes of objects more readily than others, to experience a specific emotion in regard to them, and to start on a course of action which ceases more completely at a certain specific goal activity than at any other. (1950, 199)

It can be seen from this definition that an erg has four aspects:

1. It causes selective perception; that is, it causes some things to be attended to more than others. For the hungry person, food-related events are attended to more than events unrelated to food.
2. It stimulates an emotional response to certain thoughts or objects. For example, the thought of eating is a pleasant one.
3. It stimulates goal-directed behavior. For example, the hungry person will do whatever is necessary to come into contact with food.
4. It results in some sort of consummatory response. That is, when one comes into contact with food, one will eat it.

Cattell's research has revealed eleven ergs, which are listed on the right side of Figure 8–4.

Metaergs

A **metaerg** is a dynamic source trait with an environmental origin. In other words, a metaerg is an environmental-mold, dynamic source trait. Thus, a metaerg is the same as an erg except for its origin. Both ergs and metaergs cause motivational predispositions toward certain environmental objects. But ergs are innate whereas metaergs are learned. Metaergs are divided into **sentiments** and **attitudes.** According to Cattell, sentiments are "major acquired dynamic trait structures which cause their possessors to pay attention to certain objects or classes of objects, and to feel and react in a certain way with regard to them" (1950, 161). Cattell believes that sentiments are usually centered on such things as one's career or profession, sports,

Figure 8–4.
*A dynamic lattice
showing the
relationship among
ergs, sentiments
and attitudes.*

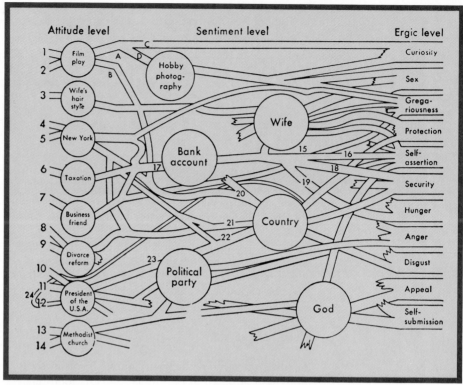

(From Cattell 1950, 158.)

religion, one's parents, one's spouse or sweetheart, or oneself. The most powerful sentiment of all, according to Cattell, is the **self-sentiment,** which organizes the entire personality.

> In the first place, the preservation of the self as a physically healthy and intact going concern is obviously a prerequisite for the satisfaction of any sentiment or erg which the individual possesses! So also is the preservation of the social and ethical self as something which the community respects. . . . Dynamically, the sentiment towards maintaining the self correct by certain standards of conduct, satisfactory to community and super-ego, is therefore a *necessary instrumentality* to the satisfaction of most other of our life interests. . . . It contributes to all sentiment and ergic satisfactions, and this accounts also for its dynamic strength in controlling, as the "master sentiment," all other structures. (1965, 272–73)

A sentiment is an acquired predisposition to respond to a class of objects or events in a certain way. An *attitude* is more specific but is derived from a sentiment, which, in turn, is derived from an erg. An attitude, according to Cattell, is a tendency to respond in a particular way in a particular situation to a particular object or event. Cattell (1957, 444) describes the manifestation of an attitude:

In these circumstances (Stimulus situation)	I (Organism)	want so much (Interest-need of a certain intensity)	to do this (Specific goal, course of action)	with that. (Object concerned in action)

Thus, an attitude is an interest, of a certain intensity, in doing something with something in a certain situation.

Subsidiation

By the term **subsidiation** Cattell means simply that sentiments are subsidiary to ergs (that is, dependent on them), and attitudes are subsidiary to sentiments. This arrangement is diagrammed in what Cattell called the **dynamic lattice,** shown in Figure 8–4.

It can be seen in Figure 8–4 that ergic desires are seldom satisfied directly. Instead, one usually goes about satisfying a basic need indirectly. For example, one may develop skills to get a job, get married, or satisfy one's sex drive. Cattell called this indirect satisfaction of an ergic impulse **long-circuiting.** Also, it can be seen that each sentiment is a function of, or subsidiary to, a number of ergs. For example, the sentiment toward wife reflects the ergs of sex, gregariousness, protection, and self-assertion. The most important point about the dynamic lattice is that it demonstrates the complexity of human motivation. Attitudes, sentiments, and ergs are constantly interacting and are constantly reflecting not only current circumstances, but also an individual's future goals.

Personality Development

Like most personality theorists, Cattell believes personality development to be a function of both motivation and learning. Motivation is responsible for many changes in perceptual and behavioral capabilities.

Learning.   Learning allows changes in the ways ergs are satisfied; that is, learning is responsible for the development of sentiments and attitudes.

Cattell believes that there are three kinds of learning: **classical conditioning, instrumental conditioning,** and **structured learning.** He defines classical conditioning as a situation in which "a new stimulus gets attached to an old response by occurring a moment before the old stimulus" (1965, 266). Instrumental conditioning (also called reward learning or operant conditioning) is learning to perform a response that will produce a reward.

Cattell feels that both classical and instrumental conditioning are relatively unimportant, because they deal with only one stimulus or one response at a time. He feels a third kind of learning, which he calls *personality* or *structural learning,* is much more important. According to Cattell, the learning process, as it occurs in real life, cannot be neatly divided into conditioned reflexes. Rather, it typically is a change in a person's entire constellation of traits. In other words, when something is learned, it influences one's entire personality structure in one way or another; thus the name "structured learning," indicating that one personality structure existed before learning took place, and that another personality structure existed after learning took place.

As an example of how structured learning is produced, Cattell shows the many adjustments that are possible if the satisfaction of an erg is blocked. He describes the various adjustment possibilities as a series of **dynamic crossroads,** which are summarized in Figure 8–5. It can be seen in Figure 8–5 that the arousal of ergic tension can result in anything from immediate satisfaction to pathological disorders, depending on the circumstances. In any case, one's trait structure is modified somewhat from the experience, and therefore structured learning has taken place.

Importance of Early Experience.   Cattell believes that early experiences exert a strong influence on the development of certain personality traits. For example, he observes that adults displaying high *affectia* (see Table 8–2) typically come from a warm, loving home where the father was cheerful, the mother was calm, and the children were controlled through reasoning rather than punishment.

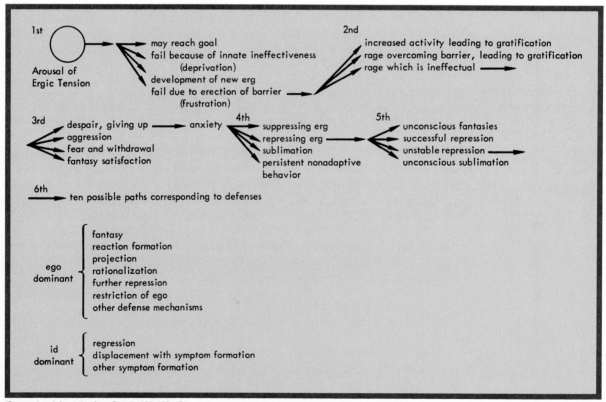

(Summarizes information from Cattell 1950, 209–47.)

Figure 8–5   *The adjustment possibilities or dynamic crossroads that follow the arousal of ergic tension.*

The same is true for adults displaying a high level of ego strength (see Table 8–2). Proneness to dominance and guilt tends to characterize adults whose parents were authoritarian, used physical punishment, and were highly critical of their offspring. (For a further discussion of how various parental behaviors relate to the development of certain source traits see Cattell 1973, 158–78).

Cattell (1973) has also studied the Adlerian contention that birth order significantly impacts personality development. In general he found that oldest children tend to be high in dominance, ego strength, and conservatism but low in self-sentiment strength. Only children tend to also be conservative but are high in self-sentiment strength. Also, children who are not the oldest tend to display surgency (see Table 8–2). Finally, Cattell found that ergic tension tends to increase as family size increases.

Heredity Versus Environment.   No other personality theorist has done more than Cattell to determine the relative contributions of heredity and environment to the development of each personality trait. To examine these contributions Cattell has created a complicated statistical procedure called *Multiple Abstract Variance Analysis* (MAVA). In general, the method compares members of the same family raised together or raised apart and unrelated persons raised either together or apart. Each person studied is given a test, or a series of tests, to assess a particular trait. More specifically, measurements are taken of identical twins raised together, identical twins raised apart, fraternal twins raised together, fraternal twins raised apart, siblings raised together, siblings raised apart, unrelated persons raised together, and unrelated persons raised apart (Cattell 1982, 90). The number of genes in common is highest for identical twins, then fraternal twins and siblings, and is lowest for unrelated persons. The logic of such research is straightforward; if a trait is genetically determined, the degree to which it is possessed by two persons should be correlated with the degree to which they share the same genes. For example, if a trait is completely genetically determined, then identical twins should possess that trait whether they are raised together or apart.

On the basis of the kind of research just described, Cattell concludes that heredity plays a significant role in the development of at least some traits. He confirmed his earlier observation that intelligence (fluid intelligence) is 65 percent genetically determined. Also the tendency to have a zestful, active disposition versus a reflective, circumspective one was found to be 70 percent genetically determined. Cattell, Schuerger, and Kline (1982) studied the heritability of three source traits: ego strength (factor C), superego strength (factor G), and self-sentiment (factor Q_3). In this particular study a ten-hour battery of tests was administered to 94 identical twins reared together, 124 fraternal twins reared together, 470 brothers reared together, and 2,973 unrelated children reared apart. Using the MAVA procedure the authors found that superego strength (factor G) is largely a function of environmental influences rather than heredity. However, ego strength (factor C) and self-sentiment (factor Q_3) were found to be strongly influenced by heredity. Cattell (1979–80, 2:58) reports the heritability of most of the other source traits. Several traits are found to have a genetic component of 30 percent or more. When the overall contribution of heredity to personality is considered, Cattell essentially confirmed his earlier conclusion that personality is about two-thirds determined by environmental influences and about one-third by heredity (Hundleby, Pawlik, and Cattell 1965).

Psychopathology and Psychotherapy

Psychopathology.   Cattell suggests two reasons for psychopathology. One is an abnormal imbalance of the normal personality traits; that is, those measured by the 16 PF. For example, an excessive amount of factor A (*affectia* versus *sizia*) could result in a manic-depressive disorder. The second reason for psychopathology is the possession of abnormal traits which are not found among normal individuals. Cattell and his colleagues have isolated twelve abnormal traits that can be used to describe various kinds of neuroses and psychoses. Cattell (1975) has devised the Clinical Analysis Questionnaire to assess those abnormal traits. The twelve abnormal traits that Cattell has discovered are listed in Table 8–3.

Cattell concludes that abnormal persons are, first of all, like normal ones in that they possess all of the normal source traits. However, they may also possess pathological traits (Cattell 1979–80, 1:73–74). In Table 8–3, the first seven abnormal traits (symbolized by the letter D) are depressive traits. The last five traits are considered relatively more powerful and more serious.

Psychotherapy.   Ideally for Cattell, psychotherapy should be preceded by a precise personality-factor assessment. Such a profile not only defines exactly what the problem is but also aids the clinician in determining the most effective treatment procedure. Furthermore, the P-technique should be used during treatment so that the changes occurring within the client, while he or she is in therapy, can be assessed. As far as therapeutic treatment is concerned, Cattell is an eclectic. He thinks that the kind of treatment should be dictated by the kind of disorder that is revealed by precise personality assessment. Severe psychoses may be best treated by drugs or electric shock; certain neuroses might be best treated by dream analysis and the reliving of traumatic experiences; and for relatively minor problems some form of behavior therapy might be most effective (behavior therapy will be discussed in the next chapter).

Table 8–3
Cattell's Twelve Abnormal Source Traits

FACTOR	LOW SCORE DESCRIPTION	HIGH SCORE DESCRIPTION
D_1	Low hypochondriasis	High hypochondriasis
D_2	Zestfulness	Suicidal disgust
D_3	Low brooding discontent	High brooding discontent
D_4	Low anxious depression	High anxious depression
D_5	High energy euphoria	Low energy depression
D_6	Low guilt and resentment	High guilt and resentment
D_7	Low bored depression	High bored depression
P_a	Low paranoia	High paranoia
P_p	Low psychopathic deviation	High psychopathic deviation
S_c	Low schizophrenia	High schizophrenia
A_s	Low psychasthenia	High psychasthenia
P_s	Low general psychosis	High general psychosis

Syntality

Cattell thinks that because much of people's behavior is determined by their group affiliations, it is important to know as much as possible about the groups to which people belong. The term personality summarizes a person's traits, whereas the term **syntality** summarizes a group's traits. Cattell studied groups such as various religions, schools, peer groups, and nations in the same way that he studied people. For example, in one study (Cattell, Breul, and Hartman 1952), forty countries were evaluated on seventy-two variables. All measures were intercorrelated and factor-analyzed. It was found that the major differences between the countries could be explained using the following four factors:

> *Factor 1:* Enlightened Affluence versus Narrow Poverty
> *Factor 2:* Vigorous Order versus Unadapted Rigidity
> *Factor 3:* Cultural Pressure and Complexity versus Direct Ergic Expression
> *Factor 4:* Size

Thus the groups that influence people have traits, too, and these traits can be uncovered by factor analysis, just as the traits characterizing people can be discovered using that technique. Once group or national traits have been discovered, a wide variety of comparisons can be made.

Specification Equation

Like Allport, Cattell is mainly interested in normal people. He is interested in being able to predict with considerable accuracy how people will respond in various situations. In arriving at his predictions, Cattell is very much a *determinist*. That is, he believes that behavior is a function of a finite number of variables, and if those variables are completely known, human behavior can be predicted with complete accuracy. Such a belief characterizes **determinism.** Cattell and other determinists realize that all of the variables influencing behavior can never be known, so the prediction of behavior will always be probabilistic. Realizing this, the determinist says that as more is known about the variables influencing human behavior, predictions of human behavior will become more accurate. According to Cattell, this is also true in the realm of personality research. The more we know about the various traits of a particular person, the better we will be able to predict his or her behavior.

What, then, is personality to Cattell? It is that which provides consistency, thus making prediction possible.

> *Personality is that which permits a prediction of what a person will do in a given situation. The goal of psychological research in personality is thus to establish*

laws about what different people will do in all kinds of social and general environmental situations. . . . Personality is . . . concerned with *all* the behavior of the individual, both overt and under the skin. (Cattell 1950, 2–3)

In general, Cattell's position can be symbolized as follows:

$$R = f(P,S)$$

in which:

> R = the person's reaction
> P = the person's personality
> S = the situation

In other words, how a person behaves is a function of both the person's personality and the given situation.

Obviously, this formula is an oversimplification of Cattell's viewpoint. To predict accurately a person's performance, what was symbolized *P* (personality) must be spelled out in greater detail. What exactly is a person's personality? According to Cattell, it is all of the traits that he or she possesses. Thus, a measure of each of a person's traits must be included in the formula. Also, because the importance of a person's traits will vary from situation to situation, the importance or weight of each trait must be specified in each situation. Such a specification is called the trait's **factor loading.** In addition to a person's stable traits, other more temporary conditions may influence behavior at certain times. For example, he or she may be sick or fatigued. Likewise, certain situations may require that the person play a role, and such a requirement will strongly influence behavior. Temporary body states such as fatigue, illness, anxiety, and required social roles are called **situational modulators,** because they are thought to modulate behavioral expressions. Concerning the influence of roles on behavior, Cattell says, "Everyone may shout lustily at a football match, less lustily at dinner, and not at all in church" (1979–1980, Vol. 1, 250).

It is complicated to predict a person's behavior. We must know what traits a person possesses, how important they are to the situation of interest, the person's present bodily state, and what roles the situation will stimulate him or her to play. The general formula just given becomes the following formula, which Cattell calls the **specification equation** (Cattell 1965, 265):

$$P_j = s_{j_A}A \ldots + s_{j_T}T \ldots + s_{j_E}E \ldots + s_{j_M}M \ldots + s_{j_R}R \ldots + s_{j_S}S$$

Where:

P_j = performance in situation j
A = ability traits
T = temperament traits
E = ergic tensions present
M = metaergs (sentiments and attitudes)
R = roles called for in the situation
S = temporary bodily states such as fatigue, illness, or anxiety
sj = a weight or "loading," indicating the importance of each of the foregoing influences in situation j.

This formula simply restates Cattell's assumption of determinism; if you want to know how a person will react to a certain situation, list his or her traits and weigh each one in terms of its relevance to the situation. For example, if the person were in a problem-solving situation, the ability trait of intelligence would be given great weight or a high factor loading. When this is done with each of a person's traits and when the situational modulators are taken into consideration, the person's behavior is thought to be highly predictable.

Evaluation

Empirical Research.   As we have seen throughout this chapter, Cattell's theory is based firmly on empirical research. Cattell and his colleagues have created hundreds of scales, inventories, tests, and questionnaires and most of them have been used extensively in research projects. We have already sampled some of the research done using Cattell's 16 PF. Although a thorough review of the research using just the 16 PF would take much more space than is available here, we will add just a few more examples of such research.

Cattell and Nesselroade (1967) used the 16 PF to determine the personality profiles of persons involved in a stable marriage and those involved in an unstable marriage. An unstable marriage was defined as one in which at least one step had been taken toward dissolution. Contrary to the old saying "opposites attract," it was found that stable marriages were characterized by similarities in traits among the couples, unstable marriages revealed dissimilar traits among the couples.

Cattell, Eber, and Tatsuoka (1970) used the 16 PF to study the personality profiles of men and women who had attempted suicide. The profiles for men and women were similar and both departed significantly from profiles generated by the general adult population. In general, those who had attempted suicide were more introverted, more anxious, and displayed lower superego strength when compared to the general adult population. The same study found that airline pilots and airline hostesses had profiles nearly opposite to those who had attempted suicide. Compared to the general adult population, airline pilots and hostesses were more extroverted, less anxious, and displayed more superego strength.

Criticisms

Too Subjective.   As scientifically rigorous as Cattell's theory appears to be a number of critics claim that it still is characterized by too much subjectivity. One source of subjectivity, say the critics, is in determining what to study about people to begin with. What comes out of a factor analysis is totally dependent on what goes into it. Subjectivity is also involved in determining what will be accepted as evidence of a factor. That is, how many variables must be correlated and how high must the correlations be? Finally, how many factors need to be postulated to account for the data? The subjective nature of the many decisions involved in Cattell's factor analytic approach to studying personality is reflected in the fact that others have not been able to replicate many of Cattell's findings. For example, Digman and

Takemoto-Chock (1981) note that many of Cattell's factors or source traits have not been found by other researchers. Also, Goldberg (1981) says that when Cattell's data are analyzed by others, they typically find five factors instead of the sixteen or more reported by Cattell.

Behavior Not as Consistent as Cattell's Theory Suggests. Even though Cattell does not ignore the influence of specific environmental situations on behavior, he still assumes a considerable amount of cross-situational consistency in behavior. Critics claim that such consistency simply does not exist (see, for example, Mischel 1968; Mischel and Peake 1982). To the extent to which it is found that behavior is not at least moderately consistent across time and similar situations, theories such as those of Allport and Cattell suffer.

Too Much Emphasis on Groups and Averages. Although Cattell developed his P-technique partially to appease Allport, Allport was still dissatisfied with the way Cattell went about discovering traits to begin with. Allport thought that Cattell's method yielded average traits that no person actually possessed.

> An entire population (the larger the better) is put into the grinder, and the mixing is so expert that what comes through is a link of factors in which every individual has lost his identity. His dispositions are mixed with everyone else's dispositions. The factors thus obtained represent only *average* tendencies. Whether a factor is really an *inorganic* disposition in any one individual life is not demonstrated. All one can say for certain is that a factor is an empirically derived component of the *average* personality, and that the average personality is a complete abstraction. This objection gains point when one reflects that seldom do the factors derived in this way resemble the dispositions and traits identified by clinical methods when the *individual* is studied intensively. (Allport 1937, 244)

Allport's point is valid only when one looks at how Cattell arrived at his sixteen basic personality traits. Most of this research did involve large groups of people and dealt with averages. Once the sixteen personality traits were isolated, however, they were used to understand the behavior of persons (P-technique) and to predict individual behavior (the specification equation). To say that Cattell was mainly interested in groups and in averages is incorrect.

Contributions

Scientific Rigor. Even with the possibility that his approach may contain a few subjective elements, Cattell has been concerned with the construction of a theory of personality that is based on precise measurement. Because so much personality research has been unscientific, Cattell's effort to quantify personality is widely appreciated. Personality is a complex topic and it makes sense that our most sophisticated, statistical technique (factor analysis) should be used to study it. It makes even more sense now that computers are available to aid in the analysis.

Applied Value. Versions of Cattell's evaluative devices have been translated into more than a dozen languages and in each language they are used extensively for both research and practical applications. Cattell's materials have been used for clinical diagnoses, personnel selection, vocational counseling, marital counseling, predicting accident proneness, predicting the possibility of heart attacks in men, and predicting scholastic performance.

Wiggens (1984), I think, is correct in his evaluation of Cattell's theory:

> Cattell's theory turns out to be a much more impressive achievement than has been generally recognized. . . . It seems fair to say that Cattell's original blueprint for personality study has resulted in an extraordinarily rich theoretical structure that has generated more empirical research than any other theory of personality. (177, 190)

Summary

Cattell's approach to the study of personality first measures a large group of individuals in as many ways as possible. The measures then are intercorrelated and displayed in a correlation matrix. The measures that are moderately or highly correlated are thought to be measuring the same attribute. This procedure is called factor analysis, and the attributes it detects are called factors or traits. Cattell describes a number of different kinds of traits. His most important distinction is between surface traits and source traits. Surface traits are those that are actually measured and are, therefore, expressed in overt behavior of some kind. Source traits are those that are the underlying causes of overt behavior. He feels that most people have about sixteen source traits. Some source traits are genetically determined and are called constitutional traits. Other source traits are shaped by one's culture and are called environmental-mold traits. Cattell also distinguishes between ability, temperament, and dynamic traits. Ability traits determine how well a task is performed. The most important ability trait is intelligence, of which Cattell describes two kinds. Fluid intelligence is general problem-solving ability and is thought to be largely genetically determined. Crystallized intelligence is the cumulated knowledge of the kind learned in school and is thus gained through experience. Although crystallized intelligence is gained through experience, one's ability to effectively utilize such information is also largely genetically determined. Temperament traits are constitutional and determine a person's emotional makeup. Dynamic traits are those that set the person in motion toward a goal; in other words, they determine a person's motivational makeup. Cattell distinguishes two categories of dynamic traits: ergs and metaergs. Ergs are roughly equivalent to instincts, biologic needs, or primary drives. Metaergs are learned drives, divided into sentiments and attitudes. Sentiments are predispositions to act in certain ways to classes of objects or events. Attitudes are specific responses to specific objects or events. Because ergs are at the core of one's motivational patterns, sentiments are said to be subsidiary to ergs, and because attitudes are dependent on sentiments, attitudes are said to be subsidiary to sentiments. Cattell diagrams the relationships among ergs, sentiments, and attitudes in what he calls the dynamic lattice. The fact that humans almost inevitably take indirect routes to satisfy ergic tensions is referred to as long-circuiting.

To explain how personality develops, Cattell postulates three kinds of learning: classical and instrumental conditioning and structured learning. The latter is by far the most important kind of learning, because it involves a change in one's entire personality. Cattell exemplifies structured learning by showing what happens at a number of choice points following the arousal of ergic tension. A series of such choice points is called the dynamic crossroads.

Cattell has shown the relationship between various early home environments and the development of various personality traits. He also found support for Adler's assertion that birth order and family size significantly impact personality development. Using his MAVA, Cattell has attempted to determine the relative contributions of heredity and environment to the development of various traits. He finds that some traits have a very strong genetic component (for example, intelligence), and some have practically none (for example, superego strength). Overall Cattell concludes that about one-third of personality is determined by genetics and two-thirds by environmental influences.

Cattell believes that psychopathology can result from either an abnormal configuration of the normal source traits, or from the possession of one or more of the twelve abnormal traits that Cattell has discovered. Cattell believes that trait analysis should precede psychotherapy because such an analysis will provide an accurate diagnosis of the problem and will suggest the most effective method of treatment. Also, trait evaluation should occur throughout therapy to determine how treatment is affecting the client's total personality.

Factor analysis yields personality traits when applied to humans, whereas it yields syntality when applied to the study of specific groups. Cattell is very much a determinist, in that he believes that when an individual's traits are specified, when these traits are weighted or loaded according to their importance in a given situation, and when temporary influences such as fatigue, illness, or anxiety are taken into consideration, a person's behavior can be predicted with considerable accuracy. Prediction is made by including as much information about a person as possible in a specification equation.

Cattell's theory rests on a solid foundation of empirical research. He uses the factor analytic technique to discover personality traits and then, once discovered, he uses them to describe and predict a wide variety of behaviors. The research done using his 16 PF questionnaire alone is vast. Perhaps no other personality theorist has performed or stimulated as much empirical research as has Cattell.

Cattell's theory has been criticized for containing too many subjective elements, for assuming that human behavior is much more consistent than it actually is, and for concentrating too much on groups and group averages at the expense of the unique individual. Cattell's theory has been praised for providing scientific rigor to the study of personality, an area that typically lacks such rigor, and providing tools that can be used in a large number of applied areas; for example, clinical diagnoses, vocational and marital counseling, and personnel selection.

EXPERIENTIAL EXERCISES

1. By referring to Table 8–2, administer Cattell's 16 PF questionnaire to yourself. Assume that a 10 is the highest score you can attain on a factor and a 1 is the lowest. A score of 5 would indicate that you think that you are about in the middle of the two extremes for any given factor. In other words, any score from 1 to 10 is possible for each of the 16 factors. Next create a personality profile for yourself like those shown in Figure 8–3. Cattell has found that, at least in the case of married couples, the more similar the profiles of two persons are, the more positive is their relationship. Have someone you are close to respond to the 16 PF questionnaire, and summarize his or her performance in a personality profile. Compare yours with his or hers. What conclusions do you draw from the comparison?

2. Give an example of how subsidiation and long-circuiting operate in your life. That is, show how a particular erg relates to one or more of your sentiments which, in turn, relates to one or more of your attitudes.

3. Approach the prediction of your own behavior as Cattell would. That is, assume that the more you know about yourself and the situation that you are in, the more accurate will be your prediction of your behavior in that situation. Take any situation that you will find yourself in shortly (for example a social event, a major test, going home for a visit with relatives) and list the kinds of information that Cattell would need to know about you and the situation to predict your behavior accurately. In other words, you are applying the specification equation to yourself. For this exercise you will need to use some of the information that you learned about yourself in experiential exercise 1. What conclusion do you reach concerning the applicability of Cattell's specification equation to the prediction of your own behavior?

DISCUSSION QUESTIONS

1. Describe the technique of factor analysis as Cattell used it to study personality.
2. Differentiate between the R- and P-factor analytic techniques.
3. Distinguish between surface traits and source traits.
4. Distinguish between ability, temperament, and dynamic traits.
5. Distinguish between fluid and crystallized intelligence.
6. Discuss ergs, metaergs, and the dynamic lattice.
7. What is meant by subsidiation?
8. What is meant by long-circuiting?
9. Discuss Cattell's concept of structured learning. Include a discussion of the dynamic crossroads in your answer.
10. Discuss Cattell's views on the significance of early home environment on personality development. Be sure to include in your answer Cattell's findings concerning the influence of birth order.
11. Summarize Cattell's findings concerning the relative contributions of heredity and environment to personality development.
12. How does Cattell account for psychopathology?
13. How, according to Cattell, should personality assessment and psychotherapy be related?
14. Discuss Cattell's concept of syntality.
15. Report and elaborate on the components of the specification equation.
16. Respond to the statement: Factor analysis is only as good as the information fed into it.
17. Summarize the essence of Cattell's theory of personality.
18. Why has Cattell's theory been criticized?
19. What are the major contributions of Cattell's theory?

SUGGESTIONS FOR FURTHER READING

CATTELL, R. B. (1950). *Personality: A Systematic Theoretical and Factual Study.* New York: McGraw-Hill.
Cattell's effort to synthesize his earlier observations and to evaluate data from theories other than his own. For example, topics include psychoanalysis, cultural and physical anthropology, and sociology.

CATTELL, R. B. (1965). *The Scientific Analysis of Personality.* Baltimore: Penguin Books.

Perhaps the most comprehensive and most readable presentation of Cattell's theory. Cattell revised this book with P. Kline and published the revision in 1976 as *The Scientific Analysis of Personality and Motivation.* New York: Academic Press.

CATTELL, R. B. (1974). "Autobiography," in *A History of Psychology in Autobiography,* vol. 6, ed. G. Lindzey. Englewood Cliffs, NJ: Prentice-Hall.

Presents the many interesting details of Cattell's personal life.

CATTELL, R. B. (1979, 1980). *Personality and Learning Theory,* vols. 1, 2. New York: Springer.

These two volumes represent Cattell's attempt to synthesize his earlier research findings and to more clearly specify the roles of environmental and biologic influences on behavior. Volume 1 (1979) is subtitled, *The Structure of Personality in its Environment* and volume 2 (1980) is subtitled, *A Systems Theory of Maturation and Structured Learning.*

CATTELL, R. B. (1982). *The Inheritance of Personality and Ability.* New York: Academic Press.

Uses the newest, most complex methodologies to assess the role of genetic factors in the determination of personality.

DREGER, R. M. (1972). (Ed.), *Multivariate Personality Research: Contributions to the Understanding of Personality in Honor of Raymond B. Cattell.* Baton Rouge: Claitor.

A volume of articles by distinguished scientists from all over the world published in honor of R. B. Cattell. This volume demonstrates the broad, deep, and varied impact of Cattell's work on the scientific study of personality.

GLOSSARY

Ability trait. A trait that determines how effectively a person works toward a desired goal. Intelligence is such a trait.

Attitude. A learned tendency to respond in a particular way in a particular situation to a particular object or event. Attitudes derive from sentiments, which in turn derive from ergs. An attitude is one kind of metaerg.

Classical conditioning. The kind of learning in which a stimulus that did not originally elicit a response is made to do so. An example would be when a dog is made to salivate at the sound of a buzzer that had been associated with food.

Cluster analysis. The systematic search of a correlation matrix in order to discover factors.

Constitutional trait. A trait that is genetically determined.

Correlation. The condition that exists when values on two variables vary together in some systematic way.

Correlation coefficient. A mathematical expression indicating the extent to which two variables are correlated. Correlation coefficients can vary from + 1.00, indicating a perfect positive correlation, to − 1.00, indicating a perfect negative correlation.

Correlation matrix. A display of the many correlation coefficients that results when many sources of information are intercorrelated.

Crystallized intelligence. The kind of intelligence that comes from formal education or from general experience. This is the kind of intelligence that most intelligence tests attempt to measure. Cattell's most recent research has indicated that the ability to benefit from experience which is reflected in crystallized intelligence is largely innate.

Culture fair intelligence test. A test designed to measure fluid intelligence rather than crystallized intelligence.

Determinism. The belief that behavior is a function of a finite number of variables, and if those variables were completely known, behavior could be predicted with complete accuracy.

Dynamic crossroads. The many possible behavior patterns that result when ergic satisfaction is blocked.

Dynamic lattice. A diagram showing the relationships among ergs, sentiments, and attitudes.

Dynamic trait. A motivational trait that sets a person in motion toward a goal. Cattell postulated the existence of two kinds of dynamic traits: ergs and metaergs.

Environmental-mold trait. A trait that is determined by experience rather than by heredity.

Erg. A constitutional dynamic source trait that provides the energy for all behavior. Much the same as what other theorists call a primary drive. Hunger and thirst are examples of ergs.

Factor. An ability or characteristic that is thought to be responsible for consistent behavior.

Factor analysis. A complex, statistical technique based on the concept of correlation, which Cattell used to discover and investigate personality traits.

Factor loading. The weight given to a factor based on its importance to a given situation.

Fluid intelligence. A general problem-solving ability that is largely innate.

Instrumental conditioning. Learning to make a response that either will make a reward available or remove an aversive stimulus.

L-data. Information about a person's everyday life. The *L* stands for life record.

Long-circuiting. The indirect satisfaction of an erg. An example is a man developing athletic ability in order to be desirable to a female who will satisfy his sexual desires.

Metaerg. An environmental-mold, dynamic source trait. Much the same as what other theorists called secondary or learned drives. See also Attitude and Sentiment.

Negative correlation. The condition that exists when, as values on one variable tend to increase, values on a second variable tend to decrease, and vice versa.

Positive correlation. The condition that exists when values on two variables tend to increase or decrease together.

P-technique. The kind of factor analysis that studies how a single individual's traits change over time.

Q-data. Information provided when people fill out a questionnaire on which they rate themselves on various characteristics. The Q stands for questionnaire.

R-technique. The kind of factor analysis that studies many things about many people.

Self-sentiment. The concern for oneself that is a prerequisite to the pursuit of any goal in life.

Sentiment. A learned predisposition to respond to a class of objects or events in a certain way. A sentiment is one kind of metaerg.

Situational modulators. The temporary conditions, such as fatigue or illness, that influence how a person will respond in a given situation.

Source traits. These traits constitute a person's personality structure and are thus the ultimate causes of behavior. Source traits are causally related to surface traits.

Specification equation. A formula listing the various factors influencing behavior in a given situation.

Structured learning. The kind of learning that results in the rearrangement of one's personality traits. According to Cattell, this is the most important kind of learning.

Subsidiation. The fact that sentiments depend on ergs and attitudes depend on sentiments.

Surface traits. The outward manifestations of source traits. These are the characteristics of a person that can be directly observed and measured.

Syntality. The description of the traits that characterize a group or a nation.

T-data. Information obtained about a person from the performance on an objective test. The T stands for test.

Temperament trait. A constitutional source trait that determines a person's emotionality.

Trait. For Cattell, the term trait refers either to a group of interrelated overt behaviors (surface trait) or to the deeper determinant of such interrelated behavior (source traits). The main usefulness of surface traits is that they provide information about source traits.

9

B. F. Skinner

■ **CHAPTER OUTLINE**

B. F. Skinner was born on 20 March, 1904 in Susquehanna, Pennsylvania. He was the older of two sons, but his younger brother died at the age of sixteen. Skinner's father was a lawyer, who wanted his son to follow in his footsteps, but that was never to be. Skinner was raised according to strict standards but was physically punished only once.

> I was never physically punished by my father and only once by my mother. She washed my mouth out with soap and water because I had used a bad word. My father never missed an opportunity, however, to inform me of the punishments which were waiting if I turned out to have a criminal mind. He once took me through the county jail, and on a summer vacation I was taken to a lecture with colored slides describing life in Sing Sing. As a result I am afraid of the police and buy too many tickets to their annual dance. (Skinner 1967, 390–91)

Perhaps this unusually small amount of physical punishment influenced Skinner's later theoretical emphasis on the positive rather than on the aversive control of behavior. As we have seen throughout this text, it is not unusual to find the seeds of a theory in the theorist's early childhood experiences.

Skinner's aptitude for creative apparatus building, for which he is now widely known, was evident in his childhood.

> I was always building things. I built roller-skate scooters, steerable wagons, sleds, and rafts to be poled about on shallow ponds. I made see-saws, merry-go-rounds, and slides. I made slingshots, bows and arrows, blow guns and water pistols from lengths of bamboo, and from a discarded water boiler a steam cannon with which I could shoot plugs of potato and carrot over the houses of our neighbors. I made tops, diabolos, model airplanes driven by twisted rubber bands, box kites, and tin propellers which could be sent high into the air with a spool-and-string spinner. I tried again and again to make a glider in which I myself might fly.
>
> I invented things, some of them in the spirit of the outrageous contraptions in the cartoons which Rube Goldberg was publishing in the *Philadelphia Inquirer* (to which, as a good Republican, my father subscribed). For example, a friend and I used to gather elderberries and sell them from door to door, and I built a flotation system which separated ripe from green berries. I worked for years on the design of a perpetual motion machine. (It did not work.) (Skinner 1967, 388)

In high school, Skinner earned money by playing in a jazz band and with an orchestra. He went to Hamilton College, a small liberal arts school in Clinton, New York. He felt that he never fit into the life of the college student, because he was terrible at sports and was "pushed around" by unnecessary requirements such as daily chapel. He wrote highly critical articles about the faculty and administration in the school paper and disrupted the campus with a number of tricks. For example, he caused the campus and the local railroad station to be jammed with people by falsely announcing a lecture by Charlie Chaplin. The college president told Skinner to quit his antics, or he would not graduate. Skinner graduated with a Phi Beta Kappa Key and a B.A. degree in English literature. It is interesting to note that Skinner never took a course in psychology as an undergraduate.

Skinner left college with a burning desire to be a writer. Part of this desire is explained by the fact that the famous American poet Robert Frost had favorably reviewed three of Skinner's short stories. Skinner's first attempt at writing was in the attic of his parents' home. This attempt failed. His next attempt was in Greenwich Village, in New York City. This attempt also failed. After two years of trying, Skinner concluded that he "had nothing important to say" and gave up the idea of becoming a writer. He spent the next summer in Europe.

While in Greenwich Village, Skinner read the works of Ivan Pavlov and J. B. Watson, which greatly influenced him. On returning from Europe in 1928, he enrolled in the graduate program in psychology at Harvard. He at last had found his niche (or as Erikson would say, his identity), and he pursued his studies with extreme intensity. Skinner described his daily routine at Harvard:

> I would rise at six, study until breakfast, go to classes, laboratories, and libraries with no more than fifteen minutes unscheduled during the day, study until exactly nine o'clock at night and go to bed. I saw no movies or plays, seldom went to concerts, had scarcely any dates and read nothing but psychology and physiology. (1967, 398)

B. F. Skinner

This high degree of self-discipline characterizes Skinner's work habits to this day.

Skinner earned his M.A. in two years (1930), his Ph.D. in three years (1931), and then remained at Harvard for the next five years as a postdoctoral fellow. He began his teaching career at the University of Minnesota in 1936 and remained there until 1945. It was during this time that Skinner established himself as a nationally prominent experimental psychologist by publishing his famous book *The Behavior of Organisms* (1938).

In 1945 Skinner moved to Indiana University as chairman of the psychology department, where he remained until 1948 when he returned to Harvard. He has been there ever since.

Skinner has been highly productive, to say the least. In 1948 he published *Walden Two*, which described a society that functioned in accordance with his principles of learning. In 1953 he published *Science and Human Behavior*, which, in this writer's opinion, is still the best overall presentation of his theory. *Verbal Behavior* was published in 1957, and in that same year he published (along with Charles B. Ferster) *Schedules of Reinforcement*. He wrote *Beyond Freedom and Dignity* in 1971, which became a best-seller and garnered reactions from a wide variety of sources, including an extremely negative one from the then vice-president of the United States, Spiro T. Agnew.

Skinner was disturbed that his position had been misunderstood by so many (including many psychologists), so he wrote another book, *About Behaviorism* (1974), that attempted to clarify his position. The titles listed here represent only a sample of Skinner's many articles and books.

*John Broadus
Watson*

(Courtesy Clark University.)

Among Skinner's many honors are an honorary doctor of science degree from his Alma mater, Hamilton College; the American Psychological Association's Distinguished Contribution Award in 1958 and its Gold Medal Award in 1971; and the National Medal of Science Award for distinguished scientific achievement in 1968.

Behaviorism

It is impossible to understand fully Skinner's view of personality without first understanding the school of psychology to which he belongs, which is **behaviorism.** To understand behaviorism, we must briefly discuss two other schools of psychology. Psychology's first school of thought was **structuralism,** which developed in Germany. The main goal of the structuralists was to study the nature of consciousness through the use of introspection or self-analysis. A well-trained subject was shown an object and was asked to describe the various sensations that the object caused. It was hoped that that process would eventually uncover the elements of thought from which all conscious experience is derived. Structuralism was short-lived for several reasons, but the main one was the growing influence of Darwinism. American psychologists embraced the doctrine of evolution enthusiastically and created America's first school of psychology around it, which was **functionalism.** As the name implies, the functionalist was concerned primarily with discovering how various processes are related to survival. For example, they studied how thinking and behaving functioned in one's adaptation to the environment. It is important to note that the functionalist studied both behavior *and* cognitive processes but did so with the goal of discovering how they enhanced adjustment to the environment.

John B. Watson took the next step. According to Watson, if psychology wanted to be truly scientific, it would have to have a subject matter that could be reliably and objectively studied. This could not be consciousness, because the study of consciousness had been notoriously unreliable and because it could be studied only indirectly, through introspection. The subject matter on which Watson insisted was behavior, and he thus founded the school of *behaviorism.* Watson insisted that the study of consciousness be abandoned completely. He also wanted to end explanations of human behavior in terms of instincts. Likewise, he thought that setting man artificially apart from the other animals made no sense. The behavior of both, he said, is governed by the same principles.

Watson believed that, with the exception of a few basic emotions that are inherited, behavior patterns are learned through experience. Therefore, if you can control a person's experiences, you can create any kind of person you wish. Watson's following statement of this belief is one of the most famous (or infamous) statements ever made by a psychologist:

> Give me a dozen healthy infants, well-formed, and my own specified world to bring them up in and I'll guarantee to take any one at random and train him to become any type of specialist I might select—doctor, lawyer, artist, merchant, chief, and yes, even beggarman and thief, regardless of his talents, penchants, tendencies, abilities, vocations, and race of his ancestors. (1926, 10)

Behaviorism became the rage in American psychology, and although its popularity is diminishing, behaviorism still is an important part of American psychology. This brings us back to B. F. Skinner, who is no doubt the most famous behaviorist in the world today.

Like most behaviorists, Skinner bypasses the internal workings of the organism (for instance, cognitive and physiological processes) and concentrates on the relationship between environmental events and behavior. For this reason, Skinner's approach has been characterized as the "empty organism" approach. Skinner believes that no information is lost by making a **functional analysis** between measurable experiences and measurable behavior and leaving out the intervening activities. In fact, he said, all of the problems inherent in a study of consciousness can be avoided.

> The mentalistic problem can be avoided by going directly to the prior physical causes while bypassing intermediate feelings or states of mind. The quickest way to do this is to confine oneself to what an early behaviorist, Max Meyer, called the "psychology of the other one": consider only those facts which can be objectively observed in the behavior of one person in its relation to his prior environmental history. If all linkages are lawful, nothing is lost by neglecting a supposed nonphysical link. Thus, if we know that a child has not eaten for a long time, and if we know that he therefore feels hungry and that because he feels hungry he then eats, then we know that if he has not eaten for a long time, he will eat. (Skinner 1974, 13)

As we shall see throughout this chapter, Skinner believes strongly that a behavioral technology based on behavioristic principles can solve many of the world's major problems. He believes, however, that many nonscientific explanations of the causes of behavior are inhibiting the utilization of such a technology. His book *Beyond Freedom and Dignity* (1971) describes this problem in great detail. The following quotation from that book nicely summarizes Skinner's concerns:

> The environment is obviously important, but its role has remained obscure. It does not push or pull, it *selects*, and this function is difficult to discover and analyze. The role of natural selection in evolution was formulated only a little more than a hundred years ago, and the selective role of environment in shaping and maintaining the behavior of the individual is only beginning to be recognized and studied. As the interaction between organism and environment has come to be understood, however, effects once assigned to states of mind, feelings, and traits are beginning to be traced to accessible conditions, and a technology of behavior may therefore become available. It will not solve our problems, however, until it replaces traditional prescientific views, and these are strongly entrenched. (25)

In the following section, we will examine how, according to Skinner, the environment *selects* some behaviors and not others.

Respondent and Operant Behavior

It should be clear from what has preceded that both John B. Watson and B. F. Skinner represent the behavioristic camp. Although it is true that they both are behaviorists, they are different kinds of behaviorists, because each emphasizes a different kind of behavior. Watson accepted the principles of learning developed by Ivan Pavlov as a model for his brand of behaviorism. Pavlov's work on learning contains the following ingredients:

Conditioned Stimulus (CS)—A stimulus that, at the beginning of training, does not elicit a predictable response from an organism.

Unconditioned Stimulus (UCS)—A stimulus that elicits an automatic, natural, and predictable response from an organism.

Unconditioned Response (UCR)—The natural and automatic response elicited by the unconditioned stimulus.

Pavlov found that if the conditioned stimulus were paired several times with the unconditioned stimulus, it gradually would develop the capacity to elicit a response similar to the unconditioned response; such a response was called a **conditioned response** (CR). Pavlovian or **classical conditioning** can be diagrammed as follows:

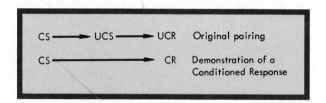

Skinner refers to behavior elicited by a known stimulus as **respondent behavior,** and all conditioned and unconditioned responses are examples. He calls Pavlovian or classical conditioning **type S conditioning,** to stress the importance of the stimulus. The important point to remember about respondent behavior is that a direct link exists between its occurrence and the stimulus that preceded it. In other words, a direct stimulus-response association occurs. All reflexes, such as pupillary constriction when light intensity is increased or pupillary dilation when light intensity is decreased, are examples of respondent behavior.

Unlike Pavlov and Watson, Skinner does not emphasize respondent behavior in his theory. Rather, he emphasizes behavior that is *not* linked to any known stimulus. He emphasizes behavior that appears to be simply emitted by the organism rather than elicited by a known stimulus, which is labeled **operant behavior.** Skinner believes that operant behavior is indeed caused by stimulation, but the source of that stimulation is not known, so that behavior *appears* to be emitted. Skinner also said that it is not important to know the origins of operant behavior. The most important characteristic of operant behavior is that it is under the control of its consequences. In other words, it is what happens *after* operant behavior is emitted that determines its fate. The name "operant" now might make more sense; operant behavior operates on the environment so as to change it in some way. The changes in the environment that it causes will determine the subsequent frequency with which the response is made. We will have much more to say about this concept in the next section, but for now suffice it to say that the conditioning of operant behavior is called **type R conditioning** to emphasize the importance of the response. Skinner's work has been, and is, primarily in the area of operant conditioning.

Operant Conditioning

Operant conditioning has been used in psychotherapy, education, and child rearing, and has been proposed as a means of redesigning cultures. A technique this powerful must be complex and not easily comprehensible, right? Wrong! Operant conditioning is summarized in the following statement: "If the occurrence of an operant is followed by presentation of a reinforcing stimulus the strength is increased" (Skinner 1938, 21). Putting this in slightly different form, we can say, if a response is followed by a reward the response will be strengthened. This enormously powerful rule could not be more simple: *If you want to strengthen a certain response or behavior pattern, reward it!*

How do we know what will act as a reinforcer or reward for a particular organism? Only through its effect on behavior. If a stimulus strengthens behavior, it is a reinforcer; if it does not, it is not.

To modify behavior, two elements are necessary—behavior and a reinforcer. Having defined operant, or type *R* conditioning, we will look in more detail at its characteristics. It should be remembered as we go through these characteristics that, according to Skinner, personality is nothing more than consistent behavior patterns that have been strengthened through operant conditioning. As we look more carefully at the principles of operant conditioning, we are at the same time examining Skinner's theory of personality.

Acquisition

To demonstrate operant conditioning, Skinner invented a small experimental chamber for use with small animals, such as rats or pigeons, that has come to be called a **"Skinner box."** Typically, the chamber contains a lever, a light, a food cup, and a grid floor. The apparatus is arranged so that when the lever is depressed, a feeder mechanism is activated, which delivers a pellet of food into the food cup. In this box the lever-press response is the operant response of interest, and the food pellet is the reinforcer. Even before the reinforcer is introduced into the situation, the animal will probably press the lever now and then just as part of its random activity. The frequency with which an operant response occurs *before* the introduction of a reinforcer is called the **operant level** of that response. When the response is followed by a reinforcer, the frequency with which it is made increases, which is what Skinner meant when he said a response has been strengthened. Operant conditioning is measured by the change in **rate of responding.** Under the conditions we have described, the rate with which the lever-press response is made will increase (relative to its operant level), by which operant conditioning is said to have been demonstrated. Note that the origins of the initial lever-press responses are not known; nor do they need to be. The situation is arranged so that when a lever-press response is made, it is reinforced, and when it is reinforced, it is strengthened in that the frequency with which it is made increases.

So much for rats in Skinner boxes; now, how about people? Remember, the behaviorist does not believe that one set of learning principles exists for humans and another set for nonhumans. It is assumed that the same principles apply to all living organisms. Such an assumption has not gone unchallenged. Greenspoon (1955) hypothesized that the therapist's "mmm-hmm" is reinforcing in a situation in which a client is talking quietly. To verify this notion, Greenspoon tested many subjects one at a time in a situation in which he uttered "mmm-hmm" each time a plural noun was spoken by the subject. This arrangement subsequently increased the frequency with which plural nouns were spoken, even though none of the subjects were aware of the fact that his or her verbal behavior was being modified.

Verplanck (1955) had his experimental class at Harvard condition a wide range of simple motor responses using points as the reinforcer.

> After finding a fellow student who was willing to be a subject, the experimenter instructed him as follows: "Your job is to work for points. You get a point every time I tap the table with my pencil. As soon as you get a point, record it on your sheet of paper. Keep track of your own points." With these instructions, it seemed likely that a tap, a "point," would prove to be a reinforcing stimulus. The method worked very well. Indeed, the experimenters were now able to condition a wide variety of simple motor behaviors, such as slapping the ankle, tapping the chin, raising an arm, picking up a fountain pen, and so on. They were further able to differentiate out, or shape, more complex parts of behavior, and then to manipulate them as responses. The data they obtained included the results on the manipulation of many of the variables whose effects were familiar in operant conditioning of rats and pigeons. Despite the fact that the experiments were carried out in a variety of situations, the experimenters were able to obtain graphical functions that could not be distinguished from functions obtained on the rat or the pigeon in a Skinner box. (Verplanck 1955, 598–99)

Verplanck and his students went on to condition the response of stating opinions (for example, "I think that," or "I believe that").

> The results of these experiments were unequivocal. In the first experiment, on opinion-statements, every one of 23 subjects showed a higher rate of giving opinion-statements during the 10-minute period when the experimenter reinforced each of them by agreeing with it, or by repeating it back to him in paraphrase, than he showed in the first 10-minute period when the experimenter did not reinforce. (Verplanck 1955, 600)

Verplanck, like Greenspoon, found that conditioning did not depend on the subject's awareness of what was happening. Most of Verplanck's subjects were totally unaware of the experimental conditions governing their behavior.

The Greenspoon and Verplanck studies represent only a sample of the hundreds of studies that have confirmed that operant principles apply to human behavior as well as to nonhuman behavior. These two studies were chosen for this book because they show the ease with which that is demonstrated.

Shaping

What does one do if the response that one wants to strengthen is not in the organism's response repertoire? The answer is that it is shaped into existence. Assume that the lever-press response is one that a rat would initially not make on its own in a Skinner box. Using the principles of operant conditioning already described, the lever-press response can be developed through a series of several steps. Using an external hand switch to trigger the feeder mechanism, the rat would be reinforced only for behavior that brings it closer and closer to making the response that is ultimately wanted, which, in this case, is the lever-press. We see that the shaping process has two components: **differential reinforcement,** which means that some responses are reinforced and some are not; and **successive approximations,** which means the responses that are reinforced are those that are increasingly close to the response ultimately desired. Hergenhahn listed the following steps as one way of **shaping** the bar-press response:

1. Reinforce the rat for being on the side of the test chamber containing the bar.
2. Reinforce him for moving in the direction of the bar.
3. Reinforce him for rising up in front of the bar.
4. Reinforce him for touching the bar.
5. Reinforce him for touching the bar with both paws.
6. Reinforce him for exerting pressure on the bar.
7. Reinforce him only for the bar-press response. (1974, 361)

Several complex human skills need to be shaped into existence over time, because they do not appear initially in fully developed form. Reading is one example. Hergenhahn suggested the following shaping procedure to encourage reading in a young child:

1. Have a number of children's books available and leave them where the child is likely to come across them.
2. If a child avoids books, reward activities related to reading, such as noticing signs, naming and/or labeling things, and so on.
3. As the activities in number 2 above are rewarded, the child will tend to do them more often, and when he does, one must become more rigorous in what is expected before giving additional rewards, for example, reading longer signs and attending to more detailed labels.
4. A next step could be to ask the child to get you certain books, such as the red one, the one with the duck on the cover, the one with the A, B, C,'s on it. When he does, he is rewarded.
5. The next step involves getting the child still more involved with the book, for example, asking him to find certain things like the red barn, the dog, and so on. Again, the child is rewarded in some way for doing this.
6. The above process is continued and refined until the child is reading on his own.
7. To maintain this interest in reading once it has been brought about through

these procedures, it is important to go on rewarding the child even when he starts reading on his own, at least to begin with. Eventually, the content of the stories will begin to be enough of a reward to maintain the child's interest in reading. (1972, 40–41)

According to operant theory, the best way to teach a complex skill is to divide it into its basic components and gradually shape it into existence one small step at a time. According to this viewpoint, the shaping process is extremely important to education and to child rearing. For example, Skinner gave the following example of how a mother may unknowingly shape undesirable behavior in her child:

The mother may unwillingly promote the very behavior she does not want. For example, when she is busy she is likely not to respond to a call or request made in a quiet tone of voice. She may answer the child only when [he or she] raises [his or her] voice. The average intensity of the child's vocal behavior therefore moves up to another level. . . . Eventually the mother gets used to this level and again reinforces only louder instances. This vicious circle brings about louder and louder behavior. . . . The mother behaves, in fact, as if she has been given the assignment of teaching the child to be annoying. (1951, 29)

Extinction

If operant behavior that is followed by a reinforcer is strengthened, it should follow that if the reinforcer is removed from the situation, the operant behavior would be weakened. This pattern is exactly what happens. If, for example, after the lever-press response was conditioned, the feeder mechanism was disconnected, thus creating a situation in which a lever-press response is no longer followed by a food pellet, eventually that response would return to its original operant level. In other words, when a reinforcer no longer follows a response, the frequency with which the response is made returns to the level it was at, before the reinforcer was introduced into the situation, and we say that **extinction** has occurred.

Extinction can be regarded as the counterpart of acquisition, and the two processes together, according to Skinner, explain much of what we call personality. Briefly stated, rewarded behavior persists, and nonrewarded behavior extinguishes. For example, an infant emits the sounds contained in every language on earth. From these random babblings the child's language is shaped. Those sounds that resemble words of the parents' language are noticed or reinforced in some way, and those utterances that are irrelevant to the parents' language are ignored. The reinforced verbal responses are strengthened and are shaped further, whereas the nonreinforced verbal responses are extinguished. So it is with all the behavior we refer to as personality.

Extinction is important to the Skinnerian view of behavior modification. This view is quite simple: *Reinforce desired behavior and ignore undesirable behavior.* Skinner looks on extinction as the proper method of dealing with undesirable behavior, *not punishment.* Skinner gave the following example:

The most effective alternative process [to punishment] is probably *extinction.* This takes time but is much more rapid than allowing the response to be forgotten.

The technique seems to be relatively free of objectionable by-products. We recommend it, for example, when we suggest that a parent "pay no attention" to objectionable behavior on the part of his child. If the child's behavior is strong only because it has been reinforced by "getting a rise out of" the parent, it will disappear when this consequence is no longer forthcoming. (1953, 192)

We will have more to say about the problems associated with punishment later in this chapter.

Spontaneous Recovery

Let us say that we have extinguished the lever press in a rat. That is, because the reinforcement for a lever press was discontinued, that response went back to its original operant level. Now we take the animal out of the Skinner box and put it back in its home cage for a period of time, say twenty-four hours. Next we put it back in the Skinner box. We usually would note that, although there was no additional training, the rate with which the lever-press response is made again will increase. This renewed burst of responding following a delay after extinction is called **spontaneous recovery.**

Behavior therapy must take spontaneous recovery into account. Both the therapist and patient, believing that an undesirable habit has been extinguished, may be disappointed when it reappears, but the reappearance of the habit may simply be spontaneous recovery. In a way, the appearance of spontaneous recovery indicates that extinction was never complete in the first place. After several extinction sessions, no spontaneous recovery will occur, even after a prolonged rest period.

Discriminative Operants

A **discriminative operant** is an operant response that is made under one set of circumstances but not under others. In describing the Skinner box, it was mentioned that it typically contains a light, which is usually above the lever. The circuitry of the Skinner box can be arranged so that a lever-press response is reinforced when the light is on but not reinforced when the light is off. Under these circumstances the rate with which the lever is pressed is much higher when the light is on than it is when the light is off. We say that the light has become a **discriminative stimulus** (S^D) for the lever-press response. In other words, the light-on condition becomes the *occasion* for the lever-press response. With S^R symbolizing a reinforcing stimulus or simply a reinforcer, the situation can be diagrammed as follows:

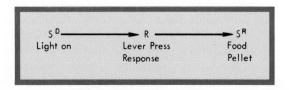

Everyday life is filled with discriminative operants. A few examples follow.

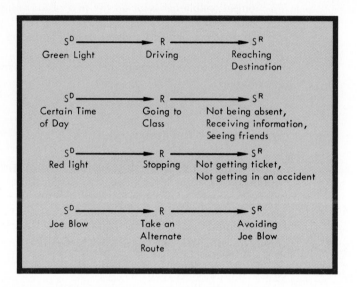

Secondary Reinforcement

At this point we must distinguish between a **primary reinforcer** and a **secondary reinforcer.** Primary reinforcers are factors related to survival, such as food, water, oxygen, elimination, and sexual activity. These factors are not biologically neutral, because if an organism (or in the case of sex, a species) goes long enough without any one of them, it will not survive. Food for a hungry animal is a natural, powerful, primary reinforcer, as is water for a thirsty animal. Secondary reinforcers are stimuli that are originally biologically neutral and thus not reinforcing but that *acquired* their reinforcing properties through their association with a primary reinforcer. This principle can be stated as follows: *Any neutral stimulus that is consistently paired with a primary reinforcer takes on reinforcing properties of its own.*

It follows that each S^D that precedes a primary reinforcer, such as food, will become a secondary reinforcer. In our example in which a light was the occasion for a lever-press response to be reinforced by food, the light became a secondary reinforcer. Once a stimulus takes on reinforcing properties, it can be used to condition a new response or it can be used to maintain the response for which it was the occasion. For example, the light in the example could be used to teach the animal a response other than the lever-press response; for example, sticking its nose in a particular corner of the Skinner box. Likewise if the light followed the lever-press response during extinction, the animal would go on responding far beyond the point at which it would stop if the light did not follow the lever-press response.

According to Skinner, most human behavior is governed by secondary reinforcers. For example, because mothers are typically associated with the satisfaction of the child's basic needs, they become secondary reinforcers. Eventually the sight of the mother is enough to pacify temporarily a hungry or thirsty child. In fact, attention alone is a powerful secondary reinforcer, because it must precede the satisfaction of almost all, if not all, basic needs. Besides attention, which is a secondary reinforcer for children and adults alike, other common secondary reinforcers include:

kind words	awards
bodily contact	recognition
glances	gifts
money	privileges
medals	points

Secondary reinforcers that do not depend on a particular motivational state are called **generalized reinforcers.** A mother, for example, is a generalized reinforcer, because her presence is associated with several primary reinforcers. Her reinforcing properties do not depend on the child's being hungry or thirsty. Money is another generalized reinforcer because, like a mother, it usually is associated with several primary reinforcers.

There are two points of agreement in Skinner's theory and Allport's theory. First, they both believe the single individual should be intensively studied; that is, they both use the idiographic approach to research. For example, Skinner stated:

> A prediction of what the *average* individual will do is often of little or no value in dealing with a particular individual . . . a science is helpful in dealing with the individual only insofar as its laws refer to individuals. A science of behavior which concerns only the behavior of groups is not likely to be of help in our understanding of the particular case. (1953, 19)

Second, they both accept the notion of functional autonomy. The notion was not nearly as important to Skinner as it was to Allport, but, nonetheless, Skinner did accept it to a certain extent. This acceptance can be detected in the following statement by Skinner:

> Eventually generalized reinforcers are effective even though the primary reinforcers upon which they are based no longer accompany them. We play games of skill for their own sake. We get attention or approval for its own sake. Affection is not always followed by a more explicit sexual reinforcement. The submissiveness of others is reinforcing even though we make no use of it. A miser may be so reinforced by money that he will starve rather than give it up. (1953, 81)

Chaining

For the Skinnerians, much complex behavior is explained using the concept of **chaining,** which involves the notion of secondary reinforcement. We mentioned that any S^D that is the occasion for primary reinforcement becomes a secondary reinforcer. It is also true that all stimuli that consistently and immediately precede primary reinforcement will take on secondary reinforcing properties. In turn, stimuli associated with those stimuli will take on reinforcing properties, and so forth. In this way, stimuli far removed from the primary reinforcement can become secondary reinforcers, and as such can influence behavior. These secondary reinforcers develop two functions: (1) they reinforce the response that preceded their appearance and (2) they act as an S^D for the next response. The secondary reinforcers act as S^Ds that ultimately bring the organism into contact with the primary reinforcer. It is the primary reinforcer that holds this entire chain of events together.

> One response can bring the organism into contact with stimuli that act as an S^D for another response, which in turn causes it to experience stimuli that cause a third, and so on. This process is referred to as *chaining*. In fact, most behavior can be shown to involve some form of chaining. For example, even the lever-press in the Skinner box is not an isolated response. The stimuli in the Skinner box act as S^Ds, causing the animal to turn toward the lever. The sight of the lever causes him to approach it and press it. The firing of the feeder mechanism acts as an additional S^D which elicits the response of going to the food cup. Consuming the food pellet acts as an S^D causing the animal to return to the lever and again press it. This sequence of events (chain) is held together by the food pellet, which, of course, is a primary positive reinforcer. It can be said that various elements of a behavior chain are held together by secondary reinforcers, but that the entire chain depends upon a primary reinforcer. (Hergenhahn 1988, 93)

The process described in the preceding quotation is diagrammed in Figure 9–1.

Chained behavior also results when two people confront each other. Typically, what one person says acts as an S^D for a response from the second person, and the second person's response not only rewards the first person's response but also acts as an S^D for another response, and so forth. An example of this process is diagrammed in Figure 9–2.

Skinner maintains that these principles also govern our behavior when we simply roam about or even when we mentally free associate.

> A response may produce or alter some of the variables which control another response. The result is a "chain." It may have little or no organization. When we go for a walk, roaming the countryside or wandering idly through a museum or store, one episode in our behavior generates conditions responsible for another. We look to one side and are stimulated by an object which causes us to move in its direction. In the course of this movement, we receive aversive stimulation from which we beat a hasty retreat. This generates a condition of satiation or fatigue in which, once free of aversive stimulation, we sit down to rest. And so on. Chaining

Figure 9–1
An example of simple chained behavior.

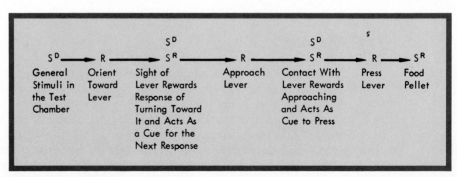

(From Hergenhahn 1988, p. 93.)

Figure 9–2
*An example of
chaining involving
two people.*

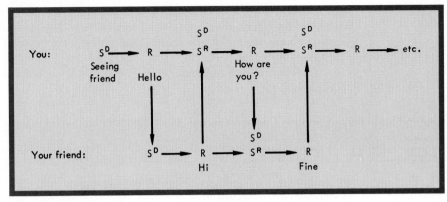

(From Hergenhahn 1988, p. 94.)

need not be the result of movement in space. We wander or roam verbally, for example, in a casual conversation or when we "speak our thoughts" in free association. (Skinner 1953, 224)

Anyone who plays a musical instrument has experienced chained behavior. When into a musical piece, playing a note both reinforces the preceding response (S^R) and stimulates the next one (S^D).

Verbal Behavior

As indicated in chapter 1, the nativism-empiricism controversy is an ancient one. The nativist maintains that important attributes, such as intelligence, creativity, or even personality, are mainly genetically determined. The empiricist, conversely, insists that such attributes are the product of experience and not of genes. As one might expect, both viewpoints are represented in the explanation of language.

Skinner falls squarely in the empiricist's camp. For him, language is simply verbal behavior that is governed by the same principles as any other behavior: Reinforced behavior persists; nonreinforced behavior extinguishes. Skinner (1957) did describe various categories of **verbal behavior,** which are distinguished by what is being done to be reinforced. The **mand** is a verbal command that specifies its own reinforcer. For example, the mand "pass the salt" is reinforced when the salt is passed. A **tact** is the accurate naming of something. For example, if a child says "doll" while holding a doll, he or she will be reinforced. **Echoic behavior** is repeating something verbatim. For example, in the early stages of language training, a parent may point to her mouth and say "mouth"; if the child responds by saying "mouth," he or she will be reinforced.

We see then that Skinner's explanation of language is simply an extension of his general principles of learning. Skinner's most severe critic has been Noam Chomsky (1959). Basically, Chomsky contends that language is simply too complex to be explained by learning. For example, it has been estimated that there are 10^{20} possible twenty-word sentences in the English language, and it would take approximately 1000 times the estimated age of the earth just to listen to them all (G. A. Miller 1965). Thus, says Chomsky, a process other than learning must be operating. Chomsky's answer is that the brain is structured in a way that causes it to generate language. In other words, our verbal skills are genetically determined. Chomsky's nativistic explanation of language is diametrically opposed to Skinner's empirical explanation.

Schedules of Reinforcement

So far we have talked as if it were necessary in modifying behavior to reinforce every desirable response that is made. That is, if we want to encourage children to read, they should be reinforced each time we observe them reading, or if we want a rat to continue to press a lever in a Skinner box, we should reinforce it with food each time it does so. If, indeed, each desirable response is followed by reinforcement, we say that the organism is on a 100 percent or **continuous reinforcement schedule.** Likewise, if a response that had been learned is now never followed by a reinforcement, we say that the organism is on a 0 percent reinforcement schedule, which leads to extinction.

Skinner observed that everyday behavior is maintained on schedules somewhere between these two extremes.

> We do not always find good ice or snow when we go skating or skiing. . . . We do not always get a good meal in a particular restaurant because cooks are not always predictable. We do not always get an answer when we telephone a friend because the friend is not always at home. . . . The reinforcements characteristic of industry and education are almost always intermittent because it is not feasible to control behavior by reinforcing every response. (Skinner 1953, 99)

A response that is sometimes followed by a reinforcer and sometimes not followed by a reinforcer is said to be on a **partial reinforcement schedule.** Many believe that the research by Ferster and Skinner (1957) on schedules of reinforcement represents a major contribution to experimental psychology. Although Ferster and Skinner studied many schedules, four have become most representative of their work. They are described briefly.

1. Fixed interval reinforcement schedule (FI)   On this schedule, the organism is reinforced for a response that is made following a certain time interval. For example, only the response made following a thirty-second interval is reinforced. After an organism has been on this kind of schedule for awhile, its behavior quickens toward the end of the time interval and then slows down drastically after reinforcement has been obtained. Individuals working for a fixed weekly or monthly salary are on this kind of schedule. Students preparing a term paper also will often wait until the deadline approaches before starting and then "work like mad" to finish. Such behavior is typical of a FI schedule. Note that with this schedule, only one response is needed to obtain reinforcement, if the response is made at just the right time.

2. Fixed ratio reinforcement schedule (FR)   On this schedule, the organism must make x number of responses before it is reinforced. For example, every fourth (FR4) response is reinforced. Such a schedule produces extremely high rates of responding and characterizes persons doing piecework or working for a commission. In both cases the harder one works the more pay one receives, because reinforcement is response-contingent instead of time-contingent.

3. Variable interval reinforcement schedule (VI)   On this schedule, the organism is reinforced at the end of variable time intervals. In other words, rather than the organism's being reinforced after a fixed interval of, say, ten seconds, it is reinforced *on the average* of every ten seconds. For example, it may be reinforced for a response made after five seconds, then after twenty seconds, then after two seconds. Bosses who believe their workers should be periodically rewarded place them on such a schedule. At various times as they were working, the boss would come along with a kind word, although they did nothing extra to deserve the kind word.

For interval schedules it is not the *number* of responses made that is important; rather, it is the *passage of time* that determines when a response will be reinforced. For ratio schedules, however, the frequency of responding has a direct relationship to the number of reinforcers the organism will receive. For ratio schedules, the faster the organism responds, the more often it will be reinforced.

4. Variable ratio reinforcement schedule (VR)   This, like the FR schedule, is response-contingent, but on this schedule, the organism is reinforced on the basis of an average number of responses. That is, instead of being reinforced for *every* fourth response, it is reinforced on the *average* of every fourth response. Thus, reinforcements could be close together or fairly far apart. On this schedule, however, the faster it responds, the more reinforcement it will obtain. This schedule produces the highest rate of responding. Gambling behavior is under the control of a VR schedule, as is the behavior of salespersons. For example, the faster one pulls the handle of a slot machine, the more often one will receive a payoff (and the faster one will go broke). With salespersons, the more contacts they make, the more likely they will be to make a sale, although exactly when a sale will be made cannot be predicted. The salesperson's schedule of reinforcement may look as follows:

No Sale, No Sale, Sale, No Sale, Sale, No Sale, No Sale, No Sale, No Sale, No Sale, Sale, Sale, and so on.

Partial reinforcement schedules have two important effects on behavior: (1) They influence rate of responding. The VR schedule produces the highest rate of responding, followed by the FR schedule, then the VI schedule, and finally the FI schedule. (2) They increase resistance to extinction. All partial reinforcement schedules produce greater resistance to extinction than does a 100 percent or continuous schedule of reinforcement, and this fact is named the **partial reinforcement effect** (PRE). That is, a response followed by reinforcement only some of the time will persist much longer when reinforcement is discontinued than will a response followed by reinforcement each time that it occurs. The PRE has implications for education and child rearing. For example, even though a 100 percent schedule may be used in the early stages of training, a response should be switched to a partial reinforcement schedule as soon as possible. This will increase the perseverance of the response. In most cases, this will happen automatically, because most behavior that occurs outside a laboratory is on some kind of partial reinforcement schedule.

Superstitious Behavior

When a response is responsible for making available a reinforcer, we say that the reinforcer is *contingent* on the response. In our earlier example, a rat had to press the lever in a Skinner box *in order to* obtain a pellet of food. This is called **contingent reinforcement;** if the appropriate response is not made, the reinforcer will not become available.

Now let us imagine what would happen if a Skinner box were arranged so that the feeder mechanism would fire automatically, providing the animal with a pellet of food *regardless of what it was doing.* Let us imagine, for example, that the feeder mechanism is arranged so that it automatically provides a pellet of food on the average of every fifteen seconds. According to the principles of operant conditioning, whatever the animal is doing when the feeder mechanism fires will be reinforced and thus tend to be repeated. As that response is being repeated, the feeder mechanism will again fire, further reinforcing the response. The end result will be that whatever the animal was "caught" doing when the feeder mechanism first fired will become a very strong habit. Strange ritualistic behavior develops under these circumstances. For example, one animal may learn to turn in a circle, another may learn to bob its head, and still another may learn to sniff air holes on the top of the Skinner box. Such behavior is called **superstitious behavior,** because it appears *as if* the animal believed its ritualistic response were responsible for producing the reinforcer, when in fact it was not. Reinforcement that occurs regardless of what the animal is doing is called **noncontingent reinforcement.** Superstitious behavior results from noncontingent reinforcement.

Numerous examples of superstitious behavior on the human level exist. A baseball player, for example, who adjusts his hat a certain way just before hitting a home run will have a strong tendency to adjust his hat that way again the next time he comes up to bat. Many actors who are wearing a certain article of clothing before giving an outstanding performance may wear that same article of clothing whenever they perform. A native who beats on a drum in response to an eclipse of the sun may have a strong tendency to beat the drum the next time an emergency develops, because his drum beating looked "as if" it brought the sun back.

Kinds of Reinforcement Contingencies

In this section we will discuss the various events that can follow a response and thus influence that response.

Positive Reinforcement

As we have already seen, a **primary positive reinforcer** is something that is related to survival. If a response produces a primary positive reinforcer, the rate increases with which that response is made. We have seen too that any biologically neutral stimulus that is paired with a primary positive reinforcer takes on positive reinforcing characteristics of its own, thus becoming a **secondary positive reinforcer.** As with primary reinforcement, if a secondary positive reinforcer follows a response, the rate with which that response is made will go up.

Negative Reinforcement

Positive reinforcement presents the organism with something it "wants," whereas **negative reinforcement** *removes* something it does not want. A **primary negative reinforcer** is a stimulus that is potentially harmful to the organism, such as an extremely loud noise, a bright light, or an electric shock. Any response that removes or reduces one of these aversive stimuli will increase in frequency and is said to be negatively reinforced. This is labeled an **escape contingency,** because the organism's response allows it to escape from an aversive situation. Any neutral stimulus consistently paired with a primary negative reinforcer becomes a **secondary negative reinforcer,** and an organism will work to escape from it just as it does from a primary negative reinforcer. Both primary and secondary negative reinforcement involve escaping from an aversive situation.

It is important to note that both positive and negative reinforcement result in an increase in response probability or in rate of responding. Both result in something the organism wants. In the case of positive reinforcement, a response produces something the organism wants. In the case of negative reinforcement, a response removes something aversive.

Avoidance

An **avoidance contingency** means engaging in behavior that prevents an aversive event from occurring. For example, opening an umbrella prevents getting wet, which is aversive. If a Skinner box is arranged so that a light precedes the onset of a shock, the animal will learn to respond to the light in such a way as to avoid the shock. With an avoidance contingency, the organism's behavior prevents it from experiencing a negative reinforcer. As with our earlier example with Joe Blow:

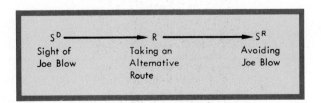

The sight of Joe Blow was a signal for an aversive encounter, and taking a route away from Joe Blow prevented or avoided that encounter. The reinforcement from negative reinforcement contingencies comes from *escaping* something aversive, whereas the reinforcement from an avoidance contingency comes from *avoiding* an aversive experience.

Punishment

Punishment involves either removing a positive reinforcer or presenting a negative reinforcer. In other words, punishment is either taking away something an organism wants or giving it something it does not want.

Over and over Skinner emphasizes his belief that behavior should be controlled using positive contingencies. He feels strongly that positive reinforcement and punishment are not opposite in their consequences. That is, although positive reinforcement strengthens behavior, punishment does not necessarily weaken it.

> Punishment is designed to remove awkward, dangerous, or otherwise unwanted behavior from a repertoire on the assumption that a person who has been punished is less likely to behave in the same way. Unfortunately, the matter is not that simple. Reward and punishment do not differ merely in the direction of the changes they induce. A child who has been severely punished for sex play is not necessarily less inclined to continue; and a man who has been imprisoned for violent assault is not necessarily less inclined toward violence. Punished behavior is likely to reappear after the punitive contingencies are withdrawn. (Skinner 1971, 61–62)

Even if punishment is effective in eliminating undesirable behavior, why use it if the same result can be accomplished with positive control? The use of punishment in controlling behavior appears to have several shortcomings. For example, it causes the punished person to become fearful; it indicates what the person should not do, instead of what he or she should do; it justifies inflicting pain on others; it often causes aggression; and it tends to replace one undesirable response with another, as when a child who is spanked for a wrongdoing now cries instead.

Skinner stresses positively reinforcing desirable behavior and ignoring undesirable behavior. This should be looked on as an ideal, however, because instances occur when punishing a child is strongly reinforcing to a parent. A child acting up in a supermarket may stop doing so immediately if spanked by a parent, and this will vastly increase the likelihood of the child's being spanked again next time it acts up. Even parents are capable of learning. As Skinner says, there are always two organisms whose behavior is being modified in a learning situation, and sometimes it is difficult to know who is the experimenter and who is the subject. This point is made in the cartoon in Figure 9–3.

Our Biggest Problem

Malott, Ritterby, and Wolf (1973, 4–2) state our biggest problem as follows:

MAN'S BIGGEST PROBLEM IS THAT
HIS BEHAVIOR IS MORE EASILY
INFLUENCED BY
SMALL, BUT IMMEDIATE AND DEFINITE
REINFORCERS
THAN IT IS BY
LARGE, BUT DISTANT AND UNCERTAIN
REINFORCERS

Figure 9–3
"Boy, have I got this guy conditioned! Every time I press the bar down he drops in a piece of food."

(From Skinner 1959, p. 378.)

It is the fact described in this quotation that keeps many people smoking cigarettes when they "know" they should not and overeating when they "know" that in the long run it will do them no good. The prospect of a long, healthy life is no contest for a small amount of nicotine or the immediate taste of food in one's mouth.

The relatively greater effect of small, immediate reinforcers compared to large distant ones is exemplified in Figures 9–4 and 9–5.

Figure 9–4
The diagram shows that smoking is under the control of immediate reinforcers rather than distant ones.

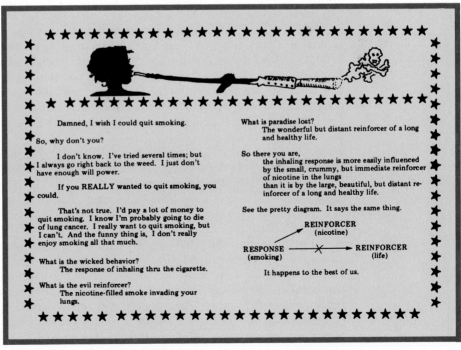

(From Malott, Ritterby, & Wolf 1973, pp. 4–3.)

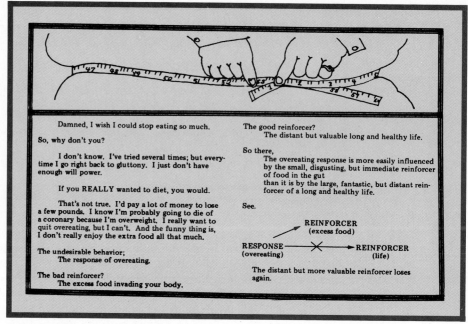

Damned, I wish I could stop eating so much.

So, why don't you?

I don't know. I've tried several times; but every-time I go right back to gluttony. I just don't have enough will power.

If you REALLY wanted to diet, you would.

That's not true. I'd pay a lot of money to lose a few pounds. I know I'm probably going to die of a coronary because I'm overweight. I really want to quit overeating, but I can't. And the funny thing is, I don't really enjoy the extra food all that much.

The undesirable behavior;
   The response of overeating.

The bad reinforcer?
   The excess food invading your body.

The good reinforcer?
   The distant but valuable long and healthy life.

So there,
   The overeating response is more easily influenced by the small, disgusting, but immediate reinforcer of food in the gut
   than it is by the large, fantastic, but distant rein-forcer of a long and healthy life.

See.

REINFORCER
(excess food)

RESPONSE————✕————▶REINFORCER
(overeating)   (life)

The distant but more valuable reinforcer loses again.

(From Malott, Ritterby, & Wolf 1973, pp. 4–3.)

Contingency Contracting.   So how do we solve "our biggest problem"? One solution is to make the future immediate, and one way to do that is through **contingency contracting.** Let us say you want to quit smoking but cannot seem to do it on your own. Let us assume further that one hundred dollars is a substantial amount of money for you. One plan is to make an agreement with another person in which you turn over the one hundred dollars to that person with the stipulation that every week that you go without smoking you will get back ten dollars. If you have even one cigarette during the week, you will lose ten dollars. Such an agreement is called a contingency contract, and many variations are possible. For example, the payoff could come on a daily basis instead of on a weekly basis, and the object of value could be such items as records or clothing instead of money. The major point is that by such an agreement you have rearranged the reinforcement contingencies in your environment so that they now encourage desirable behavior and discourage undesirable behavior. In the case of smoking, rather than waiting for old age for the effects of nonsmoking to become manifest, you need wait only a day or a week. Now your behavior is under the control of more immediate reinforcers instead of distant ones.

What happens when the contract expires? Perhaps other reinforcement contingencies will support the desired behavior. In other words, it is hoped that non-smoking will be functional in producing reinforcement. Both smoking and nonsmoking produce reinforcers. The problem is switching from one source of reinforcement to another. For example, the reinforcers that support smoking include nicotine and perhaps a degree of social approval from other smokers. The reinforcers for not smoking include saving money, feeling better, not suffering the abuse from anticancer commercials, and social approval from other nonsmokers.

Both smoking and nonsmoking are functional in producing reinforcement, and it is mainly a matter of switching from one source of reinforcement to another. Contingency contracting is one way of making the switch.

Since its early description as a behavior modification technique (for example, Homme, Csanyi, Gonzales, and Rechs 1969; and Stuart and Lott 1972), contingency contracting has been used to treat: marital problems (Jacobson 1978; Weiss, Birchler, and Vincent 1974); studying problems and other school-related behavior problems (Blechman, Taylor, and Schrader 1981; Kelley and Stokes 1982; Speltz, Shimamura, and McReynolds 1982); self-control problems, such as drug abuse (Boudin 1972; Frederiksen, Jenkins, and Carr 1976); weight control problems (Aragona, Cassady, and Drabman 1975; Mann 1972); alcoholism (P. M. Miller 1972); and heavy smoking (Paxton 1980, 1981).

Behavior Disorders and Behavior Therapy

Behavior Disorders

For the Skinnerians inappropriate behavior is learned in the same way that appropriate behavior is learned. That is, both desirable and undesirable behavior are under the control of their consequences. In other words, so-called abnormal behavior is not seen by the Skinnerians as resulting from some underlying neurophysiological disease, nor is it seen as resulting from psychic conflicts such as those among the id, ego, and superego. Like appropriate behavior, inappropriate behavior persists because it is maintained by reinforcement. Thus, according to the Skinnerians, if you want to eliminate undesirable behavior you must prevent its reinforcement. Furthermore, you should specify the behavior you want instead of the undesirable behavior and reinforce it when it occurs. **Behavior therapy** is a term used to describe any approach to psychotherapy that is based on a learning theory; however, several learning theories exist. For example, behavior therapy could be based on Pavlovian learning theory, Bandura's observational learning theory (see chapter 11), or on Skinnerian learning theory. The Skinnerian version of behavior therapy involves clearly specifying the undesirable behaviors that are to be extinguished, clearly specifying the desirable behaviors to be reinforced, and arranging reinforcement contingencies so that they are responsive to the desirable behavior but not to the undesirable behavior. Because contingency contracting incorporates all of these procedures, it can be considered an example of Skinnerian behavior therapy.

The Skinnerian version of behavior therapy has been used successfully in treating a wide range of behavior disorders such as alcoholism, drug addiction, mental retardation, autism, juvenile delinquency, phobias, speech disorders, obesity, sexual disorders, and various neuroses and psychoses. (For reviews of the applications of behavior therapy see, for example, Craighead, Kazdin, and Mahoney 1976; Masters, Burish, Hollon, and Rimm 1987.)

Token Economies

An interesting example of the Skinnerian approach to therapy is seen in **token economies.** In a token economy certain behaviors are deemed desirable, and other behaviors are deemed undesirable. When the participants in the economy act in desirable ways, they are given tokens (most often plastic disks like poker chips, but sometimes points or plastic cards are used). Because the tokens can subsequently be exchanged for items such as candy or cigarettes, they are secondary reinforcers. More specifically, the tokens are generalized reinforcers because they are paired with several primary reinforcers. Typically token economies are used in institutional settings such as schools or psychiatric hospitals. For a detailed description of the procedures, rules, and general considerations for such programs see Ayllon and Azrin 1968; Schaefer and Martin 1969; Thompson and Grabowski 1972, 1977. Krasner (1970) reported that more than one hundred token economies in more than fifty institutions existed, and no doubt many more such programs exist now.

Token economies may sound contrived and unnatural, but perhaps it is the contingencies that exist within institutions without token economies that are unnatural. Masters, Burish, Hollon, and Rimm (1987) explain.

> Token economies are not really unnatural. Indeed, any national economy with a currency system is in every sense a token economy: any currency consists by definition of token or symbolic "reinforcers" that may be exchanged for items that constitute a more direct form of reinforcement. Whereas the individual in society works to earn tokens (money) with which he purchases his dwelling place, food, recreation, and so on, most institutions provide such comforts noncontingently and hence cease to encourage many adaptive behaviors that are appropriate and effective in the natural environment. (222)

Ayllon and Azrin (1965, 1968) were among the first to use a token economy to treat maladaptive behavior. Working with psychotic patients in a mental institution, Ayllon and Azrin first spent eighteen months teaching attendants which behavior to reinforce, how much to reinforce it, and when to reinforce it. By the time the behavior modification program started, they had created a standardized list of behaviors to be changed as well as a list showing how many tokens were to be given when the patients engaged in various activities. Typically, supply and demand determined how many tokens various activities earned. Jobs that were strenuous or tedious and took a long time tended to be worth more tokens than more attractive jobs. The program allowed for individual treatment, however. For example, if, for whatever reason, the therapists wanted to encourage certain behaviors in a particular patient then those behaviors, for that patient, would earn a relatively larger number of tokens. Examples of behaviors that would earn tokens included washing dishes; helping to serve meals to other patients; cleaning tables; keeping oneself or one's room clean; proceeding to the dining room in an orderly fashion at mealtime; and washing sheets, pillow cases, and towels in the laundry. The tokens earned could be subsequently exchanged for such items as candy, cigarettes, coffee, privacy, a thirty-minute grounds pass, a private audience with the ward psychologist or a social worker, the exclusive use of a radio, or the choice of a television program.

In general, Ayllon and Azrin found that the frequency of desirable behavior increased significantly when it was reinforced by tokens. Furthermore, in another phase of the program, it was found that such behavior decreased in frequency when the tokens were withdrawn and increased again when the tokens were reinstated.

Criticisms and Shortcomings of Token Economies.   Although token economies have tended to be successful, they have not gone uncriticized. One criticism directed at all forms of behavior therapy is that it treats only symptoms and not the causes of those symptoms. Admittedly, say the critics, getting a psychotic patient to groom himself or herself, or to choose a television program is an improvement; however, the real problem, the psychosis itself, remains intact. Other critics complain that it may be unethical to deprive patients of goods and services to which they are legitimately entitled and then to provide those items selectively when the patients act in only appropriate ways.

A shortcoming of token economy programs is that the effects of the programs often do not generalize to extratreatment conditions such as the home, the community, or the place of employment (see for example, Kazdin 1977; Kazdin and Bootzin 1972). A study by Becker, Madsen, Arnold, and Thomas (1967) even suggests that behaviors learned in a token economy program during one part of the day do not spontaneously generalize to other parts of the day. These and other studies indicate that people in fact learn desirable behavior when such behavior leads to reinforcement but will stop engaging in that behavior when the reinforcement is no longer forthcoming. Gagnon and Davison (1976) suggest that token economies actually do the participants a disservice because within the program certain behaviors are inevitably followed by reinforcement, whereas in the real world reinforcement is not nearly as predictable.

Finally, it seems that in some cases token economies simply do not work. For example, one token economy was designed to reduce the disruptive behavior of nine adolescent boys in a psychiatric hospital school. It turns out that disruptive behavior actually increased among the group when two of the boys realized the nature of the program. These two boys declared themselves "on strike" and labeled any boy willing to cooperate in the program "a fool" (Santogrossi, O'Leary, Romanczyk, and Kaufman 1973).

The Skinnerians say that even with their possible shortcomings, token economies have made many institutions much more livable than they otherwise had been. Also, they have made various rehabilitation programs much more accessible to many patients. Even if this result is all token economies do, they say, they are well worth the effort.

Implications for Child Rearing

The major lesson from Skinner's theory is: Control reinforcement contingencies, and you control behavior. This statement is especially important in child rearing, because parents have at least the potential for controlling the reinforcement contingencies governing their child's behavior. Hergenhahn summarizes how reinforcement theory can be used in child rearing:

1. Decide the major personality characteristics you want your child to possess as an adult. Let's say, for example, you want the child to grow up to be a creative adult.
2. Define these goals in behavioral terms. In this case you ask, "What is a child doing when he is being creative?"
3. Reward behavior that is in accordance with these goals. With this example, you would reward instances of creativity as they occurred.

4. Provide consistency by arranging the major aspects of the child's environment so that they too reward the behavior you have deemed important. (1972, 152–53)

This plan of action oversimplifies the situation, however, because anyone attempting to follow it will run into at least the following problems:

1. Often it will not be clear what behavior you want from the child.
2. Your ideas concerning what constitutes desirable behavior may change.
3. You may want different things at different times.
4. Just because you want certain things from your child does not mean everyone else will want the same things.
5. It is not always easy to know what will be rewarding to a child.
6. Often what you reward will depend upon your mood.
7. Sometimes you will get the behavior you want from the child, but at the wrong time or place.
8. It is difficult to reward others when you are not adequately rewarded yourself. (Hergenhahn 1972, 16–17)

The situation is further complicated by the fact that children constantly are learning from the television they watch, the books they look at or read, and the games they play. A major influence of television seems to come from **modeling.** Children will model or imitate the behavior of someone they see being reinforced; thus they receive **vicarious reinforcement.** If children see a gunfighter on television being reinforced with power, money, and recognition, they may imitate this behavior and in so doing experience those reinforcers indirectly. This result means that parents wishing to direct their children's emerging personality will need to consider all of the children's major experiences, which is a monumental task.

According to the Skinnerians, it is never a question of whether children's lives should be controlled or not, because they always are controlled. It is simply a matter of who or what is going to do the controlling.

Walden Two

The purposive manipulation of reinforcement contingencies so that they encourage certain behaviors is called **contingency management.** We just saw how contingency management could be applied to child rearing. Skinner believes it can be used on a much larger scale. In fact, he defines **culture** itself as a set of reinforcement contingencies, which encourages certain behaviors and discourages others. It follows that cultures, like experiments, can be designed to produce certain effects.

A culture is very much like the experimental space used in the analysis of behavior. Both are sets of contingencies of reinforcement. A child is born into a culture as an organism is placed in an experimental space. Designing a culture is like designing an experiment; contingencies are arranged and effects noted. In an experiment we are interested in what happens, in designing a culture with whether it will work. (Skinner 1971, 153)

When contingency management is used to design a culture, the effort is called **cultural engineering.** In 1948, Skinner published a book called ***Walden Two,*** in which he described a utopian culture designed in accordance with the principles of operant conditioning.

Walden Two is a fictitious community of 1000 people. A few of the community's characteristics follow: No private homes exist; rather, the inhabitants live in apartment complexes. Children do not live with their parents; they first live in a nursery and later in a dormitory, and they move to their own apartment when they are about thirteen years old. No living quarters have cooking facilities; all meals are in community dining halls, which assures a healthy diet and frees people from the drudgery of preparing meals. Women of Walden Two are not burdened by cooking, cleaning, or mothering and are thus able to realize their full potential along with men. Marriage and child bearing are encouraged in the mid-teens. Marriages tend to last, because couples are matched by interests, money is no problem, and child rearing is no burden. Children do not live with their parents; rather, they are raised by experts, because average parents do not have the knowledge or the facilities to raise children properly. The goal is "to have every adult member of Walden Two regard all the children as his own and to have every child think of every adult as his parent" (Skinner 1948, 142)

Education is individualized, in that every child progresses at his or her own pace. No "formal" education exists, and teachers act only as guides. Education is provided in the actual workshops and laboratories in the community. Even at the college level, students are merely "taught to think" and are left to learn anything else on their own. No grades or diplomas are given.

Virtually no money exists in Walden Two. Instead, each person is responsible for 1,200 labor credits per year. This amounts to about four hours of work per day, although some jobs are worth more labor credits than others. For example, an unpleasant job such as garbage collecting or sewer cleaning would be worth more labor credits than a more pleasant job would. Thus, by engaging in unpleasant work, the member would need to work fewer hours than someone doing more pleasant work.

Each member of the community is provided with all of his or her basic needs. For example, the following are provided: food, leisure activities, clothing, medical services, education, and security against old age and ill health. This allows the members to concentrate on such areas as the arts, the sciences, the exercise of skills, the satisfaction of curiosities, and on self-actualization.

No prisons, taverns, unemployment, narcotics, mental institutions, wars, or crime exist. Is such an "ideal" society possible? Frazier, the hero of the novel, who to many represents Skinner himself, said:

> The one fact that I would cry from every housetop is this: the Good Life is waiting for us. . . . It does not depend on a change in government or on the machinations of world politics. It does not wait upon an improvement in human nature. At this very moment we have the necessary techniques, both material and psychological, to create a full and satisfying life for everyone. (1948, 193)

Skinner believes that using the ideas contained in *Walden Two* may actually solve several of our major problems.

It is now widely recognized that great changes must be made in the American way of life. Not only can we not face the rest of the world while consuming and polluting as we do, we cannot for long face ourselves while acknowledging the violence and chaos in which we live. The choice is clear: Either we do nothing and allow a miserable and probably catastrophic future to overtake us, or we use our knowledge about human behavior to create a social environment in which we shall live productive and creative lives and do so without jeopardizing the chances that those who follow us will be able to do the same. Something like a *Walden Two* would not be a bad start. (1978, 66)

Several experimental communities have been designed according to the suggestions found in *Walden Two*. One of these communities, in Virginia, publishes a newsletter that describes its progress (Twin Oaks; Louisa, VA 23093). The history of this particular project is summarized in a book by K. Kinkade (1973). In an article entitled "Easing Toward Perfection at Twin Oaks," Cordes (1984) gives a progress report on the Twin Oaks experiment after seventeen years of existence.

Beyond Freedom and Dignity

As we have just seen Skinner believes strongly that cultural engineering need not be fictional, but before such engineering will be possible, we need to develop a technology of behavior.

What we need is a technology of behavior. We could solve our problems quickly enough if we could adjust the growth of the world's population as precisely as we adjust the course of a spaceship, or improve agriculture and industry with some of the confidence with which we accelerate high-energy particles, or move toward a peaceful world with something like the steady progress with which physics has approached absolute zero (even though both remain presumably out of reach). But a behavioral technology comparable in power and precision to physical and biological technology is lacking, and those who do not find the very possibility ridiculous are more likely to be frightened by it than reassured. That is how far we are from "understanding human issues" in the sense in which physics and biology understand their fields, and how far we are from preventing the catastrophe toward which the world seems to be inexorably moving. (Skinner 1971, 5)

What prevents the development of a technology of behavior? According to Skinner, the main barrier is the traditional view of human nature, which depicts people as autonomous. Autonomous people are free to do as they choose, and therefore are worthy of praise and dignity when they accomplish something. If those same accomplishments could be ascribed to outside influences, they would lose their meaning.

We recognize a person's dignity or worth when we give him credit for what he has done. The amount we give is inversely proportional to the conspicuousness of the causes of his behavior. If we do not know why a person acts as he does, we attribute his behavior to him. We try to gain additional credit for ourselves by concealing the reasons why we behave in given ways or by claiming to have acted for less powerful reasons. We avoid infringing on the credit due to others by controlling them inconspicuously. We admire people to the extent that we cannot explain what they do, and the word ''admire'' then means ''marvel at.'' What we may call the literature of dignity is concerned with preserving due credit. It may oppose advances in technology, including a technology of behavior, because they destroy chances to be admired and a basic analysis because it offers an alternative explanation of behavior for which the individual himself has previously been given credit. The literature thus stands in the way of further human achievements. (Skinner 1971, 58–59)

The trouble with the notion of autonomous people, according to Skinner, is that it explains nothing about human behavior; that is, in autonomous people the causes of behavior are mystical. As our knowledge about human behavior has increased, says Skinner, more and more of what once was attributed to autonomous people has been attributed to the environment. As we learn more, this trend will continue.

If it were autonomous people who needed to be understood and improved before we could solve our problems, then, says Skinner, we would be in trouble.

Fortunately, the point of attack is more readily accessible. It is the environment which must be changed. A way of life which furthers the study of human behavior in its relation to that environment should be in the best possible position to solve its major problems. This is not jingoism, because the great problems are now global. In the behavioristic view, man can now control his own destiny because he knows what must be done and how to do it. (Skinner 1974, 251)

Evaluation

Empirical Research

Skinner's theory has no problem with empirical validation. Throughout this chapter we have sampled research generated by Skinner's theory, and the studies we have mentioned indeed constitute only a sample. Because so many researchers follow Skinnerian principles, they have formed their own division of the American Psychological Association (Division 25, The Division of the Experimental Analysis of Behavior). In addition, the Skinnerians have two journals in which to publish their research, *The Journal of Applied Behavior Analysis* and *Journal for the Experimental Analysis of Behavior*. With the possible exception of Cattell's, no personality theory considered in this text thus far is so intimately tied to experimental research as Skinner's.

Criticisms

Too Much Generalization from Nonhuman Animals to Humans.   Skinner and his followers believe that much, if not all, of what is learned by studying nonhuman animals applies to humans as well. For example, they believe that the behavior of all animals is controlled by its consequences. Therefore, if you can control consequences you can control behavior; whether the behavior in question is that of a rat, a pigeon, or a human. Many of the attributes thought to be uniquely human are essentially ignored in the Skinnerian analysis. For example, intentions, sense of self, thinking, reasoning, feeling, choosing, and reflecting have little or no place in Skinnerian theory. In fact, cognitive processes of any kind are actively avoided by most Skinnerians.

Other critics agree with Skinner that some of the principles of learning that apply to nonhuman animals can be generalized to humans. They believe that he goes too far, however, when he uses those principles in social, religious, economic, cultural, and philosophical speculations.

Radical Environmentalism.   The brand of determinism that Skinner embraces is called radical environmentalism because he assumes that behavior is caused by reinforcement contingencies found in the environment. We have seen throughout this chapter that all Skinnerian efforts to modify behavior involve changing reinforcement contingencies. Critics say that this view reduces humans to mindless automatons (or say some critics, large white rats). Where in the Skinnerian analysis of behavior, ask the critics, is the explanation for such phenomena and experiences as suicide, depression, love, wonder, hope, purpose, and awe?

Who Controls the Controllers?   This reaction to Skinner's writings is more of a concern than a criticism. Skinner believes strongly that operant principles can be, and should be, applied in the area of cultural engineering. He believes that an entire society could be arranged like a token economy. That is, desirable behavior would be defined and would be reinforced with such items as tokens, money, goods, or services. Because behavior is controlled by its consequences, members of this society would soon be acting as the dispensers of the reinforcers want them to act. Who, however, are the dispensers of the reinforcers? Who decides what behavior is desirable and what behavior is undesirable? Skinner argues that the people in the society could determine the answers to these questions and could institute methods for countercontrolling the controllers. Many critics are not convinced, however, and continue to believe that the possibility of serious abuse exists within Skinner's notion of cultural engineering.

Contributions

Applied Value.   Throughout this chapter we have seen how Skinnerian principles have been applied to education, child rearing, therapy, personal improvement, and societal problems. More and more, his ideas are being used in prison reform, in which positive control is being explored as an alternative to negative control (see for example, Boslough 1972). A good theory explains, synthesizes large amounts of information, generates new information, and can be used as a guide in solving practical problems. Skinner's theory gets high marks in all of these categories. The criticisms that he generalizes too readily from the animal level to the human level and from the laboratory to the "real world" seem minor when compared to what has been accomplished using his theory as a guide.

Scientifically Rigorous Explanation of Human Behavior. In an area such as personality theory it is not uncommon to encounter terms, concepts, beliefs, and speculations that are difficult, if not impossible, to validate empirically. Skinner's theory (like Cattell's) is an exception. All of the elements in Skinner's theory grew out of his laboratory research. The question concerning Skinner's theory is not whether or not it is correct. The question is not even whether it can be generalized to humans. The question is *to what extent* it can be employed to explain human behavior.

How popular is Skinner among psychologists? Davis, Thomas, and Weaver (1982) provide an answer to this question. They sent surveys to chairpersons of departments with graduate programs in psychology. The chairpersons were asked in 1966 and again in 1981 to first rank from 1 to 10 the greatest psychologists of all time and then rank only living psychologists. (A rank of 1 was the highest rating.) In 1966, Freud was ranked 1 on the all-time great list and Skinner ranked 9. In 1981, Freud still ranked 1, but Skinner was ranked 2. Among living psychologists Skinner ranked 1 in both 1966 and 1981. The authors also observe that the distance between Freud and Skinner on the all-time great list suggests that Skinner may soon replace Freud in the top position.

Summary

Skinner's position falls into the behavioristic camp, because it stresses the study of overt behavior and not internal mental or physiological events. He recognized two major categories of behavior, respondent behavior, which is elicited by a known stimulus, and operant behavior; which appears to be emitted rather than elicited. Respondent behavior is controlled by the events that *precede* it, and operant behavior is controlled by the events that *follow* it. Skinner's work has been mainly on operant behavior. If an operant response is followed by a reinforcer (either positive or negative), the rate at which it occurs will increase. An operant response is acquired by following the desired response with a reinforcer. If the desired response does not occur naturally, it can be shaped into existence using differential reinforcement and successive approximations. If the reinforcement for an operant response is discontinued, the rate eventually will return to its operant level, and extinction will have occurred. Following a delay after extinction, the conditioned operant response will again appear, which is called spontaneous recovery. The situation can be arranged so that an operant response will be made under one set of circumstances but not under another set of circumstances. For example, a rat could be trained to press the bar in a Skinner box when the light is on but not when it is off. Under these conditions, we say that the light has become the occasion or the discriminative stimulus (S^D) for the bar-press response, and that the rat has learned a discriminative operant. Any neutral stimulus consistently paired with a primary reinforcer becomes a secondary reinforcer, and thus all S^Ds become secondary reinforcers. A stimulus that is paired with more than one primary reinforcer becomes a generalized reinforcer.

Much complex behavior is explained using the concept of chaining. Chaining occurs when one response by an organism brings it into proximity with a reward, which both reinforces that response and triggers the next one. Chaining can also involve two people when the response of one triggers the response in the other. Verbal behavior or language is thought to be governed by the same principles as any other behavior is. Those utterances that are reinforced are repeated; those that are not reinforced, extinguished. Thus, Skinner is on the empiricism side of the empiricism-nativism debate. A response that is followed by a reinforcer on only some occasions is said to be on a partial reinforcement schedule. A response that is reinforced each time it occurs is said to be on a continuous or 100 percent reinforcement schedule. A response that has been on a partial reinforcement schedule takes much longer to extinguish than one that has been on a continuous schedule, which is called the partial reinforcement effect (PRE).

When a response makes available a reinforcer, we say that the reinforcer is contingent on the response. When a reinforcer appears independent of any response, we refer to it as noncontingent reinforcement. The ritualistic responses labeled superstitious behavior result from noncontingent reinforcement. A primary positive reinforcer is something that contributes to survival. A secondary positive reinforcer is anything that has been consistently paired with a primary positive reinforcer. A primary negative reinforcer is anything that is physically harmful to the organism. A secondary negative reinforcer is anything that has been consistently paired with a primary negative reinforcer. Positive reinforcement occurs when a response adds a primary or secondary positive reinforcer to the situation. Negative reinforcement occurs when a response removes a primary or secondary negative reinforcer from the situation. Punishment occurs when a response adds a primary or secondary negative reinforcer to the situation or removes a primary or secondary positive reinforcer. Skinner opposes the use of punishment in the control of behavior and stresses control through positive reinforcement.

A major problem that humans have is that our behavior is controlled by small, immediate reinforcers instead of by larger, more distant reinforcers. One way to remedy this problem is to use contingency contracting, which rearranges the reinforcement contingencies in the environment. According to the Skinnerians, both appropriate and inappropriate behavior is maintained by reinforcement. Their version of behavior therapy, then, involves arranging reinforcement contingencies so that they strengthen appropriate behavior and weaken inappropriate behavior. Token economies exemplify the Skinnerian approach to behavior therapy. The Skinnerian belief that behavior can be directed by controlling reinforcement contingencies, has special relevance to child rearing, because parents have considerable control over their child's environment. Skinner wrote a utopian novel, entitled *Walden Two*, which described a society designed in accordance with the principles of operant conditioning. Skinner believes strongly, however, that cultural engineering need not be fictitious. We now have the knowledge that would allow us to develop a technology of behavior that could be used to solve many of our major problems. It is the traditional view of autonomous people with their freedom and dignity that is the major barrier to the development of such a technology of behavior.

Skinner's theory grew out of empirical research and has generated a massive amount of empirical research since its inception. His theory has been criticized for generalizing his findings too readily from the nonhuman to the human level and for insisting that even complex human behavior can be explained in terms of reinforcement contingencies. His notion of cultural engineering has also raised questions concerning decisions as to which behaviors will be deemed desirable and which undesirable, and who will control the controllers. Among the contributions of Skinner's theory are its widespread applied value and scientifically rigorous attempt to understand personality. Evidence suggests that Skinner may soon surpass Freud as the most highly ranked psychologist of all time by chairpersons of departments with graduate programs in psychology.

EXPERIENTIAL EXERCISES

1. Assume that Skinner is correct in his assumption that frequently occurring behavior is maintained by reinforcement. First, note an activity that you engage in with considerable frequency, and then attempt to specify the reinforcers that are maintaining that activity.

2. According to the Skinnerians you need only two elements to modify behavior: behavior and reinforcement. With this point in mind, attempt to modify someone's behavior. First, choose a behavior that occurs with some moderate frequency and that is easy to measure. Examples would be the utterance of plural nouns, opinionated statements, various hand gestures, or laughter. When the person whose behavior you are attempting to modify engages in the behavior you have chosen, reinforce him or her with interest and attention. Arrange some kind of a barrier between you and the person so that you can note the frequency with which the behavior occurs initially and then as it is reinforced. Make tally marks on a sheet of paper each time the behavior occurs in three-minute intervals. After fifteen minutes discontinue the reinforcement, but continue to count the occurrence of the behavior. Did the frequency of the response increase as a function of reinforcement? If it did, what conclusions do you reach about human behavior? If it did not, what conclusions do you reach?

3. Using the information in this chapter, work out a contingency contract with a friend to deal with some behavior thought by him or her to be undesirable. Describe the behavior, what will be used to reinforce abstaining from that behavior, and the conditions under which the reinforcers will be dispensed. For example, if your friend wants to quit smoking, what will be used to reinforce abstaining from smoking and how often will such nonsmoking behavior be reinforced? Describe in detail your contingency contract program and how it came out.

4. Modify your own behavior using Skinnerian principles. First, make a list of those items that you find reinforcing. The list should contain large reinforcers like going on vacation; medium-sized reinforcers like going to the movies, a play, or a concert; and small reinforcers like a snack, a cup of coffee, or watching a television program. Next, make a list of some of the qualities you would like to improve about yourself. Perhaps you would like to study longer, not smoke so much, not spend so much time socializing, or spend more time reading. Now arrange your life so that you need to do something you do not enjoy to get something you do enjoy. For example, decide that you will not have the cup of coffee that you desire until after you have studied for forty-five minutes. In that way you create an incentive for yourself to do something that you otherwise would not enjoy doing. Describe and summarize your experience with the modification of your own behavior.

DISCUSSION QUESTIONS

1. Describe the essential features of behaviorism.

2. Differentiate between respondent and operant behavior and between type S and type R conditioning.

3. Discuss how you would go about shaping a response that an animal did not ordinarily make.

4. What is a discriminative operant? Give several examples from everyday life.

5. Discuss the concept of secondary reinforcement. Indicate its importance to the control of human behavior. Include in your answer a definition of generalized reinforcers, and give a few examples of them.

6. Discuss the concept of chaining, and give a few examples of chained behavior on the human level.

7. Describe the nativism-empiricism debate as it applies to verbal behavior. Summarize Skinner's explanation of verbal behavior.

8. Describe the various schedules of reinforcement. Describe the partial reinforcement effect, and discuss its relevance to everyday life.

9. What is superstitious behavior? Include in your answer a discussion of contingent and noncontingent reinforcement.

10. List and describe the various kinds of reinforcement contingencies.

11. Discuss the concept of punishment from the Skinnerian viewpoint.

12. Describe "our biggest problem" and offer a possible way of solving it.

13. How, according to the Skinnerians, does inappropriate or undesirable behavior originate?

14. Summarize the Skinnerian approach to behavior therapy.

15. Describe the token economy approach to dealing with behavior problems. What are the criticisms of token economies?

16. Describe how Skinner's theory might be applied to child rearing.

17. Discuss cultural engineering from Skinner's viewpoint. Give examples of what he thinks could be done now.

18. According to Skinner, what must be done before we can begin to solve our major problems? What does Skinner think is the major factor inhibiting us from making progress in this area?

19. Summarize the criticisms of Skinner's theory.

20. Summarize the contributions of Skinner's theory.

SUGGESTIONS FOR FURTHER READING

KAZDIN, A. E. (1980). *Behavior Modification in Applied Settings.* Homewood, IL: The Dorsey Press.

> Provides an excellent summary of operant conditioning procedures and reviews the many ways that these principles have been used. The author also discusses the ethical and legal issues involved in modifying behavior.

SKINNER, B. F. (1948). *Walden Two.* New York: Macmillan.

> Skinner's utopian novel in which he describes a community designed in accordance with operant principles.

SKINNER, B. F. (1953). *Science and Human Behavior.* New York: Macmillan.

> An early but still perhaps the best introduction to Skinner's theory.

SKINNER, B. F. (1967). Autobiography. In E. G. Boring & G. Lindzey (Eds.), *A History of Psychology in Autobiography* (Vol. 5) (pp. 387–413). New York: Appleton-Century-Crofts.

> A short, readable, and often humorous autobiography.

SKINNER, B. F. (1968). *The Technology of Teaching.* New York: Appleton-Century-Crofts.

> Skinner's provocative effort to explain why our educational system is typically so ineffective and his recommendations for improvement.

SKINNER, B. F. (1971). *Beyond Freedom and Dignity.* New York: Alfred A. Knopf.

> Skinner's widely acclaimed and highly criticized best seller in which he claimed many of our problems could be solved by employing a technology of behavior based on operant principles. According to Skinner, however, before such a technology could be successfully employed, several traditional conceptions of humans must be dispelled (for example, the notions that humans are free, and worthy of praise or blame).

SKINNER, B. F. (1974). *About Behaviorism.* New York: Alfred A. Knopf.

Addresses what Skinner believes are twenty common misconceptions about behaviorism.

SKINNER, B. F. (1976). *Particulars of My Life*. New York: Alfred A. Knopf.

In this, the first volume of his three volume autobiography, Skinner describes the first twenty-four years of his life including his years at Hamilton College, his encounter with Robert Frost, and his stay in Greenwich Village, New York. The other two volumes in Skinner's three-volume autobiography are: *The Shaping of a Behaviorist* (1979), New York: Alfred A. Knopf; and *A Matter of Consequences* (1983), New York: Alfred A. Knopf.

SKINNER, B. F. (1978). *Reflections on Behaviorism and Society*. Englewood Cliffs, NJ: Prentice Hall.

Contains several extremely interesting and diverse articles including "Are We Free to Have a Future?"; "Humanism and Behaviorism"; "Walden Two Revisited"; "The Free and Happy Student"; "Designing Higher Education"; and "Freedom and Dignity Revisited."

SKINNER, B. F. (1987). *Upon Further Reflection*. Englewood Cliffs, NJ: Prentice Hall.

Contains several of Skinner's most recent articles including "Why We Are Not Acting to Save the World"; "What Is Wrong with Daily Life in the Western World?"; "The Shame of American Education"; and "How to Discover What You Have to Say: A Talk to Students."

SKINNER, B. F., & VAUGHAN, M. E. (1983). *Enjoy Old Age*. New York: Norton.

This book offers advice to the elderly on how to manage their environments so that they can maximize their enjoyment of old age despite declines in their physical prowess and health.

GLOSSARY

Acquisition. That part of operant conditioning in which an operant response is followed by a reinforcer, thereby increasing the rate with which the response occurs.

Avoidance contingency. The situation in which the organism can avoid an aversive stimulus by engaging in appropriate activity.

Behavior therapy. The approach to treating behavior disorders that is based on any one of several learning theories. For example, some behavior therapies are based on the theories of Pavlov, Skinner, and Bandura.

Behaviorism. A school of psychology, founded by J. B. Watson, whose members believe that the only scientifically valid subject matter for psychology is measurable behavior.

Chaining. The situation in which one response brings the organism into contact with stimuli that (1) reinforce that response and (2) stimulate the next response. Chaining can also involve other people; for example, one person's response can both reinforce another person's response and determine the next course of action.

Classical conditioning. The kind of conditioning studied by Ivan Pavlov and used by J. B. Watson as a model for his version of behaviorism.

Conditioned response (CR). A response similar to an unconditioned response that is elicited by a previously neutral stimulus (CS).

Conditioned stimulus (CS). A stimulus that, before classical conditioning principles are applied, is biologically neutral; that is, it does not elicit a natural reaction from an organism.

Contingency contracting. An agreement between two people that when one acts in an appropriate way, the other one gives him or her something of value. For example, each time the first goes a week without smoking, the second gives him or her ten dollars.

Contingency management. The purposive manipulation of reinforcement contingencies so that they encourage certain behaviors.

Contingent reinforcement. The situation in which a certain response must be made before a reinforcer is obtained; that is, no response, no reinforcer.

Continuous reinforcement schedule. A schedule of reinforcement that reinforces a desired response each time that it occurs. Also called a 100 percent schedule of reinforcement.

Cultural engineering. The use of contingency management in designing a culture.

Culture. According to Skinner, a set of reinforcement contingencies.

Differential reinforcement. The situation in which some responses are reinforced and others are not.

Discriminative operant. An operant response that is made under one set of circumstances but not under others.

Discriminative stimulus (S^D). A cue indicating that if a certain response is made it will be followed by reinforcement.

Echoic behavior. The accurate repeating of what someone else had said.

Escape contingency. A situation in which an organism must respond in a certain way to escape from an aversive stimulus. All negative reinforcement involves an escape contingency.

Extinction. The weakening of an operant response by removing the reinforcer that had been following the response during acquisition. When a response returns to its operant level, we say that it has extinguished.

Fixed interval reinforcement schedule (FI). The reinforcement schedule that reinforces a response that is made only after a specified interval of time has passed.

Fixed ratio reinforcement schedule (FR). The reinforcement schedule that reinforces every nth response. For example, every fifth response the organism makes is reinforced (FR5).

Functional analysis. Skinner's approach to research that attempts to relate measurable environmental experiences to measurable behavior and bypasses cognitive and physiological processes altogether.

Functionalism. America's first school of psychology. The major goal of the functionalist was to relate various behavior and psychological processes to survival.

Generalized reinforcers. A class of secondary reinforcers that have been paired with more than one primary reinforcer. A mother, for example, is a generalized reinforcer because she is associated with the satisfaction of several biologic needs.

Mand. A verbal response that demands something and is reinforced when what is demanded is obtained.

Modeling. The imitation of the behavior of someone who is seen obtaining reinforcement.

Negative reinforcement. The kind of reinforcement that occurs when a response removes a primary or secondary negative reinforcer.

Negative reinforcer. Anything that when removed from the situation by a response increases the rate with which that response is made.

Noncontingent reinforcement. The situation in which no relationship exists between an organism's behavior and the availability of reinforcement.

Operant behavior. Behavior that cannot be linked to any known stimulus and therefore appears to be emitted rather than elicited.

Operant conditioning. The modification of response strength by manipulation of the consequences of the response. Responses that are followed by a reinforcer gain in strength; responses not followed by a reinforcer become weaker. Also called type R conditioning.

Operant level. The frequency with which an operant response is made before it is systematically reinforced.

Partial reinforcement effect (PRE). The fact that a partially or intermittently reinforced response will take longer to extinguish than a response on a continuous or 100 percent schedule of reinforcement.

Partial reinforcement schedule. A schedule of reinforcement that sometimes reinforces a desired response and sometimes does not. In other words, the response is maintained on a schedule of reinforcement somewhere between 100 percent and 0 percent.

Positive reinforcement. The kind of reinforcement that occurs when a response makes available a primary or secondary positive reinforcer.

Positive reinforcer. Anything that when added to the situation by a response increases the rate with which that response is made.

Primary negative reinforcer. A negative reinforcer that is related to an organism's survival—for example, pain or oxygen deprivation.

Primary positive reinforcer. A positive reinforcer that is related to an organism's survival—for example, food or water.

Primary reinforcer. Something an organism must have to survive—for example, food, water, and oxygen.

Punishment. Either removing a positive reinforcer or presenting a negative reinforcer.

Rate of responding. Used by Skinner to demonstrate operant conditioning. If a response is followed by a reinforcer, the rate or frequency with which it is made will go up; if a response is not followed by a reinforcer, its rate of frequency either will stay the same (if it is at its operant level) or will go down.

Respondent behavior. Behavior that is elicited by a known stimulus.

Respondent conditioning. Another term for classical or Pavlovian conditioning. Also called type S conditioning.

Secondary negative reinforcer. A negative reinforcer that derives its reinforcing properties through its association with a primary negative reinforcer.

Secondary positive reinforcer. A positive reinforcer that derives the reinforcing properties through its association with a primary positive reinforcer.

Secondary reinforcer. Objects or events that acquire reinforcing properties through their association with primary reinforcers.

Shaping. The gradual development of a response that an organism does not normally make. Shaping requires differential reinforcement and successive approximation.

Skinner box. A small experimental chamber that Skinner invented to study operant conditioning.

Spontaneous recovery. The reappearance of a conditioned response following a delay after extinction had occurred.

Structuralism. Psychology's first school of thought. The goal of the structuralist was to study the nature of consciousness through the use of introspection.

Successive approximations. The situation in which only those responses that are increasingly similar to the one ultimately wanted are reinforced.

Superstitious behavior. Behavior that develops under noncontingent reinforcement in which the organism seems to believe that a relationship exists between its actions and reinforcement, when in fact no such relationship exists.

Tact. That part of verbal behavior that accurately names objects and events in the environment.

Token economies. An example of Skinnerian behavior therapy that usually occurs within an institutional setting, such as a psychiatric hospital or a school. Within a token economy, desirable behavior is reinforced by tokens (or sometimes points or cards) that can subsequently be traded for desirable objects or events, such as food, cigarettes, privacy, or a choice of a television program.

Type R conditioning. The term used by Skinner to describe the conditioning of operant or emitted behavior to emphasize the importance of the response (R) to such conditioning. Also called operant conditioning.

Type S conditioning. The term Skinner used to describe classical conditioning to emphasize the importance of the stimulus (S) to such conditioning. Also called respondent conditioning.

Unconditioned response (UCR). The natural, automatic response elicited by an unconditioned stimulus (UCS).

Unconditioned stimulus (UCS). A stimulus that elicits an automatic, natural response from an organism. Also called a primary reinforcer, because conditioning ultimately depends on the presence of a UCS.

Variable interval reinforcement schedule (VI). The reinforcement schedule in which a certain average time interval must pass before a response will be reinforced. For example, the organism is reinforced on the average of every thirty seconds.

Variable ratio reinforcement schedule (VR). The reinforcement schedule in which a certain average number of responses need to be made before reinforcement is obtained. For example, the organism is reinforced on the average of every fifth response.

Verbal behavior. Skinner's term for language.

Vicarious reinforcement. The kind of reinforcement that comes from imitating the behavior of someone who is seen engaging in activities that are reinforced.

Walden Two. The name of a novel written by Skinner to show how his learning principles could be applied to cultural engineering.

10

John Dollard
Neal Miller

Neal Miller

Neal E. Miller was born in Milwaukee, Wisconsin, on 3 August, 1909. He received his B.S. degree from the University of Washington in 1931. While at the University of Washington he studied with the famous learning theorist Edwin Guthrie. He received his M.A. degree from Stanford in 1932 and his Ph.D. degree from Yale in 1935. While at Yale he studied with another famous learning theorist, Clark L. Hull. As we shall see, Hull had a major influence on Miller's theory of personality. Miller undertook what Hull himself expressed an interest in doing but never did—that is, to explore the relationship between Hull's theory of learning and Freud's theory of personality.

Shortly after obtaining his Ph.D., Miller went to Europe as a Social Science Research Council Traveling Fellow. While in Europe he was psychoanalyzed by Heinz Hartman at the Vienna Institute of Psychoanalysis. From 1936 to 1941 he was an instructor, assistant professor, and associate professor at Yale's Institute of Human Relations. From 1942 to 1946 he directed psychological research for the Army

Neal Miller

Air Force. In 1946 he returned to Yale, and in 1952 he became the James Rowland Angell Professor of Psychology.

Miller remained at Yale until 1966, when he went to Rockefeller University to become professor of psychology and head of the laboratory of physiological psychology. Through the years Miller has been a courageous researcher, who has been willing to apply the rigorous methods of science to the more subjective aspects of human experience, such as conflict, language, and unconscious mechanisms. This boldness continues today at Rockefeller University, where Miller is currently exploring the conditions under which people can learn to control their own internal environment. His pioneer research in this area of *biofeedback* is but one area in which Miller has stimulated research and to which he has made significant contributions. Most recently Miller has been concerned with the relatively new topic of *behavioral medicine*, which, to a large extent, is an outgrowth of his research on biofeedback (see for example, Miller 1983, 1984).

Among Miller's many honors are included the presidency of the American Psychological Association, a position he held during 1960–61; the Warren Medal from the Society of Experimental Psychologists in 1957; and the U.S. President's Medal of Science in 1965.

John Dollard

John Dollard was born in Menasha, Wisconsin, on 29 August, 1900. He received his B.A. degree from the University of Wisconsin in 1922, and his M.A. in 1930 and Ph.D. in sociology in 1931 from the University of Chicago. In 1932 he became assistant professor of anthropology at Yale University, and in 1933 he became an assistant professor of sociology in the newly formed Institute of Human Relations at Yale. In 1935 he became research associate at the institute, and in 1948 was appointed research associate and professor of psychology. Dollard remained at Yale, where he became professor emeritus in 1969.

Dollard was truly a generalist. Besides teaching anthropology, sociology, and psychology, he also was trained in psychoanalysis at the Berlin Institute. He wrote *Caste and Class in a Southern Town* (1937), which is now considered a classic field study of the black person's social role in the South during the 1930s. Miller (1982) comments on the impact of Dollard's book *Caste and Class*:

> Today it is difficult to realize the courage that it took to make such a study and to write such a book. Southern whites, and some Northern white scholars as well, felt that it was despicable to describe such facts. The book was banned in South Africa and in Georgia. If conditions in this country are considerably better today, it is partly due to the long-term effects of the early insights provided by Dollard's classic study of *Class and Caste*. (587)

A companion volume, *Children of Bondage* (1940) was coauthored with the black social anthropologist, Allison Davis, and was based on the study of black youths in New Orleans, Louisiana, and Natchez, Mississippi. During World War II, Dollard conducted a psychological analysis of military behavior, which resulted in two books: *Victory over Fear* (1942) and *Fear in Battle* (1943). This list is only a sample of Dollard's publications.

John Dollard

In 1939 Dollard and Miller (along with Doob, Mowrer, and Sears) published a book entitled *Frustration and Aggression*, which attempted to analyze frustration and its consequences in terms of learning principles. Shortly afterward, Miller and Dollard published *Social Learning and Imitation* (1941), which analyzed several complex behavior problems within the context of learning principles. In 1950 Dollard and Miller published *Personality and Psychotherapy: An Analysis in Terms of Learning, Thinking and Culture*. Much of this chapter is based on that book. John Dollard died on 8 October, 1980 at 80 years of age.

The combined efforts of Dollard and Miller created a framework within which complex topics such as personality and psychotherapy could be understood more clearly than they had ever been before. As we shall see, they took two preexisting systems—namely, Freud's and Hull's—and synthesized them, thus creating a more comprehensive and more useful theoretical structure than either Freud's theory or Hull's theory alone had been.

Goal of Dollard and Miller.   Dollard and Miller dedicated their 1950 book, *Personality and Psychotherapy*, to "Freud, Pavlov and their students." The first paragraph of this book reads:

This book is an attempt to aid in the creation of a psychological base for a general science of human behavior. Three great traditions, heretofore followed separately, are brought together. One of these is psychoanalysis, initiated by the genius of

Freud and carried on by his many able students in the art of psychotherapy. Another stems from the work of Pavlov, Thorndike, Hull, and a host of other experimentalists. They have applied the exactness of natural-science method to the study of the principles of learning. Finally, modern social science is crucial because it describes the social conditions under which human beings learn. The ultimate goal is to combine the vitality of psychoanalysis, the rigor of the natural-science laboratory, and the facts of culture. We believe that a psychology of this kind should occupy a fundamental position in the social sciences and humanities—making it unnecessary for each of them to invent its own special assumptions about human nature and personality. (3)

Dollard and Miller set as their goal combining the genius of Freud's insights with the rigors of scientific method as exemplified by the work of the learning theorists to understand more clearly human behavior in a cultural setting.

Why the emphasis on learning principles? It is because Dollard and Miller believe that most human behavior is learned. In their earlier book, *Social Learning and Imitation* (1941), which was dedicated to Clark Hull, they explained:

Human behavior is learned; precisely that behavior which is widely felt to characterize man as a rational being, or as a member of a particular nation or social class, is acquired rather than innate. To understand thoroughly any item of human behavior—either in the social group or in the individual life—one must know the psychological principles involved in its learning and the social conditions under which this learning took place. It is not enough to know either principles or conditions of learning; in order to predict behavior both must be known. The field of psychology describes learning principles, while the various social science disciplines describe the conditions. (1)

It is not just simple overt behavior that Dollard and Miller believe is learned, but also the complex processes such as language and the processes described by Freud such as repression, displacement, and conflict. Because they believe that most important behavior is learned, they also believe that an understanding of the principles of learning is essential if human behavior is to be understood.

Hull's Theory of Learning

In the preceding chapter we saw that Skinner defined a reinforcer as anything that modified either the probability of a response or the rate of responding. Hull (1943) was more specific about the nature of **reinforcement.** He said that for a stimulus to be a reinforcer it must reduce a drive. Therefore Hull is said to have a **drive reduction** theory of learning. A stimulus capable of reducing a drive is a reinforcer, and the actual drive reduction is the reinforcement.

The cornerstone of Hull's theory is the concept of **habit,** which is an association between a stimulus and a response. If a stimulus (S) leads to a response (R), which, in turn, produces a reinforcer, the association between that stimulus (S) and that response (R) becomes stronger. We say that the habit of performing that response in the presence of that stimulus becomes stronger. Because habits describe relationships between stimuli and responses, Hull's theory has been called an S-R theory of learning.

In addition to the concepts of drive and habit, Dollard and Miller borrowed many other concepts from Hull's theory of learning. Among them are the concepts of response hierarchies, stimulus generalization (which Hull borrowed from Pavlov), primary and secondary drives, primary and secondary reinforcers, anticipatory goal responses, and cue-producing responses.

A few of the Freudian concepts that Dollard and Miller attempt to explain or equate with learning principles are the pleasure principle, the relationship between frustration and aggression, the importance of early childhood experience to the formation of adult personality, conflict, repression, and the importance of the unconscious mind to the generation and maintenance of neurotic behavior. Dollard and Miller also attempt to explain many of the effective procedures in psychotherapy in terms of Hullian learning principles.

For the remainder of this chapter we will review certain aspects of Freudian theory and place them within the context of **Hull's theory of learning.** First, however, we will note some similarities and differences between Hull's and Skinner's theories of learning.

Relationship to Skinner's Position

Skinner's position is antitheoretical. As we saw in the last chapter, his approach to research was to make a **functional analysis** between environmental conditions and behavior. He is said to study the "empty organism," because, for his purposes, he did not care about the physiological or cognitive processes that occur between environmental events and the behavior they produce. Skinner even refused to speculate on the nature of reinforcement.

Hull's approach to learning theory was very different. His formulations were highly theoretical. In fact, most of Hull's theory is concerned with hypothetical events that were believed to influence either learning or performance. Hull's theory attempted to explain both cognitive and behavioral events, and therefore it provided a more useful framework for Dollard and Miller to use than a theory such as Skinner's could have. For example, it would have been impossible to explain concepts such as repression without a theory that provided for mediational processes such as thinking and reasoning. Hull's theory provides such processes; Skinner's does not.

Like Skinner, the Hullians, including Dollard and Miller, see nothing wrong with studying lower animals, such as the rat, to learn about human behavior. In fact, Dollard and Miller believe rather strongly that two of the best sources of information about the normal human personality are the rat and neurotic humans who seek professional help. They think that studying rats is useful because their histories (both genetic and environmental) can be controlled, they are less complex than humans, and the simple behavioral "units" found in rats are also the ingredients of human behavior.

Dollard and Miller think that studying neurotics is useful because: They seek help and therefore can be observed under controlled conditions; their behavior can be systematically studied during a fairly long period of time; they are more willing than normal people to speak openly about sensitive and highly personal aspects of their lives; and the same variables govern both neurotic and normal behavior, but the variables appear in exaggerated form in neurotics, making them easier to observe. Dollard and Miller do caution, however, that any generalizations from rats or neurotics applied to normal humans should be checked empirically to test their validity. Dollard and Miller believe that a combination of psychotherapy and laboratory experimentation offers the best means of studying personality.

Like Skinner, Dollard and Miller also acknowledge the importance of culture in determining certain personality attributes. In the last chapter we saw that Skinner defined culture as a set of reinforcement contingencies; Miller and Dollard say about the same in the following quotation:

> No psychologist would venture to predict the behavior of a rat without knowing on what arm of a T-maze the feed or the shock is placed. It is no easier to predict the behavior of a human being without knowing the conditions of his "maze," i.e., the structure of his social environment. Culture, as conceived by social scientists, is a statement of the design of the human maze, of the type of reward involved, and of what responses are to be rewarded. It is in this sense a recipe for learning. This contention is easily accepted when widely variant societies are compared. But even within the same society, the mazes which are run by two individuals may seem the same but actually be quite different. . . . No personality analysis of two . . . people can be accurate which does not take into account these cultural differences, that is, differences in the types of responses which have been rewarded. (1941, 5–6)

Drive, Cue, Response, and Reinforcement

Dollard and Miller's theory of personality relies heavily on four concepts, which they borrowed from Hull's theory of learning. The four concepts are drive, cue, response, and reinforcement. Each will be discussed in the following sections.

Drive

A **drive** is any strong stimulus that impels an organism to action and whose elimination or reduction is reinforcing. Drives may be *internal*, such as hunger or thirst, or they may be *external*, such as a loud noise or intense heat or cold. A drive may be *primary*, in that it is directly related to survival—for example, hunger, thirst, pain, sex, and elimination—or it may be *secondary*, or learned, such as fear, anxiety, or the need to be successful or attractive. Secondary drives are usually culturally determined, whereas primary drives are not. It is important to note that primary drives are the building blocks of personality, and all acquired drives ultimately depend on them. This concept is similar to Freud's position that many of the everyday behaviors we see in people are indirect manifestations of basic drives such as sex or aggression.

Drive is the motivational concept in Dollard and Miller's theory. Drive is the energizer of personality. The stronger the stimulus, the stronger the drive and the greater the motivation.

> A drive is a strong stimulus which impels action. Any stimulus can become a drive if it is made strong enough. The stronger the stimulus, the more drive function it possesses. The faint murmur of distant music has but little primary drive function; the infernal blare of the neighbor's radio has considerably more. (Miller & Dollard 1941, 18)

Cue

A **cue** is a stimulus that indicates the appropriate direction that an activity should take. Drives energize behavior, whereas cues guide behavior.

> The drive impels a person to respond. Cues determine when he will respond, where he will respond, and which response he will make. Simple examples of stimuli which function primarily as cues are the five o'clock whistle determining when the tired worker will stop, the restaurant sign determining where the hungry man will go, and the traffic light determining whether the driver will step on the brake or on the accelerator. (Dollard & Miller 1950, 32)

Any stimulus can be thought of as having certain drive properties, depending on its strength, and certain cue properties, depending on its distinctiveness.

Response

Responses are elicited by the drive and cues present, which are aimed at reducing or eliminating the drive. In other words, the hungry (drive) person seeing a restaurant (cue) must get into the restaurant (response) before the hunger drive can be reduced. In Dollard and Miller's theory (and in Hull's) a **response** can be *overt*—it can be directly instrumental in reducing a drive—or it can be *internal*, entailing the thinking, planning, and reasoning that will *ultimately* reduce a drive. Dollard and Miller refer to internal responses as cue-producing responses. We will have more to say about such responses later in the chapter.

Some responses are more effective than others in reducing a drive and are the ones that should occur when next the drive occurs. New responses must be learned to new situations, and old responses must be discouraged if they are no longer maximally effective. The rearrangement of response probabilities as new conditions emerge or as old conditions change is called **learning.** We will say more about the circumstances under which response probabilities change in the next section.

Reinforcement

As we said earlier, reinforcement, according to Dollard and Miller, is equated with drive reduction. Any stimulus that causes drive reduction is said to be a reinforcer.

A reinforcer can be primary, in which case it satisfies a need related to survival, or it can be secondary. A secondary reinforcer, as in Skinner's theory, is a previously neutral stimulus that has been consistently paired with a primary reinforcer. A mother, for example, becomes a powerful secondary reinforcer because of her association with the reduction of primary drives.

If a cue leads to a response and the response leads to reinforcement, the association between the cue and the response will be strengthened. If this process is repeated, eventually we can say that the organism has developed a strong habit.

It should be pointed out that the nature of reinforcement is a highly controversial issue among learning theorists, of which Dollard and Miller are aware. Like good scientists, they use the definition of reinforcement that they think is the best available but would be happy to discard that definition if a better one came along.

> The stimulus-reduction hypothesis of reinforcement could be discarded without having an appreciable effect on the rest of my theoretical formulations. I take this occasion to urge attempts to formulate and rigorously test competing hypotheses, and time permitting, may even join in that activity myself. However unsatisfactory, the drive-reduction hypothesis is not likely to be abandoned as long as it is the best thing of its kind that we have. The decisive way to kill it is with a superior alternative. (Miller 1959, 257)

As we have seen, Dollard and Miller set as their goal the explanation of human personality in terms of learning theory. Having discussed the concepts of drive, cue, response, and reinforcement, we are now in a position to understand what, according to Dollard and Miller, learning theory is.

> What, then, is learning theory? In its simplest form, it is the study of the circumstances under which a response and a cue stimulus become connected. After learning has been completed, response and cue are bound together in such a way that the appearance of the cue evokes the response. . . . Learning takes place according to definite psychological principles. Practice does not always make perfect. The connection between a cue and a response can be strengthened only under certain conditions. The learner must be driven to make the response and rewarded for having responded in the presence of the cue. This may be expressed in a homely way by saying that in order to learn one must want something, notice something, do something, and get something. Stated more exactly, these factors are drive, cue, response and reward. (Miller & Dollard 1941, 1–2)

The best summary of what the learning theorists call **reinforcement theory** is the preceding statement: "in order to learn one must want something, notice something, do something, and get something."

Response Hierarchies

Every cue elicits several responses simultaneously, which vary in terms of their probability of occurrence. This group of responses elicited by a cue is what Hull called the **habit family hierarchy,** which can be diagrammed as follows:

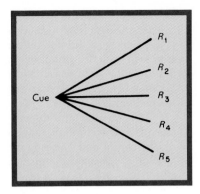

In the preceding diagram, R_1 is the most likely response to be made when the cue is encountered, R_2 is next likely, and so forth. If R_1 is prevented, R_2 would be made, and if R_1 and R_2 were blocked, R_3 would be made, and so on.

When a newborn child experiences an irritation, a set of responses is triggered that, because no learning is involved, is called the **innate hierarchy of responses.** This hierarchy is a genetically determined set of responses that is triggered by certain drive conditions. The hungry infant first may become restless, then cry, and then toss violently while screaming. Note that the innate hierarchy of responses exists for only a short period of time. As certain responses in the hierarchy are reinforced, they change their position in the hierarchy. The response most likely to occur is called the **dominant response** in the hierarchy and is the one that has been most successful in bringing about drive reduction.

Learning is constantly rearranging responses in the various habit family hierarchies. Prior to a learning experience, the arrangement of responses elicited by a cue is called the **initial hierarchy of responses.** After learning has occurred, the revised arrangement of responses is called the **resultant hierarchy of responses.** It should be noted that what is called the initial hierarchy of responses refers to either an innate hierarchy of responses or to a hierarchy that resulted from prior learning. In either case, it is the hierarchy that exists before a *new* learning experience that will rearrange the hierarchy, thus creating a resultant hierarchy of responses. The term *initial* then, refers to clusters of response probabilities that exist *before* a learning experience, whether those probabilities are determined by genetics or by prior learning experience.

It is also important to note that if the dominant response in a hierarchy always reduced the existing drive, no learning would ever occur. If, for example, the innate response of blinking always removed stray particles from one's eye, no need would exist to learn to rub the eye or roll it or wash it. According to Dollard and Miller, all learning, which we can now equate with the rearrangement of response hierarchies, depends on failure. This concept is labeled the **learning dilemma,** and has vast implications for both education and child rearing.

> In the absence of a dilemma, no new learning of either the trial-and-error or the thoughtful problem-solving type occurs. For example, a mother was worried because her child seemed to be retarded in learning to talk. Brief questioning revealed that she was adept at understanding the child's every want as expressed by

its gestures. Having other successful means of responding, the child was not in a dilemma. He learned only his old habits of using gestures more thoroughly, and consequently he did not perform the type of random vocal behavior which would lead to speech. By gradually pretending to become more stupid at understanding gestures, the mother put the child in a dilemma and probably facilitated the learning of speech. At least, under these modified conditions, this child rapidly learned to talk.

The absence of a dilemma is one of the reasons why it is often difficult to teach successful people new things. Old, heavily rewarded habits must be interrupted before new learning can occur. When the accustomed rewards are withdrawn by unusual circumstances such as revolution, new responses may occur and, if rewarded, may be learned; Russian Counts *can* learn to drive taxicabs and Countesses to become cooks. (Dollard & Miller 1950, 45–46)

Fear as an Acquired Drive

We have looked in detail at the complexities of Dollard and Miller's concepts of response and reinforcement. In this section we will focus on their concept of drive, and in the next section we will discuss in more detail some additional properties of cues.

We mentioned earlier that two kinds of drives exist—primary and secondary. Primary drives are biologically determined, and secondary drives are learned or culturally determined. One of the most important secondary drives is fear, because it is so important to both adaptive and maladaptive human behavior. Freud observed that fear could serve as a warning of impending danger. For example, events that accompanied a painful experience, when re-encountered, would cause fear or anxiety, thus warning the person to be careful. For example, a child who was burned by a hot stove would experience fear when next seeing a stove even though there was no pain in merely seeing the stove.

In 1948 Miller performed his now-famous experiment exploring the acquisition of fear. His apparatus consisted of an experimental chamber with black and white compartments. When a rat was allowed to roam freely, it showed no aversion to either the white or the black compartment. Next, Miller shocked the rat in the white compartment, and it was allowed to escape the shock by running into the black compartment. The rat quickly learned to escape the shock by leaving the white compartment. Later when the animal was placed in the white compartment without being shocked, it urinated, defecated, crouched, and ran into the black compartment. The animal had learned to fear the white compartment, because it had been associated with shock.

Miller next arranged the experiment so that the animal could escape the white compartment only by first turning a small wheel. The animal learned to do this, even though no additional shocks were given. Miller replaced the wheel with a lever and found the animal quickly extinguished the wheel-turning response, which was now ineffective, and learned the lever-pressing response, again with no further shocks. The animal had developed a **conditioned fear reaction** to the white chamber.

The most important point about Miller's experiment is that it demonstrates that fear itself becomes a drive that can be reduced, resulting in reinforcement. It was the reduction of fear, not pain, that caused the animal to learn the wheel-turning and the lever-pressing responses. Such behavior is highly resistant to extinction, because as long as fear is present, its reduction will be highly reinforcing. Note that, under these circumstances, the animal does not stay in the situation long enough to learn that it will not receive additional shocks and thereby extinguish its fear reaction. It keeps behaving "as if" it will be shocked again if it lingers in the situation.

It is Dollard and Miller's contention that phobias, anxieties, and other irrational fear responses are produced by similar experiences on the human level. Such behavior looks irrational to the observer because the history of its development is not known as it is with the rat. It could be that because of harsh physical punishment for sexual behavior in early childhood, a person has an aversion to sexual activities and sexual thoughts. For this person, even approximating such activities or thoughts elicits fear, which is reduced by escape or avoidance. Like the rat in Miller's experiment, this person never dwells long enough in the anxiety-provoking situation to learn that he or she will no longer be punished for such thoughts or activities. As with the rat, extinction of the fear reaction is extremely difficult. As we shall see later in this chapter, the main job of psychotherapy, as Dollard and Miller see it, is to provide a situation in which the client is encouraged to experience threatening thoughts without punishment and, in that way, to finally extinguish them. This goal is similar to what Freud was attempting to do when he used free association and dream analysis to discover repressed thoughts.

Stimulus Generalization

If an association exists between S_1 and R_1, not only will S_1 elicit R_1, but so will various stimuli similar to S_1. The greater the similarity of a stimulus to S_1, the greater will be the tendency for it to elicit R_1. This is called **stimulus generalization.** In Miller's experiment on fear, we would expect not only the white compartment to elicit fear but also various shades of gray compartments to elicit fear. The lighter the shade of the compartment, however, the greater will be the fear response, because it was the white compartment that was originally associated with pain.

All learned responses generalize to other stimuli. If a child learns to fear snakes, she probably will also, at least at first, fear rope. If an adolescent fears his father, he will also tend to fear men who look like his father. A woman who is raped may shortly thereafter hate all men. With further experience, however, most normal humans learn to discriminate. **Discrimination** is the opposite of generalization. Thus, the child learns that some snakes are to be feared but that ropes are safe. The adolescent learns that his father perhaps should be feared under some circumstances but that men of similar appearance pose no threat, and the rape victim realizes that her attacker was not typical of all men. Therefore, generalization causes the initial tendency for learned responses to be elicited by a wide range of stimuli, but further experience allows the person to discriminate and thus respond selectively to stimuli. This is true, at least, of normal people. As we shall see later in this chapter, neurotics often lose their ability to discriminate and therefore tend to overgeneralize their anxieties.

Dollard and Miller distinguish two kinds of generalization: primary and secondary. **Primary generalization** is based on the physical similarity among stimuli. The closer two stimuli are in their physical attributes, the greater the probability is that they will elicit the same response. Primary generalization is innate and governed by a person's sensory apparatus. **Secondary generalization** is based on verbal labels, not on the physical similarity among stimuli. Thus, one responds to all individuals labeled "friendly" in a similar way. Likewise the word "dangerous" equates many dangerous situations, which tend to elicit similar kinds of responses. Secondary generalization is what Dollard and Miller call learned equivalence, which is mediated by language. It is important to realize that secondary generalization is not based on physical attributes; in fact, it can counteract primary generalization by labeling one event "good" and another event "bad," although the two events are physically similar.

Conflict

One of Freud's concepts that Miller studied intensively was that of **conflict.** Lewin (1935) had studied the concept earlier, and Miller borrowed from both Freud and Lewin. It was Miller, however, who experimentally analyzed in depth the concept of conflict. Freud had talked about the continuous conflict between libidinal desires and the demands of the superego. To Freud, a person could be both attracted to an object and repelled by it at the same time. This was later called an approach-avoidance conflict and is one of four kinds of conflict studied by Miller. Each of the four now will be described.

Approach-Approach Conflict

Here the conflict is between two positive goals that are equally attractive at the same time. Such a conflict can be diagrammed as follows:

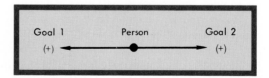

An **approach-approach conflict** exists when two equally attractive people ask for a date on the same night or when one is both hungry and sleepy. Such conflicts can become severe—witness the proverbial ass that starved to death between two equally desirable bales of hay. Typically, however, this kind of conflict is easily solved by attaining first one goal and then the other; for example, one could first eat and then go to bed.

Avoidance-Avoidance Conflict

Here the person must choose between two negative goals. For example, the child must eat her spinach or be spanked, the student must do his arithmetic homework or get low grades, or a person must either go to a job he dislikes or lose his income. A person having such a conflict is "damned if he does and damned if he doesn't"; he can also be said to be "caught between the devil and the deep blue sea." Such a conflict can be diagrammed as follows:

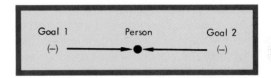

Two kinds of behavior typically characterize an organism having an **avoidance-avoidance conflict:** (1) vacillation or indecision and (2) escape. Escape can be either actually leaving the conflict situation, or it can be mental escape such as daydreaming or mental preoccupation with other thoughts.

Approach-Avoidance Conflict

Here the person is both attracted to and repelled by the *same goal.* A job may be attractive because of the money it will earn but be unattractive because it is boring, or because it keeps the person from doing more enjoyable activities. The young woman may be attracted to the idea of marriage because of the security it would bring to her life but may be anxious about her sexual role in marriage. Such a conflict can be diagrammed as follows:

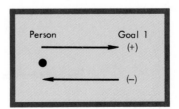

Miller listed the following as the most significant features of the **approach-avoidance conflict:**

A. The tendency to approach a goal is stronger the nearer the subject is to it.

B. The tendency to avoid a feared stimulus is stronger the nearer the subject is to it.

C. The strength of avoidance increases more rapidly with nearness than does that of approach.

D. The strength of tendencies to approach or avoid varies directly with the strength of the drive upon which they are based.

E. Below the asymptote of learning, increasing the number of reinforced trials will increase the strength of the response tendency that is reinforced.

F. When two incompatible responses are in conflict, the stronger one will occur (Miller 1959, 205–206)

It is on the approach-avoidance conflict that Miller has done his most extensive research (for example, 1944, 1959, and 1964). Figure 10–1 summarizes many of these characteristics of the approach-avoidance conflict.

Among the many deductions that can be made from Figure 10–1 is that as long as the approach gradient is higher than the avoidance gradient, the person will approach the goal. As soon as the avoidance gradient becomes higher, the person will avoid the goal.

Therefore, because the approach gradient becomes higher the farther one is from the goal, a strong approach tendency will occur. As one approaches the goal, however, the avoidance tendency increases and eventually is stronger than the approach tendency. At that point, the person will retreat from the goal. Thus, we would expect vacillation at the point at which the two gradients cross. We all know couples who have doubts about their relationship and who are constantly breaking up and going back together. While apart, the favorable aspects of their relationship are dominant, and therefore they are driven back together. Once reunited, however, they confront the negative aspects of their relationship and are once again driven apart.

Figure 10–1
Diagram of an approach-avoidance conflict.

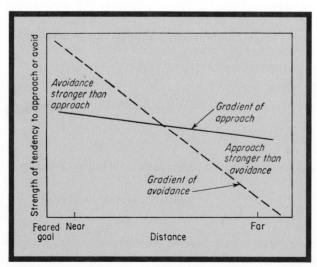

(From Miller 1959, p. 206.)

We will have more to say about the approach-avoidance conflict in subsequent sections of this chapter.

Double Approach-Avoidance Conflict

Here the person has ambivalent feelings about two goal objects. Such a conflict can be diagrammed as follows:

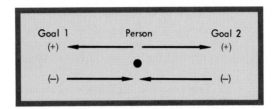

One example of a double approach-avoidance conflict comes from the female child's position relative to her parents in Freudian theory. She is attracted to her mother because the mother satisfies her biologic needs but is repelled by the mother because she is thought responsible for denying the girl a penis. She is attracted to her father because he possesses the valued organ and yet is envious of him because he does. According to Freud, the female child has ambivalent feelings about both parents.

According to Dollard and Miller, most neurotic behavior involves conflict. For example, when a neurotic person begins to engage in activities or thoughts that will lead to the reduction of a strong drive such as sex, he is overwhelmed with anxiety. The closer he comes to approaching a goal that will satisfy his need for sex, the stronger his anxiety will become, until eventually he retreats from the goal. Because his original need was not satisfied, however, he again approaches sex-related goals, only to be eventually driven from them by anxiety, and on it goes. Only psychotherapy, or its equivalent, will rescue this person from this vicious circle.

Displacement

Another Freudian concept that is explored thoroughly by Dollard and Miller is that of **displacement.** One of the most important aspects of Freud's theory was his contention that frustrated drives do not simply go away but rather show up in disguised form. In other words, if a need could not be satisfied directly, it was displaced and satisfied indirectly. As we saw in chapter 2, Freud's term for the displacement of the sex drive to more socially acceptable activities such as hard work, and creativity in general, was sublimation.

Miller's first step was to verify experimentally the phenomenon of displacement. To do this, Miller (1948b) placed two rats in an apparatus and shocked them both until they started fighting, at which point the shock was turned off. In other words, the aggressive act of fighting was reinforced by escape from shock. Training continued in this manner until the animals began fighting immediately after the shock was turned on. At this point, a doll was placed in the apparatus, and the animals were shocked. Again they fought with each other and ignored the doll. This is shown in Figure 10–2.

When only one animal was placed in the apparatus and shocked, however, it attacked the doll. This is shown in Figure 10–3. When the object of aggression was not available to the animal, it aggressed toward a substitute object—that is, the doll. Thus, **displaced aggression** was demonstrated.

To show that displacement occurs is important, but it leaves unanswered questions as to what determines which objects are involved in displacement and why. For example, if an employee cannot aggress toward her boss after being refused a raise, toward what object or objects will she aggress? Miller (1959, 218–19) reached the following conclusions about displacement:

1. When it is impossible for an organism to respond to a desired stimulus, it will respond to a stimulus that is most similar to the desired stimulus. For example, if a woman is prevented from marrying the man she loved because of his death, she will tend to marry someday a man similar to him.

2. If a response to an original stimulus is prevented by conflict, displacement will occur to an intermediate stimulus. For example, if a girl leaves her boyfriend after a quarrel, her next boyfriend will tend to be similar to her original boyfriend in many ways and yet also different from him.

3. If there are strong avoidance tendencies to an original stimulus, displacement will tend to occur toward dissimilar stimulus. For example, if a girl's original romance was negative, her next sweetheart would tend to be much different from the first.

Figure 10–2
The figure shows two rats that have been trained to fight each other to terminate an electric shock.

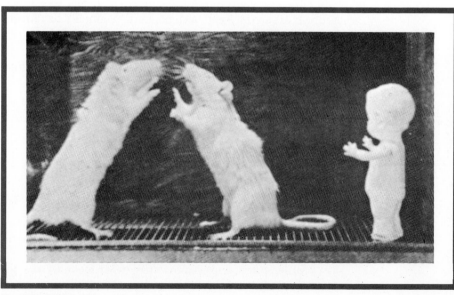

(From Miller 1948b, p. 157.)

Figure 10–3
*The figure shows
the displacement of
an aggressive
response.*

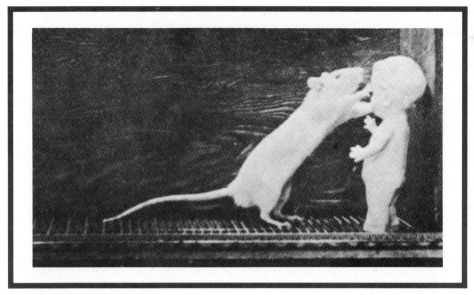

(From Miller 1948b, p. 157.)

If displacement occurs because of conflict, the strength of the conflicting responses will determine where displacement occurs. Figure 10–4 shows the nature of displacement when a weak conflicting response and a strong conflicting response occur.

We can see in Figure 10–4, for example, that if a desire to aggress toward a goal and a weak fear of punishment exist, a tendency to displace to an object similar

Figure 10–4
*The figure shows
that with a weak
avoidance tendency,
fear is not
experienced until
objects very near or
very similar to the
goal are
encountered. When
there is a strong
avoidance tendency,
however, fear is
caused by objects
more distant from
and more dissimilar
to the goal.*

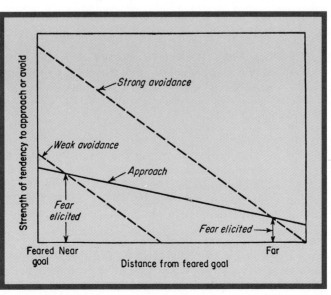

(From Miller 1959, p. 208.)

to the original goal will occur. If a desire exists to aggress toward a goal and there is a strong fear of punishment, however, the expression probably will be to objects dissimilar to the original goal. In other words, increasing a person's fear will decrease the tendency to displace the response to similar objects, and decreasing a person's fear increases the tendency to displace the response to similar objects. For example, if an employee has no fear of her boss and her boss frustrates her, she will aggress directly toward the boss. If an employee has a mild fear of her boss and the boss frustrates her, she will not aggress toward the boss but will aggress toward someone similar to the boss—for instance, the vice-president or manager. If an employee has a strong fear of her boss and the boss frustrates her, she will aggress toward objects dissimilar to the boss, such as other cars on the way home from work, her husband and children, or perhaps her pet.

One could also expect students who are frustrated by poor academic performance and who are fearful of teachers and school authorities to be among those who would commit acts of vandalism against their school. Their aggression caused by the frustration of poor academic performance is displaced from those directly responsible for their frustration to an object that is related but less threatening, the school itself.

We see, then, that if an object of choice is not available and no conflict exists, displacement is simply a matter of stimulus generalization. That is, an object most like the one not available will be chosen. If a conflict exists, however, displacement will be governed by the net of the approach and avoidance tendencies.

Frustration-Aggression Hypothesis

In 1939 Dollard and Miller (along with Doob, Mowrer, and Sears) published their first book together, entitled *Frustration and Aggression*. In this book they analyzed the Freudian notion that frustration leads to aggression, better known as the **frustration-aggression hypothesis.** Dollard, Doob, Miller, Mowrer, and Sears made the following assumption:

> This study takes as its point of departure the assumption that *aggression is always a consequence of frustration.* More specifically, the proposition is that the occurrence of aggressive behavior always pre-supposes the existence of frustration and, contrariwise, that the existence of frustration always leads to some form of aggression. (1939, 1)

Frustration was defined as "that condition which exists when a goal-response suffers interference," and *aggression* was defined as "an act whose goal-response is injury to an organism (or organism-surrogate)" (1930, 11). It was assumed that the disruption of goal-directed behavior causes frustration, and frustration causes aggression toward the person or object acting as a barrier between the person and his or her goal.

Dollard and others (1939, 28–32) conclude that three main factors determine how much aggression will result from frustration:

1. Drive level associated with the frustrated response.   In other words, the more intensely the person wants to attain a goal, the more frustrated he or she will be when the goal-directed activity is blocked, and thus the more aggressive that person will become.

2. Completeness of the frustration.   Goal responses that are only partially blocked will lead to less frustration and therefore less aggression than produced by goal responses that are completely blocked.

3. Cumulative effect of minor frustrations.   Minor frustrations or interferences will eventually add up to produce considerable frustration and therefore considerable aggression. If on the way to a restaurant to eat, for example, one first is interrupted by a friend who wants to chat, then by unusually heavy traffic, and then finds the restaurant closed, one is likely to become more frustrated than one would have been if one had gone directly to the restaurant and found it closed.

In all of these points, the message is always the same—the strength of aggression is a function of the magnitude of frustration.

In the last section we learned that as the threat of punishment for a direct act of aggression increases, the tendency for the act of aggression to be displaced to less threatening people or objects also increases. According to Dollard and others, "It follows that the *greater the degree of inhibition specific to a more direct act of aggression, the more probable will be the occurrence of less direct acts of aggression*" (1939, 40).

Through the years the relationship between frustration and aggression has been found to be less direct than originally thought. For example, Miller and Dollard (1941) concluded that aggression is only one result of frustration. Other possible reactions to frustration are withdrawal or apathy, regression, and fixation (stereotyped behavior). Most researchers still believe, however, that aggression is one of the most common and important reactions to frustration and that the relationship between the two has many implications for penal reform, child rearing, and behavior modification in general.

Importance of Language

Earlier in the chapter we listed "response" as one of the four essential ingredients in Dollard's and Miller's theory. The other three are drive, cue, and reinforcement. Two kinds of responding were mentioned, instrumental or overt and internal or thinking. Both kinds of responses were considered important by Dollard and Miller, which is a major distinction between their theory and Skinner's. Although Skinner did not avoid the topic of language, to him, language was simply verbal behavior that was governed by the same laws as any other behavior. Dollard and Miller were much more willing to speculate on the nature of internal thought processes and their relationship to language than Skinner was. Furthermore, Dollard and Miller analyzed the Freudian notions of repression and neurosis in terms of internal response mechanisms. Dollard and Miller think that people's ability to use language accounts for their higher mental processes, which are part of both neurotic and normal functioning.

Many years ago, Pavlov referred to physical stimuli that elicit conditioned responses as the **first signal system.** That is, through experience we learn to respond to certain environmental objects in certain ways, depending on the nature of our experience with them. For example, we avoid hot stoves and salivate when we are hungry and see food. In addition, according to Pavlov, we develop conditioned responses to *symbols* of environmental events. For example, we become fearful when we hear words like "fire," "danger," or "enemy." Likewise, we feel good when we hear the name of a loved one or hear such words as "love," "peace," or "friend." Pavlov called these conditioned responses the **second signal system.**

Dollard and Miller follow Pavlov in believing that language becomes a symbolic representation of reality. As this set of symbols develops, one can "think through" experiences without actually needing to have them. Thinking, then, is a kind of talking to oneself about several behavioral possibilities. Dollard and Miller call images, perceptions, and words **cue-producing responses,** because they generally determine what the next response in a sequence will be. Counting, for example, is a series of cue-producing responses because the response "one" triggers the response "two," and so forth. Thoughts constitute responses, but they also act as cues in eliciting further responses.

Two of the most useful functions of cue-producing responses are **reasoning** and **planning.** Reasoning replaces overt behavioral trial and error with cognitive trial and error. The latter is far more efficient, because *mentally* a problem can be approached from various viewpoints and no set sequence needs to be followed.

Figure 10–5 shows the advantage of reasoning in problem solving. In this example of reasoning, the driver in the black car is blocked from making a left turn by the traffic jam in the left lane. In the distance he sees the cars in the much lighter traffic coming from the opposite direction making the right turn easily on to the road he wants to take. He thinks, "If I were only going the other way." This stimulates him to think of how he could be going the other way. He pulls out into the right lane, passes the cars ahead, turns around, comes back the other way, and makes a right turn on to the highway. (The small circle at the center intersection indicates a traffic light.)

When cue-producing responses are part of solving an immediate problem, the process is called reasoning. When the cue-producing responses are directed at the solution of a future problem, the process is called planning.

In this section we have emphasized Dollard and Miller's analysis of language in normal functioning. Later in this chapter we will see how language functions in the mechanism of repression and in neuroses in general.

Unconscious Mind

Like Freud, Dollard and Miller consider unconscious processes to be extremely important in determining behavior. They describe two major categories of unconscious material: (1) experiences that were never verbally labeled and (2) experiences that have been repressed.

Experiences That Were Never Verbalized

Learning that occurs before language is developed is not labeled or recorded in a way that allows it to be recalled, and therefore, such learning becomes part of the unconscious.

Figure 10–5
An example of how reasoning replaces behavioral trial and error in a problem-solving situation.

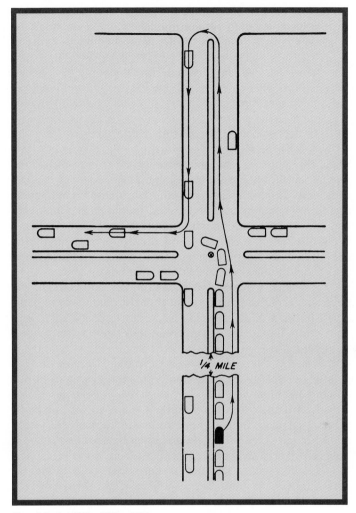

(From Dollard and Miller 1950, p. 112.)

> According to our hypothesis, drives, cues, and responses that have never been labeled will necessarily be unconscious. One large category of this kind will be experiences that occurred before the child learned to talk effectively. Since the effective use of speech develops gradually and may not be established for certain categories until long after the child has learned to say "Mamma," the period during which major parts of social learning are unconscious extends over a considerable number of years and has no set boundaries. (Dollard & Miller 1950, 198)

At the time in life thought by Freud to be most critical to adult personality development, experiences are unlabeled and thus cannot be recalled. These early experiences have a profound effect on one's later conscious life, and yet they themselves remain unconscious.

The young child does not notice or label the experiences which it is having at this time. It cannot give a description of character traits acquired during the first year of life nor yet of its hardships, fears, or deep satisfactions. What was not verbalized at the time cannot well be reported later. An important piece of history is lost and cannot be elicited by questionnaire or interview. Nevertheless, the behavioral record survives. The responses learned occur and may indeed recur in analogous situations throughout life. They are elicited by unlabeled cues and are mutely interwoven into the fabric of conscious life. (Dollard & Miller 1950, 136)

Experiences That Have Been Repressed

Some thoughts are uncomfortable because they cause anxiety. A few examples would be: thinking about an automobile accident in which a loved one was killed or injured; thinking about sex after learning how evil some believe such thoughts are; thinking about how you would like to steal something from a store; thinking about how you would like to caress your teacher or minister. Anxiety is a negative drive, just as pain, hunger, and thirst are, and therefore anything that reduces anxiety will be reinforcing. In other words, *anything that terminates an anxiety-provoking thought will be learned as a habit.*

If suddenly during a conversation you find yourself wanting your best friend's boyfriend, you may find such a thought anxiety-provoking because of your early moral training. If so, you may respond by consciously "putting the thought out of your mind." Such a conscious and deliberate effort to stop an anxiety-provoking thought is called **suppression.** Suppression is learned just like any other response; that is, because it is followed by drive reduction (in this case, anxiety is reduced), it gains in strength. Suppression is a common way of stopping thoughts that cause one to be anxious.

Eventually the suppression of anxiety-provoking thoughts becomes *anticipatory* in that such thoughts are terminated automatically before they can cause anxiety. When a potentially painful thought is aborted before it enters consciousness, the process is called **repression.** Repression is the learned response of *not thinking* thoughts that are unpleasant. In repression, early thoughts act as signals that, if a line of thought is continued, it will result in the experience of anxiety. Therefore the line of thought is terminated long before it can become painful. For this reason, repression is said to be anticipatory, and because it prevents the experience of anxiety, it is said to be a conditioned avoidance response. Suppression allows *escape* from anxiety-provoking thoughts, whereas repression allows *avoidance* of them. In other words, repression is triggered when unacceptable material starts to emerge from the unconscious, and suppression is triggered when such material is already conscious. Both processes are learned responses, which are maintained by the elimination, reduction, or prevention of anxiety.

It may appear that a process such as repression is beneficial because it allows a person to avoid many painful thoughts, and this certainly is true. Repression also has its negative side. A thought that is repressed cannot be treated rationally, because it does not enter consciousness. As we saw in the preceding section, it is conscious mechanisms that are part of the problem-solving processes of reasoning and planning. If a category of experience is repressed, it cannot be considered logically, and the activities related to it will tend to be unreasoned and stupid. Furthermore, any attempt to bring repressed material into consciousness is typically met with great resistance, which is the case during psychoanalysis.

As the reader may have guessed by now, the mechanism of repression is thought by Dollard and Miller (as it was by Freud) to be causally related to most neurotic behavior. The goal of psychotherapy is to free certain thoughts from repression so that they may be treated logically and realistically.

Neurosis and Symptom Formation

Dollard and Miller follow Freud in assuming that conflict is at the heart of neurotic behavior, and that this conflict is unconscious and usually learned in childhood.

> An intense emotional conflict is the necessary basis for neurotic behavior. The conflict must further be unconscious. As a usual thing, such conflicts are created only in childhood. How can it be that neurotic conflicts are engendered when there is no deliberate plan to do so? Society must force children to grow up, but it does not idealize neurosis and makes no formal provision in its system of training for the production of neurotic children. Indeed we deplore the neurotic and recognize him as a burden to himself and to others. How then does it happen? Our answer is that *neurotic conflicts are taught by parents and learned by children.* (Dollard & Miller 1950, 127 [italics added])

Beyond stating that neurotic behavior is unconsciously motivated by a conflict with its origin in childhood, it is difficult to state further exactly what **neurosis** is.

> Most people, even scientists, are vague about neurosis. Neither the neurotic victim nor those who know him seem able to state precisely what is involved. The victim feels a mysterious malady. The witness observes inexplicable behavior. The neurotic is mysterious because he is *capable* of acting and yet he is *unable* to act and enjoy. Though physically capable of attaining sex rewards, he is anesthetic; though capable of aggression he is meek; though capable of affection, he is cold and unresponsive. As seen by the outside witness, the neurotic does not make use of the obvious opportunities for satisfaction which life offers him. (Dollard and Miller 1950, 12)

Although the term neurosis is hard to define precisely, it is clear that the neurotic is miserable, stupid about certain aspects of his or her own existence, and often develops physical symptoms that are only manifestations of the repressed conflict.

If children are severely punished for sexual activities, they will learn to repress sexual behaviors and thoughts as adults. They will therefore need to live with a sex drive that strongly impels them to engage in sexual activities but with a strong fear of punishment if they do so. As we saw in the last section, thoughts of sexual activity will be repressed under these circumstances, and as a result, this strong approach-avoidance conflict will remain unconscious, so that language cannot be used to describe and analyze it.

> Without language and adequate labeling, the higher mental processes cannot function. When these processes are knocked out by repression, the person cannot guide himself by mental means to a resolution of his conflict. Since the neurotic

cannot help himself, he must have the help of others if he is to be helped at all—though millions today live out their lives in strong neurotic pain and never get help. The neurotic, therefore, is, or appears to be, stupid because he is unable to use his mind in dealing with certain of his problems. He feels that someone should help him, but he does not know how to ask for help since he does not know what his problem is. He may feel aggrieved that he is suffering, but he cannot explain his case. (Dollard & Miller 1950, 15)

The neurotic, therefore, is caught in an unbearable conflict between frustrated drives, on the one hand, and the fear connected with the approach responses that would bring about their satisfaction, on the other.

Symptom Formation

Neurotics often develop symptoms such as phobias, inhibitions, avoidances, compulsions, and physical disorders such as paralysis or nervous tics. Although it is common for neurotics to think that their symptoms constitute their problem, they do not. Neurotic symptoms are only manifestations of a repressed conflict. As an example, Dollard and Miller (1950) cite the case of Mrs. A., who was an orphan, born of unknown parents in a southern city. She was raised by foster parents, who gave her very repressive sex training. Although she had strong sexual appetites, sex became a dirty, loathsome activity about which it was painful for her to talk or think. Eventually she developed several phobias and a preoccupation with her heartbeat. In analysis it was learned that her preoccupation with her heartbeat was used as a means of preventing sex-related thoughts. Dollard and Miller summarized the case of Mrs. A. as follows:

> When on the streets alone, her fear of sex temptation was increased. Someone might speak to her, wink at her, make an approach to her. Such an approach would increase her sex desire and make her more vulnerable to seduction. Increased sex desire, however, touched off both anxiety and guilt, and this intensified her conflict when she was on the street. . . . When sexy thoughts came to mind or other sex stimuli tended to occur, these stimuli elicited anxiety. . . . Since [heartbeat] counting is a highly preoccupying kind of response, no other thoughts could enter her mind during this time. While counting, the sexy thoughts which excited fear dropped out. Mrs. A. "felt better" immediately when she started counting, and the counting habit was reinforced by the drop in anxiety. (1950, 21)

Neurotic symptoms are learned because they reduce fear or anxiety. Such symptoms do not solve the basic problem any more than repression does, but they make life temporarily more bearable.

> The symptoms do not solve the basic conflict in which the neurotic person is plunged, but they mitigate it. They are responses which tend to reduce the conflict, and in part they succeed. When a successful symptom occurs it is reinforced because it reduces neurotic misery. *The symptom is thus learned as a habit* [italics added]. One very common function of symptoms is to keep the neurotic person away from those stimuli which would activate and intensify his neurotic conflict. Thus, the combat pilot with a harrowing military disaster behind him may walk

away from the sight of any airplane. As he walks towards the plane his anxiety goes up; as he walks away it goes down. Walking away is thus reinforced. It is this phobic walking away which constitutes his symptom. If the whole situation is not understood, such behavior seems bizarre to the casual witness. (Dollard & Miller 1950, 15–16)

We have seen that neurotics are miserable and stupid about the nature of their problem and therefore are unable to help themselves. In the next section we will see how the professional therapist attempts to help neurotics, using Freudian notions as interpreted by Dollard and Miller.

Psychotherapy

The major assumption that Dollard and Miller make about neurosis is that it is learned, and if it is learned, it can be unlearned. **Psychotherapy** provides a situation in which neurosis can be unlearned.

If neurotic behavior is learned, it should be unlearned by some combination of the same principles by which it was taught. We believe this to be the case. Psychotherapy establishes a set of conditions by which neurotic habits may be unlearned and nonneurotic habits learned. Therefore, we view the therapist as a kind of teacher and the patient as a learner. In the same way and by the same principles that bad tennis habits can be corrected by a good coach, so bad mental and emotional habits can be corrected by a good psychotherapist. There is this difference, however. Whereas only a few people want to play tennis, all the world wants a clear, free, efficient mind. (Dollard & Miller 1950, 7–8)

As we have seen, the only way for a learned response to be extinguished is for it to occur and not be followed by reinforcement. For unrealistic fears to be extinguished they must occur and then not be followed by the kind of events that produced the fears in the first place. As previously mentioned, however, the person has learned to repress such fears, thus preventing their expression and therefore their subsequent extinction. Psychotherapy can be regarded as a situation in which the expression of repressed thoughts is encouraged. If the patient can be made to express these painful thoughts, the therapist is extremely careful to be encouraging, positive, and not punitive. Dollard and Miller (1950) explain:

In addition to permitting free speech, the therapist commands the patient to say everything that comes to mind. By the free-association technique the therapist sets the patient free from the restraint of logic. The therapist avoids arousing additional anxiety by not cross-questioning. By encouraging the patient to talk and consistently failing to punish him, the therapist creates a social situation that is the exact opposite of the one originally responsible for attaching strong fears to talking and thinking. The patient talks about frightening topics. Since he is not punished, his fears are extinguished. This extinction generalizes and weakens the motivation to repress other related topics that were originally too frightening for the patient to discuss or even to contemplate. Where the patient cannot say things for himself, the therapist helps by attaching a verbal label to the emotions that are being felt and expressed mutely in the transference situation. (230)

To persuade a patient to express a repressed thought is no easy matter, however, and typically a procedure similar to successive approximations is used. Let us imagine that a patient, for whatever reason, has learned to fear his mother to the point at which he cannot talk about her or about anything directly related to her. The therapist using Dollard and Miller's theory would not confront the patient directly with a conversation about his mother. Rather, the therapist would begin the discussion with events only indirectly related to the patient's mother. How indirect this needs to be depends on the magnitude of the avoidance the patient has toward his mother. As the therapist and patient discuss events only remotely related to the mother *in a nonthreatening environment*, a small amount of the avoidance of the mother is extinguished, or there occurs what Freud called catharsis. With the avoidance response somewhat reduced, the therapist can steer the conversation a bit closer to the mother but still stay a safe distance away. When doing so, the avoidance response is further reduced, and the therapist can move still closer to the ultimate target, the mother. Gradually, usually over several sessions, the therapist moves closer and closer to a discussion of the mother and then, when the avoidance response is sufficiently reduced, to a discussion of the mother herself. Now with most of the avoidance gone, the patient can talk about his mother phobia openly and logically.

We see, then, that psychotherapy, as seen by Dollard and Miller (and also by Freud) is a process of gradual extinction that depends on generalization, because the events discussed must be related in some way to the object, person, or event of ultimate concern. It also can be said that avoidance is displaced onto objects similar to the one that is avoided the most, so that not only will the patient avoid his mother, but he will also avoid people who look like her (primary generalization) or all mothers (secondary generalization); he may even be mildly apprehensive of women in general. Thus, conflict, extinction, generalization, and displacement all are part of the therapeutic process.

Psychotherapy usually does not stop when repressions have been released. Because the patient has spent such a large amount of his or her life with repressed thoughts, and because it is impossible to deal effectively with repressed material, there will be important gaps in the person's life even after successful therapy. For example, a person who is suddenly able to ponder her sex drive at the age of thirty-five will need to be given some guidance as to how best to adjust to the relative absence of inhibition. Such guidance also is considered by Dollard and Miller to be essential to the therapeutic process.

Murray and Berkun Experiment

We saw earlier in this chapter that Dollard and Miller and their followers see nothing wrong with using rat research to learn about humans or to verify hunches about principles that have come from observing humans. The experiment by Murray and Berkun (1955) clearly demonstrated this philosophy. Essentially, Murray and Berkun created a situation analogous to psychotherapy, only they used rats as patients. First, they created an approach-avoidance conflict in the rats by feeding the animals in a goal box and then shocking the animals in the same goal box. Thus the animals had a strong approach tendency to the goal box because they had been fed there and a strong avoidance tendency because they had been shocked in the same goal box.

Training took place in the apparatus shown in Figure 10–6. Some of the animals received their approach-avoidance training in the white runway, and others received their training in the black runway. As can be seen in Figure 10–6, there are escape doors all along the three runways. One runway was white, one was medium gray, and one was black. After the initial approach-avoidance training, no further shocks were given.

The purpose of the experiment was to test how conflict, generalization, displacement, and extinction operate in a situation roughly analogous to psychotherapy. Based on conflict theory, one would predict that the animal experiencing an approach-avoidance conflict would approach the goal until it reached the point at which the avoidance gradient became stronger than the approach gradient (see Figure 10–1). At that point the animal should displace to a similar but less threatening object if one were available. In this case, one would expect the animal to

Figure 10–6
The apparatus used by Murray and Berkun to train their rats.

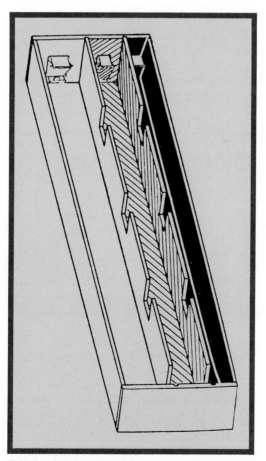

(From Murray & Berkun 1955, p. 50.)

leave the runway in which it had been shocked and enter the gray runway. Because the gray runway is not the same color runway in which the animal was shocked, however, one would expect the animal to go farther toward the goal box in the gray runway than in the runway in which it was shocked. Even in the gray runway, however, the animal should eventually experience enough fear to cause it to displace to the black runway (if it were trained on the white runway). Because the black runway is so dissimilar to the one in which the animal was originally shocked, it probably will go all the way to the goal box. Because the black runway has some similarities to the white runway, however, and because the animal was not shocked when it made a goal response in the black runway, one might expect some of the fear of the white runway to be extinguished. The situation is not unlike the one described in the last section in which some of the patient's fear of his mother was reduced when he talked about events related to his mother without being punished for doing so.

The behavior of one rat across five trials is shown in Figure 10–7. Notice that because of the animal's nonshocked goal responses in runway 3, it was eventually able to make a goal response in the runway in which it was originally shocked. Murray and Berkun concluded: *"Goal responding in displaced situations will have a therapeutic effect on the original conflict.* This is shown simply by the fact that 10 of the 10 animals who made goal responses in the gray or farthest alleys eventually made goal responses in the alley of original training" (1955, 53).

Murray and Berkun then related their findings to human psychotherapy and gave an example of what they had found using rats in a verbatim account of a therapeutic process. Their experiment bolstered Dollard and Miller's contention

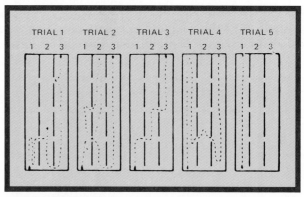

(From Murray & Berkun 1955, p. 51.)

Figure 10–7
A single rat's record of trial-by-trial behavior. The behavior of a rat in the Murray and Berkun experiment showing the "therapeutic effect" of displaced responses. Original training took place in alley 1; alley 2 and 3 are the alleys of diminishing similarity. The goals are at the top of the diagram. Each trial was begun by placing the rat at the starting point, shown here by the open circle. The rat was removed when it made a response at a goal, shown by the solid circle.

that most effective psychotherapy uses generalization, displacement, and extinction.

Four Critical Training Situations of Childhood

As we have seen throughout this chapter, Dollard and Miller agreed with Freud that most neuroses have their origin in early childhood. This is an especially vulnerable time because children have no verbal labels for their feelings and experiences and are not aware of time; for example, they do not know that "in a little while" their hunger, thirst, or pain will be reduced. Their lives vacillate from extreme discomfort to bliss and back again. Also, infants, because of their helplessness, are completely at the mercy of their parents for the satisfaction of their needs, and how the parents go about satisfying their infants' needs will make the difference between a normal healthy adult and a neurotic. Dollard and Miller (1950, 132–156) describe four critical training situations that they feel have a profound influence on adult personality.

1. Feeding Situation The conditions under which the hunger drive is satisfied will be learned and generalized into personality attributes. If, for example, children are fed when active, they may become active people; if they are fed while quiet and passive, they may become passive or apathetic individuals. If their hunger drives are satisfied in an unpredictable manner, they may grow up believing the world is an unpredictable place. If children are left alone for long periods when they are hungry, they may develop a fear of being alone. If the mother is harsh and punitive during the feeding situation, the child may grow up disliking other people and avoid them at all costs. If, however, the mother is kind, warm, and positive during the feeding situation, the child may grow up with a positive attitude toward other people and seek them out as friends. All of this is very similar to what Freud, Horney, and Erikson said about early childhood experiences and their influence on subsequent personality development.

2. Cleanliness Training Dollard and Miller, like Freud, believe the events surrounding toilet training to be extremely important to personality development. If the parents respond negatively to children's inability to control their bladder or bowels, the children may not be able to distinguish between parental disapproval of what they have done and disapproval of themselves.

> The child may not be able to discriminate between parental loathing for its excreta and loathing for the whole child himself. If the child learns to adopt these reactions, feelings of unworthiness, insignificance, and hopeless sinfulness will be created—feelings which sometimes so mysteriously reappear in the psychotic manifestations of guilt. (Dollard & Miller 1950, 139–40)

Although it is necessary to toilet-train a child, how it is done may have a profound influence on the child's emerging personality.

3. Early Sex Training The first sex training a child normally receives in our culture is related to the child's early efforts to masturbate. Typically, such behavior elicits physical punishment or such terms as "nasty" and "dirty." So it is with most sexually oriented activities in which the child engages. There are probably more taboos in our culture related to sexual matters than there are for any other kind of activity, and these taboos are all part of our child-rearing practices. No wonder sexual conflict is such a common theme in the analyst's office. The sex drive is innate, but the fear of sexual thoughts and activities is learned in childhood.

4. Anger-Anxiety Conflicts   Frustration is inevitable in childhood (and at any other age), and as we learned earlier, the most common reaction to frustration is aggression. However, aggressive behavior on the part of the children in our culture is usually met with parental disapproval or punishment. Children are placed in still another approach-avoidance conflict; that is, they want to be aggressive but inhibit this impulse because of the fear of punishment. This may result in being too passive to compete successfully in modern society.

> After this learning has occurred, the first cues produced by angry emotions may set off anxiety responses which "outcompete" the angry emotional responses themselves. The person can thus be made helpless to use his anger even in those situations where culture does permit it. He is viewed as abnormally meek or long-suffering. Robbing a person of his anger completely may be a dangerous thing since some capacity for anger seems to be needed in the affirmative personality. (Dollard & Miller 1950, 149)

The importance of child rearing to personality development has been a common theme throughout this book, and Dollard and Miller's theory is no exception. According to them, how needs surrounding hunger, elimination, sex, and anger are treated by parents will make the difference between a normal, mentally healthy, creative adult on the one hand or a miserable neurotic on the other. Dollard and Miller have described the kinds of childhood experiences that they believe lead to adult neuroses, and their message is: *Change these childhood conditions, and neuroses can be eliminated.*

> As a learning theorist sees it, the existence of neuroses is an automatic criticism of our culture of child rearing. Misery-producing, neurotic habits which the therapist must painfully unteach have been as painfully taught in the confused situation of childhood. A system of child training built on the laws of learning might have the same powerful effect on the neurotic misery of our time as Pasteur's work had on infectious diseases. (1950, 8)

Evaluation

Empirical Research

Dollard and Miller's theory is firmly grounded in empirical research. Almost without exception, when a concept is used in their theory, several experiments are cited that empirically verify that concept. Dollard and Miller's theory is, to a large extent, an extension of Hullian learning theory, which itself is one of the most scientifically rigorous theories in psychology's history. Throughout this chapter we have reviewed experiments that Dollard, Miller, or their colleagues have run to verify or test their theoretical concepts. For example, research was cited showing how fear is acquired; how fear and other tendencies generalize; how various conflicts impact behavior; how fear and other tendencies are displaced; how frustration and aggression are related; how physical symptoms partially reduce neurotic conflict; and how learning principles operate in the therapeutic process.

Dollard and Miller's theory earns marks as high as the theories of Cattell and Skinner in its effort to validate empirically the terms, principles, and concepts that it contains.

Criticisms

Unsuccessful Marriage between Hullian Learning Theory and Psychoanalysis. Prominent members of both camps have complained that Dollard and Miller's attempt to synthesize the Hullian learning theory and psychoanalysis did not work. Learning theorists such as Bandura (whose theory we will review in the next chapter) and Skinner have complained that no need exists to use nebulous, subjective psychoanalytic terminology in explaining personality. Bandura and Skinner (and others) claim that learning principles alone can do the job. As we saw in the last chapter, Skinner goes so far as to say that personality can be understood without reference to mental events *of any kind.*

Skinner believes that even Dollard and Miller's use of such "hypothetical fictions" as cues, drives, conflicts, and cue-producing responses is not only unnecessary but may, in fact, interfere with a true understanding of personality. In the next chapter we shall see that Bandura's analysis *does* allow, even emphasizes, mental events, but those events are not the unconscious variety stressed by the psychoanalysts.

Many psychoanalysts were equally unimpressed by the efforts of Dollard and Miller. Their argument was that the dynamics of the human mind are far more complicated than Dollard and Miller's analysis suggests. To them phenomena such as displacement, repression, conflict, and neuroses are much too complex to be understood in terms of a few principles of learning. Furthermore, they say, it is foolish to suggest that the processes occurring during psychotherapy (especially psychoanalysis) could be demonstrated by a rat running a maze.

Too Much Generalization From Nonhuman Animals to Humans. Like Skinner, Dollard and Miller have been criticized for assuming that the principles observed in nonhuman animals also apply to humans. What good, ask the critics, are all of the carefully controlled laboratory experiments on nonhuman animals if a tenuous assumption concerning the generalizability of the findings must be made? Insofar as humans are different from rats and pigeons, the findings from such research is irrelevant. In fairness to Dollard and Miller, however, it must be noted that they stressed that any such generalizations should be carefully investigated; they did do a considerable amount of research on humans as well as nonhuman animals.

Overly Simplistic Approach. Some critics say that a theory such as Dollard and Miller's that stresses only environmental stimuli, a few mental events, and overt responses misses the richness and complexity of human personality. Love, despair, the importance of the future, meaning of life, and the experience of the self, are just a few of the human experiences that are not addressed by such a theory. In addition to suggest that bad mental or emotional habits can be corrected by a therapist in much the same way that a good coach corrects bad tennis habits is just too simplistic, say the critics.

Contributions

Synthesis of Hullian Learning Theory and Psychoanalysis.   As so often happens, what some find to be a weakness in a theory, others see as a strength. For many, Dollard and Miller's synthesis of Hullian learning and psychoanalysis was a milestone in the history of psychology. The synthesis achieved two goals: It broadened the application of an otherwise limited theory of learning to a wide array of human phenomena; and it made many psychoanalytic concepts much more testable than they had been. Until Dollard and Miller's efforts the gulf between the research laboratory and the clinical consulting room was enormous. Their work provided a bridge across that gulf, and ideas have been flowing back and forth ever since. In fact, Dollard and Miller were the first theorists to explore the role of learning in personality development specifically, a role now accepted by most theorists as substantial.

Scientifically Respectable Approach to the Study of Personality.   In an area of personality in which the early theories were difficult to test empirically, a scientifically rigorous theory is welcomed. Most of the terms and concepts in Dollard and Miller's theory are defined precisely enough to allow them to be empirically verified. In terms of testability, Dollard and Miller's theory ranks high along with the theories of Cattell and Skinner.

Clear Description of Therapeutic Process.   By describing traditional psychotherapeutic procedures in terms of learning principles, Dollard and Miller have been able to account for much successful therapy and to make sound recommendations for the improvement of the therapeutic process. It is now widely accepted that anxiety is an acquired drive, and once acquired it causes a person to avoid thoughts or events that elicit it. It is, according to Dollard and Miller, this avoidance that causes anxiety-provoking thoughts to persist. Effective therapy creates a situation in which such thoughts can be expressed without experiencing the unpleasant consequences originally associated with them. As this change occurs, extinction gradually takes place, and the thoughts that were once too anxiety provoking to entertain can now be dealt with rationally. All of these elements of the therapeutic process were discussed by Freud but restating them using the terminology of learning theory makes them clearer and more testable. What has become known as behavior therapy has been given a tremendous boost by the work of Dollard and Miller.

Dollard and Miller have provided information that is certainly helpful in treating neuroses and that information may also someday be responsible for a reduction in their frequency of occurrence. If this is true, one can forgive them for favoring animal research and for having a deterministic model of human nature. Every theory must be judged by its ultimate effectiveness, not by origins or by its assumptions.

Summary

Dollard and Miller's goal was to combine learning theory, mainly Hullian, with Freud's theory. Hull's theory of learning equated reinforcement with drive reduction and defined a habit as a strong association of a stimulus (cue) and a response. Hull, unlike Skinner, was willing to speculate on the nature of reinforcement and of the nature of mediational processes such as thinking and reasoning. Skinner was content to make a functional analysis between environmental events and behavior. Central to Dollard and Miller's theory are the concepts of drive, cue, response, and reinforcement. Drive impels an organism to action, cue directs its behavior, response is what the organism does either overtly or internally, and reinforcement occurs when the motivational drive is either reduced or terminated. In other words, in order to learn, the organism must want something, notice something, do something, and get something.

Every cue elicits several responses arranged in accordance with their probability of occurrence. This set of responses is called the habit family hierarchy. Shortly after birth, before learning has occurred, this is called the innate hierarchy of responses. The hierarchy that exists before new learning occurs is called the initial hierarchy of responses. The hierarchy that exists after learning has occurred is called the resultant hierarchy of responses. The most likely response to any situation is called the dominant response. The learning dilemma refers to the fact that old learned responses or innate responses must fail to solve a problem before learning can take place. Thus, all learning depends on failure.

Dollard and Miller demonstrated that events associated with the experience of pain themselves will become feared, and an organism will learn responses that will allow it to escape from those fear-producing cues. Stimulus generalization refers to the fact that a learned response will be elicited not only by the cue in the actual learning, but by a variety of similar stimuli as well. The more similar a cue is to the one actually used in training, the greater the probability is that it will elicit the same response. Primary generalization is determined by the physical properties of stimuli. Secondary generalization is caused by using the same verbal label to describe things. For example, one responds to all things labeled "dangerous" in a similar fashion. Discrimination is the opposite of generalization.

Dollard and Miller studied four kinds of conflict: approach-approach conflicts, in which the organism is attracted to two things at the same time; avoidance-avoidance conflicts, in which the organism is repelled by two things at the same time; approach-avoidance conflicts, in which the organism is attracted and repelled by the same object; and double approach-avoidance conflicts, in which the organism is both attracted and repelled by two objects at the same time. Dollard and Miller did most of their research on approach-avoidance conflict and found that at great distances from the goal the approach tendency is strongest, but as one approaches the goal, the avoidance tendency becomes stronger. This causes vacillation at the point that the two tendencies have about equal strength.

If the goal object of choice is not available, the organism will choose a substitute goal object, which is called displacement. If one cannot aggress toward the object, event, or person that caused frustration, one will aggress toward a substitute object; this is called displaced aggression. If one is fearful of aggressing toward an object, event, or person causing frustration, displacement will be toward dissimilar objects, events, or people. If little fear exists, displacement will be to more similar things.

The frustration-aggression hypothesis originally stated that aggression followed from frustration and that frustration always resulted in aggression. This was later modified, however, to state that aggression was just one result of frustration, instead of the only one.

Language is important to Dollard and Miller's theory. Thinking is essentially talking to oneself. Thinking allows for cognitive trial and error to replace behavioral trial and error. Dollard and Miller call images, perceptions, and words "cue-producing responses" because they determine what the next response in a series will be. Thinking consists of a series of cue-producing responses. Two important kinds of thinking are reasoning, which is directed at solving a current problem, and planning, which is directed at solving a future problem.

The unconscious mind, according to Dollard and Miller, consists of experiences that were never verbalized and experiences that have been repressed. Repression is considered "a response of not thinking," which is reinforced because it prevents an anxiety-provoking thought from becoming conscious. Suppression is the act of driving an anxiety-provoking thought out of consciousness. Repressed thoughts are practically immune to extinction, because they are not experienced consciously long enough for the person to realize that they are no longer followed by negative consequences.

Most neurotic conflicts are learned in childhood and therefore are not verbally labeled. Neurotics are miserable and stupid about matters related to their repressions. Neurotics often develop symptoms that stem from their repressed conflict. Symptoms such as phobias, compulsions, or physical disorders temporarily relieve neurotics' distress because they act as a barrier between them and anxiety-provoking situations. For example, by becoming obese, a person can decrease the likelihood of confronting sexual situations. Thus, for the person with a repressed sexual conflict, being obese is reinforcing. The desire for sex does not go away, however, so the conflict continues to manifest itself in strange ways. Both repressions and neurotic symptoms are learned for the same reason; they temporarily reduce or prevent anxiety.

Psychotherapy is a situation in which patients are encouraged to label their conflicts verbally and to confront them gradually. The therapist is encouraging and nonthreatening, so that if and when repressed material emerges, it will extinguish. Therapy usually starts by discussing objects, people, or events that are only indirectly related to those causing strong anxiety. As distant, but related, events are discussed, a certain amount of anxiety is extinguished, and gradually the person can talk directly about events that previously were too anxiety provoking. Psychotherapy, as Dollard and Miller see it, treats conflict and repression using the processes of generalization, displacement, and extinction.

Dollard and Miller believe that neurotic conflicts are learned in childhood. The difference between a mentally healthy normal adult and a neurotic adult is thought to be fairly well determined by how parents handle the four critical training periods of childhood; namely, the feeding situation, cleanliness training, sex training, and anger-anxiety training.

Dollard and Miller's theory is firmly grounded in empirical research but has been criticized for failing to synthesize Hullian learning theory and psychoanalysis successfully; generalizing too freely from nonhuman animals to humans; and being too simplistic in its account of personality and of the therapeutic process. Their theory has been praised for combining Hullian learning theory and psychoanalytic theory, thereby making both more useful; clarifying the processing that is actually involved in effective psychotherapy; and being scientifically rigorous.

EXPERIENTIAL EXERCISES

1. Give at least one example of an approach-approach, avoidance-avoidance, and approach-avoidance conflict that you have experienced and state how you resolved each conflict. In the case of the approach-avoidance conflict, did your experiences conform to Miller's description? That is, did you experience a great deal of vacillation and indecision as the goal was approached?

2. Give an example of displaced aggression in your life. That is, describe a situation in which you could not aggress directly toward a source of frustration so you aggressed, in some way, toward a person or a thing other than the one that actually frustrated you. Explain, in terms of Dollard and Miller's theory, why you chose the object or person that you did to aggress toward.

3. Privately ponder an idea or topic that you could not openly discuss without experiencing considerable anxiety. Review the way that Dollard and Miller suggest such anxiety-provoking thoughts should be approached and resolved. Do you believe that by following their procedure of systematic extinction your anxiety-provoking thought would become increasingly more tolerable? Why or why not?

4. Ask someone who would know (e.g., your mother) how the four critical training situations of feeding, cleanliness, sex and anger-anxiety were handled in your life. Do notable relationships exist between these early training experiences and your current personality characteristics? If they do, describe them. If they do not exist, try to explain why.

DISCUSSION QUESTIONS

1. Dollard and Miller's theory is often called a blending of Hullian learning theory and Freudian psychoanalytic theory. Explain why their theory is identified this way. Give several examples of such a blend.

2. Compare and contrast Dollard and Miller's theory of personality with Skinner's.

3. Discuss the concepts of drive, cue, response, and reinforcement. Give both the formal definition and a concrete example of each.

4. Discuss the concept of habit family hierarchy. Include in your answer definitions of innate, initial, and resultant hierarchies.

5. What did Dollard and Miller mean by the term *learning dilemma*? Discuss the implications of this concept for education and child rearing.

6. Outline the procedures that Miller used to demonstrate that fear was an acquired drive.

7. Discuss the topic of stimulus generalization. Include in your answer a discussion of both primary and secondary generalization.

8. Compare discrimination to generalization, and explain why both processes are important when adjusting to the world.

9. Give the formal definitions and then examples of each of the following kinds of conflict: approach-approach, avoidance-avoidance, approach-avoidance, and double approach-avoidance.

10. List the characteristics of an approach-avoidance conflict.

11. What effect do you think the ingestion of alcohol would have on an approach-avoidance conflict? For example, do you think it would raise or lower the avoidance gradient? Explain why you think the way you do.

12. Define displacement and then discuss it in relation to generalization. Describe several variables influencing displacement.

13. Outline the procedures Miller followed to demonstrate displaced aggression.

14. What is the frustration-aggression hypothesis? How was it first stated by Dollard and Miller and how was it later revised?

15. Discuss the status of language in Dollard and Miller's theory. Include in your answer the terms cue-producing responses, reasoning, and planning.

16. Of what, according to Dollard and Miller, does the unconscious mind consist? Give examples.

17. Describe what Dollard and Miller meant when they referred to repression as the conditioned avoidance response of not thinking.

18. Differentiate between suppression and repression.

19. Explain how, according to Dollard and Miller, neuroses typically develop.

20. Explain what Dollard and Miller mean when they say neurotic symptoms have drive-reducing properties.

21. Give a specific example of how early childhood experiences can produce neurotic conflict.

22. Explain what is meant when the kind of psychotherapy that is prescribed by Dollard and Miller is said to involve conflict, generalization, displacement, and extinction. Describe a theoretical therapeutic situation in which each of these concepts is involved.

23. Summarize the Murray and Berkun experiment.

24. Summarize the four critical training periods of childhood as described by Dollard and Miller. Explain why what a child experiences during each of these periods is so important.

25. Compare what Dollard and Miller said about the importance of early childhood experiences with what Horney and Erikson said. On which points do the three theories agree and on which do they differ?

SUGGESTIONS FOR FURTHER READING

DOLLARD, J., & MILLER, N. E. (1950). *Personality and Psychotherapy: An Analysis in Terms of Learning, Thinking, and Culture*. New York: McGraw-Hill.

Dollard and Miller's seminal attempt to synthesize Hullian learning theory and Freudian psychoanalysis. Still highly informative and well worth reading.

EVANS, R. I. (1976). *The Making of Psychology: Discussions with Creative Contributors*. New York: Alfred A. Knopf.

Contains an interesting interview of Neal Miller as well as several other theorists covered in this text (Skinner, Allport, Rogers, Bandura, Jung, and Erikson).

MILLER, N. E. (1959). Liberalization of basic S-R concepts: Extensions to conflict behavior, motivation and social learning. In S. Koch (Ed.), *Psychology: A Study of a Science* (Vol. 2) (pp. 196–292). New York: McGraw-Hill.

An updating and polishing of many of the terms and concepts that Miller employed in his earlier writings. Includes a detailed analysis of conflict.

MILLER, N. E., & DOLLARD, J. (1941). *Social Learning and Imitation*. New Haven, CT: Yale University Press.

In this book Miller and Dollard make an early effort to apply Hullian learning theory to the explanation of human social behavior. Much of the discussion concentrates on the variables influencing relatively simple, imitative learning, but the authors also extend their analysis to such phenomena as crowd behavior and lynching.

WACHTEL, P. L. (1977). *Psychoanalysis and Behavior Therapy: Toward An Integration*. New York: Basic Books.

A more recent attempt to do what Dollard and Miller attempted to do in 1950. That is, to synthesize psychoanalytic theory and learning theory.

GLOSSARY

Acquired drive. A drive that is learned, not innate. Fear is an example of an acquired drive.

Anger-anxiety conflicts. One of the four training situations in childhood that, if not handled properly, could result in neurotic conflict.

Approach-approach conflict. The situation that exists when a person must choose between two equally attractive goals.

Approach-avoidance conflict. The situation that exists when a person is both attracted to and repelled by the same goal.

Avoidance-avoidance conflict. The situation that exists when a person must choose between two equally aversive goals.

Cleanliness training. One of the four critical training situations in childhood that, if not handled properly, could lead to neurotic conflict.

Conditioned fear reaction. Learning to fear something that was not previously feared.

Conflict. The situation in which two or more incompatible response tendencies exist simultaneously.

Cue. A stimulus that indicates the appropriate direction that an activity should take.

Cue-producing responses. Images, perceptions, and words, the main functions of which are to determine subsequent behavior. Thinking is an example of a cue-producing response.

Discrimination. The opposite of generalization. That is, stimuli similar to the stimulus in the learning process do *not* elicit a learned response.

Displaced aggression. Aggressing toward a substitute person or object when the actual object of aggression is either not available or is feared.

Displacement. The act of substituting one goal for another when the primary goal is not available.

Dominant response. That response in a habit family hierarchy that has the greatest probability of occurrence.

Double approach-avoidance conflict. The situation that exists when a person has both positive and negative feelings about two goals.

Drive. Any strong stimulus that impels an organism to action and whose elimination or reduction is reinforcing.

Drive reduction. Constitutes reinforcement in Hull's theory of learning.

Early sex training. One of the four critical training situations in childhood that if not handled properly, could result in neurotic conflict.

Feeding situation. One of the four critical training situations in childhood that, if not handled properly, could result in neurotic conflict.

First signal system. The term used by Pavlov to describe the conditioned responses that we develop to physical objects.

Frustration-aggression hypothesis. Originally the contention that frustration always leads to aggression and aggression results only from frustration. Later modified to state that aggression is only one of several possible reactions to frustration.

Functional analysis. Skinner's approach to research, which notes the relationship between certain environmental events and behavior.

Habit. An association between a stimulus and a response.

Habit family hierarchy. The group of responses elicited by a single stimulus that are arranged in accordance with their probability of occurrence.

Hull's theory of learning. The theory of learning that Dollard and Miller synthesized with Freud's theory. Hull's theory equates reinforcement with drive reduction. In other words, for learning to take place, the organism must engage in an activity that leads to the elimination or reduction of a need.

Initial hierarchy of responses. The hierarchy of responses elicited by a cue before new learning.

Innate hierarchy of responses. A habit family hierarchy that is genetically determined.

Learning. According to Dollard and Miller, the rearrangement of response probabilities that results when certain responses are reinforced and others are not.

Learning dilemma. The contention that for learning to occur, both innate responses and previously learned responses must be ineffective in solving a problem. Therefore, learning is said to depend on failure.

Neurosis. A condition that causes a person to function at less than maximal efficiency, which typically results from unconscious conflict that originated in early childhood.

Planning. The use of cue-producing responses (thinking) in attempting to solve some future problem.

Primary generalization. Generalization that is determined by the physical properties of stimuli.

Psychotherapy. For Dollard and Miller, a situation in which repressed conflicts can be unlearned; that is, extinguished.

Reasoning. The attempted solution of an immediate problem through the use of cue-producing responses (thinking) rather than of overt trial and error.

Reinforcement. In Hull's theory of learning, drive reduction constitutes reinforcement.

Reinforcement theory. Any theory of learning that states that reinforcement must occur before learning can take place.

Reinforcer. A stimulus capable of reducing a drive.

Repression. The learned response of "not thinking" an anxiety-provoking thought. The reinforcement for this response comes from the avoidance of anxiety.

Response. Any overt or internal action elicited by a stimulus.

Resultant hierarchy of responses. The hierarchy of responses elicited by a cue after learning has taken place.

Second signal system. The term used by Pavlov to describe the conditioned responses we develop to words and other symbols.

Secondary generalization. Generalization that is based on verbal labels (words), not on the physical similarity among stimuli.

Stimulus generalization. The tendency for stimuli other

than the stimulus actually in the learning process to elicit a learned response. The more similar these stimuli are to the one actually in the learning process, the greater the probability is that they will elicit a learned response.

Suppression. Actively putting an anxiety-provoking thought "out of one's mind." Suppression is reinforced by the escape from anxiety.

Symptom formation. The neurotic's tendency to develop such things as phobias, compulsions, or physical disorders because they reduce anxiety temporarily.

11

Albert Bandura
Walter Mischel

■ **CHAPTER OUTLINE**

Although Bandura and Mischel have not collaborated on major books, as did Dollard and Miller, their positions are so similar that we can consider them together. The theory of Bandura and Mischel has been referred to as **social learning theory.** As we shall see, it differs in several important ways from the theories of Skinner and Dollard and Miller. We will begin this chapter with Bandura's description of social learning theory, which will provide an overview of several points we shall elaborate on in this chapter.

> Social learning theory emphasizes the prominent roles played by vicarious, symbolic, and self-regulatory processes in psychological functioning. . . . The extraordinary capacity of humans to use symbols enables them to represent events, to analyze their conscious experience, to communicate with others at any distance in time and space, to plan, to create, to imagine, and to engage in foresightful action. . . . [Another] distinctive feature of social learning theory is the central role it assigns to self-regulatory processes. People are not simple reactors to external influences. They select, organize, and transform the stimuli that impinge upon them. . . . Social learning theory approaches the explanation of human behavior in terms of a continuous reciprocal interaction between cognitive, behavioral, and environmental determinants. Within the process of reciprocal determinism lies the opportunity for people to influence their destiny as well as the limits of self-direction. This conception of human functioning then neither casts people into the role of powerless objects controlled by environmental forces nor free agents who can become whatever they choose. Both people and their environment are reciprocal determinants of each other. (1977, vii)

We see that the emphasis of social learning theory is clearly cognitive, and this differentiates it from Skinner's position. Social learning theory also emphasizes the self-regulation of behavior and thus de-emphasizes the importance of external reinforcers. The stressing of intrinsic (self-) reinforcement as opposed to extrinsic (environmental) reinforcement differentiates social learning theory from both the Skinnerian position and the position of Dollard and Miller. Perhaps the most important difference between social learning theory and the positions of Skinner and Dollard and Miller concerns the importance of reinforcement for learning. For Skinner and for Dollard and Miller, external reinforcement is necessary for learning to occur. For Bandura and Mischel, however, learning occurs independently of reinforcement. According to them, we learn what we observe. As we shall see later in this chapter, observational learning is at the heart of social learning theory.

Biographical Sketches

Albert Bandura

Albert Bandura was born on 4 December, 1925 in Mundare, a small town in the province of Alberta, Canada. His parents were wheat farmers of Polish heritage. The

Albert Bandura

high school that he attended had only twenty students and two teachers. He obtained his B.A. from the University of British Columbia in 1949. He then went to the University of Iowa, where he obtained his M.A. in 1951 and his Ph.D. in 1952. After a year's clinical internship at the Wichita, Kansas Guidance Center, he moved to Stanford University, where he has been ever since.

After arriving at Stanford, Bandura began working on the familial causes of aggression, with his first graduate student, Richard Walters. It was during this work that Bandura became aware of the importance of modeling and observational learning for personality development. A section on observational learning appears later in this chapter. Bandura's first book (coauthored with Richard Walters) was *Adolescent Aggression* (1959). His second book (also written with Richard Walters) was *Social Learning and Personality Development* (1963). Subsequent books were *Principles of Behavior Modification* (1969), *Aggression: A Social-Learning Analysis* (1973), *Social Learning Theory* (1977) and *Social Foundations of Thought and Action: A Social Cognitive Theory* (1986). In addition to his books, Bandura has written many influential journal articles.

Included among Bandura's many honors are a Guggenheim fellowship (1972); a Distinguished Scientist Award from Division 12 of the American Psychological Association (1972); a Distinguished Scientific Achievement Award from the California Psychological Association (1973); presidency of the American Psychological Association (1974); the James McKeen Cattell Award (1977); and the Distinguished Scientific Contribution Award from the American Psychological Association for "masterful modeling as researcher, teacher, and theoretician" (1980).

Walter Mischel

Walter Mischel

Walter Mischel was born in 1930 in Vienna, within walking distance of Freud's house. When he was nine years old, he and his family were forced by Nazism to leave Europe. They relocated in New York City, where Mischel eventually attended City College and became a social worker. Mischel believed that Freud's theory was the best explanation of human behavior, but after he attempted to apply it in his work with juvenile delinquents, he changed his mind.

Mischel did his graduate work at Ohio State University, where he came under the influence of George Kelly and Julian Rotter. Rotter's work emphasized the importance of expectancies in human behavior, and Kelly stressed the importance of the formulation of mental concepts (personal constructs) in dealing with the world. Both Rotter and Kelly emphasized cognitive events in dealing with current situations and de-emphasized the importance of traits and early developmental experience. The influence of both men is seen in Mischel's work. George Kelly's theory will be covered in the next chapter.

After finishing graduate school, Mischel held several faculty posts, including one at Harvard, before joining Bandura at Stanford University in 1962. In 1983, he returned to New York City, where he joined the faculty at Columbia University. There Mischel continues to pursue his long-standing interests in delay of gratification and self-control.

In 1978 Mischel received a Distinguished Scientist award from the clinical division of the American Psychological Association. His books include *Personality and Assessment* (1968) and *Introduction to Personality*, first published in 1971 and revised in 1976, 1981, and 1986.

Consistency of Human Behavior

Through the years, most, if not all, personality theorists have assumed that a person's behavior is fairly consistent over time and across similar situations. That is, it was assumed that how people act at one time in their lives will be more or less how they act at other times, and that they will tend to respond to similar situations in similar ways. For example, if a person was outgoing in one social situation, it was assumed that he or she would be outgoing in other situations and will continue to respond in that characteristic way throughout most of his or her life. It was also assumed that scores on various personality tests and questionnaires would correlate significantly with actual behavior. That is, if a person scored high on a scale intended to measure introversion, he or she would tend to be introverted in social situations. The question was never whether or not behavior was consistent; rather, theorists wanted to know how best to account for consistent behavior. Psychoanalytic theory attempted to account for it by postulating repressed experiences, complexes, fixations, or internalized values. Within psychoanalytic theory, however, the conclusion of consistency can sometimes only be reached by a trained psychoanalyst, because it is assumed that sometimes extreme aggression really means passivity, love sometimes really means hate, and repulsion sometimes really means attraction, to give but a few examples. Trait theory postulated enduring traits to explain why, for example, a neat person tended to be neat in a wide variety of situations. Learning theory emphasized the role of reinforcement. That is, behavior that was reinforced tended to persist and to transfer to situations similar to the one in which the reinforcement had occurred.

Traditionally, personality theory has attempted to account for individual differences among people, but it was always assumed that although people differ from one another, the behavior of any given individual tended to be consistent across similar situations and over time. It was this assumption of consistency that Mischel challenged in his book *Personality and Assessment* (1968). In this volume, Mischel reviewed many studies designed to measure consistency of behavior across situations or to measure the relationship between performance on personality questionnaires and actual behavior. He found the typical correlation to be about 0.30. Mischel called this weak correlation the **personality coefficient,** and he argued that the weakness of the coefficient was not due to problems in measuring such characteristics as traits or behavior but, rather, to the fact that human behavior is simply not very consistent.

Thus, according to Mischel, although traits and various other inner states have been used to describe behavior for a long time, they are of limited use in actually predicting behavior. The use of traits to describe and explain behavior, says Mischel, often indicates what the theorist thinks *should be* the case rather than what actually is the case.

Mischel's major criticism of traditional personality theories is that they emphasize **person variables** and de-emphasize **situation variables.** Person variables are those aspects of a person, like traits, habits, and repressed experiences, that are assumed to cause the person to act consistently in a variety of similar situations. According to those theories emphasizing person variables, behavior is consistent because variables inside the person are enduring and thus continue to generate the same behavior patterns. Situation variables consist of the environmental circumstances the person finds himself or herself in.

Although Mischel believes that situation variables have been de-emphasized by most personality theories, he believes they have been overemphasized by certain behavioristic theories—for instance, Skinner's. According to Mischel, Skinner's attempt to explain behavior entirely in terms of environmental conditions overlooks the significant contributions made by the person to his or her own behavior. What is needed, says Mischel, is a theory that considers the contributions of both the person *and* the situation.

The position taken by the social learning theorist is called **reciprocal determinism,** which means person variables, situation variables, and behavior all continuously interact with one another. Situation variables provide the setting in which a person behaves, person variables determine how a situation is analyzed and which behaviors are chosen, and behavior both provides information concerning the person's analysis of the situation and modifies the environment. Bandura (1986, p. 24) diagrams reciprocal determinism as follows, where P is the person, E is the environment and B is the person's behavior:

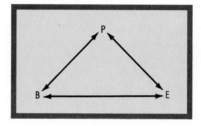

Social learning theory, then, does not exclude person variables. In fact, they are considered extremely important. The person variables postulated, however, are not the traditional kind. Rather, they are cognitive and are related to information-processing strategies. Furthermore, they are important only insofar as they manifest themselves in the present. Mischel (1986) says:

> Social behavior theory searches for causes in the current conditions that demonstrably control the person's present behaviors. This emphasis contrasts with traditional dynamic theories, which infer the person's motives, conflicts, and dispositions from behavioral "signs" and which construe behaviors as being in the service of underlying motives and their dynamic transformations. . . .
>
> The focus of social behavior theory is on what people are doing in the "here and now" rather than on reconstructions of their psychic history. There is a refusal to hypothesize drives, forces, motives, and other broad dispositions as explanations, and an emphasis on the individual's potential for change. (313–14)

It is to a discussion of the person variables that social learning theory assumes operate in the "here and now" that we turn next.

Cognitive Social Learning Person Variables

Social learning theory views the interaction between the person and the environment as highly complex and individualistic. Each individual brings to each situation the remnants of previous experience, which are used in dealing with the present situation. The outcome of the negotiations with the present situations will, in turn, influence how similar situations are dealt with in the future. How a given individual will interact with a situation is determined by what Mischel calls **cognitive social learning person variables** (1986, p. 305). It is these variables that determine which of the myriad stimuli confronted by a person are perceived, selected, interpreted, and used. Unlike the traditional person variables such as traits, habits, and repressed experiences, the person variables in social learning theory are active cognitive processes that operate in the present. These variables provide for a dynamic, reciprocal relationship between the person and the environment. We see again that the environment influences the person, and the person influences the environment.

Mischel (1986, 305–13) describes five social learning person variables.

1. Competencies   Through observational learning, which will be discussed later, the person acquires information about the physical and social worlds and his or her relationship to them. The person develops skills, concepts, and problem-solving strategies that are actively used in dealing with the environment. Mischel stresses the fact that these **competencies** are not static memories that are mechanically activated by environmental stimuli. Rather, they are active processes that can be used by the person to generate a wide variety of creative constructions or responses to any given situation. Competencies, then, are seen as tools available to the individual in doing commerce with the environment. Like any tools, what can be done with them is limited only to the imagination of those using them. Competencies refer to what a person knows and what he or she is capable of doing.

2. Encoding strategies and personal constructs   People not only select different aspects of the environment to attend to, but they also assign different meanings to the stimuli selected. Mischel (1986) says:

> People differ greatly in how they encode (represent, symbolize) and group information from stimulus inputs. The same "hot weather" that upsets one person may be a joy for another who views it as a chance to go to the beach. A stimulus perceived as "dangerous" or "threatening" by one person may be seen as "challenging" or "thrilling" by the one next to her. (309)

Here we see the influence of George Kelly (see chapter 13) on Mischel. Kelly suggested that any given event can be construed (interpreted) in any number of ways and that people are free to choose the constructs (concepts, symbols, or words) with which they interpret their experiences. This means that in the same physical situation, people will encode it, construe it, and respond to it differently. Furthermore, because person variables are dynamic, no reason exists to assume that even for a given person the same situation will be construed the same way twice. It is a person's **encoding strategies and personal constructs** that provide some consistency in behavior, but the fact that both can be changed by the individual at any time at least partially accounts for the fact that cross-situational behavior is not very consistent. Encoding strategies and personal constructs determine what aspects of the world are attended to and how they are interpreted.

3. Expectancies   The two person variables discussed thus far described what a person is *capable* of doing and how one categorizes experience. At some point, however, people must actually act on the environment. The most important variable for actual performance is a person's expectations. For example, in a given situation, the person hypothesizes, "If I act in this way, it will have the following result." This is called a **behavior-outcome expectancy.** In the absence of any information about a specific situation, one will tend to create **expectancies** based on past experience with similar situations. If specific information is available, however, one's expectations change accordingly. In preparation for a job interview, for example, if one hears that the job interviewer is especially impressed by assertiveness, one might expect that acting assertively would increase the probability of getting the job, and then would act on this newly formed expectancy. In fact, Mischel refers to people who cannot modify their expectations in light of changing circumstances as "maladaptive" and gives the following example:

> Adaptive performance requires the recognition and appreciation of new contingencies. To cope with the environment effectively, we must identify new contingencies as quickly as possible and reorganize behavior in the light of the new expectancies. Strongly established behavior-outcome expectancies may handicap our ability to adapt to changes in contingencies. Indeed, "defense reactions" may be seen in part as a failure to adapt to new contingencies because one is still behaving in response to old contingencies that are no longer valid. For example, if on the basis of past experiences a man overgeneralizes and becomes convinced that people will take advantage of him unless he is hostile toward everyone, his own suspicious, aggressive behavior may prevent him from ever being able to disconfirm his belief, even when people are trying to be considerate. The "maladaptive" individual is behaving in accord with expectancies that do not adequately represent the actual behavior-outcome rules in his current life situation. (1986, 310)

Mischel refers to a second kind of hypothesis we formulate in dealing with our experience as a **stimulus-outcome expectancy.** We learn that if event 1 occurs, event 2 is likely to follow. For example, if we hear a siren, we expect a speeding emergency vehicle will soon be seen; or, noting that it is six o'clock, it is expected that dinner will soon be available.

A third kind of hypothesis we use in dealing with the world is called a **self-efficacy expectancy.** It is one thing to know what behavior would be effective in a given situation and another to be able to perform that behavior. One's ability to perform the behaviors called for in a particular situation is called self-efficacy. Because what one can actually do often differs from what one thinks he or she is capable of doing, social learning theory places great stress on **perceived self-efficacy,** which is what a person thinks he or she is capable of doing in various situations. We will return to a discussion of self-efficacy later in the chapter.

In general, the person variable of "expectancies" answers the questions, "What should I expect if I act in a certain way?"; "If I see one thing, what should

I expect to see next?"; and "Am I capable of doing what I think needs to be done?"

As the emphasis on personal constructs showed the influence of George Kelly on social learning theory, the emphasis on expectancies shows the influence of Julian Rotter.

4. Subjective values   Even if a person has a strong behavior outcome expectancy and a strong self-efficacy expectancy, he or she may decide not to translate those expectancies into behavior, because what would be gained simply is not seen as worth the effort. For example, a student may know exactly what needs to be done to write an outstanding term paper, and may believe he or she has the ability to do what is necessary but may decide that getting an A on a term paper is not worth the time and effort. Another student in the same situation may value an A more, and thus expend the time and energy and engage in the behaviors necessary to obtain it. Likewise, a given student may, at one time, under certain conditions, decide an A is worth pursuing and at another time, under different circumstances, decide that it is not. One's values will to a large extent determine whether or not the other person variables will be translated into performance. The **subjective values** of a person determine what is worth having or doing.

5. Self-regulatory systems and plans   According to social learning theory, human behavior is largely self-regulated. Performance standards are established, and when actual performance meets or exceeds those standards, one feels good; when it does not, one feels bad. Behavior, then, is seen as influenced more by **intrinsic** (internal) **reinforcement** and punishment than it is by **extrinsic** (external) **reinforcement** and punishment.

Humans also set future goals and then plan the events in their lives so that they are compatible with those goals. Typically, a major future goal is approached by first reaching a sequence of lesser short-term goals. For example, the goal of obtaining a college degree is met by doing well in high school, graduating from high school, applying for admission into a college, surviving the first term in college, and so on. Thus social learning theory sees much human behavior as teleological; that is, purposive. **Self-regulatory systems and plans** make it possible to attain those goals deemed important. We will say more about self-regulated behavior later in this chapter.

Thus far we have said little about the origins of such things as competencies, encoding strategies, personal constructs, expectancies, values, and performance standards and goals. According to social learning theory, these person variables are acquired through observational learning. We turn to that topic next.

Observational Learning

At the heart of social learning theory is the notion of **observational learning.** The most important fact about observational learning is that it requires no reinforcement. According to Bandura and Mischel, humans learn what they attend to, and therefore, for them, learning is a perceptual process. Thus, social learning theory is in sharp contrast with the theories of Skinner and of Dollard and Miller, which rely heavily on the concept of reinforcement.

Although within social learning theory, reinforcement is not believed to influence learning, it is believed to be importantly related to *performance* and to perceptual processes. In other words, reinforcement is thought to influence what is attended to, and thus learned, and, more important, it is thought to determine which aspect of what has been learned is translated into behavior.

The distinction between learning and performance is nicely illustrated in a study performed by Bandura (1965). In this experiment a film was shown of a **model** aggressing toward a large BoBo doll. In social learning theory a model is anything that conveys information—for instance, a person, television, a film, a demonstration, or instructions. In this experiment, the model was an adult human. One group of children was shown the model's being reinforced for his aggressiveness. A second group of children was shown the model's being punished for his aggressiveness. For a third group of children, the model was neither reinforced nor punished. The children were then exposed to a doll similar to that in the film, and their aggressiveness toward it was measured. Results indicated that the group who saw the model being reinforced for aggressiveness was most aggressive; the group who saw the model punished for aggressiveness showed the least amount of aggressiveness; and the group who saw neutral consequences was between the other two groups in aggressiveness.

This much of Bandura's study was interesting because it was shown that children performed on the basis of what they had seen happen to someone else. That is, rather than performing on the basis of direct reinforcement and punishment, they were responding to **vicarious reinforcement** and **vicarious punishment.** To put this in terms of the person variables described earlier, it was as if the children had formulated behavior-outcome expectancies on the basis of what they had seen in the film. The children seeing the model's aggressiveness reinforced appeared to develop the hypothesis that if they acted aggressively, they, too, could expect to be reinforced. Those children seeing the model punished for aggressiveness expected similar behavior on their part would yield similar results.

The first phase of Bandura's study seemed to indicate that reinforcement was still important for learning, but that it could be vicariously experienced and need not be contingent on one's own behavior. This finding alone was in contradiction to the theories of Skinner and Dollard and Miller, which state that for reinforcement to be effective, it must be contingent on one's own behavior. In their view, seeing someone else's behavior being reinforced or punished should have no effect on one's own behavior.

The results of the second phase of Bandura's study were even more surprising. In this phase, all the children were offered an attractive incentive to act as the model had acted in the film. Remember that in the various films the model was always shown aggressing toward the doll, but the consequences of the model's aggression varied according to what group the children were in. When offered the incentive to replicate the model's behavior, *the children in all three groups did so.* This means that all the children had learned what they had observed—that is, the model's being aggressive—but they had translated what had been learned into the kind of behavior that they expected would be either reinforced or at least not punished. Bandura's experiment shows that indeed what is observed is learned, and that how what is learned is translated into performance depends on the learner's behavior-outcome expectancies. The behavior-outcome expectancies in this case came from observing the consequences of a model's behavior or vicariously.

Bandura and Rosenthal (1966) showed that emotional responses can also be learned vicariously. It was found that when a model was shown reacting with pain, presumably in response to extreme electric shock, following the sound of a buzzer, the observer, too, would develop an emotional response to the buzzer. Physiological measures indicated that after observing a model experience what appeared to be a buzzer-shock relationship, the observer responded emotionally when the buzzer sounded even when the model was no longer present. Thus, a conditioned emotional response was developed on the basis of what appeared to be happening to another person.

Although it is accurate to say that, according to social learning theory, what is observed is learned, certain processes influence what is attended to, what is retained, how what is learned is translated into behavior, and why it is translated into behavior. Bandura (1986) describes four such processes.

Attentional Processes

These processes include aspects of the environment that influence attention, such as the complexity, distinctiveness, and prevalence of the stimulation. For example, screeching brakes attract almost everyone's attention. Certain characteristics of models determine the extent to which they are observed. For instance, it has been found that models are attended to more if they are seen as similar to oneself, are respected, are considered powerful, or are attractive.

Attentional processes also include observer characteristics such as sensory capacities. Blind and deaf people, for example, do not respond to the same stimuli as people with normal sight and hearing.

Also, the consequences of past behavior can create a perceptual set in the observer. For example, if attending to certain stimuli in the past resulted in positive consequences, a tendency will exist to attend to similar stimuli in similar situations.

Retentional Processes

What is learned by observation is of no value unless it is retained. We saw earlier that how information is encoded and construed varies from person to person, but in general, Bandura (1986) says that experiences are stored either imaginally or verbally. That is, we either retain an actual cognitive picture of what was experienced or we retain the words that describe the experience. These memories make **delayed modeling** possible. Delayed modeling refers to the fact that often information gained by observational learning is first translated into behavior long after the time that it had been learned.

Motor Reproduction Processes

To translate learning into performance, one needs to have the necessary motor apparatus. Also, even if one has the necessary motor apparatus, one can be temporarily prevented from performing because of injury, fatigue, or illness. Even with the necessary motor system available and functioning well, complex skills cannot simply be observed and immediately translated into performance. First, with complex skills, many observations may be required before all of the relevant information can be attended to. Second, if all the relevant information is learned, many rehearsals that attempt to match performance with what had been learned and retained may be necessary. Hergenhahn (1988) says:

> Bandura maintains that even if one is equipped with all of the physical apparatus to make appropriate responses, a period of cognitive rehearsal is necessary before an observer's behavior can match that of a model. According to Bandura, the symbols retained from a modeling experience act as a template with which one's actions are compared. During this rehearsal process individuals observe their own behavior and compare it to their cognitive representation of the modeled experience. Any observed discrepancies between one's own behavior and the memory of the model's behavior trigger corrective action. This process continues until there is an acceptable match between the observer's and the model's behavior. Thus, the symbolic retention of a modeling experience creates a "feed-back" loop which can be used to gradually match one's behavior with that of a model's by utilizing self-observation and self-correction. (327)

Motivational Processes

No matter how much one has learned, and no matter what one's capabilities are, learning will not be translated into performance unless there is an incentive to do so. Observational learning may create potentially effective behavior-outcome expectations, but unless the person feels that behavior will yield something valued, no behavior will be emitted. According to social learning theory, reinforcement, either direct or vicarious, provides the *information* necessary for the development of effective behavior-outcome expectancies. Even with direct reinforcement, however, it is assumed that learning is observational and not an automatic, unconscious strengthening of response tendencies, as Skinner and Dollard and Miller had assumed. According to social learning theory, a person learns from *observing* the consequences of either his or her own behavior (direct reinforcement) or from observing the consequences of other people's behavior (vicarious reinforcement). In either case, information is provided about what behaviors lead to what consequences.

In addition to providing information concerning what behaviors lead to what consequences, reinforcement provides an *incentive* for action. Within social learning theory, reinforcement is equated with something of value to the person under existing circumstances. People, then, are motivated to act in ways that provide things they value and that allow them to avoid things considered aversive. The variables affecting observational learning and the translation of that learning into behavior are summarized in Figure 11–1.

It is important to note that within social learning theory, anticipated *environmental* consequences constitute only one determinant of behavior. Another determinant is the feelings that various actions cause a person to have. As we shall see in the next section, the intrinsic reinforcement that governs self-regulated behavior is at least as important, if not more important, in determining behavior than extrinsic or environmental consequences.

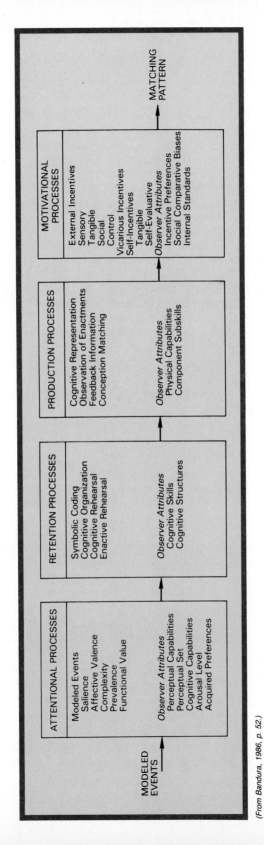

(From Bandura, 1986, p. 52.)

Figure 11–1. *The processes thought by Bandura to influence observational learning.*

Self-Regulated Behavior

As we have seen, direct and vicarious reinforcement and punishment are important because they allow us to create behavior outcome expectancies that we use while interacting with the environment. External reinforcements and punishments, however, cannot explain all human behavior. Bandura (1977) says:

> If actions were determined solely by external rewards and punishments, people would behave like weathervanes, constantly shifting in different directions to conform to the momentary influences impinging upon them. They would act corruptly with unprincipled individuals and honorably with righteous ones, and liberally with libertarians and dogmatically with authoritarians. (128)

Social learning theory maintains that much, if not most, human behavior is **self-regulated.** Through cumulative direct and vicarious experience, people develop **performance standards**, which they use to evaluate their own behavior. Almost constantly, the person is comparing what he or she does in a situation with some performance standard. If performance meets or exceeds the standard, the person experiences intrinsic reinforcement. If performance falls short of a standard, the person experiences intrinsic punishment.

Modeling has been found to influence the formulation of one's performance standards. Bandura and Kupers (1964), for example, found that children exposed to models who set high performance standards reinforced themselves only for superior performance, whereas children exposed to models accepting minimal performance standards reinforced themselves for minimal performance. It would be expected, then, that relevant people in a child's life—for instance, parents, siblings, and peers—would have a profound influence on the development of a child's performance standards.

Goals and *plans* extend self-directed behavior over long periods of time. Once a future goal has been established, one organizes his or her experiences so that they increase the probability of the goal's being attained. Experiences that keep the person on track toward the goal result in self-reinforcement; those that are incompatible with the goal cause self-punishment. As mentioned earlier, major goals are seldom accomplished all at once. Rather, a series of subgoals are established, and as they are attained, one approximates the major goal. Personal frustration and depression can occur if goals are either too distant or too difficult. Goals must be related to one's capabilities and must be attainable through the achievement of reasonable subgoals that are of moderate difficulty relative to a person's competencies. Performance standards, too, must be realistic. If they are too lenient, they will be too easily met, and little, if any, self-reinforcement will result from performing in accordance with them. If they are too stringent, one will experience frustration or worse. Bandura (1986) says: "In its more extreme forms, harsh standards for self-evaluation give rise to depressive reactions, chronic discouragement, feelings of worthlessness, and lack of purposefulness" (358).

The situation is best if one's performance standards are modified as a function of one's accomplishments and failures. Bandura (1986) notes:

> One's previous behavior is continuously used as a reference against which ongoing performance is judged. In this referential process, self-comparison supplies the

measure of adequacy. Past attainments affect self-appraisal mainly through their effects on standard setting. . . . After a given level of performance has been attained, it is no longer challenging, and people seek new self-satisfactions by means of progressive improvement. Hence, people tend to raise their performance standards after success and to lower them to more realistic levels after repeated failure. (347–48)

Self-Efficacy

An important variable in determining self-regulated behavior is **self-efficacy,** which describes what a person is capable of doing. Even more important, however, is what a person *thinks* he or she is capable of doing, or perceived self-efficacy. Perceived self-efficacy is influenced by several factors—for example, personal accomplishments and failures, seeing models perceived as similar to oneself succeed or fail at various tasks, and verbal persuasion. Through verbal persuasion, persons can often be encouraged to try to achieve goals they would otherwise avoid; an example would be when a coach "fires up" his team before a game. The effects of verbal persuasion are short-lived, however, if the resulting perceived self-efficacy is not manifested in real performance. In general, people with high perceived self-efficacy are better off than those with low perceived self-efficacy. Hergenhahn (1988) says:

> Persons with high perceived self-efficacy try more, accomplish more and persist longer at a task than persons with low perceived self-efficacy. People with high perceived self-efficacy also tend to experience less fear than people with low perceived self-efficacy. Bandura . . . speculates that this is because people with high perceived self-efficacy tend to have more control over the events in their environment and therefore experience less uncertainty. Since individuals tend to fear events over which they have no control, and therefore are uncertain of, those individuals with high perceived self-efficacy tend to experience less fear. (332)

Within social learning theory, anxiety is experienced when a person has an expectation of pain or injury, and at the same time believes he or she is incapable of doing anything to prevent it. In other words, anxiety results from perceived inefficacy in the face of danger.

As with goals and performance standards, the situation is best when one's perceived self-efficacy is in line with one's true capabilities. Thinking one can do more than one can actually do results in frustration. Thinking that one is not capable of doing something that one is actually capable of doing inhibits personal growth and experience. Both distortions of one's self-efficacy result in dysfunctional (erroneous) self-expectancies, which, if severe enough, can cause a person to seek psychotherapy. A growing volume of research exists that supports Bandura's contention that one's perceived self-efficacy accurately predicts one's behavior. For example, Baer, Holt, and Lichtenstein (1986) studied subjects enrolled in a program to help them quit smoking. At the end of the program it was found that those subjects who believed strongly that they could quit smoking for six months were much more able to do so than subjects who were less confident. Likewise, Mitchell and Stuart (1984) found that people with low perceived self-efficacy, regarding their ability to lose weight, were much more likely to drop out of a Weight Watchers program than those with high perceived self-efficacy regarding that ability. Concerning the importance of perceived self-efficacy, Bandura says, "Among the different aspects of self-knowledge, perhaps none is more influential in people's everyday lives than conceptions of their personal efficacy" (1986, 390).

Moral Conduct

Standards of right and wrong are also highly personal and are also derived from one's direct and vicarious experience. As with performance standards, moral principles are usually modeled by a child's parents and are eventually internalized. Once internalized, these moral principles determine which behaviors and thoughts are self-sanctioned and which result in self-contempt. Thus, moral behavior comes to be self-regulated and is maintained independently of, and in many cases despite, environmental consequences. Bandura (1977) says: "The anticipation of self-reproach for conduct that violates one's standards provides a source of motivation to keep behavior in line with standards in the face of opposing inducements. There is no more devastating punishment than self-contempt" (154).

Certain cognitive mechanisms, however, allow a person to act contrary to his or her moral principles without experiencing self-contempt. These **self-exonerating mechanisms,** suggested by Bandura, are summarized by Hergenhahn (1988, 333–35).

1. **Moral justification.** One's otherwise reprehensible behavior becomes a means to a higher purpose and therefore is justifiable. "I committed the crime so that I could provide food for my family."
2. **Euphemistic labeling.** By calling an otherwise reprehensible act something other than what it really is, one can engage in an act without self-contempt. For example, nonaggressive individuals are far more likely to aggress toward another person when doing so is called a game.
3. **Advantageous comparison.** By comparing one's self-deplored acts with even more heinous acts, it makes one's own reprehensible acts look trifling by comparison. "Sure I did that, but look at what he did."
4. **Displacement of responsibility.** Some people can readily depart from their moral principles if they feel a recognized authority sanctions their behavior and takes responsibility for it. "I did it because I was ordered to do so."
5. **Diffusion of responsibility.** A decision to act in an otherwise reprehensible manner which is made by a group is easier to live with than an individual decision. Where everyone is responsible, no single individual feels responsible. "I couldn't be the only one saying no."
6. **Disregard or distortion of consequences.** Here people ignore or distort the harm caused by their conduct and therefore there is no need to experience self-contempt. The farther people remove themselves from the ill effects of their immoral behavior the less pressure there is to censure it. "I just let the bombs go and they disappeared in the clouds."
7. **Dehumanization.** If some individuals are looked upon as subhuman, they can be treated inhumanly without experiencing self-contempt. Once a person or a group has been dehumanized, they no longer possess feelings, hopes, and

concerns, and they can be mistreated without risking self-condemnation. "Why not take their land, they are nothing but savages without souls."

8. **Attribution of blame.** One can always choose something that a victim said or did and claim that it caused one to act in a reprehensible way.

The self-exonerating mechanisms provide another reason why human behavior appears to be inconsistent. Even if a person's moral principles were known with certainty, employing one or more of these mechanisms would make the person's moral behavior unpredictable to the outside observer. Such behavior would undoubtedly seem consistent and logical to the person himself or herself, however. In fact, it seems that humans have a strong tendency to believe that their personality is consistent over time even when actual behavior or thought processes do not support that belief. According to Mischel (1969), it is not only traditional personality theorists who need to believe that personality is stable over time, but most nonprofessionals as well.

> Clinically, it seems remarkable how each of us generally manages to reconcile his seemly diverse behaviors into one self-consistent whole. A man may steal on one occasion, lie on another, donate generously to charity on a third, cheat on a fourth, and still construe himself readily as "basically honest and moral." Just as the personality theorist who studies them, our subjects also are skilled at transforming their seemingly discrepant behavior into a constructed continuity, making unified wholes out of almost anything. (1012)

Delay of Gratification

That aspect of self-regulated behavior called **delay of gratification** is considered by Mischel to be necessary for civilization itself. Without the **self-control** involved in delaying gratification, humans would be as impulsive as the lower animals, and goal-oriented behavior would be impossible. Mischel (1986) says:

> The ability to voluntarily refuse immediate gratification, to tolerate self-imposed delays of reward, is at the core of most philosophical concepts of "will power" and their parallel psychological concept of "ego strength." It is hard to imagine civilization without such self-imposed delays. Learning to wait for desired outcomes and to behave in the light of expected future consequences is essential for the successful achievement of long-term distant goals. Every person must learn to defer impulses and to express them only under special conditions of time and place, as seen in toilet training. Similarly, enormously complex chains of deferred gratification are required for people to achieve the delayed rewards provided by our culture's social system and institutions.
>
> Consider, for example, the self-imposed deferrals of pleasure required to achieve occupational objectives such as careers in medicine or science. The route leading to such a goal involves a continuous series of delays of gratification, as seen in the progression from one grade to the next, and from one barrier to another in the long course from occupational choice to occupational success. In social relationships, the culture also requires delays, as seen in the expectation that people should postpone sexual relations, marriage, and children until they are "ready for them." Although judgments of what constitutes such readiness differ

greatly across cultures and among different people, some norms concerning appropriate timing are found in every society. (414)

If the ability to delay gratification is at the core of civilized behavior, what about people who cannot delay gratification? Mischel (1986) says that such people typically cause trouble either for themselves or for others:

Inadequate delay patterns often are partial causes of antisocial and criminal behavior (including violence and physical aggression). People who cannot delay gratification also may fail to achieve reasonable work and interpersonal satisfactions. . . . Thus while some personal and social problems stem from excessive frustration, others result from the failure of individuals to learn and practice appropriate patterns of delay and restraint. Indeed, deficiencies in voluntary delay may cause frustration and may victimize the individual by guaranteeing an endless chain of failure experiences in our culture. Consider, for example, the "high school dropout" who leaves school because he cannot tolerate postponing pleasures and working for more distant goals. His school failure in turn may sentence him to future vocational hardships and prevent him from achieving durable satisfaction. (415)

The willingness to delay gratification has been found to be related to several factors, such as one's faith that the future goal will, in fact, materialize, one's previous experience with delaying gratification, the value of the future goal, and one's belief that he or she can perform the skills necessary to attain a future goal (perceived self-efficacy). Mischel (1986) says, "If you really expect to get the delayed reward, and want it, you are more likely to wait for it" (422).

To measure the stability of the ability to delay gratification, Mischel (1984) obtained parental ratings of seventy-seven adolescents (average age: sixteen years, eight months) who had participated in delay of gratification studies twelve years before (average age: four years, six months). It was found that subjects who had tolerated long delays as preschoolers tended, as adolescents, to be able to think and plan ahead, to act self-confidently, resourcefully, and trustworthily. Adolescents who demonstrated a weak ability to delay gratification as preschoolers, tended to be immature, unpredictable and prone to stress. Three years later, when the average age of the group was about eighteen years, it was found that delayers were able to concentrate, form friendships, and cope better than nondelayers. They also scored higher on the Scholastic Aptitude Test (Fisher 1988). Because the ability to delay gratification is a beneficial attribute, the questions become how best to create delayers and to convert nondelayers into delayers? One answer seems to be to use modeling.

As with other factors influencing self-regulated behavior, it has been found that the willingness to delay gratification can be learned by observing models. For example, Bandura and Mischel (1965) gave 250 children fourteen opportunities to choose between receiving a small candy bar immediately or a larger one sometime in the future. For each child a delay-of-gratification score was computed based on the number of choices for the immediate reward as opposed to the larger future reward. From the original 250 children, sixty (thirty boys and thirty girls) with the strongest preference for immediate gratification and sixty (thirty boys and thirty girls) with the strongest preference for larger delayed rewards were selected for further study. The former constituted the low-delay group, and the latter constituted the high-delay group. Next, ten boys and ten girls from each of the two groups were assigned to one of three experimental conditions. The first was a **live modeling** condition, in which an adult was shown choosing between immediate or delayed gratification. For the low-delay group, the adult selected delayed rewards and commented on the virtues of delayed gratification. For the high-delay group, the adult selected immediate rewards and commented on the benefits of immediate gratification. In each case, the model was acting *opposite* the way the children had acted. The second group was assigned to a **symbolic modeling** condition, in which the choices available to an adult were described and an account of the model's choices along with the model's comments were read by the children. Again, the model's behavior was opposite that of the children's. The third group involved a *no model condition*, in which children were simply shown the choices available to the model. The experimental design can be summarized as follows:

LOW-DELAY CHILDREN *(30M, 30F)*	*HIGH-DELAY CHILDREN* *(30M, 30F)*
Live Adult Models High-Delay (10M, 10F)	*Live Adult Models Low-Delay (10M, 10F)*
Symbolic Modeling Describes High-Delay (10M, 10F)	Symbolic Modeling Describes Low-Delay (10M, 10F)
No-Model Condition Only Describes Choices (10M, 10F)	No-Model Condition Only Describes Choices (10M, 10F)

After the foregoing treatments, each child was again given fourteen choices between a small immediate reward and a large distant reward. In addition, to test how long the effects of the experiment lasted, each child was tested again four to five weeks after the experiment. Results indicated that high-delay children significantly shifted their choices toward immediate gratification and that they continued to make low-delay responses four to five weeks later. Although both live and symbolic modeling significantly influenced the behavior of high-delay children, live modeling had the greatest effect. Likewise, low-delay children significantly changed to high-delay responses as a result of both live and symbolic modeling, and the effects persisted for four to five weeks following the experiment. For low-delay children, however, live and symbolic modeling were equally effective.

The results of the Bandura and Mischel (1965) study demonstrate that modeling (both live and symbolic) can easily cause children to reverse the response preferences with which they started the experiment which again shows the volatility of behavior-outcome expectancies. That this volatility does not pertain only to children is demonstrated by an experiment by Stumphauzer (1971) in which the foregoing procedures were used on eighteen- to twenty-year-old prison inmates. The results obtained were essentially the same as those found by Bandura and Mischel (1965).

Dysfunctional Expectancies and Psychotherapy

According to social learning theory, psychological problems result from **dysfunctional expectancies** (that is, erroneous, nonfunctional, or faulty expectancies), and any kind of therapy that corrects them—that is, brings them in line with reality—will be, by definition, effective.

If, for example, one believes that developing a close relationship with a member of the opposite sex will bring pain and frustration, one will avoid such relationships. Such expectancies are usually based on real experiences, but they are overgeneralized, and, when they are, keep the person from having the kinds of experiences that would disconfirm them. The defensive behavior based on a dysfunctional expectancy is therefore often difficult to remedy. Bandura (1986) says:

> Once established, defensive behavior is difficult to eliminate even when the hazards no longer exist. This is because protective avoidance prevents individuals from learning that what they perceive to be dangerous is actually quite safe. When expected adversities do not follow a defensive act believed to forestall them, their nonoccurrence is viewed as a confirming consequent that the defense works rather than being seen as a nonhappening. The nonoccurrence of expected adversities functions as a positive outcome. . . . Hence, the failure of anticipated calamities to materialize becomes confirmatory evidence strengthening the belief that the defensive maneuvers forestalled them. This process of subjective confirmation is captured by the apocryphal case of a compulsive who, when asked by his therapist why he snapped his fingers ritualistically, replied that it kept ferocious lions away. When informed that obviously there were no lions in the vicinity to ward off, the compulsive replied, "See, it works!" (189)

Some dogs do bite, some airplanes do crash, some intimate relationships do result in pain and frustration, some members of minorities do commit crimes, and some men and some women are insensitive. To generalize on the basis of a few cases to all possible experiences, however, does not accurately represent reality. People forming strong expectancies on the basis of limited experiences need to have further experiences with the same kinds of objects, events, or people without those experiences being negative. Bandura (1986) remarks:

> Beliefs that have little basis in reality would ordinarily be amenable to change through accurate information. But expectations of vulnerability are not entirely groundless. Situations usually contain uncertainties, and circumstances can arise that swamp coping capabilities. Some animals do bite, automobiles crash from time to time, and assertiveness is sometimes punished, despite the best of efforts. When injurious consequences occur irregularly and unpredictably, beliefs about one's coping capabilities and potential hazards are not easily altered. If self-doubting persons do not fully trust what they have been told, as happens in severe cases, they continue to behave in accordance with their beliefs rather than risk painful consequences, however improbable they may be. What such individuals need in order to relinquish their erroneous beliefs are powerful disconfirming experiences, which verbal assurances alone do not provide. (189–90)

Another kind of dysfunctional expectancy concerns perceived self-efficacy. As we have seen, if people believe they are incapable of doing something, they will not try to do it. If one believes he or she cannot touch dogs, cats, snakes, children, or members of the opposite sex, that person will not do so regardless of his or her true capabilities. Likewise, a person who feels he or she is incapable of handling success will avoid success. Thus, according to social learning theory, the goal of **psychotherapy** is to change the client's perceived self-efficacy. The assumption is that if a person's perceived self-efficacy becomes more realistic, behavior will become more adaptive.

The assumption that perceived self-efficacy relates directly to behavior was tested by Bandura, Adams, and Beyer (1977). Seven men and twenty-six women who suffered a chronic snake phobia were recruited through newspaper advertisements. Before treatment, each person was given a Behavioral Avoidance Test, which consisted of twenty-nine performance tasks requiring increasingly close interactions with a red-tailed boa constrictor. Self-efficacy expectancies were also measured before treatment. Each person was given a list describing various interactions with a snake and was asked to indicate which ones he or she would be able to perform. Subjects were also asked to indicate the certainty with which they believed they could or could not engage in various interactions with the snake.

After pretesting, Bandura, Adams, and Beyer (1977) randomly assigned subjects to one of three treatment groups. The first was the **participant modeling** condition in which first a live model handled a boa constrictor in a series of interactions ranging from mildly threatening to extremely threatening. Then subjects were asked to perform these same interactions. The time required for these interactions ranged from forty minutes to seven hours, with the average time being one and a half hours. In some cases, the fear of a subject was so intense that a baby boa had to be used initially. The second group was called the *modeling condition*, where subjects observed a model engage in a series of interactions with the snake, but the observer did not actually come into contact with the snake himself or herself. In the *control condition*, the pretreatment measures were made but no treatment was given.

After the various treatments, subjects were again given the Behavior Avoidance Test, the final step of which was to let the boa constrictor crawl on the subject's lap while his or her hands were held passively at one's side. Results indicated that both the participant modeling and the modeling conditions significantly reduced avoidance behavior, but the participant modeling condition was the more effective of the two treatments.

Efficacy expectations were measured again after conclusion of treatment. It was found that the participant modeling condition and the modeling condition significantly changed the self-efficacy expectations of being able to handle a snake. Again, although both techniques were effective, the participant modeling technique was most effective in changing self-efficacy expectations. Most important, however, was the finding that self-efficacy expectations were accurate predictors of behavior. Those subjects who indicated that they now believed they could handle a snake *actually did so.* The relationship between perceived self-efficacy and actual performance existed for subjects in all groups. In almost every case, the kind of interactions a person believed that he or she could engage in were those that he or she actually engaged in. Maximal efficacy expectations, however, did not always result from maximal interactions with the snake; that is, some of the individuals in the participant modeling group who were able to perform the most threatening interactions with the snake during treatment did not form the expectation that they would be able to interact that way with a snake on subsequent occasions, and they were not able to. The formation of efficacy expectations, then, is based on more than one's experience with successful performance, although successful performance has a powerful influence on the formation of efficacy expectations.

Further measures indicated that the reduction of avoidance caused by the treatments generalized to other snakes, that the results of the experiment persisted over time, and that the results generalized positively into other aspects of the subjects' lives. For instance, in some cases, improvement was reported in dealing effectively with other animal and social threats.

In another study, Bandura, Blanchard, and Ritter (1969) tested the effectiveness of various techniques in dealing with snake phobia. In this experiment, adults and adolescents were divided into four groups: symbolic modeling, in which subjects were shown a film showing models interacting with a snake; live modeling with participation in which subjects interacted with a snake along with the model; **systematic desensitization,** in which subjects were asked to imagine interactions with a snake ranging from low-anxiety-producing interactions to those producing great anxiety. Subjects, starting with imagining low-anxiety scenes, continued to imagine each scene until it no longer caused anxiety, and continued in this manner until the scenes that previously caused the greatest amount of anxiety no longer did so. The last group was the *control condition,* in which subjects received no treatment. The ability to interact with a snake was measured for all subjects before and after the experiments. Results are shown in Figure 11–2.

It can be seen that again live modeling with participation was most effective, followed by symbolic modeling and desensitization. Subjects in the control condition showed little or no improvement in their ability to interact with a snake. Follow-up research again indicated that the effects of the experiment endured and generalized positively into other areas that had produced fear prior to the experiment.

Many other experiments have shown the effectiveness of modeling in dealing with a wide variety of dysfunctional expectancies. In all of this research, the emphasis is on the person's current perceptions and expectancies. There is no mention of traits, reinforcement histories, or internal conflicts. In fact, Bandura (1986) believes those therapists looking for such things tell us more about themselves than they tell us about the source of their client's problem:

> Advocates of theoretical orientations repeatedly discover their chosen motivators at work but rarely find evidence for the motivators emphasized by the proponents of competing viewpoints. Hence, one can predict better the types of insights and unconscious motivators that persons are apt to discover in themselves in the course of psychodynamic analysis from knowledge of the therapists' conceptual belief system than from the clients' actual psychological status. (5)

Figure 11–2.
The ability to interact with a snake before and after various kinds of therapeutic treatments.

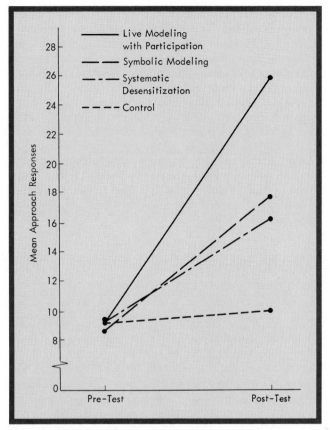

(From Bandura, Blanchard, & Ritter, 1969, p. 183. Copyright 1969 by The American Psychological Association. Reprinted by permission.)

Social Learning Theory View of Human Nature

According to social learning theory, certainly nothing fixed exists about people. We are not locked into a life-style because we possess certain traits, have had certain early experiences or reinforcement histories, or for any other reason. Each person is thought to develop information-processing strategies that apply to current situations. Although external reinforcement may be informative and thereby influence the formation of expectancies, intrinsic reinforcement is more important, because most human behavior is self-regulated.

Mischel (1981) nicely summarizes the image of **human nature** generated by social learning theory:

> This image is one of the human being as an active, aware problem-solver, capable of profiting from an enormous range of experiences and cognitive capacities, possessed of great potential for good or ill, actively constructing his or her psycho-

logical world, interpreting and processing information in potentially creative ways, influencing the world but also being influenced by it lawfully—even if the laws are difficult to discover and hard to generalize. It views the person as so complex and multi-faceted as to defy classifications and comparisons on any single or simple common dimensions, as multiply influenced by a host of determinants, as uniquely organized on the basis of prior experiences and future expectations, and yet as studyable by the methods of science, and continuously responsive to stimulus conditions in meaningful ways. It is an image that has moved a long way from the instinctual drive-reduction models, the static global traits, and the automatic stimulus-response bonds of earlier times. . . . It is an image that highlights the shortcomings of all simplistic theories that view behavior as the exclusive result of any narrow set of determinants, whether these are habits, traits, drives, constructs, instincts, genes, or reinforcers. And yet it is an image that is sure to shift in still unpredictable directions as our understanding and knowledge increase. (532–33)

Evaluation

Empirical Research

Like the theories of Cattell, Skinner, and Dollard and Miller, the theory of Bandura and Mischel is well grounded in empirical research. Throughout this chapter we have sampled numerous experimental studies that Bandura and Mischel, and their colleagues have run to test their concepts. Social learning theory continues to generate an enormous amount of research. Also, Mischel's book, *Personality Assessment* (1968) triggered a debate among personality theorists concerning the consistency of human behavior that has lasted to the present time. This debate has stimulated many research programs designed to answer the question as to whether human behavior is consistent or not and, if so, to what extent, and in what areas? It now appears that whether behavioral consistency is found or not depends on what is meant by consistency and how the research is performed. For example, if *average* behavior is measured, it pools together those behaviors that are consistent with those that are not. The result would tend to support the notion that behavior is inconsistent. Bowers (1973), and Bem and Allen (1974) argue that research on consistency should be correlational rather than experimental, because the correlational method preserves individual differences. Bem and Allen tested the hypothesis that "individuals who identify themselves as consistent on a particular trait dimension will in fact be more consistent cross-situationally than those who identify themselves as highly variable" (512). The hypothesis was supported, indicating that some people are consistent on some traits and others are not; further, people themselves know whether or not they are consistent.

After reviewing the literature and the arguments on consistency versus inconsistency, Pervin (1984) reaches the following conclusion:

Perhaps the conclusion that makes most sense is that most people are consistent in their behavior some of the time and variable in their behavior the rest of the time. . . . In other words, each person can be expected to be consistent in ways that are salient or meaningful for him or her. The areas of consistency differ with different individuals. Thus, for example, for some individuals it may be important to be always honest while for others it may be important to be always dominant. Each individual may have many or few such areas in which there exists cross-situational consistency. Sampling of a large group of individuals on any one characteristic might suggest little cross-situational consistency since it is unlikely that more than a small proportion of the total sample will be consistent in that particular area. The consistency of a subgroup in the population can be masked by the situational specificity of the larger group: this is true for every personality characteristic that is assessed. The conclusion might then be that behavior is situationally specific rather than that behavior is stable in some ways for some individuals and in other ways for other individuals. What appears to be needed is a more differentiated picture of consistency and of the relationship between person and situational determinants. (17)

The information just summarized refutes the position of neither the social learning theorist nor the trait theorist. Although the position that Mischel took in 1968 tended toward situationalism, by claiming that the probability of reward or punishment in any situation is the most powerful determinant of behavior, he never said that behavior was entirely inconsistent; if it were, he said, memory would have no value (1977, 333). In any case, regardless of Mischel's early position, he is now an **interactionist,** who stresses the importance of both person and situation variables. Just as showing consistency of behavior is no longer a valid argument against social learning theory, finding inconsistency in behavior is not necessarily an argument against trait theory. We saw in chapter 7 that Allport believed that the possession of personality traits did not cause a person's behavior to be "fixed and stable." Rather, Allport viewed traits as representing "ranges of possible behavior." He believed that it was differing situations that determined which behavior, in the possible range of behaviors, occurred. Thus, Allport's theory was in fact close to the interactionism of social learning theory. The major differences would be in Allport's use of the term *trait* and his belief that a person's behavior must occur within a specified range of possibilities. Also, we saw in chapter 8 that Cattell believed that traits interact with "situational modulators" to produce behavior in any given situation. Thus, neither Allport nor Cattell believed that behavior was entirely consistent or that it could be predicted on the basis of personality traits alone.

Criticisms

Behavior Is More Consistent Than Social Learning Theory Claims.   A great deal of criticism was triggered by Mischel's early book (1968), which seemed to emphasize situation variables almost to the exclusion of person variables and in which he suggested that little consistency exists in human behavior. Since that time, however, Mischel has accepted an interactionist position, in which both the person and the environment are considered important. Also, Mischel claims that his earlier statements about the consistency of behavior were misunderstood. He notes that he never said *no* consistency existed; rather, he argued that the amount of consistency predicted by trait and psychoanalytic theories did not exist.

Mental Events Cannot Cause Behavior.   Radical behaviorists, such as Skinner, take issue with any theory that contains mentalistic concepts. They believe that mental events are irrelevant to an understanding of human behavior. Terms like *perceived self-efficacy* and *functional and dysfunctional expectancies,* say the radical behaviorists, confuse the study of human behavior rather than clarify it. Also, say the Skinnerians, *observational learning* is probably just a special case of operant conditioning in which acts of imitation sometimes lead to reinforcement and are thus repeated. Therefore, observational learning is under the control of reinforcement not independent of it as the social learning theorists claim (see for example, Gewirtz 1971).

Social Learning Theory Is No Better at Predicting Behavior Than the Theories That It Criticizes.   Psychoanalytic, trait, and learning theorists all claim that their theories predict human behavior at least as well as social learning theory does. Much current research is currently attempting to substantiate or refute these claims.

Criticism of Psychoanalytic Theory.   The social learning theorists have been harshly critical of both traditional psychoanalytic theory, and Dollard and Miller's attempt to synthesize psychoanalytic theory and Hullian learning theory. Social learning theorists claim that no need exists to employ the nebulous language of psychoanalytic theory, because the clearly defined terms from social learning theory work as well, if not better. Psychoanalytic theorists believe that this position is naïve and misses the complex interplay between the conscious and unconscious mind. It is because social learning theory does not understand the workings of the human mind, say the critics, that it can only deal with relatively simple psychological problems such as phobias, and with nothing more complex.

Important Aspects of Personality Neglected.   We just saw that the psychoanalysts criticize social learning theory because it does not recognize the importance of unconscious motivation. Another important area neglected by social learning theory is development. Other theorists have found that maturational factors are important in determining the feelings that people experience and how they process information. Little is said in social learning theory about the biologic, hormonal, or maturational influences on personality development. Other topics neglected or minimized by social learning theory include motivation and conflict. Motivation appears to be covered by the social learning theorists mainly in relationship to goal formulation and in the formulation of plans to reach goals. Also the concept of conflict, so important to so many personality theorists (e.g., Freud, and Dollard and Miller), does not even appear in the index of Bandura's most recent book (1986).

Social Learning Theory Is Not a Unified One.   Social learning theory has been criticized for being neither systematic nor unified. Several important topics have been studied extensively (e.g., the variables governing observational learning, perceived self-efficacy, and the self-regulation of behavior), but how these topics are related to each other is not clear. The same is true for Mischel's cognitive social learning person variables; they are simply listed and described, but little discussion occurs on how they relate to each other, let alone social learning theory in general.

Contributions

Emphasis on Human Empirical Research. One reason that social learning theory is currently so popular among personality psychologists is because its terms are defined precisely enough to be empirically verified. Bandura and Mischel, and their colleagues have always been associated with active research programs. Furthermore, Bandura and Mischel have avoided the touchy problem of generalizing research on nonhumans to humans by performing all of their research on humans. Likewise, they have avoided the problem of generalizing from simple behavior to complex behavior by doing research on complex behavior to begin with. By concentrating on human subjects and on complex behavior, social learning theory skirts many of the criticisms of Skinner's, and Dollard and Miller's theories.

Applied Value. Social learning theory has been enormously heuristic. It has provided information about topics of vital importance in today's world: aggression; moral behavior; delay of gratification; the influence of models (e.g., parents, television, films, and rock stars) on behavior; dysfunctional expectancies and how to correct them; self-regulation of behavior; and the importance of perceived self-efficacy.

For many, the social learning theory view of humans as thinking, planning, reasoning, expecting, and reflecting organisms is much more realistic than the more mechanistic, simplistic view of humans derived from animal research. Social learning theory recognizes the importance of language, symbols, and cognitive information-processing mechanisms; the research it generates is usually directed at something relevant; it views humans optimistically, and it emphasizes either the here and now or the future, rather than the past.

With its emphasis on cognitive processes, the here and now and the future, and its belief in the individual's potential for change, social learning theory has much in common with the existential/humanistic theories, to which we turn in chapters 13–16.

Summary

The major spokespersons for social learning theory today are Albert Bandura and Walter Mischel. Social learning theory stresses cognitive factors in learning and in performing, and states that behavior in any given situation is a function of both the characteristics of the person and the situation. Early in his career, Mischel took both trait and psychoanalytic theories to task because he found that human behavior was not nearly as consistent as it should be if it was determined by factors thought to exist within the person, such as traits or repressed experiences. Although in 1968 Mischel was basically a situationalist, in that he believed the probability of reward or punishment was the strongest determinant of behavior in any given situation, he later became an interactionist, who saw the importance of both person and situation variables and their interaction. Bandura labeled the interactionist's position "reciprocal determinism," which states that the person influences the environment and the environment influences the person. Mischel replaced the traditional person variables such as traits and internal conflicts with what he called cognitive social learning person variables: competencies, or the various skills a person possesses; encoding strategies and personal constructs, or how experiences are retained and categorized; expectancies, or what a person expects will happen if he or she behaves in a certain way or sees a certain event; subjective values, or what a person believes is worth having or doing and self-regulatory systems and plans, which determine what people will reward and punish themselves for, and how they will organize their lives to attain future goals.

According to social learning theory, we learn what we observe. We learn by either observing the consequences of our own behavior or by observing the consequences of other people's behavior. That is, we learn from either direct or vicarious reinforcement and punishment. Even though learning is an almost continuous process, we only translate what we have learned into performance when there is an incentive to do so. According to Bandura, observational learning is influenced by four variables: attentional processes, which determine what we can and do attend to; retentional variables, which determine how experience is encoded in memory; motor reproduction processes, which determine what behaviors can be performed; and motivational processes, which determine the circumstances under which learning is translated into performance.

Most human behavior is, according to social learning theory, self-regulated. Performance standards are established, and if one's behavior meets or exceeds those standards, one experiences self-reinforcement; if they are not, one experiences self-punishment. Humans also formulate future goals and then plan their lives so as to increase the probability of attaining those goals. Usually, future goals are approached by first attaining a series of smaller, more immediate subgoals. A great deal of self-regulated behavior is influenced by one's perceived self-efficacy or one's own view of what he or she is capable of doing. Those people with high perceived self-efficacy try more, do more, persist longer, and are less anxious than those with low perceived self-efficacy. Moral conduct is governed by internalized moral principles, which, if violated, cause a person to experience self-contempt. Self-contempt can be escaped, however, by using one of the self-exonerating mechanisms. The ability to tolerate delay of gratification is necessary for civilization, and therefore, those who demand immediate gratification often engage in antisocial behavior. Like the other variables involved in self-regulated behavior, the ability to delay gratification has been shown to be influenced by modeling.

Psychological and behavioral problems result from dysfunctional expectancies. Such erroneous or ineffective expectancies can result from the overgeneralization of a single or small number of negative personal experiences or from modeling. Within social learning theory, psychotherapy is seen as a means of changing self-efficacy expectations. If a person does not believe he or she can handle a snake, for example, a film of a model interacting with a snake can be shown (symbolic modeling), a live model can be shown interacting with a snake (live modeling), or a model and the client can interact with a snake together (live modeling with participation). Although all forms of modeling have been found effective in treating many kinds of phobias, live modeling with participation is usually found to be the most effective. It has been shown that modeling changes a person's perceived self-efficacy, which, in turn, results in a change in behavior.

Social learning theory sees humans as thoughtful problem solvers who are dealing with the present but also planning for the future. Although we may enter each situation with certain expectations, those expectations are easily modified if new relevant information becomes available. Unlike many other personality theories, social learning theory sees people as highly modifiable.

Social learning theory is firmly grounded in empirical research but has been criticized for claiming human behavior is more inconsistent than it actually is; suggesting that mental events can cause behavior; not being any better at predicting behavior than the theories it criticizes; being too critical of psychoanalytic theory and thus missing the importance of unconscious motivation; neglecting important aspects of personality such as development, motivation, and conflict; and not being a systematic, unified theory. Social learning theory has been praised for emphasizing empirical research using human subjects; performing research on complex, socially relevant topics; and for recognizing the many cognitive processes that differentiate humans from nonhuman animals.

EXPERIENTIAL EXERCISES

1. According to social learning theory most human behavior is self-regulated. For example, it is claimed that much of our behavior is guided by internalized performance and moral standards. If performance meets or exceeds these standards we feel good about ourselves, and if it does not we feel bad. Give two examples of how such standards guide your behavior. Do you agree with the social learning contention that intrinsic reinforcement has more of an impact on behavior than extrinsic reinforcement? Explain. Also, attempt to account for the origins of your moral and performance standards.

2. A key concept within social learning theory is perceived self-efficacy. Discuss how your *perceptions* of your abilities influence your behavior. That is, how do they influence what you try, how long you persist, and what you avoid doing? Discuss how you think your perceived self-efficacy originated and the circumstances under which you think it can be changed. Do you agree with the contention of the social learning theorists that changing dysfunctional expectancies is largely a matter of changing perceived self-efficacy? Explain.

3. Another important concept within social learning theory is that of modeling. Describe a person who has acted as an influential model in your life. What important values did you learn from this person? Discuss the topic of observational learning as it applies to this modeling experience.

4. Evaluate your own behavior in terms of consistency. List two of your personality characteristics that have remained stable during the past few years and two that have changed. Also evaluate your consistency across similar situations. For example, do you tend to act the same way at all social events? If not, why not? What conclusion do you reach concerning the consistency of your own behavior?

5. Give an example of each of Mischel's five cognitive social learning person variables as they apply to you. Those variables are competencies; encoding strategies and personal constructs; expectancies; subjective values; and self-regulatory systems and plans.

6. Describe someone you know who has a strong ability to delay gratification (perhaps yourself), and someone you know who has a weaker ability. Other than the strong ability or the weak ability to delay gratification, what are some of the other characteristics that differentiate the two people?

DISCUSSION QUESTIONS

1. What was Mischel's basic argument with trait and psychoanalytic theories?

2. List and describe the cognitive social learning person variables.

3. What is reciprocal determinism? Give an example.

4. Define and give an example of each of the following: behavior-outcome expectancy, stimulus-outcome expectancy, and self-efficacy expectancy.

5. List and give an example of the four variables influencing observational learning.

6. Discuss the role of reinforcement in social learning theory. In your answer, state whether reinforcement is a learning or a performance variable.

7. Why, according to social learning theory, are we able to learn by observing the consequences of the behavior of others?

8. What determines the circumstances under which a person will experience self-reinforcement? Self-punishment?

9. How, according to social learning theory, do people formulate and attain future goals?

10. What influences a person's perceived self-efficacy? What are some differences between people with high perceived self-efficacy and people with low perceived self-efficacy?

11. What, according to social learning theory, determines a person's moral conduct? Describe the mechanisms that a person can employ to escape self-contempt.

12. Discuss the relationship between being able to delay gratification and the ability to plan and live in society. What influences one's ability to delay gratification?

13. What are dysfunctional expectancies? Give examples.

14. Summarize some of the techniques used by social learning theorists to treat dysfunctional expectancies. Which of these techniques is generally found to be most effective?

15. What do the social learning theorists mean when they say that for therapy to be effective it must change perceived self-efficacy?

16. How does the social learning theorist see human nature?

17. Summarize the criticisms that have been made of social learning theory and indicate which ones you agree with and which ones you disagree with and why.

18. Do you think that the social learning theorist would be concerned about the content of television programs? Explain.

19. Describe the strengths of social learning theory.

20. Describe child-rearing practices that you think would increase the probability of a child growing up with the ability to delay gratification.

SUGGESTIONS FOR FURTHER READING

BANDURA, A. (1973). *Aggression: A Social Learning Analysis.* Englewood Cliffs, NJ: Prentice Hall.
    An application of social learning theory to an analysis of aggressive behavior.

BANDURA, A. (1977). *Social Learning Theory.* Englewood Cliffs, NJ: Prentice Hall.
    An early sketch of Bandura's theory, which was greatly expanded in his 1986 book.

BANDURA, A. (1986). *Social Foundations of Thought and Action: A Social Cognitive Theory.* Englewood Cliffs, NJ: Prentice Hall.
    Bandura's most recent, complete statement of his theory.

MISCHEL, W. (1968). *Personality and Assessment.* New York: Wiley.
    This book, by pointing out the inadequacies of many personality theories, stimulated many counterattacks from personality theorists and has led to several conceptual and methodological revisions in the field. To a large extent the current popularity of the interactionist approach to studying personality can be attributed to this book.

MISCHEL, W. (1986). *Introduction to Personality.* New York: Holt, Rinehart and Winston. Mischel presents the more traditional approaches to explaining personality and compares them with his own cognitive-social learning approach.

GLOSSARY

Attentional processes. Processes that determine what is attended to and therefore what is learned through observation.

Behavior-Outcome expectancy. The belief that acting a certain way in a certain situation will have a certain consequence.

Cognitive social learning person variables. Those variables thought by Mischel to determine how a person selects, perceives, interprets, and uses the stimuli confronting him or her. Those variables are competencies; encoding strategies and personal constructs; expectancies; subjective values; and self-regulatory systems and plans.

Competencies. The cognitive social learning person variable that describes what a person knows and what he or she is capable of doing.

Delay of gratification. The postponement of an immediate reinforcer usually to obtain a larger, more distant reinforcer.

Delayed modeling. Refers to the fact that there is often a long delay between when something is learned observationally and when that learning is translated into behavior.

Dysfunctional expectancies. Expectancies that do not result in effective interactions with the environment. Such expectancies can result from inaccurate modeling, from overgeneralization of nonrepresentational personal experience, or from distorted perceived self-efficacy.

Encoding strategies and personal constructs. The cognitive social learning person variable that determines which aspects of the environment are selected for attention and how those aspects are interpreted by the individual.

Expectancies. The cognitive social learning person variable that determines how individuals anticipate events in their lives (see also behavior-outcome-expectancy, self-efficacy expectancy, and stimulus-outcome expectancy).

Extrinsic reinforcement. Reinforcement that results from sources outside of the person.

Human nature. Social learning theory sees human nature as highly flexible, because it is not set by traits, genetics, early experience, repression, or reinforcement history. Human behavior is seen as oriented toward the present or the future, cognitively determined, and largely self-regulated.

Interactionist. Any theorist who contends that it is the interaction of person variables and situation variables that determines behavior at any given moment.

Intrinsic reinforcement. Self-reinforcement.

Live modeling. Modeling involving the physical presence of a human being.

Model. Anything that conveys information to an observer.

Moral conduct. Behavior that is in accordance with internalized moral principles. When a person acts in accordance with internalized moral principles, he or she experiences self-praise. If not, the person experiences self-contempt.

Motivational processes. Those processes that determine the circumstances under which learning is translated into behavior. Such a translation will not occur unless the person has an adequate incentive.

Motor reproduction processes. Those processes that determine what behavior a person is actually capable of performing.

Observational learning. Learning that results from attending to something. Such learning is said to occur independently of reinforcement.

Participant modeling. The kind of modeling that requires the observer to participate in the modeling experience. Typically, both the model and the observer engage in activities together that are anxiety-provoking to the observer. This kind of modeling is generally found to be the most effective.

Perceived self-efficacy. What a person *thinks* he or she is capable of doing.

Performance standards. Those standards that must be met or exceeded before one experiences self-reinforcement. If a person's performance does not meet or exceed a performance standard, he or she experiences self-punishment.

Person variables. Variables contained within the person that determine how he or she responds to a situation.

Personality coefficient. Mischel's quantification of the amount of consistency found in human behavior. He found that the correlation of behavior across time, across similar situations, and between personality questionnaires and behavior was about 0.30. This weak correlation suggested that human behavior was not nearly as consistent as it had been widely assumed to be.

Psychotherapy. With social learning theory, any procedure that corrects dysfunctional expectancies. Typically, the procedure used is some kind of modeling.

Reciprocal determinism. The contention that person variables, situation variables, and behavior constantly interact with one another. For example, the person influences the environment, the environment influences the person, and the consequences of one's behavior change both the person and the environment.

Reinforcement. Within social learning theory, reinforcement (either direct or vicarious) provides information concerning what behavior will be effective in a given situation. Also, reinforcement provides an incentive for translating learning into performance.

Retentional processes. Those processes that determine how experiences are encoded into memory for possible future use.

Self-Control. The ability to tolerate a delay in gratification.

Self-Efficacy. What a person is actually capable of doing.

Self-Efficacy expectancy. The expectancy one has concerning his or her ability to engage in effective behavior (see also self-efficacy and perceived self-efficacy).

Self-Exonerating mechanisms. Cognitive mechanisms that a person can employ to escape the self-contempt that ordinarily results when one acts contrary to an internalized moral principle.

Self-Regulated behavior. Behavior that is governed by intrinsic reinforcement and punishment. Self-regulated behavior is often directed at some major future goal, which is approached through a series of subgoals. Once goals are set, an individual organizes his or her life so as to increase the probability of their attainment. Also, much of a person's self-directed behavior is determined by his or her perceived, self-efficacy (see also delay of gratification and moral conduct).

Self-Regulatory systems and plans. The cognitive social learning person variable that determines the circumstances under which an individual experiences self-reinforcement and self-punishment. This variable also determines the setting of future goals and the formulation of plans (strategies) used in attaining those goals.

Situation variables. Variables in the environment that provide the setting in which person variables manifest themselves.

Social learning theory. As presented by Bandura and Mischel, it refers to a theory that emphasizes vicarious, symbolic, and self-regulatory processes and a continuous interaction among cognitive, behavioral, and environmental determinants of behavior. Such a theory avoids the problem of generalizing from research on nonhuman animals to humans by conducting experiments with only humans as subjects. Furthermore, the research typically is on relevant, complex human behavior.

Stimulus-Outcome expectancy. The belief that one environmental event will be followed by another specific event that has been consistently associated with the first event in the past.

Subjective values. The cognitive social learning person variable that determines under what circumstances a person will translate what has been learned into behavior. Subjective values determine what is worth having or aspiring for, and what is not.

Symbolic modeling. Modeling involving something other than a live human; for instance, a film, television, instructions, reading material, or a demonstration.

Systematic desensitization. The therapeutic procedure whereby a client is asked to imagine a series of interrelated anxiety-provoking scenes until they no longer cause anxiety.

Vicarious punishment. The punishment that comes from observing the negative consequences of another person's behavior.

Vicarious reinforcement. The reinforcement that comes from observing the positive consequences of another person's behavior.

12

Edward O. Wilson
David P. Barash

I n 1975, Edward O. Wilson published *Sociobiology: The New Synthesis* which marked the formal beginning of the discipline of **sociobiology.** In his book Wilson defines sociobiology as "The systematic study of the biological basis of all social behavior" (1975, 4). The major contention of the sociobiologists is that certain social behaviors have been selected by evolution because they contribute to the biologic fitness of those who engage in them. In other words, just as various bodily structures and physiological processes are the products of the natural selection that has occurred in our evolutionary past, so too are patterns of social behavior.

According to the sociobiologists, humans are born with several behavioral tendencies that have been naturally selected during our long evolutionary past. These tendencies are part of human nature. How various persons express, or inhibit, these tendencies is, however, to a large extent culturally determined. To understand personality, then, one must understand both biologic factors (nature) and cultural factors (nurture).

Sociobiologists attempt to demonstrate a biologic basis for such social phenomena as love, altruism, warfare, athletic and other forms of competition, societal rules and regulations, religion and morality, indoctrinability, marital systems, male and female strategies for mate selection, territoriality, child-rearing strategies, xenophobia, patriotism, aggression, nepotism, male and female societal roles, parent-child conflicts, sibling rivalry, and the female orgasm.

Although this chapter will discuss the work of several authors, it will feature the works of Edward O. Wilson and David P. Barash.

Biographical Sketches

Edward O. Wilson

Wilson was born in Birmingham, Alabama, on 10 June, 1929. He was an only child. Wilson had many colorful relatives. On his father's side, the men were mainly shipowners and river pilots, although his grandfather was a railroad engineer. During the Civil War, his paternal great-grandfather (William "Black Bill" Wilson) used his ship to smuggle guns past a federal blockade until he was captured by Admiral Farragut and sent to prison in Tampa (Wilson 1985, 466). On his mother's side his relatives were mainly farmers from northern Alabama.

Wilson's mother and father divorced when he was seven, and he was raised by his father and stepmother. His father was a federal employee whose job required him to move frequently. Between the first and twelfth grades Wilson attended sixteen schools. The numerous school changes, along with the fact that Wilson skipped third grade because of exceptional performance, steered him in the direction of his later career choice. Because he was a perpetual newcomer, without siblings, and younger than his classmates, he took to the woods and fields, where he found surrogate companionship in the organisms he discovered and studied there (Wilson 1985, 465).

Wilson fell in love with the outdoors and the organisms found there; he could

Edward O. Wilson

easily have become a zoologist if it were not for a childhood accident. At the age of seven he lost the sight in his right eye by accidentally jerking a fish fin into it. As a result of his monocular vision, he found it difficult to locate birds and mammals in the field. The vision in his left eye, however, became, and remains, exceptionally acute. "I am the last to spot a hawk sitting in a tree, but I can examine the hairs and contours of an insect's body without the aid of a magnifying glass" (Wilson 1985, 466).

Wilson was also slightly hearing impaired. So, not only was he unable to see various species of birds, he was also unable to hear their songs. Thus, it was Wilson's love of nature combined with his monocular vision and his hearing difficulty that led him in the direction of **entomology** (the study of insects).

Wilson majored in biology at the University of Alabama, where he obtained his B.S. in 1949 and his M.S. in 1950. He received his Ph.D. in biology from Harvard in 1955. Wilson joined the Harvard faculty in 1956, was promoted to full professor in 1964, and became Frank B. Baird, Jr., Professor of Science in 1976. He was given the National Medal of Science by President Carter in 1977. In *The Insect Societies* (1971) Wilson attempted to explain the behavior of social insects using principles from physiology, population biology, and evolutionary theory. Wilson extended these principles to all organisms in *Sociobiology: The New Synthesis* (1975). Only the last chapter of Wilson's 1975 book pertained to humans, whereas in *On Human Nature* (1978) Wilson focused exclusively on human social behavior. Wilson was awarded the Pulitzer Prize for *On Human Nature* in 1979. He is currently the curator in entomology at the Museum of Comparative Zoology at Harvard. As of July 1987 Wilson had authored or coauthored ten books and about 310 technical articles focusing mainly on social insects and evolutionary theory. Barash (1982) says affectionately of Wilson "Long before jogging became a national fad, E. O. Wilson was an enthusiastic runner—both with his legs and with new concepts in evolutionary biology" (5).

David P. Barash

Barash was born in New York City on 9 January, 1946. He obtained his B.A. in biology in 1966 from the State University of New York (SUNY) Binghamton (then known as Harpur College), and his M.A. in 1968 and his Ph.D. in 1970 from the University of Wisconsin. Barash taught for three years at SUNY, Oneonta, before moving to the University of Washington in 1973, where he has been ever since. Barash is currently professor of psychology at the University of Washington.

Barash's books *The Whisperings Within* (1979), *Evolution and the Origin of Human Nature* (1979), and *Sociobiology and Behavior* (2d ed., 1982) have done much to extend and popularize sociobiology. In the foreword of the latter book, E. O. Wilson said, "*Sociobiology and Behavior* is the best introductory textbook available on the subject, and it is not likely to be surpassed in the near future" (xi). Currently Barash's general concern is with specifying the problems that result when cultural evolution proceeds at a much faster rate than biologic evolution. This concern is addressed in his book *The Hare and the Tortoise* (1986). The "hare" is fast-moving cultural evolution, and the "tortoise" is slow-moving biologic evolution. Barash believes that much of what is wrong with humanity today stems from the incompatibility between human culture and human biology. "This incongruity (literally: an inability to fit): between our biology, which has evolved by the labo-

David P. Barash

rious process of natural selection, and our culture, which has appeared with explosive speed through cultural evolution, is the root of nearly every human difficulty'' (60). Barash is especially concerned with the problems that result when prenuclear thought processes and brain mechanisms are used to deal with a world in which nuclear weapons are a reality. With his psychiatrist wife, Judith Eve Lipton, Barash wrote *Stop Nuclear War! A Handbook* (1982) and *The Caveman and the Bomb* (1985). Most recently he has published *The Arms Race and Nuclear War* (1987).

Darwin's Theory of Evolution

Because to a large extent, sociobiology is an effort to apply Darwinian evolutionary theory to the explanation of human social behavior, we will spend a moment reviewing Darwinian theory.

Darwin observed that all species of living organisms are capable of producing more offspring than environmental resources can support. When this happens a **struggle for survival** occurs. Because individual differences exist among members of a species in terms of the traits necessary for survival, only those persons possessing traits allowing **adaptation** (successful adjustment) to the environment survive and reproduce. If the traits that allow adaptation to an environment are at least partially heritable, the offspring of parents who previously survived in that environment will also tend to possess traits conducive to survival. This tendency will continue to be true as long as the environment does not radically change. The term **survival of the fittest** refers to the fact that only those members of a species who are best adapted to their environment survive and reproduce. **Fitness,** then, is measured by an organism's ability to survive and reproduce, and nothing else. Crawford (1987) cautions us not to confuse fitness with social standing: "It is essential to distinguish biological fitness from social standing. Michelangelo, Isaac Newton, and Leonardo da Vinci had zero reproductive fitness since they apparently did not leave offspring. However, their social standing is beyond question" (16). Also fitness is often equated with such factors as physical size, strength, or aggressiveness. As we have just seen, however, an organism's fitness is determined only by its ability to survive and reproduce in a given environment, and this ability often involves complex behavior patterns that are anything but aggressive. As we shall see, the tendencies to like and eat ripe fruit, to love children, and to cooperate with fellow humans can all be fitness enhancing, but none involves aggression. Within Darwinian theory, any anatomic structure, physiological process, or pattern of behavior is said to be adaptive if it contributes to an organism's ability to survive and reproduce. The term **natural selection** refers to the fact that only organisms possessing adaptive traits in a given environment are "selected" to survive and reproduce. Naturally selected characteristics, then, are those that increase the chances of survival in the struggle for existence.

Inclusive Fitness

When Darwin published his theory of evolution he knew nothing about genes. All that he knew was that persons possessing adaptive characteristics tended to leave more persons like themselves in future generations than persons possessing fewer adaptive characteristics. For Darwin, fitness was assessed by counting the number of offspring produced by a person. If Darwin had known about genes he may have defined fitness in terms of the number of *genes* (or more accurately, replicas of genes) that a person leaves in subsequent generations; however, he did not. The difference between defining fitness in terms of offspring or in terms of gene replicas is a highly significant one. It is true that the most direct way to perpetuate one's genes is to produce offspring, but it is not the only way because one's offspring are not the only persons carrying one's genes. One's brothers and sisters, nieces and nephews, and aunts and uncles also carry one's genes. Thus, in addition to producing offspring, another way of perpetuating one's genes is to help one's relatives survive and reproduce.

The fact that persons can perpetuate their genes into subsequent generations either by having offspring or by helping relatives survive and reproduce significantly expands traditional Darwinian theory. It is this expanded theory of evolution that is accepted by sociobiology. Instead of concentrating exclusively on a person's ability to survive and create offspring (fitness), sociobiology concentrates on the many other ways that a person can increase the probability of his or her genes being represented in subsequent generations. This expanded notion of gene reproduction is called **inclusive fitness,** which Silverman (1987) describes as "undoubtably the most heuristic, sociobiological principle of the past two decades" (214). The concept of inclusive fitness, although suggested by others earlier, including Darwin himself (1859, 250–57), was most fully developed in two highly influential papers by W. D. Hamilton (1964). The notion of inclusive fitness is used by the sociobiologists to explain various social phenomena and we will, therefore, return to it often throughout this chapter.

Basic Assumptions of Sociobiology

Perpetuation of the Genes

According to the sociobiologists, whether we know it or not, our primary goal in life is to perpetuate our genes into the next generation, which was also true of our ancestors. It is because of the natural selection of genes that we now possess the kinds of brains, minds, bodies, and behavioral tendencies that we do.

Even though the perpetuation of our genes is the master motive in life, it controls much of what we do without our being aware of that control. "Genes need not know what they are doing in order to function effectively, and—here is the painful part—neither need we. We can spend a whole lifetime serving their purposes without ever knowing it" (Barash 1979, 25).

This assumption, then, underlies all of sociobiology: *We live to pass our genes into the next generation.* Everything we do serves this goal, or, if not, is deleterious to us. Those experiences that are neither biologically helpful nor harmful are irrelevant. One may argue, however, that life seems to involve so much more than doing those things necessary to perpetuate one's genes. Perhaps it does just *seem* that way. Wallace (1979) comments:

So what does all this make us? Genetic caretakers? Temporary housings for chromosomes? Slaves to tiny, coiled molecules that operate us by remote control? Ponderous robots, full of rationalizations, explanations, superstitions, and excuses but blindly following the Reproductive Imperative? What about the fact that we are learning classical guitar? That we have an interest in tap dancing and may start lessons soon? That we are very tidy and responsible and hold darned good jobs? That we have read Camus and don't pronounce the "s"? That we have good, really good, friends? That we are fine people and our parents are proud of us? How about all that? Chromosomes make us do all that? "No," comes the answer from the mountain, "but they don't care if you do"—*as long as* it doesn't interfere with your reproduction. Being such a splendid person may even help you find a mate more easily and leave *more* genes. (183)

Natural Selection Shapes Social Behavior

A second basic assumption that sociobiologists make is that evolution selects certain patterns of social behavior just as it selects certain anatomic structures or physiological mechanisms. Lumsden and Wilson (1981) say: "The central tenet of sociobiology is that social behaviors are shaped by natural selection" (99). The assumption is that complex social behaviors such as courting, associating with friends, and caring for children can be as much related to fitness as are certain anatomic or physiological characteristics. That is, people who are *socially* effective are more adaptive than those who are not. If this assumption is correct, it means that much of our current social behavior is engaged in because similar behavior was adaptive for our ancestors.

This sociobiologic view of human social behavior may be disturbing to some, but the fact that it is disturbing does not mean that it is necessarily incorrect and should be rejected. Any objective seeker of truth cannot disregard facts simply because they are not to his or her liking. Barash (1979) comments:

> We human beings like to think we are different. We introspect, we are confident that we know what we are doing, and why. But we may have to open our minds and admit the possibility that our need to maximize our fitness may be whispering somewhere deep within us and that, know it or not, most of the time we are heeding these whisperings. (31)

Because sociobiology may be disturbing does not mean that it is necessarily correct either. The objective inquirer will weigh the actual evidence offered to support or refute sociobiology (or any other theory), and arrange his or her beliefs accordingly.

Nature of Human Nature

A theory of human nature attempts to describe what it means to be human. Theories of human nature are extremely important within the realm of personality theory because every theory of personality accepts a theory of human nature either explicitly or implicitly. Here we will discuss only two theories of human nature: the empirical and the sociobiologic.

Empirical Theory

The **empirical theory of human nature** maintains that what characterizes a person at any given time is a function of what that person has experienced in his or her lifetime. Although John Locke (1631–1704) was not the first to offer an empirical view of human nature, his was among the most clearly articulated. According to Locke, the mind is a *tabula rasa* (a blank tablet) at birth and experience writes on that tablet. For Locke, what you become as a person depends on what you experience. According to this view of human nature the environment is all important in determining human behavior. Other than this capacity to become whatever you experience, a concept of human nature does not exist. We come equipped with *no* inherited predispositions. In chapter 9 we noted that J. B. Watson believed that if he could control the environments of healthy infants he could make them into any kind of adult you may specify. Other learning theorists, for example, Dollard and Miller, and Skinner, are a bit more specific in that they claim that behavior is controlled by the reinforcement contingencies found in the environment. Reinforcement theorists also accept an empirical theory of human nature, because they believe that if you change the environment (reinforcement contingencies) you change the person.

Sociobiologic Theory

The sociobiologists strongly disagree with the empirical theory of human nature. Their entire theory is built on the assumption that the human mind is much more than a blank tablet at birth. Instead, they see the mind as programmed by evolution to cause its possessor to act in certain ways and not in others. Sociobiologists are interested in **cultural universals** because they assume that if a category of social behavior appears in every culture, chances are good that it is genetically influenced. Such a category of behavior could not have been transmitted from one culture to another because, in many cases, no way could have existed for cultures to communicate with each other. Exactly how a particular category of experience is responded to may vary from culture to culture, but the category itself is responded to in some way and is therefore a cultural universal. Barash (1979) explains:

> Human beings are, after all, still human beings, and as such, there is a certain range within which their behavior will fall. They may develop distinctive customs of dress and adornment, perhaps parrot feathers in one place, strange patterns of head shaving in another, the ritual carving of deep scars on cheeks and foreheads in yet another, but some pattern of dress and adornment is always found. Similarly, marriage in one place might be sanctified by a ceremonial sharing of food, or maybe by the union of menstrual blood with semen, or by the payment of tokens from one partner to the other or by signing a document and uttering officially approved words, but some ritualized sanctioning of male-female association seems almost always to take place. . . . While it is true that culture makes people, people

also make cultures, and there is much to gain by looking at what remains the same about people underneath their customs and habits. (4–5)

Biogrammar.   According to Barash (1979, 10), just as a grammar structures our verbal behavior, a **biogrammar** structures our social behavior. The rules of grammar allow ideas to be expressed in many ways without the essential meaning of those ideas being lost. Biogrammar allows innate social behavior tendencies to be expressed in many ways without the essential function of that behavior being lost. People may learn different languages in different cultures, but *the capacity for humans to learn some language* is universal.

The sociobiologists believe that social science has provided little information as to why people act as they do, and the reason for this failure is social science's widespread acceptance of the empirical theory of human nature. For the sociobiologists, the empirical view of human nature has not been informative, heuristic, or flattering.

> If we maintain that there is no "us" located inside, beneath or beyond our customs, we are in danger of missing ourselves altogether. For anyone concerned about human dignity I would happily recommend a sociobiological recognition of human nature grounded in evolution over the extreme social science view that people are merely empty shells waiting for culture to fill them up, ghostly actors waiting for their lines. (Barash 1979, 13)

So for the sociobiologists, a human nature indeed exists. During our long evolutionary past those of our ancestors that possessed genes that caused them to engage in adaptive behavior survived and reproduced. The genes that caused adaptive behavior were perpetuated, those that did not, were not. Thus, according to the **sociobiologic theory of human nature** each human being is well endowed at birth with the genetically determined behavioral tendencies that allowed his or her ancestors to survive and reproduce.

Proximate versus Ultimate Causation

What one seeks and accepts as a cause of behavior also varies with one's conception of human nature. Those accepting the empirical theory of human nature tend to seek the causes of an organism's behavior in its immediate environment, its current motivational state, its memories of past experiences, or in some combination of the three. These environmental, physiological, and experiential factors constitute the **proximate causation** of behavior. Social scientists tend to explain human behavior in terms of proximate causation. For example, in answer to the question "What causes learning?" the learning theorist might say that learning occurs when, in a given environmental situation, an organism does something that produces a result that it wants, or that learning occurs when two stimuli are consistently experienced together. These and other explanations of learning offered by learning theorists stress proximate causation.

In contrast, the sociobiologists attempt to explain why a characteristic was selected and maintained by evolutionary pressures. That is, the sociobiologists seek to discover the adaptive significance of various behaviors, sensory capabilities, and physiological mechanisms. Why, they ask, does the human body maintain its temperature within certain limits? Why do humans, and other animals, have the ability to learn from experience? Why are some experiences learned more easily than others? Why, for example, are some phobias so easy to learn and so difficult to forget? Why do some species of animals learn with ease what other species learn with great difficulty or not at all? Why can we see some colors, hear some sounds, taste some tastes, smell some odors, and not others? Why do we tend to love children, especially our own? By seeking the evolutionary significance of abilities and behaviors, sociobiologists are seeking their **ultimate causation.**

The sociobiologists believe, however, that a complete explanation of behavior must involve both proximate and ultimate explanations. It is important to know under what circumstances a behavior occurs in an organism's lifetime (proximate causation), but it is equally important to know why that behavior potential exists in that organism's behavioral repertoire to begin with (ultimate causation).

Why Are Some Behaviors "Sweeter" Than Others?

In his book *The Whisperings Within* (1979) Barash addresses the question "Why is sugar sweet?" He first answers the specific question and then turns to a question of crucial importance to sociobiologists: "Why are some behaviors sweeter (more desirable, likely) than other behaviors?" First, Barash's explanation as to why sugar is sweet to us.

> The reason is clear enough: we are primates, and some of our ancestors spent a great deal of time in trees, where they ate a great deal of fruit. Ripe fruit is more nutritious than unripe, and one thing about ripe fruit is that it contains sugars. It doesn't take much imagination to reconstruct the evolutionary sequence that selected for a strong preference among our distant ancestors for the taste that characterized ripe fruit. Genes that influenced their carriers to eat ripe fruit and reject the unripe ultimately made more copies of themselves than did those that were less discriminating. (Barash 1979, 39)

Now we will address the more crucial question: "Why are some *behaviors* sweeter than others?" What really is being asked is why, under certain circumstances, does acting one way feel better, more natural, or more satisfying than acting another way? The answer to this question offered by the sociobiologists forms the heart of sociobiology. Their answer is that our evolutionary past has genetically programmed us to respond to certain situations with any one of a certain range of possible responses. Those behaviors compatible with our biogrammar will be sweet, those incompatible will not be. Barash puts the matter as follows: "The process of evolution, operating on human beings, has produced a creature for whom certain behaviors just don't go at all, whereas others go very well indeed" (1979, 11). According to the sociobiologists, then, those behaviors that we find sweet are those that increased the fitness of our ancestors. Sweetness and fitness go hand in hand. For example, it is sweet for us to love our children and for them to love us, but why is it sweet? Barash (1979) answers:

> Here we are back in the realm of evolutionary events, where human inclinations are so often revealed as the handmaidens of fitness. We love our children "be-

cause" it is adaptive for us to do so. Love of parent for child is an evolutionary strategem insuring that parents will invest in the child in a manner that maximizes each parent's fitness. The child, of course, is equally motivated to love its parents "because" such an attachment to appropriate adults enhances its own chances of ultimate evolutionary success. In other words, parental and filial love, solicitude and care are ultimately selfish. (94)

All of the usual reasons given by parents for loving their children, such as, because they are so cute, or helpless, or because it feels good to love them, constitute proximate causes of parental love. The ultimate cause, however, is the fact that surviving offspring perpetuate the genes of the parents.

According to the sociobiologists, then, any behavior that increases a person's inclusive fitness will be sweet and will therefore be preferred over other behaviors. If this sounds selfish it is because it is selfish. It is assumed that everything living organisms do is selfish, humans included.

What Is Inherited?

It is extremely important to note that the sociobiologists do not say that the genes are the only cause of human social behavior, or even that they are the primary cause. Rather, they say that we inherit behavioral *tendencies*, and that these tendencies are always modified by culture. Social behavior, then, is always the result of the *interaction* between biologic and cultural influences. For the title of his book, *The Whisperings Within* (1979), Barash chose the term **"whisperings"** to describe our inherited predispositions; he did not choose terms such as, "shoutings," "yellings," "cravings," or "urges." A whisper is a whisper. It is a slight biologic push to act in some general way as opposed to others. It is even possible for culture to inhibit many of these behavioral tendencies altogether. What the genes provide, according to the sociobiologists, is a **behavioral potentiality** and not a strict **biologic determinism.** The sociobiologists, therefore, do not draw a direct cause-and-effect relationship between genes and behavior.

Our biogrammar, then, provides only a general game plan for social behavior. A genetic tendency exists to adorn one's body, but how it is adorned is culturally determined. A genetic tendency exists to learn a language, but which language one learns is culturally determined. A genetic tendency exists to attend to a child's needs, but how children are reared is culturally determined.

The sociobiologists fully appreciate the contributions of both biology and culture in determining human social behavior. Barash (1979) urges all who attempt to explain such behavior to avoid **nothing butism,** which is:

The notion that just because we are animals we are nothing but animals. And, again, the opposite is equally misleading: beware the notion that we are "nothing but" the products of social learning. For too long social science and biological science have pursued "nothing but" approaches. Sociobiology may just help redress that imbalance. (45)

Relationship between Biology and Culture

Innate Tendency to Create Culture

According to the sociobiologists, one of our whisperings predisposes us to create and participate in a culture of some sort. Barash (1979) says: "Culture is, in fact, one of our most important biologic adaptations, and it therefore need not be opposed to biology. In behaving culturally, we are also behaving biologically. Our culture is natural to us, just as quills are natural to a porcupine" (221).

Limitations of Culture as a Modifier of Human Behavior

Culture is a powerful modifier of human behavior, but it is not all-powerful. The range of behaviors that can occur within a category of social behavior is often vast, but a range still exists. In other words, our biologic heritage places a limit on the extent to which our behavior is modifiable by culture. Wilson (1978) warns what might happen if we tried to live in accordance with social systems that were too incompatible with our biologic nature.

> It is inconceivable that human beings could be socialized into the radically different repertories of other groups such as fishes, birds, antelopes, or rodents. Human beings might self-consciously *imitate* such arrangements, but it would be a fiction played out on a stage, would run counter to deep emotional responses and have no chance of persisting through as much as a single generation. To adopt with serious intent, even in broad outline, the social system of a nonprimate species would be insanity in the literal sense. Personalities would quickly dissolve, relationships disintegrate, and reproduction cease. (21–22)

We have seen that the sociobiologists believe that human nature can be described in terms of whispers or a biogrammar, which is reflected in cultural universals. Because we inherit only behavioral tendencies from our evolutionary past, human culture can, and does, take many forms. For a culture to last and for the people living under its influence to remain mentally healthy, however, a reasonable compatibility must occur between that culture and the human biogrammar. As we saw earlier, Barash, in his book *The Hare and the Tortoise: Culture, Biology, and Human Nature* (1986), discusses the many problems that result from the fact that human culture is evolving much faster than is human biology. Barash (1986) sees the increasing discrepancy between human culture and human biology as the cause of many, if not most, of our interpersonal, international, environmental, and societal problems.

> The hare and the tortoise: culture and biology have been racing within us throughout our history. In recent years the hare has been accelerating mightily and the gap between the two has been widening. Reworking the analogy: we have one foot on the tortoise and the other on the hare. As they get farther apart, we are stretched more and more. It's getting awfully uncomfortable. (319)

The discrepancy between our biology and our culture is especially disturbing to Barash in the area of modern warfare as is evidenced in the title of the book that he coauthored with his wife, Judith Eve Lipton, *The Caveman and the Bomb: Human Nature, Evolution, and Nuclear War* (1985).

Leash Principle.   In fact, our biogrammar normally functions to keep culture compatible with our biologic makeup. This is because we are genetically predisposed to seek experiences and establish institutions that enhance our genetic fitness. Wilson (1980) describes his **leash principle:** "The genes hold culture on a leash. In some categories of behavior—eating, voiding, and the basic facial expressions, the predisposition toward sexual behavior—the leash is short and tight. In others—the form of dress, religious ritual, artistic expression—it is very long and flexible" (64). We will have more to say about the leash principle when we discuss "mind-body relationships" shortly.

Hypertrophy.   One way for biology and culture to be incompatible is for biology to be overrepresented in culture. The tendency for a relatively weak biologic tendency to be amplified out of proportion in culture is what Wilson calls **hypertrophy.** Wilson (1978) defines hypertrophy as: "The cultural inflation of innate human properties" (172). Wilson (1978) believes that civilization itself exemplifies hypertrophy: "In my opinion the key to the emergence of civilization is *hypertrophy*, the extreme growth of preexisting structures. . . . the basic social responses of the hunter-gatherers have metamorphosed from relatively modest environmental adaptation into unexpectedly elaborate, even monstrous forms in more advanced societies" (92).

What Wilson calls hypertrophy Barash (1986) calls *cultural hyperextension* about which Barash says: "Rather than setting itself in opposition to innate human inclinations, culture often seeks to mimic and extend these inclinations, in the process outdoing nature itself and going too far" (58). According to Barash (1986) the male physical and behavioral traits that led to the male domination over women were selected because, at the time, male aggressiveness, competitiveness, and defense of the family enhanced male fitness. Under current circumstances, however, these traits are essentially obsolete. Barash (1986) elaborates:

> We are stuck, saddled with an outdated biological system, rendered anachronistic by our rapidly evolving culture, and unacceptable by our expanding social consciousness. We possess physical characteristics and behaviors such as male dominance and aggressiveness that are offensive, inappropriate, and often down right dangerous. . . . It seems especially likely that society, seizing on a degree of evolutionary reality, has hyperextended it, making awkward, unjust, and offensive cultural mountains out of what may, in essence, be biological molehills. Men and women are indeed different, but in most cases they are less different than human social traditions have demanded them to be. Give cultural evolution a hand in such cases, and it takes the whole arm, ultimately, perhaps, to the detriment of all concerned. (105–106)

Human biology, then, can be underrepresented in culture, and it can be overrepresented; in either case, problems can result. In general, it seems best if biology is adequately represented in culture. As we shall see, however, that does not mean that what is natural is necessarily good. The sociobiologists believe that in certain instances, cultures should expend resources to inhibit natural human tendencies. We will see examples of such times later in this chapter.

Mind-Body Relationship

As we noted in chapter 1, determining how the mind and body are related has been a persistent problem in psychology's history. As the reader may recall, the problem is determining how something purely mental (for example, consciousness, ideas, awareness, or rationality) can result from something purely physical (for example, the brain). Unlike most who study human behavior the sociobiologists tackle the mind-body problem enthusiastically. Barash (1979) says:

> The mind-body problem is an ancient one: a tremendous gap seems to exist between our unique, personal thoughts and emotions on the one hand and the cells, chemicals and electrical circuits that make up our brains on the other. Yet the human mind—its conscious as well as its unconscious aspects, its thoughts as well as its emotions—springs somehow from the concrete, impersonal human brain, and that brain is the product of evolution. . . . Our bodies . . . are the vehicles created by our genes in the service of themselves. And our minds are among the devices that serve to control those bodies. Both the cellular structure of the brain and the psychic structure of consciousness are the results of millions of generations of evolution, during which genes that were more successful at reproducing themselves prospered at the expense of those that were less adept. Our genes have programmed us and every other living thing to do what is best for them. Our minds are likely to serve that ultimate end no less than are our hands or our kidneys. (199–200)

Epigenetic Rules. In *Genes, Mind, and Culture: The Coevolutionary Process* (1981), Lumsden and Wilson describe how they believe the genes influence the mind. It is postulated that environmental experience is filtered through and mediated by innate **epigenetic rules** before one cognitively experiences and acts on environmental information. Lumsden and Wilson (1981) discuss two kinds of epigenetic rules: **primary epigenetic rules,** which determine what kinds of sensory experiences and perceptions we can have; and **secondary epigenetic rules,** which determine how those sensations and perceptions are evaluated and responded to emotionally. Both levels of information processing are the product of evolution and therefore have adaptive significance. The first level, for example, determines what can be a biologic stimulus for a human being. Primary epigenetic rules determine what can be seen, heard, smelled, tasted and felt. Secondary epigenetic rules determine which of those sensations or perceptions are attended to, retained, learned, and responded to with an appropriate emotional response. Secondary epigenetic rules also determine what courses of action, if any, will be taken in response to various sensations or perceptions.

According to Lumsden and Wilson (1981), it is the epigenetic rules (mainly the secondary ones) that hold culture on a leash. Because they are innate in all humans, the epigenetic rules will always make some decisions, evaluations, emotional responses, learning experiences, and memories more likely than others. Wilson (1980) says: "Long-term defections from the innate censors and motivators of the brain can only produce an ultimate dissatisfaction of the spirit and eventually social instability and massive losses in genetic fitness'' (69).

Prepared Learning.   Among other things, the secondary epigenetic rules predispose humans to learn some experiences much more easily than others. The fact that we are biologically disposed to learn with ease those experiences that enhance fitness is referred to as **prepared learning.** Thus we readily learn the rules and regulations that characterize our culture, we learn a language, we learn incest avoidance, we learn those qualities necessary to attract a mate, and we learn to distrust strangers. The development of phobias also exemplifies prepared learning.

> The preparedness of human learning is most clearly manifested in the case of phobias, which are fears defined by a combination of several traits. They are first of all extreme in response. . . . They typically emerge full-blown after only a single negative reinforcement [and] they are exceptionally difficult to extinguish. . . . It is a remarkable fact that the phenomena that evoke these reactions consistently (closed spaces, heights, thunderstorms, running water, snakes, and spiders) include some of the greatest dangers present in mankind's ancient environment, while guns, knives, automobiles, electric sockets, and other far more dangerous perils of technologically advanced societies are rarely effective. It is reasonable to conclude that phobias are the extreme cases of irrational fear reactions that gave an extra margin needed to ensure survival during the genetic evolutions of human epigenetic rules. Better to crawl away from a cliff, nauseated with fear, than to casually walk its edge. (Lumsden & Wilson 1981, 84–85)

Thus, according to the sociobiologists, the structure and processes of our mind exist because they were adaptive to our ancestors; that is, they enhanced their fitness.

Altruism

If human behavior is ultimately selfish why do we spend so much time doing things that benefit our fellow humans? Is the unselfish, or altruistic, nature of these actions illusory? According to the sociobiologists the answer is yes, it is illusory. Barash (1979) says: "Real, honest-to-God altruism simply doesn't occur in nature" (135). This statement does not mean that people do not help each other; clearly they do. According to the sociobiologists, however, they do so for reasons that are ultimately selfish. The sociobiologists discuss two kinds of **"altruism"**: one that involves blood relatives (kin) and one that does not.

Kin Altruism

In his theory, Darwin emphasized an organism's ability to adapt to its environment and to successfully reproduce. The sociobiologists have emphasized, however, the fact that because our relatives possess copies of many of our genes, we have reason to be concerned with their survival and reproduction. The closer the degree of genetic relationship, the deeper will be our concern and the greater will be our willingness to help them. The offering of help to genetic relatives is called **kin altruism.** This is not true altruism, because, in looking out for one's relatives, we are actually looking out for ourselves (or more accurately, for our genes).

As we saw earlier, when fitness is seen as perpetuating one's genes into future generations by producing offspring or by helping relatives survive and reproduce, it is called *inclusive fitness.* When a person's genes are perpetuated (or selected) because that person confers advantages on his or her relatives, the process is called **kin selection.** Thus, kin selection is accomplished through kin altruism. **Nepotism** is another term for kin altruism. Both terms refer to the tendency to show favoritism toward one's relatives. Because this tendency is culturally universal, the sociobiologists suggest that it has a biologic basis.

> In maximizing its inclusive fitness, each living thing is expected to devalue relatives proportionately as they are more distantly related—that is, as they share fewer genes with the would-be altruist. A brother or child "counts" one-half as much as one's self, a cousin one-eighth, and so on. (Barash 1979, 136)

Reciprocal Altruism

Altruism among nonrelatives is called **reciprocal altruism** (Trivers 1971), and it is based on the evolutionary fact that humans who cooperate with one another have a better chance of surviving than those who do not. In primitive times, humans who cooperated in the hunting of large animals or in defending their village had a better chance of surviving than those who did not. Reciprocal altruism is based on the assumption that if I help you, you, at some time in the future, will help me. With reciprocal altruism you "do unto others as you would have others do unto you," and you are willing to "scratch another person's back" if you are convinced that someday he or she will scratch yours. The person returning the help may be the same one who received it (*direct reciprocity*) or it may be returned by someone else in the social group (*indirect reciprocity*). Indirect reciprocity is more likely to occur within a social system in which helping others is encouraged by rules and regulations, and accepting help without offering it to others (cheating) is actively discouraged or punished.

Wilson argues that it is the human capacity for reciprocal altruism that makes civilized society possible. He describes what the human condition would be like if only kin altruism existed.

> Altruism based on kin selection is the enemy of civilization. If human beings are to a large extent guided by programmed learning rules and canalized emotional development to favor their own relatives and tribe, only a limited amount of global harmony is possible. International cooperation will approach an upper limit, from which it will be knocked down by the perturbations of war and economic struggle, canceling each upward surge based on pure reason. The imperatives of blood and territory will be the passions to which reason is slave. (1978, 163–64)

Cheating.   With reciprocal altruism there is always the possibility that **cheating** will occur. That is, someone will take and not give or take more than they give. Barash (1979) elaborates:

A system of this sort is vulnerable, as any good con man knows. Why not take the altruism from another, then refuse to pay it back? If this happens, genes for altruism are at a disadvantage, since they incur a cost but no benefit. And cheaters gain doubly, since they profit once from the others' altruism and again by never incurring the cost of repayment. Perhaps crime does pay.

Of course, the evolutionary process can be as calculating as the cheater, maybe more so. If selfish individuals are cheating in a reciprocal system, selection would favor those altruists who could discriminate true reciprocators from those who had cheated the last time around. It could become a never-ending spiral: greater care by would-be reciprocators selects for greater slyness on the part of the cheaters, which in turn selects for greater discrimination by the altruists, and so on. Where does it all lead? Just look around. (158–59)

In everyday life we usually develop a sense of a person's willingness to play according to the rules—that is, to take from others only if he or she is willing to give. Cheaters are trying to get more than they give and we label such persons as sleazy, selfish, inconsiderate, liars, or just plain cheats. If possible, such persons are avoided. Also, society does whatever it can to reward reciprocators and punish cheaters. The sociobiologists believe that many ethical, moral, and religious systems have developed as ways of dealing with, or preventing, cheating in a system of reciprocal altruism.

Thus, according to the sociobiologists, we agree to help our close relatives because in doing so we are promoting our own fitness, and we agree to help non-relatives because we expect that they, or some other member of the community, will help us in return. In neither case is true altruism (giving help and expecting nothing in return) involved. True altruism, however, seems to occur on some occasions. What about the famous Japanese kamikaze pilots who flew to their deaths by diving into American ships during World War II? Because these pilots were sacrificing their lives for their country, should one consider their actions truly altruistic? Before deciding, Barash (1979, 168) asks that the following facts be considered: The kamikazes were promised eternal life if they died for their country, they were given national recognition and special privileges (including sexual privileges), and their families gained status. Also, when the moment for self-sacrifice came, if they refused to fly they were shot. If they did take off they had no parachute and only enough gasoline to make it to their target. Barash (1979) concludes: "Perhaps there is a question here whether the bargain these men were making was a fully altruistic one" (168).

Male and Female Criteria for Mate Selection

As should be vividly clear by now, the sociobiologists believe that the master motive for every living organism (including humans) is to perpetuate its genes into the next generation. A major variable determining whether or not one's genes will be perpetuated is mate selection. The question here is, do men and women choose mates in the same way and for the same reasons? The answer, according to the sociobiologists, is that they do not. Although the major goal of both males and females is to produce healthy offspring successfully, they use different strategies in attempting to reach that goal because of the biologic differences between them. What happens if a man and a woman copulate? Wallace (1979) facetiously describes the experience from the man's viewpoint: "A male can make up the energy expended in a sexual episode by eating a grape. His cost is low, and—who knows?— perhaps it will result in a child for him" (74). If pregnancy does result from copulation, however, the consequences for the woman are enormous. Barash (1979) explains:

> Eggs are fertilized by sperm, not vice versa. And women become pregnant, not men. It is the woman who must produce a placenta and nourish her unborn child; who must undergo the metabolic and hormonal stresses of pregnancy; who must carry around an embryo that grows in bulk and weight, making her more and more ungainly as her pregnancy advances; and who, when the child is born, must nurse it.
>
> Because women become pregnant, they simply cannot produce as many children as can men. We may regret this fact, glory in it or simply accept it, but it remains, nevertheless, an indelible part of our biology. (47).

What does all this have to do with male and female criteria for mate selection? A lot! Women have a much greater stake in any one reproductive act than do men.

> In virtually all species males are selected to be aggressive—sexual advertisers— while females are selected to be choosier—comparison shoppers. Again, these behaviors follow directly from the biology of what it is to be male or female. For males, reproduction is easy, a small amount of time, a small amount of semen, and the potential evolutionary return is very great if offspring are produced. On the other hand, a female who makes a "bad" choice may be in real evolutionary trouble. If fertilization occurs, a baby is begun, and the ensuing process is not only inexorable but immensely demanding. . . . Small wonder that females in virtually every species are more discriminating than males in the choice of sexual partners. . . . For males, a very different strategy applies. The maximum advantage goes to individuals with fewer inhibitions. A genetically influenced tendency to "play fast and loose"—"love 'em and leave 'em"—may well reflect more biological reality than most of us care to admit. (Barash 1979, 48)

Wilson (1978) makes similar points.

> If a man were given total freedom to act, he could theoretically inseminate thousands of women in his lifetime. . . . In most species, assertiveness is the most profitable male strategy. During the full period of time it takes to bring a fetus to term, from the fertilization of the egg to the birth of the infant, one male can fertilize many females but a female can be fertilized by only one male. . . . It pays males to be aggressive, hasty, fickle, and undiscriminating. In theory it is more profitable for females to be coy, to hold back until they can identify males with the best genes. In species that rear young, it is also important for the females to select males who are more likely to stay with them after insemination.
> Human beings obey this biological principle faithfully. (129–30)

Double Standard

The sexual activities of men and women are often evaluated differently. For example, male promiscuity is almost universally accepted and is often encouraged, whereas female promiscuity is simply not tolerated. Barash (1979) reviews the possible biologic reasons for this **double standard.**

> Compare these two situations: (1) you are a male animal, paired with a single female, and your "wife" goes around copulating with other males; (2) you are a female animal, paired with a single male, and your "husband" goes around copulating with other females. In which case is your fitness likely to be lower? In the first situation, if you (as male) remain faithful to your "swinging" spouse, she will eventually conceive offspring via other males, and you will have lost out in the evolutionary sweepstakes. However, in the second case, if you (as female) remain faithful to your mate, you can still breed successfully despite his philandering, provided he includes you among his girlfriends. This is the basic biology of the double standard: males are expected to be sexually less discriminating, more aggressive and more available than females. They are also expected to be more intolerant of infidelity by their wives than wives will be of infidelity by their husbands. (53)

We expect men to "come on" to women, and in most cases the man will be rejected. This reflects the fact that through the eons men have had little to lose by copulating, whereas women had much to lose if copulation was not with the right man under the right circumstances. Wallace (1979) describes a fictitious experiment that clearly reflects the double standard.

> I once facetiously suggested that my students in an "adult" class perform an experiment in which members of a pair (man and wife) would enter a crowded bar and see which sex could persuade a stranger to copulate with them first. We decided that the success of most women could be measured with a stopwatch but that the men might well require a calendar. (71)

Female Criteria for Mate Selection.   In general, women tend to seek men with quality genes (for example, genes that will produce an offspring with survival and reproductive potential); with adequate resources (for example, food, territory, shelter, and protection); and with a willingness to invest some of those resources in them and their offspring. A man's resources, then, tend to be important to females. According to Buss (1987): "In humans, resources can take many forms . . . [for example] income, occupational and social status, possessions, networks of alliance, and family background. Personality characteristics such as hard-working, ambitious, energetic, industrious, and persevering also appear to be correlated with achievement potential" (340). Women will tend to reject sexual overtures until all or most of the preceding criteria are met.

Because women can produce only a relatively small number of offspring in their lifetimes, and because they choose only men with special characteristics as mates, women tend to be a limited resource and therefore a source of male competition. Under these circumstances attractive women can choose men with the greatest resources. **Hypergamy,** or the widespread tendency for women to benefit themselves through marriage (marrying up) appears to have its roots in biology. After reviewing the data on the subject Buss (1987) concludes: "Physically attractive females tend to marry high-status males who have access to resources" (347).

Male Criteria for Mate Selection.   For many men the most important attribute in a mate is **reproductive value,** which Buss (1987) defines as: "The extent to which persons of a given age and sex (and other features) will contribute, on the average, to the ancestry of future generations" (340). According to Buss (1987) it is important to differentiate between reproductive value and **fertility:** "Fertility reflects immediate probability of reproduction, while reproductive value reflects long-term probability of reproduction" (341).

According to Buss (1987), men seeking a temporary sex partner will tend to seek women with the highest fertility (early twenties in the United States). Men seeking a long-term relationship will tend to seek women with the highest reproductive value (mid-teens in the United States). The question is: What cues do males use in assessing a woman's reproductive capability? Buss suggests that the two strongest cues are *age* and *health.* How, in our evolutionary past, however, was age determined?

> In our evolutionary past prior to the development of counting systems . . . age was not a characteristic that could be evaluated directly. Instead, cues that correlated with age and health could be used by males to identify reproductively capable females. Physical appearance probably provides the strongest set of cues, and these include features such as clear, smooth, and unblemished skin, lustrous hair, white teeth, clear eyes, and full lips. . . . Behavioral cues such as spritely gait and high activity level also provide cues to youth.
>
> According to this evolutionary argument, males should come to value and view as attractive those physical and behavioral cues in potential mates that correlate with female reproductive capability. (Buss 1987, 341)

By contrast, age should be less of a factor in female mate selection because age does not provide a reliable cue concerning a man's ability to fertilize eggs. Much data need to be collected and analyzed before the predictions based on evolutionary theory concerning mate selection can be accepted or rejected. Some data, however, already appear to substantiate the predictions suggested earlier. Buss (1987) reviews seven studies of mate selection criteria that occurred during a period of more than forty years. These studies and their major findings are summarized in Table 12–1. The data support the contention that for women the most important variables in mate selection are those qualities directly or indirectly related to resources, and for men, the variables all involve physical attractiveness.

About the results of these studies, Buss (1987) says: "This sex difference does not appear to be a transient generational phenomenon, and the magnitude of this sex difference does not appear to have changed over the past 40 years. . . . The findings are so consistent across studies that they qualify as among the most robust and consistently replicated psychological findings that have been documented across several generations" (344).

Biology of Mating Arrangements

As we have seen, the most effective reproductive strategy for men is to mate with as many women as possible. As far as marital arrangements are concerned this means that **polygyny,** the reproduction system in which one man mates with more

Table 12–1.
Summary of Seven
Studies on Sex
Differences in Mate
Selection Criteria
Done during a
Period of More Than
Forty Years

AUTHORS	YEAR	SAMPLE SIZE	METHOD	FEMALES VALUE MORE	MALES VALUE MORE
Hill	1945	600	Ratings	Ambition & industrious; good financial prospect	Good looking
Langhorne & Secord	1955	5000	Nominations	Getting ahead; ambitious; enjoys work; high-status profession; good provider; wealth	Physical attractiveness
McGinnis	1958	120	Ratings	Ambition & industrious; favorable social status; good financial prospect	Good looks
Hudson & Henze	1969	566	Ratings	Ambition & industrious; favorable social status; good financial prospect	Good looks
Buss	1985	162	Rankings	Good earning capacity	Physical attractiveness
Buss & Barnes*	1986	186	Ratings	Good earning capacity; ambitious & career-oriented	Good looking Physically attractive
Buss & Barnes	1986	100	Rankings	Good earning capacity	Physically attractive

* This sample was composed of married couples between the ages of twenty and forty-two.

(From Buss 1987, p. 345.)

than one woman is probably the most natural one for men. Such an arrangement is also conducive to the woman's fitness because it allows each woman involved to reproduce. **Polyandry,** the reproductive system in which one woman mates with more than one man is very rare.

> About three-fourths of all human societies permit the taking of multiple wives, and most of them encourage the practice by law and custom. In contrast, marriage to multiple husbands is sanctioned in less than one percent of societies. The remaining monogamous societies usually fit that category in a legal sense only, with concubinage and other extramarital stratagems being added to allow *de facto* polygyny. (Wilson 1978, 130)

About **monogamy,** a reproductive system consisting of one man and one woman, Barash (1979) says:

> Monogamy is rare in mammals, almost unheard of in primates, and, despite our
> Judeo-Christian fondness for the "nuclear family," it appears to be a relatively
> recent invention of certain human cultures. Our biology may permit this social
> form, but it certainly doesn't demand it—and may not even like it. (65–66)

Thus, according to the sociobiologists, not only are men biologically inclined
toward multiple mates but, typically, the marital arrangement sanctioned by a
society reflects this male inclination. That is, in most societies men can legally have
more than one mate and in cultures in which such an arrangement is not sanctioned,
many men follow their promiscuous urges illegally—another manifestation of the
double standard.

Biology of Parenting

Barash (1979) points out that parenting has been, and is, largely the job of the
women.

> There is no human society, historically or in recent times, in which women have
> not borne the primary responsibility for child care. Parenting is a largely sex-
> linked occupation. In all societies, men do men things and women are left holding
> the babies. But why does this occur? Since one-half of the genes making up every
> individual have been contributed by each parent, then each parent should have
> the same interest in each child. Right? Wrong. (108)

According to the sociobiologists, a major reason for this inequality in involvement in parenting is the fact that each child reflects a large proportion of the
mother's total reproductive potential and a large investment of her time and energy.
As we have seen, for the man the investment is only a tiny amount of sperm. For
these reasons women tend to be much more committed to a child's survival than are
their mates. A second major reason why women tend to be more devoted parents
than are men concerns certainty of parenthood. When a child is born, only the
woman knows with certainty that her genes have been passed on. Therefore, the
woman knows that everything that she invests in her offspring is ultimately to her
own evolutionary benefit. Men have no such guarantee and, therefore, it is always
possible that investing in an offspring might turn out to be a wasted effort in terms
of the man's fitness.

Jealousy.   According to the sociobiologists, the emotion of **jealousy** suggests
some important male-female differences in criteria in mate selection and mate
retention. In general, men experience jealousy when they feel that their mate's
activities may result in the perpetuation of someone else's genes—that is, when her
activities raise doubts about their parenthood. A woman, conversely, tends to experience jealousy when she feels that another woman is threatening the resources
that her mate is providing to her and her offspring. According to Wallace (1979),
"We must realize that, on an evolutionary basis, jealousy is important. Women
must see to it that they and their offspring are the sole recipients of a male's
services. The male must see to it that he does not raise someone else's chromosomes" (63).

Involvement of Men in Parenting.   First of all, relative to most other living organisms, human infants remain dependent on adults for an incredibly long period of time. During this period of dependency a mother's chances of successfully rearing a child are greatly increased if she has someone to help her obtain food, and to protect her and her offspring from harm. The mother, therefore, has good reasons for attempting to entice the father into sharing child-rearing responsibilities. What does she use to entice him? The answer appears to be sex. Human women are unique among primates in that they are not sexually receptive only at time of ovulation or estrus. Human women remain sexually receptive throughout their entire menstrual cycle. Wilson (1978) explains why this may be the case.

> Why has sexual responsiveness become nearly continuous? The most plausible explanation is that the trait facilitates bonding; the physiological adaptation conferred a Darwinian advantage by more tightly joining the members of primitive human clans. Unusually frequent sexual activity between males and females served as the principal device for cementing the pair bond. . . . Love and sex do indeed go together. (146–47)

Barash (1979) also suggests that the evolution of the female orgasm may have occurred because it helps to keep the father of a child close.

> What about the female orgasm, another uniquely human trait?. . . Non-reproductive sex could represent an evolutionary strategy for keeping the male nearby, but not simply as an appeal to pleasure. . . . Female sexual receptivity throughout the reproductive cycle may actually be a loving form of deceit. . . . If women enjoy making love and are motivated to do so (enter: the female orgasm), men might not want to stay away too long. They will remain nearby and look after their genetic investment. (88–89)

Elsewhere, Barash (1986) says: "Orgasm, then, gives women a direct stake in copulation, making regular sexual activity more likely and with it, the increased coordination of male-female behavior that is the evolutionary payoff" (66).

Although it appears that shared sexual activity can create a bond between a male and a female, it does little to create a bond between a father and his offspring. If a man agrees to share in the responsibilities of parenting, he must be convinced to do so by the mother or encouraged by considerable social pressure. "My guess is that male parenting in human beings, as in virtually all mammals, is not nearly as innate as modern sexual egalitarians might wish it to be" (Barash 1979, 88).

Stepparenting.   It comes as no surprise to the sociobiologists that more problems involve children in homes with stepparents than in homes with natural parents. Barash (1979) elaborates:

> If human parental behavior is influenced by actual genetic relatedness to the children in question, we would expect real differences between parents and step-parents in such behavior. Psychologists Martin Daly and Margo Wilson have examined statistics compiled at the National Center for Child Abuse, in Denver, Colorado. They find that children in families containing at least one stepparent are significantly more likely to be abused or neglected than are children living with both biological parents.

Psychologists have given considerable attention to the difficulties faced by a child in adjusting to loss of a parent or in accepting a new one. Virtually no one has considered the adjustment required of a stepparent. In nearly all cases, the stepparent who joins a single parent and child(ren) does so because of his or her relationship with that parent, and not with the children. (104–105)

Adoption.   Do the preceding observations mean that the sociobiologists believe that only natural parents can be good parents? On the contrary, they believe that humans are capable of developing as much love for an adopted child as they feel toward their own children. Barash suggests that humans may even have a natural inclination to adopt children. This natural inclination may have developed because for much of evolutionary history humans lived in small groups of about fifty people who were all probably closely genetically related. Under such circumstances if a child was orphaned he or she could be adopted by one or more adults in the band who would likely be the child's uncle, aunt, or cousin. Adoption, then, becomes a way of increasing the adopter's inclusive fitness.

It seems, however, that such an evolutionary history makes adoption acceptable or tolerable, but not optimal. Barash (1979) explains:

Adoption is rarely as smooth and trouble free as many would think, or wish. If we take a hard, unromanticized look at adoption in Western culture two significant facts stand out. First, despite a great deal of social approval, adoption is overwhelmingly a second choice of parents. Given the option, most people prefer to produce their own children. Although extended-family members—grandparents, aunts and uncles, cousins—may sincerely attempt not to treat the adopted child differently, it is notable that such effort is required at all. A second fact about adoption is that our society subjects would-be adoptive parents to intensive scrutiny, while extending virtually none to would-be biological parents. It is remarkable that we require a license to drive an automobile but none to carry out the much more difficult task of having and raising a child. (106–107)

The reason that would-be adoptive parents are scrutinized so thoroughly is because it is assumed that biologic parents will naturally care for their offspring, but adoptive parents must prove that they are capable and willing to do so. Barash (1979) says: "In fact, there is probably real wisdom involved in this assumption; in scrutinizing the motives and suitability of would-be adopters, child welfare agencies may be good sociobiologists without being aware of it" (107).

Intentional Childlessness.   According to Barash (1979) intentional childlessness is a sociobiologic puzzle. He says: "Women may have been less than wildly enthusiastic about spending a large percentage of their adult lives either pregnant or nursing, yet as long as they ultimately became pregnant, such feelings had no real evolutionary consequences" (107). Now, however, because of the existence of various contraceptive devices, women have the opportunity to act on whatever ambivalence they may feel toward child bearing. This opportunity may create an approach-avoidance conflict toward having children, however. On the one hand, to choose not to have children would help to alleviate the world overpopulation problem and would spare one the physical, psychological, and financial expense of having and rearing them. Conversely, such a choice runs contrary to the tendency to have children that has developed during billions of years of evolution.

Barash believes that it will be interesting to study the long-term consequences (both costs and benefits) of deciding not to become a parent. He also believes that the long-term genetic consequences of intentional childlessness must also be considered, "Because, by definition, selection will favor those people who wish to have children, and any genetically influenced tendency for lesser reproduction will eventually disappear, leaving us with a population of even more eager breeders" (Barash 1979, 108).

Male Dominance

Wilson (1978) believes that anatomic and temperamental differences between men and women have resulted in male dominance over women.

> Anatomy bears the imprint of the sexual division of labor. Men are on the average 20 to 30 percent heavier than women. Pound for pound, they are stronger and quicker in most categories of sport. The proportion of their limbs, their skeletal torsion, and the density of their muscles are particularly suited for running and throwing, the archaic specialties of the ancestral hunter-gatherer males. . . . Women as a group are less assertive and physically aggressive. The magnitude of the distinction depends on the culture. . . . But the variation in degree is not nearly so important as the fact that women differ consistently in this qualitative manner regardless of the degree.
>
> The physical and temperamental differences between men and women have been amplified by culture into universal male dominance. History records not a single society in which women have controlled the political and economic lives of men. Even when queens and empresses ruled, their intermediaries remained primarily male. . . . Men have traditionally assumed the positions of chieftains, shamans, judges, and warriors. Their modern technocratic counterparts rule the industrial states and head the corporations and churches. (131–33)

Earlier we saw that Barash believes that current male domination of women results from cultural hyperextension. That is, male-female differences that were functional during the hundreds of thousands of years when humans were hunter-gatherers, still exist in us as whisperings, and these whisperings are amplified all out of proportion by culture. Thus, although male dominance has a biologic basis, that fact alone cannot explain the current widespread domination of men over women. That domination, according to Barash, is much more cultural than it is biologic.

Furthermore, even if it can be demonstrated conclusively that male-female societal roles and opportunities have their roots in biology, that does not mean the situation cannot be modified by cultural influences. Time and time again, the sociobiologists go out of their way to avoid committing the **naturalistic fallacy,** which is believing that just because something is natural it is necessarily good. Barash (1979) says: "No claim is made that what is natural is therefore good. 'Smallpox is natural,' Ogden Nash pointed out. 'Vaccine ain't.' And there is very little good that anyone can see in smallpox" (15).

Comments such as those made concerning male dominance have led some to accuse the sociobiologists of sexism. We will review their reaction to this criticism in the evaluation section at the end of the chapter.

Aggression, Territoriality, and Warfare

Are Humans Innately Aggressive?

Although the sociobiologists believe that humans are innately aggressive, an important difference exists between what they mean by that contention and what Freud meant by it. In explaining his version of innate human aggressiveness Freud followed a drive-discharge model. The **drive-discharge model of aggression** assumes that humans, like other animals, have a need to be aggressive that must be periodically satisfied. Freud believed that the human aggressive need could be, and should be, displaced so that its satisfaction would not be harmful and may even be beneficial to society. Satisfaction of the need to aggress through competitive sports is but one example. According to Freud, humans have a need to be aggressive just as they have a need for food or water. Being deprived of any of these things too long builds up a drive that must eventually be discharged. The sociobiologists believe that the analysis of aggression by Freud is incorrect.

The sociobiologic explanation of aggression emphasizes the interaction between genetic potential and learning. This explanation assumes that humans have the inherited potential to be aggressive, but it is through learning (culture) that we learn what form our aggression should take and under what circumstances it should occur. According to the sociobiologists, we engage in aggressive behavior when it is advantageous for us to do so.

Barash (1979) summarizes the sociobiologist's view of aggression.

> Competition will be selected only when its benefits outweigh its costs. Struggling with others expends both time and energy and, when push comes to shove, it may even be quite dangerous. Discretion is invariably the better part of valor, unless there are good—that is, fitness-enhancing—reasons to behave aggressively. . . . Aggression is a highly risky business for the organism and not something to be undertaken lightly. It is resorted to only after all possible factors are considered. Some of these factors are contained in our genes. Some are in the environment, made available to us through experience. Our genes advise us when aggression is an appropriate (fitness-maximizing) response to our experience. In this sense, and only in this sense, can we be considered "instinctively" aggressive. (171–72)

According to the sociobiologist, then, aggressive behavior will occur when it maximizes fitness—that is, when the benefits of such behavior exceed the costs. In fact, the terms *strategy* and *cost-benefit analysis* are popular ones in sociobiology suggesting that humans, consciously or unconsciously, weigh various alternatives before deciding on a course of action.

Territoriality and Warfare

The sociobiologists define a **territory** as any defended area (Barash 1982, 394). Thus, a territory could be an area of land, a house, a country, or even a person. According to Wilson (1978): "Each culture develops its own particular rules to safeguard personal property and space" (112). Wars occur when some humans do not respect the rules and regulations by which the territories of other humans can be penetrated. Wilson (1978) elaborates: "War can be defined as the violent rupture of the intricate and powerful fabric of the territorial taboos observed by social groups" (113). A major reason for territoriality is the feeling of kinship that one has toward either his or her relatives or toward those with whom he or she shares beliefs. Wilson (1978) says: "The force behind most warlike policies is ethnocentrism, the irrationally exaggerated allegiance of individuals to their kin and fellow tribesman" (113–14).

Organized aggression directed toward those perceived as threatening one's territory evolved into warfare and warfare as a means of defending and expanding one's territory was effective indeed.

> Primitive men cleaved their universe into friends and enemies and responded with quick, deep emotion to even the mildest threats emanating from outside the arbitrary boundary. With the rise of chiefdoms and states, this tendency became institutionalized, war was adopted as an instrument of policy of some of the new societies, and those that employed it best became—tragically—the most successful. The evolution of warfare was an autocatalytic reaction that could not be halted by any people, because to attempt to reverse the process unilaterally was to fall victim. A new mode of natural selection was operating at the level of entire societies. (Wilson 1978, 119)

Sociobiologists believe that the primitive tendencies described above are still whispering within us and, therefore, we are in trouble. We are dealing with a complex, modern world with behavioral tendencies that developed hundreds of thousands of years ago. The dangers of dealing with modern conflicts with a primitive brain are explored by Barash and Lipton in *The Caveman and the Bomb: Human Nature, Evolution and Nuclear War* (1985). In their book Barash and Lipton suggest that because of our biologic heritage we still respond aggressively to real or perceived threats to our territory, making war more likely than peace.

> Those old Neanderthal cravings are still alive and well, running just beneath the surface, needing only the slightest provocation to erupt, even in the most sophisticated and presumably civilized societies. Just let some Americans be taken hostage in Iran, or a Korean airliner violate Soviet airspace, and suddenly the cavemen are at it again and the old predictable tribal bellowing resumes. *Homo*, called *sapiens*, is all but drowned in an atavistic avalanche of anger, distrust, and intolerance. The structures of peace, built up with such care and needing such nur-

turance, seem woefully delicate and fragile before the crude, easily evoked Neanderthal onslaught. (266)

Is there hope? Wilson (1978) says yes, but improvement will not come easily.

The learning rules of violent aggression are largely obsolete. We are no longer hunter-gatherers who settle disputes with spears, arrows, and stone axes. But to acknowledge the obsolescence of the rules is not to banish them. We can only work our way around them. To let them rest latent and unsummoned, we must consciously undertake those difficult and rarely travelled pathways in psychological development that lead to mastery over and reduction of the profound human tendency to learn violence. (123)

Finally, Barash (1979) asks: "Can we recognize that, because of modern technology, the rules of the game have been changed? Can we use our understanding and our reason to overrule our dangerously outmoded whisperings from within? We had better do so" (198).

Rape, Incest, and Suicide

Rape

As we have seen, social scientists tend to study the proximate causes of behavior and sociobiologists tend to study the ultimate causes. When studying rape then, the social scientists would seek the physiological and cultural variables leading to such behavior, whereas the sociobiologists would seek an explanation based on evolutionary principles.

Thornhill and Thornhill (1983, 1987b) attempt to explain the phenomenon of rape in evolutionary terms by assuming that rape is engaged in by men who cannot successfully compete for the resources and status necessary to attract and successfully reproduce with a desirable mate. In other words, rapists are losers in the competition for available women. Thornhill and Thornhill (1987b) say: "When female mate choice is based importantly on resources and male striving for resources produces losers and winners, forced copulation may be a viable alternative for losers" (277).

Thornhill and Thornhill discuss the two most common explanations of rape offered by social scientists. The first is that rape represents a behavior pathology that somehow grew out of modern industrial societies. This hypothesis is rejected because the evidence indicates that rape is probably culturally universal. The second hypothesis, derived from feminist ideology, is that rape is used by men to dominate women. Thornhill and Thornhill (1987b) give the reasons that they reject the second hypothesis: "The feminist hypothesis seems to predict that men will rape powerful, older women. . . . This is false. Rape is directed primarily at young poor women. . . . The feminist view would also predict that rapists will derive equally from all walks of life and adult age categories. This appears to be false in all human societies for which there are data. Rapists primarily are young, poor men" (283–84).

Thus, the sociobiologic explanation of rape is based on the assumption that rape is an effort to reproduce on the part of men who cannot successfully compete for mates. If this assumption is correct, the typical targets of rape will tend to have certain characteristics. Earlier in this chapter we distinguished between the reproductive value of a woman and her current fertility. Female reproductive value peaks sometime in the mid-teens and fertility in the early twenties in the United States. According to Thornhill and Thornhill (1987b): "Rapists in particular are expected to unconsciously evaluate fertility of potential victims to a greater degree than reproductive value because fertility is most closely related to the probability that a copulation will lead to conception and successful gestation and live birth" (284–85).

Do the data support the sociobiologic explanation of rape? Thornhill and Thornhill (1987b) report the following.

> We compared the ages of rape victims with ages of females in the general population of the U.S. Statistically, young women are greatly overrepresented and older women are greatly underrepresented in the data on victims of rape. The peak in rape victims in relation to age corresponded with ages of high reproductive capacity. We also examined all major data sets on ages of rape victims in the U.S. The same pattern is revealed by all data sets: Young females of high reproductive capacity are raped most often. . . . It is interesting that ages of rape victims seem to follow fertility distributions to a greater extent than reproductive value distributions.
>
> Clearly our prediction about female age in relation to rape victimization was supported, and there is suggestion that fertility of females is more important than reproductive value in rape victimization. (285)

Thornhill and Thornhill tested several other predictions concerning the characteristics of rapists and rape victims, and in each case the data supported an evolutionary explanation. Thornhill and Thornhill (1987b) conclude: "The general conclusion that emerges is that evolutionary theory is very relevant to any attempt to understand rape and any of its ramifications. . . . In fact, it appears that significant understanding of rape will derive primarily from the evolutionary approach" (287).

Incest

If persons who are closely genetically related mate (for example, parents and offspring, siblings, and half siblings) there is a high probability that any resulting offspring will be genetically defective. Therefore, it makes good evolutionary sense to avoid such mating arrangements. In fact, an inherited tendency should exist to avoid incestual sexual relationships, and indeed an inherited mechanism does appear to discourage incest. If such an innate inhibitory mechanism against incest exists, however, why do so many cultures, including our own, spend so much time and energy discouraging incestual sexual relationships? In his effort to explain why both culture prohibitions and an innate inhibitory mechanism are involved in incest avoidance, Van den Berghe (1987) first reviews the statement on incest made by Freud (1913/1958) and the one made by Westermarck (1891).

Freud (1913/1958) took the position that cultural incest taboos were necessary to counteract the strong sexual attractions that occur between members of a nuclear family. In other words, Freud believed that a natural tendency toward incest existed that needed to be inhibited by cultural rules and regulations. Westermarck (1891) took the opposite viewpoint. According to Westermarck, close association among young children (apparently between the ages of two and six) inhibits the development of sexual attraction between them. This avoidance of sex by those who experienced each other as young children is called the **Westermarck effect** and it results in a natural avoidance of at least brother-sister incestual relationships. As Lumsden and Wilson (1985) say: "To put the matter simply, little children who use the same potty do not, in later life, fall in love" (355).

Israeli anthropologist Joseph Shepher (1971) studied the eventual marriages of people who grew up together in a kibbutz in which they had been treated as if they were all members of one large family. Of the 2,769 marriages studied, only six were between members of the same kibbutz who had been together since birth despite the fact that such marriages were actively encouraged by the authorities. Wolf and Huang (1980) report similar findings. *Shim-pua* marriages in China involve adopting a young girl and raising her together with the family's biologic children, with the understanding that she will marry one of the family's sons. Although such marriages were sanctioned by society, they failed at an incredible rate. Often the married couples had to be forced to occupy the same room. Also, adultery and divorce for these couples were much higher than the average, and birth rate was much lower.

The fact that the Westermarck effect occurs whether those involved are related or not, and the fact that it comes from *experience*, seems to suggest that it is learned rather than an inherited disposition. Trigg (1982), however, suggests that this is not the case.

> The absence of genetic ties in such a case might seem to be an argument against a sociobiological explanation but it can in fact easily be taken to confirm it. Natural selection will have found it simpler to favour those who behave towards others as if they are genetically related when they *normally* would be. The alternative would involve a discrimination perhaps amounting to conscious understanding of when people were genetically related and when they were not. It may even demand some knowledge of the significance of this. Such an enterprise would be ridiculously complicated. Simple instinctive reactions in what would usually be the appropriate situations would further genetic fitness just as well, even if such reactions sometimes occurred when they were unnecessary. (122)

Some believe that the Westermarck effect will occur only if the interacting persons are between two and six (for example, Shepher 1983). If true, the Westermarck effect would explain incest avoidance only among those who experienced each other as young children (for example, brother-sister incest). Others, however, believe that anyone, of any age, who interacts with a young child will develop a sexual aversion to that child as a child and later as an adult. For example, Thornhill and Thornhill (1987a) respond to the contention that the Westermarck effect results only when young children interact:

We disagree and suggest that a more parsimonious hypothesis is that cosocialization of an individual of any age with a child who is experiencing the sensitive stage [two to six years of age], should lead to sexual aversion between them. This eliminates the need for hypothesizing complex mechanisms of mother/son and father/daughter incest avoidance. . . . When cosocialization does *not* occur during the sensitive stage it appears that the mechanism for close inbreeding is not learned, and incest might occur. (377)

Wilson (1978) also accepts the more comprehensive view of the Westermarck effect.

When two persons form one kind of strong bond between themselves, they find it emotionally difficult to join in certain other kinds. Teachers and students are slow to become colleagues even after the students surpass their mentors; mothers and daughters seldom change the tone of their original relationship. And incest taboos are virtually universal in human cultures because fathers and daughters, mothers and sons, and brothers and sisters find their primary bonds to be nearly all-exclusive. People, in short, are deterred from learning the precluded bonds. (71)

We now return to the question, with such a powerful natural mechanism preventing incestual relationships why are there so many cultural prescriptions against them, and why do they still occur so often? Van den Berghe provides a reasonable explanation. Van den Berghe (1987) examined several societies and found some of them encouraged sexually permissive relationships among family members and some did not. In those that did allow such relationships, the Westermarck effect occurred; when such relationships were discouraged the Westermarck effect did not occur. Thus, according to Van den Berghe (1987) both Freud and Westermarck were correct.

In short, sexually permissive, relaxed, unsegregated societies foster natural immunity to incest through intimate childhood association between siblings and parents and offspring of opposite sex, and therefore need not taboo and punish that which is unlikely to occur. Repressive, segregated cultures, by leaving open the possibility of sexual attraction between close kin through lack of childhood intimacy, have to fall back on strong taboos and heavy sanctions. It is presumably the latter kind of culture in which Freud grew and which led him to his formulation. (354)

Presumably, it is also in the more restricted society in which incest will occur more frequently, because many people may not have learned the cultural rules concerning incestual behavior or may ignore them if they were learned. It appears to be much more difficult to avoid a natural inhibitory mechanism than it is to avoid those created by society.

Suicide

Living organisms generally act in ways that are conducive to their survival. They will seek food, water, and safety, and will actively escape or avoid experiences that threaten their continued existence. Natural selection easily explains such tendencies; organisms that display them are far more likely to survive and reproduce than those that do not. Thus, over many generations, any predispositions toward self-preservation are passed on, whereas predispositions not conducive to self-preservation are not. It is assumed that humans also have evolved in this way, but if humans have such a propensity for self-preservation why do so many of us engage in self-destructive behavior—suicide being the most dramatic example? De Catanzaro (1987) indicates how widespread the act of suicide is.

> It has been estimated that discrete acts of suicide account for at least 1–2% of all deaths in modern cultures . . . and this may well be an underestimate because of equivocal circumstances surrounding many deaths and biases in reporting. . . . Suicide occurs in virtually every culture in which a careful survey has been conducted. . . . Historical evidence suggests that it was not uncommon in the classical civilizations . . . and in ancient India . . . and the Orient. . . . It is also particularly significant that suicide has been observed in a variety of less technologically developed or "primitive" cultures. . . . As well as discrete suicidal acts, there are untold numbers of cases where individuals bring about or hasten their own deaths through excessive risk-taking or "accidents." . . . Researchers have long suspected that many accidents may be suicides, and that other individuals with subsuicidal motives may simply be careless. . . . We must also consider the various ways in which some individuals engage in "chronic suicide," for example through chronic drug abuse. (313–14)

As we have often seen, the concept of inclusive fitness is central to sociobiology. De Catanzaro emphasizes this concept in his analysis of suicide.

He asks: Do circumstances exist under which a person's genes would have a better chance of being perpetuated if that person ceased to exist? De Catanzaro (1987) answers in the affirmative: "It could be predicted that once an individual is postreproductive or otherwise excluded from reproduction, and has no further role to play in nurturance of its progeny, self-preservation is of little or no value for the individual's inclusive fitness" (316). De Catanzaro (1987) elaborates:

> Any genetic predispositions favoring a self-preserving orientation of behavior, when expressed prior to or during reproductive (including nurturant) phases of the life cycle, would confer a strong selective advantage for the individual. However, expression of such predispositions after all reproductive opportunities had passed would have no positive reproductive consequences. *In fact, to the extent that postreproductive or nonreproductive individuals consumed resources that otherwise would be available to potential reproducing kin, their self-preservation could actually have adverse effects upon their inclusive fitnesses* [italics added]. . . . Wherever the continued existence of one individual impedes the reproduction of close kin . . . more than it enhances the reproduction of the individual himself, self-destructiveness is at least theoretically possible. (317)

So much for the predictions concerning suicide based on sociobiologic theory; what do the facts show? De Catanzaro (1987) reports that suicide typically occurs among people whose capacity to promote inclusive fitness is seriously impaired. That is, suicide is related to diminished reproductive potential, absence of or unfavorable relations to one's kin or one's social group, or the lack of coping skills.

One of the best predictors of true suicidal intent is the feeling of hopelessness or desperation. According to de Catanzaro, such a feeling usually means that a person finds himself or herself incapable of engaging in reproductive and productive behavior that would promote his or her inclusive fitness.

> An examination of certain high risk populations also supports this notion. Suicide is very common in the terminally ill and those with permanently debilitating handicaps ... such individuals are relatively incapable of engaging in future reproductive and productive behavior. Suicide is also very common in the chronically unemployed and others with severe economic difficulties ... such difficulties may engender problems in attracting a mate and supporting offspring, rendering the individual incapable of reproducing, and may preclude other activity that indirectly advances the individual's inclusive fitness. (de Catanzaro 1987, 319)

Among the other variables that de Catanzaro (1987) found to be related to suicide were social isolation (a socially isolated person would be relatively incapable of engaging in productive or reproductive behavior); age (suicide is rare in children under fourteen, but in adolescence and early adulthood, suicide is a major cause of death); sex (men are much more likely to commit suicide than women); marital status (people in a stable marriage are less likely to commit suicide than those who are single, divorced, widowed, or have an unstable marriage); and culture (learning may provide the means by which one commits suicide, but the ultimate cause of such an act must be understood in evolutionary terms).

Other Forms of Self-Destructive Behavior

Many persons smoke, drink alcohol, take drugs, or overeat; these activities are not conducive to self-preservation. In their attempt to explain behavior that appears to be contrary to self-preservation, the sociobiologists tend to (1) show that the self-abusive behavior is actually conducive to the person's inclusive fitness (for example, suicide); or (2) stress the fact that the environment in which we evolved is, in many ways, different from the one in which we now live. Barash (1979) gives the following examples.

> Most of us over-indulge in foods that are high in saturated fats and cholesterol, despite the fact that these materials are clearly harmful and may in fact be life threatening when consumed in sufficient quantities. Fats cause our arteries to clog up and lead to heart disease, the foremost killer in the United States today. This dietary imprudence is aggravated by our tendency to avoid exercise. We drive when we could walk, use the elevator when we could take the stairs and so on. . . . Dangerous Western eating and exercise habits may well be the effects of our cultural developments outstripping our biological evolution. Human beings evolved as part-time carnivores, probably on the African savannah. There is every reason to suspect that we are programmed to relish animal fat, a very concentrated food source and, not surprisingly one that is prized by all meat-eating animals. Most wild game is actually quite lean, and a fatty meal would therefore be a rare and sought-after treat. Because we undoubtedly got more than enough exercise

during our long African evolution, any opportunity to avoid exercise and to leave ourselves with enough physical activity to keep our bodies in good order would be seized upon.

But nowadays we fatten our livestock in feedlots; slather butter and oils on everything; and compound the problem by adding unnecessary calories through sugar, candies and other worthless confections. For a savannah-bred protohuman, this diet would be heaven. For us, it may well be lethal. Having provided us with an opportunity to satisfy (in excess) our primitive needs, modern culture then adds to the villainy by designing all sorts of "labor-saving devices" that enable us to avoid the exercise that might otherwise be our bodily salvation. (228–29)

Religion

Artifacts have been found indicating that Neanderthals engaged in religious practices 60,000 years ago and since that time humans have produced about 100,000 religions (Wilson 1978, 176). Religion is culturally universal, uniquely human, and, according to the sociobiologists, part of human nature (that is part of our biogrammar). Wilson (1978) says: "The predisposition to religious belief is the most complex and powerful force in the human mind and in all probability an ineradicable part of human nature" (176).

According to Wilson, religion plays a vital role in allowing humans to live in groups such as tribes or nations. Wilson (1978) says "Religion is above all the process by which individuals are persuaded to subordinate their immediate self-interest to the interests of the group" (183). Religion does this in several ways but one way is to generate a feeling of kinship among persons who share common beliefs. By holding similar beliefs people, at least symbolically, become related and, feeling related they are much more likely to engage in reciprocal altruism. Furthermore, religions almost always sanctify the principles by which believers should conduct themselves. Wilson (1978) says: "To sanctify a procedure or a statement is to certify it as beyond question and imply punishment for anyone who dares to contradict it" (191). Rules concerning reciprocal altruism, for example, "Do unto others as you would have them do unto you," are a vital part of religion as are the procedures used to deal with cheaters. Thus, society depends on reciprocal altruism, and religion encourages its practice and creates fear or guilt in those who are inclined to cheat.

Another important function of religion is to simplify life, and religion does this in several ways. In addition to giving believers a feeling of kinship, religion also encourages the human tendency to divide humans into two categories such as believers and nonbelievers, members of the ingroup and members of the outgroup, and friends and enemies. We seem to be willing to accept any doctrine that simplifies life, and the dichotomization of people is one way to do just that. Related to the strong human tendency to dichotomize is **xenophobia,** the intense fear of strangers. From our distant past comes the tendency to distrust anyone who is not like us—for example, someone not from the same clan, village or tribe, someone who lives life according to different (and therefore inferior) rules. Such a person is at least a potential enemy and should be treated as such.

Need for Rules and Regulations

Social living requires rules and regulations and historically it has been religion, in one form or another, that has furnished and enforced them. Although it appears necessary that these rules and regulations encourage reciprocal altruism, give a sense of kinship to members of the community, and discourage any practice that is not conducive to survival and reproduction, they can provide these functions in a wide variety of ways. In other words, rules and regulations are necessary for societal living, but any number of systems of rules and regulations are possible.

The willingness to accept a system of rules and regulations, and to live according to them, may have a biologic basis. Perhaps we are born to be team players as long as the game does not stray too far from our biologic makeup. Thus Wilson (1975) says: "The enduring paradox of religion is that so much of its substance is demonstrably false, yet it remains a driving force in all societies. Men would rather believe than know. . . . Human beings are absurdly easy to indoctrinate—they seek it" (561–62). In other words, humans readily embrace any beliefs that simplify their lives and allow cooperative living, and it appears that the ultimate validity of those beliefs is irrelevant as long as they have pragmatic value. Furthermore, because good "team players" are more likely to survive and reproduce, parents eagerly pass on the rules of societal living to their offspring, and the offspring are eager to learn them. Lumsden and Wilson (1981) say: "Adults are strongly prone to provide complex instructions, and the young are predisposed to follow them" (5). Smith (1987) compares the typical goals toward which parents socialize their children with the goal suggested by the sociobiologist.

> In Western culture, these goals [according to parents] often involve producing polite, active, law-abiding adults who will have the skills to secure fulfilling, lucrative employment and a similarly socialized spouse. An evolutionary perspective views these end-points of socialization as intermediate steps in achieving the real goal of parenting: the maximization of inclusive fitness through the maximal production of grandchildren. (235)

Wilson (1978) comments on the ease with which humans are indoctrinated, the tendency to dichotomize humans, interest in professional sports, and conflicts among nations.

> The genius of human sociality is in fact the ease with which alliances are formed, broken, and reconstituted, always with strong emotional appeals to rules believed to be absolute. The important distinction is today, as it appears to have been since the Ice Age, between the ingroup and the outgroup, but the precise location of the dividing line is shifted back and forth with ease. Professional sports thrive on the durability of this basic phenomenon. For an hour or so the spectator can resolve his world into an elemental physical struggle between tribal surrogates. The athletes come from everywhere and are sold and traded on an almost yearly basis. The teams themselves are sold from city to city. But it does not matter; the fan identifies with an aggressive ingroup, admires teamwork, bravery, and sacrifice, and shares the exultation of victory.
>
> Nations play by the same rules. During the past thirty years geopolitical alignments have changed from a confrontation between the Axis and the Allies to

one between the Communists and the Free World, then to oppositions between largely economic blocks. The United Nations is both a forum for the most idealistic rhetoric of humankind and a kaleidoscope of quickly shifting alliances based on selfish interests. (170–71)

When you come to think of it, it is remarkable how emotionally involved some persons can become in the victories or losses of "their" school team or of a team representing their state or nation. When a team wins the World Series or the Super Bowl, for example, tens of thousands of the inhabitants of the city with which the team is affiliated are whipped into an emotional frenzy that can last for many hours and even days. Why? Why should one care if one's high school or college team wins or loses a game? For that matter why should the team care? It is quite possible that the explanation of such emotional involvement, as the sociobiologists suggest, lies deep within our biogrammar.

Biology of Ethics

Every human society has some ethical code of behavior for its members to follow and even though ethical codes vary significantly from society to society, there do seem to be common elements among them. All encourage reciprocal altruism and specify punishment for cheaters, all promote patriotism ("My country, or tribe, right or wrong"), and all encourage behaviors that are conducive to the survival and reproductive success of its members. Religion typically functions to strengthen and maintain the ethical code by which a society functions; therefore, it is not surprising to find that all of the major religions make strong statements about reciprocal altruism. In his book *The Expanding Circle: Ethics and Sociobiology*, Singer (1981) summarizes several of these statements.

> In Judaism the rule is to love your neighbor as yourself; a rule which Jesus elevated to the status of one of the two great commandments. About the same time, Rabbi Hillel said: "What is hateful to you do not do to your neighbor; that is the whole Torah, the rest is commentary thereof." Jesus also put it another way: "As you would that men should do to you, do ye also to them likewise." When Confucius was asked for a single word which could serve as a rule of practice for all one's life, he replied: "Is not reciprocity such a word? What you do not want done to yourself, do not do to others." In Indian thought we find the Mahabharata saying: "Let no man do to another that which would be repugnant to himself; this is the sum of righteousness." (136)

In his book *The Genesis Factor*, Wallace (1979) says all life must obey the **reproductive imperative,** which is: "*Reproduce, and leave as many offspring as possible*" (17). In time, according to Wallace, those activities conducive to the reproductive imperative made up the norm of a society and became formally encoded by tradition, laws, religions, and ethics. Those activities not conducive to the reproductive imperative became crimes, sins, or in some other way discouraged. According to Wallace, activities contrary to the reproductive imperative include oral and anal sex, masturbation, necrophilia (a sexual attraction to dead bodies), pederasty (sexual relations between a man and a boy), sex with young children in general, adultery, rape, fornication, and incest. All of the activities listed either cannot produce offspring and are therefore wasted activities or they may produce offspring that have a low probability of being cared for and therefore may not survive. Adultery (sexual activity with someone outside of the family unit), fornication (copulation involving unmarried persons), and rape all appear on the list of crimes against the reproductive imperative because they may produce offspring that may not be cared for adequately.

Barash (1979) also says that it is the responsibility of society to keep humans from following their selfish, biologic inclinations.

> If our "human nature" impels us to behave more selfishly than society would like, it is not surprising that societies everywhere have developed techniques to bend us to their will. No human society is without its shoulds and should-nots, its moral injunctions that coax, cajole, warn, threaten and punish. . . . There may be real wisdom to the Ten Commandments and other such moral codes—from society's viewpoint, if not from that of each citizen. Perhaps we have to be told not to steal, murder or covet our neighbor's wife because those are just the sorts of things our internal whisperings are telling us to do, if they profit us and if we can get away with them. (168–69)

Homosexuality.   The reader may have noticed that homosexuality did not appear on the list of sexual activities that violate the reproductive imperative. Indeed, Wallace (1979, 58) lists homosexuality as a practice that does violate the reproductive imperative. In fact, the relatively widespread practice of homosexuality seems to run contrary to a genetic account of sexual preferences. That is, if homosexuality is at least partially genetically determined, how can it be perpetuated since homosexuals tend not to leave offspring? Wilson (1978) answers this question by once again employing the concept of *inclusive fitness*. Wilson suggests that homosexuals perpetuate their genes by helping their relatives rear and protect their children. Because it is assumed that those closely related to homosexuals carry homosexual genes, homosexuals who assist their relatives in child-bearing and child-rearing actually enhance their own inclusive fitness. Wilson (1978) summarizes his view of homosexuality:

> How can genes predisposing their carriers toward homosexuality spread through the population if homosexuals have no children? One answer is that their close relatives could have had more children as a result of their presence. The homosexual members of primitive societies could have helped members of the same sex, either while hunting and gathering or in more domestic occupations at the dwelling sites. Freed from the special obligations of parental duties, they would have been in a position to operate with special efficiency in assisting close relatives. They might further have taken the roles of seers, shamans, artists, and keepers of tribal knowledge. If the relatives—sisters, brothers, nieces, nephews, and others were benefitted by higher survival and reproduction rates, the genes these individuals shared with the homosexual specialists would have increased at the expense of alternative genes. Inevitably, some of these genes would have been those that predisposed individuals toward homosexuality. A minority of the population would consequently always have the potential for developing homophilic preferences. Thus it is possible for homosexual genes to proliferate through collateral lines of descent, even if the homosexuals themselves do not have children.

This conception can be called the "kin-selection hypothesis" of the origin of homosexuality. (150–51)

Thus, according to Wilson, homosexuality is not abnormal or unnatural and it is perpetuated genetically via kin selection.

Importance of Myth

In addition to encouraging and enforcing codes of conduct, and giving persons a sense of group identity, religion also provides simple answers to complex questions. Typically, religion provides the answers to the most perplexing questions such as "Where did we come from?"; "Why are we here?"; and "What is our ultimate fate?" in the form of myths. For example, the universe is divided into heaven and hell; human existence is viewed as a struggle between good and evil; various gods or spirits control natural events, for example, volcanos, earthquakes, and storms; and a God, gods, spirits, or demons are available to enforce whatever societal taboos exist. Lastly, religion, again through myth, explains why its adherents have a special place in the world.

The myths offered by religion to answer complex questions and to make believers feel special will vary with the listener's ability to understand them. The sophistication of many modern humans has not rendered myths obsolete, it has just meant that our myths have become more sophisticated. Wilson (1978) says, "It is obvious that human beings are still largely ruled by myth. Furthermore, much of contemporary intellectual and political strife is due to the conflict between three great mythologies: Marxism, traditional religion, and scientific materialism" (198–99).

Wilson places scientific materialism within the realm of mythology because he believes the evolutionary epic lies at its core. About the evolutionary epic Wilson (1978) says:

> Its narrative form is the epic: the evolution of the universe from the big bang of fifteen billion years ago through the origin of the elements and celestial bodies to the beginnings of life on earth. The evolutionary epic is mythology in the sense that the laws it adduces here and now are believed but can never be definitely proved to form a cause-and-effect continuum from physics to the social sciences, from this world to all other worlds in the visible universe, and backward through time to the beginning of the universe. Every part of existence is considered to be obedient to physical laws requiring no external control. (200)

So humans need myths, even modern humans. Education, science, and rationality do not eliminate the human need to mythologize. Wilson (1978) puts the matter as follows.

> When blind ideologies and religious beliefs are stripped away, others are quickly manufactured as replacements. If the cerebral cortex is rigidly trained in the techniques of critical analysis and packed with tested information, it will reorder all that into some form of morality, religion, and mythology. If the mind is instructed that its pararational activity cannot be combined with the rational, it will divide

itself into two compartments so that both activities can continue to flourish side by side. (208)

Religion, then, facilitates societal living in several ways. On the negative side, however, is the fact that religions are seldom tolerant of each other. Wilson (1978) says: "The one form of altruism that religions seldom display is tolerance of other religions" (182–83). This is as true for ancient religions as it is for more modern religions. Each religion is made up of rules, regulations, myths, and ceremonies and rituals. Each religion sanctifies a particular way of societal life, provides answers to the great mysteries of life, and makes its adherents believe that they are special in some way, for example, that they are God's favorite people. All of this would be fine if only one religion generated one way of life, but when more than one religion exists trouble often occurs. After all, only one set of sanctified rules and regulations can be the correct set, and only one group of people can be God's favorite. Many wars have already been fought attempting to straighten out such matters, and no doubt others will occur.

Sociobiology and Freudian Theory

In their article "Freudian Psychoanalysis and Sociobiology: A Synthesis" Leak and Christopher (1982) outline several points of agreement between Freud's theory and sociobiology.

Id

Like the gene, the id is inherited from our evolutionary past, is ultimately selfish, is totally unconscious, and has as its goal the survival and reproductive success of the person.

Ego

Because neither the genes nor the id come into contact with social and physical reality, they need to use a mediating structure to satisfy their selfish needs. In sociobiology this mediating mechanism is that cortical region of the brain responsible for consciousness; for Freud it was the ego. In both cases, the mechanisms are responsible for allowing the person to deal effectively with physical reality in meeting his or her survival and reproductive needs. Thus, for both Freud and the sociobiologists much human behavior and most cognitive processes are rooted in biology.

Furthermore, both Freud and the sociobiologists view humans as flexible problem solvers whose primary goal is to maximize fitness under varied and changing circumstances. Leak and Christopher (1982) say:

The concept of the ego as a reality-oriented system that maximizes instinctual gratification while minimizing punishment accords perfectly with the cost-benefit-analyzing, fitness-maximizing view of behavior derived from natural selection theory. (317)

Leak and Christopher (1982) continue:

Since the advent of sociobiology, *strategy* has become a ubiquitous term in the literature of animal behavior. The implication that organisms exercise choices among an array of options is quite deliberate. In this . . . sociobiology and psychoanalytic theory seem . . . congruent. Freud argued that although individuals work toward similar goals, their methods of obtaining them differ according to historical and situational factors. This is a position sociobiologists find easy to defend. (321)

Superego

As we have seen, it is often adaptive to conform to norms and standards of a group even when doing so seems in opposition to one's own selfish biologic interests. It is also advantageous to help fellow humans if they will probably help you in return. In Freudian theory it is the superego that accounts for altruistic behavior. The values of the culture are instilled into children, usually via their parents, by rewarding "appropriate" behavior (resulting in the ego ideal) and punishing "inappropriate" behavior (resulting in the conscience). Once instilled, these values will make the person have positive feelings when doing what is culturally appropriate and negative feelings (for example, guilt) when doing what is inappropriate. Getting along with others, conforming to societal norms, and helping others in times of need are among the behaviors usually considered appropriate, and, according to Freud, all of these actions are learned. The sociobiologists would reject the heavy emphasis on learning in the Freudian analysis of altruism and other forms of social behavior. According to them, if learning is involved at all it is *prepared learning*. That is, the person is biologically prepared to learn such behavior and, therefore, learns it with ease.

Both Freud and the sociobiologists believe that it is the experience of various emotions that cause a person to conform to the norms and standards of a group. Leak and Christopher (1982) summarize the importance of emotions for altruistic behavior.

It is possible to view emotions such as guilt, gratitude, sympathy, and pride as proximate mechanisms which motivate appropriately adaptive behavior. For example, guilt may in fact be a selfishly motivated emotion that causes a cheater to make reparations, hence increasing the cheater's chances of being allowed to remain in the altruism network and reap its benefits. Similarly, moral indignation is a way of galvanizing the person into taking appropriate action against a cheater. . . . The reliance on norms and customs may be a way of simplifying the problem of identifying cheaters, and the tendency to conform may increase one's chances of being perceived as a genuine altruist, one worth trusting. (317)

Leak and Christopher (1982, 317) speculate that perhaps the id reflects tendencies developed before humans lived in social groups, and the superego reflects tendencies that developed to enhance living in social groups.

Aggression

As we have already seen, Freud viewed aggression as a tension that must be periodically relieved. The sociobiologists strongly disagree with the Freudian position on aggression, arguing instead for an interactionist position that stresses the importance of both genes and the environment. The sociobiologic position is that humans inherit the capacity to act aggressively but will only do so when it maximizes fitness. For example, humans would be likely to fight among themselves in environments where valuable resources are scarce. Should circumstances change and resources become more plentiful, aggression among humans would decrease. Unfortunately, many occasions have occurred in human history when aggression has been effective in protecting or expanding one's resources. So, although Freud and the sociobiologists disagree on the exact nature of human aggression, they do agree that a great deal of aggression characterizes the human animal.

Unconscious

The notion of the unconscious mind is at the heart of Freudian theory and it also plays a prominent role in sociobiologic theory. According to the sociobiologists, remaining unconscious of one's true motives makes good evolutionary sense. As we have seen, the sociobiologists assume that all human motives are ultimately selfish. Yet, for practical reasons we must cooperate with our fellow humans. This whole process might be facilitated if one's selfish motives remained unconscious and only more altruistic motives were entertained consciously. This kind of self-deception might even be fitness enhancing, because the person would believe that he or she is motivated by social rather than individual motives.

Irrationality and Rationality

Finally, Freud believed that although it is extremely difficult, unconscious motives could be made conscious and thereby dealt with rationally. Although Freud believed that most human behavior was unconsciously motivated, he also believed that it did not need to be. In fact, he hoped his theory would provide the information necessary for human behavior to become more rational. Assuming that what Barash calls whisperings are unconscious and realizing that they have a different origin than the unconscious motives in Freud's theory, Freud and the sociobiologists seem to be making the same point. To know which whisperings to allow full expression, which to encourage, and which to discourage, we must first know what those whisperings are. It may not be possible to eliminate a whispering without somehow changing our genetic makeup, but, once known, like unconscious motives made conscious, they can be dealt with rationally.

Jungian Theory

Similarity exists between Jung's concept of archetypes and what the sociobiologists call the whisperings within (or the biogrammar). Both Jung and the sociobiologists stress general inherited predispositions to respond to certain categories of experience. According to the sociobiologists, these predispositions were selected by evolution because of their survival value. Jung does not give a mechanism for the perpetuation of these predispositions, but he does say that they represent the collective memory of universal human emotional experiences. The important similarity between Jung and the sociobiologists is that both say our behavior is strongly influenced by what has happened to our species throughout its evolutionary history. Also, both agree that neither specific ideas or specific behavior patterns are inherited. Rather, a general tendency to respond to certain categories of experience is inherited from our distant past.

Science and Politics

Unfortunately it is often difficult—if not impossible—to separate science and politics. Morris (1983) gives an example.

> There is one particular kind of predisposition that has cropped up again and again. Environmentalism [empirical conception of human nature] has been associated with liberal and radical political outlooks, while hereditarian interpretations have been bound up with conservative viewpoints. Although we would like to believe that science and politics should be divorced from each other, they frequently have not been. (164–65)

Our concern in this chapter has been to present the young science of sociobiology as its creators and adherents view it. When sociobiology is thoroughly tested, what is found to be true should be accepted and what is found to be false should be revised or abandoned. Optimally, this should be true for any theory. In reality, however, theories are sometimes accepted or rejected for other than objective reasons. A particular theory may be accepted by some because conceptually it supports their biases and rejected by others because it does not. Although sociobiology has been criticized for valid scientific reasons, it has also been attacked for emotional and political reasons. Morris (1983) explains:

> It should come as no surprise that sociobiology, a theory (or discipline) that embraces hereditarian outlooks, should have aroused the ire of the left. Some of the most vehement criticisms that have been heaped upon Wilson and his colleagues have come from a group affiliated with the radically oriented Science for the People. This group, a collective calling itself the Sociobiology Study Group, was made up primarily of Harvard professors and students. It began to publish attacks on Wilson's *Sociobiology* shortly after the book was published. Although some of the charges were reasoned scientific objections, others were unabashedly political in nature. (165)

On the political side, the study group associated sociobiology with past theories that promoted or supported sterilization laws, restrictive immigration laws, eugenics, and even the gas chambers of Nazi Germany. Wilson responded by saying that sociobiology contains no political message and that the study group has seriously distorted his ideas, which, in many cases, they had. The damage had been done, however, and for a period of time Wilson experienced intimidation, harsh labels (for example, a dangerous racist), and hostile questioning following his public lectures.

Other criticisms of sociobiology were more reasonable and we will consider them shortly.

Evaluation

Empirical Research

If what is meant by empirical research is controlled experimental research, not much exists to substantiate sociobiology. It should be realized, however, that, sociobiologists study behavior in the natural environment. Therefore, much of the research offered to support sociobiology is based on naturalistic observations. Such research *is* empirical, but it is not experimental. A major problem with naturalistic observation is that it is difficult to determine, with any degree of certainty, the causes of the behavior that is observed. Because the causes of complex, naturally occurring behavior are hard to specify, they are, to a large extent, a matter of speculation. For example, the explanation of the social behavior observed by the sociobiologists based on evolutionary theory is only one possible explanation. As we shall see, some critics of sociobiology maintain that everything that it explains in evolutionary terms can be better explained in terms of learning.

Criticisms

Sociobiology Is Not Falsifiable.   In chapter 1 we saw that, according to Karl Popper, for a theory to be considered scientific it must be falsifiable. That is, it must make risky predictions. If no conceivable observation would refute or falsify the theory, then the theory is not scientific. According to Harvard paleontologist Stephen Jay Gould (1978), sociobiology is like Christian fundamentalism because for both no possible negative cases, exceptions, or refutations exist. In other words, neither can be falsified. According to Gould, whenever sociobiologists want to demonstrate that a current form of social behavior has been naturally selected because it has adaptive value they make up a "just-so story." A just-so story is an explanation of behavior that sounds plausible, and, in fact, may be true but is not supported by any solid evidence.

Sociobiology Is Based on Adaptationism.   Related to their criticism of sociobiology's tendency to tell just-so stories to substantiate its claims, Gould and Lewontin (1979) also criticize sociobiology for accepting an *adaptationist program*. The adaptationists believe that if a structure or a behavioral tendency exists now, it must have been conducive to the survival of our ancestors. That is, it characterizes humans now because of the natural selection that had occurred in our evolutionary past. Gould and Lewontin (1979) find three faults with the adaptationism of the sociobiologists: (1) factors other than adaptation cause evolutionary change (genetic drift and genetic mutations are two examples); (2) a trait is not adaptive in our present environment because it was adaptive in the environments of our distant relatives; and (3) a characteristic may have evolved for specific reasons in the past but may be used in totally different ways in the modern world. The way the brain functions, for example, is a result of its evolution, but the computing powers of the brain are now used to solve the problems of modern living that are often unlike any experienced in our evolutionary past.

Gould and Lewontin (1979) also say that accepting an adaptationist program results in believing that this must be "The best of all possible worlds." This is because human social behavior is the product of millions of years of evolution and should, therefore, be maximally adaptive. Lewontin, Rose, and Kamin (1984) also make this point.

> The claim that genetically determined social organization is a product of natural selection has the further consequence of suggesting that society is in some sense optimal or adaptive. While genetic fixity in itself is logically quite sufficient to support the status quo, the claim that present social arrangements are also optimal adds to their palatability. It is rather a handy feature of life that what must be is also the best. (237)

As we have seen, however, this concept is *not* what the sociobiologists believe. Rather they believe that many of the tendencies that we inherit are obsolete, troublesome, or even dangerous, and that such tendencies should be actively inhibited. Surely the sociobiologists see that the world is anything but perfect. The criticism that the sociobiologists suggest that this is the best of all possible worlds is closely related to the criticism that sociobiology legitimizes the status quo, which we shall consider next.

Sociobiology Legitimizes the Status Quo. It is often claimed that sociobiology legitimizes the status quo by insisting that the patterns of human social behavior that exist do so because they were naturally selected. Lewontin, Rose, and Kamin (1984) say:

> The general appeal of sociobiology is in its legitimation of the *status quo.* . . . If men dominate women, it is because they must. If employers exploit their workers, it is because evolution has built into us the genes for entrepreneurial activity. If we kill each other in war, it is the force of our genes for territoriality, xenophobia, tribalism, and aggression. Such a theory can become a powerful weapon in the hands of ideologues who protect an embattled social organization by "a genetic defense of the free market." It also serves at the personal level to explain individual acts of oppression and to protect the oppressors against the demands of the oppressed. It is "why we do what we do" and "why we sometimes behave like cavemen." (236–37)

As we have seen throughout this chapter, however, the sociobiologists do not believe that just because something is natural, it is necessarily good. Believing that would be committing the naturalistic fallacy. They do say, however, that natural behaviors are learned and maintained much easier than unnatural behavior. In other words, if a culture decides that unnatural behavior is more desirable than natural behavior, that culture will need to expend vast resources developing and maintaining the unnatural behavior.

Sociobiology Accepts a Rigid, Biologic Determinism.   Some have criticized sociobiology for accepting the position that humans are "hard wired" by genetics to respond to specific situations in specific ways.

Because the sociobiologists spend so much time emphasizing that human behavior is *always* the result of the *interaction* between biologic predispositions *and* culture, it is hard to understand how they can be accused of accepting a strict biologic determinism. As we have seen, Barash pleads with students of human behavior not to follow "nothing butism"—that is, believing that human behavior is nothing but genetically determined, or that it is nothing but culturally determined.

After reading the following quotation from Barash (1986), it is difficult to understand how anyone can accuse him of either being a rigid biologic determinist or of legitimizing the status quo.

> Fortunately, there is some good news. Human beings, intelligent primates that we are, can exercise choice. We can overcome our primitive limitations and short-sightedness. We can learn all sorts of difficult things, once we become convinced that they are important, or unavoidable. We can even learn to do things that go against our nature. A primate that can be toilet trained could possibly even be planet trained someday. (254)

Sociobiology Is Racist.   According to the sociobiologists, the more closely related we are to someone, the more likely we are to help that person. This, as we have seen, is called kin altruism. Reciprocal altruism, conversely, involves nonrelatives and is based on an agreement (either implicit or explicit) that one's helpful gesture will be reciprocated. The probability of cheating in such an arrangement goes down as the people involved are known to each other. Therefore, according to the sociobiologists, we will be most friendly toward, and most comfortable with, those humans with whom we are either related or familiar. The reverse is also true. The more unfamiliar a person is, the more we tend to fear him or her. According to the sociobiologists, then, xenophobia, or the fear of strangers, is genetically influenced. Barash (1979) says:

> People of different races *are* different. Although we are all one species and quite capable of exchanging genes, the fact remains that members of any race seem likely to share more genes with each other than with individuals of a different race. Physical resemblance almost certainly has some correlation with genetic resemblance, and, accordingly, we can expect the principles of kin-selected altruism to operate on this fact. More to the point, we can expect the other side of the coin—antagonism—toward those who are different. (153)

In this situation, what is "natural" is not good, and society must commit resources to encourage what is better.

Sociobiology Is Sexist.   Sociobiology does specify many biologically based male-female differences—for example, those involved in parental investment, mate selection strategies, and aggressiveness. Because of these observations sociobiology has been criticized for being sexist. To *describe* male and female traits, say the sociobiologists, is not the same as the differential *valuing* of those traits, however (for example, claiming that one sex is somehow better than the other). Disciplines such as anatomy and physiology describe male-female differences without being accused of sexism; so it should be with sociobiology.

In response to the question "Is sociobiology sexist?" Barash (1979) says:

> Evolution simply *is*—or better yet, evolution *does*. It says nothing whatever about what ought to be. . . . If females appear to be scheming and yet basically passive, males are nasty and aggressive, sometimes ridiculous and, given modern weaponry, very, very dangerous. There is probably a risk that the sociobiological understanding of male-female differences will be used to justify sexist attitudes to defend the view that it is only "natural" for men to be aggressive and for women to be more passive, and all the rest. But, as we've said before, what is natural is not necessarily what is good. Furthermore, the inclinations predicted by sociobiology are just that: inclinations! They are not certainties. . . . To my thinking, sexism occurs when society differentially values one sex above another, providing extra opportunities for one (usually the males) and denying equal opportunities for the other (usually the females). As such, it has nothing to do with sociobiology. On the other hand, sexism is also sometimes applied to the simple identification of male-female differences, and on this count sociobiology is, I suppose sexist. No one would think it awful to state that a man has a penis and a woman, a vagina. Or that a man produces sperm and a woman, eggs. But when we begin exploring the behavioral implications of these facts somebody is sure to cry "Foul." If male-female differences are sexist, we should put the blame where it really belongs, on the greatest sexist of all: "Mother" Nature! (90)

Contributions

Scientific Framework to Study Human Social Behavior. The social sciences have long suffered from what biologist Joel Cohen calls **physics envy** (Barash 1979, 3). That is, social sciences are impressed by how much reliable information physics can generate using only a few scientifically rigorous theoretical principles. The social scientists have no such structure. As a result, Barash (1979) says:

> The "essence" of human beings has escaped their analysis, and indeed the social sciences have never been able to agree on even the most basic principles governing their work. They have much to envy in physics.
>
> The real strength of physics, and to a lesser extent the other natural sciences, lies in their intellectual coherence. In most cases, good science derives from a small number of relatively simple but enormously powerful ground rules. Indeed, it is remarkable how simplicity and explanatory power often go together. By contrast, the social sciences have erected an incredibly intricate but rickety Tower of Babel. Theories have proliferated with almost the abundance of their expounders, and there has been over the years a succession of Spencerians, Durkheimians, Weberians, Marxists, Freudians, Adlerians, Jungians, Piagetians, Skinnerians—and countless others. (3)

Barash and the other sociobiologists believe that evolutionary theory can provide the theoretical underpinning that the social sciences need.

Responding to the usefulness of sociobiology as a scientific theory, Buss (1987) says:

Among the valuable attributes of any psychological theory are the power to array known and sometimes disparate observations in an orderly and coherent fashion; to generate clear predictions and phenomena not yet discovered; and to render sensible otherwise anomalous or incomprehensible findings. Evolutionary theory carries the promise of possessing these valuable attributes. (335)

Likewise, Wallace (1979) says:

One would wish that the sociobiological paradigm will simply provide our introspective species with one more window into itself. After all, we need all the windows we can get. We are altering our world with dizzying and accelerating rapidity. And we are placing ourselves in the peculiar position of having to adapt to what we have made. Yet we know so little about ourselves, our motivations, our goals, our heritage. You can't even predict what *you* will do under this or that circumstance. If we are ignorant about ourselves individually, how little we must know about our species. Our efforts to understand the human condition have been met too often with abysmal failure. Perhaps we need a fresh approach. Sociobiology can provide such an approach. (16)

Sociobiology Is Heuristic.   Many believe that sociobiology will provide several new, important, and interesting avenues of research in psychology. For example, Symons (1987) says:

The potential contribution of Darwinism to psychology does not lie merely in assigning ultimate causes to psychological mechanisms. Rather . . . Darwinism can aid our understanding of the mind: It guides research, prevents certain kinds of errors, inspires new questions, and calls attention to aspects of the mind that are normally too mundane or uniform to be noticed. . . . Even such a modest contribution to the formidable task of understanding the most complex thing in the known universe, the human brain/mind, surely will be welcomed. (143–44)

Crawford, Smith, and Krebs (1987) describe what they see as sociobiology's heuristic potential.

As a synthesis of ideas from behavioral ecology, population genetics, ethology, comparative psychology and behavior genetics, sociobiology offers the opportunity of integrating ideas from biology into the social sciences and even into the humanities. Some believe that its eventual impact may be as great as that of psychoanalysis and behaviorism. (xi)

Summary

The formal beginning of sociobiology is marked by the publication of Wilson's book *Sociobiology: The New Synthesis* in 1975. To a large extent sociobiology is based on Darwin's theory of evolution. Darwin's theory includes the important concepts of struggle for survival, survival of the fittest, and natural selection. Unlike traditional Darwinian theory, sociobiology emphasizes inclusive fitness—that is, perpetuating one's genes either by producing offspring, or by assisting close relatives so that they can survive and reproduce.

The two basic assumptions of sociobiology are (1) the primary motive for every living organism, including humans, is to perpetuate its genes into the next generation; and (2) adaptive social behavior is shaped by natural selection just as anatomic features and physiological mechanisms are. The empirical theory of human nature assumes that what a person is at any given moment is determined by his or her cumulative experiences. Most social scientists accept the empirical theory of human nature, and therefore, for them culture (learning) is all important in determining human social behavior. The sociobiologists disagree with the empirical theory of human nature saying instead that humans are born with a biogrammar (whisperings, innate predispositions) that has been selected by evolution. The sociobiologists offer cultural universals as evidence that the human mind is not a blank tablet at birth. Because most social scientists accept the empirical theory of human nature they seek the causes of human behavior in a person's internal or external environment, or in his or her life's experiences (for example, learning and memory). Such causes of behavior are called proximate. The sociobiologists, conversely, seek the reasons why certain behaviors were perpetuated by the evolutionary process. Such reasons constitute the ultimate causes of behavior. According to the sociobiologists, the reason why some behaviors are "sweeter" than others is because they are conducive to survival and reproduction.

What we inherit from our evolutionary past are general tendencies or predispositions to act in some ways instead of others. Because these tendencies are always modified by culture, human social behavior must always be seen as resulting from an interaction between innate tendencies and cultural influences. To say that culture has a powerful influence on human behavior, however, is not to say that culture is all-powerful. Culture must always maintain a reasonable relationship to human biology. If culture strays too far from human biology, social behavior will disintegrate and eventually reproduction will cease. Human biology, then, holds culture on a leash, sometimes a long leash, but a leash nonetheless. Wilson calls this the "leash principle." Both Wilson and Barash believe that much in culture represents the extension or amplification of slight biologic tendencies. Wilson calls the cultural exaggeration of biologic tendencies hypertrophy, and Barash calls it cultural hyperextension.

According to the sociobiologists, both the human mind and the human body are the products of evolution. This means that mental processes, both conscious and unconscious, exist as they do in us today because they enhanced the survival and reproduction of our ancestors. The genes influence cognitive processes through epigenetic rules. Primary epigenetic rules determine what kinds of sensations and perceptions we can have. Secondary epigenetic rules determine which sensations or perceptions are selected for further processing, and how they are evaluated intellectually and emotionally and then acted on. Evaluation via the secondary epigenetic rules is always done relative to survival and reproduction. Secondary epigenetic rules also account for prepared learning.

We are willing to help our close relatives because in doing so we are increasing our inclusive fitness. Through the preferential treatment of relatives (kin altruism or nepotism) we perpetuate our genes through kin selection. We agree to help nonrelatives, because it is understood that if and when we need help we too will receive it. Altruism involving nonrelatives is called reciprocal altruism. The help you receive may come from the very person you helped (direct reciprocity) or from someone else in the community (indirect reciprocity). With reciprocal altruism the possibility of cheating always exists—that is, taking but not giving or giving less than what you had received. In every human society rules and regulations reward reciprocal altruism and punish cheaters. The sociobiologists conclude that true altruism (giving and expecting nothing in return) does not exist.

For men a sexual act may result in an offspring and, therefore, would enhance their fitness. This being the case, the more women a man can inseminate, the greater is his fitness. For the woman, being inseminated involves an enormous investment of time, energy, and resources. To make the most of her substantial investment, a woman tends to seek a man as a mate who carries genes that are likely to create healthy offspring, has resources that would enhance the survival of her and her offspring, and would be willing to share those resources. The optimal female strategy for mate selection, then, is to discriminate among men. The optimal male strategy is to be promiscuous. The difference between these strategies for mate selection is believed by the sociobiologists to be the basis for the double standard. Because men have such a small investment in reproduction and because they can never be absolutely certain that an offspring carries their genes, they tend not to get very involved in parenting. According to the sociobiologists, women tend to experience the emotion of jealousy when another woman threatens to reduce the resources being provided to her by a man. Men tend to become jealous when their mates see other men, thereby bringing into question the authenticity of their parenthood. The fact that men become involved in parenting at all may be explained by the mate's sexual availability. Apparently frequent sex creates a bond between partners. For men, the most natural mating arrangement appears to be polygyny (having more than one mate). Polyandry (women having more than one mate) is extremely rare, and monogamy, (having one mate) may be biologically "unnatural" for men.

Humans are interested in their own genes but not very interested in those of others. This explains why stepparents tend to have more problems with children than do natural parents and why adoption is an overwhelming second choice among parents. The sociobiologists suspect that intentional childlessness could cause some psychological or emotional damage, because such a decision runs contrary to millions of years of evolution. In general, the tendency of men to be anatomically larger and more emotionally aggressive than women has led directly or indirectly to male dominance over women in all past and present societies. In most cases, men have held, and now hold, the most powerful and influential positions within a society. To say that male dominance over women is "natural," however, is not to say that such dominance is good. To argue that because something is natural it is therefore good, is to commit the naturalistic fallacy.

The sociobiologists do not accept the drive-discharge model of aggression offered by Freud. Rather, they say that humans are capable of acting aggressively but will do so only when it is justified. That is, humans engage in a cost-benefit analysis before deciding to act aggressively or not. Often organisms will act aggressively in defense of their territories. Members of a tribe or nation may even engage in war if they believe that their territory is threatened.

According to the sociobiologic analysis of rape, rapists tend to be men who are losers in the competition with other men for women. Rape, then, is seen as a desperate attempt to perpetuate one's genes when one is not chosen by a woman.

This theory of rape predicts that rapists will tend to be poor, young men, and rape victims will tend to be fertile, young women. Research has supported both predictions.

A high probability exists that an offspring resulting from an incestuous relationship will be genetically defective. Therefore, it makes good evolutionary sense to avoid such relationships and taboos against incest are culturally universal. Freud believed that incest taboos were necessary to inhibit strong sexual attractions among family members. Westermarck believed that at least brother-sister incest was naturally inhibited if brother and sister interacted closely as young children. The avoidance of sex by those who interacted as young children is called the Westermarck effect. Van den Berghe found that in societies in which close, intimate contact is encouraged between children and between children and adults, the Westermarck effect operates to inhibit incestuous relationships. In societies in which close, intimate contact among family members is discouraged (such as the one in which Freud grew up), strong taboos appear to be needed to inhibit incestuous relationships.

De Catanzaro speculates that people who commit suicide are those whose continued existence would not contribute to their inclusive fitness and may even operate against it. Groups with a high risk of suicide include the terminally ill; the chronically unemployed; the socially isolated; and those who are single, divorced, widowed, or in an unstable marriage. Other forms of self-destructive behavior, such as overeating, smoking, drinking alcohol, or taking drugs are thought to result from the incompatibility between the conditions under which humans evolved and those under which we now live.

Religion plays several important roles in human society: It gives its adherents a sense of kinship; it sanctifies the rules and regulations governing social life, including those related to reciprocal altruism; it simplifies life by dichotomizing the people in the world into friends and enemies, and by providing myths that offer simple answers to complex questions; and it encourages people to subordinate their selfish interests to those of the community. Humans then are remarkably easy to indoctrinate because in our evolutionary past conformity and survival were closely related. In general, religion functions to encourage behavior conducive to survival and to discourage behavior that is not. For this reason, many religions contain sanctions against nonreproductive sexual behavior.

Freud and the sociobiologists agree that humans are basically selfish; the unconscious mind is important; humans are flexible problem solvers; emotional experience guides behavior; and self-deception plays a significant role in behavior. Freud and the sociobiologists disagree on the origin of the superego and in their explanations of human aggression. Both Jung and the sociobiologists believe that much current human behavior can be understood in terms of our evolutionary past.

Sociobiology has been criticized for accepting or supporting an array of radical, political viewpoints; not being falsifiable; accepting an adaptationist program; accepting a rigid biologic determinism; legitimizing the status quo; supporting racism; and being sexist. The contributions of sociobiology include providing the social sciences a solid scientific base from which to study human behavior and providing many new avenues of research.

EXPERIENTIAL EXERCISES

1. List those aspects of your life that are of special importance right now. For example, relationships, education, health, employment, or finances. Which of these areas of concern could have a biologic basis? That is, which of them could reflect a "whispering" within you. Explain.

2. Ponder a few members of the opposite sex that you find especially attractive. Determine what characteristics those persons have in common. Are the characteristics that you find attractive in accordance with the predictions made by sociobiology? Explain.

3. Has it been your experience that women are more committed to parenting than men? Do you think that our culture values mothers more than fathers as parents? Are your observations in accordance with sociobiology or not? Explain.

4. List the ten people about whom you care the most. For example, for whom would you be most willing to make a sacrifice? According to sociobiology, your list should be dominated by persons with whom you are either genetically related or with whom you are bonded through sexual intimacy. How does your list compare to the one predicted by sociobiology?

5. Do you agree with the sociobiologists that all human behavior is ultimately selfish? Explain why you do or do not agree.

6. Based on your own life's experiences, describe the conditions under which women and men experience jealousy. Are the reasons the same? Different? Are the reasons in accordance with those suggested by sociobiology? Explain.

7. Summarize aspects of sociobiology with which you agree or disagree. Do you agree that sociobiology offers a valuable framework with which to study human behavior? Explain.

DISCUSSION QUESTIONS

1. What is sociobiology?

2. Explain why applying evolutionary principles to the study of human behavior might be disturbing to some people.

3. Briefly discuss the following terms: *struggle for survival, adaptation, survival of the fittest, fitness, natural selection.*

4. What are the two basic assumptions made by sociobiologists?

5. Distinguish between the empirical and the sociobiologic theories of human nature.

6. Distinguish between the terms *biologic determinism,* and *inherited behavior potentiality.* Which of the two does sociobiology accept? Explain.

7. Distinguish between proximate and ultimate causation of behavior and give an example of each.

8. Describe the relationship between cultural and biologic evolution. According to the sociobiologists, what might happen if the discrepancy between the two becomes too great? Include in your answer a discussion of Wilson's "leash principle."

9. First define hypertrophy (cultural hyperextension) and then give an example of it.

10. Define and give examples of primary and secondary epigenetic rules.

11. What is prepared learning? Give an example.

12. According to Barash, why are some behaviors and experiences "sweeter" than others?

13. Why, according to the sociobiologists, are we willing to help those genetically related to us? Those who are not?

14. Compare and contrast the strategies used by men and women to perpetuate their genes?

15. According to the sociobiologists, what do

women tend to look for in a mate? What do men tend to look for in a mate?

16. First define the double standard and then discuss what the sociobiologists think might be its biologic basis.

17. According to the sociobiologists, what mating arrangements are probably best for men? Why do they think that this is the case?

18. What is the *naturalistic fallacy?*

19. Why, according to the sociobiologists, have human women developed the ability to be sexually receptive throughout their menstrual cycle? Why have they developed the ability to have an orgasm?

20. Summarize the differences between men and women in relation to parenting.

21. According to the sociobiologists, under what circumstances do women experience jealousy? Men?

22. Summarize the views of the sociobiologists concerning stepparents, adoption, and intentional childlessness.

23. What, according to the sociobiologists, are the reasons that humans go to war? What, if anything, can be done to reduce the probability of war?

24. Summarize the sociobiologic explanation of rape.

25. Compare and contrast Freud's thinking on incest with that of Westermarck.

26. According to de Catanzaro, what are the circumstances under which a person may commit suicide?

27. In general, how do the sociobiologists account for self-abusive behavior?

28. Compare and contrast sociobiology and Freudian theory.

29. Discuss how religion is instrumental in facilitating cooperative living among humans.

30. Discuss how a scientist's personal beliefs may influence what kinds of information he or she accepts or rejects.

31. First describe each of the following criticisms of sociobiology, and then indicate whether you accept or reject it and why: Sociobiology is not falsifiable, sociobiology is based on adaptationism, sociobiology accepts a rigid biologic determinism, sociobiology legitimizes the status quo, sociobiology is racist, and sociobiology is sexist.

32. Summarize what the author of your text lists as the contributions of sociobiology and indicate whether or not you agree.

SUGGESTIONS FOR FURTHER READING

BARASH, D. P. (1979). *The Whisperings Within: Evolution and the Origin of Human Nature.* New York: Penguin Books.

> The most readable, nontechnical introduction to sociobiology. Barash's sense of humor makes this book entertaining as well as informative.

BARASH, D. P. (1982). *Sociobiology and Behavior* (2d ed). New York: Elsevier.

> The book that Edward Wilson described as "The best introductory textbook available on [sociobiology], and it is not likely to be surpassed in the near future." More comprehensive and more technical than *The Whisperings Within* but still very readable.

BARASH, D. P. (1986). *The Hare and the Tortoise: Culture, Biology, and Human Nature.* New York: Penguin Books.

> Discusses the many problems that result when cultural evolution outpaces biologic evolution.

BARASH, D. P., AND LIPTON, J. E. (1985). *The Caveman and the Bomb: Human Nature, Evolution, and Nuclear War.* New York: McGraw-Hill.

> Chapters include "Paranoia: The Individual," "Paranoia: The Nation," "Propaganda: Lies We Love to Believe," and "Deterrence: The Last Tango."

WILSON, E. O. (1975). *Sociobiology: The New Synthesis.* Cambridge, MA: Harvard University Press.

> The book that founded sociobiology. Highly technical and focuses mainly on the behavior of nonhuman animals (only the last chapter discusses the implications of sociobiology for humans). Best suited for the advanced student with considerable background in biology.

WILSON, E. O. (1978). *On Human Nature.* New York: Bantam.

Wilson's Pulitzer Prize–winning book in which he discusses such topics as aggression, sex, altruism, religion, and hope in sociobiologic terms.

GLOSSARY

Adaptation. Any anatomic structure, physiological process, or behavior pattern that enhances an organism's chances of surviving and reproducing; and the process of successfully adjusting to the environment.

Altruism. Making a sacrifice of some kind to help someone else without expecting anything in return. Although the sociobiologists use the term *altruism,* they do not believe that true altruistic behavior occurs among living organisms, including humans. (See also kin altruism and reciprocal altruism.)

Behavioral potentiality. The ability to respond with any one of a range of behaviors to a category of environmental experience.

Biogrammar. The genetic program that is responsible for culturally universal human behavior. Our biogrammar structures our social behavior just as grammar structures our verbal behavior.

Biologic determinism. In the strong sense, the inherited predisposition to respond in a specific way to specific categories of environmental experience. In the weak sense, the predisposition to respond in any one of several ways to categories of environmental experience. Weaker biologic determinism assumes that behavioral potentiality is inherited. It is the weaker form of biologic determinism that is accepted by sociobiology.

Cheating. Accepting help from someone without the intention of reciprocating. The cheater either takes and does not give, or takes much more than he or she gives.

Cultural universal. A category of human social behavior that is found in all human cultures.

Double standard. The fact that male and female sexual activity is evaluated differently. For example, male promiscuity is generally tolerated much more so than is female promiscuity.

Drive-discharge model of aggression. The view that the need to act aggressively increases in magnitude if it is not periodically satisfied. According to this view the need to act aggressively must be satisfied just like the hunger and thirst drives must be satisfied. Freud held such a view of aggression.

Empirical theory of human nature. The contention that the human mind is blank at birth and becomes furnished by experience. According to this conception of human nature, no inherited predispositions exist, and, therefore, what a person becomes in his or her lifetime is determined by his or her empirical (sensory) experience.

Entomology. The scientific study of insects.

Epigenetic rules. The innate rules that mediate between experience and the processes of the mind. Primary epigenetic rules determine which aspects of the physical environment can be sensed or perceived. Secondary epigenetic rules determine how information provided by the primary epigenetic rules is evaluated, responded to emotionally, learned and remembered, and how decisions are made with regard to that information.

Fertility. For a woman, the current ability to become pregnant. For a man, the current ability to cause a woman to become pregnant.

Fitness. The ability to survive and reproduce.

Hypergamy. The tendency for women to benefit themselves through their selection of a mate.

Hypertrophy. (Also called cultural hyperextension.) The cultural exaggeration of innate human predispositions.

Inclusive fitness. A person's success in perpetuating his or her genes into subsequent generations either by producing offspring himself or herself, by helping relatives survive and reproduce, or both.

Jealousy. According to the sociobiologists, the emotion that women experience when the resources that men provide them and their offspring are threatened; and that men experience when the activities of their mates raise questions concerning the authenticity of their parenthood.

Kin altruism. The offering of help to genetically related individuals. The closer the genetic relatedness, the stronger is the tendency to offer preferential treatment.

Kin selection. The increase in one's inclusive fitness that results from the preferential treatment of one's relatives.

Leash principle. Wilson's contention that the genes function to maintain a reasonable relationship between our culture and our biologic makeup. If culture becomes too incompatible with our biologic makeup, widespread deterioration of social behavior would perhaps lead to the extinction of the human species.

Monogamy. The reproductive system whereby one man mates with one woman.

Natural selection. The fact that only organisms who possess adaptive traits in a given environment survive and reproduce.

Naturalistic fallacy. The mistaken belief that what naturally "is" is also what "ought" to be.

Nepotism. The same as kin altruism.

Nothing butism. Barash's term describing those who take extreme positions when attempting to explain human behavior. For example, those who say that all human social behavior is nothing but learned (culturally determined), or those who say that all human social behavior is nothing but genetically determined.

Physics envy. The dismay expressed by many social scientists over the fact that physics is a rigorous science with a few highly heuristic explanatory principles and the social sciences are not.

Polyandry. The reproductive system whereby one woman mates with more than one man.

Polygyny. The reproductive system whereby a man mates with more than one woman.

Prepared learning. The kind of learning that occurs rapidly and with ease because it involves learning information and skills that enhance an organism's inclusive fitness.

Proximate causation. The immediate factors, such as the organism's motivation state, the organism's previous experience in the situation, and various environmental events that are responsible for a particular response being made.

Reciprocal altruism. The willingness to help genetically unrelated people, which is based on the understanding that those people (direct reciprocity), or other members of the community (indirect reciprocity), will help you when the need arises.

Reproductive imperative. According to Wallace, the biologic mandate to reproduce and leave as many offspring as possible.

Reproductive value. A person's long-term ability to produce offspring. In general, a young person will have higher reproductive value than an older person, because the younger person will be capable of reproduction during a longer period of time.

Sociobiologic theory of human nature. The contention that humans are born with tendencies to behave in ways that enhanced the fitness of our ancestors. For the sociobiologists the human mind is well stocked with behavioral predispositions at birth and, therefore, is anything but blank.

Sociobiology. The systematic study of the biologic basis of social behavior, including that of humans.

Struggle for survival. The competition for survival that results among members of a species when the number of organisms exceeds that which could be sustained by environmental resources.

Survival of the fittest. The fact that only those organisms that possess adaptive traits survive and reproduce.

Territory. An area or property that is perceived as one's own and is therefore defended if penetrated by an uninvited person or persons.

Ultimate causation. Those causes of an organism's behavior that reflect the evolutionary history of the organism. Ultimate causes of behavior reflect the behavior's adaptive significance.

Westermarck effect. The tendency to avoid a sexual relationship later in life with someone with whom one had a close relationship when he or she was a young child.

Whisperings. Barash's term for inherited behavioral predispositions.

Xenophobia. The fear of strangers.

George Kelly

George Alexander Kelly was born on a farm near Perth, Kansas, on 28 April 1905. He was an only child. Kelly's father had been trained as a Presbyterian minister but, because of poor health, gave up the ministry and turned to farming. In 1909, Kelly's father converted a lumber wagon into a covered wagon and used it to move his family to Colorado, where they staked a claim to a plot of land offered free to settlers. They moved back to their farm in Kansas, however, when they were unable to find water on their claim. Kelly never seemed to lose the pioneer spirit derived from his early experiences. He remained a practical person throughout his life; his overriding concern with an idea or a device was whether it worked or not; if it did not, he had no time for it. Furthermore, Kelly was strongly influenced by his parents' deep religious convictions and remained an active member of the church.

Kelly's early education consisted of attending a one-room schoolhouse and being tutored by his parents. When he was thirteen, he was sent to Wichita, where he eventually attended four different high schools. After the age of thirteen, Kelly seldom lived at home again. On graduation from high school, he enrolled in the Friends University in Wichita, a Quaker school. After three years he moved to Park College, where he earned his B.A. degree in physics and mathematics in 1926. Kelly remembered his first psychology class as totally unimpressive. For the first few weeks he waited in vain for something interesting to be said. One day the instructor began to discuss stimulus-response psychology and placed "S→R" on the blackboard. Finally, Kelly thought, they were getting to the crux of the matter. Kelly (1969) recalled his disappointment.

> Although I listened intently for several sessions, after that the most I could make of it was that the "S" was what you had to have in order to account for the "R" and the "R" was put there so the "S" would have something to account for. I never did find out what that arrow stood for—not to this day—and I have pretty well given up trying to figure it out. (47)

Kelly had originally planned on a career as an engineer, but decided such a career would not allow him to deal with social problems, with which he was becoming increasingly interested. As a result, he enrolled in the M.A. program at the University of Kansas, with a major in educational sociology and a minor in labor relations. For his master's thesis, he studied how workers in Kansas City spent their leisure time. He was awarded an M.A. degree in 1928. It was during his graduate training at the University of Kansas that Kelly decided it was time for him to become acquainted with the writings of Freud. He was about as impressed by Freud's theory as he was by S→R psychology. "I don't remember which one of Freud's books I was trying to read, but I do remember the mounting feeling of incredulity that anyone could write such nonsense, much less publish it" (Kelly 1969, 47).

The next year was a busy one for Kelly. He taught part-time in a labor college in Minneapolis, speech classes for the American Bankers Association, and an Americanization class to immigrants wishing to become citizens. Finally, in the winter

George Kelly

of 1928, he joined the faculty at a junior college in Sheldon, Iowa, where he met his future wife, Gladys Thompson. Among his other duties, he coached dramatics, which, as we shall see, may have influenced Kelly's later theorizing.

In 1929, Kelly was awarded an exchange scholarship, which enabled him to spend a year at the University of Edinburgh, in Scotland, where he worked closely with Sir Godfrey Thomson. Sir Godfrey was largely responsible for Kelly's developing an interest in psychology. In 1930, Kelly earned a degree in education from the University of Edinburgh. His thesis, under the supervision of Sir Godfrey, was on predicting teaching success.

On returning to the United States in 1930, he enrolled in a psychology program at Iowa State University, where he earned his Ph.D. in 1931. His dissertation was on the common factors in speech and reading disabilities. Two days after graduation, he married Gladys Thompson, and they eventually had two children. By the time Kelly obtained his Ph.D. in psychology at the age of 26, he had already studied physics, mathematics, sociology, education, labor relations, economics, speech pathology, cultural anthropology, and biometrics.

Kelly's academic career began at Fort Hays Kansas State College, in the midst of the Great Depression. He learned soon that his interest in physiological psychology, which he pursued at Iowa State University, would do him little good under his present circumstances. He noted that the people with whom he had contact simply did not know what to do with their lives—they were confused. Kelly, therefore, switched his interests to clinical psychology, for which there was a great need. It turns out that Kelly had a great advantage at this point, in that *he was not formally trained in any particular clinical technique.* This, along with his practical nature, gave him great latitude in trying a variety of approaches in treating emotional problems. What worked was salvaged; what did not work was discarded. Kelly had read some of Freud and did try some of his ideas, but found them basically ineffective and boring.

During his thirteen-year (1931 to 1943) stay at Fort Hays, Kelly developed traveling clinics, which serviced the state's public school system. This service allowed Kelly and his students to experience a wide range of psychological problems and to experiment with ways of treating them. It was during this time that Kelly made two observations that were to have a profound influence on his later theory. First, Kelly found that even if he made up a radical explanation for a client's problem, the client would accept it and usually improve. In other words, Kelly noted that anything that would cause clients to look at themselves or their problems differently caused improvement in the situation. Logic, or "correctness," seemed to have little to do with it. Kelly described his experiment with psychotherapy as follows:

> I began fabricating "insights." I deliberately offered "preposterous interpretations" to my clients. Some of them were about as un-Freudian as I could make them— first proposed somewhat cautiously, of course, and then, as I began to see what was happening, more boldly. My only criteria were that the explanation account for the crucial facts as the client saw them, and that it carry implications for approaching the future in a different way. (1969, 52)

Second, Kelly noted that a teacher's complaint about a student often said more about the teacher than it did about the student. It was the way the teacher was *seeing things* that determined the nature of the problem, rather than some objective event that everyone could experience. It was observations like these that stimulated Kelly to develop perhaps one of the boldest theories of personality since Freud's theory.

At the beginning of World War II, Kelly was in charge of a local civilian pilot-training program. Eventually he joined the navy as a psychologist in the Bureau of Medicine and Surgery and was stationed in Washington, D.C. While in the service, he did much to improve the quality and effectiveness of clinical psychology in the armed forces. Kelly remained active in a number of government programs related to clinical psychology until his death.

In 1945, when the war ended, Kelly was appointed associate professor at the University of Maryland, where he remained for one year. In 1946 he became professor of psychology and director of clinical psychology at Ohio State University. Although the department was extremely small, Kelly, along with Julian B. Rotter, himself destined to become a prominent psychologist, developed a clinical psychology program that many considered to be the best in the country. It was during his nineteen years at Ohio State that Kelly refined and tested his theory of personality. As was mentioned in the previous chapter, Walter Mischel was a student of Rotter's and Kelly's and their influence is clearly seen in social learning theory.

During 1960–61, Kelly and his wife received a grant from the Human Ecology Fund that allowed them to travel around the world lecturing on the relationship between Kelly's theory and various international problems. Their journey carried them to Madrid, London, Oslo, Louvain, Copenhagen, Prague, Warsaw, Moscow, the Caribbean area, and South America. It was quite an adventure for someone who claimed never to have gotten all the Kansas mud off his shoes.

In 1965, Kelly left Ohio State to accept an appointment to an endowed chair at Brandeis University. Kelly died on 6 March 1967 at the age of sixty-two.

Among Kelly's honors were the presidencies of both the clinical and counseling divisions of the American Psychological Association. He also played a major role in formulating the American Board of Examiners in Professional Psychology; an organization whose purpose it is to upgrade the quality of professional psychologists. He served as president of the Board of Examiners from 1951 through 1953.

Kelly was remembered by his students and colleagues as a warm, accepting person. George Thomson, a former colleague of Kelly's shared the following reflection on the occasion of Kelly's death:

> At the 1963 Convention of the American Psychological Association, some 40 former students of George Kelly attended a dinner to pay tribute to their good teacher and warm friend. These professors, scientists, and therapists came from all parts of the United States. All of them knew that here was a man who helped them find their ways to more productive lives. Many others who could not attend wrote letters of appreciation for his wise counsel and guidance. (1968, 22–23)

Compared to the other theorists covered in this book, Kelly wrote relatively little. The major presentation of his theory is found in his two-volume work, entitled, *The Psychology of Personal Constructs* (1955). In the preface to volume one of this work Kelly gave his readers fair warning about what they were about to read. We reproduce Kelly's warning here to give the flavor of his writing style, to show his iconoclastic approach to psychology, and to provide an overview of his theory of personality.

> It is only fair to warn the reader about what may be in store for him. In the first place, he is likely to find missing most of the familiar landmarks of psychology books. For example, the *learning*, so honorably embedded in most psychological texts, scarcely appears at all. That is wholly intentional; we are for throwing it overboard altogether. There is no *ego*, no *emotion*, no *motivation*, no *reinforcement*, no *drive*, no *unconscious*, no *need*. There are some words with brand-new psychological definitions, words like *foci of convenience, preemption, propositionality, fixed-role therapy, creativity cycle, transitive diagnosis,* and *the credulous approach. Anxiety* is defined in a special systematic way. *Role, guilt,* and *hostility* carry definitions altogether unexpected by many; and to make heresy complete, there is no extensive bibliography. Unfortunately, all this will make for periods of strange, and perhaps uncomfortable, reading. Yet, inevitably, a different approach calls for a different lexicon; and, under its influence, many old terms are unhitched from their familiar meanings.
>
> To whom are we speaking? In general, we think the reader who takes us seriously will be an adventuresome soul who is not one bit afraid of thinking unorthodox thoughts about people, who dares peer out at the world through the eyes of strangers, who has not invested beyond his means in either ideas or

vocabulary, and who is looking for an ad interim, rather than an ultimate, set of psychological insights. He may earn his living as a psychologist, an educator, a social worker, a psychiatrist, a clergyman, an administrator—that is not particularly relevant. He may never have had a course in psychology, although if he has not been puzzling rather seriously over psychological problems he will most certainly be unhappy with his choice of this book. (x–xi)

Categorization of Kelly's Theory

As already mentioned, Kelly started as a clinical psychologist without any formal clinical training. In other words, he was not indoctrinated in any particular school of thought. Kelly was confronted by people with problems and, because he had no clinical skills, had to improvise his own techniques. He had no mentor to guide him; he came from no department with a particular philosophical leaning; and he was not surrounded by a group of colleagues who steered him in a certain direction. He therefore "played it by ear." Thus, if Kelly's theory resembles anyone else's, it is not Kelly's fault; it is a coincidence. As we shall see, Kelly believed that a person's present personality need not be tied to his or her past. He believed the same to be true of personality theories; that is, to be valid, a theory need not grow out of those theories already in existence. Kelly's theory of personality is probably as independent of other theoretical positions as a theory can be. The similarities between his and other theories have been noted mainly by other people; Kelly did not care much about them.

Kelly's theory, however, can be classified in certain ways. First, Kelly was a **phenomenologist.** Phenomenologists believe that intact conscious experience should be psychology's focus of attention. It should not matter where such experiences originate; the important thing to study, the phenomenologists believe, is a person's own individual conscious experiences, without breaking them down into component parts or attempting to determine their origin. Although Kelly can be labeled a phenomenologist because he studied intact conscious experience, it should be noted that he was only interested in such experience in relationship to objective reality. That is, unlike many phenomenologists, Kelly was interested in how thought processes were used while interacting with the environment.

Kelly's theory also can be labeled cognitive, because it emphasizes mental events. It is not a behavioral theory, because the emphasis is not on behavior and its causal relationships to the environment; it is not a psychoanalytic theory, because it does not stress unconscious mechanisms or early experience in the determination of adult personality; and it is not a trait theory, because it does not attempt to categorize people in terms of their traits. It is a **cognitive theory,** because it stresses how people *view* and *think about* reality.

Kelly's theory also can be considered an **existential theory** because it emphasizes the present and the future rather than the past, and because it assumes that humans are free to choose their own destinies. In general, existentialism assumes that humans are free and future oriented, that their subjective feelings and personal experience are extremely important, and that they are concerned with the meaning of life. The existentialists also believe that, because humans are free, they are also responsible for their own destinies. Generally, existentialists examine the problems of human existence. The statement that man "is what he wills to be," by the famous existential philosopher Jean-Paul Sarte (1956, 291), fairly well summarizes both Kelly's and the existentialist's position.

Last, Kelly's theory can be considered a **humanistic theory** because it stresses the human capacity for improvement. Kelly urged each person to continue to explore new possibilities for living; possibilities that may turn out to be more effective than those already tried. Both Kelly and the humanists believed that humans sought, and were capable of, better personal, sociological, and international conditions.

Kelly's theory, then, can be labeled phenomenological because it focuses on *intact* subjective experience, cognitive because it emphasizes the study of mental events, existential because it stresses the present and the future and humans' ability to choose their own destinies, and humanistic because it is optimistic about humans in that it emphasizes humans' creative abilities, which can be directed at solving individual or sociological problems.

Basic Postulate—People as Scientists

Kelly took the scientist as the model for describing all humans. He noted that scientists are constantly seeking clarity and understanding in their lives by developing theories that will allow them to predict future events; in other words, *the scientist's main goal is to reduce uncertainty.* Kelly believed that, like scientists, all humans are attempting to clarify their lives by reducing uncertainty, and therefore the distinction between the scientist and the nonscientist is not a valid one.

> It is as though the psychologist were saying to himself, "I, being a *psychologist*, and therefore a *scientist*, am performing this experiment in order to improve the prediction and control of certain human phenomena; but my subject, being merely a human organism, is obviously propelled by inexorable drives welling up within him, or else he is in gluttonous pursuit of sustenance and shelter." (Kelly 1955, 5)

According to Kelly, all humans are like scientists in that they are interested in the future and use the present only to test a theory's ability to anticipate events. "Anticipation is not merely carried on for its own sake; it is carried on so that future reality may be better represented. It is the future which tantalizes man, not the past. Always he reaches out to the future through the window of the present" (Kelly 1955, 49).

The major tool a person uses in anticipating events is the **personal construct.** Personal constructs are used by individuals to **construe** or interpret, explain, give meaning to, or predict experiences. A construct is an idea or thought that a person uses when attempting to interpret his or her own personal experiences. A construct is like a miniscientific theory, in that it makes predictions about reality. If the predictions generated by a construct are confirmed by experience, it is useful; if the predictions are not confirmed, the construct must be revised or abandoned. "Man looks at his world through transparent patterns or templets which he creates and then attempts to fit over the realities of which the world is composed. . . . Let us give the name *constructs* to these patterns that are tentatively tried on for size. They are ways of construing the world" (Kelly 1955, 8–9).

We will have much more to say about constructs in the next section, but it is important to note that they are usually verbal labels that a person applies to environmental events and then tests with subsequent experience with those events. For example, on meeting a person for the first time, one might construe that person with the construct of "friendly." If the person's subsequent behavior is in accordance with the construct of friendly, then the construct will be useful in anticipating that person's behavior. If the new acquaintance acts in an unfriendly manner, he or she will need to be construed either with different constructs or by using the other pole (see the *Dichotomy Corollary* in the next section) of the friendly-unfriendly construct. The major point is that constructs are used to anticipate the future, so they must fit reality. Arriving at a **construct system** that corresponds fairly closely to reality is largely a matter of trial and error. According to Kelly, a person's **personality** refers to the collection of constructs that constitute his or her construct system at any given time.

Kelly emphasized the fact that each person *creates his or her own constructs* for dealing with the world. Kelly believed that, although all people have the goal of reducing future uncertainty, they are free to construe reality any way they wish. He called this belief **constructive alternativism,** which he described as follows: "We take the stand that there are always some alternative constructions available to choose among in dealing with the world. No one needs to paint himself into a corner; no one needs to be completely hemmed in by circumstances; no one needs to be the victim of his biography" (1955, 15).

Although it is true that no one *needs* to "paint himself into a corner," it does not mean that people do not do so. Here we have an interesting distinction between freedom and determinism. Although Kelly believed that individuals are free to create their own construct systems, he also believed that they are controlled by them after they are created. In other words, a person's life is strongly influenced by the way he or she construes experiences, and some ways of construing things are better than others. According to Kelly, some individuals arrive at inflexible convictions about the world and become slaves to them. The lives of such individuals are dominated by rules and regulations, and they live within a narrow range of highly predictable events. Others have a broader perspective. Their lives are lived in accordance with flexible principles rather than the rigid rules. Such individuals live a richer life because of their openness to experience.

> Ultimately a man sets the measure of his own freedom and his own bondage by the level at which he chooses to establish his convictions. The man who orders his life in terms of many special and inflexible convictions about temporary matters makes himself the victim of circumstances. Each little prior conviction that is not open to review is a hostage he gives to fortune; it determines whether the events of tomorrow will bring happiness or misery. The man whose prior convictions encompass a broad perspective, and are cast in terms of principles rather than rules, has a much better chance of discovering alternatives which will lead eventually to his emancipation. (Kelly 1955, 21–22)

Thus, according to Kelly, whether one lives an open, creative life or a restrictive one is largely a matter of personal choice. Likewise, some people can look at a situation positively, and others can look at the same situation negatively. Again, it is a matter of personal choice. Kelly's position on this matter is nicely summarized by the old saying, "Two men looked out from prison bars, one saw mud and the other saw stars." This brings us to the fundamental postulate in Kelly's theory: "*A person's processes are psychologically channelized by the ways in which he anticipates events*" (Kelly 1955, 46). In other words, an individual's activities (behavior and thoughts) are guided in certain directions by the personal constructs used to predict future events. We will explore several of Kelly's elaborations of this postulate.

Elaborations—The Eleven Corollaries

Kelly embellished his basic postulate by adding eleven corollaries.

1. Construction Corollary. "A person anticipates events by construing their replications" (Kelly 1955, 50).

Events in one's life occur with some regularity; for example, a friendly person will tend to remain friendly; day follows night; it tends to be cold in winter; and the physical objects in one's environment will tend to remain in place—for instance, the refrigerator probably will still be in the kitchen tomorrow. Although no two events are ever exactly the same ("No man ever steps into the same river twice"), nonetheless, themes running through events bind them together. It is on the basis of these themes that constructs are formed and that predictions about the future are made. In other words, if the events in our lives did not occur with some regularity, it would be impossible to form constructs that represent them.

2. Individuality Corollary. "Persons differ from each other in their construction of events" (Kelly 1955, 55).

This corollary cannot be stressed too much; it is the essence of Kelly's theory. According to Kelly, not only is beauty in the eye of the beholder; so is everything else. Reality is what we perceive it to be. This, of course, is a restatement of Kelly's notion of constructive alternativism, which says that we are free to construe events as we wish. This freedom is thought to apply not only to our interpretation of external reality but to ourselves as well.

> On occasion I may say of myself . . . "I am an introvert." "I," the subject, "am an introvert," the predicate. The language form of the statement clearly places the onus of being an introvert on the subject—me. What I actually am, the words say, is an introvert.
>
> The proper interpretation of my statement is that *I construe* myself to be an introvert, or, if I am merely being coy or devious, I am inveigling *my listener into construing me* in terms of introversion. The point that gets lost in the shuffle of words is the psychological fact that I have identified myself in terms of a personal construct—"introversion." (Kelly 1958, 38)

This corollary has implications for Kelly's version of psychotherapy, which we will cover later in the chapter. To place this corollary within the context of social learning theory, it can be applied to perceived self-efficacy. Very often whether an act is performed or not depends on whether a person perceives (construes) himself or herself as capable of performing it. For example, people will not sign up for a college-level course if they perceive themselves to be incapable of performing at the college level. If people are, in fact, capable of performing an act but decide not to because of perceived self-inefficacy, they need to change the way they construe themselves.

3. Organization Corollary. "Each person characteristically evolves, for his convenience in anticipating events, a construction system embracing ordinal relationships between constructs" (Kelly 1955, 56).

Not only do individuals differ in the constructs they use to construe events, but they also differ in how they organize their constructs. According to Kelly, personal constructs are arranged in a hierarchy, some being more comprehensive than others. For example, the construct extrovert-introvert subsumes such constructs as likes people-dislikes people and likes parties-dislikes parties. A construct that subsumes other constructs within it is called a **superordinate construct,** and the constructs that are subsumed under it are called **subordinate constructs.**

Neimeyer (1985a) discusses a female patient who viewed herself as "businesslike" as opposed to "emotional." When asked why she chose to be viewed as businesslike she said that she regarded it as a "mature approach to life" as opposed to an "unstable" one. When asked her definition of maturity she said that it meant "being in control" as opposed to "being controlled by others." When asked why it was important to be in control, she answered that her very "survival" depended on it and the opposite of survival was viewed as "just death." Figure 13-1 summarizes the constructs the patient used to describe herself and shows that some of those constructs were superordinate and some were subordinate.

Kelly believed that without this hierarchical arrangement of constructs, one would experience contradictions and would make inaccurate predictions of events. Because this is undesirable, a person organizes constructs in a way that reduces contradictions and increases predictive efficiency.

4. Dichotomy Corollary. "A person's construction system is composed of a finite number of dichotomous constructs" (Kelly 1955, 59).

According to Kelly, all constructs are bipolar or dichotomous. He believed that for a construct to be significant, it must indicate at least two elements that are similar to each other and a third element that is different from those two. One might say that two people are beautiful because they possess certain attributes and that a third person is ugly because he or she lacks those attributes. It is important to note, however, that for Kelly not only is the choice of the constructs used to construe reality a personal matter but so is the choice of the poles of a construct. The dichotomous poles of a construct are not determined by logic or convention; they are whatever a person views them to be. For example, for one person, one pole of a construct may be beautiful and the contrasting pole may be insensitive. For another person beautiful might be contrasted with ugly. For still another person beautiful might be contrasted with unsexy. Because it is these personally defined constructs that a person uses to construe his or her world, if one is ever going to know another person, one must know his or her construct system. For Kelly, then, a construct is a personal way of construing certain experiences as being alike and yet different from other experiences.

5. Choice Corollary. "A person chooses for himself that alternative in a

Figure 13-1.
Shows the superordinate and subordinate constructs used by a female patient to describe herself. The "P" indicates the pole of the construct with which the patient aligned herself.

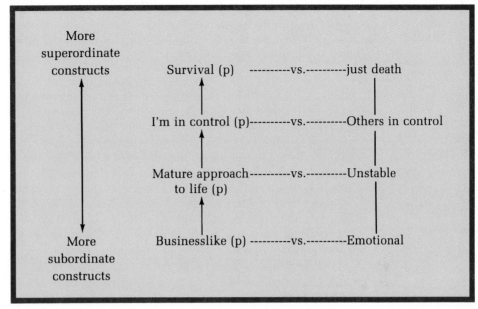

More
superordinate
constructs

Survival (p) ----------vs.----------just death

I'm in control (p)----------vs.----------Others in control

Mature approach----------vs.----------Unstable
to life (p)

More
subordinate
constructs

Businesslike (p) ----------vs.----------Emotional

(From Neimeyer, 1985a, p. 281.)

dichotomized construct through which he anticipates the greater possibility for extension and definition of his system" (Kelly 1955, 64).

Here the person can either be safe or take a risk. If a person applies constructs to a new situation that have been accurate in the past when applied to similar situations, one is merely seeking further validation of one's construct system. Kelly referred to this relatively safe path as **definition,** because such experiences further define or validate a construct system. Conversely, the person can use the occasion to try new constructs, which, if validated, would further expand the person's construct system, thereby making it better able to assimilate experiences that before were foreign to it. Kelly referred to this as **extension.** The danger in extension, as opposed to definition, is the possibility of failure. When choosing a construct, the person is torn between "security" and "adventure." One can make safe predictions or one can attempt to expand one's construct system, thereby making an ever-increasing number of experiences understandable. In Kelly's words, "One may anticipate events by trying to become more and more certain about fewer and fewer things [definition] or by trying to become vaguely aware of more and more things on the misty horizon [extension]" (1955, 67). According to Kelly, too much emphasis on definition may result in too much certainty and in a very restricted view of life. Conversely, too much emphasis of extension may result in too much uncertainty and confusion. *A middle ground seems best.*

6. Range Corollary. "A construct is convenient for the anticipation of a finite range of events only" (Kelly 1955, 68).

A construct such as hot versus cold cannot be applied to a situation that requires a good versus bad judgment. Each construct has a **range of convenience,** which includes all of the events to which the construct is relevant.

Suppose, for example, A and B are men, C is a woman, and O is the time of day. We abstract an aspect of A, B, and C which we may call *sex.* Sex, then is our z. Sex is not applicable to O, the time of day; at least most of us would not so abstract it. The time of day, O, does not fall within the range of convenience of sex, z. Now, with respect to sex, z, the two men, A and B, are alike and in contrast to the woman, C. (Kelly 1955, 60)

The events within the range of convenience for which a construct is maximally pertinent define the construct's **focus of convenience.** For example, if one sees a wild animal rapidly approaching, the construct of danger-safe may be a useful one to employ in construing the situation. Certainly the event of being charged by a wild animal would fall within the range of convenience of the danger-safe construct. Furthermore, the notion of very dangerous would seem especially appropriate within that construct. In this situation, the construct of danger-safe would be employed, and the notion of very dangerous would be the focus of convenience within that construct's range of convenience. Constructs such as nice weather–bad weather or politically liberal–politically conservative would seem irrelevant to the situation. In other words, the range of convenience of the latter constructs would not include the situation at hand.

7. Experience Corollary. "A person's construction system varies as he successively construes the replications of events" (Kelly 1955, 72).

Experience alone was unimportant to Kelly; what was important was the construing of experience.

Experience is made up of the successive construing of events. It is not constituted merely by the succession of events themselves. A person can be a witness to a tremendous parade of episodes and yet, if he fails to keep making something out of them, or if he waits until they have all occurred before he attempts to reconstrue them, he gains little in the way of experience from having been around when they happened. It is not what happens around him that makes a man experienced; it is the successive construing and reconstruing of what happens, as it happens, that enriches the experience of life. . . . The person who merely stands agog at each emerging event may experience a series of interesting surprises, but if he makes no attempt to discover the recurrent themes, his experience does not amount to much. It is when man begins to see the orderliness in a sequence of events that he begins to experience them. (Kelly 1955, 73–74)

Thus, for Kelly, experience alone is not the best teacher but the active construing of experience is.

8. Modulation Corollary. "The variation in a person's construction system is limited by the permeability of the constructs within whose range of convenience the variants lie" (Kelly 1955, 77).

Some constructs are more **permeable**—that is, open to experience—than are others. "A construct is permeable if it will admit to its range of convenience new elements which are not yet construed within its framework" (Kelly 1955, 79).

For example, a person's construct nice people–awful people might be defined in terms of certain individuals, nice people consisting of a circle of close friends and awful people consisting of everyone else. Such a person is not open to experience, because one pole of the construct nice people–awful people is not permeable. Thus, even if the individual encountered a person with several admirable characteristics, that person could not be assimilated into the individuals construct system, because of its lack of permeability.

A person who has several permeable constructs will be in a better position to extend his or her construct system than a person who has an abundance of impermeable constructs will. The former person can be characterized as "open-minded," and the latter as "close-minded."

9. Fragmentation Corollary. "A person may successively employ a variety of construction subsystems which are inferentially incompatible with each other" (Kelly 1955, 83).

Kelly said that a person's construct system is in a state of continual flux. Different constructs are constantly being tested, and new elements are constantly entering into one's more permeable constructs. Likewise, one is constantly reorganizing one's construct system so that the most reliable predictions are made. This experimentation with one's construct system creates the possibility for inconsistent behavior. One may not respond in a consistent way to the same event each time that it is encountered. For example, the interaction with one's boss on the job and in a local bar may be totally different. One may act differently because the situation has changed, one's constructs have changed, or the organization of one's constructs has changed. Kelly felt that a certain number of inconsistencies were inevitable because construct systems "are in flux," but he felt that even with minor inconsistencies, the overall outcome was still consistent. "We can say that while a person's bets on the turn of minor events may not appear to add up, his wagers on the outcome of life do tend to add up" (Kelly 1955, 88).

10. Commonality Corollary. "To the extent that one person employs a construction of experience which is similar to that employed by another, his psychological processes are similar to the other person" (Kelly 1955, 90).

With this corollary Kelly emphasized the point that it is not common experiences that make people similar, but the fact that they construe their experiences in a similar way. Two people can have the same physical experiences but construe them differently. Likewise, it is conceivable that two similar construct systems can result from distinctly different sets of physical experiences.

> It is important to make clear that we have not said that if one person has experienced the same events as another he will duplicate the other's psychological processes. . . . One of the advantages of this position is that it does not require us to assume that it would take identical events in the lives of two people to make them act alike. Two people can act alike even if they have each been exposed to quite different phenomenal stimuli. It is in the similarity in the construction of events that we find the basis for similar action, not in the identity of the events themselves. (Kelly 1955, 90–91)

11. Sociality Corollary. "To the extent that one person construes the construction processes of another, he may play a role in a social process involving the other person" (Kelly 1955, 95).

The concept of **role** was very important to Kelly's theory, but he did not use the concept in the traditional way. Kelly defined role as "an ongoing pattern of behavior that follows from a person's understanding of how the others who are associated with him in the task think" (1955, 97–98).

In other words, playing a role is acting in accordance with the expectations of others. To play a role one must understand at least one other person's construct system. For example, if a man wants to play the role of "husband" to his wife, he must first understand her expectations for the construct "husband" and then act accordingly. Kelly called our understanding of another person's outlook and expectations a **role construct;** how we act in light of this understanding is called a role. "A *role* is a psychological process based upon the role player's construction of aspects of the construction systems of those with whom he attempts to join in a social enterprise" (Kelly 1955, 97).

This corollary was Kelly's major statement on social behavior. He said that if we want to engage in constructive interactions with other people, we must first determine how other people see things and then take their perceptions into consideration when dealing with them. The deepest kind of social interaction occurs when this role playing is reciprocal.

CPC Cycle

According to Kelly, the **CPC cycle** characterizes the actions of a person confronted with a novel situation. The initials CPC symbolize the three phases of the cycle: circumspection, preemption, and control.

Circumspection Phase

In this phase, the person ponders several **propositional constructs,** which could possibly be used to interpret the situation. The thinking during this phase is hypothetical and tentative, and might be labeled cognitive trial and error.

Preemption Phase

In this phase, the person chooses from all the constructs pondered in the preceding phase the one construct that seems especially relevant to the situation. In other words, one cannot go on pondering the situation forever; one must choose a strategy for dealing with one's experience.

Control Phase

During the preemption phase a choice was made concerning which construct would be used to construe the situation. In the **control phase,** the person decides which pole of the dichotomous construct chosen during the preemption phase is most relevant to the situation. Thus the CPC cycle involves pondering several possible constructs with which to construe a situation, deciding on one of those constructs, and then deciding which pole of that construct seems best for construing the situation. Once the final choice is made, subsequent experience will either validate or invalidate the person's predictions.

We again can use the example of our being attacked by a wild animal to demonstrate the CPC cycle. On seeing the animal approaching, the person being attacked enters the circumspection phase of the CPC cycle by pondering several constructs that seem to be pertinent to the situation—for example, stand still–run, fight–not fight, or hide–not hide. In the preemption phase the person chooses from the constructs pondered in the preceding phase. Let us say the person decided on the construct stand still–run. In the control phase, he or she will choose that pole of the chosen construct that seems most useful under the circumstances and will then act on it. Let us say the person chooses to run. Because the whole idea was to predict personal safety, if the person's course of action had gotten him or her out of trouble, the construct stand still–run would be validated and would thus tend to dominate that person's thinking if again attacked by a wild animal.

Creativity Cycle

The **creativity cycle** is employed when one seeks innovating solutions to problems or a fresh way of viewing something. The creativity cycle, like the CPC cycle, involves three phases.

Loosened Construction Phase

According to Kelly, creative thinking involves a loosening of one's construct system. A loosened construct system allows varying alignments of elements and constructs. Thus bananas can be thought of as blue, loud, or intelligent. A teacher can be thought of as a paintbrush, a door stopper, or a hat. A loosened construct system allows for cognitive experimentation. The thinking during this phase can often be preposterous.

Tightened Construction Phase

The whole idea of the preceding stage is to discover solutions to problems or interpretations of situations that may not be obvious. For a loosened construct system to be useful, however, it must eventually be tightened. That is, a construct system is loosened to explore new ideas, but once an idea that may be useful is discovered the cognitive experimentation must stop and the idea must be evaluated. Kelly (1955) said:

> Just as a person who uses tight constructions exclusively cannot be creative, so a person who uses loose constructions exclusively cannot be creative either. He would never get out of the stage of mumbling to himself. He would never get around to setting up a hypothesis for crucial testing. The creative person must have the important capacity to move from loosening to tightening. (529)

Test Phase

The creative idea discovered in the loosened construction phase is submitted to a test and if validated by subsequent experience it is retained as part of one's construct system. If not, it is discarded and the creativity cycle is repeated.

Kelly's Interpretation of Traditional Psychological Concepts

As we have seen, in the preface of volume one of his 1955 book, Kelly warned the reader that he has ignored many traditional concepts, has redefined others, and has invented several new ones. In this section we will review a sample of the traditional psychological concepts that Kelly redefined in accordance with his personal construct theory.

Motivation

Kelly strongly disagreed with most of the traditional views of **motivation.** He thought that they looked on humans as naturally inert and therefore in need of being set in motion by something. In other words, traditional theories of motivation claimed that humans needed a drive, a need, a goal, or a stimulus to set them in motion. Kelly thought that this was nonsense. He believed that humans are born motivated, and nothing more needs to be said. Every person, according to Kelly, is motivated "for no other reason than that he is alive" (1958, 49).

> Motivational theories can be divided into two types, push theories, and pull theories. Under push theories we find such terms as drive, motive, or even stimulus. Pull theories use such constructs as purpose, value, or need. In terms of a well-known metaphor, these are the pitchfork theories on the one hand and the carrot theories on the other. But our theory is neither of these. Since we prefer to look to the nature of the animal himself, ours is probably best called a jackass theory. (Kelly 1958, 50)

Examples of what Kelly called **push theories** would include those of Freud, Skinner, and Dollard and Miller. Examples of what Kelly called **pull theories** would include those of Jung and Adler. Other "jackass theories" include those of Rogers, Maslow, and May, to which we turn in the next three chapters. As far as motivation is concerned, social learning theory, too, is more like a jackass theory than it is a push or pull theory.

Anxiety

Kelly defined **anxiety** as "the recognition that the events with which one is confronted lie outside the range of convenience of one's construct system" (1955, 495).

As we have seen, the ability to predict the future accurately is everyone's goal. The extent to which our predictions are invalid is the extent to which we experience anxiety.

> We become anxious when we can only partially construe the events which we encounter and too many of their implications are obscure. Sex for the chaste, adulthood for the adolescent, books for the illiterate, power for the humble and death for nearly all of us tend to provoke anxiety. It is the *unknown* aspects of things that go bump in the night that give them their potency. (Bannister & Fransella 1971, 35)

In the extreme, life can become so unpredictable that the only certain thing that one can imagine is death. For some this may stimulate suicide. "For the man of constricted outlook whose world begins to crumble, death may appear to provide the only immediate certainty which he can lay his hands on" (Kelly 1955, 64). Anxiety is caused by the uncertainty that results when one's construct system does not permit the accurate construing of life's experiences. In some extreme cases the certainty of death may be preferred to the uncertainty of the future.

Hostility

Kelly defined **hostility** as the *"continued effort to extort validational evidence in favor of a type of social prediction which has already proven itself a failure"* (1955, 510).

Hostility is related to anxiety. Anxiety is experienced when one's predictions are incorrect. According to Kelly, anxiety is to be avoided. When it is clear that one's construct system has failed to construe the situation properly (that is, when anxiety is inevitable), one may refuse to accept this fact and attempt to demand validation from the environment. Such demands characterize hostility. Bannister and Fransella (1971) say:

> There are times when, if his construct system is to be preserved, a person simply cannot afford to be wrong. If he acknowledges that some of his expectations are ill-founded, this might involve the modification or abandonment of the constructions on which those expectations were based. If, in turn, these constructions are central to the whole of his system, he might well be faced with chaos, having no alternative way of viewing his situation. In such a position the person is likely to become *hostile*, to extort evidence, to bully people into behaving in ways which confirm his predictions, to cook the books, to refuse to recognize the ultimate significance of what is happening. (35)

Aggression

Kelly (1955) defined **aggression** as "the active elaboration of one's perceptual field" (508). Thus, according to Kelly, the aggressive individual opts to extend his construct system rather than define it (see the choice corollary). He or she seeks adventure rather than security. He or she seeks to expand his or her construct system so that it includes an increasing range of events. Aggression, then, in Kelly's theory, is the opposite of hostility. Bannister and Fransella (1971) put it as follows:

> It is interesting to note that Kelly is here attempting to define aggression (and similarly attempts to define hostility) in terms of what is going on *within the individual* rather than in terms of other people's reaction to him. Thus, a person is being aggressive when he actively experiments to check the validity of his construing; when he extends the range of his constructions (and thereby his activities) in new directions; when he is exploring. Obviously from the point of view of the people around and about such a person, this can be a very uncomfortable process and they may well see it as an attack upon them and handle it as such. But in terms of the aggressive person's construction system it is essentially an extending and elaborating process and thereby the opposite of hostility. (37–38)

To Kelly, hostility was the unwillingness to give up an ineffective system, and aggression is an attempt to expand one's construct system to an ever-increasing range of events.

Guilt

Kelly defined **guilt** as the "*perception of one's apparent dislodgement from his core role structure*" (1955, 502). The term **core role structure** refers to the roles we play while interacting with the relevant individuals and groups in our lives. According to Kelly, "Guilt arises when the individual becomes aware that he is alienated from the roles by which he maintains his most important relationships to other persons" (1963, 228). Thus, if a man construes his relationship with his wife as loving, reliable, and caring, he will feel guilty if he acts in an unloving, unreliable, and uncaring way toward her.

In Kelly's view the experience of guilt has nothing to do with good versus evil or right versus wrong. It has to do with the consistency or inconsistency with which one interacts with significant people or groups in one's life. It is inconsistency in these relationships that causes guilt. Even as Kelly defined it, however, guilt can be devastating.

> If you find yourself doing, in important respects, those things you would not have expected to do if you are the kind of person you always thought you were, then you suffer from guilt. . . . To live in a world where you cannot understand and predict others can be terrifying—how much more terrifying is it to find that one cannot understand and predict oneself. (Bannister & Fransella 1971, 36)

Some similarity exists between Kelly's concept of guilt and Freud's concept of moral anxiety. According to Kelly, we experience guilt when a discrepancy exists between how we think we will act in a situation and how we actually act. According to Freud, we internalize values, which act as a guide in determining what is right and what is wrong in our lives. When we act contrary to one or more of these internalized values, we experience moral anxiety. For both Kelly and Freud, when we depart from the behavior that is expected from us, we experience discomfort; guilt for Kelly, moral anxiety for Freud.

Threat

Kelly defined **threat** as the *"awareness of imminent comprehensive change in one's core structures"* (1955, 489).

Just as we have a core role structure that governs our significant interpersonal relationships, we have other constructs for predicting external events on which we rely heavily. These **core structures** are used to make sense out of life. They become the heart of what others may call our "belief system." When these basic core constructs suddenly seem no longer to be validated by experience, we feel threatened. To challenge our core constructs is to challenge our very existence, and that could be dangerous.

> We are threatened when our major beliefs about the nature of our personal, social and practical situation are invalidated and the world around us appears about to become chaotic. Threat is an extremely important construct for anyone engaged in attempts to help other people. For example, the psychotherapist in his enthusiasm to change what he considers to be the restrictive and poorly developed ideas of his client may plunge the client into over-hasty experimentation and thereby threaten him. The client may then either become hostile and resist all change or may plunge into the kind of chaos that earns him the title of psychotic. By threatening, in the construct theory sense of the term, we do psychological violence to a person. (Bannister & Fransella 1971, 37).

For Kelly, guilt is experienced when the constructs we use to predict our significant interpersonal relationships are not validated, and we feel threatened when previously validated constructs for dealing with external events lose their validity. For example, a person who spent most of his life avoiding alcohol would feel guilty if he accepted a drink at a party; if a person looked out her window in the middle of summer and saw snow, she would feel threatened.

Fear

Fear, according to Kelly, is similar to threat but less severe. Fear results when a peripheral element of one's construct system is invalidated rather than one's core constructs. *"Fear is like threat, except that, in this case, it is a new incidental construct, rather than a comprehensive construct, that seems about to take over"* (Kelly 1955, 494). A person may experience fear if a previously friendly dog growls at him. The change this experience necessitates in one's construct system is a minor one; for instance, a friendly dog now becomes a friendly dog that sometimes growls.

Unconscious

Kelly felt that constructs could be described in terms of their "cognitive awareness." Constructs with low cognitive awareness could be considered more or less as **unconscious.** According to Kelly, there are three kinds of constructs with low cognitive awareness: preverbal, submerged, and suspended.

Kelly defined a **preverbal construct** as *"one which continues to be used even though it has no consistent word symbol"* (1955, 459). Preverbal constructs typically are formed early in life, before language is available. Even though words are not available to infants, they still describe and anticipate events in terms of nebulous, nonverbal constructs, such as feelings of warmth and security. Because verbally labeling a construct makes it much easier to use, preverbal constructs are less definite and more cumbersome than those that are verbally labeled.

As we saw earlier, every construct has two poles. Sometimes a person will act as if only one of the two poles exists, however; for example, to believe that "all people are good" or "everything is living." Emphasizing one pole of a construct and ignoring the other pole is what Kelly called **submergence.** "There is the *likeness* and the *contrast* end. Sometimes one of these two ends is less available than the other. When this is markedly true we may refer to the less available end as the *submerged* end" (Kelly 1955, 467). An anxious person may choose not to entertain one pole of a construct because doing so would challenge his or her construct system. Kelly's notion of submergence is similar to Freud's notion of repression.

Another way by which an element of experience can have low cognitive awareness is through **suspension.** An element of experience is suspended when it cannot be used constructively in one's construct system. It is as if an experience is kept in a holding pattern until a construct system that can assimilate it is created.

> Our theory does not place the emphasis upon remembering what is pleasant or forgetting what is unpleasant; rather, it emphasizes that one remembers what is structured and forgets what is unstructured. In contrast with some notions of repression, suspension implies that the idea or element of experience is forgotten simply because the person can, at the moment, tolerate no structure within which the idea would have meaning. Once he can entertain such a structure the idea may become available within it. (Kelly 1955, 473).

For Kelly, then, what others call the unconscious is explained in terms of preverbal constructs, submergence, and suspension.

Learning

Learning, for Kelly, was the constant alteration of one's construct system with the goal of increasing its predictive efficiency. Any change in one's construct system exemplifies learning.

Reinforcement

Kelly replaced what others call reinforcement or reward with the concept of **validation.** According to Kelly, people do not seek reinforcement or the avoidance of pain. People seek validation of their construct systems. If a person predicts that something unpleasant is going to occur and it does, his or her construct system will have been validated even though the experience was a negative one. Again, according to Kelly, the primary goal in one's life is to reduce uncertainty by accurately predicting future events. "Confirmation and disconfirmation of one's predictions

[have] greater psychological significance than rewards, punishments, or . . . drive reduction" (Kelly 1970, 11).

Psychotherapy

According to Kelly, neurotic people are like bad scientists; they keep making the same predictions in the absence of validating experiences. "From the standpoint of the psychology of personal constructs, we may define a disorder as any personal construction which is used repeatedly in spite of consistent invalidation" (Kelly 1955, 831). In other words, a neurotic's construct system does not adequately predict future events, and therefore anxiety is inescapable. What the neurotic person needs is a more adequate construct system, and psychotherapy is a procedure designed to help that person develop one. For Kelly, **psychotherapy** provides a person with an opportunity to examine and reformulate his or her construct system. In other words, psychotherapy trains people to be better scientists.

Role Construct Repertory Test

Because psychotherapy must deal with a client's constructs, the therapist must first discover what those constructs are. Kelly devised the **Role Construct Repertory Test** to identify the constructs a client uses to construe the relevant people in his or her life. This test has come to be called the *Rep test*. A typical form used in administering the Rep test is shown in Figure 13-2.

The first step in administering the Rep test is to ask the client to fill in the grid portion of the form, numbered 1–22, with the names of twenty-two persons relevant to his or her life. The client taking the test usually is asked to place the names of the following people in the blanks above the numbers on the test sheet:

BLANK NUMBER

1. The name of the client taking the test.
2. Mother's first name (or the person who acted as your mother).
3. Father's name (or the person who acted as your father).
4. Brother nearest to you in age, or if no brother, a boy near your age most like a brother.
5. Sister nearest to you in age, or if no sister, a girl near your age most like a sister.
6. Your wife or husband, or if not married, your closest friend of the opposite sex.
7. Closest friend of the opposite sex after the person listed in item 6.
8. Closest friend of your own sex.
9. A person who was once a close friend but no longer is.
10. A religious leader, for example, a minister, priest, or rabbi to whom you would be willing to discuss your feelings about religion.

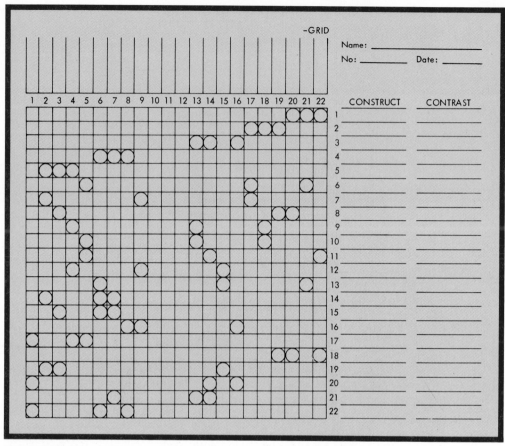

(From Kelly 1955, 270)

Figure 13-2   *A typical form used for Kelly's Role Construct Repertory (Rep) Test.*

11. Your medical doctor.
12. The neighbor you know best.
13. A person you now know who dislikes you.
14. A person for whom you feel sorry and would like to help.
15. The person with whom you feel most uncomfortable.
16. A recent acquaintance whom you would like to know better.
17. Your most influential teacher when you were in your teens.
18. The teacher with whom you disagreed the most.
19. An employer or supervisor under whom you worked while you were experiencing stress.
20. The most successful person whom you know personally.
21. The happiest person whom you know personally.
22. The most ethical person whom you know personally.

When the names have been furnished, the client is asked to compare them in groups of three. The three names that are to be compared are indicated by circles on the test sheet. For example, the first comparison is of the individuals whose names appear in blanks, 20, 21 and 22. The second comparison is of the individuals whose names appear in blanks 17, 18, and 19, and so on. For each triad the client is asked to choose a word or phrase that describes how two of the three individuals are alike and a word or phrase that describes how the third person is different from the other two. The way in which the two people are the same is listed under construct, and the way in which the third person is different is listed under contrast. An X is placed in the circles of the two people who are alike, and the circle of the person thought to be different is left blank. A partially completed Rep test is shown in Figure 13-3.

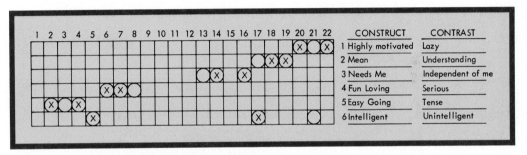

Figure 13-3 *An example of a partially completed Rep test. Typically the client is asked to make twenty-two comparisons instead of the six indicated in the figure.*

It can be seen in Figure 13-3 that the client felt that individuals 20 and 22 were highly motivated but that individual 21 was lazy; individuals 18 and 19 were thought to be mean, whereas individual 17 was thought to be understanding, and the like.

By analyzing the client's performance on the Rep test, the psychotherapist can answer a number of questions about a client's construct system. For example, which constructs are used? What aspects of people do they emphasize, for example, physical characteristics and social characteristics? Which people are seen as most like or different from the client? Does the client have many constructs available or only a few?

How valid is the Rep test? The answer depends on whom you ask. In an interview with Evans, Bannister, who is one of Kelly's disciples, describes his experience with the Rep test as follows:

> I arrived at this brain-crunching chapter on the grid and set to work to do one on me. Then I scored it. It was a fairly murderous task, taking about three weeks to get through it all. Then when I looked at it it seemed ridiculous. I wasn't, I said to myself, the overemotional bigoted bastard portrayed there, so I stuck it in a file and did other things. About two weeks later I took it out again and said "Yes, I *am* the overemotional bigoted et cetera portrayed in the grid." It was a troubled time for me personally and the grid had picked it up. (Evans 1978, 7)

The Rep test was only one tool that Kelly used to learn about his clients' construct systems. Another tool was simply to ask the clients about themselves. Kelly adopted what he called a **credulous attitude** toward his clients. In other words, he felt that the information they furnished about themselves could be trusted. *"If you don't know what's wrong with a client, ask him; he may tell you"* (Kelly 1955, 201). What a client reports may not be true in an objective sense, but what a client believes to be true *is* true in at least a subjective sense. Because it is these personal beliefs or perceptions that determine the client's behavior, they must be understood by the therapist.

> A person may misrepresent a real phenomenon, such as his income or his ills, and yet his misrepresentation will itself be entirely real. This applies even to the badly deluded patient: What he perceives may not exist, but his perception does. (Kelly 1955, 8)

In keeping with his credulous attitude, Kelly often had his clients write a **self-characterization.**

> I want you to write a character sketch of Harry Brown (i.e., client's name), just as if he were the principal character in a play. Write it as it might be written by a friend who knew him very *intimately* and very *sympathetically*, perhaps better than anyone every really could know him. Be sure to write it in the third person. For example, start out by saying, "Harry Brown is . . . " (Kelly 1955, 323).

Again, as with the Rep test, the purpose of this sketch was to help the therapist see how clients construed themselves and their interactions with the world and with other people.

Fixed-Role Therapy

Kelly believed that one way to cause clients to explore different ways of construing things is to have them pretend they are different people. In **fixed-role therapy** the therapist presents the client with a personality sketch and asks the client to act it out, just as an actor would play a part in a play. To enhance the development of new constructs, the personality of the person the client is asked to play is markedly different from the client's own personality. Kelly asked the client to try on a new personality as one would try on a new suit of clothes. Under these circumstances the therapist becomes a supporting actor. Kelly said the therapist must "play in strong support of an actor—the client—who is continually fumbling his lines and contaminating his role" (1955, 399).

The client plays his role for about two weeks, during which time he lives "as if" he were the person in the role he is playing. The therapist, during this time, responds to the client "as if" he were the person in the part and offers encouragement and validating experiences for the new constructs with which the client is experimenting. The therapist must give the client enough courage to overcome the threat involved in giving up his core constructs and developing new ones.

What I am saying is that it is not so much what man is that counts as it is what he ventures to make of himself. To make the leap he must do more than disclose himself; he must risk a certain amount of confusion. Then, as soon as he does catch a glimpse of a different kind of life, he needs to find some way of overcoming the paralyzing moment of threat, for this is the instant when he wonders what he really is—whether he is what he just was or is what he is about to be (Kelly 1964, 147).

By providing validating data in the form of responses to a wide variety of constructions on the part of the client, some of them quite loose, fanciful, or naughty, the clinician gives the client an opportunity to validate constructs, an opportunity which is not normally available to him. (Kelly 1955, 165)

We see, then, that Kelly maintained his cognitive viewpoint even in psychotherapy. Emotional problems are *perceptual* problems. To resolve a perceptual problem, one must be made to *look at* experiences differently. Psychotherapy is a process by which a client is encouraged to look at experiences differently, while the therapist attempts to minimize the anxiety in doing so.

Kelly suggested that neurotics have lost their ability to make believe, and the therapist tries to help them regain it. Healthy people make believe all the time. In fact, in Kelly's opinion, brilliant novelists and brilliant scientists do much the same thing; that is, they make believe.

Both [the novelist and the scientist] employ . . . human tactics. The fact that the scientist is ashamed to admit his phantasy probably accomplishes little more than to make it appear that he fits a popular notion of the way scientists think. And the fact that a novelist does not continue his project to the point of collecting data in support of his portrayals and generalizations suggests only that he hopes that the experiences of man will, in the end, prove him right without anyone's resorting to formal proof.

But the brilliant scientist and the brilliant writer are pretty likely to end up saying the same thing—given, of course, a lot of time to converge upon each other. The poor scientist and the poor writer, moreover, fail in much the same way— neither of them is able to transcend the obvious. Both fail in their make-believe. (Kelly 1964, 140)

On Being Oneself

Kelly took issue with the advice that encourages people to be "themselves." In fact, his advice is quite the opposite:

A good deal is said these days about being oneself. It is supposed to be healthy to be oneself. While it is a little hard for me to understand how one could be anything else, I suppose what is meant is that one should not strive to become anything other than what he is. This strikes me as a very dull way of living; in fact, I would be inclined to argue that all of us would be better off if we set out to be something other than what we are. Well, I'm not so sure we would all be *better* off—perhaps it would be more accurate to say life would be a lot more *interesting*. (Kelly 1964, 147)

Construct Systems and Paradigms

In many ways Kelly's view of personality is similar to Kuhn's view of science. Kelly maintains that the way in which an individual construes reality is only one of many possible ways, but for that particular individual his or her construct system *is* reality, and it is sometimes difficult for him or her to imagine other constructions. For Kuhn, as we saw in chapter 1, a paradigm is a way of looking at a subject matter, and scientists doing research while following a paradigm are said to be doing "normal science." Such scientists, according to Kuhn, are often blinded to other, perhaps more effective, ways of looking at a body of information.

It seems that the most important similarity between Kelly and Kuhn is that they both emphasize *perceptual mechanisms*. For Kelly, a construct system is a set of personal constructs that result in a person's construing the world in a certain way. Likewise, Kuhn's paradigm is a perceptual habit shared by several scientists that causes them to *view* their subject matter in a similar way.

Both Kelly and Kuhn insist that there are many equally valid interpretations of reality, not just one. Whereas Kelly took this view of an individual's adjustment to the world and Kuhn took this view of science, we take the same view of personality theory. One of the main functions of this book is to offer the various personality theories, not as "truths" but as *ways of viewing* personality. In other words, we believe that, like reality in general, personality can be construed in several equally valid ways. It is hoped that the student's construct for personality is permeable enough to allow various viewpoints to enter it.

We end our coverage of Kelly's theory with the following quotation, which seems to summarize Kelly's philosophy of the individual, Kuhn's philosophy of science, and this book's approach to personality theory: "Whatever nature may be, or howsoever the quest for truth will turn out in the end, the events we face today are subject to as great a variety of constructions as our wits will enable us to contrive" (Kelly 1970, 1).

Evaluation

Current Status

A relatively small but highly productive group of Kellians currently exist (Jankowicz 1987). A clearinghouse for research generated by Kelly's theory is at the University of Nebraska, Lincoln, headed by Al Landfield. The clearinghouse issues a newsletter and publishes bibliographies of recent research on personal construct theory. Similar clearinghouses are scattered throughout the world. Worldwide membership in these clearinghouses has risen from 112 in 1970 to about 500 currently.

Although interest in Kelly's theory is increasing in the United States, the theory is most popular in England. A major reason for the theory's popularity in England is the fact that Kelly's former student and prominent clinical psychologist,

Donald Bannister, has been effectively promoting it there for many years. The recently opened London-based Centre for Personal Construct Psychology, under the direction of Fay Fransella, is also influential in disseminating Kelly's ideas in England. So popular is Kelly's theory in England that exposure to it is required in most clinical programs approved by the British Psychological Society (Jankowicz 1987, 483).

A major reason that Kelly's theory did not become more popular in the United States was that it was extremely critical of the other approaches to psychology that were so popular at the time—for example, behaviorism and psychoanalysis. Because Kelly actively avoided forming links between his theory and those of others, they, in turn, avoided forming links to his. As American psychology has become more cognitive in nature, however, Kelly's theory has become more popular. In fact, for many, Kelly is viewed as having been ahead of his time.

Empirical Research

Almost every aspect of Kelly's theory has received some research attention, but most of that attention has involved the Rep test. An early research project using the Rep test was conducted by James Bieri, one of Kelly's students. Using the Rep test, Bieri (1955) was able to distinguish between a **cognitively complex person** and a **cognitively simple person.** A cognitively complex person has many highly differentiated constructs available to him or her. As a result, such a person can cast other people into many categories and can see much variety among them. Conversely, a cognitively simple person has a limited, poorly differentiated construct system. As a result, such a person casts all of humanity into a few categories, such as good–bad. Bieri was able to substantiate Kelly's assumption that the more constructs that one has available, the better one will be at predicting future events. Bieri found that cognitively complex people are far better at predicting the behavior of others than cognitively simple ones. As we shall see when we discuss the applications of Kelly's theory shortly, the Rep test has been used for various clinical purposes. For further examples of how the Rep test has been used as a research tool see Bannister and Mair (1968); Landfield and Leitner (1980); and Mancuso and Adams-Webber (1982).

Recently the Rep test has been found useful in the area of industrial-organization psychology. Bannister and Fransella (1971) pointed out that the Rep test need not only be used to evaluate the set of fixed role titles that Kelly had suggested. Rather, it could be used to evaluate how individuals construe most anything. A recent nonclinical application of the Rep test is in the area of market research. Because consumer behavior is largely determined by consumer perceptions it makes sense to use the Rep test to determine how consumers perceive (construe) various products. Stewart and Stewart (1982) give several examples of how the Rep test is applied to the world of business. For example, one study explored the constructs used by a panel of home testers to describe a range of cosmetics and perfumes. Knowing the constructs that consumers use in evaluating and comparing products is extremely important, because it is on the basis of those constructs that consumers make purchasing decisions; it is to those constructs that advertisers must appeal. Jankowicz (1987) gives several examples of how personal construct theory is being used by industrial-organizational psychologists, management development specialists, and occupational counselors. Jankowicz (1987) concludes that, "In all these fields of psychology, finding out what the other person thinks, as a guide to discovering why he or she acts, is a central undertaking" (481).

We see then that Kellian psychology has a substantial base of empirical research. Furthermore, this empirical base appears to be growing rapidly.

> There have been over 1000 publications in construct theory, three-quarters of which represent data-based research reports. . . . Moreover, the vitality of the field is reflected in the fact that the rate of construct theoretical publications has increased exponentially since the mid-1970s. From the standpoint of the sociology of science, construct theory can be characterized as an established speciality having multiple research fronts and a broad international base of support. (Neimeyer 1985a, 276)

Criticisms

Limited Empirical Research.   Although Kelly's theory has generated a considerable amount of empirical research, most of it has involved the Rep test. Little research has been designed to test the theory of personal constructs on which the Rep test is based. Because little has been done to extend the theory it remains more or less as Kelly originally proposed it in 1955.

Important Aspects of Personality Neglected or Denied.   In his effort to create a new way of viewing personality, Kelly may have gone too far in his rejection of other theoretical approaches. In his rather flippant rejection of learning, motivation, and the developmental aspects of personality, Kelly may have discarded information that is vital to a comprehensive understanding of personality. Others think that his treatment of the unconscious mind and of human emotions was superficial, at best. For example, his theory excluded such lofty human emotions as love, hate, despair, and those associated with human sexuality. For many, Kelly's emphasis on the rational, intellectual aspects of humans does not accord well with life as it really is.

Difficulty in Predicting Behavior.   For Kelly, construing was a private, creative process. Furthermore, construct systems are constantly being tested and revised. These features of Kelly's theory make it practically impossible to predict what a person will do in a particular situation. In fact, Kelly insisted that unpredictability is an important characteristic of a healthy person. For many, this violates the scientific definition of understanding. That is, if something is truly understood its behavior can be predicted and controlled. Kelly focused his attention on the unique person almost as much as Allport did. When one seeks to understand an individual, one does not seek the general laws that govern human behavior. Thus, for many, a focus on individual behavior violates the tenets of science.

Too Many Unanswered Questions.   Kelly left unanswered such basic questions as: Why do some people have more constructs available to them than others? Why do some people opt for the definition of their construct systems and others opt for extension? What is the origin of a personal construct? What causes people to construe the same situation differently? Is the model of humans as scientists really an accurate one? That is, do people really spend that much time trying to accurately predict future events?

Contributions

Emphasis on Cognition. Just as Kelly has been criticized for emphasizing the cognitive aspects of humans too much, others have praised him for doing just that. Both the psychoanalysts and the behaviorists (for different reasons) played down the kind of rational thought that Kelly made the cornerstone of his theory. As other personality theorists were attempting to explain human behavior in terms of repressed memories, stimuli and responses, reinforcement, habits, ego-defense mechanisms or the built-in tendency toward self-actualization, Kelly was attempting to explain it in terms of cognitive hypotheses testing. It is a tribute to Kelly that the newer theories (e.g., information processing psychology) are more like his own that those that he opposed. His theory is even compatible with the popular interactionist position because it stressed both person variables (e.g., constructs and construct systems) and situation variables (those events people construe). One with the other would have been meaningless to Kelly. In fact, as we have seen, Kelly rejected pure phenomenology because it was concerned only with subjective reality and he rejected behaviorism because it was concerned only with objective reality. Kelly's concern was with the relationship between subjective and objective reality and that concern is now very much in vogue.

Applied Value. Beyond furnishing a new theory with which to explore human personality and new methods for treating disturbed people, Kelly's ideas have been applied to a number of different areas. As we have seen, his ideas are now widely used in industrial-organizational settings. Other areas in which Kelly's ideas are either applied or researched or both include friendship formation; developmental psychology; person perception; education; political science; and environmental psychology (Adams-Webber 1979; Mancuso and Adams-Webber 1982).

Examples of clinical areas to which construct theory had been applied include suicide (Neimeyer 1984; Parker 1981); obsessive-compulsive disorder (Rigdon & Epting, 1983); drug abuse (Dawes 1985; Rivers and Landfield 1985); childhood disorders (Agnew 1985); physical illness (Robinson & Wood 1984; Viney 1983, 1984); couples in conflict (Neimeyer & Hudson 1984); and other relationship disorders (Leitner 1984; Neimeyer & Neimeyer 1985).

Starting with practically no formal training in clinical psychology, Kelly ended up developing a unique theory of personality and psychotherapeutic procedures that were both innovative and effective. Kelly's belief that truth is mainly a way of looking at things both freed him from the dogma of the past and gave him latitude to experiment with his own theory. We agree with Pervin's eloquent evaluation of Kelly's theory:

> George Kelly, then, was a person who refused to accept things as black or white, right or wrong. He was a person who liked to test new experiences; a person who dismissed truth in any absolute sense and, therefore, felt free to reconstrue or reinterpret phenomena; a man who challenged the concept of "objective" reality and felt free to play in the world of "make-believe"; a person who perceived events as occurring to individuals and, therefore, was interested in the interpretations of these events by individuals; a person who viewed his own theory as only a tentative formulation and who, consequently, was free to challenge views that others accepted as fact; a man who experienced the frustration and challenge, the threat and joy, of exploring the unknown. (Pervin 1989, 235)

The criticisms of Kelly's theory should not disturb the reader who found it enlightening. No personality theory—indeed, no theory of any kind—is without valid criticism. As Kelly would have said, every theory, like any construct, has a range of convenience and a focus of convenience, and that includes his own theory as well.

As we have seen, many aspects of Kelly's theory are found in social learning theory, which is very popular today. Kelly's theory also has much in common with existential-humanistic theories, which are also very popular today. We can conclude that the influence of Kelly's work will be felt in the realm of personality theory for a long time to come.

Summary

Kelly was born in the Midwest and raised by educated, religious parents. From his early pioneering experiences with his parents came a practical, flexible outlook, which characterized Kelly all of his life. Kelly's theory can be categorized as phenomenological because it studied intact, significant cognitive experiences; cognitive because it studied mental events; existential because it emphasized the future and people's freedom to choose their own destinies; and humanistic because it emphasized people's creative powers and was optimistic about people's ability to solve their problems.

Kelly's major premise was that all humans act like scientists in that they attempt to reduce uncertainty by developing theories (construct systems), which allow them to anticipate future events accurately. People construe—that is, interpret, explain or predict—the events in their lives by utilizing constructs. A construct is a category of thought that describes how events are similar to one another and yet different from other events. All individuals are free to create whatever constructs they choose, in their attempts to give meaning to their experiences. This freedom to choose constructs is called constructive alternativism. People are free to choose constructs but are more or less bound to them once they have been selected.

Kelly elaborated his theory through eleven corollaries. The construction corollary states that constructs are formed on the basis of the common themes in our experiences. The individuality corollary states that all individuals construe their experiences in their own unique way. The organization corollary states that some constructs are subsumed under other constructs. The dichotomy corollary states that each construct must describe how certain events are similar and also how those events are contrasted with other events. The choice corollary states that those constructs are chosen that have the best chance of either defining (validating) or extending (generalizing) one's construct system. The range corollary states that each construct has a range of convenience consisting of the events to which the construct is relevant and a focus of convenience to which the construct is maximally relevant. The experience corollary states that it is not physical experience that is important but the active construing of physical experiences. It is construing that provides for the testing and revision of one's construct system. The modulation corollary states that some constructs are more permeable—that is, more open to experience—than other constructs. The fragmentation corollary states that while trying new constructs people may at times be inconsistent, but if the larger picture is viewed, people tend to be consistent. The commonality corollary states that in order for two individuals to be considered similar they must construe their experiences in a similar manner. The sociality corollary states that in order to play a role, one must first determine what another person's expectations are and then act in accordance with those expectations.

When individuals are confronted with a novel situation, they apply the CPC cycle. In the circumspection phase of the cycle people ponder a number of constructs that they feel may be appropriate to the situation. In the preemption phase they choose that construct that seems to be the most relevant. In the control phase they choose the pole of the dichotomous construct chosen during the preemption phase and act on it. The creativity cycle is used where an innovative idea is sought, and it too involves three phases: Loosening of the construct system to experiment with new ideas; tightening of the construct system so that the cognitive experimentation of the previous phases comes to an end; and testing the innovative idea arrived at in the first phase.

Kelly redefined several traditional psychological concepts in terms of his theory. The concept of motivation was thought unnecessary, because humans are born motivated. Anxiety was defined as the feeling one gets when it is recognized that what is being experienced lies outside one's construct system. Hostility was defined as an attempt to force the validation of one's construct system when it is clear that it is generating inaccurate predictions. Aggression was defined as the attempt to expand one's construct system. The aggressive person, according to Kelly, is one who typically seeks new experiences. Guilt, according to Kelly, is experienced when one's core role structure is threatened; in other words, when one acts contrary to the role he or she typically plays in relation to a significant person or group in his or her life. Threat was defined as the feeling one experiences when one's core structures are invalidated. Fear was defined as the feeling one has when constructs other than core constructs are invalidated. The unconscious, to Kelly, was explained in terms of preverbal constructs; submergence, in which one pole of a construct is emphasized; and suspension, in which certain elements of experience are ignored until they can be made to fit into one's construct system in a constructive way. Learning was defined as any change in one's construct system.

Kelly compared a neurotic person to a bad scientist, because he or she keeps making inaccurate predictions in the absence of validating experiences. Psychotherapy, to Kelly, was a process in which a client could try out different, potentially more effective, construct systems. In order to discover what constructs a client used in dealing with experiences, Kelly devised the Role Construct Repertory Test, better known as the Rep test. Kelly maintained a credulous attitude toward his clients, believing that they could provide a great deal of valid information about themselves. For example, he often had his clients write a self-characterization, in which they described themselves in the third person. Kelly used fixed-role therapy, in which he had clients act "as if" they were different people and in which the therapist was much like a supporting actor. Such a procedure allowed clients to test an alternative construct system, while the therapist provided encouragement and validating experiences.

Kelly's theory was compared to Kuhn's notion of scientific paradigms, in that both emphasize that reality can be viewed in several equally valid ways.

Currently Kelly's theory has a relatively small but highly productive group of supporters scattered throughout the world. The empirical research generated by

Kelly's theory has concentrated on the Rep test, but almost all aspects of Kelly's theory have generated some research. Currently there is a rather widespread application of Kelly's ideas to industrial–organizational psychology, management development, and occupational counseling.

Kelly's theory has been criticized for generating a limited amount of empirical research; neglecting or denying important aspects of personality; having difficulty in predicting behavior; and leaving too many important questions unanswered. Kelly's theory has been praised for refocusing the study of personality back on the rational, intellectual aspects of human behavior; and for having considerable applied value. Because many aspects of Kelly's theory are found in both social learning theory and in existential-humanistic theory, it promises to continue to be an influential one.

EXPERIENTIAL EXERCISES

1. Choose an issue in your life about which you feel strongly. Write down the issue and how you feel about it. Possibilities include abortion, capital punishment, the existence of God, American involvement in Central America, women's rights, and so on. Next, try taking a stand that is diametrically opposed to your own. Try to think about the issue as would those with views contrary to your thinking. Can you "see" their viewpoint? Is one viewpoint clearly correct and others clearly incorrect? With regard to this exercise, comment on Kelly's contention that "truth" is largely a viewpoint.

2. Describe in a few words the roles that you have assumed while interacting with the relevant people or groups in your life. For example, what role describes your relationship with your parents, your loved one, and your closest friends? Kelly claimed one experiences guilt when one acts contrary to the role one assumes while interacting with the significant others in one's life. Explain why you agree or disagree with Kelly.

3. Take the Role Construct Repertory Test found earlier in this chapter yourself. Carefully note the number and the variety of the constructs that you use in construing other people. Also note what you listed as the two poles of your constructs. What does the Rep test tell you about your construct system? Next, administer the Rep test to someone you are very close to and compare responses. Summarize your observations.

4. To experience what fixed-role therapy might be like, write a self-characterization of yourself in the third person. Next, write a description of a person very much unlike yourself. For the next few days keep this fictitious description in mind. As you have various experiences, note not only how you interpret and respond to them, but try to imagine how the fictitious person might construe and respond. Remember Kelly's clients were instructed to *actually* construe and respond as if they were the fictitious person. Do you think it would be easy to try on a new personality as one would try on a new set of clothes? Explain.

5. To what extent do you feel arguments, or even wars, result because people construe events with different construct systems? What can be done to reduce such confrontation? What can be done to improve the interpersonal relationships in your own life? Explain.

6. Kelly suggested that if you do not like the way something looks, you should look at it differently. Try his advice. Isolate a source of frustration, anger, or discouragement in your life. Attempt to view that negative aspect of your life positively. For example, if lack of adequate finance is a source of frustration in your life, try to see the positive aspects of having limited funds. Describe the outcome of your experience with constructive alternativism.

1. Describe the categories into which Kelly's theory fits.

2. Explain how Kelly used the model of the scientist to explain the psychological processes of all humans.

3. Define the term construct as Kelly used it. List the various characteristics of constructs.

4. Explain how Kelly accounts for inconsistencies in a person's behavior.

5. According to Kelly, what is required before we can call two people similar?

6. Describe the CPC cycle.

7. Describe the creativity cycle.

8. Discuss each of the following terms from Kelly's point of view: motivation, anxiety, hostility, aggression, guilt, threat, fear, learning, and reinforcement.

9. What, in Kelly's theory, corresponds to the concept of the unconscious in other theories?

10. Describe the procedures in administering the Rep test.

11. What did Kelly mean when he said that he maintained a credulous attitude toward his clients?

12. Summarize the procedures of fixed-role therapy.

13. According to Kelly, what is the goal of psychotherapy?

14. Elaborate on Kelly's contention that playing a role requires that one's behavior be guided by the perception of another person's expectations.

15. How did Kelly differentiate between a healthy person and an emotionally disturbed person?

16. Answer the following question as if you were Kelly: "If playing different parts is so useful in calling different construct systems to the attention of a client, why is it that there seems to be so many emotionally disturbed actors and actresses? Are they not experimenting with different construct systems all the time?"

17. Describe those theories of motivation that Kelly labeled "pitchfork" theories and those that he labeled "carrot" theories. Why did Kelly refer to his own theory of motivation as a "jackass" theory?

18. In chapter 1 it was pointed out that all cognitive theories have the problem of explaining how something cognitive is translated into behavior. This is one manifestation of the mind-body problem. Discuss this problem as it relates to Kelly's theory.

19. Compare the terms motivation, anxiety, and aggression as they are used in Freudian theory with the way they are used in Kellian theory.

20. Assuming that anxiety is a basic ingredient of humor, what types of things, according to Kelly, should make us laugh? Does Kelly's suggestion coincide with your experience with humor? Explain.

21. Summarize the criticisms of Kelly's theory.

22. Summarize the contributions of Kelly's theory.

BANNISTER, D. (Ed.) (1984). *Further Perspectives in Personal Construct Theory.* New York: Academic Press.

    A collection of papers on construct theory written by English, Canadian, and American psychologists and philosophers.

BANNISTER, D., AND FRANSELLA, F. (1971). *Inquiring Man: The Theory of Personal Constructs.* New York: Penguin Books.

    A brief introduction to Kelly's ideas written by two of his closest supporters. The book explores the implications of construct theory for such areas as behavior therapy, social psychology, and schizophrenia.

KELLY, G. A. (1955). *The Psychology of Personal Constructs* (Vols. 1 & 2). New York: Norton.

    These two volumes present the basics of Kelly's theory. Volume 1 discusses his theory of personality, the Role Construct Repertory

Test, the self-characterization, and fixed-role therapy. Volume 2 deals mainly with the client–therapist relationship and how to induce movement (improvement) during therapy.

KELLY, G. A. (1963). *A Theory of Personality: The Psychology of Personal Constructs*. New York: Norton.

The first three chapters of Kelly's 1955 text are offered in this text as a brief introduction to his theory.

KELLY, G. A. (1964). The Language of Hypotheses: Man's Psychological Instrument. *Journal of Individual Psychology, 20,* 137–152.

Discusses the importance of make-believe for scientists, professional writers, and anyone else who wants to live a more effective, interesting life. Kelly argues that it is not what one *is* that is important, rather, it is what one can *become*. In this article, Kelly discusses the close relationship between his ideas and Hans Vaihinger's philosophy of "as if" which was so influential in Adler's theorizing.

MAHER, B. (Ed.). (1969). *Clinical Psychology and Personality: The Selected Papers of George Kelly*. New York: Wiley.

When Kelly died, he was in the process of editing a collection of his most recent papers, most of which had not been published before. Brendan Maher, one of Kelly's most distinguished students, finished the editing job and the result is this volume. Among the many interesting articles is "The Autobiography of a Theory," which traces the origins of Kelly's theory.

NEIMEYER, R. A. (1985b). *The Development of Personal Construct Psychology*. Lincoln: University of Nebraska Press.

Traces the development of Kelly's theory from the time when it reflected the ideas of just one person (Kelly) to recent times when a network of social scientists are applying construct theory to problems in clinical, personality, social and developmental psychology as well as to cultural anthropology and urban planning. Neimeyer evaluates construct theory's current status and its prospects for the future.

GLOSSARY

Aggression. The effort to expand one's construct system so that it is capable of assimilating a greater range of experiences.

Anxiety. The feeling one has when it is realized that an experience lies outside one's construct system.

Choice corollary. States that people will choose a construct that will either further define or extend their construct system. See also definition and extension of a construct system.

Circumspection phase. That phase of the CPC cycle in which a person ponders several constructs that might be useful in construing a novel situation.

Cognitive theory. Any theory that focuses on the study of mental events.

Cognitively complex person. A person with many well-differentiated constructs in his or her construct system.

Cognitively simple person. A person with only a few poorly differentiated constructs in his or her construct system.

Commonality corollary. States that people can be considered similar, not because of similar physical experiences, but because they construe their experiences in a similar fashion.

Construct. See personal construct.

Construct system. A collection of constructs used by a person at any given time to construe the events in his or her life.

Construction corollary. States that constructs are formed on the basis of the recurring events in one's life.

Constructive alternativism. A term that reflects Kelly's belief that there are numerous ways of construing one's experience and therefore one is free to choose from a number of construct systems.

Construe. One's active effort to interpret, explain, and give meaning to experiences.

Control phase. That phase of the CPC cycle in which people choose a pole of the construct chosen in the preemptive phase of the cycle and act in accordance with that pole.

Core role structure. The roles we play while interacting with the important people and groups in our lives.

Core structures. Those constructs on which we rely most heavily when construing experience—that is, those that have been most consistently validated.

CPC cycle. The series of activities engaged in by a person confronted with a novel situation. See also circumspection phase, control phase, and preemption phase.

Creativity cycle. A three-phase cycle in which innovative ideas are sought. Phase 1 involves the loosening of one's construct system to allow realignments of elements and constructs. Phase 2 involves the retightening of one's construct system after an innovative idea has been found. Phase 3 involves testing the idea and retaining it if it is found useful and discarding it if not.

Credulous attitude. The assumption that the information provided by clients about themselves can be trusted as accurate and valid.

Definition of a construct system. The choice of a construct, in construing a situation, that has already been successful in construing similar situations. Such a choice has the effect of further validating one's construct system.

Dichotomy corollary. States that each construct has two poles, one of which describes what characteristics the events to which the construct is relevant have in common, the other of which describes events without those characteristics. For example, if one pole of a construct describes beautiful things, the other pole may describe things without beauty, or ugly things.

Existential theory. Any theory that focuses on the nature of, or the problems related to, human existence.

Experience corollary. States that mere passive experience is unimportant. It is the active construing of experience that ultimately results in a more effective construct system.

Extension of a construct system. The choice of a construct, in construing a situation, that has never been tried before. Such a choice has the potential effect of extending one's construct system so that it is capable of assimilating a greater range of experience.

Fear. The feeling one has when a relatively unimportant construct is about to be invalidated, thus requiring a minor change in one's construct system.

Fixed-Role therapy. The clinical technique that asks clients to act as if they were other people. Thus clients become actors, and the therapist becomes a supporting actor. The idea is to have the clients try different ways of construing their experiences in a nonthreatening situation as the therapist provides validating information about their new construct systems.

Focus of convenience. The events within the range of convenience of a construct to which that construct is maximally significant.

Fragmentation corollary. States that as a construct system is being tested, revised, or extended, certain inconsistencies in behavior may result.

Guilt. The feeling one has when one acts contrary to a role he or she has assumed while interacting with a significant person or group in his or her life.

Hostility. The attempt to force the validation of a prediction that has already proved to be erroneous.

Humanistic theory. Any theory that assumes that humans are basically good and rational and that their behavior is purposive.

Individuality corollary. States that each person is unique in his or her manner of construing experience.

Jackass theory of motivation. Kelly's description of his own theory, since it focused on the nature of the organism itself rather than on the events that either push or pull the organism.

Learning. Any change in one's construct system.

Man the scientist. A statement reflecting Kelly's belief that all humans act like scientists in that they attempt to devise "theories" that allow them to predict future events, thereby reducing uncertainty in their lives.

Modulation corollary. States that a construct system is more likely to change if the constructs contained in it are permeable. See also permeable construct.

Motivation. For Kelly, a synonym for life.

Organization corollary. States that constructs are arranged in a hierarchy from most general to most specific. See

also superordinate construct and subordinate construct.

Permeable construct. A construct that easily assimilates new experiences.

Personal construct. An idea or thought that a person uses when construing personal experience. Sometimes simply called a construct.

Personality. For Kelly, the term personality refers to a person's construct system.

Phenomenologist. One who studies intact, subjective, conscious, and personal experience.

Phenomenology. The study of intact, subjective, conscious and personal experience.

Preemption phase. That phase of the CPC cycle in which people decide which construct they are going to use to construe a novel situation.

Preverbal construct. A construct that was formulated early in one's life, before language was adequately developed. Although such a construct cannot be labeled verbally it can still be used to construe one's experiences.

Propositional construct. A construct that is cognitively tested as one that might be useful in construing a novel situation.

Psychotherapy. Because Kelly equated people suffering emotional problems with bad scientists, therapy was regarded as a setting in which the client could learn to be a better scientist—that is, learn to develop a more effective construct system.

Pull theories of motivation. Those theories that emphasize terms such as purpose, value, or need. Kelly also called these carrot theories.

Push theories of motivation. Those theories that emphasize terms such as drive, motive, and stimulus. Kelly also called these pitchfork theories.

Range corollary. States that a construct is relevant to only a finite range of events. See also range of convenience and focus of convenience.

Range of convenience. The finite range of events to which a particular construct is relevant.

Role. For Kelly, a role is acting in accordance with another person's expectations of how one will act.

Role construct. The awareness of another person's expectations. In a sense, a role construct involves seeing the world through someone else's eyes.

Role Construct Repertory Test (Rep test). A test developed by Kelly to identify the constructs clients use to construe the relevant people in their lives.

Self-Characterization. The sketch that Kelly sometimes had his clients write about themselves (in the third person) in order to learn what constructs they used to construe themselves and other people.

Sociality corollary. States that to engage in constructive social interaction with another person, one must first understand how that person construes his or her experiences. Only then can one play a role in that person's life. See also role.

Submergence. The situation in which one pole of a construct is used, but the other pole tends not to be. The unused pole is said to be submerged or unconscious.

Subordinate construct. A construct that is subsumed under a more general construct.

Superordinate construct. A general construct that subsumes other constructs.

Suspension. The situation in which an experience has low cognitive awareness because it is incompatible with one's current construct system. If one's construct system is changed so that it can assimilate the experience, it (the experience) will enter full awareness; that is, it will no longer be suspended.

Threat. The awareness that one or more of the constructs depended on most in construing experience is going to be invalidated, thus requiring a major change in one's construct system. See also core structures.

Unconscious. Constructs with low cognitive awareness. See also submergence and suspension.

Validation. Results when a construct or a construct system is successful in anticipating an experience.

14

Carl Rogers

C arl Ranson Rogers was born on 8 January 1902 in Oak Park (a Chicago suburb), Illinois, and was the fourth of six children. Because his father was a successful civil engineer and contractor, there were no economic problems in Rogers's early life. Rogers described himself as "the middle child in a large, close knit family, where hard work and a highly conservative (almost fundamentalist) Protestant Christianity were about equally revered" (1959, 186). Rogers's parents discouraged the development of friendships outside their home because, it was argued, nonfamily members engaged in questionable activities. Rogers commented:

> I think the attitudes toward persons outside our large family can be summed up schematically in this way: Other persons behave in dubious ways which we do not approve in our family. Many of them play cards, go to movies, smoke, drink, and engage in other activities—some unmentionable. So the best thing to do is to be tolerant of them, since they may not know better, and to keep away from any close communication with them and live your life within the family. (1973, 3)

As a result of the attitude toward "outsiders" he described, Rogers spent a great deal of time by himself, reading everything he could get his hands on, including encyclopedias and a dictionary.

When he was twelve years old, Rogers and his family moved to a farm about thirty miles from Chicago. It was here that Rogers first developed an interest in science. Because his father insisted that the farm be run scientifically, Rogers read about many agricultural experiments. He also developed an interest in a species of moth about which he read and which he captured, raised, and bred. This interest in science is something that never left Rogers, although he worked in one of the more subjective areas of psychology all of his professional life.

Rogers's tendency toward solitude lasted all through high school, during which time he only had two dates. He was an excellent student and obtained almost straight A's. His main interests were English and science.

In 1919, Rogers enrolled at the University of Wisconsin, which both his parents, two brothers, and a sister had attended, and chose to study agriculture. Rogers was very active in church work through his early years in college. In 1922, he was one of ten college students selected to attend the World Student Christian Federation Conference in Peking, China. This six-month trip had a profound effect on Rogers. Having experienced, firsthand, people of different cultures with different religions, Rogers (1961) reflected on an insight that he had aboard ship on his way back from China: "It struck me one night in my cabin that perhaps Jesus was a man like other men—not divine! As this idea formed and took root, it became obvious to me that I could never in any emotional sense return home. This proved to be true" (351). Rogers wrote to his parents declaring his independence from their conservative, religious viewpoint. Rogers found his declaration of independence intellectually refreshing but it seems he had to pay an emotional price for his new-found freedom. Shortly after he returned from the Orient, he was increasingly troubled by abdominal pains that were diagnosed as being due to a duodenal ulcer. Rogers was hospitalized for several weeks and received intensive treatment for six months. On returning to the University of Wisconsin, he changed his major from agriculture to history. Rogers received his B.A. degree in 1924.

After graduation, Rogers married (despite strong parental disapproval) his childhood sweetheart, Helen Elliott, and they later had two children. Also in 1924, Rogers enrolled in the liberal Union Theological Seminary in New York. Although by now Rogers was interested in helping people with problems, he was increasingly doubtful that the best vehicle for help was to be found in religious doctrine. After two years at the seminary, Rogers transferred to Columbia University to study clinical and educational psychology. He received his M.A. in 1928 and his Ph.D. in 1931. His dissertation was on the measurement of personality adjustment in children.

On receiving his Ph.D., Rogers accepted a position as psychologist in the Child Study Department of the Society for the Prevention of Cruelty to Children in Rochester, New York, where he had worked as an intern while pursuing his Ph.D. It was here that Rogers had a number of experiences that greatly influenced his later theory of personality and his approach to psychotherapy. First, he learned that the psychoanalytic approach to therapy, which dominated the department, was often ineffective. Second, because of the vastly different approaches to therapy he had studied at Columbia and in the Child Study Department, he learned that so-called

Carl Rogers

authorities could not agree on what constituted the best treatment for a troubled person. Third, he learned that looking for an "insight" into a problem is often met with frustration. Rogers described one situation in which he felt that a mother's rejection of her son was the cause of his delinquent behavior. He tried his best to share this "insight" with the mother but failed.

> Finally I gave up. I told her that it seemed we had both tried, but we had failed. . . . She agreed. So we concluded the interview, shook hands, and she walked to the door of the office. Then she turned and asked, "Do you ever take adults for counseling here?" When I replied in the affirmative, she said, "Well then, I would like some help." She came to the chair she had left, and began to pour out her despair about her marriage, her troubled relationship with her husband, her sense of failure and confusion, all very different from the sterile "case history" she had given before. Real therapy began then. . . .
>
> This incident was one of a number which helped me to experience that fact—only fully realized later—that it is the *client* who knows what hurts, what directions to go, what problems are crucial, what experiences have been deeply buried. It began to occur to me that unless I had a need to demonstrate my own cleverness and learning, I would do better to rely upon the client for the direction of movement in the process. (Rogers 1961, 11–12)

Rogers wrote his first book while at the Child Study Department; it was entitled *The Clinical Treatment of the Problem Child* (1939). In 1940, Rogers moved from a clinical setting to an academic setting, by accepting a faculty position in clinical psychology at Ohio State University. It was here that Rogers began to formulate and test his own approach to psychotherapy.

> I found that the emerging principles of therapy, which I had experienced largely on an implicit basis, were by no means clear to well-trained, critically minded graduate students. I began to sense that what I was doing and thinking in the clinical field was perhaps more of a new pathway than I had recognized. The paper I presented to the Minnesota Chapter of Psi Chi in December, 1940 (later Chapter 2 of *Counseling and Psychotherapy*) was the first conscious attempt to develop a relatively new line of thought. Up to that time, I had felt that my writings were essentially attempts to distill out more clearly the principles which "all clinicians" were using. (Rogers 1959, 187)

In 1942, Rogers published his now-famous book, *Counseling and Psychotherapy: Newer Concepts in Practice*, which many thought described the first major alternative to psychoanalysis. The publisher was reluctant to publish this book, believing that it would not sell 2,000 copies, the number necessary to break even. By 1961 it had sold more than 70,000 copies, and it is still going strong.

In 1945, Rogers left Ohio State to become professor of psychology and director of counseling at the University of Chicago. It was during his stay at the University of Chicago that Rogers published what many consider to be his major work, *Client-Centered Therapy: Its Current Practice, Implications, and Theory* (1951).

In 1957, Rogers left the University of Chicago to return to the University of Wisconsin, where he held the dual position of professor of psychology and professor of psychiatry. In 1963, he resigned his positions at the University of Wisconsin to become a member of the Western Behavioral Sciences Institute (WBSI) in La

Jolla, California. In 1968, Rogers, and several of the more humanistically oriented members of WBSI, left that organization to form the Center for the Studies of the Person, also in La Jolla.

Many of Rogers's moves were coupled with a shift in his interests, techniques, or philosophy. His last move stressed his interest in the individual as he or she experiences the world. Rogers explained, "We are deeply interested in persons but are rather 'turned-off' by the older methods of studying them as 'objects' for research" (1972a, 67). In his later years, Rogers worked with encounter groups and taught sensitivity training. He was mainly interested in discovering the conditions under which a person can fully develop his or her full potentialities. Also toward the end of his life, Rogers became intensely interested in promoting world peace. He organized the Vienna Peace Project that brought leaders of thirteen countries together in 1985, and conducted peace workshops in Moscow in 1986. Rogers continued to work on these and other projects until his death on 4 February 1987 from cardiac arrest following surgery for a broken hip.

Rogers served as president of the American Psychological Association in 1946–47, and in 1956 he received the first Distinguished Scientific Contribution Award presented by the American Psychological Association. The latter award moved Rogers to tears because he felt that his colleagues viewed his efforts as nonscientific. In 1972, Rogers received the Distinguished Professional Contribution Award from the American Psychological Association, making him the first psychologist in that organization's history to receive both the Distinguished Scientific and Professional Contribution Awards.

Through the years Rogers has maintained that the most important resource that people have is their actualizing tendencies, and it is to a discussion of that tendency that we turn next.

Actualizing Tendency

Rogers postulated one master motive, which he calls the **actualizing tendency.**

> The organism has one basic tendency and striving—to actualize, maintain, and enhance the experiencing organism. (Rogers 1951, 487)

> There is one central source of energy in the human organism; that is a function of the whole organism rather than some portion of it; and that it is perhaps best conceptualized as a tendency toward fulfillment, toward actualization, toward the maintenance and enhancement of the organism. (Rogers 1963, 6)

According to Rogers, all humans, as well as all other living organisms, have an innate need to survive, grow, and enhance themselves. All biologic drives are subsumed under the actualizing tendency, because they must be satisfied if the organism is to continue its positive development. This "forward thrust of life" continues despite many obstacles. For example, children first learning to walk stumble again and again, but, despite the pain, press on with their attempts to walk. There are numerous examples of humans who, while living under dire circumstances, not only survive but continue to enhance their lives.

One might ask: Toward what is the actualizing tendency moving? Rogers's answer to this question specifies a view of human nature that is essentially the opposite of the view suggested by Freud. Freud viewed humans as having the same needs, drives, and motives as any other animal has. Therefore, humans' tendencies toward uninhibited sex and aggression must be controlled by society. Rogers believed that humans are basically good and therefore need no controlling. In fact, he believed that it is the attempt to control humans that makes them "act" bad. Rogers's view of human nature places him in the humanistic camp.

> I have little sympathy with the rather prevalent concept that man is basically irrational, and that his impulses, if not controlled, will lead to the destruction of others and self. Man's behavior is exquisitely rational, moving with subtle and ordered complexity toward the goals his organism is endeavoring to achieve. (Rogers 1961, 194–95)

> I am inclined to believe that fully to be a human being is to enter into the complex process of being one of the most widely sensitive, responsive, creative, and adaptive creatures on this planet.
> So when a Freudian such as Karl Menninger tells me (as he has, in a discussion of this issue) that he perceives man as "innately evil" or more precisely, "innately destructive," I can only shake my head in wonderment. (quoted in Kirschenbaum 1979, 250)

Rogers was aware that people sometimes act in unfortunate ways. But, he claimed, such actions are not in accordance with human nature. Such actions result from fear and defensiveness.

> I do not have a Pollyanna view of human nature. I am quite aware that out of defensiveness and inner fear individuals can and do behave in ways which are incredibly cruel, horribly destructive, immature, regressive, anti-social, and hurtful. Yet one of the most refreshing and invigorating parts of my experience is to work with such individuals and to discover the strongly positive directional tendencies which exist in them, as in all of us, at the deepest levels. (Rogers 1961, 27)

The actualizing tendency, which is the driving force in everyone's life, causes the person to become more differentiated (complex), more independent, and more socially responsible. We will say more about the goals of the actualizing tendency when we describe the fully functioning person in a later section of this chapter.

Organismic Valuing Process

All of the organism's experiences are evaluated using the actualizing tendency as a frame of reference. Rogers called this method of evaluation of one's experiences the **organismic valuing process.** Those experiences that are in accordance with the actualizing tendency are satisfying and therefore are approached and maintained. Those experiences that are contrary to the actualizing tendency are unsatisfying and therefore are avoided or terminated. The organismic valuing process, therefore, creates a feedback system that allows the organism to coordinate its experiences with its tendency toward self-actualization. This means that people can trust their *feelings.* Rogers believed that even infants, if given the opportunity, will choose what is best for them.

> The simplest example is the infant who at one moment values food, and when satiated, is disgusted with it; at one moment values stimulation, and soon after, values only rest; who finds satisfying the diet which in the long run most enhances his development. (Rogers 1959, 210)

In his own life, Rogers learned the value of acting on his own feelings.

> One of the basic things which I was a long time in realizing, and which I am still learning, is that when an activity *feels* as though it is valuable or worth doing, it *is* worth doing. Put another way, I have learned that my total organismic sensing of a situation is more trustworthy than my intellect.
>
> All of my professional life I have been going on directions which others thought were foolish, and about which I have had many doubts myself. But I have never regretted moving in directions which "felt right," even though I have often felt lonely or foolish at the time. . . . *Experience is, for me, the highest authority.* . . . Neither the Bible nor the prophets—neither Freud nor research—neither the revelations of God nor man—can take precedence over my own experience. (1961, 22–24)

Phenomenological Field

The following quotation identifies Rogers as a phenomenologist and shows a kinship between his position and that of Kelly.

> The only reality I can possibly know is the world as *I* perceive and experience it at this moment. The only reality you can possibly know is the world as *you* perceive and experience it at the moment. And the only certainty is that those perceived realities are different. There are as many "real worlds" as there are people! (Rogers 1980, 102)

According to Rogers then, all people live in their own subjective world, which can be known, in any complete sense, only to themselves. It is this **phenomenological reality,** rather than the physical world, that determines people's behavior. In other words, how people see things is, for them, the only reality. This private reality will correspond in varying degrees to physical reality, depending on the individual. It is this subjective, phenomenological reality that the therapist, according to Rogers, must attempt to understand. Again, a great deal of similarity exists on this point between Rogers's theory and Kelly's. They both stressed the individual's singular subjective interpretation of experience, and that is why they both are labeled phenomenologists. The major difference between Rogers and Kelly is in the actualizing tendency. Kelly's major point was that people keep trying out new constructs in order to find the set which best anticipates the future. There was, for Kelly, no innately determined condition toward which all humans were evolving. Rather, each individual, in a sense, invented his or her personality rather than having its major features genetically determined. The view of the social learning theorist is similar to Kelly's.

Rogers differentiated between **experience** and **awareness.** Experience is all that is going on within the organism's environment at any given moment, which is potentially available to awareness. When these potential experiences become *symbolized*, they enter awareness and become part of the person's phenomenological field. The symbols that act as vehicles for experiences to enter awareness are usually words, but they need not be. Rogers believed that symbols also could be visual and auditory images. The distinction between experience and awareness was important to Rogers, because, as we shall see, certain conditions cause people to deny or distort certain experiences, thereby preventing them from entering their awareness.

Emergence of the Self

Rogers confessed to having resisted using the concept of self because he felt it was not scientific. It was the fact that his clients used the term so much that gradually changed his mind.

> Speaking personally, I began my work with the settled notion that the "self" was a vague, ambiguous, scientifically meaningless term which had gone out of the psychologist's vocabulary with the departure of the introspectionists. Consequently I was slow in recognizing that when clients were given the opportunity to express their problems and their attitudes in their own terms, without any guidance or interpretation, they tended to talk in terms of the self. Characteristic expressions were attitudes such as these: "I feel I'm not being my real self." "I wonder who I am, really." "I wouldn't want anyone to know the real me." "I never had a chance to be myself." "It feels good to let myself go and just *be* myself here." "I think if I chip off the plaster facade I've got a pretty solid self—a good substantial brick building, underneath." It seemed clear from such expressions that the self was an important element in the experience of the client, and that in some odd sense his goal was to become his "real self." (Rogers 1959, 200–201)

Since this early reluctance, however, the concept of self has become the cornerstone of Rogers's theory. In fact, his theory of personality is often labeled a "self theory."

At first, infants do not distinguish between events in their phenomenological field; they are all blended together in a single configuration. Gradually, however, through experiences with verbal labels such as "me" and "I," a portion of their phenomenological field becomes differentiated as the **self.** At this point, a person can reflect on one's self as a distinct object of which one is aware.

The development of the self is a major manifestation of the actualizing tendency, which, as stated earlier, inclines the organisms toward greater differentiation or complexity. The actualizing tendency that, prior to the development of the self, characterized the organism as a whole, now characterizes the self as well. In other words, those experiences seen as enhancing one's self-concept are positively valued; those seen as detrimental to the self-concept are negatively valued.

Need for Positive Regard

With the emergence of the self comes the **need for positive regard,** which Rogers believed was universal, although not necessarily innate (whether it was learned or innate was unimportant to Rogers). Positive regard means receiving such things as warmth, love, sympathy, care, respect, and acceptance from the relevant people in one's life. In other words, it is the feeling of being "prized" by those people who are most important to us.

As a typical part of the socialization process, children learn there are things they can do and things they cannot do. Most often parents will make positive regard contingent on desirable behavior on the part of their children. That is, if the children do certain things, they will experience positive regard; if they do other things, they will not. This creates what Rogers called **conditions of worth,** which specify the circumstances under which children will experience positive regard. Through repeated experiences with these conditions of worth, children internalize them, making them part of their self-structure. Once internalized, they become a "conscience," or "superego," which guides the children's behavior even when the parents are not around.

From the need for positive regard comes the **need for self-regard.** That is, children develop the need to view themselves positively. In other words, children first want others to feel good about them and then they want to feel good about themselves. The conditions that make relevant people in their lives regard them positively are "introjected" into their self-structure and thereafter they must act in accordance with those conditions in order to regard themselves positively. The children are now said to have acquired conditions of worth. Unfortunately, when conditions of worth have been established, the only way children can view themselves positively is by acting in accordance with someone else's values, which they have internalized. Now children's behavior is no longer guided by their organismic valuing process but by the conditions in their environment that are related to positive regard. Rogers stated that the infant:

> Comes to be guided in his behavior not by the degree to which an experience maintains or enhances the organism, but by the likelihood of receiving maternal love. (Rogers 1959, 225)
>
> In order to hold the love of a parent, the child introjects as his own values and perceptions which he does not actually experience. He then denies to awareness the organismic experiencings that contradict these introjections. Thus, his self-concept contains false elements that are not based on what he is, in his experiencing. (Rogers 1966, 192)

Whenever there are conditions of worth in children's lives, they may be forced to deny their own evaluations of their experiences in favor of someone else's evaluation, and this causes an alienation between people's experiences and their self. This alienation creates a condition of incongruence, which we will discuss in the next section.

Even when people turn to others for positive regard, they will not experience it consistently. For example, parents may not be consistent in what they reward and punish. In order to increase the likelihood of experiencing more consistent positive regard, people may affiliate themselves with a group in which the conditions of worth are relatively stable; for example, a fundamentalist religion, the American Legion, the Elks, the Lions, the League of Women Voters, or a small group of predictable acquaintances. In so doing, people do not come any closer to their own organismic valuing process, they just have specified more clearly the conditions of worth that allow them to experience positive regard. For Rogers, each person's ultimate goal is to be true to his or her own feelings, not someone else's.

The only way not to interfere with children's actualizing tendencies is to give them **unconditional positive regard,** which allows them to experience positive regard no matter what they do.

> If an individual should *experience* only *unconditional positive regard*, then no *conditions of worth* would develop, *self-regard* would be unconditional, the needs for *positive regard* and *self-regard* would never be at variance with *organismic evaluation*, and the individual would continue to be *psychologically adjusted*, and would be fully functioning. (Rogers 1959, 224)

This does not mean that Rogers believed that children should be allowed to do whatever they please. He believed that a rational, democratic approach to dealing with behavior problems is best. Since, according to Rogers, it is conditions of worth that are at the heart of all human adjustment problems, they should be avoided at all costs. Rogers suggested the following strategy for dealing with a misbehaving child:

> If the infant always felt prized, if his own feelings were always accepted even though some behaviors were inhibited, then no conditions of worth would develop. This could at least theoretically be achieved if the parental attitude was genuinely of this sort: "I can understand how satisfying it feels to you to hit your baby brother (or to defecate when and where you please or to destroy things) and I love you and am quite willing for you to have those feelings. But I am quite willing for me to have my feelings, too, and I feel very distressed when your brother is hurt, . . . and so I do not let you hit him. Both your feelings and my feelings are important, and each of us can freely have his own. (1959, 225)

In other words, Rogers felt that the following message should be conveyed to the child: "We love you deeply as you are but what you are doing is upsetting and therefore we would be happier if you would stop." The child should always be loved, but some of his or her behaviors may not be.

Incongruent Person

Incongruency exists when people are no longer using their organismic valuing process as a means of determining whether or not their experiences are in accordance with their actualizing tendency. If people do not use their own valuing process for evaluating their experiences, then they must be using someone's introjected values in doing so. That is, conditions of worth have replaced their organismic valuing process as the frame of reference for evaluating their experiences. This results in an alienation between the self and experience, because, under these circumstances, what may truly be satisfying to the person may be denied awareness because it is not in accordance with the person's introjected conditions of worth. Rogers (1959, 226) summarized the development of incongruence between the self and experience as follows:

1. Once conditions of worth develop, people respond to their experiences selectively. Those experiences that are in accordance with their conditions of worth are perceived and are symbolized accurately in awareness. Those experiences that are not in accordance with their conditions of worth are distorted or are denied awareness.

2. After conditions of worth develop, people must edit out of their awareness those experiences which are contrary to those conditions. Thus, the self is denied experiences which may be beneficial to it.

3. Selective perception creates an incongruence between the self and experience because certain experiences that may be conducive to positive growth may be distorted or denied. Once this incongruence between self and experience exists, people are vulnerable, and psychological maladjustment may result.

Rogers looked on incongruence as the cause of all human adjustment problems. It follows then, that eliminating incongruence will solve those problems.

> This, as we see it, is the basic estrangement of man. He has not been true to himself, to his own natural organismic valuing of experience, but for the sake of preserving the positive regard of others has now come to falsify some of the values he experiences and to perceive them only in terms based upon their value to others. Yet this has not been a conscious choice, but a natural—and tragic—development in infancy. The path of development toward psychological maturity . . . is the undoing of this estrangement in man's functioning . . . the achievement of a self which is congruent with experience, and the restoration of a unified organismic valuing process as the regulator of behavior. (Rogers 1959, 226–27)

When an incongruency exists between self and experience the person is, by definition, maladjusted and is vulnerable to anxiety and threat and therefore is defensive.

Anxiety results when people "subceive" an experience as being incompatible with their self-structure and its introjected conditions of worth. In other words, anxiety is experienced when an event is encountered that *threatens* the existing self-structure. Note that Rogers said that the event is *subceived* rather than *perceived*. **Subception** is the detection of an experience before it enters full awareness. This way a potentially threatening event can be denied or distorted before it causes anxiety. According to Rogers, the process of **defense** consists of editing experiences, via the mechanisms of **denial** and **distortion,** to keep them in accordance with the self-structure. It is important to note that an experience, according to Rogers, is not denied **symbolization** because it is "sinful" or "naughty" or contrary to cultural mores, as Freud believed. It is denied symbolization because it is contrary to the self-structure. For example, if a person's introjected conditions of worth include being a poor student, then receiving a good grade on a test would be threatening, and the experience would tend to be distorted or denied. The person may say, for example, that he or she was just lucky or that the teacher made a mistake.

According to Rogers, almost all individuals experience incongruency and therefore defend against certain experiences being symbolized in awareness. It is only when the incongruency is severe that adjustment problems occur.

We see that any given experience can have any one of three fates: (1) it can be symbolized accurately in awareness; (2) it can be distorted so that it no longer threatens the self-structure; or (3) it can be denied symbolization. If either 2 or 3 occurs, incongruency will result, and if the incongruency is pronounced enough, psychological maladjustment will result.

> When man's unique capacity of awareness is thus functioning freely and fully, we find that we have, not an animal whom we must fear, not a beast who must be controlled, but an organism able to achieve, through the remarkable integrative capacity of its central nervous system, balanced, realistic, self-enhancing . . . behavior as a resultant of all these elements of awareness. To put it another way, when man is less than fully man—when he denies to awareness various aspects of his experience—then indeed we have all too often reason to fear him and his behavior, as the present world situation testifies. But when he is most fully man, when he is his complete organism, when awareness of experience, that peculiarly human attribute, is most fully operating, then he is to be trusted, then his behavior is constructive. (Rogers 1961, 105)

Next we turn to the procedures that Rogers recommended for eliminating or reducing incongruency.

Psychotherapy

Like Freud's and Kelly's, Rogers's notions of personality came from his therapeutic practice. It has been therapy that has always been most important to Rogers; his personality theory developed only as he tried to become more effective as a therapist and as he tried to comprehend the principles that were operative during the therapeutic process.

Through the years, Rogers's description of the therapeutic process has changed. First, he referred to his approach to therapy as **nondirective therapy,** which emphasized clients' ability to solve their own problems if they were given the proper atmosphere for doing so. Next, Rogers labeled his technique **client-centered therapy.** Now therapy was regarded as a joint venture deeply involving both client and therapist. Instead of simply providing an atmosphere in which clients could gradually see more clearly the nature of their problems, as was the case in the earlier stage, the therapist's job now was to attempt *actively* to understand the client's phenomenological field, or **internal frame of reference.** The next stage was called the **experiential stage.** It was during this stage in the evolution of Rogers's thinking that the therapist became as free as the client. Now the deep personal feelings of both therapist and client were equally important, and the therapeutic process was regarded as a struggle to put these feelings into words.

The last stage in Rogers's thinking was labeled the **person-centered stage.** During this stage, Rogers's theory was extended to many areas beyond the therapeutic process. A sample of the areas to which his theory has been applied includes education, marriage and the family, encounter groups, problems of minority groups, and international relations. Rogers believed, however, that it is not the greater applicability that is most important to this stage of development; rather, it is the emphasis on the *total person,* instead of looking at an individual as merely a client or a student.

> The shift in emphasis to person-centered points out more than the widespread applicability of the theory. It attempts to emphasize that it is as *person,* as *I am,* as *being,* and not just in terms of some role identity as client, student, teacher, or therapist that the individual is the unit of all interactions. The name change conveys the full complexity of each person; it indicates that each individual is more than the sum of the parts that make the person. (Holdstock & Rogers 1977, 129)

With all the changes in Rogers's thinking through the years, however, certain basic components of his theory have remained unchanged. These are the importance of the actualizing tendency, the importance of the organismic valuing process as a frame of reference in living one's life, and the importance of unconditional positive regard in allowing a person to live a rich, full life.

Rogers (1959, 213) summarized the six conditions he thought were necessary for effective therapy.

1. The client and the therapist must be in psychological contact; that is, they both must make a difference in the phenomenological field of the other.
2. The client must be in a state of incongruence and therefore vulnerable or anxious.
3. The therapist must be in a state of congruency in relation to the client.
4. The therapist must give the client unconditional positive regard.
5. The therapist must seek an empathic understanding of the client's internal frame of reference.
6. The client must perceive the fact that the therapist is giving him or her unconditional positive regard and is attempting to understand empathetically his or her internal frame of reference.

If the conditions necessary for effective therapy have been met, then, according to Rogers (1959, 216), the following changes in the client should be observed.

1. Clients will express their feelings with increased freedom.
2. Clients become more accurate in their description of their experiences and of the events around them.
3. Clients will begin to detect the incongruity between their concept of self and certain experiences.

4. Clients will feel threatened as incongruity is experienced, but the unconditional positive regard of the therapist allows them to go on experiencing incongruent experiences without the necessity of distorting or denying them.

5. Clients eventually will be able to symbolize accurately, and thus be aware of, feelings which in the past had been denied or distorted.

6. Clients' concepts of self become reorganized and thus are able to include those experiences which had previously been denied awareness.

7. As therapy continues, clients' concepts of self become increasingly congruent with their experience; that is, they now include many experiences which were previously threatening. As clients feel less threatened by experience, they become less defensive.

8. Clients become increasingly able to experience, without feeling threatened, the therapist's unconditional positive regard.

9. Clients feel an increasing amount of unconditional positive self-regard.

10. Therapy is successful if, in the end, clients' experiences are evaluated in terms of their organismic valuing process and not in terms of conditions of worth.

The process of therapy, as Rogers saw it, brings clients ever closer to using their own organismic valuing process in living their lives. Rogers described what he hoped would happen to a client as the result of therapy: "He will *be*, in more unified fashion, what he organismically *is*, and this seems to be the essence of therapy" (1955, 269). In psychotherapy, the client "begins to drop the false fronts, or the masks, or the roles, with which he has faced life. He appears to be trying to discover something more basic, something more truly himself" (1961, 109).

Rogers shared the reactions of one of his clients after several therapeutic sessions.

> I find that many individuals have formed themselves by trying to please others, but again, when they are free, they move away from being this person. So one professional man, looking back at some of the process he has been through, writes, toward the end of therapy: "I finally felt that I simply had to begin doing what I wanted to do, not what I thought I should do, and regardless of what other people feel I should do. This is a complete reversal of my whole life. I've always felt I had to do things because they were expected of me, or more important, to make people like me. The hell with it! I think from now on I'm going to just be me—rich or poor, good or bad, rational or irrational, logical or illogical, famous or infamous. So thanks for your part in helping to rediscover Shakespeare's 'To Thine Own Self be True.' " (1961, 170)

Therapy, then, is designed to eliminate incongruity between experience and the self. When the person is living in accordance with his organismic valuing process, rather than conditions of worth, the defenses of denial and distortion are no longer needed and the individual is referred to as a **fully functioning person.**

Fully Functioning Person

In many ways the fully functioning person is like a young infant, because he or she is living in accordance with his or her own organismic valuing process rather than conditions of worth. It is this "being true to oneself" that described the good life to Rogers. Happiness is not the tranquility that comes when all of one's biologic needs are satisfied or when one attains a sought-after goal, such as a house, a large amount of money, or a college degree. Happiness comes from the active participation in the actualizing tendency, which is a continuous process. It is important to note that Rogers stressed the actualizing tendency, and not the *state* of self-actualization.

We have seen that to use one's organismic valuing process as a guide for living one's life, it is necessary to exist in an unconditional environment. Rogers felt that unconditional positive regard was an essential ingredient of psychotherapy, but one need not undergo psychotherapy in order to experience unconditional positive regard.

A few lucky people experience it in their home, in their marriage, or with their close friends. In 1980, Rogers extended the conditions that he felt must be present in any human relationship if growth is going to occur.

> There are three conditions that must be present in order for a climate to be growth promoting. These conditions apply whether we are speaking of the relationship between therapist and client, parent and child, leader and group, teacher and student, or administrator and staff. The conditions apply, in fact, in any situation in which the development of the person is a goal. . . . The first element could be called *genuineness, realness,* or *congruence.* . . . The second attitude of importance in creating a climate for change is *acceptance,* or *caring,* or *prizing*—what I have called "*unconditional positive regard.*" . . . The third facilitative aspect of the relationship is *empathic understanding.* . . . This kind of sensitive, active listening is exceedingly rare in our lives. We think we listen, but very rarely do we listen with real understanding, true empathy. Yet listening, of this very special kind, is one of the most potent forces for change that I know. (Italics added; 115–16)

If people are fortunate enough to have a generous portion of the three kinds of experiences just described they will be free to act in accordance with their own feelings—that is, in accordance with their organismic valuing process. Such people will be fully functioning and, according to Rogers (1959, 234–35), they will have at least the following characteristics.

1. They will be open to experience—that is, they will exhibit no defensiveness. Therefore, all their experiences will be accurately symbolized and thus available to awareness.
2. Their self-structures will be congruent with their experiences and will be capable of changing so as to assimilate new experiences.
3. They will see themselves as the locus of evaluation of their experiences. In other words, their organismic valuing process is used to evaluate their experiences instead of conditions of worth.

4. They will experience unconditional self-regard.

5. They will meet each situation with behavior that is a unique and creative adaptation to the newness of that moment. In other words, they meet each new experience with honest spontaneity instead of with preconception of what those experiences should mean.

6. They will live in harmony with others because of the rewarding nature of reciprocal unconditional positive regard.

Q–sort Technique

One of the many interesting aspects of Rogers's theory is that he stressed the importance of the completely subjective phenomenological field of the individual, on the one hand, and the importance of scientific methodology, on the other.

> Therapy is the experience in which I can let myself go subjectively. Research is the experience in which I can stand off and try to view this rich subjective experience with objectivity, applying all the elegant methods of science to determine whether I have been deceiving myself. The conviction grows in me that we shall discover laws of personality and behavior which are as significant for human progress or human understanding as the law of gravity or the laws of thermodynamics. (Rogers 1961, 14)

It is not the emphasis on scientific method that differentiated Rogers's theory from theories such as those of Skinner, Dollard and Miller, and Bandura and Mischel. Rather, it was Rogers's insistence that research be directed to phenomenological experience rather than to overt behavior.

As a therapist with an inclination toward science, Rogers could not accept on faith the changes that were *supposed* to occur during therapy, or the changes that *appeared* to take place. Like any good scientist, Rogers had to find a way to *quantify* the extent to which a client changed as a function of therapy. The technique that Rogers found most useful was one developed by William Stephenson, a colleague of Rogers at the University of Chicago. The method was called the **Q–sort technique.**

The Q–sort technique can be administered in a number of different ways, but all of them use the same basic concepts and assumptions. First, it is assumed that the client can describe himself or herself accurately, and this is called the **real self.** Second, it is assumed that a person can describe those attributes that he or she would like to possess but currently does not; this is called the **ideal self.** Typically, when therapy begins, there is a great discrepancy between a person's real self (what he or she is) and the ideal self (what he or she would like to be).

The procedures used in administering the Q–sort are as follows.

1. The client is given 100 cards, each containing a statement such as the following.

I have a warm, emotional relationship with others.
I put on a false front.

I am intelligent.

I have a feeling of hopelessness.

I despise myself.

I have a positive attitude toward myself.

I often feel humiliated.

I can usually make up my mind and stick to it.

I express my emotions freely.

I am afraid of sex.

2. The client is asked to choose those statements that best describe the way he or she is. This creates the **self-sort.** To facilitate the statistical analysis of the results of the various Q–sorts, the client is asked to select cards in a manner that creates a normal distribution. This is done by asking the client to place the cards in nine piles. The piles are arranged to reflect those statements that are most like the client, on one extreme, to the statements least like the client, on the other. Statements placed in the middle pile are those for which the client cannot decide whether the trait listed is like him or her or not; that is they are neutral. The number of piles and the number of cards the client is asked to place in each pile are shown in Table 14-1.

Table 14-1
A typical Q-sort arrangement.

Pile No.	LEAST LIKE ME			UNDECIDED			MOST LIKE ME		
	0	1	2	3	4	5	6	7	8
No. of Cards (Total: 100)	1	4	11	21	26	21	11	4	1

3. Next, the client is asked to sort the cards again, but this time in such a way that they describe the person he or she would most like to be. This creates the **ideal-sort.**

These procedures allow the therapist to examine several features of the therapeutic process. Most importantly, the therapist can examine the relationship between the person's real self and his or her ideal self at the beginning, during, and at the end of therapy. The most common way of quantifying these changes is by using the correlation coefficient. When two sets of scores are perfectly correlated in a positive direction, the correlation coefficient is $+1.00$. When there is a perfect negative or inverse relationship, the correlation coefficient is -1.00. When there is no relationship, the correlation coefficient is .00. The stronger the tendency is for two sets of measures to be positively related, the higher the positive correlation coefficients will be. For example, $+.95$, $+.89$, and $+.75$ all represent high positive correlations. The stronger the tendency is for two sets of measures to be inversely related, the higher the negative correlation coefficient will be. For example, $-.97$, $-.85$, and $-.78$ all represent high negative correlations.

Rogers (1954) reported the following correlation coefficients between a self-sort for a client before therapy and a self-sort for that client at the following points during the therapeutic process:

After seventh session .50
After twenty-fifth session .42
After therapy .39
Twelve months after therapy .30

The above correlation coefficients indicate that the self-concept of the client became increasingly *unlike* the self-concept the client had when he or she started therapy. Rogers also correlated the ideal-sort *after therapy* with the self-sort at various stages of therapy and obtained the following coefficients:

Before therapy .36
After seventh session .39
After twenty-fifth session .41
After therapy .67
Twelve months after therapy .79

The foregoing correlation coefficients clearly indicate that the self-concept became increasingly like the ideal self-concept as therapy progressed, with the tendency continuing even after therapy had terminated. In other words, the client was becoming more like the person he or she had described as ideal. It seems clear that in this case, based on the aforementioned data, therapy was accomplishing exactly what Rogers had hoped it would.

In addition to being the first therapist actually to measure the effectiveness (or ineffectiveness) of therapy, Rogers was also the first to record and film therapy sessions. He did this, with the client's permission, so that one would not need to rely on the therapist's memory (perhaps selective) of what happened, in order to evaluate the session. In addition, recording and filming allows the careful analysis of aspects of behavior such as speech mannerisms and physical gestures as possible indicators of the extent to which the client was experiencing stress or anxiety.

It is somewhat paradoxical that the theorist who insisted that the only way to know a person is to attempt to understand his or her private, unique, subjective world is also the theorist who had done the most to stimulate the scientific evaluation of the therapeutic process.

Rogers-Skinner Debate

On 4 September 1955, members of the American Psychological Association held their breath as two of the world's most influential psychologists climbed on stage at the association's annual meeting in Chicago to engage in debate. What psychologist could ask for more? In one corner was Carl Rogers, representing the phenomenological, subjective approach to understanding humans, who claimed the master motive behind human action is the actualizing tendency. Rogers also represented the belief in the innate goodness of the individual, whose freedom comes from within. In the other corner was B. F. Skinner, representing the behavioristic, objective approach to understanding humans. Skinner also represented the belief that what a person becomes is explained in terms of environmental reinforcement contingencies, not of a built-in actualizing tendency. The stage was set for a massive philosophical confrontation. What actually happened was less than a battle; in fact, there was about as much agreement between the two men as there was disagreement.

Both Rogers and Skinner agreed that humans always have attempted to understand, predict, and control human behavior. Both agreed that the behavioral sciences have made vast progress in developing the ability to predict and control human behavior. Both stated their commitment to the further development of the behavioral sciences.

The most important difference between Rogers and Skinner was over the idea of cultural engineering. Skinner felt that behavioral principles should be used in designing a culture that was more efficient in satisfying human needs. To Rogers that notion raised the following important questions: "Who will be controlled? Who will exercise control? What type of control will be exercised? Most important of all, toward what end or what purpose, or in the pursuit of what value, will control be exercised?" (1956b, 1060).

Rogers proposed a model of humans that emphasizes the actualizing tendency and creative powers. Rather than controlling human behavior from the outside, Rogers suggested that principles developed in the behavioral sciences be applied to the creation of conditions that would release and facilitate humans' inner strengths.

> It is quite clear that the point of view I am expressing is in sharp contrast to the usual conception of the relationship of the behavioral sciences to the control of human behavior. . . .
>
> 1. It is possible for us to choose to value man as a self-actualizing process of becoming; to value creativity, and the process by which knowledge becomes self-transcending.
> 2. We can proceed, by the methods of science, to discover the conditions which necessarily precede the processes and, through continuing experimentation, to discover better means of achieving these purposes.
> 3. It is possible for individuals or groups to set these conditions, with a minimum of power to control. According to present knowledge, the only authority necessary is the authority to establish certain qualities of interpersonal relationship.
> 4. Exposed to these conditions, present knowledge suggests that individuals become more self-responsible, making progress in self-actualization, become more flexible, and become more creatively adaptive.
> 5. Thus such an initial choice would inaugurate the beginnings of a social system or subsystem in which values, knowledge, adaptive skills, and even the concept of science would be continually changing and self-transcending. The emphasis would be upon man as a process of becoming. (Rogers 1956b, 1063–64)

Another major difference between Rogers and Skinner was over the issue of whether human behavior is free or determined. Skinner maintained that human behavior is determined by the reinforcement contingencies in the environment. Rogers, however, maintained that the existence of choice cannot be denied. He agreed that science must assume determinism, but felt this in no way should conflict with the existence of responsible choice on the individual level.

Behavior, when it is examined scientifically, is surely best understood as determined by prior causation. This is one great fact of science. But responsible personal choice, which is the most essential element in being a person, which is the core experience in psychotherapy, which exists prior to any scientific endeavor, is an equally prominent fact in our lives. To deny the experience of responsible choice is, to me, as restricted a view as to deny the possibility of a behavioral science. That these two important elements of our experience appear to be in contradiction has perhaps the same significance as the contradiction between the wave theory and the corpuscular theory of light, both of which can be shown to be true, even though incompatible. We cannot profitably deny our subjective life, any more than we can deny the objective description of that life. (Rogers 1956b, 1064)

My experience in therapy and in groups makes it impossible for me to deny the reality and significance of human choice. To me it is not an illusion that man is to some degree the architect of himself . . . for me the humanistic approach is the only possible one. It is for each person, however, to follow the pathway—behavioristic or humanistic—that he finds most congenial. (Rogers 1974, 118)

Skinner maintained that his major argument with Rogers was over method, because they both wanted to see approximately the same kind of person in the future.

The whole thing is a question of method. That's the crux of my argument with Carl Rogers; I'd like people to be approximately as Rogers wants them to be. I want independent people, and by that I mean people who don't have to be told when to act or who don't do things just because they've been told they're the right things to do. . . . We agree on our goals; we each want people to be free of the control exercised by others—free of the education they have had, so that they profit by it but are not bound by it, and so on. (Evans 1968, 67–68)

As already mentioned, Rogers agreed with Skinner that the behavioral sciences are, and should be, advancing, but to have such knowledge is not necessarily to know how to use it. It was Rogers's contention that, depending on how this information is used, we will experience great positive growth or destruction.

So I conclude that knowledge in the science of psychology will in the near future be used and exploited as fully as knowledge in the physical sciences is used today. The challenge for educators is unreal only if we are looking a year or two ahead. From the long view I know of no problem holding greater potentiality of growth and of destruction than the question of how to live with the increasing power the behavioral sciences will place in our hands and the hands of our children. (Rogers 1956c, 322)

One change that Rogers wanted to see in our society is the development of a better educational system. He wanted to see a system that gives students the "freedom to learn" rather than having information imposed on them by an authority figure in a highly structured learning environment. Different kinds of learning environments create different kinds of people, so in choosing how to teach we are deciding what kind of person we find desirable.

We know how to influence and mold behavior and personality in a great many significant ways. We also have available the choice of whether to set the conditions which develop a suggestible, submissive, unsure individual who can be easily influenced to behave in any way that "we" think wise, or the conditions which will develop an open, adaptive, independent, free-thinking, self-respecting individual. It is this latter person who will perhaps be able to use with intelligence and sensitivity to human values the enormous powers which the physical and behavioral sciences are putting at his disposal. The issue of what choice to make in this regard constitutes, I believe, the challenge of tomorrow both for education and for our whole culture. (Rogers 1956c, 322)

Freedom to Learn

Rogers was highly critical of the American educational system and suspected that the worst would happen unless our educational system was changed radically. He believed strongly that education in our country was based on faulty assumptions about the learner. For example, it is widely believed that students must have information given to them and digested for them, while they remain passive in the process. Instead of basing education on these or other faulty assumptions, Rogers believed that education would be vastly improved if it took into consideration the following facts about the learning process (Rogers 1969, 157–63):

1. Humans have a natural potential for learning.
2. Learning is best when the student sees relevance in what is being learned.
3. Some learning may require a change in the learner's self-structure, and such learning may be resisted.
4. Learning which necessitates a change in the learner's self-structure occurs more easily in a situation in which external threats are at a minimum.
5. When threats to the learner's self-concept are small, experience can be perceived in great detail, and learning will be optimal.
6. Much learning takes place by doing.
7. Learning proceeds best when the student participates responsibly in the learning process.
8. Self-initiated learning which involves the whole person, that is, both intellect and feelings, is the most long-lasting learning.
9. Independence and creativity are facilitated when self-criticism and self-evaluation are of primary importance, and evaluation by others is of secondary importance.
10. The most useful kind of learning is the learning to learn, which results in a continuing openness to experiences and a tolerance of change.

Rogers thought the term **"teacher"** was unfortunate, because it suggests a person who dispenses information to students. Instead, Rogers suggested the term "facilitator," to emphasize the fact that the person is there to create an atmosphere conducive to learning. A **facilitator of education** acts on the principles of learning we have listed, and thereby treats each student as a unique person with feelings of his or her own, rather than as an object to be taught something.

We see that Rogers's approach to education was not unlike his approach to psychotherapy. In both cases, he insisted that it must be recognized that each person is unique, each person has feelings, and each person has an actualizing tendency that functions best when experiencing unconditional positive regard and freedom. The reader will no doubt note a discrepancy between the educational conditions that Rogers considered optimal and those that generally now exist.

Modern Marriage

Statistics show that the institution of marriage in our culture is in deep trouble, and according to Rogers, it is in trouble for good reason. Too often marriages are based on outdated, superficial or selfish assumptions. Rogers (1972b) offered examples of statements that he felt were danger signals as far as a marriage lasting or being satisfying were concerned.

> "I love you"; "We love each other.". . . "I commit myself wholly to you and your welfare" . . . "I am more concerned for you than I am for myself.". . . "We will work hard on our marriage.". . . "We hold the institution of marriage sacred, and it will be sacred for us" . . . "We pledge ourselves to each other until death do us part.". . . "We are destined for each other." (199–200)

According to Rogers, all of the preceding statements miss the important point that for marriage to work it must be egalitarian, enriching, and satisfying for *both* partners. Marriage should be a dynamic process within which both partners continually grow. The only pledge that made any sense to Rogers is, "We each commit ourselves to working together on the changing process of our present relationship, because that relationship is currently enriching our love and our life and we wish it to grow" (1972b, 201). A good marriage is one that is mutually beneficial to the partners involved.

Rogers observed some themes running through the apparently successful marriages of couples who had learned the person-centered philosophy from discussion groups, encounter groups, or individual therapy. Rogers summarized those themes.

> *Difficulties already present in the partnership are brought into the open. . . . Communication becomes more open, more real, with more mutual listening. . . . The partners come to recognize the value of separateness. . . . The woman's growing independence is recognized as valuable in the relationship. . . . There is increasing recognition of the importance of feelings, as well as reason, of emotions as well as intellect. . . . There is a thrust toward the experiencing of greater mutual trust, personal growth, and shared interests. . . . Roles, and role expectation, tend to drop away and are replaced by the person choosing her own way of behaving. . . . There is a more realistic appraisal of the needs each can meet in the*

other. . . . So-called satellite relationships may be formed by either partner, and this often causes pain as well as enriching growth. (1977, 45–52)

Rogers (1977) elaborated on the point concerning **satellite relationships.**

Satellite relationship means a close secondary relationship outside the marriage which may or may not involve sexual intercourse, but which is valued for itself. . . . When two persons in a partnership learn to look upon each other as separate persons, with separate as well as mutual interests and needs, they are likely to discover that outside relationships are one of those needs. (52–53)

The notion of satellite relationships brings jealousy to mind. For Rogers, however, jealousy suggested possessiveness.

To the extent that jealousy is made up of a sense of possessiveness, any alteration in that feeling makes a profound difference in the politics of the marriage relationship. To the degree that each partner becomes truly a free agent, then the relationship only has permanence if the partners are committed to each other, are in good communication with each other, accept themselves as separate persons, and live together as persons, not roles. This is a new and mature kind of relationship toward which many couples are striving. (1977, 55)

Rogers (1977) described a married couple that apparently had overcome possessiveness and its related feeling of jealousy.

Fred and Trish endeavored to make their marriage a relationship in which primary value is placed on each of them as persons. They have tried to share in decision-making, the desires of each having equal weight. Each seems to have avoided, to an unusual degree, any need to possess or control the other. They have developed a partnership in which their lives are both separate *and* together. They have each developed relationships outside of marriage, and these intimate interactions have often been sexual in nature. They have communicated openly about these relationships and appear to have accepted them as a natural and rewarding part of their individual lives and of their marriage. They like their life-style. Theirs is a marriage both person-centered and far from conventional. (205)

Permitting an intimate satellite relationship within a marriage is apparently easier to accept intellectually than it is emotionally because so many of the couples that have tried one or more of them have ended up in the divorce court. For it to work, according to Rogers, the idea must be acceptable to both marital partners on both intellectual and emotional levels.

Person of Tomorrow

Rogers believed that a "new person" is emerging who has many of the characteristics of a fully functioning person. Such a person is humanistically oriented rather than technologically oriented. It was because of the emergence of such a person that Rogers was optimistic about the future.

In all candor I must say that I believe that the humanistic view will in the long run take precedence. I believe that we are, as a people, beginning to refuse to allow technology to dominate our lives. Our culture, increasingly based on the conquest of nature and the control of man, is in decline. Emerging through the ruins is the new person, highly aware, self-directing, an explorer of inner, perhaps more than outer, space, scornful of the conformity of institutions and the dogma of authority. He does not believe in being behaviorally shaped, or in shaping the behavior of others. He is most assuredly humanistic rather than technological. In my judgment he has a high probability of survival. (1974, 119)

Where will these humanistic, person-centered individuals of the future come from? According to Rogers (1980) many of them are already here.

Where have I found them? I find them among corporation executives who have given up the gray-flannel rat race, the lure of high salaries and stock options, to live a simpler new life. I find them among young men and women in blue jeans who are defying most of the values of today's culture to live in new ways. I find them among priests and nuns and ministers who have left behind the dogmas of their institutions to live in a way that has more meaning. I find them among women who are vigorously rising above the limitations that society has placed on their personhood. I find them among blacks and Chicanos and other minority members who are pushing out from generations of passivity into an assertive, positive life. I find them among those who have experienced encounter groups, who are finding a place for feelings as well as thought in their lives. I find them among creative school dropouts who are thrusting into higher reaches than their sterile schooling permits. I realize, too, that I saw something of this person in my years as a psychotherapist, when clients were choosing a freer, richer, more self-directed kind of life for themselves. (349)

Rogers, (1980, 350–52) enumerated twelve characteristics that he thought persons of tomorrow will possess. As you can see, the person of tomorrow shares many characteristics with the fully functioning individual described earlier. According to Rogers, the person of tomorrow will display:

1. An openness to both inner and outer experience.
2. A rejection of hypocrisy, deceit, and double talk. In other words, a desire for authenticity.
3. A skepticism toward the kind of science and technology that has as its goal the conquest of nature or the control of people.
4. A desire for wholeness. For example, equal recognition and expression of the intellect and the emotions.
5. A wish for shared purpose in life or intimacy.
6. A tendency to embrace change and risk taking with enthusiasm.
7. A gentle, subtle, nonmoralistic, nonjudgmental caring.
8. A feeling of closeness to, and a caring for, nature.
9. Antipathy for any highly structured, inflexible, bureaucratic institution. They believe that institutions should exist for the people, not the other way around.
10. A tendency to follow the authority of their own organismic valuing process.

11. An indifference toward material comforts and rewards.

12. A desire to seek a meaning in life that is greater than the individual. Rogers referred to this characteristic as "a yearning for the spiritual."

Rogers believed that the emergence of the humanistic person of the future will not go unopposed. Rogers summarized what he considered to be the sources of opposition to such a person in the form of slogans.

> 1. "The State above all.". . . 2. "Tradition above all.". . . 3. "The intellect above all.". . . 4. "Human beings should be shaped.". . . 5. "The status quo forever.". . . 6. "Our truth is the truth." (1980, 353–55)

Rogers was confident that person-centered individuals will prevail, however, and the result will be a more humane world.

Evaluation

Empirical Research

Among Rogers's accomplishments is the fact that he, more than any other therapist, exposed the psychotherapeutic process to scientific examination. Using techniques such as the Q-sort, Rogers and his colleagues were able to examine a client's tendency toward congruency as a function of therapy. We have already seen examples of how the Q-sort has been used to measure therapeutic effectiveness. Further evidence that the Q-sort can be used to measure therapeutic success is provided by Butler and Haigh (1954). These researchers found that the average correlation between real self and ideal self for twenty-five clients before therapy was $-.01$, indicating essentially no relationship. Following therapy, the average correlation between real self and ideal self rose to $+.34$, indicating significant movement toward the clients' ideal selves. A control group consisting of sixteen people not undergoing therapy did the Q-sort at the same time as the twenty–five clients undergoing therapy. For the control group, the first Q-sort showed an average correlation between the real and ideal selves was $+.58$ and the second Q-sort yielded an average correlation of $+.59$. The latter correlations showed that the people not involved in therapy showed less of a discrepancy between their real and ideal selves than the clients involved in therapy and that this small discrepancy persisted over time.

Rogers was also responsible for creating encounter groups (sometimes called sensitivity groups or T-groups) and there have been several studies designed to determine their effectiveness. For example, Dunnette (1969) found that people were found to be more empathetic following an encounter group experience, and Diamond and Shapiro (1973) found that encounter group participants subsequently felt more in control of their own lives.

The Q-sort has also been widely used as a research tool outside of the therapeutic situation. Turner and Vanderlippe (1958) studied the relationship among the discrepancy between the real self and the ideal self, general effectiveness, and degree of satisfaction for 175 college students. These investigations found that the students for whom the discrepancy between the real and ideal selves was small were active, sociable, emotionally stable, and had higher scholastic averages, as compared to students displaying a wider discrepancy between their real and ideal selves. Rosenberg (1962) found that small discrepancies between the real and the ideal selves related to a variety of measures of successful living. Mahoney and Harnett (1973) found that a measure of self-actualization correlated with degree of congruence. That is, as the discrepancy between the real and ideal selves became smaller, the tendency to display the characteristics of a self-actualizing person became greater.

A great deal of research has been performed in an effort to validate Rogers's claim that empathy, unconditional positive regard, and genuineness are the necessary ingredients for personal growth. Aspy and Roebuck (1974) tested the Rogerian hypothesis in the realm of education. These researchers recorded over 3,500 hours of student-teacher interactions involving 550 primary and secondary school teachers in various parts of this country and abroad. It was found that the most important variable in producing favorable educational outcomes was teacher empathy, or the effort to understand the meaning of the school experience from the student's viewpoint. Unconditional positive regard and genuineness were also found to be important. Taken together, empathy, unconditional positive regard, and genuineness produced the most powerful effect. The presence of these three conditions correlated highly with academic achievement, positive self-concepts in the students, decreased discipline problems, decreased truancy, and higher student morale, creativity, and problem-solving ability. In the realm of psychotherapy, Truax and Mitchell (1971) found that the extent to which genuineness, unconditional positive regard, and empathy characterized the therapeutic process, it was successful. Likewise, Gurman (1977) reviewed twenty-two studies in which clients' perceptions of their therapists were obtained. It was found that those clients who perceived their therapist as displaying empathy, unconditional positive regard, and genuineness tended also to be the clients who perceived their therapy as effective. Because empathy is such an important characteristic of effective therapy and other forms of helping relationships, it is important to know if it is something that can be learned or if it is something one is born with. Research strongly suggests that it can be learned (Aspy 1972; Aspy and Roebuck 1974; and Goldstein and Michaels 1985).

Many studies have also been performed to investigate the Rogerian hypotheses that incongruent individuals must defend themselves by denying or distorting certain experiences. For example, using male undergraduates as subjects, Chodorkoff (1954) tested the hypotheses that congruent people will display less perceptual defense and will be better socially adjusted than incongruent individuals. Both hypotheses were confirmed. Incongruent subjects took significantly longer to identify emotional words (for example, whore, bitch, or penis) than they did to identify neutral words (for example, tree, house, or book). For congruent subjects there was no difference in time of recognition. Also, using clinically experienced judges and a variety of measures it was found that the congruent people were better socially adjusted than incongruent people. Cartwright (1956) and Suinn, Osborne, and Winfree (1972) also supported the Rogerian contention that congruent individuals tend to be open to experience, whereas incongruent individuals tend to experience more selectively.

Criticisms

Overly Simplistic and Optimistic Approach.   Many believe that Rogers's assumption that humans are basically good and born with a tendency toward self-actualization is nothing more than wishful thinking. Real people, say some critics, experience hate as much as love and are often motivated by intense sexual desires. Moreover, except for subception, the importance of unconscious motivation is denied by Rogers. For those who experience bizarre dreams, intense conflict, deep depression, anger, or psychosomatic illness, the Rogerian view of humans does not ring true. Also, considered simplistic is Rogers's heavy reliance on self-reports that others have found to be notoriously unreliable. Many have criticized Rogers for a kind of simplicity that is opposite to the kind of simplicity of which Kelly was accused. Rogers emphasizes the emotional aspect of personality by saying that what truly feels good is the best guide for action. For Rogers, emotions were more important than the intellect. For Kelly, the opposite was true.

Failure to Credit Those Who Have Influenced His Theory.   Many elements are similar in Rogers's and Adler's theories. Both emphasized the whole individual, conscious experience, and an innate drive toward harmonious relationships with fellow humans. A strong relationship also exists between Rogers's theory and Horney's. The crux of Horney's theory was that psychological problems begin when the healthy real self is displaced by the unhealthy idealized self, with its associated tyranny of the should. For Horney, the way to make unhealthy people healthy is to bring them back in touch with their real selves so that the real self, instead of the externally imposed idealized self, would be used as a guide for living. Except for slight differences in terminology, Rogers and Horney were saying about the same thing. Despite these similarities, Rogers gave little recognition to the influence of such theorists as Adler and Horney on his own thinking.

Important Aspects of Personality Ignored or Denied.   We have seen that Rogers simply dismissed the darker side of human nature (for example, aggressive, hostile, selfish, and sexual motives). He also said very little about the development of personality. Except for the fact that for some the organismic valuing process is displaced by conditions of worth, Rogers said very little about the developmental experiences that are conducive to healthy growth.

Contributions

Alternative, Positive View of Humans.   Rogers helped to illuminate a facet of human nature that was previously obscure. He contributed to the development of a "third force" in psychology, which is rapidly becoming more influential than psychology's other two dominant forces, behaviorism and psychoanalysis. This third force within psychology has been named humanistic psychology because of its emphasis on the goodness of human nature and its concern with the conditions that allow humans to reach their full potential. These concerns run through every aspect of Rogers's writings.

New Form of Therapy.   No one since Freud has had more influence on psychotherapy than Rogers. His positive, humanistic approach to counseling and therapy have become extremely popular. Three reasons for its popularity are (1) it is effective; (2) the approach does not require long, tedious training that psychoanalysis does; and (3) it is positive and optimistic about human nature. Not only did Rogers create a new form of therapy, but he created methods for evaluating the effectiveness of therapy as well. By recording therapeutic sessions, making recordings and transcripts available to other professionals, and developing objective measures of personality change as a function of the therapeutic experience, Rogers, for the first time, made research on psychotherapy scientifically legitimate.

Applied Value.   Again, no one since Freud has had more of an impact on both psychology and on other disciplines. Rogers's person-centered psychology has been applied in such diverse areas as: Religion, nursing, dentistry, medicine, law enforcement, social work, race and cultural relations, industry, politics, and organizational development (for the various applications of person-centered psychology see, for example, Levant and Schlien, 1984). In an interesting paper, Rogers and Ryback (1984) show how person-centered psychology might be used on the global level to reduce or avoid international conflict. More specifically, McGaw, Rice, and Rogers (1973) discussed how person-centered psychology might be used to ease the tension between Catholics, Protestants, and the English in Northern Ireland. Lastly, Rogers (1969, 1983) showed how his person-centered principles might be used to improve education at all levels.

So who was Carl Rogers? Rogers himself offered an answer.

So, who am I? I am a psychologist whose primary interest, for many years, has been in psychotherapy. . . . I rejoice at the privilege of being a midwife to a new personality—as I stand by with awe at the emergence of a self, a person, as I see a birth process in which I have had an important and facilitating part. (1961, 4–5)

In his comments on the occasion of Rogers's death, Gendlin (1988), succinctly described the kind of person Rogers was. "He cared about each person—but not about institutions. He did not care about appearances, roles, class, credentials, or positions, and he doubted every authority including his own" (127).

Summary

Rogers was born into a financially successful, religious family. He spent his adolescent years on a farm, where he first became interested in science. A trip to the Far East while in college was very influential, in that it introduced Rogers to several different cultures, with their own religions and philosophies.

The main premise of Rogers's theory is that all people are born with an actualizing tendency, which causes them to seek those experiences that will maintain and enhance their lives. This tendency drives individuals toward greater complexity, independence, creativity, and social responsibility. Ideally, all individuals evaluate their experiences using the organismic valuing process, which indicates whether or not experiences are in tune with the actualizing tendency. Those experiences that cause satisfaction are sought; those that are not are unsatisfying and avoided. Healthy people use their organismic valuing processes as guides in living their lives.

All people live in their own subjective reality, called their phenomenological field. It is according to this field that people act, rather than according to objective reality; that is, physical reality. Experience was defined as all of those events happening around people of which they could be aware. However, only a small portion of those events is symbolized, thus, entering awareness. Gradually, a portion of the phenomenological field becomes differentiated as the self. The self-concept emerges as a result of repeated experiences involving such terms as "I," "me," and "mine."

With the emergence of the self comes the need for positive regard, which is receiving such things as warmth, love, sympathy, and respect from the relevant people in one's life. The need for positive regard expands into the need for self-regard. This means that now, in addition to children needing relevant individuals to respond to them positively, they also need to respond positively to themselves. Typically, adults do not give positive regard to children regardless of what they do. Rather, they respond selectively according to what children are doing. In other words, children experience positive regard after certain behaviors but not after other behaviors. This sets up conditions of worth that specify how children must behave or feel in order to be positively regarded. These conditions of worth are introjected into children's self-concept and thereby control their self-regard. Now, even in the absence of adults, children must act in accordance with those conditions of worth in order to feel good about themselves. The only way to escape imposing conditions of worth on children is to give them unconditional positive regard.

Conditions of worth create an incongruent person because they force the person to live in accordance with introjected values rather than his or her own organismic valuing process. The incongruent person is vulnerable, because he or she must constantly watch out for experiences or feelings that violate one's conditions of worth. Such experiences threaten self-structure and therefore cause anxiety. When an experience is perceived or subceived as threatening, it is either distorted or denied symbolization. Thus, incongruent people, because they are not living in accordance with their true feelings, are more likely to experience anxiety and to perceive experiences selectively.

According to Rogers, the goal of psychotherapy is to make the incongruent person congruent again. His approach to therapy, which was originally called nondirective, then client-centered, then experiential, and finally person-centered, emphasizes unconditional positive regard, which presumably will reduce threat, eliminate conditions of worth, and bring the person back in tune with his or her own organismic valuing process, thereby becoming a fully functioning person, who is open to experience, not defensive, and is capable of living with others in maximum harmony. Rogers concluded that in addition to unconditional positive regard, genuineness and empathy must characterize any human relationship in which positive growth is sought.

Rogers had two major interests in his professional life: One was to encourage the phenomenological person-centered approach in psychology, and the other was to study scientifically the changes that occur in a person as a function of therapy. His most frequently used method for accomplishing the latter goal was the Q-sort technique. Using this technique, the client is asked to sort 100 cards containing trait descriptions into nine piles. Into which pile a card goes depends on the extent to which the trait on the card is thought, by the client, to be like or unlike him or her. First, the client is asked to sort the cards in a way that describes how he or she is at the moment; this creates a self-sort. Next, the client is asked to sort the cards so that they describe the kind of person he or she would like to become; this creates an ideal-sort. These two sorts allow the therapist to make many comparisons; for example, real self-concept before therapy versus real self-concept after therapy, or real self-concept after therapy versus ideal self-concept after therapy. Many other comparisons are possible. Research has indicated that Rogerian therapy is effective in changing a client's self-concept in a positive direction.

In 1955, Rogers debated with B. F. Skinner, the world's leading behaviorist. Both men agreed that the behavioral sciences had been growing exponentially, and both agreed that that was a good thing. However, the two parted company when they discussed how the principles generated by the behavioral sciences should be used. Skinner maintained that they should be used as a guide in creating an environment that would encourage desirable behavior and satisfy human needs. His approach emphasized control of behavior from the outside. Rogers maintained that the principles should be used to avoid control from the outside; rather, they should be used to create an environment that gives humans as much freedom as possible so that their actualizing tendencies can function without interference. Skinner suggested that both he and Rogers wanted to see the same kind of people but differed in the methods they would employ in producing them.

Rogers felt that, generally speaking, our educational system is in poor shape. It treats the student as an object to be taught and the teacher as an authority figure who dispenses information in a highly structured environment. Rogers believed such an education system is based on faulty assumptions about human nature. He felt that it would be more constructive if we assumed that each human wants to learn and that each human will learn if placed in a nonthreatening learning environment characterized by unconditional positive regard. Also, learning will occur much faster and will be retained better if the material to be learned has personal relevance to the learner. Rogers opposed the term "teacher" and felt that the term "facilitator of education" was better.

Rogers thought that many marriages fail because they are based on outdated, superficial, or selfish assumptions. He thought that for a marriage to work it must be viewed as a dynamic, mutually satisfying relationship by both partners. Because in such a relationship both partners must remain free, autonomous individuals, one or both may choose to develop a satellite relationship, which is a close relationship with someone other than one's marital partner.

Rogers saw a new kind of person emerging that displays many of the characteristics of a fully functioning person. Such a person rejects hypocrisy, has a respect for nature and other people, and resists any attempt to control his or her thoughts or behavior externally. The emergence of such a person, according to Rogers, will be resisted by those who want to maintain the status quo, withhold tradition, emphasize the intellect over emotions, or believe that they possess the one truth that everyone else should act in accordance with.

A considerable amount of empirical research has been generated by Rogers's theory and most of it has been supportive. Rogers's theory has been criticized for portraying an overly simplistic and optimistic view of humans; not giving proper credit to other theories on which his is based; and ignoring important aspects of personality. His theory has been praised for developing a theory that promoted a positive view of humans, as opposed to the more negative views of behaviorism and psychoanalysis; creating a new form of therapy as well as methods that could be used to test its effectiveness; and creating a theory that had widespread usefulness in psychology and in many other fields.

1. Rogers thought that any relationship that is characterized by unconditional positive regard, empathy, and genuineness is conducive to positive growth. On the other hand, relationships characterized by conditions of worth stifle positive growth. First, describe a relationship within which you *receive* unconditional positive regard, empathy, and genuineness and another one in which conditions of worth are placed on you. Do you agree with Rogers that the former is more conducive to your positive growth than the latter? Next, describe what you feel you *give* in an important relationship. Ask the person involved in this relationship with you whether or not he or she agrees with your assessment. What was his or her response?

2. Explain why you agree or disagree with Rogers's assertion that humans are basically good and if left alone to live in accordance with their organismic valuing process, would live in peace and harmony with their fellow humans. Include in your response how you think Rogers would explain the fact that some humans engage in criminal activities. What, in your opinion, would Rogers recommend as the most effective way of dealing with criminals? In other words, what would likely reduce the probability of them again committing a criminal act?

3. Make a list of at least fifteen statements that you feel accurately describe you as you really are. Some possibilities include:

I am basically lazy.
I am overly sensitive.
I am very moody.
I am optimistic.

I am intelligent.
I am able to express my feelings openly.
I feel others control me too much.
I am reliable.
I am pessimistic.
I make new friends easily.
I often feel phony.
I am confused about my future.
I understand myself quite well.
I frequently feel guilty.
I am too critical of myself.

Next, make a list of at least fifteen statements that describe the kind of person that you would ideally like to become. Carefully examine the two lists. If the two lists have many characteristics in common, Rogers would say that you are a congruent person. If the lists are quite different, he would say you are an incongruent person. Which are you? In either case, does Rogers's description of the congruent or the incongruent person (whichever applies to you) accurately describe you? Explain.

4. Review the characteristics of a fully functioning person. How many of those characteristics do you display? Relate your response to your answer to the previous question.

5. Explain why you do or do not agree with Rogers's thoughts on marriage. Be sure to include in your answer a reaction to his thoughts on satellite relationships.

6. Do you share Rogers's hope that a new kind of person ("the person of tomorrow") will emerge and eventually populate the world? Explain.

1. First define "the actualizing tendency" and then discuss its importance to Rogers's theory. Include in your answer a discussion of the "organismic valuing process."

2. Explain why Rogers's theory is labeled humanistic and existential. Could it also be labeled cognitive? Explain.

3. What did Rogers mean by the term "phenomenological field"? Include in your answer a discussion of the terms experience, awareness, and symbolization.

4. Explain how the self becomes differentiated within the phenomenological field.

5. First describe the need for positive regard, the need for self-regard, and conditions of worth, and then explain how the three are interrelated.

6. Under what circumstances is a person incongruent?

7. Discuss the terms vulnerability, threat, anxiety, defense, distortion, and denial as they apply to the incongruent person.

8. Discuss psychotherapy as Rogers viewed it. What is its goal and what procedures are followed to attain that goal?

9. Describe the fully functioning person.

10. Describe the usual procedures in using the Q-sort technique. List a few of the more important comparisons that can be made using this technique.

11. Summarize the Rogers-Skinner debate.

12. Indicate why Rogers was so critical of the American educational system and what he proposed to improve the situation.

13. Describe what would characterize the self-actualized person if Freud's view of human nature were correct and Rogers's were wrong.

14. Rogers's theory is sometimes called the mirror image of Skinner's theory. Explain why you think this is either true or not.

15. How did Rogers suggest that discipline problems with a child be handled?

16. Summarize the conditions that Rogers thought must exist if a marriage is going to be successful. Also, describe what Rogers thought were faulty justifications for marriage.

17. Summarize the characteristics that Rogers thought the "person of tomorrow" will possess. Who, according to Rogers, will oppose the emergence of such a person?

18. Describe one experiment that was run to test some aspect of Rogers's theory.

19. For what has Rogers's theory been criticized?

20. What are the contributions of Rogers's theory thought to be?

KIRSCHENBAUM, H. (1979). *On Becoming Carl Rogers*. New York: Dell.

> A highly sympathetic biography of Rogers.

ROGERS, C. R. (1961). *On Becoming A Person*. Boston: Houghton Mifflin.

> In this highly influential book, Rogers shares his experiences as a man, a husband, a father and a professional as they influenced the development of his theory. He also discusses the implications of person-centered psychology for family life, education, and interpersonal and intergroup communication.

ROGERS, C. R. (1967). Autobiography. In E. G. Boring and G. Lindzey (Eds.), *A History of Psychology in Autobiography* (Vol. 5, 343–384). New York: Appleton-Century-Crofts.

> An extremely interesting autobiographical sketch.

ROGERS, C. R. (1969). *Freedom to Learn*. Columbus, OH: Merrill.

> According to Rogers our education system is authoritarian and coercive and therefore in dire need of reform. This book describes the changes that need to be made if our education system is to encourage the development of fully functioning individuals.

ROGERS, C. R. (1970). *Carl Rogers on Encounter Groups*. New York: Harper & Row.

Rogers discusses: The history of the use of encounter groups, the various ways in which encounter groups can be arranged, who can be a group facilitator, areas in which encounter groups would be useful, and what the research shows as to the effectiveness of encounter groups.

ROGERS, C. R. (1972b). *Becoming Partners: Marriage and Its Alternative*. New York: Delacorte.

Rogers examines several marriages and attempts to specify the reasons why some marriages work and others do not.

ROGERS, C. R. (1977). *Carl Rogers on Personal Power*. New York: Delacorte.

This book describes the revolutionary impact that widespread acceptance of Rogers's person-centered philosophy would have on family life, education, management, and politics.

ROGERS, C. R. (1980). *A Way of Being*. Boston: Houghton Mifflin.

In this book Rogers reflects on his own experiences with aging, discusses the building of person-centered communities, suggests that education in the future must encompass both ideas and feelings, and speculates about the world and the person of the future.

GLOSSARY

Actualizing tendency. The innate tendency in all humans to maintain and enhance themselves.

Anxiety. Results when a person perceives or subceives an experience as being incompatible with his or her self-structure and its introjected conditions of worth.

Awareness. Characterizes the events in one's experience that have been symbolized and therefore have entered consciousness.

Client-centered therapy. Description of Rogers's second approach to therapy, in which the therapist makes an active effort to understand the client's subjective reality.

Conditions of worth. The conditions under which a person will experience positive regard.

Defense. The effort to change a threatening experience through distortion or denial.

Denial. The refusal to allow threatening experiences to enter awareness.

Distortion. The modification of a threatening experience so that it is no longer threatening.

Experience. All the events of which a person *could* be aware at any given moment.

Experiential stage. The third stage in the evolution of Rogers's approach to therapy, in which the feelings of the therapist became as important as the feelings of the client.

Facilitator of education. A term that Rogers thought was better than teacher, because it suggests someone who is helpful and uncritical and who will provide the freedom that is necessary for learning to take place.

Fully functioning person. A person whose locus of evaluation is his or her own organismic valuing process rather than internalized conditions of worth.

Ideal self. A client's description of how he or she would like to be.

Ideal-sort. The statements chosen by a client as best describing the person he or she would most like to be. Part of the Q-sort technique.

Incongruency. Exists when a person is no longer using the organismic valuing process as a means of evaluating experiences. The person, under these conditions, is no longer acting honestly toward his or her own self-experiences.

Internal frame of reference. The subjective reality, or phenomenological field, according to which a person lives his or her life.

Introjected values. The conditions of worth that are internalized and become the basis for one's self-regard.

Need for positive regard. The need to receive such things as warmth, sympathy, care, respect, and acceptance from the relevant people in one's life.

Need for self-regard. The need a person develops to feel positively about himself or herself.

Nondirective therapy. Description of Rogers's first approach to therapy, in which the emphasis was on the client's ability to solve his or her own problems.

Openness to experience. One of the chief characteristics of a fully functioning person.

Organismic valuing process. The frame of reference that allows an individual to know whether or not his or her experiences are in accordance with his or her actualizing tendency. Those experiences that maintain or enhance the person are in accordance with this process; other experiences are not.

Person-centered stage. The final stage in Rogers's thinking, in which the emphasis was on the understanding of the *total* person, not on understanding the person merely as a client.

Phenomenological field. That portion of experience of which an individual is aware. It is this subjective reality, rather than physical reality, that directs a person's behavior.

Phenomenological reality. A person's private, subjective perception or interpretation of objective reality.

Psychological maladjustment. Results from severe incongruence.

Psychotherapy. To Rogers, an experience designed to help an incongruent person become congruent again.

Q-sort technique. The method Rogers used to determine

how a client's self-image changed as a function of therapy. See also self-sort and ideal-sort.

Real self. A client's description of how he or she currently sees himself or herself.

Rogers-Skinner debate. A debate held in 1955 between Rogers and Skinner over how best to use the principles discovered by the behavioral sciences.

Satellite relationships. Close relationships with individuals other than one's marital partner.

Self. That portion of the phenomenological field that becomes differentiated because of experiences involving terms such as "I," "me," and "mine."

Self-sort. The statements chosen by a client as best describing the person as he or she actually is at the moment. Part of the Q-sort technique.

Subception. The detection of an experience before it enters full awareness.

Symbolization. The process by which an event enters the individual's awareness.

Teacher. A term that Rogers felt was unfortunate, because it connotes an authoritarian figure who dispenses information to passive students.

Threat. Anything that is thought to be incompatible with one's self-structure.

Unconditional positive regard. The experience of positive regard without conditions of worth. In other words, positive regard is not contingent on certain acts or thoughts.

Vulnerability. The increased likelihood of experiencing anxiety because a person is incongruent.

Abraham Maslow

A braham Harold Maslow was born on 1 April 1908 in Brooklyn, New York. He was the first of seven children. His parents were Jewish immigrants from Russia. Being the only Jewish boy in his neighborhood, he was alone and unhappy much of the time. Like Rogers, Maslow took refuge in books. Maslow described his childhood as follows: "With my childhood, it's a wonder I'm not psychotic. I was a little Jewish boy in the non-Jewish neighborhood. It was a little like being the first Negro enrolled in the all-white school. I was isolated and unhappy. I grew up in libraries and among books, without friends" (Hall 1968, 37).

Unfortunately, not all of Maslow's problems were outside of his home. Maslow recalled his father as loving whiskey, women, and fighting (Wilson 1972, 131) and thinking of his son (Maslow) as ugly and stupid. Once, at a large family gathering, his father, Samuel, asked, "Isn't Abe the ugliest kid you've ever seen?" Hoffman (1988) describes the impact of such remarks on young Maslow, "Such thoughtless remarks affected the boy's self-image so much that for a time he sought out empty cars when riding the subway, 'to spare others the sight' of him, as though he were horribly disfigured" (6).

If anything, Maslow's mother, Rose, was worse than his father.

[Maslow] grew to maturity with an unrelieved hatred for her and never achieved the slightest reconciliation. He even refused to attend her funeral. He characterized Rose Maslow as a cruel, ignorant, and hostile figure, one so unloving as to nearly induce madness in her children. In all of Maslow's references to his mother—some uttered publicly while she was still alive—there is not one that expresses any warmth or affection. (Hoffman 1988, 7)

One reason for Maslow's bitterness toward his mother was the miserly way in which she ran her household.

[Maslow] recalled bitterly that she kept a bolted lock on the refrigerator, although her husband was making a good living. Only when she was in the mood to serve food would she remove the lock and permit her children to take something to eat. Whenever the young Maslow had a friend over to the house, she was especially careful to keep the refrigerator bolted. (Hoffman 1988, 7)

Maslow eventually made peace with his father and often spoke of him kindly. Not so, however, with his mother.

In an effort to please his father, Maslow began college by studying law, but after only two weeks he decided that his interests were elsewhere. He left home to study a variety of things, first at Cornell University. After two years, he transferred to the University of Wisconsin, where he received his B.A. in 1930, his M.A. in 1931, and his Ph.D. in 1934.

It was shortly before he moved to the University of Wisconsin that he married his childhood sweetheart, Bertha Goodman, and they eventually had two children. Maslow claimed that his life really did not start until he married and moved to Wisconsin. He was twenty years old at the time, and Bertha was nineteen.

Abraham H. Maslow

As strange as it now seems, Maslow decided to study psychology when he discovered the behaviorism of J. B. Watson. He described his excitement over his discovery:

> I had discovered J. B. Watson and I was sold on behaviorism. It was an explosion of excitement for me. . . . Bertha came to pick me up and I was dancing down Fifth Avenue with exuberance; I embarrassed her, but I was so excited about Watson's program. It was beautiful. I was confident that here was a real road to travel, solving one puzzle after another and changing the world. (Hall 1968, 37)

This infatuation with behaviorism ended when Maslow and his wife had their first child.

> Our first baby changed me as a psychologist. It made the behaviorism I had been so enthusiastic about look so foolish I could not stomach it anymore. That was the thunderclap that settled things. . . . I was stunned by the mystery and by the sense of not really being in control. I felt small and weak and feeble before all this. I'd say anyone who had a baby couldn't be a behaviorist. (Hall 1968, 55)

While at the University of Wisconsin, Maslow became the first doctoral student of Harry Harlow, the famous experimental psychologist, who was just in the process of developing a primate laboratory to study the behavior of monkeys.

Maslow's dissertation was on the establishment of dominance in a colony of monkeys. He noted that dominance seemed to result from a kind of "inner confidence" or "dominance-feeling" rather than through physical aggression.

After receiving his Ph.D. in 1934, Maslow returned to New York, first to Columbia University as a Carnegie Fellow where he worked for eighteen months with the eminent learning theorist, E. L. Thorndike. He then moved to Brooklyn College, where he stayed until 1951. During many of these years, besides being the plant manager of his family's barrel factory from 1947 to 1949, he extended his research on dominance to the human level. He found that high-dominance individuals tended to be unconventional, less religious than low-dominance individuals and extroverted. Also, they tended *not* to be anxious, jealous, or neurotic.

Maslow found that the high-dominance female was attracted to the high-dominance male, who was described as "highly masculine, self-confident, fairly aggressive, sure of what he wants and able to get it, generally superior in most things" (1942, 126). Low-dominance women, conversely, were attracted to men who were kind, friendly, gentle, faithful, and showed a love for children.

We see that in Maslow's early work, he was concerned with the healthy, exceptional, dominant specimen. It was but a minor step from these early interests to a concern for the most outstanding human beings. This step in the evolution of Maslow's concerns was stimulated by the tragedy of World War II. Maslow explained:

> I gave up everything I was fascinated with in a selfish way around 1941. I felt I must try to save the world and to prevent these horrible wars and this awful hatred and prejudice.
>
> It happened very suddenly, you know. One day just after Pearl Harbor I was driving home and my car was stopped by a poor, pathetic parade.
>
> Boy Scouts and fat people and old uniforms and a flag and someone playing a flute off-key. . . . As I watched, tears began to run down my face. I felt we didn't understand—not Hitler, nor the Germans, nor Stalin, nor the communists. We didn't understand any of them. I felt that if we could understand, then we could make progress. I had a vision of a peace table, with people sitting around it, talking about human nature and hatred and war and peace and brotherhood.
>
> I was too old to go into the army. It was at that moment that I realized that the rest of my life must be devoted to discovering a psychology for the peace table.
>
> That moment changed my whole life and determined what I have done since. . . . I wanted to prove that human beings are capable of something grander than war and prejudice and hatred. I wanted to make science consider all the problems that nonscientists have been handling—religion, poetry, values, philosophy, art.
>
> I went about it by trying to understand great people, the best specimens of mankind I could find. (Hall 1968, 54–55)

Maslow was in New York in the late 1930s and early 1940s, when the best minds in Europe were arriving in this country to escape Nazi Germany. Among those individuals whom Maslow sought out and learned from were Alfred Adler, Max Wertheimer, Karen Horney, and Erich Fromm.

Also among those having a strong influence on Maslow at this time was the American anthropologist Ruth Benedict. In fact, it was Maslow's deep admiration for Max Wertheimer, the founder of the school of Gestalt psychology, and Ruth Benedict that finally stimulated his interest in self-actualizing people. Maslow described how his efforts to understand these two individuals evolved into what became his life's work:

> My investigations on self-actualization were not planned to be research and did not start out as research. They started out as the effort of a young intellectual to try to understand two of his teachers whom he loved, adored, and admired, and who were very, very wonderful people. It was a kind of high-IQ devotion. I could not be content simply to adore, but sought to understand why these two people were so different from the run-of-the-mill people in the world. These two people were Ruth Benedict . . . and Max Wertheimer. They were my teachers after I came with a Ph.D. from the West to New York City, and they were most remarkable human beings. My training in psychology equipped me not at all for understanding them. It was as if they were not quite people but something more than people. My own investigation began as a prescientific or nonscientific activity. I made descriptions and notes on Max Wertheimer, and I made notes on Ruth Benedict. When I tried to understand them, think about them, and write about them in my journal and my notes, I realized in one wonderful moment that their two patterns could be generalized. I was talking about a kind of person, not about two noncomparable individuals. There was wonderful excitement in that. I tried to see whether this pattern could be found elsewhere, and I did find it elsewhere, in one person after another.
>
> By ordinary standards of laboratory research, that is of rigorous and controlled research, this simply was not research at all. (1971, 41–42)

By 1951, when Maslow went to Brandeis University, he was completely dedicated to the study of the most psychologically healthy people he could find. It was during these years that Maslow emerged as the leader of the humanistic movement in American psychology. He stayed at Brandeis until 1969, at which time he became resident fellow of the Laughlin Foundation in California. His job there was to explore the implications of **humanistic psychology** for a philosophy of politics, economics, and ethics. During this time, Maslow also became interested in sensitivity groups and was one of the founders of the Esalen Institute of California. Maslow died on 8 June 1970 of a heart attack. Among Maslow's many honors is included election to the presidency of the American Psychological Association in 1967.

Although it is clear that a number of personality theorists fall into the humanistic camp (for instance Allport, Kelly, and Rogers), it is Maslow who emerged as spokesman for humanistic psychology. It was Maslow who took the development of humanistic psychology on as a cause, and he did so with a religious fervor.

Third-Force Psychology

As noted earlier, Maslow believed that his training in psychology did not equip him to understand the positive qualities of people whom he considered remarkable. By viewing humans as victims of animal instincts and of the conflicts caused by culture, the psychoanalytic camp told only part of the story. Likewise, the behaviorists, who viewed humans as creatures whose behavior is molded by the environment, shed only limited light on the mysteries of human existence. In fact, Maslow believed that all of psychology had concentrated on the dark, negative, sick, and animalistic aspects of humans. By emphasizing the study of psychologically crippled individuals, we have created a "crippled" psychology. "It becomes more and more clear that the study of crippled, stunted, immature, and unhealthy specimens can yield only a cripple psychology and a cripple philosophy" (Maslow 1970, 180).

It was hoped by Maslow that humanistic psychology would attend to humans' positive aspects and thus provide information that could be used in formulating a complete theory of human motivation, a theory that would include both the positive and the negative aspects of human nature. "Health is not simply the absence of disease or even the opposite of it. Any theory of motivation that is worthy of attention must deal with the highest capacities of the healthy and strong man as well as with the defensive maneuvers of crippled spirits" (Maslow 1970, 33).

Maslow felt that the typical **reductive-analytic approach to science,** which reduces human beings to a collection of habits or conflicts, overlooks the essence of human nature. The **holistic-analytic approach to science,** which studies the person as a thinking, feeling, totality, is more likely to yield valid results. If, said Maslow, the standard scientific techniques cannot be applied to the study of the whole person, throw them out and develop techniques that can be used. It is the understanding of humans that is important, and if traditional scientific procedures do not aid in gaining that understanding, so much the worse for them. Maslow even suggested that some scientists are preoccupied with the reductive-analytic approach because it serves as a defense against knowing their own nature. In other words, some scientists in the name of "scientific rigor" cut themselves off from the poetic, romantic, tender, and spiritual aspects of themselves and other people. Maslow said that such scientists **desacralize** people by making them less marvelous, beautiful, and awesome than they really are.

> Briefly put, it appears to me that science and everything scientific can be and often is used as a tool in the service of a distorted, narrowed, humorless, de-eroticized, de-emotionalized, desacralized, and de-sanctified *Weltanschauung* [world view]. This desacralization can be used as a defense against being flooded by emotion, especially the emotions of humility, reverence, mystery, wonder and awe. (Maslow 1966, 139)

Maslow's goal, then, was to round out psychology by making it focus on a subject that it had ignored through the years, that is, the healthy, fully functioning human being. This effort was to become psychology's **third-force,** with psychoanalysis and behaviorism constituting the other two forces.

In 1962, Maslow, along with several other humanistically oriented psychologists (including Carl Rogers), established the American Association of Humanistic Psychology, which operated in accordance with the following principles.

1. The primary study of psychology should be the experiencing person.
2. Choice, creativity, and self-realization, rather than mechanistic reductionism, are the concern of the humanistic psychologist.

3. Only personally and socially significant problems should be studied—significance, not objectivity, is the watchword.

4. The major concern of psychology should be the dignity and enhancement of people.

A humanistic science of psychology would consider these principles, and the result would be *less* external prediction and control of human behavior, but greater self–knowledge.

> If humanistic science may be said to have any goals beyond sheer fascination with the human mystery and enjoyment of it, these would be to release the person from external controls and to make him *less* predictable to the observer (to make him freer, more creative, more inner determined) even though perhaps more predictable to himself. (Maslow 1966, 40)

Hierarchy Of Needs

The backbone of Maslow's position is his theory of motivation. He contended that humans have a number of needs that are **instinctoid,** that is, innate. Maslow chose the term "instinctoid" instead of "instinctive" to demonstrate the difference between our biologic heritage and that of lower animals.

> This inner core, even though it is biologically based and "instinctoid," is weak in certain senses rather than strong. It is easily overcome, suppressed or repressed. It may even be killed off permanently. Humans no longer have instincts in the animal sense, powerful, unmistakable inner voices which tell them unequivocally what to do, when, where, how and with whom. All that we have left are instinct-remnants. And furthermore, these are weak, subtle and delicate, very easily drowned out by learning, by cultural expectations, by fear, by disapproval, etc. (Maslow 1968, 191)

Maslow also assumed that our needs are arranged in a hierarchy in terms of their potency. Although all needs are instinctoid, some are more powerful than others. The lower the need is in the hierarchy, the more powerful it is. The higher the need is in the hierarchy, the weaker it is and the more distinctly human it is. The lower, or basic, needs in the hierarchy are similar to those possessed by other "lower" animals, but no other animal, except humans, possesses the higher needs.

Maslow (1970, 98–100) summarized the differences between the higher and lower needs:

1. The higher the need, the later it emerges in the evolutionary process.

2. Higher needs occur relatively late in an individual's development. Typically, some of the higher needs will not occur until middle age, if at all.

3. The higher needs are less directly related to survival than the lower needs are, thus there is less urgency associated with their satisfaction.

4. Even though the higher needs are not directly related to survival, their satisfaction is more desirable than the satisfaction of a lower need is. Satisfaction of the higher needs produces deep happiness, peace of mind, and a richer inner life.

5. The higher needs require more preconditions for their emergence and satisfaction than do the lower needs. They also require better environmental conditions for their functioning.

As one climbs the hierarchy of needs, one becomes less animal-like and more human. A person progresses from one need level to the next by first satisfying the cluster of needs characteristic of one level in the hierarchy. This point will become clearer as we discuss the five levels of needs in the hierarchy.

Physiological Needs. These are the needs directly related to survival, which we share with other animals. Included here are the needs for food, water, sex, elimination, and sleep. If one of the physiological needs is not met, it will completely dominate the individual's life.

> For our chronically and extremely hungry man, Utopia can be defined simply as a place where there is plenty of food. He tends to think that, if only he is guaranteed food for the rest of his life, he will be perfectly happy and will never want anything more. Life itself tends to be defined in terms of eating. Anything else will be defined as unimportant. Freedom, love, community feeling, respect, philosophy, may all be waved aside as fripperies that are useless, since they fail to fill the stomach. Such a man may fairly be said to live by bread alone. (Maslow 1970, 37)

Obviously, such needs are extremely important and should be heeded. But, according to Maslow, psychology has overemphasized the importance of such needs in determining the behavior of humans in a modern society. For most humans, these needs are easily satisfied. The real question, to Maslow, was what happens *after* the physiological needs are satisfied. "It is quite true that man lives by bread alone—when there is no bread. But what happens to man's desires when there is bread and when his belly is chronically filled?" (Maslow 1970, 38). Maslow's answer was that the individual is then dominated by the next level or cluster of needs. It is important to note that Maslow did not feel that one set of needs had to be completely satisfied before the individual was released to deal with the next level. Rather, he felt that one set of needs had to be consistently and substantially satisfied. In other words, a person can be periodically hungry or thirsty and still be able to deal with higher needs, but the person's life cannot be *dominated* by hunger or thirst.

Safety Needs. When the physiological needs are satisfactorily met, the safety needs emerge as dominant motives. Included here are the needs for structure, order, security, and predictability. The person operating at this level is very Kellian, in that the primary goal is to reduce uncertainty in his or her life. These needs are most clearly seen operating in children, who typically show great fear when confronted with novel (unpredictable) events. The satisfaction of the safety needs assures individuals that they are living in an environment that is free from danger.

Belongingness and Love Needs. With the physiological and safety needs essentially satisfied, the person now is driven by the need for affiliation. Humans need to love and to be loved. If this need is not met, the person will feel alone and empty. Maslow believed that the failure to satisfy needs at this level is a major problem in America today, and explains why so many people are seeking psychotherapy and joining sensitivity or encounter groups. Maslow described the typical person joining such a group as:

> Motivated by unsatisfied hunger for contact, for intimacy, for belongingness and by the need to overcome the widespread feelings of alienation, aloneness, strangeness, and loneliness, which have been worsened by our mobility, by the breakdown of traditional groupings, the scattering of families, the generation gap, the steady urbanization and disappearance of village face-to-faceness, and the resulting shallowness of American friendship. (Maslow 1970, 44)

Esteem Needs. If one has been fortunate enough to satisfy one's physiological, safety, and belongingness and love needs, the need for esteem will begin to dominate one's life. This group of needs requires both recognition from other people, which results in feelings of prestige, acceptance, status, and self-esteem, which results in feelings of adequacy, competence, and confidence. Both kinds of feelings usually result from engaging in activities considered to be socially useful. Lack of satisfaction of the esteem needs results in discouragement and feelings of inferiority.

Self-Actualization. If all the lower needs have been adequately satisfied, the person is in a position to become one of the rare people who is self-actualized.

> So far as motivational status is concerned, healthy people have sufficiently gratified their basic needs for safety, belongingness, love, respect, and self-esteem so that they are motivated primarily by trends to self-actualization [defined as ongoing actualization of potentials, capacities and talents, as fulfillment of mission (or call, fate, destiny, or vocation), as a fuller knowledge of, and acceptance of, the person's own intrinsic nature, as an unceasing trend toward unity, integration or synergy within the person]. (Maslow 1968, 25)

> Musicians must make music, artists must paint, poets must write if they are to be ultimately at peace with themselves. What humans *can* be, they *must* be. They must be true to their own nature. This need we may call self-actualization. (Maslow 1987, 22)

We will have more to say about the characteristics of self-actualized people later in this chapter. Maslow's hierarchy of needs is diagrammed in Figure 15–1.

Exceptions in the Hierarchy of Needs. Maslow believed that most people progress through the hierarchy of needs in the order shown in Figure 15-1. Exceptions occur, however. For example, some people have gone so long with their psychological needs only partially satisfied that they lose all desire to ever progress beyond them. For the rest of their lives these people may be satisfied if only they can get enough food to eat. Something similar may happen with the need for love. If a person is starved for love in his or her early childhood, the desire for and the ability to give affection may be lost forever. In both of these cases, something similar to a Freudian fixation occurs. In the first case, the person would be "fixated" on the physiological level of the hierarchy, and in the second case, on the belong-

Figure 15-1
*Maslow's Hierarchy
of Needs.*

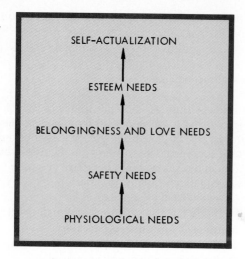

SELF-ACTUALIZATION

ESTEEM NEEDS

BELONGINGNESS AND LOVE NEEDS

SAFETY NEEDS

PHYSIOLOGICAL NEEDS

ingness and love level. Maslow (1987, 26) also suggested that the creativity of some innately talented people does not seem to require the satisfaction of the preself-actualization needs. Rather, their creativity seems to occur despite such satisfaction.

Degrees of Satisfaction.   We saw earlier that one set of needs does not require complete satisfaction before the next higher set is reached. It is also true that no matter what set of needs in the hierarchy a person is concentrating on, he or she is also addressing other sets of needs at the same time. Maslow (1987) explained:

> So far, our theoretical discussion may have given the impression that these five sets of needs—physiological, safety, belongingness, esteem, and self-actualization—are somehow in such terms as the following: If one need is satisfied, then another emerges. This statement might give the false impression that a need must be satisfied 100 percent before the next need emerges. In actual fact, most members of our society who are normal are partially satisfied in all their basic needs and partially unsatisfied in all their basic needs at the same time. A more realistic description of the hierarchy would be in terms of decreasing percentages of satisfaction as we go up the hierarchy of prepotency. For instance, to assign arbitrary figures for the sake of illustration, it is as if the average citizen is satisfied perhaps 85 percent in physiological needs, 70 percent in safety needs, 50 percent in love needs, 40 percent in self-esteem needs, and 10 percent in self-actualization needs.
>
> As for the concept of emergence of a new need after satisfaction of the prepotent need, this emergence is not a sudden, saltatory phenomenon, but rather a gradual emergence by slow degrees from nothingness. For instance, if prepotent need A is satisfied only 10 percent, then need B may not be visible at all. However, as this need A becomes satisfied 25 percent need B may emerge 5 percent, as need A becomes satisfied 75 percent need B may emerge 50 percent, and so on. (27–28)

It should also be noted that no matter how far one has progressed up the hierarchy, if lower needs are frustrated for a considerable length of time, the person will regress to the level of the hierarchy corresponding to those needs and will remain there until those needs are satisfied. Thus, no matter what one has accomplished in life, if the need for food is suddenly unsatisfied, that need will again dominate one's life.

Desire to Know and Understand

Maslow believed that the desire to know and understand was related to the satisfaction of the basic needs. In other words, knowing and understanding were thought to be tools used in solving problems and overcoming obstacles, thereby allowing the satisfaction of the basic needs.

> If we remember that the cognitive capacities (perceptual, intellectual, learning) are a set of adjustive tools, which have, among other functions, that of satisfaction of our basic needs, then it is clear that any danger to them, any deprivation or blocking of their free use, must also be indirectly threatening to the basic needs themselves. Such a statement is a partial solution of the general problems of curiosity, the search for knowledge, truth, and wisdom, and the ever persistent urge to solve the cosmic mysteries. Secrecy, censorship, dishonesty, blocking of communication threaten *all* the basic needs. (Maslow 1970, 47)

The Aesthetic Needs

These are the needs for such things as order, symmetry, closure, structure, and for completion of the act, which are seen in some adults and almost universally in children. Maslow believed that evidence exists for such needs in every culture as far back as the cavepeople.

Although the physiological, safety, love and belongingness, and esteem needs and the need for self-actualization form a hierarchy, and the needs to know and understand are functionally related to their satisfaction, it is not clear how the aesthetic needs relate to other needs. Two things are clear, however. First, Maslow believed that the aesthetic needs are instinctoid, and second, that they are given their fullest expression in self-actualizing individuals.

Being Motivation

What happens to an individual when all of the basic needs have been met to a satisfactory degree, and he or she enters the realm of self-actualization? Maslow's answer was that, in a sense, the person becomes qualitatively different from those who are still attempting to meet their basic needs. The self-actualizing person's life is governed by **being values** (B-values), which Maslow also labeled **metamotives.** "Self-actualizing people are not primarily motivated (i.e., by basic needs); they are primarily metamotivated (i.e., by metaneeds = B-values)" (Maslow 1971, 311). Because being motivation affects personal inner growth, it is also called **growth motivation.** Examples of B-values are beauty, truth, and justice.

The lives of nonactualizing people are governed by deficiency motives (D-motives); in other words, they are influenced by the absence of things that they need, such as food, love, or esteem. The perception of a nonactualizing person is also influenced by his or her deficiencies and is therefore called **need-directed perception** (also called **D-perception or D-cognition**). "Need-directed perception is a highly focused searchlight darting here and there, seeking the objects which will satisfy needs, ignoring everything irrelevant to the need" (Jourard 1974, 68).

Being cognition (B-cognition), on the other hand, is qualitatively different from need-directed perception. "Being-cognition . . . refers to a more passive mode of perceiving. It involves letting oneself be reached, touched, or affected by what is there so that the perception is richer" (Jourard 1974, 68).

As an example of the difference between D-motivation and B-motivation, Maslow used the concept of love. He differentiated between D-love and B-love. D-love is motivated by the lack of fulfillment of the need for love and belonging-ness. A person in such a need-state craves love as a hungry person craves food. Such love is said to be selfish, because, when obtained, it satisfies a personal deficiency. In contrast to D-love, Maslow (1968, 42–43) listed some of the charac-teristics of B-love.

1. B-love is non-possessive.
2. B-love is insatiable, it can be enjoyed without end. It usually grows stronger rather than disappearing. D-love, however, can be satiated.
3. The B-love experience is often described as having the same effect as an aesthetic or mystic experience has.
4. B-love has a profound and widespread therapeutic effect.
5. B-love is a richer, higher, and more valuable experience than D-love is.
6. There is a minimum of anxiety and hostility in B-love.
7. B-lovers are more independent of each other, less jealous, less needful, more interested, and more autonomous than D-lovers are. Also, they are more eager to help the other toward self-actualization and are more proud of the other's triumphs.
8. B-love makes the truest, most penetrating perception of the other possible.
9. B-love in a sense, creates the partner. It offers self-acceptance and a feeling of love-worthiness, both of which permit the partner to grow. Perhaps full hu-man development cannot occur without the experience of B-love.

The list of fifteen B-values that Maslow felt dominated the lives of self-actualizing people is shown in Table 15-1. The condition that results if the value is not given expression is shown under the column labeled "pathogenic deprivation."

The B-values are not arranged in a hierarchy and thus are given equal value, but Maslow felt that all the B-values influenced one another. In other words, to be truly self-actualized, a person would need to give expression to all the B-values.

> It is my (uncertain) impression that any B-Value is fully and adequately defined by the total of the other B-Values. That is, truth, to be fully and completely defined, must be beautiful, good, perfect, just, simple, orderly, lawful, alive, comprehen-sive, unitary, dichotomy-transcending, effortless, and amusing. . . . It is as if all the B-Values have some kind of unity, with each single value being something like a facet of this whole. (Maslow 1971, 324)

Table 15-1
B-Values, Condition That Exists If a B-Value is Not Satisfied (Pathogenic Deprivation), and The Effect That Not Satisfying a B-Value Has in One's Life. (Specific Metapathologies)

B-VALUES AND SPECIFIC METAPATHOLOGIES

B-Values	Pathogenic Deprivation	Specific Metapathologies
1. Truth	Dishonesty	Disbelief; mistrust; cynicism; skepticism; suspicion
2. Goodness	Evil	Utter selfishness; hatred; repulsion; disgust; reliance only on self and for self; nihilism; cynicism
3. Beauty	Ugliness	Vulgarity; specific unhappiness, restlessness, loss of taste, tension, fatigue; philistinism; bleakness
4. Unity; wholeness	Chaos, atomism, loss of connectedness	Disintegration; "the world is falling apart"; arbitrariness
4A. Dichotomy-Transcendence	Black-and-white dichotomies; loss of gradations, of degree; forced polarization; forced choices	Black-and-white thinking, either/or thinking; seeing everything as a duel or war, or a conflict; low synergy; simplistic view of life
5. Aliveness; process	Deadness; mechanization of life	Deadness; robotizing; feeling oneself to be totally determined; loss of emotion; Boredom (?); loss of zest in life; experiential emptiness
6. Uniqueness	Sameness; uniformity; interchangeability	Loss of feeling of self and of individuality; feeling oneself to be interchangeable, anonymous, not really needed
7. Perfection	Imperfection; sloppiness; poor workmanship, shoddiness	Discouragement (?): hopelessness; nothing to work for
7A. Necessity	Accident; occasionalism; inconsistency	Chaos, unpredictability; loss of safety; vigilance
8. Completion; finality	Incompleteness	Feelings of incompleteness with perseveration; hopelessness; cessation of striving and coping; no use trying
9. Justice	Injustice	Insecurity; anger; cynicism; mistrust; lawlessness; jungle world-view; total selfishness
9A. Order	Lawlessness; chaos, breakdown of authority	Insecurity; wariness; loss of safety, of predictability; necessity for vigilance, alertness, tension, being on guard
10. Simplicity	Confusing complexity; disconnectedness; disintegration	Overcomplexity; confusion, bewilderment, conflict, loss of orientation
11. Richness; totality; comprehensiveness	Poverty; coarctation	Depression; uneasiness; loss of interest in world
12. Effortlessness	Effortfulness	Fatigue, strain, striving, clumsiness, awkwardness, gracelessness, stiffness
13. Playfulness	Humorlessness	Grimness; depression; paranoid humorlessness; loss of zest in life; cheerlessness; loss of ability to enjoy
14. Self-sufficiency	Contingency; accident; occasionalism	Dependence on (?) the perceiver (?); it becomes his responsibility
15. Meaningfulness	Meaninglessness	Meaninglessness; despair; senselessness of life

(From Maslow 1971, pp. 318–319).

Even though B-values are metaneeds, they are still needs, and, as such, they must be satisfied if a person is to experience full psychological health. Failure to satisfy a metaneed (B-value) causes what Maslow called a **metapathology.** A description of the metapathologies caused by the failure to satisfy the various B-values is shown in Table 15-1.

Moments of intense B-cognition cause feelings of ecstasy or rapture. Maslow called these mystic or oceanic feelings **peak experiences,** and we will have more to say about them in the next section, as we consider the characteristics of self-actualizing people.

Characteristics of Self-Actualizing People

As noted earlier, Maslow's interest in self-actualizing people began with his great admiration for Ruth Benedict and Max Wertheimer. After discovering that these two people had much in common, he began to search for others with the same qualities. He searched for people who seemed to be operating at full capacity, that is, doing the best that they were capable of doing. Such people were found among his students, his personal acquaintances, and historical figures. The group that he finally isolated for more detailed study consisted of forty-eight persons: twelve "probable" actualizers, ten "partial" actualizers, and twenty-six "potential or possible" actualizers. Among the public and historical figures included in his study were the following.

Jane Addams	Johann Wolfgang von Goethe
Ludwig van Beethoven	William James
Albert Einstein	Thomas Jefferson
George Washington Carver	Abraham Lincoln
Eugene V. Debs	Fritz Kreisler
Thomas Eakins	Eleanor Roosevelt
Sigmund Freud	Franklin D. Roosevelt
Albert Schweitzer	Henry David Thoreau
Baruch Spinoza	Walt Whitman

The reader may be interested to know that Maslow listed the following public or historical figures as probably self-actualized: Einstein, Eleanor Roosevelt, Jane Addams, William James, Schweitzer, Aldous Huxley, Spinoza, Lincoln, and Jefferson.

Maslow realized full well that his "research" on self-actualizers was not "scientific" and could be criticized on several levels, but he was so startled by what he found that he felt obliged to share his observations with others.

> [This] study . . . is unusual in various ways. It was not planned as ordinary research; it was not a social venture but a private one, motivated by my own curiosity and pointed toward the solution of various personal, moral, ethical, and scientific problems. I sought only to convince and to teach myself rather than to prove or demonstrate to others.
>
> Quite unexpectedly, however, these studies have proved to be so enlightening to me, and so laden with exciting implications, that it seems fair that some

sort of report should be made to others in spite of its methodological shortcomings. (Maslow 1970, 149).

Maslow compared his method of gathering data on his self-actualizing individuals to the gradual development of a global impression of a friend or acquaintance. In other words, the impression came from a large number of informal observations, under a wide variety of circumstances, rather than from controlled observations under laboratory conditions. This, along with the fact that his conclusions were based on such a small sample, has stimulated much criticism of Maslow's work.

From his informal research, Maslow concluded that self-actualizing people exhibit the following characteristics:

1. They perceive reality accurately and fully Their perceptions are not colored by specific needs or defenses. In other words, their perception of the world is characterized by B-cognition rather than by D-cognition.

2. They demonstrate a greater acceptance of themselves, others, and of nature in general Self-actualizers accept themselves as they are. They lack defensiveness, phoniness, and are not burdened by undue guilt, anxiety, or shame. "Self-actualizing people tend to be good animals, hearty in their appetites and enjoying themselves without regret or shame or apology. They seem to have a uniformly good appetite for food; they seem to sleep well; they seem to enjoy their sexual lives without unnecessary inhibition and so on for all the relatively physiological impulses" (Maslow 1987, 131). Similarly, they are accepting of others and have no need to instruct, inform, or convert them. Not only can they tolerate weakness in others but they are not threatened by their strengths. Nature is also accepted as it is.

3. They exhibit spontaneity, simplicity, and naturalness Self-actualizers tend to be true to their feelings; what they really feel they tend to say or experience. They do not hide behind a mask and do not act in accordance with social roles. They are true to themselves.

4. They tend to be concerned with problems rather than with themselves Self-actualizers are typically committed to some task, cause, or mission toward which they can direct most of their energies. This is contrasted with the preoccupation with oneself often found in non-actualizers.

5. They have a quality of detachment and a need for privacy Because self-actualizing individuals depend on their own values and feelings to guide their lives, they do not need to be in constant contact with other people.

> It is often possible for them to remain above the battle, to remain unruffled, undisturbed by that which produces turmoil in others. They find it easy to be aloof, reserved, and also calm and serene; thus it becomes possible for them to take personal misfortunes without reacting violently as the ordinary person does. They seem to be able to retain their dignity even in undignified surroundings and situations. Perhaps this comes in part from their tendency to stick by their own interpretation of a situation rather than to rely upon what other people feel or think about the matter. This reserve may shade over into austerity and remoteness. (Maslow 1970, 160)

6. They are autonomous and therefore tend to be independent of their environment and culture Because self-actualizers are B-motivated rather than D-motivated, they are more dependent on their own inner world than on the outer world.

Deficiency-motivated people *must* have other people available, since most of their main need gratifications (love, safety, respect, prestige, belongingness) can come only from other human beings. But growth-motivated [B-motivated] people may actually be *hampered* by others. The determinants of satisfaction and of the good life are for them now inner-individual and *not* social. They have become strong enough to be independent of the good opinion of other people, or even of their affection. The honors, the status, the rewards, the popularity, the prestige, and the love they can bestow must have become less important than self-development and inner growth. (Maslow 1970, 162)

7. They exhibit a continued freshness of appreciation Self-actualizers continue to experience the events of their lives with awe, wonder, and pleasure. Every baby or sunset is as beautiful and exciting as the first they had seen. Marriage is as exciting after forty years as it was in the beginning. Generally such individuals derive great inspiration and ecstasy from the basic experiences of everyday life.

8. They have periodic mystic or peak experiences Maslow believed that all humans had the potential for peak experiences, but only self-actualizers could have them full-blown, because such people were not threatened by them and therefore would not inhibit or defend against them in any way. Generally, peak experiences are the embracing of B-values.

Feelings of limitless horizons opening up to the vision, the feeling of being simultaneously more powerful and also more helpless than one ever was before, the feeling of great ecstasy and wonder and awe, the loss of placing in time and space with, finally, the conviction that something extremely important and valuable had happened, so that the subject is to some extent transformed and strengthened even in his daily life by such experiences. (Maslow 1970, 164)

One of Maslow's own peak experiences involved imagining he was part of the greatest commencement exercise of all time.

I was in a faculty procession here at Brandeis. I saw the line stretching off into a dim future. At its head was Socrates. And in the line were the ones I love most. Thomas Jefferson was there. And Spinoza. And Alfred North Whitehead. I was in that same line. Behind me that infinite line melted into the dimness. (Hall 1968, 35)

Maslow concluded that some self-actualizers peak more often than others. The *nonpeakers* (low frequency of peak experiences) tend to be practical, effective people. *Peakers* (relatively high frequency of peak experiences) tend to be more poetic, aesthetically oriented, transcendent, and mystical.

9. They tend to identify with all of mankind The concerns that self-actualizers have for other people do not extend only to their friends and family but to all people in all cultures throughout the world. This feeling of brotherhood extends also to individuals who are aggressive, inconsiderate, or otherwise foolish. Self-actualizers have a genuine desire to help the human race.

10. They develop deep interpersonal relations with only a few individuals Self-actualizers tend to seek out other self-actualizers as their close friends. Such friendships are few in number but are deep and rich.

11. They tend to accept democratic values Self-actualizers do not respond to individuals on the basis of race, status, or religion. "They can be and are friendly with anyone of suitable character regardless of class, education, political belief, race, or color. As a matter of fact it often seems as if they are not even aware of these differences, which are for the average person so obvious and so important" (Maslow 1970, 167)

12. They have a strong ethical sense Although their notions of right and wrong are often unconventional, self-actualizers, nonetheless, almost always know the ethical implications of their own actions.

13. They have a well-developed, unhostile sense of humor Self-actualizers tend not to find humor in things that injure or degrade other humans. Rather, they are more likely to laugh at themselves or at human beings in general.

14. They are creative Maslow found this trait in all of the self-actualizers.

> This is a universal characteristic of all the people studied or observed. . . . There is no exception. . . . This creativeness appears in some of our subjects not in the usual forms of writing books, composing music or producing artistic objects, but rather may be much more humble. It is as if this special type of creativeness, being an expression of healthy personality, is projected out upon the world or touches whatever activity the person is engaged in. In this sense there can be creative shoemakers or carpenters or clerks. (Maslow 1970, 170–71)

This creativity comes from the fact that self-actualizers are more open to experience and more spontaneous in their feelings. It is directly related to B-motivation.

15. They resist enculturation Self-actualizers tend to be nonconformists because they are inner-directed people. If a cultural norm is contrary to their personal values, they simply will not adhere to it.

Negative Characteristics of Self-Actualizing People

Most people would list these fifteen characteristics as positive, but Maslow wanted to make it clear that self-actualizing people were far from perfect.

> Our subjects show many of the lesser human failings. They too are equipped with silly, wasteful, or thoughtless habits. They can be boring, stubborn, irritating. They are by no means free from a rather superficial vanity, pride, partiality to their own productions, family, friends, and children. Temper outbursts are not rare.
> Our subjects are occasionally capable of an extraordinary and unexpected ruthlessness. It must be remembered that they are very strong people. This makes it possible for them to display a surgical coldness when this is called for, beyond the power of the average man. The man who found that a long-trusted acquaint-

ance was dishonest cut himself off from this friendship sharply and abruptly and without any observable pangs whatsoever. Another woman who was married to someone she did not love, when she decided on divorce, did it with a decisiveness that looked almost like ruthlessness. Some of them recover so quickly from the death of people close to them as to seem heartless. (Maslow 1970, 175)

Maslow concluded that as healthy, creative, democratic, and spontaneous as his self-actualizers were, *"there are no perfect human beings!"* (Maslow 1970, 176).

Why Self-Actualization Is Not Universal

Why, if the tendency toward self-actualization is innate, is not every mature adult self-actualized, instead of Maslow's estimate that only one percent of them are? Maslow felt that there were four basic explanations for this fact.

1. Because self-actualization is at the top of the hierarchy, it is the weakest of all the needs and therefore easily impeded. "This inner nature is not strong and overpowering and unmistakable like the instincts of animals. It is weak and delicate and subtle and easily overcome by habit, cultural pressure, and wrong attitudes toward it" (Maslow 1968, 4).

2. Most people fear the kind of knowledge about themselves that self-actualization requires. Such knowledge requires giving up the known and entering a state of uncertainty.

More than any other kind of knowledge we fear knowledge of ourselves, knowledge that might transform our self-esteem and our self-image. . . . While human beings love knowledge and seek it—they are curious—they also fear it. The closer to the personal it is, the more they fear it. (Maslow 1966, 16)

Maslow referred to this fear and doubt of one's own abilities and potentialities as the **Jonah complex.** To become self-actualized requires enough courage to sacrifice safety for personal growth.

3. The cultural environment can stifle one's tendency toward actualization by imposing certain norms on segments of the population. For example, defining "manly" in the way that our culture does tends to prevent the male child from developing such traits as sympathy, kindness, and tenderness, all of which characterize the self-actualized individual.

4. As indicated in item 2, in order to become self-actualized one must choose growth rather than safety. Maslow observed that children from warm, secure, friendly homes are more likely to choose experiences that lead to personal growth than are children from insecure homes. Thus, childhood conditions influence the probability of a person's becoming self-actualized. Maslow characterized what he felt was the optimal set of circumstances for a child as **freedom within limits.** He believed that too much permissiveness was almost as harmful as too much control. What is needed, he thought, was a proper mixture of the two.

Conditions Necessary for Self-Actualization

In addition to satisfying the physiological needs, the safety needs, and the love and belongingness needs, an environment must have several other characteristics before self-actualization can occur. These characteristics, according to Maslow, include freedom of speech, freedom to do what one wants to do as long as it harms no one else, freedom of inquiry, freedom to defend oneself, order, justice, fairness, and honesty. Later Maslow added "challenge" (proper stimulation) as a characteristic of an environment conducive to self-actualization.

With these environmental prerequisites in mind, along with the four reasons why more people are not self-actualized cited earlier, it becomes easier to understand why only about one percent of the population becomes self-actualized. Most of the rest of us live out our days somewhere between the love and belongingness and self-esteem needs.

Eupsychia

Because Maslow believed that all human needs, including the need for self-actualization, were instinctoid, it must be the environment (society, culture) that determines how far up the hierarchy of needs one will be able to climb. Maslow rejected the Freudian notion that humans and society had to be engaged in constant conflict. Rather, he believed that at best society could be designed so as to maximize the probability of self-actualization. Because Maslow believed that people's needs are good rather than bad (as the Freudians believed), their satisfaction should be encouraged rather than discouraged.

Maslow speculated on the kind of utopia that would be developed if 1,000 healthy families moved to a deserted island, where they could determine their own destiny. He called this potential utopia **Eupsychia** (pronounced Yew-sígh-key-a), which can be broken down as follows: Eu = good, psych = mind, and ia = country. In Eupsychia there would be complete **synergy**, a concept he borrowed from Ruth Benedict: syn = together and ergy = working. Thus, in Maslow's utopia, there would be complete cooperation, or working together.

What other features would characterize Eupsychia?

What kind of education would they choose? Economic system? Sexuality? Religion?

I am very uncertain of some things—economics in particular. But of other things I am very sure. One of them is that this would almost surely be a (philosophically) anarchistic group, a Taoistic [nature-oriented] but loving culture, in which people (young people too) would have much more free choice than we are used to, and in which basic needs and metaneeds would be respected much more than they are in our society. People would not bother each other so much as we do, would be much less prone to press opinions or religions or philosophies or tastes in clothes or food or art or women on their neighbors. In a word, the inhabitants of Eupsychia would tend to be more Taoistic, nonintrusive, and basic need-gratifying (whenever possible), would frustrate only under certain conditions that I have not attempted to describe, would be more honest with each other than we are, and would permit people to make free choices wherever possible. They would be far less controlling, violent, contemptuous, or overbearing than we are. Under such conditions, the deepest layers of human nature could show themselves with greater ease. (Maslow 1970, 277–78)

In 1962, Maslow went to Non-linear Systems, Inc. as a Visiting Fellow. His experiences at this voltmeter factory resulted in his book **Eupsychian Management,** (1965). The basic message in the book was that if industrial management were more aware of human needs and what it takes to satisfy those needs, both the worker and the industry would be far healthier. "Eupsychian . . . conditions of work are often good not only for personal fulfillment, but also for the health and prosperity of the organization, as well as for the quantity and quality of the products or services turned out by the organization" (Maslow 1971, 237). Eupsychian management, then, is an attempt to create a working situation that is conducive to the satisfaction of human needs as Maslow described them. It should be clear that Maslow believed not only that industry would run better if it became more humanistic, but our entire country would too.

Ashrams—Places for Personal Growth

For hundreds of years, India has had **ashrams,** or retreats, where people could escape the anxieties associated with everyday life. The pace of living in the ashram is radically slowed down, so that individuals can meditate and reflect on the meaning of their lives. Each ashram is led by a **guru** (spiritual teacher) who acts as a guide for those seeking inner peace. People stay in the ashram for a day, a week, months, or, in some cases, even years. Others, however, use the ashram as a church is used in our country; that is, they visit for a few hours, and then return to their regular, routine lives.

In 1963, Michael Murphy developed the first equivalent to the Indian ashram in this country, in Big Sur, California. The philosophy of the ashram was directly in accordance with Maslow's view that psychology should concentrate more on *healthy* people than on sick ones. Ashrams were places where nonneurotic individuals could go and search themselves and reflect on their own values and thus could become even more effective in their daily lives. Whereas psychotherapy is available to the emotionally disturbed, ashrams are places where the already healthy person can become healthier. It is not surprising, then, that Maslow was the first to conduct seminars at this newly founded ashram, which was named the **Esalen Institute,** after the Esalen Indians, who once inhabited the Big Sur region.

The Western version of the Indian ashram has come to be called a **growth center.**

Since Esalen Institute first came into being, the idea of a center devoted to personal growth has become widespread, and there are several hundreds in existence around the Western world. Although growth centers are not identical with Indian ashrams, there is a similarity in that there is the commitment to self-exploration, to reinvention of one's life, and to radical honesty in one's relationships with others. The people who operate Esalen Institute bake the bread, cook the meals, conduct encounter groups and offer Rolfing sessions and massage. They live a kind of communal life and serve as exemplars of ways to be "in one's body," and ways to be with one another, which are believed to be most life-giving and conducive to personal growth. (Jourard 1974, 342)

Transpersonal Psychology

Toward the end of his life, Maslow began to realize that even humanistic psychology could not adequately explain certain aspects of humans. For example, various mystical, ecstatic, or spiritual states were viewed by Maslow as experiences beyond self-actualization. They were experiences that transcended the customary limits of personal identity and experience. Maslow believed that the study of such phenomena would constitute a fourth force in psychology that he called **transpersonal psychology.** In the preface of his book *Toward a Psychology of Being* (1968) he summarized his views on transpersonal psychology.

I consider Humanistic, Third Force Psychology to be transitional, a preparation for a still "higher" Fourth Psychology, transpersonal, transhuman, centered in the cosmos rather than in human needs and interest, going beyond humanness, identity, self-actualization, and the like. . . . These new developments may very well offer a tangible, usable, effective satisfaction of the "frustrated idealism" of many quietly desperate people, especially young people. These psychologies give promise of developing into the life-philosophy, the religion-surrogate, the value-system, the life-program that these people have been missing. Without the transcendent and the transpersonal, we get sick, violent, and nihilistic, or else hopeless and apathetic. We need something "bigger than we are" to be awed by and to commit ourselves to in a new, naturalistic, empirical, nonchurchly sense. (iii–iv)

Maslow lived to see the founding of the *Journal of Transpersonal Psychology* in 1969. This journal was organized by Anthony Sutich, the same person who founded the *Journal of Humanistic Psychology*. Following is Sutich's statement of the purpose of the *Journal of Transpersonal Psychology*, a statement that was enthusiastically endorsed by Maslow.

The emerging Transpersonal Psychology ("Fourth Force") is concerned specifically with the empirical, scientific study of, and responsible implementation of the findings relevant to, becoming, individual and species-wide meta-needs, ultimate values, unitive consciousness, peak experiences, B-values, ecstasy, mystical experience, awe, being, self-actualization, essence, bliss, wonder, ultimate meaning, transcendence of the self, spirit, oneness, cosmic awareness, individual and species-wide synergy, maximal interpersonal encounter, sacralization of everyday life, transcendental phenomena, cosmic self humor and playfulness, maximal sensory awareness, responsiveness and expression, and related concepts, experiences, and activities. (Sutich 1976, 13–14)

Maslow's "The Farther Reaches of Human Nature" was the lead article in the first issue of the new journal. By 1985, there were 1,200 members in the Association for Transpersonal Psychology and the International Transpersonal Association has sponsored conferences on transpersonal psychology throughout the world.

With the emergence of transpersonal psychology in this country came an appreciation for non-Western psychologies, philosophies, and religions. It was realized that such views have offered ways of inducing and understanding the "higher" states of consciousness for centuries, for example, through intense meditation.

Evaluation

Empirical Research

A major criticism of Maslow's theory has concerned the subjective way that he and his colleagues described and studied self-actualizing people. One response to this criticism has been the development of the *Personal Orientation Inventory* (POI) by Everett Shostrom (Shostrom 1963, 1964, 1974; Shostrom, Knapp, and Knapp, 1976). The POI consists of 150 items which are self-administered. Each item consists of two statements and the respondent simply chooses the statement which most consistently applies to him or her. For example, the choices corresponding to one item may be "my ethical standards are dictated by society" and "my ethical standards are self-determined." For another item, the choices may be "I find some people to be uninteresting," and "I never find people to be uninteresting." The test yields two overall scores. One is for *inner directed support,* or the degree to which a person is his or her own source of support. The other is *time competence,* or the degree to which a person lives in the present. In addition to the two overall scores, ten subscales measure values important to the development of a self-actualizing person; they are self-actualizing values, existentiality, feeling reactivity, spontaneity, self-regard, self-acceptance, nature of humans, synergy, acceptance of aggression, and capacity for intimate contact.

The POI has proved to be a reliable measure of the extent to which an individual is self-actualized, as Maslow had defined the term (Shostrom 1966; Klavetter and Mogar 1967; Ilardi and May 1968). The POI has also proven to be a valuable research tool. For example, Dosamantes-Alperson and Merrill (1980), administered the POI to groups of people before and after they participated in several group therapy sessions. Control groups (those waiting for therapy but not yet participating in the program) were also given the POI at the same times as the groups receiving group therapy. Results indicated that those receiving therapy became more inner directed, spontaneous, and self-accepting—that is, they became more self-actualizing. POI scores have also been found to be positively correlated with academic achievement (Stewart 1968; LeMay and Damm 1968), teaching effectiveness (Dandes 1966), and the effectiveness of psychotherapists (Foulds 1969).

Graham and Balloun (1973) found support for Maslow's concept of the hierarchy of needs. Thirty-seven participants were asked to describe the most important things in their lives. Judges rated these responses on a scale ranging from "very high" to "little or no" desire expressed for physiological, safety, love and belongingness, and self-actualization needs. Results supported Maslow's hypothesis that individuals at different levels of the hierarchy would show greater satisfaction of the needs below their level than of the needs above it. Lester, Hvezda, Sullivan, and Plourde (1983) found a significant positive relationship between the satisfaction of the basic needs and psychological health. Maslow's concept of the hierarchy of needs has also received some attention in the area of industrial-organizational psychology. For example, Marrow, Bowers, and Seashore (1967) found that providing conditions that gratify higher needs produces improvement in both employee production and morale.

Maslow's notion of peak experiences has been studied rather extensively. For example, Panzarella (1980) found that artistically and musically oriented people claim that peak experiences have deepened their appreciation of music or art and that such mystical moments provide them with a sense of renewal and an urge to be creative. Ravizza (1977) had twenty athletes in twelve different sports describe their "greatest moments" as athletes. Their descriptions had much in common with Maslow's description of peak experiences. During their greatest moments the athletes felt no fear; were totally immersed in their activity; had a God-like feeling of control; felt a sense of self-validation; felt a unity with the experience and with the universe; viewed themselves as passive and their activity as effortless; and described their activity in terms of awe, ecstasy, and wonder. Mathes, Zevon, Roter, and Joerger (1982) developed the Peak Scale to measure the tendency to have peak experiences. Several studies using the Peak Scale yielded results consistent with Maslow's theorizing. For example, those scoring high on the scale tended to have experiences of a mystical nature as well as feelings of intense happiness. High scorers also reported living in terms of B-values (for example, truth, beauty, and justice) instead of D-values.

Criticisms

Too Many Exceptions.   Too many people seem to be highly productive and creative even though their basic needs do not seem to have been satisfied. Although Maslow noted such exception to his theory, he did little to account for them.

Unscientific Approach.   Maslow has been accused of using uncontrolled and unreliable research techniques, basing his conclusions about self-actualizing people on a small sample of people; accepting as valid the conscious, self-reports of his subjects, using his own intuitive criteria as to what constitutes a self-actualizing person; and of using ambiguous terms in his theory such as metaneed, metapathology, love, beauty, and peak experience.

Overly Optimistic View of Human Nature.   Like Rogers, Maslow has been criticized for assuming that humans have an innate tendency toward self-actualization. Critics say that many humans are too violent, insensitive, and inhumane to justify such an assumption. To these critics, theories such as those of Freud, Jung, and the sociobiologists present a more realistic picture of humans, and the theories of Rogers and Maslow represent wishful thinking rather than fact.

Too Many Unanswered Questions.   For example, who can become self-actualized? Most, if not all, of Maslow's subjects were highly intelligent, and financially successful. What about less intelligent and financially successful persons? Can they also become self-actualized? Are feeble-minded persons capable of using their full potential to become self-actualized? Also, can people intentionally become self-actualized or is it something that must occur naturally? That is, if one knows the criteria for self-actualization, can one adopt those characteristics and thus be self-actualized? Finally, as we have seen, Maslow was vague about how much satisfaction must be achieved at a given level of the hierarchy before the next higher needs become prominent in a person's life.

Contributions

Vastly Increased Domain in Psychology.   Maslow took a position essentially opposite Freud's. In discussing Freud, we pondered a view of humans as animals in conflict with a society that imposes restrictions on their animal impulses. When we considered Maslow, we pondered a view of humans as basically good, nonaggressive seekers of such things as truth, beauty, and perfection. For Freud, given complete freedom, humans would become sexually promiscuous and aggressive. For Maslow, given complete freedom, humans would create Eupsychia, a loving, harmonious, and nonaggressive society. The views of human nature held by Freud and Maslow are about as different as two views of human nature can be.

There is no doubt that Maslow's contention that psychology had traditionally focused on the darker side of human nature was valid. Of course, there have been theorists whose works have been exceptions to this; for example, Adler, Allport, Bandura, Mischel, Rogers, and Kelly. In general, however, psychology has been preoccupied with either the importance of the physiological drives in determining behavior or the conditions under which neuroses and psychoses develop. Maslow did about as much as one person could have done to extend the domain of psychology to the study of healthy humans. His efforts, along with those of other theorists such as Rogers, have indeed created a viable third force in psychology.

Applied Value.   In addition to its impact on psychology, Maslow's theory has been highly influential in the areas of education, business, religion, and child rearing.

We conclude this chapter with the last entry that Maslow made in his diary before he died. The entry, dated 7 May, 1970, attempts to explain why he was willing to take so many unpopular positions and what he was attempting to accomplish in his life.

> Somebody asked me the question . . . How did a timid youngster get transformed into a (seemingly) "courageous" leader and spokesman? How come I was willing to talk up, to take unpopular positions, while most others didn't? My immediate tendency was to say: "Intelligence—just realistic seeing of the facts," but I held that answer back because—alone—it's wrong. "Good will, compassion *and* intelligence," I finally answered. I think I added that I'd simply *learned* a lot from my self-actualizing subjects and from their way of life and from their metamotivations, which have now become *mine*. So I respond emotionally to the injustice, the meanness, the lies, the untruths, the hatred and violence, the simplistic answers. . . . So I feel cheap and guilty and unmanly when I *don't* talk up. So then, in a sense, *I have to.*
>
>   What the kids *and* the intellectuals—and everybody else too—need is an ethos, a scientific value system and way of life and humanistic politics, *with* the

theory, the facts, etc., all set forth soberly. . . . So *again* I must say to myself: to work! (Lowry 1979, Vol. II, 1309)

Summary

Maslow survived the many negative experiences of his early years by taking refuge in books. He claimed that his life did not really begin until he married and moved to the University of Wisconsin.

Maslow's early research on dominance in monkeys led to research on dominance in humans and then finally to an interest in "the good specimen" or actualizing humans. His interest in the latter was stimulated by his efforts to understand two individuals whom he admired very much, Ruth Benedict and Max Wertheimer. He was distressed that his training in psychology had not equipped him to understand truly healthy, well-adjusted individuals. He concluded that the reason for this was that psychology had been preoccupied with either the study of lower animals, children, or maladjusted adults. Psychology also had borrowed the reductive-analytic approach from the natural sciences. This approach attempts to understand things by breaking them down into small elements. When applied to the study of humans, this technique is desacralizing, because it denies or distorts many positive human qualities. Instead, Maslow suggested a holistic-analytic approach that studies the total person. Such an approach is humanistic because it emphasizes the positive qualities of humans. Humanistic psychology is also called "third force" psychology, because it is seen as an alternative to the psycholanalytic and behavioristic models of man. Maslow had no argument with the psychoanalysts or the behaviorists; he just felt that they did not tell the whole story. He thought that humans had several positive attributes that had been ignored by psychology.

Human nature, according to Maslow, consists of a number of instinctoidal (innate but weak) needs that are arranged in a hierarchy according to their potency. The nature of these needs is such that as one group of needs is satisfied, the next group in the hierarchy comes to dominate a person's life until they too are satisfied, at which time the next group becomes dominant, and so on. The needs from the most basic to the least basic are physiological needs, safety needs, belongingness and love needs, esteem needs, and the need for self-actualization.

Self-actualizing people are no longer motivated by deficiencies (D-motivation); they are motivated by being values (B-motivation). B-values include such things as truth, goodness, beauty, justice, and perfection. B-values are also called metamotives. D-motivated people search for specific need-related events in their environment; this is called D-perception (or D-cognition) because it is need-motivated. B-motivated people perceive their environments more fully, because they are not looking for anything in particular; this is called B-perception (or B-cognition). Failure to give expression to a B-value results in a metapathology.

Maslow attempted to correct the fact that psychology had concentrated too much on unhealthy humans by studying the characteristics of the healthiest individuals he could find. Some of these people were his friends, some were famous living people, and some were famous historical figures. He found that self-actualizing people tended to have in common the following characteristics: They perceive reality accurately; show great acceptance of themselves, others, and nature; are spontaneous; are problem-oriented rather than self-oriented; tend to be detached and private; are autonomous; exhibit continued freshness of appreciation; have peak experiences; identify with all of humanity; have only a few, deep friendships; accept democratic values; have a strong ethical sense; have a well-developed sense of humor that is not hostile; are creative; and tend to be nonconformists. In addition to these positive qualities, self-actualizers also show some negative qualities, such as vanity, pride, partiality, silliness, temper outbursts, and a coldness toward death.

Although the tendency toward actualization was thought by Maslow to be innate, it is not universally experienced, because the need is so weak that it is easily impeded; it takes considerable courage to be self-actualized (this fear of self-development is called the Jonah complex); cultural norms are often incompatible with the self-actualizing process; and early childhood experiences must instill enough security in the child so that he or she is willing to grow rather than constantly seeking safety, but such childhood experiences are uncommon.

Maslow described a utopian society that he speculated a group of healthy people might design. He called this society Eupsychia. He thought that there would be complete synergy, or working together, in Eupsychia because all human needs would be recognized, respected, and gratified. When an industry attempts to consider human needs, as Maslow defined them, the process is known as Eupsychian management.

In his later years, Maslow contributed to the development of an ashram in California, which came to be called the Esalen Institute. An ashram is a place where already healthy individuals can fully explore themselves and thus revitalize their lives. There are now several hundred of these centers for personal growth in the Western world.

Also later in his life, Maslow became interested in transpersonal or fourth force psychology. Such psychology examines the human relationship to the cosmos and the various emotional experiences that an awareness of such a relationship creates.

The *Personal Orientation Inventory* has been used successfully to determine the extent to which individuals are self-actualized. Other research has supported Maslow's notion of the hierarchy of needs and of peak experiences. Maslow's theory has been criticized for having too many exceptions to its predictions, being unscientific, being overly optimistic about human nature, and leaving too many important questions unanswered. His theory has been praised for vastly increasing psychology's domain and having substantial applied value.

EXPERIENTIAL EXERCISES

1. At what level of Maslow's hierarchy of needs do you think you are currently operating? Justify your answer.

2. Evaluate your personality in terms of the fifteen characteristics of the self-actualizing person. Indicate which of the fifteen characteristics you possess to some degree and which you do not. If you do not possess all fifteen characteristics, would you like to? Explain.

3. Review Maslow's distinction between D-love and B-love and then evaluate a loving relationship that you have had, or are having, in light of that distinction.

4. As part of his research on peak experiences,

Maslow (1968) gave 190 college students the following instructions:

> I would like you to think of the most wonderful experience or experiences of your life; happiest moments, ecstatic moments, moments of rapture, perhaps from being in love, or from listening to music or suddenly "being hit" by a book or a painting, or from some great creative moment. First list these. And then try to tell me how you feel in such acute moments, how you feel differently from the way you feel at other times, how you are at the moment a different person in some ways. (71)

Respond to Maslow's instructions by listing a peak experience or two and then discussing the significance of such experiences in your life.

5. Respond to Maslow's utopian society (Eupsychia). Which aspects of this society do you agree with and which ones do you disagree with? Do you believe that such a society is even theoretically possible? Explain.

DISCUSSION QUESTIONS

1. Describe the evolution of Maslow's research from monkeys to self-actualizing humans.
2. What is "third-force" psychology? Why did Maslow feel that this "third force" was needed? Include in your answer the difference between the reductive-analytic approach to science and the holistic-analytic approach. Also discuss the term desacralization.
3. Discuss the hierarchy of needs. Which needs are included and how are they related to one another?
4. Differentiate between deficiency motivation (D-motivation) and being motivation (B-motivation).
5. What causes a metapathology? Give an example.
6. List the positive characteristics of self-actualizing people.
7. List the negative characteristics of self-actualizing people.
8. Discuss peak experiences. What are they, who has them, and what consequence do they have?
9. If the tendency toward self-actualization is innate, why is it that self-actualization is not universal?
10. Discuss Eupsychia and synergy.
11. Discuss Eupsychian management.
12. Discuss ashrams and Maslow's involvement in them.
13. Summarize the criticisms of Maslow's theory.
14. Summarize the contributions of Maslow's theory.
15. Compare Maslow's view of human nature with Freud's.
16. Give an example of how Maslow's theory might be used to improve our public-school system.
17. Explain how Maslow's theory might be used as a guide to child rearing.
18. Why did Maslow refer to human needs as instinctoid?

SUGGESTIONS FOR FURTHER READING

CHIANG, H., and MASLOW, A. H. (Eds.). (1977). *The Healthy Personality* (2d ed.). New York: D. Van Nostrand.
    An extremely interesting collection of readings in humanistic psychology including those authored by Allport, Rogers, Maslow, May, Alan Watts, Aldous Huxley, and Albert Schweitzer. The book includes a verbatim report of a workshop on self-knowledge conducted by Maslow.

HOFFMAN, E. (1988). *The Right to be Human: A Biography of Abraham Maslow*. Los Angeles: Tarcher.

A very interesting and readable biography of Maslow.

LOWRY, R. (Ed.). (1979). *The Journals of Abraham Maslow* (2 vols.). Monterey, CA: Brooks/Cole.

Beginning in 1959 and continuing until a month before his death, Maslow recorded his thoughts, opinions, and feelings. Included in these diaries are his social activities, important conversations, and concerns about his health.

MASLOW, A. H. (1964). *Religions, Values and Peak Experiences*. Columbus, OH: Ohio State University Press.

Maslow proposed that values and religious experience can be, and should be, studied scientifically. He believed that a better understanding of the need for spiritual expression could be obtained by scientifically studying peak or religious experiences.

MASLOW, A. H. (1966). *The Psychology of Science: A Reconnaissance*. New York: Harper & Row.

Maslow criticizes the use of the traditional scientific method in studying humans. Such methods have as their goal the prediction and control of behavior. Maslow argues for a more humanistic science, one capable of studying and understanding the many mysteries of human existence. Maslow argues for a Taoistic science that is noninterfering, passive, and receptive.

MASLOW, A. H. (1968). *Toward A Psychology of Being*. New York: Van Nostrand Reinhold.

Maslow presents some of his basic ideas. For example, the difference between deficiency and growth motivation, peak experiences, and creativity in self-actualizing people.

MASLOW, A. H. (1971). *The Farther Reaches of Human Nature*. New York: Viking.

In this interesting book, Maslow comments on such topics as: Self-actualizing and beyond, fusion of facts and values, notes on innocent cognition, various meanings of transcendence, and religions, values, and peak experiences.

MASLOW, A. H. (1987). *Motivation and Personality* (3d ed.). New York: Harper & Row.

This is probably Maslow's most important book. In it he discusses the hierarchy of needs, the characteristics of self-actualizing people, love in self-actualizing people, and suggested methodologies for a human science. This edition was under the editorship of Frager, Fadiman, McReynolds, and Cox, and sections on "The Influence of Abraham Maslow" and "The Rich Harvest of Abraham Maslow" have been added.

GLOSSARY

Acceptance of democratic values. Characterizes the self-actualizing person.

Acceptance of self, others, and nature. Characterizes the self-actualizing person.

Accurate and full perception of reality. Characterizes the self-actualizing person.

Aesthetic needs. The innate need for such qualities as symmetry, closure, and order, seen most clearly in children and in self-actualizing adults.

Ashrams. Retreats in India where ordinary citizens can go for various periods of time and search themselves and the meaning of their lives.

B-cognition. See being cognition.

Being cognition. (Also called B-perception or B-cognition.) Thinking or perceiving that is governed by B-values rather than by D-motives. Such cognition is richer and fuller than D-cognition.

Being motivation. Motivation that is governed by the pursuit of B-values instead of by the satisfaction of basic deficiencies. See also being values. Also called growth motivation.

Being values (B-values). Those higher aspects of life pursued by self-actualizing individuals. Included are such values as truth, goodness, beauty, justice, and perfection. Also called metamotives.

Belongingness and love needs. The third cluster of needs in the hierarchy of needs. Included are the needs for affiliation with others and for the feeling of being loved.

B-perception. See being cognition.

Continued freshness of appreciation. Characterizes the self-actualizing person.

Creativity. Characterizes the self-actualizing person.

D-cognition. See need-directed perception.

Deep friendships with only a few people. Characterizes the self-actualizing person.

Deficiency motivation (D-motivation). Motivation that is governed by the basic needs. Characterizes the lives of individuals who are not self-actualizing.

Deficiency motive (D-motive). Any need or deficiency that exists in the hierarchy of needs prior to the level of self-actualization.

Desacralization. Any process that distorts human nature and makes it less marvelous and dignified than it is.

Desire to know and understand. Innate curiosity that Maslow felt was functionally related to the ability to satisfy the basic needs.

Detachment and a need for privacy. Characterizes the self-actualizing person.

D-perception. See need-directed perception.

Esalen Institute. An institute in California modeled after the Indian ashram in that it is a place where nonneurotic, healthy people can go and further develop their inner resources.

Esteem needs. The fourth cluster of needs in the hierarchy of needs. Included are the needs for status, prestige, competence, and confidence.

Eupsychia. Maslow's name for the utopia that he felt a community of healthy adults could create.

Eupsychian management. Industrial or societal management that attempts to consider the basic human needs as Maslow saw them.

Fourth-force psychology. See transpersonal psychology.

Freedom within limits. Maslow's description of what he considered the optimal psychological atmosphere for a child to experience.

Growth center. The Western equivalent of the Indian ashram. A place where nonneurotic, healthy individuals can go to expand their potentialities. See also Esalen Institute.

Growth motivation. See being motivation.

Guru. The spiritual leader of an ashram.

Hierarchy of needs. The arrangement of the needs from lowest to highest in terms of their potency.

Holistic-analytic approach to science. The strategy of studying an object of interest as a totality rather than attempting to reduce it to its component parts.

Humanistic psychology. An approach to psychology that emphasizes the experiencing person, creativity, the study of socially and personally significant problems, and the dignity and enhancement of people.

Identification with all of humanity. Characterizes the self-actualizing person.

Independence from the environment and culture. Characterizes the self-actualizing person.

Instinctoid. The term Maslow used to describe the nature of the human needs. An instinctoidal need is innate but weak and easily modified by environmental conditions.

Jonah complex. The fear of and doubt about one's own abilities and potentialities, which result in a resistance to personal growth.

Metamotives. See Being values.

Metapathology. A psychological disorder that results when a being motive is not allowed proper expression.

Need-Directed perception (also called D-perception or D-cognition). Perception that is motivated by a search for objects or events that will fulfill a basic need; for example, a hungry person looks for food.

Nonconformity. Characterizes the self-actualizing person.

Peak experience. A mystical, oceanic experience that is accompanied by a feeling of ecstasy or rapture. Such experiences were thought by Maslow to reach their full magnitude as B-values are fully embraced.

Physiological needs. The most basic cluster of needs in the hierarchy of needs. Included are the needs for water, food, oxygen, sleep, elimination, and sex.

Problem-oriented rather than self-oriented. Characterizes the self-actualizing person.

Reductive-analytic approach to science. The strategy of reducing an object of interest to its component parts in order to study and understand it.

Safety needs. The second cluster of needs in the hierarchy of needs. Included is the need for order, security, and predictability.

Self-Actualization. The highest level in the hierarchy of needs, which can be reached only if the preceding need levels have been adequately satisfied. The self-actualizing individual operates at full capacity and is B-motivated rather than D-motivated.

Sense of humor that is unhostile. Characterizes the self-actualizing person.

Spontaneity, simplicity, and naturalness. Characterize the self-actualizing person.

Strong ethical sense. Characterizes the self-actualizing person.

Synergy. Working together. The individuals in a community characterized by synergy would work in harmony and would not be in conflict with their society.

Third-force psychology. Humanistic psychology, which was seen by Maslow and others as an alternative to psychoanalysis and behaviorism.

Transpersonal psychology. (Also called fourth-force psychology.) Psychology that examines the human relationship to the cosmos or to something "bigger than we are" and the mystical, spiritual, or peak experiences that the realization of such a relationship produces.

16

Rollo Reese May

■ **CHAPTER OUTLINE**

Although the theories of Kelly, Rogers, and Maslow have a clear existential orientation, in that they are concerned with the meaning of human life, it is May's theory that is most compatible with existential philosophy. In fact, May has been as responsible as anyone for incorporating European existential philosophy into American psychology.

Biographical Sketch

Rollo May was born in Ada, Ohio on 21 April 1909, and grew up in Marine City, Michigan. He obtained his B.A. degree from Oberlin College in Ohio in 1930; his B.D. from Union Theological Seminary in New York in 1938; and his Ph.D. in clinical psychology from Columbia University in New York in 1949.

Following graduation from Oberlin College, May pursued his interest in art by roaming through Europe with a group of artists. He remained in Europe from 1930 to 1933, and during that time, in addition to studying art, he taught at an American college in Greece and took summer-school classes from Alfred Adler.

In 1934, May returned to the United States and enrolled in the Union Theological Seminary—not, May says, to become a preacher but to study the basic questions related to human existence. It was at this time that May met Paul Tillich, the existentialist philosopher, who was a recent refugee from Germany and a faculty member at the seminary. Tillich became May's lifelong friend, and in 1973 May wrote *Paulus: Reminiscences of a Friendship* as a tribute to Tillich, who died in 1966. It was through Tillich that May was exposed to existential thought, although he had already concluded, after his exposure to Adler's thinking, that he could never accept a mechanistic, deterministic view of humans. May, then, was ready for the existential view of humans, and he embraced that view enthusiastically.

May's first book was *The Art of Counseling* (1939), and his second was *The Springs of Creative Living: A Study of Human Nature and God* (1940). Both books were religiously oriented, but neither endorsed blind obedience to religious dogma. May considered religions that required blind acceptance of dogma to be unsound and unhealthy. Healthy religion allows for creative living, which May defines as follows (1940).

> Creative living is that attitude . . . which welcomes each day with calm enthusiasm instead of melancholy boredom. It is that state of soul by which one can work with success and satisfaction and occasionally a little joy, can love and move through love into a happy marriage and then enjoy the simple pleasures of a family. The creative person can affirm life in its three dimensions—affirm himself, affirm his fellow-men and affirm his destiny. To him life has meaning. He is warmed by the friendship of his fellows and cheered by the confidence that he is of worth to them. Love can be supreme pleasure to him precisely because it is more than pleasure. His work can be satisfying precisely because it is part of a creative purpose larger than any particular work. All of which means that life's fundamental question receives a positive answer: the person has confidence in meaning in his destiny. (19)

Rollo Reese May

Also in this early book, May indicates his belief in the compatibility of psychoanalysis and the realm of human values, a belief that May has retained to this day.

It is in this aiding of people to find meaning for their lives that religion and depth-psychology [another term for psychoanalytic theory] are in partnership. The field of meaning in life is essentially the religious area, but the technique of discovering why persons fail to find meaning—why they suffer hindrances, complexes, irrational fears—is the modern contribution of depth-psychology. (19)

May, from the beginning, thought that Freud had made a significant contribution to the understanding of humans. Freud, like the existentialists, attempted to free humans from illusions about themselves, and both attempted to bring the irrational elements of human existence under rational control. May, however, disagreed with Freud's contentions that anxiety results from conflict, guilt results from the violation of internalized values, and the unconscious is a storehouse of repressed experiences. We shall review May's analyses of these concepts elsewhere in this chapter.

Contrasted with unhealthy religion, true, healthy religion is defined as follows (1940). "Call it confidence in the universe, trust in God, belief in one's fellow-men, or what not, the essence of religion is the belief that something matters—the *presupposition that life has meaning.*" (19–20)

So, in general, the religious person is one who has found meaning in life, and an *atheist* is one who cannot, or has not, found it. May (1940) gives a description of a college student who described himself as a "complete atheist."

> [The student] went on in the next breath to assure me that life was a terribly boring affair and that the only relief he could find from the monotony of existence was getting drunk and using women as his playthings. He was intelligent and widely read, but he looked forward to no vocation; he was on the flunking line in his college courses, and was so unhappy that his physical health was suffering. Friendship had no meaning for him, he stated, and since women were useful only as sources of sensuous pleasure, there was no point in falling in love.
>
> This is a vivid picture of the general neurotic attitude toward life. The young man could not affirm himself; hence the drunkenness, which he practiced several times a week as a lift from the depths of meaninglessness. He could not affirm his fellow-men; hence friendship was a bankrupt business and women were chiefly prostitutes. He could not affirm his human world; hence no vocation to prepare for and no feeling of the worth of his energies. And finally, he could not affirm his destiny; the total scheme of things was senseless, and hence he must state himself to be an atheist. This is a life without purpose and meaning. It is the kind of life in which atheism and neurotic tendencies are so intertwined that one is inclined to suspect that at bottom they may be the same thing.
>
> Let us say immediately that we are defining atheism here as a denial of meaning in life. . . . (29–30)

May goes on to say the following (1940).

> Denying the worth of other people, one cannot love with joy; denying purposiveness in the world, one cannot work with gratification; and denying meaning in the total scheme of things, one cannot face one's own destiny with courage. True atheism is a drying up of the springs of life, and the individual must increasingly stagnate until he breaks in a neurotic crisis. His atheism will not be met by religious preaching, but rather by understanding the reasons why he now distrusts his fellow-men, cannot fall in love, and has no satisfactory vocation, and particularly the reason why he regards the whole scheme of life as set against him. (31–32)

Although these early comments do not yet contain the formal terminology of existential philosophy, the emphasis on meaning, the future, the individual, courage, and interpersonal harmony is clearly compatible with that philosophy and shows May's predisposition toward it.

In the 1940s, May studied psychoanalysis at the William Alanson White Institute of Psychiatry, Psychoanalysis, and Psychology in New York. May remained affiliated with the institute in a variety of capacities for many years. May became a practicing psychoanalyst in 1946, and it was about this time that he contracted tuberculosis and lived for a few years in a sanitorium in upstate New York. His close brush with death had a profound influence on his thinking and brought him still closer to existential philosophy.

During his illness, May read both Kierkegaard's and Freud's analyses of anxiety. Soren Kierkegaard (1813–1855) was a Danish theologian and philosopher, who rejected the attempts of other philosophers to view humans as totally rational and logical. He viewed humans as largely emotional and as free to choose their own destinies. Although May agreed with Freud on many points, he agreed more with Kierkegaard's conclusion that anxiety results from a threat to one's existence. This definition of anxiety has become a focal point in May's theory and therefore will be elaborated later in this chapter. May's analysis of anxiety was submitted to Columbia University as his Ph.D. dissertation and was ultimately published as *The Meaning of Anxiety* (1950). In 1949 May was granted the first Ph.D. in clinical psychology ever awarded by Columbia University. The following is a list of May's major books.

Man's Search for Himself (1953)

Existence: A New Dimension in Psychiatry and Psychology (coedited with Ernest Angel and Henri Ellenberger) (1958)

Existential Psychology (ed.) (1961)

Psychology and the Human Dilemma (1967)

Love and Will (1969)—winner of the Ralph Waldo Emerson award, given by Phi Beta Kappa

Power and Innocence: A Search for the Sources of Violence (1972)

The Courage to Create (1975)

Freedom and Destiny (1981)

The Discovery of Being: Writings in Existential Psychology (1983)

Almost from the beginning, May's writings have described humans as free and responsible. Also, he has contended that as self-awareness expands, so does one's personal freedom. To expand his own awareness, May has read and experienced widely, and this fact is evident in his work. Clement Reeves concludes his book *The Psychology of Rollo May* (1977) with the following statement.

The work of a man of wide reading and of broad, interdisciplinary interests, May's writings abound with allusions to and illustrations from art and literature, both ancient and modern, and with references to psychological and psychoanalytic work. His preferences seem to be those artists and authors who offer a direct insight into man's contemporary predicament and into the psychological and cultural pressures of modern living. He cites Sophocles, Aeschylus, Auden, Eliot, and Ibsen, for example. He sees illustrations of the tragic, destructive side of human existence in Picasso and sends the reader to study form and space in the paintings of Cézanne. He shows that he is all the while concerned that readers, in particular those involved in psychological studies or therapy, should try to see deeply into the meaning, richness, and breadth of human beings into what it is that responsible human becoming is at its best and most creative. (261–62)

Existentialism

As we have seen, elements of existential philosophy were in several of the theories we have reviewed—for instance, in those of Adler, Allport, Bandura and Mischel, Kelly, Rogers, and Maslow. It is May's theory, however, that has the most in common with existential philosophy. Therefore, to review the major concepts of existentialism is also to review much of May's theory of personality. The concepts and terms that follow have come from various sources, including the writings of such great existential thinkers as Kierkegaard, Nietzsche, Heidegger, Jaspers, Sartre, Camus, and Tillich.

Dasein

Dasein literally means to be there (*Da* = there; *sein* = to be). This term indicates that the focus of interest for the existentialist is a particular person experiencing and interpreting the world at a particular time in a particular place. It is the study of a person as a being-in-the-world. The world and the person exist simultaneously and cannot be separated.

Three Modes of Existence

Many existential writers divide human existence into three categories: the **umwelt,** which means the physical aspects of the internal and external environments; the **mitwelt,** which is the realm of interpersonal relationships; and the **eigenwelt,** which consists of a person's own consciousness. Each person is thought to live in all three worlds simultaneously, and only the three worlds taken together give a full account of human existence.

Freedom

The most important human attribute, and the attribute that makes humans unique, is freedom of choice. **Freedom** exists only as a potentiality, however, and can be underdeveloped in some people, or even denied. One increases freedom by expanding consciousness. It is through freedom of choice that the person can transcend his or her immediate circumstances, so no human needs to be a victim of environment, genetics, early experiences, or anything else. In the words of Sartre, "We are what we choose to be."

Responsibility

Because "We are what we choose to be" we must assume full **responsibility** for what we become. No other person(s), circumstances, or fate can be praised or blamed for the nature of our existence; we alone are responsible.

Ontology

Literally the study of being. The ontologist attempts to describe the core of human existence, to discover what it is that makes humans human. The existentialists are ontologists.

Phenomenology

The existentialists all use the person's own consciousness as their subject matter. Awareness of all kinds is analyzed—for instance, awareness of the external world, awareness of bodily events, and awareness of awareness. It is generally assumed by the existentialists that humans are the only animals that are aware and know that they are aware. Furthermore, consciousness is studied as an intact, meaningful phenomenon, and is not divided or compartmentalized for further study.

Authenticity

If a person exercises his or her free will to expand consciousness further, to establish values that minimize anxiety and provide positive relationships with fellow humans, and to create the challenges necessary for further personal growth, then he or she is living an authentic life. If, however, a person lives in accordance with someone else's values and does not exercise his or her free will to enhance personal growth and effective living, the person is said to be living an inauthentic life. Living an authentic life necessarily involves risk, and therefore such a life takes **courage**— thus, the title of Paul Tillich's book *The Courage To Be* (1952).

Death

Most existentialists emphasize the importance of the fact that humans are aware that they must someday die. **Death** represents nothingness and is the polar opposite of the rich, full, creative life. It therefore represents the opposite of what most existentialists are urging people to become. No one can escape this dichotomy: We seek a full life, but at the same time we are aware that we must die. The knowledge of our mortality causes anxiety, but this anxiety need not be negative; it can be (and should be) used to motivate people to get as much out of life as they can in the time available to them. Furthermore, death is not seen as an all-or-nothing phenomenon. People can die symbolically, by degrees, each time one of their established values is threatened. Such a threat is perceived as an attack on one's existence, and therefore it too causes anxiety.

Thrownness

Thrownness (also called facticity and ground of existence) refers to the facts that characterize a person's existence over which he or she has no control. Examples include being born male or female, short or tall, attractive or unattractive, financially rich or poor, American or Russian, or during peace or wartime. It is the familial, historical, and cultural conditions into which one is born that, to a large extent, constitute the *da* of *dasein*. It is thrownness that determines the conditions under which we exercise our personal freedom. That is, some facts characterizing our existence are impossible for us to control; how we interpret, value, and act on those facts, however, is a matter of personal choice.

All of the foregoing terms and concepts are found in May's theory of personality. Next, we will turn to some of May's more specific applications of existential philosophy to psychology.

Human Dilemma

May (1967) states that the **human dilemma** is the fact that humans are capable of viewing themselves as both subject and object at the same time. May has described the **object-subject dichotomy** in various ways, which have not always been consistent (see Reeves 1977, 198–201). In general, however, May says that humans are capable of seeing themselves as an object to which things happen. For example, as people, we are influenced by the physical environment, the presence or absence of other people, genetics (we are tall, short, male, female, light-skinned, dark-skinned, and so on), and by social or cultural variables. These objective events that influence us are those things that deterministically oriented theories stress as the causes of behavior. That is, because we are stimulated in certain ways, we respond in certain ways. As subjects, however, we are aware of the fact that these things are happening to us. We perceive, ponder, and act on this information. We determine which experiences are valuable and which are not, and then act according to these personal formulations.

May says that **self-relatedness** is what distinguishes humans from the rest of nature. It is "man's capacity to stand outside himself, to know he is the subject as well as the object of experience, to see himself as the entity who is acting in the world of objects" (1967, 75). As humans, we view the world, and we can view ourselves viewing. It is this self-relatedness, or consciousness of self, that allows humans to escape determinism and have some say in what they do. "Consciousness of self gives us the power to stand outside the rigid chain of stimulus and response, to pause, and by this pause to throw some weight on either side, to cast some decision about what the response will be" (May 1953, 161).

Here we have the concept of dasein in May's theory. "Being there" is to be understood as a being who is there. The "there" is whatever deterministic forces are present in a given situation, whereas the being (the person) brings to bear on these forces his or her own freedom, values, interpretations, and so forth. For May, then, both ends of the dichotomy need to be taken into consideration to reach a full understanding of a person—that is, both one's physical circumstances (the objective part) and how one subjectively structures and values those circumstances (the subjective part).

May believes that it is a mistake to stress one pole of the object-subject dichotomy at the expense of the other pole. "Curiously enough, both these alternatives—being purely free and purely determined—amount to the same kind of playing God in the respect that we arrogantly refuse to accept the dilemma which is our fate and our great potentiality as humans" (May 1967, 9).

May thinks that Skinner and Rogers represent two psychologists who emphasize one side of the dilemma at the expense of the other. Skinner avoids subjective experience, but May asks: "Is it not a fact that people *do* react to an inner experience of their environment, *do* see their environment in terms of their past experiences, and *do* interpret it in terms of their own symbols, hopes and fears?" (May 1967, 15).

May criticizes Rogers for both his emphasis on subjectivity and for omitting from his analysis the negative components of human existence, such as the emotions of anger, aggression, hostility, and rage. "We need, therefore, to put the question, Does not Rogers' emphasis on rationality, and his belief that the individual will simply choose what is *rational* for him, leave out a large section of the spectrum of human experience, namely, all the *irrational* feelings?" (May 1967, 18).

As we shall see when we discuss the daimonic later in this chapter, May believes that the potential for evil is part of human nature and must be taken into consideration in fully understanding humans.

Intentionality

In *Love and Will* (1969), May speaks of **intentionality** as the means by which the dichotomy between subject and object is partially overcome. Intentionality is the human tendency to selectively perceive and to assign meaning to objects and events in the world. Once a structure of meaning has been developed, we respond to specific experiences in terms of it. Thus, an experience is responded to with joy, fear, or indifference, for example, depending on the structure of meaning that a person has constructed. Likewise, the same environmental event will be responded to differently depending on what meaning is assigned to it under the circumstances. May (1969) gives the following example:

> First, what does the term mean? We shall define it [intentionality] in two stages; the preliminary stage is the fact that our intentions are decisive with respect to how we perceive the world. This afternoon, for instance, I go up to see a house in the mountains. Suppose, first, that I am looking for a place which some friends can rent for the summer months. When I approach the house, I shall question whether it is sound and well-built, gets enough sun, and other things having the meaning of "shelter" to me. Or suppose I am a real-estate speculator: then what will strike me will be how easily the house can be fixed up, whether it will bring a price attractively higher than what I shall have to pay for it, and other things meaning "profit." Or let us say that it is the house of friends I am visiting: then I shall look at it with eyes which see it as "hospitality,"—its open patio and easy chairs which will make our afternoon talk more pleasant. Or, if this is a cocktail party at the house of friends who have snubbed me at a party at my house, I find myself seeing things that indicate that anyone would prefer my cottage to theirs, and other aspects of the invidious envy and "social status" for which we human beings are notorious. Or, finally, if this afternoon I am outfitted with my watercolor materials and bent on doing a sketch, I shall see how the house clings to the side of the mountain, the patterns of the lines of the roof leading up to the peaks above and sweeping away into the valley below, and, indeed, how I even prefer the house ramshackle and run down for the greater artistic possibilities this gives me.
>
> In each one of these five instances, it is the same house that provides the stimulus, and I am the same man responding to it. But in each case, the house and experience have an entirely different meaning.

But this is only one side of intentionality. The other side is that it also does come from the object. Intentionality is the bridge between these. It is the structure of meaning which makes it possible for us, subjects that we are, to see and understand the outside world, objective as it is. In intentionality, the dichotomy between subject and object is partially overcome. (224–25)

Thus, for May, intentionality elaborates an important aspect of *dasein*. As beings-in-the-world, our interactions with the physical world are highly personal and dynamic. Each person responds to the world in terms of his or her personal structure of meaning (for example, beliefs, values, and expectations). It is this structure of meaning that provides intentionality, which can be interpreted as the general human ability to form intentions (that is, goals, aspirations, and purposes). It is these intentions that influence how we perceive, interpret, and act on events in the world.

Will and wish are closely related to intentionality. May defines **will** as "The capacity to organize oneself so that movement in a certain direction or toward a certain goal may take place" (1969, 218). He defines **wish** as "The imaginative playing with the possibility of some act or state occurring" (1969, 218). Thus, given a person's structure of meaning, he or she will use his or her imagination to ponder several possible future courses of action. It is this wishing that provides vitality, imagination, and innovation to the personality. From the many possible courses of action the person chooses those that are possible and most meaningful, and organizes his or her life so that the chosen goals can be attained (will).

Intentionality, wish, and will are three of the most important concepts in May's theory, because they relate to several other human attributes. Reeves (1977) says: "It is, then, asserts May, in intentionality and will, in the broad reach of human orientation toward meaning, decision, and act, in the weighing, deciding, and acting on possibilities sensed, that the individual person experiences his identity, exercises his freedom, and senses his being" (158).

Anxiety and Guilt

Most existential thinkers assume that the experience of **anxiety** is part of the human condition, and May is no exception.

While living in a sanitorium because of his tuberculosis, May studied the works of Kierkegaard (*The Concept of Anxiety*, 1844) and Freud on anxiety. May rejected Freud's interpretation of anxiety as resulting from a conflict between one's biologic needs and the demands of society. For May, Freud's analysis of anxiety was too biologic and compartmentalized. That is, for Freud, some anxiety was seen as related to the id, superego, and ego.

Instead of accepting Freud's complex and ultimately biologic explanation of anxiety, May accepted Kierkegaard's existential definition. For Kierkegaard, human freedom and anxiety go hand in hand. When freedom is threatened, as it always is, anxiety results.

The distinctive quality of human anxiety arises from the fact that man is the valuing animal, the being who interprets his life and world in terms of symbols and meanings, and identifies these with his existence as a self. . . . It is the threat to these values that causes anxiety. Indeed, I define anxiety as *the apprehension cued off by a threat to some value which the individual holds essential to his existence as a self.* The threat may be to physical life itself, i.e., death; or to psychological life, i.e., loss of freedom. Or it may be to some value the person identifies with his existence as a self: patriotism, the love of a special person, prestige among one's peers, devotion to scientific truth or to religious belief. (May 1967, 72)

May points out that it is a uniquely human characteristic that we sometimes prefer death to the giving up of a cherished value.

Death is the most obvious threat cueing off anxiety, for unless one holds beliefs in immortality, which is not common for our culture, death stands for the ultimate blotting out of one's existence as a self. But immediately we note a very curious fact: some people *prefer to die rather than to surrender some other value.* The taking away of psychological and spiritual freedom was not infrequently a greater threat than death itself to persons under the dictatorships of Europe. "Give me liberty or give me death" is not necessarily histrionic or evidence of a neurotic attitude. Indeed, there is a reason for believing . . . that it may represent the most mature form of *distinctively human* behavior. (May 1967, 73)

Normal Anxiety

To grow as a person, one must constantly challenge one's structure of meaning, which is the core of one's existence, and this necessarily causes anxiety. Thus, to be human is to have the urge to expand one's awareness, but to do so causes anxiety. Such anxiety is not only inescapable; it is normal and healthy. "All growth consists of the anxiety-creating surrender of past values as one transforms them into broader ones. Growth, and with it normal anxiety, consists of the giving up of immediate security for the sake of more extensive goals." (May 1967, 80–81).

Normal anxiety, then, is seen as part of the growth process, and no attempt should ever be made to eliminate it from a person's experience. May strongly disagrees with those psychotherapists who have as their goal the elimination of anxiety.

Neurotic Anxiety

A certain amount of anxiety is normal, but nonetheless it is still anxiety, and some people attempt to escape from it. People who decide to conform to values arrived at by others, for example, give up their own personal freedom and the possibility for personal growth by seeking "security" in conformity. Such attempts to escape normal anxiety, which is healthy, result in **neurotic anxiety,** which is unhealthy. It is neurotic anxiety that must be dealt with by a psychotherapist. May (1967) distinguishes between normal and neurotic anxiety.

Normal anxiety is anxiety which is proportionate to the threat, does not involve repression, and can be confronted constructively on the conscious level. . . .

Neurotic anxiety, on the other hand, is a reaction which is disproportionate to the threat, involves repression and other forms of intrapsychic conflict, and is managed by various kinds of blocking-off of activity and awareness. The anxiety connected with the "loneliness at the top" and the "loneliness of the long distance runner" which the movies tell us about can be seen as *normal* anxiety. The anxiety that comes from conforming, to escape this loneliness, is the *neurotic* transformation of the original, normal anxiety.

Actually, neurotic anxiety develops when a person has been unable to meet normal anxiety at the time of the actual crisis in his growth and the threat to his values. Neurotic anxiety is the end result of previously unmet normal anxiety. (80)

Normal and Neurotic Guilt

If one does not live up to his or her potentialities as a human, one feels guilty; therefore, all humans experience a certain amount of **guilt.** May refers to guilt as ontological, because it, like anxiety, is part of the human condition. Guilt, according to May, does not result from violating a generally accepted moral code; rather, it results from not approaching or striving toward one's full potential as a human. "Ontological guilt does not consist of I-am-guilty-because-I-violated-parental-prohibitions, but arises from the fact that I can see myself as the one who can choose or fail to choose. Every developed human being would have this ontological guilt" (May, Angel, and Ellenberger 1958, 55).

Normal guilt is part of a healthy existence and can be used constructively. Guilt, however, if not recognized and dealt with, can, like anxiety, become neurotic and debilitating.

A strong relationship exists between the soundness of one's values and one's ability to deal with anxiety, and it is to that relationship that we turn next.

Importance of Values

Values summarize in symbolic form those classes of experience that we have deemed especially important. Valuing some experiences more than others cannot be avoided, because the valuing process is considered part of human nature. A person's value system determines how much meaning an experience will have, how much emotionality it elicits, and what is worth aspiring to in the future. To a large extent, how much anxiety a person experiences will be determined by the adequacy of his or her value system. "A person can meet anxiety to the extent that his values are stronger than the threat" (May 1967, 51).

According to May, a developmental pattern in the formation of values exists. Following birth, the things valued most are the love, care, and nourishment, provided by the mother. Any threat to these causes the infant to experience anxiety. As the child matures, typically such matters as approval, success, and status among peers are valued. Mature values, however, are not seen as outgrowths of previously held values. Rather, they reflect basic human nature, by emphasizing freedom, the future, and the betterment of the human condition.

The criteria for mature values follow from the distinctive characteristics of the human being ... mature values are those which transcend the immediate situation in time and encompass past and future. Mature values transcend also the immediate in-group, and extend outward toward the good of the community, ideally and ultimately embracing humanity as a whole.... The more mature a man's values are, the less it matters to him whether his values are literally satisfied or not. The satisfaction and security lie in the *holding* of values. To the genuine scientist or religious person or artist, security and confidence arise from his awareness of his devotion to the *search* for truth and beauty rather than the finding of it. (May 1967, 82)

For May, the **Oedipal conflict** is not an attraction toward one parent and a feeling of hostility toward the other, as Freud had proposed. Rather, it is a struggle between dependence and independence. That is, as young children our needs for food, shelter, and safety are satisfied by our parents. We have a tendency to go on depending on them, or others, for need satisfaction even when it is no longer necessary to do so. To approximate our potential as humans, we must give up the dependence that we value in our early years. This is not easy to do, and yet it is a prerequisite for positive growth.

When conditions remain stable for a long period of time, it is possible for people to develop values that are effective in dealing with the world and also in manifesting themselves as human beings. It is even possible for many people to hold more or less the same values. This was the case in America's pioneer days, when individualism and pragmatism were widely accepted.

In our modern world, however, conditions have changed so rapidly that we have not had time to evolve values that are adequate for coping with modern life. "In a period of transition, when old values are empty and traditional mores no longer viable, the individual experiences a particular difficulty in finding himself in his world" (May 1967, 25).

When we do not have values with which to embrace the world, we lose our sense of identity, worth, and significance. "Is not one of the central problems of modern Western man that he experiences himself as without significance as an individual? Let us focus on that aspect of his image of himself which is his doubt whether he can act and his half-aware conviction that even if he did act it would do no good" (May 1967, 25).

May contends that the "identity crisis" of the 1950s has developed into an even more serious problem.

Persons of all sorts these days, especially younger people, diagnose their trouble when they come to a counselor or therapist as an "identity crisis"—and the fact that the phrase has become trite should not lead us to overlook the fact that it may also be importantly true. ... My thesis is that the problem of identity in the 1950's has now become, more specifically, the crisis of the loss of the sense of significance. ... The feeling tends to be, "Even if I did know who I am, I couldn't make any difference as an individual anyway." (1967, 26)

According to May, people today are confronted with "mass" everything—for example, mass communication and mass education. The emphasis is on sameness, not individuality. Yet we were brought up believing in the power and worth of the individual. Thus, the values we learned as children do not fit the modern world, and therefore we feel insignificant, alone, and anxious. Without functional values, one has nothing to be committed to, and therefore one feels helpless. Without a strong value system, it is difficult, if not impossible, for a person to choose a course of action or a way of life. According to May, then, the major problem of our time is that "the younger generation . . . do not have viable values available in the culture on the basis of which they can relate to their world" (1967, 42).

In this age of transition, young people try to overcome their anxiety in several ways. One approach is to use sex as a means of gaining a sense of security. May (1967) says:

> One area in which anxiety shows itself is in sexuality and the choosing of a mate. Sex in our day is often used in the service of security: it is the readiest way to overcome your own apathy and isolation. The titillation of the sexual partner is not only an outlet for nervous tension, but demonstrates one's own significance; if a man is able to arouse such feelings in the other, he proves he is alive himself. The "going steady" . . . and the tendency toward early marriage of many students are similarly often used in the service of overcoming anxiety—"togetherness" gives at least a temporary security and sense of meaning. But togetherness easily gets empty and boring, particularly when it begins so early the young people have not given themselves the chance to develop their capacities to be interesting as partners. Sex is always something we can do when we run out of conversation. Thus going steady tends toward the meaninglessness of promiscuity, which is the substitution of *bodily intimacy* for *personal relationship*. The "body" is asked to fill the hiatus left when the "person" abdicates. And early marriage, which is the second result of using sex for security, tends toward the equally frustrating emptiness of premature commitment with the haunting possibility of a boring marital future. Both are ways of "shrinking consciousness" at the time, speaking from the viewpoint of psychophysical development, when the young person should be exploring and developing his capacity to know different members of the opposite sex, that he may eventually choose one with whom he has some possibility of a lasting and meaningful partnership.
>
> The use of sex in the service of security tends understandably to make sex increasingly *impersonal*. Indeed, the impersonal element—one must prove he can perform sexually without getting involved, without commitment—is the element investigators and writers on the problem are most concerned about. The impersonality has the effect of placing a premium on *sensation* without *sensitivity*, *intercourse* without *intimacy*, and in a strange perverse way makes the denial of feeling a preferred goal. It is exactly this loss of the feeling of being one's self in relation to one's interpersonal world that we are indicating constitutes destructive anxiety. (42–43)

Without an adequate system of values, people tend to be outer directed. That is, people with inadequate values depend on things outside of themselves to indicate their significance—for instance, social mores, peer evaluation, church dogma, teachers' opinions, and grades. Those people with strong values know they are significant independently of these external events and are therefore able to experience these things in a much different perspective. Peer approval may be valued, for example, but it is not depended on for a sense of worth. For May, as well as many other existential thinkers, values and **commitment** go hand in hand. Mature values, as we have seen, allow a person not only to deal effectively with present events, but to consider the feelings and values of others and therefore to form deep, meaningful interpersonal relationships. Also, mature values allow one to become future oriented. Such values give a person hope and therefore a reason to commit himself or herself to a course of action. A person without an adequate value system has no reason to be committed to anything. For this reason, the existentialists include commitment as an ontological human characteristic; that is, commitment characterizes every normal, healthy, mature human being.

A person's values determine how he or she acts, and because values are consciously and freely chosen, one is fully responsible for one's actions. May summarizes his views on values in the last chapter of his book *Psychology and the Human Dilemma* (1967).

> It is in the act of valuing that consciousness and behavior become united. One can take over rote values ... from the church, or the therapist, school, American Legion, or any other group in the culture. But the act of valuing, in contrast, involves a commitment on the part of the individual which goes beyond the "rote" or automatic situation. This, in turn, implies some conscious choice and responsibility. (220)

Nature of Love

May (1953) defines **love** as "a delight in the presence of the other person and an affirming of his value and development as much as one's own" (206). Massey (1981) nicely summarizes many of May's views on love.

> Love grows in proportion to the capacity for independence, for only when we can stand alone can we give ourselves and lose ourselves in ecstasy. In love, the two sexes can accentuate the characteristics of their counterparts. In the love act, the sexes can deepen consciousness in four ways: through tenderness, because of awareness of the other's needs and feelings; through affirmation of a meaningful identity; through enrichment and fulfillment of personality by being carried beyond ourselves, possibly even through procreation; and through realizing that one's own full pleasure in lovemaking flows not from releasing tension with sexual objects, but from giving to the other person. Females and males differ, and this makes at least one kind of relatedness possible. Sexual intercourse actualizes and symbolizes a universal polar rhythm of approach, entrance, union, separation and reunion, intimacy and withdrawal, touch and retreat, giving and being autonomous, participating and retiring. (462)

For May, then, love is clearly much more than biologic sex, although sex is certainly an important part of love. In his book *Love and Will* (1969), May describes four kinds of love and states that authentic love is a blending of the four. The four kinds of love are sex, eros, philia, and agapé.

Sex

Sex is one of our biologic drives, and it can be satisfied by engaging in sexual intercourse, just as eating a meal can satisfy the hunger drive. Both sexual intercourse and eating can be almost automatic activities triggered by a need and the availability of an object that will satisfy that need. "Sex can be defined fairly adequately in physiological terms as consisting of the building up of bodily tensions and their release" (May 1969, 73). Many in the modern world have equated sex with love, and, for May, this is most unfortunate.

Eros

Eros is the desire for union with another person. With sex the goal is termination, gratification, and relaxation. In contrast, we seek to continue the experience of eros.

> Eros seeks union with the other person in delight and passion, and the procreating of new dimensions of experience which broaden and deepen the being of both persons. . . . It is common experience, backed up by folklore, as well as the testimony of Freud and others, that after sexual release we tend to go to sleep—or, as the joke puts it, to get dressed, go home, and *then* go to sleep. But in eros, we want just the opposite; to stay awake thinking of the beloved, remembering, savoring, discovering ever-new facets of the prism of what the Chinese call the "many-splendored" experience. . . . It is this urge for union with the partner that is the occasion for human tenderness. For eros—not sex as such—is the source of tenderness. Eros is the longing to establish union, full relationship. . . . A sharing takes place which is a new Gestalt, a new being, a new field of magnetic force. (May 1969, 74–75)

Not only does eros cause us to seek a tender, creative relationship within the context of sexual experience, but it is also responsible for humans' seeking such a relationship with the world and with people in general. Eros is the human drive to seek wholeness or interrelatedness among all of our experiences. Seeking such feelings in a sexual relationship is but one manifestation of eros.

Eros is complicated by the existence of the **daimonic,** which May defines as:

> *Any natural function which has the power to take over the whole person.* Sex and eros, anger and rage, and the craving for power are examples. The daimonic can be either creative or destructive and is normally both. . . . The daimonic is the urge in every being to affirm itself, assert itself, perpetuate and increase itself. The daimonic becomes evil when it usurps the total personality without regard to the integration of that self, or to the unique forms and desires of others and their need for integration. It then appears as excessive aggression, hostility, cruelty—the things about ourselves which horrify us most, and which we repress whenever we can, or more likely, project on others. But these are the reverse side of the same assertion which empowers our creativity. All life is a flux between these two aspects of the daimonic. (1969, 123)

The term *daimonic* comes from the Greek word meaning both divine and diabolic. Thus, we have forces within us that in moderation lead to personal growth and creativity, but when allowed to dominate become negative and destructive. So it is with eros. One must be assertive to have a loving union with another person, but when assertiveness dominates one is in danger of exploiting one's partner by taking more than is being given. May (1969) says:

There is required a self-assertion, a capacity to stand on one's own feet, an affirmation of one's self in order to have the power to put one's self into the relationship. One must have something to give and be able to give it. The danger, of course, is that he will overassert himself. . . . But this negative side is not to be escaped by giving up self-assertion. For if one is unable to assert oneself, one is unable to participate in a genuine relationship. . . .

In its right proportion, the daimonic is the urge to reach out toward others, to increase life by way of sex, to create, to civilize, it is the joy and rapture, or the simple security of knowing that we matter, that we can affect others, can form them, can exert power which is demonstrably significant. . . .

When the daimonic takes over completely, the unity of the self and the relationship is broken down. (146)

The existence of daimonic forces within humans provides the continuing potential for cruel, irrational, and inhumane behavior. It is impossible for humans to rid themselves of these forces, and it is not necessary for them to do so. What is important is to keep daimonic urges under control and to use them for good rather than to harm.

Philia

The third kind of love is **philia,** which is what is ordinarily called friendship, or brotherly love. According to May, eros cannot last for long without philia, because the tension of continuous attraction and passion would be too great. May (1969) explains philia further.

Philia is the relaxation in the presence of the beloved which accepts the other's being as being; it is simply liking to be with the other, liking to rest with the other, liking the rhythm of the walk, the voice, the whole being of the other. This gives a width to eros, it gives it time to grow; time to sink its roots down deeper. Philia does not require that we do anything for the beloved except accept him, and enjoy him. It is friendship in the simplest, most direct terms. (317)

For May, then, for a loving relationship to be deep, the partners must truly like each other as persons in addition to seeking a creative union with them. To be able to say honestly, "I like you" to one's partner is an important part of authentic love.

Agapé

The fourth kind of love is **agapé,** which May (1969) defines as:

Esteem for the other, the concern for the other's welfare beyond any gain that one can get out of it; disinterested love, typically, the love of God for man. It is an analogy—though not an identity—with the biological aspect of nature which makes the mother cat defend to her death her kittens, and the human being love his own baby with a built-in mechanism without regard for what that baby can do for him. (310)

Agapé, then, is an unselfish giving of one's self to another; a giving of one's self without any concern of what one will get in return. May's concept of agapé is close to what Rogers called unconditional positive regard. In both cases, the love offered to another has no conditions placed on it.

As we have seen, May believes that in modern times many have had an unfortunate tendency to equate love with sex. For May, however, authentic love must involve a blending of sex, the biologic component of love; eros, the seeking of a creative union with another human, the sharing and combining of the two selves; philia, friendship, a simple liking of one's partner even when sex and eros are not involved; and agapé, the unselfish concern for one's partner, the aspect of love that is unconditional.

Psychotherapy

For May, the goal of **psychotherapy** is *not* to eliminate anxiety or guilt but rather to convert neurotic anxiety or guilt to normal anxiety or guilt, which are part of being human and are necessary for personal growth.

> Our chief concern in therapy is with the potentiality of the human being. The goal of therapy is to help the patient actualize his potentialities. . . . The goal of therapy is not the absence of anxiety, but rather the changing of neurotic anxiety into normal anxiety, and the development of the capacity to live with and use normal anxiety. The patient after therapy may well bear more anxiety than he had before, but it will be conscious anxiety and he will be able to use it constructively. Nor is the goal the absence of guilt feeling, but rather the transformation of neurotic guilt into normal guilt, together with the development of the capacity to use this normal guilt creatively. (May 1967, 109)

May uses the term **unconscious** to describe cognitive experiences that are denied awareness because a person is not living an authentic life. May's treatment of the unconscious is close to Kelly's. Kelly said that certain experiences are suspended because they do not fit into a person's construct system. For May, certain experiences are denied because they would cause too much anxiety if experienced. For both Kelly and May, repression in the Freudian sense is not involved, because the person is at least partially aware of these experiences, but they are denied full conscious expression.

For May, effective therapy cannot occur if the therapist views the client as an object and attempts to explain his or her problem in terms of various causes—for example, past experiences. Rather, the therapist must try to determine what the client is attempting to express via his or her "problem."

> From the ontological approach . . . we see *that sickness is precisely the method that the individual uses to preserve his being.* We cannot assume in the usual oversimplified way that the patient automatically wants to get well; we must assume, rather, that he cannot permit himself to give up his neurosis, to get well, until other conditions in his existence and his relation to his world are changed. (May 1967, 95)

May uses the term **encounter** to describe the therapeutic process. By encounter May means two selves coming together and sharing aspects of their existence.

> Encounter is what really happens; it is something much more than a relationship. In this encounter I have to be able, to some extent, to experience what the patient is experiencing. My job as a therapist is to be open to his world. He brings his world with him and therein we live for fifty minutes. . . . In addition, the therapeutic encounter requires that we ourselves be human beings in the broadest sense of the word. This brings us to a point where we can no longer talk about it merely psychologically, in any kind of detached way, but must "throw" ourselves into the therapeutic encounter. In this it helps to realize that we also have gone through similar experiences, and though perhaps not involved in them now, we know what they mean. (1967, 108)

We see then, that both Rogers and May view empathetic understanding as a key ingredient in effective therapy.

May's approach to psychotherapy includes all the terms and concepts of his theory of personality. Humans, he believes, have the potential to be free and to live authentic lives, but many factors can inhibit this freedom and authenticity. People who have adequate values can see their normal anxiety and guilt constructively and creatively. People without adequate values must block out various categories of experience, and healthy anxiety and guilt become neurotic. Such people cannot reach their full potential as human beings. The job of the therapist is to help the client see ways in which his or her full potential can be approximated. The therapist's job, according to May, is to help the client to live an authentic life. What May means by authenticity is much the same as what Rogers called congruency and what Maslow called self-actualization.

New Science of Humans

Unlike many existential thinkers, May is not antiscience. What is needed, according to May, is an approach to the study of humans that does not reduce us to collections of habits, brain functions, genetically determined traits, early experiences, or environmental events. We need a science of humans based on the ontological characteristics of humans. That is, we need a science that takes into consideration human freedom; the importance of phenomenological experience; the use of symbols; the ability to consider the past, present, and future in making decisions; and the valuing process. Such a science would emphasize the wholeness and uniqueness of each individual. A science of humans based on existential philosophy would be different from what is now called scientific psychology. Animal research would be irrelevant, and elementism of any kind would be avoided. May (1967) summarizes his views on this **new science of humans** as follows.

> The outlines of a science of man we suggest will deal with man as the symbol-maker, the reasoner, the historical mammal who can participate in his community and who possesses the potentiality of freedom and ethical action. The pursuit of this science will take no less rigorous thought and wholehearted discipline than

the pursuit of experimental and natural science at their best, but it will place the scientific enterprise in a broader context. Perhaps it will again be possible to study man scientifically and still see him whole. (199)

The kind of human science envisioned by May is similar to that proposed by Maslow (1966).

Evaluation

Empirical Research

Most existential theorists are not concerned with the empirical validation of their concepts. They believe that the place to validate their concepts is in the arena of everyday life, or in the therapeutic situation, and not with systematic laboratory or field investigations. Van Kaam (1966), an existential psychologist, summarizes this viewpoint. "Experiences such as responsibility, dread, anxiety, despair, freedom, love, wonder or decision cannot be measured or experimented with. . . . They are simply there and can only be explicated in their givenness" (187).

Some have made efforts to validate existential concepts empirically, however. Gendlin and Tomlinson (1967) have created the *Experiencing Scale*, designed to measure the extent to which a person is in touch with his or her own true feelings. Because a major goal of psychotherapy is to encourage persons to recognize, accept, and live in accordance with their feelings, the scale can be used to measure the extent to which therapy is effective (Gendlin, Beebe, Cassens, Klein, and Oberlander 1968). Crumbaugh (1968) devised the Purpose-in-Life Test to measure the extent to which a person's life is meaningful. It was found that persons scoring low on the test tended to have world views that were negative and lacking purpose. Also, the test was found to be positively correlated with a scale of depression. That is, people who scored high on the Purpose-in-Life Test displayed little depression, whereas people scoring low displayed considerable depression. Thorne and Pishkin (1973) developed the Existential Study, which consists of seven scales: self-status, self-actualization, existential morale, existential vacuum, humanistic identification, existence and destiny, and suicidal tendency. Thus, the scales are designed to quantify several terms and concepts from existential theory.

Even though a few have made attempts to quantify existential concepts, most existentialists believe that attempting to study and understand humans by using the traditional methods of science is misguided. May (1967) describes what might eventually happen to psychologists who attempt to study humans using the traditional scientific methodology of such disciplines as physics and physiology. In other words, to psychologists who overlook those qualities that are truly important about humans and instead study simple, meaningless behavior because it can be more easily measured.

A psychologist—any psychologist, or all of us—arrives at the heavenly gates at the end of his long and productive life. He is brought up before St. Peter for the customary accounting. . . . An angel assistant in a white jacket drops a manila folder on the table which St. Peter opens and looks at, frowning. Despite the awesome visage of the judge, the psychologist clutches his briefcase and steps up with commendable courage.

But St. Peter's frown deepens. He drums with his fingers on the table and grunts a few nondirective "uhm-uhm"s as he fixes the candidate with his Mosaic eyes.

The silence is discomfiting. Finally the psychologist opens his briefcase and cries, "Here! The reprints of my hundred and thirty-two papers."

St. Peter slowly shakes his head.

Burrowing deeper into the briefcase the psychologist offers, "Let me submit the medals I received for my scientific achievement."

St. Peter's frown is unabated as he silently continues to stare into the psychologist's face.

At last St. Peter speaks. "I'm aware, my good man, how industrious you were. It's not sloth you're accused of. Nor is it unscientific behavior." . . .

Now St. Peter slaps his hand resoundingly down on the table, and his tone is like Moses breaking the news of the ten commandments: "You are charged with *nimis simplicandum* [oversimplification]!"

"You have spent your life making molehills out of mountains—that's what you're guilty of. When man was tragic you made him trivial. . . . When he suffered passively, you described him as simpering; and when he drummed up enough courage to act, you called it stimulus and response. . . . You made man over into the image of your childhood Erector Set or Sunday School maxims—both equally horrendous.

In short, we sent you to earth for seventy-two years to a Dantean circus, and you spent your days and nights at sideshows! (3–4)

Criticisms

Philosophy Not Psychology. Historically, concepts such as values, responsibility, and commitment have been studied by philosophers and theologians, not by psychologists. Many critics of existential psychology would like this historical trend to continue.

Unscientific Approach. As we have seen, most existential psychologists reject traditional scientific methodology as a valid way of studying humans. Such methodology, say the existentialists, treats humans as passive objects, not as authors of their own existence. Furthermore, the existentialists reject the assumption of determinism that is made by traditional science. Human behavior, the existentialists say, is freely chosen, not determined. Critics say that the rejection of scientific methodology and the assumption of determinism represent a throwback to psychology's prescientific past—a throwback to the time when psychology, philosophy, and religion were indistinguishable. Existential psychology, then, say the critics, is jeopardizing the scientific respectability that psychology has gained since its prescientific era.

Nebulous Terminology. It is extremely difficult to define precisely terms such as freedom, responsibility, commitment, guilt, intentionality, love, and courage. Often the meanings of these and other terms change from one existential theorist to another, and sometimes for the same theorist at different times. This lack of precision makes understanding difficult and quantification practically impossible.

Contributions

Call for Human Science. Like Maslow, May does not reject the idea of objectively studying humans; it is only that traditional scientific methodology is not appropriate for doing so. What is needed is an approach that studies humans as whole, unique, complex beings. Many welcome May's idea of developing a science more appropriate to the study of humans—one *not* based on the assumptions and techniques of the natural sciences.

Important, New Way of Conceptualizing Personality. For many, the existential description of humans rings true: We do seek meaning in our lives and seem lost without it; some humans do seem to grow constantly by exercising their choices, whereas others seem to escape from their freedom; most humans are aware of and disturbed by our finitude; and humans do differ in the experiences they seek and in their interpretations of these experiences. According to Hergenhahn (1986) it is because of the existential-humanistic influence that psychologists are now "concerned not only with how people learn, think, and mature biologically and intellectually, but with how people formulate plans to attain future goals and why people laugh, cry, and create meaning in their lives" (393). Many believe that the existential view of humans has breathed new life into psychology. Hall and Lindzey (1978) exemplify such a belief.

> Whatever the future of existential psychology may be—and at the present time it appears to have sufficient vigor and vitality to last a long time—it has already served at least one very important function. That function is to rescue psychology from being drowned in a sea of theories that have lost contact with the everyday world and with the "givens" of experience. . . . Existentialism is helping to revitalize a science that many feel has become theoretically moribund. It has done this by insisting on using a strictly phenomenological methodology. It has tried to see what is actually there and to describe human existence in concrete terms. . . . Whatever the future of existential psychology may be . . . it is clear that now it offers a profoundly new way of studying and comprehending human beings. For this reason, it merits the closest attention by serious students of psychology. (343–44)

Summary

Under the influence of Freud, Kierkegaard, and Tillich, and with a special interest in the nature and causes of anxiety, May developed a theory of personality based on existential philosophy. From existential philosophy, May accepted the following: (1) the term *dasein*, which is the study of a particular person in the world at a particular time and existing under a particular set of circumstances; (2) a description of three modes of human existence; the *umwelt*, or our interactions with the physical world, the *mitwelt*, or our interactions with other humans, and the *eigen-welt*, which is one's interactions with oneself; (3) the belief that each person is free to choose the meaning of his or her own existence; (4) responsibility, which goes hand in hand with freedom; (5) ontology, which is the study of the ultimate nature of humans—that is, an attempt to discover those features of humans that make them humans; (6) the importance of phenomenology, or the study of intact, meaningful conscious experience *without* dividing it or reducing it for study or analysis; (7) authenticity, or the emphasis on living one's life in accordance with self-developed values chosen in accordance with one's ontological nature, not in accordance with values imposed on one from the outside; (8) and the importance of death in the ontology of humans. For example, death is the ultimate state of nonbeing, and to ponder the inevitability of one's death is a source of great anxiety; and (9) thrownness, referring to the circumstances of our lives over which we have no control.

May describes the human dilemma as our ability to view ourselves as both an object in the world to which things happen and as a subject who acts on things by interpreting them, valuing them, projecting them into the future, and thus transforming them. May believes that to develop a complete understanding of humans, both aspects, humans as objects and as subjects, must be studied. May believes that a theory like Skinner's stresses the objective side of humans too much, whereas a theory like Rogers's stresses the subjective side too much. Also, Rogers, according to May, ignores the irrational, evil aspects of human existence.

By intentionality May means the ability to form intentions that then guide our perceptions and influence how we interpret our experiences. Will is the commitment to action. After a structure of meaning has been developed and intentions formulated, we must act on those intentions. Will is directly related to action. Wish is the imaginative playing with possible courses of action (intentions) before actually committing ourselves to one.

According to May, to be human is to experience anxiety and guilt. Normal anxiety results when we ponder death or when our values our threatened. Because humans are mortal, and because to grow psychologically, our values must constantly be challenged, normal anxiety cannot be avoided. Likewise, when we become aware that we are not living up to our full potential, we experience guilt, and because no human ever lives up to his or her full potential, normal guilt is unavoidable. Some people, instead of using normal anxiety and guilt for personal growth, attempt to escape them by conforming to external values, or by refusing to acknowledge that such anxiety and guilt exist. When normal anxiety and guilt are not dealt with in a conscious, constructive manner, they become neurotic. Neurotic anxiety and guilt cause a person to deny vast areas of personal experience and therefore stifle personal growth. It is neurotic anxiety and guilt that typically cause a person to need psychotherapy.

Our values summarize those experiences that we have deemed to be most valuable. Mature values seek a harmony among people and are future oriented. Because each person can freely choose his or her own values, each person is responsible for the actions derived from them. Values require a commitment to action, and it is the person who is responsible for his or her value structure, and the actions that they necessitate. For some people, some values are so important that they would rather die than give them up. The amount of anxiety that one experiences is directly related to one's values. If one's value structure is adequate, one will experience only normal anxiety. Value structures must be dynamic, however, because an unwillingness to change values stifles personal growth and results in excessive guilt. The healthy human is constantly *becoming* more than he or she has been.

May describes four kinds of love. Sex is the attraction toward a member of the opposite sex based solely on biology. Eros seeks a union and a sharing of one's self with one's lover. Philia, which is the friendship that holds two people closely together even when sex and eros are not involved, means liking as well as loving the other person. Agapé, the last type of love, means caring for the other person even when one gets nothing in return. Authentic love, according to May, involves a blending of all four kinds of love. One must be aware of the daimonic, however, which has the power to destroy our relationships with other humans. The daimonic is any human function that has the power to dominate a person. If sex dominates a relationship, for example, authentic love is lost, because one's lover is nothing more than an object used to satisfy one's biologic sex drive. Likewise, if eros is allowed to dominate one's seeking of a union, the partner's individuality is ignored, and the union is at the expense of one's partner. It is the daimonic that provides the potential for evil in human existence.

For May, effective psychotherapy cannot occur if the client is viewed as a collection of habits, past experiences, or genetically determined dispositions or test scores. Rather, it must result from an encounter between two humans. The therapist must attempt to see what the client is trying to do or say through an emotional problem. In other words, the therapist must try to see experiences as the client does. When this is done, the therapist attempts to help the client find ways of overcoming neurotic anxiety and guilt, and thereby be in a position to realize more of his or her potential.

For May, the unconscious is not a storehouse of repressed memories. Rather, it consists of several potential experiences that must be denied because of various defenses a person has used to avoid normal anxiety, or because the person is using a very restrictive value structure. When those barriers are overcome, the person becomes more open to experience, becomes aware of previously denied possibilities, and in general, becomes freer as a human being.

May believes that psychology needs a new model for a science of humans. The old one, based on mechanistic determinism, had as its primary goals the seeking of the objective causes of behavior, and the prediction and control of behavior. Within this model, humans are viewed as the objects of the physical forces acting on them. For May, a better model would be one based on existential philosophy, a model that addresses the human capacities for freedom, valuing, and loving.

Few have made attempts to verify existential concepts empirically, but most existential psychologists believe that the place to verify their concepts is in the arena of everyday life or in the therapeutic situation. May's theory has been criticized for representing philosophy (or perhaps religion) instead of psychology, being unscientific, and containing nebulous terminology. May's theory has been praised for calling for the development of a human science and offering a new way of conceptualizing personality.

EXPERIENTIAL EXERCISES

1. May defines an atheist as a person with little or no meaning in his or her life. According to May's definition, are you an atheist? Explain.

2. List your important values and describe how you organize your life around them.

3. According to the existentialists' definition of authenticity, would you consider yourself an authentic or an inauthentic person? Explain.

4. Analyze a loving relationship that you have, or have had, in terms of May's four-part definition of love. Indicate whether you agree or disagree with May's description of love.

5. Using the existentialists' definitions of anxiety and guilt, describe the circumstances under which you have experienced these two emotions. Have you ever experienced what the exis-

tentialists call neurotic anxiety or neurotic guilt? Explain.

6. Give an example of how intentionality, wish, and will have combined and manifested themselves in your life.

7. According to the existentialists, some people accept the challenge of their individual freedom with courage and live authentic lives. Others, however, escape from their freedom and live inauthentic lives. From the people that you know or have known, describe one person that you think is (or was) authentic and one that is (or was) inauthentic.

8. Briefly describe your personal reactions to May's theory.

DISCUSSION QUESTIONS

1. Briefly describe the following terms from existential philosophy: dasein, umwelt, mitwelt, eigenwelt, ontology, phenomenology, responsibility, and thrownness.

2. Discuss the importance of death and of personal freedom in existential philosophy.

3. What, according to May and other existentialists, is an authentic life?

4. What, according to May, is the human dilemma? Give an example.

5. First define intentionality, will, and wish, and then give an example showing how the three are related.

6. Differentiate between normal and neurotic anxiety, and discuss the origins of both.

7. Differentiate between normal and neurotic guilt, and discuss the origins of both.

8. According to May, the amount of anxiety one experiences is directly proportional to the adequacy of one's value system. Explain why May believes this point, and describe the character-

istics of values that May considers mature and healthy.

9. What does May mean by "authentic love"? Include in your answer the roles played by sex, eros, philia, and agapé.

10. What is the daimonic? Explain what May meant when he said that it accounts for the human potential for evil. Also explain how it can interfere with authentic love.

11. For May, what is necessary before effective psychotherapy can occur? Include in your answer a definition of the term *encounter*.

12. For May, what is the goal of psychotherapy?

13. What did May mean by the unconscious? How does May's use of the term *unconscious* differ from Freud's?

14. Describe the model of humans that May thinks current scientific psychology is using, and then describe the model that May would replace it with.

15. Summarize the criticisms of May's theory.

16. Summarize the contributions of May's theory.

SUGGESTIONS FOR FURTHER READING

MAY, R. (1953). *Man's Search for Himself.* New York: Norton.

A most interesting presentation of what May calls the human predicament. Topics discussed include the loneliness and anxiety of modern people, roots of our malady, self-contempt, a substitute for self-worth, the struggle to be, and religion as a source of strength or weakness.

MAY, R. (1967). *Psychology and the Human Dilemma.* New York: Van Nostrand.

This presentation of May's version of existential psychology is short, interesting, and informative. Topics covered include modern people's loss of significance, personal identity in an anonymous world, freedom and responsibility re-examined, questions for a science of people, and social responsibilities of psychologists.

MAY, R. (1969). *Love and Will.* New York: Norton.

May's best-selling, highly influential statement on the nature of love. Topics covered include paradoxes of sex and love; eros in conflict with sex, love and death; the relation of love and will; and the meaning of care.

MAY, R. (1972). *Power and Innocence: A Search for the Sources of Violence.* New York: Norton.

May offers his solutions to such problems as drug addiction, racial tension, police brutality, and youth and campus unrest.

MAY, R. (1973). *Paulus: Reminiscences of a Friendship.* New York: Harper & Row.

May's touching account of his long friendship with Paul Tillich, the famous existential philosopher.

MAY, R. (1975). *The Courage to Create.* New York: Norton.

May describes many aspects of courage and shows how courage is a necessary ingredient of the creative act.

MAY, R. (1981). *Freedom and Destiny.* New York: Norton.

This work discusses the relationships among freedom, values, and destiny. Topics covered include the crisis of freedom, the paradoxes of freedom, human destiny, destiny and death, mistaken paths to freedom, dizziness of freedom, and freedom and destiny in illness and health.

MAY, R. (1983). *The Discovery of Being: Writings in Existential Psychology.* New York: Norton.

May's most recent book includes such topics as origins and significance of existential psychology, to be or not to be, the three modes of the world, and transcending the immediate situation.

REEVES, C. (1977). *The Psychology of Rollo May.* San Francisco: Jossey-Bass.

This work is a thorough analysis of May and his theory.

GLOSSARY

Agapé. The unselfish giving of one's self in a loving relationship. One loves but expects nothing in return.

Anxiety. To be human is to experience anxiety. Anxiety is the experience we have when our existence as an individual is threatened. To ponder one's inevitable death causes anxiety, as does the threat to one's values. To grow, one must have one's values threatened. Therefore, anxiety is an unavoidable component of a normal, healthy life (see also normal anxiety and neurotic anxiety).

Authenticity. If people live their lives in accordance with values that are freely chosen, they are living authentic lives. If, however, people conform to values established by others, they have not exercised their personal freedom and are therefore living inauthentic lives. Inauthenticity is causally related to neurotic anxiety and guilt and the feelings of aloneness, ineffectiveness, self-alienation, and despair.

Commitment. One must exist in the world and therefore act on it. Values are meaningless unless they are manifested in behavior. The formulation of values, therefore, also commits people to a course of action. Behavioral commitment to self-formulated, future-oriented, human values characterizes the authentic life.

Courage. An authentic life involves creating for oneself a structure of meaning that will guide one's thoughts and actions. Such a life requires courage because it means that often one's beliefs and actions will be contrary to those that are widely accepted.

Daimonic. The potential for evil or harm that is part of human nature. The daimonic occurs when any natural function that in moderation is positive, dominates the individual—for example, when assertiveness becomes aggression or hostility or when eros causes one to dominate one's lover and thereby destroy his or her individuality.

Dasein. The study of the individual as a being in the world. The emphasis is on an individual's existence at a certain time under certain circumstances. The conditions a person finds oneself in can never be separated from the person himself or herself. The two must be seen as a whole. The individual as an object and as a subject can never be separated.

Death. Because humans are mortal, and because death is the ultimate state of nonbeing, awareness of one's inevitable death causes anxiety. This source of anxiety is part of human existence and cannot be avoided. The awareness of death, however, can add vitality to life by motivating a person to get as much out of life as possible in the limited time available.

Eigenwelt. The intrapersonal world. An individual's self-awareness.

Encounter. The meeting of two selves. Seeing things as the other sees them and vice versa. An honest sharing of one's self with another person. For May, an encounter is a necessary component of successful psychotherapy. The client must be understood as a total human being, not as a collection of test scores or repressed experiences or as an object that fits into some diagnostic category.

Eros. The desire to form a union with or to feel at one with one's partner in love. Through the sharing of two selves, both experience new things and both expand their consciousness. With sex, the goal is satisfaction and termination; with eros, the goal is to prolong the loving experience as long as possible.

Existentialism. The philosophy that studies the essence of human nature. The emphasis is on freedom, individuality, and phenomenological experience.

Freedom. Not the absence of negative conditions, but the potential to set future-oriented goals and then to act in accordance with them. According to the existential philosopher Sartre, "We are our choices," or, "We are what we choose to be." Freedom exists only as a potential and must be attained over time, by increasing one's self-awareness. Because freedom necessarily involves anxiety and responsibility, many people deny, minimize or escape from their personal freedom.

Guilt. The feeling we have when it is realized that we are not living up to our full potential (see also normal guilt and neurotic guilt).

Human dilemma. The capacity of humans to see themselves as objects to which things happen, and as subjects who act on their experiences and thereby give them meaning.

Intentionality. The human capacity to form intentions that, in turn, guide perceptions and actions and influence the evaluation of one's experiences.

Love. True or authentic love involves a harmonious blending of sex, eros, philia, and agapé (see also agapé, eros, philia, and sex).

Mitwelt. The world of human interactions.

Neurotic anxiety. The anxiety that results from not being able to deal adequately with normal anxiety. For example, if one conforms or develops inflexible values to avoid normal anxiety, the normal anxiety is converted into neurotic anxiety, which causes a person to live life within narrow limits and inhibit various experiences that are necessary for healthy growth. The person experiencing neurotic anxiety is shut off from many of his or her potentialities (see also anxiety and normal anxiety).

Neurotic guilt. If normal guilt is not recognized and dealt with constructively, it can overwhelm a person, causing one to block out the very experiences conducive to personal growth.

New science of humans. Rather than a science of humans based on determinism and elementism and one that has as its goal the prediction and control of behavior, May proposes a science of humans based on existential philosophy. Such a science would take into consideration the human use of symbols, the human sense of time, the importance of values, the uniqueness of each human, and the importance of freedom.

Normal anxiety. The anxiety that results from the revisions of one's value system and from the awareness of one's inevitable death. To grow as a person requires taking risks, which causes normal anxiety.

Normal guilt. The feeling experienced when one recognizes the difference between what one is and what one could be. Because we can always be more than we are, normal guilt is unavoidable (see also guilt and neurotic guilt).

Object-subject dichotomy. The fact that as humans we are both the objects of experience and the interpreters, transformers, and originators of experience (see also human dilemma).

Oedipal conflict. Rather than interpreting the Oedipal conflict as an attraction toward one parent and hostility toward the other, as Freud did, May interprets the conflict as a struggle between dependence and independence.

Ontology. The study of being. Attempts to discover the basic structures or core of human existence. An effort to isolate the basic attributes that characterize human existence.

Phenomenology. The study of conscious experience as it exists for the person, without any attempt to reduce, divide, or compartmentalize it in any way.

Philia. The experience of friendship or companionship with one's loved one even when sex and eros are not involved. Simply liking to be with your loved one.

Psychotherapy. For May, effective psychotherapy can only result from an encounter between two humans. The therapist must attempt to see things as the client does and try to understand how the client is using a "problem" to maintain his or her identity as a person. The goal of therapy is to free the client from neurotic anxiety and guilt, so that the person will be more free to actualize more of his or her potential (see also encounter).

Responsibility. Because we are free to choose our own existence, we are also entirely responsible for that existence. We can praise or blame no one but ourselves for whatever we become as people.

Self-relatedness. To be aware of one's existence as a being in the world who is both to have experiences and to transform them. To be conscious of the fact that one is both the object and subject of experience.

Sex. The biologic aspect of love. To satisfy the sexual aspect of love requires only sexual activity with a partner. In such cases, the partner becomes the object by which the need for sex is satisfied.

Thrownness. (Also called facticity and ground of existence.) Those facts that characterize a person's life over which he or she has no control. Such facts include the biologic, historical, and cultural events that characterize one's life.

Umwelt. The physical, objective world. The world that is studied by the physical and biologic sciences.

Unconscious. For May, the unconscious is not a "cellar" in which repressed experiences reside, as it was for Freud. Rather, it consists of the experiences denied awareness, because of inflexible values or because of the restrictive influence of neurotic anxiety and guilt. When values become more flexible and neurotic anxiety and guilt are overcome, the person is again open nothing needs to be denied awarenes

Values. Those categories of experience most important to the person. Typically life involve the love, security, and no vided by one's mother; later values incl ...us and success. Mature values are future oriented, independently arrived at, and concerned with other humans.

Will. A commitment to action.

Wish. The cognitive exploring of possible courses of action before actually committing oneself to one particular course.

17

A Final Word

A fter our review of the major theories of personality in the preceding chapters, the following four conclusions seem warranted.

1. Personality theories often reflect the biographies of their authors.
2. Much about personality remains unknown.
3. The best available explanation of personality comes from a composite of all the major theories (rather than from any single theory or paradigm).
4. Each person must judge for himself or herself what information from each theory is useful or not useful.

Personality Theories Often Reflect the Biographies of Their Authors

Students sometimes wonder why so many different personality theories exist. One reason is that personality is so complex that different theories can focus on different aspects of it. Given the fact that personality can be defined and studied in several different ways, the question remains, however, what causes a *particular* theorist to choose one approach to defining and studying personality over others? The answer seems to be that, at least in part, personality theories are biographical. That is, they often reflect the significant experiences of the particular theorist. Most notably this point was true of Freud, Jung, Adler, Horney, Erikson, Allport, Cattell, Kelly, and Maslow. It appears that many personality theorists tend to develop theories that make sense to them personally, and it is their own personalities and lifes' circumstances that, to a large extent, determine what they believe needs to be explained and what constitutes an explanation.

Does the fact that personality theories reflect the personalities and experiences of their authors invalidate the theories? Not at all. A theory can be valid or invalid, useful or useless, regardless of what motivated its origin. For example, much in Freud's theory reflects his personal experiences and concerns, yet most would agree that his is among the most influential theories ever constructed. We should realize, however, that because any particular theory is partly biographical, it will tend to apply more to certain kinds of people than to others, and it will "ring true" more to some people than to others—presumably to those with a personality most like that of the theorist. Perhaps this reason is why, at the end of a course such as this one, different students have different "favorite" theories. Thus, tastes in personality theories might also be biographical.

Much About Personality Remains Unknown

The theories covered in this text, individually or collectively, do not adequately account for personality. Although each theory illuminates part of what we call personality, much remains in darkness. Existing theories need to be extended, and new theories need to be developed, before we will be able to approximate a thorough understanding of personality.

To test how much you have learned about personality and how much remains unknown, just attempt one day to account for your own actions and the actions of others by using what you have learned in this text. Perhaps you will have a better understanding of many events now. No doubt, you will encounter examples of repression (evidenced by such examples as slips of the tongue, dreams, and humor) and other ego-defense mechanisms such as projection, identification, and reaction formation. You may find that the emotion-producing symbols found in art, music, and religion reflect our evolutionary experiences as a species. You may see parents instilling either basic anxiety or basic trust in their children. You may conclude that the consistent patterns of behavior observed in people reflect underlying traits and you may see examples of how reinforcement contingencies influence behavior. You may see people showing favoritism toward their relatives, and you may observe that many apparent acts of altruism are actually selfish. You may see that much of life is a matter of interpretation or attitudinal. You may see different people struggling to satisfy different levels of needs, and perhaps you will see a person who appears to be self-actualizing. You may observe that some people have been more successful than others in developing their own values with which to deal with the world.

At the end of the day, many behaviors that were previously a mystery will have been at least partially explained, but many mysteries will remain. Their solution will need the work and imagination of future personality theorists.

Composite of All Major Theories Best Explains Personality

The position we have taken throughout this text is that all the major personality theories add to our understanding of personality, and therefore it is not necessary to search for *the* correct theory or even the *most* correct theory. As mentioned in chapter 1, just as a carpenter would not attempt to build a house with only one tool, a person cannot hope to understand personality with only one theory. It is nonsensical to say that a screwdriver is any more correct or useful than a hammer. It is just that different tools have different functions; the same is true for personality theories. In other words, which personality theory is "best" depends on which aspect of personality one is attempting to explain. This position is **eclecticism,** which means taking the best from several different viewpoints. The eclectic is not bound to any single theory but chooses useful information from any theory or theories.

Is it not possible that society forces people to repress sexual and aggressive urges, and that such repressed urges manifest themselves indirectly in a person's life, as Freud and Dollard and Miller maintain? Is it not possible that we are born with predispositions to respond emotionally to the major categories of existence, such as birth, death, and members of the opposite sex, and to symbols of perfection, as Jung suggested? Is it not possible that most of us choose a life-style with which to strive for perfection or superiority, and for the betterment of society, as Adler suggested? Does not evidence exist that some neurotics attempt to adjust to life by moving toward people, others by moving away from people, and still others by moving against people, as Horney suggested? Does not evidence exist that life consists of various stages, each characterized by different needs and potential accomplishments, and that one of the most significant events in one's life is the development of an identity, as Erikson suggested? Does it not make sense to say that each person is unique, and that some adult motives are no longer tied to their earlier origins, as Allport proposed? Is it not possible that the many variables affecting human behavior, including constitutional, learning, and situational variables, can be stated in a single equation that can be used in predicting behavior, as Cattell suggests? Is there not evidence that reinforcement contingencies exert a powerful influence on behavior as Skinner maintains? Is it not possible to think of the various ego-defense mechanisms and neurotic symptoms as learned, because they temporarily reduce anxiety, as Dollard and Miller suggest? Is it not also possible that we learn some things simply by observing them, and that modeling experiences are extremely important to personality development, as Bandura and Mischel maintain? Is it not possible that various dating, mating, and child-rearing practices, the tendency to protect what belongs to us, and differential male-female parenting can be explained, at least in part, by urges within us that have been shaped by natural selection, as the sociobiologists claim? Is it not possible that the reduction of uncertainty is a major motive in human behavior, as Kelly suggested? Does not the possibility exist that much of our behavior is in accordance with our own subjective reality rather than with physical reality, as both Kelly and Rogers maintained? Is it not possible to confirm Rogers's contention that because of our need for positive regard and for self-regard many of us internalize conditions of worth that become our frame of reference for living rather than our own organismic valuing process? Is there not evidence for Maslow's contention that the motives of people with their basic needs satisfied are qualitatively different from the motives of people still struggling to satisfy their basic needs? Lastly, is it not possible to find persons attempting to live the kind of authentic life that May describes and to find others turning their back on such a life by blindly conforming to values established by others?

What the realm of personality theory needs is a grand synthesizer, a person who could coordinate the various terms and concepts from all the various theories. This person would look carefully at all the theories that discuss developmental stages—for example, Freud, Erikson, and Allport—and attempt to derive a more comprehensive picture of personality development. If our contention is true that all of the various theories add something different to our knowledge of personality, it would make sense for a person like Newton to come along and somehow put it all together. Because such a synthesis does not seem possible in the foreseeable future, however, one can only make the best use of the existing paradigms or perhaps create new ones. The more beams of light, the better.

You Are the Final Judge

As we have seen, each theory of personality has generated at least some empirical research that supports it. It is also true that at least some empirical research refutes each theory of personality. Because the results of the empirical research performed to evaluate the various theories of personality are equivocal, they cannot be used as a basis for accepting or rejecting a theory. This situation may change as more studies are performed, and they collectively suggest acceptance or rejection of a theory or of parts of a theory. As it is now, however, not enough unambiguous empirical research is not available to help decide what is valid or invalid in the realm of personality theory. How, then, does one know what information to accept or reject? It seems that under existing circumstances, Buddha gave the best answer to this question.

> Believe nothing on the faith of traditions, even though they have been held in honour for many generations, and in diverse places. Do not believe a thing because many speak of it. Do not believe on the faith of the sages of the past. Do not believe what you have imagined, persuading yourself that a god inspires you. Believe nothing on the sole authority of your masters or priests. After examination, believe what you yourself have tested and found to be reasonable, and conform your conduct thereto. (Hawton 1948, 200).

Summary

Four conclusions seem justified after our review of the major personality theories: (1) Most, if not all, of the theories of personality reflect the biographies of their authors; (2) although the major theories of personality illuminate many aspects of personality, much about personality remains unknown; (3) the best available explanation of personality comes from using the best of all the theories rather than attempting to use one or a few of them; and (4) until more unambiguous empirical research is available, the best one can do is to evaluate the various theories personally, and to accept concepts that make sense and reject those that do not. This guideline means that valid and useful theories will vary from person to person.

EXPERIENTIAL EXERCISES

1. Suppose you were the "grand synthesizer" mentioned in this chapter; describe how you might go about your task of synthesizing the various personality theories.

2. Review the theory of personality that you formulated as part of the experiential exercises for chapter 1. Reformulate your original theory using what you have learned about personality since your original formulation. Summarize the major differences between your first and second formulations.

References

ADAMS, G. R., & FITCH, S. A. (1982). Ego stage and identity status development: A cross-sequential analysis. *Journal of Personality and Social Psychology, 43,* 547–583.

ADAMS, G. R., RYAN, J. H., HOFFMAN, J. J., DOBSON, W. R., & NIELSON, E. C. (1985). Ego identity status, conformity behavior, and personality in late adolescence. *Journal of Personality and Social Psychology, 47,* 1091–1104.

ADAMS-WEBBER, J. R. (1979). *Personal construct theory: Concepts and applications.* New York: Wiley.

ADLER, A. (1917). *Study of organ inferiority and its physical compensation: A contribution to clinical medicine* (S. E. Jeliffe, Trans.). New York: Nervous and Mental Disease Publication. (Original work published 1907)

ADLER, A. (1930a). *The education of children.* South Bend, IN: Gateway Editions.

ADLER, A. (1930b). Individual psychology. In C. Murchison (Ed.), *Psychologies of 1930.* Worcester, MA: Clark University Press.

ADLER, A. (1956). *The individual psychology of Alfred Adler: A systematic presentation of selections from his writings.* H. L. Ansbacher & R. R. Ansbacher (Eds.). New York: Basic Books.

ADLER, A. (1956). The neurotic character. In H. L. Ansbacher & R. R. Ansbacher (Eds.), *The individual psychology of Alfred Adler.* New York: Harper. (Original work published 1912)

ADLER, A. (1956). The psychology of hermaphroditism in life and in neurosis. In H. L. Ansbacher & R. R. Ansbacher (Eds.), *The individual psychology of Alfred Adler.* New York: Basic Books. (Original work published 1910)

ADLER, A. (1956). The use of heredity and environment. In H. L. Ansbacher & R. R. Ansbacher (Eds.), *The individual psychology of Alfred Adler.* New York: Basic Books. (Original work published 1935)

ADLER, A. (1958). *What life should mean to you.* New York: Capricorn Books. (Original work published 1931)

ADLER, A. (1964). *Problems of neurosis.* New York: Harper & Row. (Original work published 1929)

ADLER, A. (1964). *Social interest: A challenge to mankind.* New York: Capricorn Books. (Original work published 1933)

ADLER, A. (1969). *The science of living.* New York: Doubleday. (Original work published 1929)

ADLER, A. (1979). The structure of neurosis. In H. L. Ansbacher & R. R. Ansbacher (Eds.), *Superiority and social interest: A collection of Alfred Adler's later writings.* New York: Norton. (Original work published 1932)

AGNEW, J. (1985). Childhood disorders. In E. Button (Ed.), *Personal construct theory and mental health: Theory, research, and practice.* Beckenham, England: Croom Helm.

ALLPORT, G. W. (1937). *Personality: A psychological interpretation.* New York: Holt, Rinehart & Winston.

ALLPORT, G. W. (1942). *The use of personal documents in psychologial science.* Bulletin 49. New York: Social Science Research Council.

ALLPORT, G. W. (1950). *The individual and his religion.* New York: Macmillan.

ALLPORT, G. W. (1954). *The nature of prejudice.* Cambridge, MA: Addison-Wesley.

ALLPORT, G. W. (1955). *Becoming: Basic considerations for a psychology of personality.* New Haven: Yale University Press.

ALLPORT, G. W. (1960). *Personality and social encounter: Selected essays.* Boston: Beacon Press.

ALLPORT, G. W. (1961). *Pattern and growth in personality.* New York: Holt, Rinehart & Winston.

ALLPORT, G. W. (1962). The general and the unique in psychological science. *Journal of Personality, 30,* 405–422.

ALLPORT, G. W. (1965). *Letters from Jenny.* New York: Harcourt Brace Jovanovich.

ALLPORT, G. W. (1967). Autobiography. In E. G. Boring & G. Lindzey (Eds.), *A history of psychology in autobiography* (Vol. 5, pp. 1–25). New York: Appleton-Century-Crofts.

ALLPORT, G. W., & ALLPORT, F. H. (1921). Personality traits: Their classification and measurement. *Journal of Abnormal and Social Psychology, 16,* 6–40.

ALLPORT, G. W., & CANTRIL, H. (1934). Judging personality from voice. *Journal of Social Psychology, 5,* 37–55.

ALLPORT, G. W., & ODBERT, H. S. (1936). Trait names: A psycholexical study. *Psychological Monographs, 47*(211), 1–171.

ALLPORT, G. W., & POSTMAN, L. (1947). *The psychology of rumor.* New York: Holt, Rinehart & Winston.

ALLPORT, G. W., & VERNON, P. E. (1933). *Studies in expressive movement.* New York: Macmillan.

ALLPORT, G. W., VERNON, P., & LINDZEY, G. (1960). *A study of values* (3rd ed.). Boston: Houghton Mifflin.

ALTMAN, K. E. (1973). The relationship between social interest dimensions of early recollections and selected counselor variables (Doctoral dissertation, University of South Carolina). *Dissertation Abstracts International, 34,* 5613A. (University Microfilms No. 74-05, 364)

ANSBACHER, H. L. (1983). Individual psychology. In R. J. Corsini & A. J. Marsella (Eds.), *Personality theories, research, and assessment.* Itasca, IL: Peacock.

ANSBACHER, H. L., & ANSBACHER, R. R. (Eds.). (1956). *The individual psychology of Alfred Adler*. New York: Basic Books.

ANSBACHER, H. L., & ANSBACHER, R. R. (Eds.). (1964). *Superiority and social interest by Alfred Adler*. Evanston, IL: Northwestern University Press.

ANSBACHER, H. L., & ANSBACHER, R. R. (Eds.). (1979). *Superiority and social interest*. New York: Norton.

ARAGONA, J., CASSADY, J., & DRABMAN, R. S. (1975). Treating overweight children through parental training and contingency management. *Journal of Applied Behavior Analysis, 8,* 269–278.

ASPY, D. (1972). *Toward a technology for humanizing education*. Champaign, IL: Research Press.

ASPY, D., & ROEBUCK, F. (1974). From human ideas to humane technology and back again, many times. *Education, 95,* 163–171.

AYLLON, T., & AZRIN, N. H. (1965). The measurement and reinforcement of behavior of psychotics. *Journal of the Experimental Analysis of Behavior, 8,* 357–383.

AYLLON, T., & AZRIN, N. H. (1968). *The token economy: A motivational system for therapy and rehabilitation*. New York: Appleton-Century-Crofts.

BAER, J. S., HOLT, C. S., & LICHTENSTEIN, E. (1986). Self-efficacy and smoking reexamined: Construct validity and clinical utility. *Journal of Consulting and Clinical Psychology, 54,* 846–852.

BALMARY, M. (1979). *Psychoanalyzing psychoanalysis: Freud and the hidden fault of the father*. Baltimore: Johns Hopkins Press.

BANDURA, A. (1965). Influence of models' reinforcement contingencies on the acquisition of imitative responses. *Journal of Personality and Social Psychology, 1,* 589–595.

BANDURA, A. (1969). *Principles of behavior modification*. New York: Holt, Rinehart & Winston.

BANDURA, A. (1973). *Aggression: A social-learning analysis*. Englewood Cliffs, NJ: Prentice-Hall.

BANDURA, A. (1977). *Social learning theory*. Englewood Cliffs, NJ: Prentice-Hall.

BANDURA, A. (1986). *Social foundations of thought and action: A social cognitive theory*. Englewood Cliffs, NJ: Prentice-Hall.

BANDURA, A., ADAMS, N. E., & BEYER, J. (1977). Cognitive processes mediating behavioral change. *Journal of Personality and Social Psychology, 35,* 125–139.

BANDURA, A., BLANCHARD, E. B., & RITTER, B. (1969). Relative efficacy of desensitization and modeling approaches for inducing behavioral, affective, and attitudinal changes. *Journal of Personality and Social Psychology, 13,* 173–199.

BANDURA, A., & KUPERS, C. J. (1964). The transmission of patterns of self-reinforcement through modeling. *Journal of Abnormal and Social·Psychology, 69,* 1–9.

BANDURA, A., & MISCHEL, W. (1965). Modification of self-imposed delay of reward through exposure to live and symbolic models. *Journal of Personality and Social Psychology, 2,* 698–705.

BANDURA, A., & ROSENTHAL, T. L. (1966). Vicarious classical conditioning as a function of arousal level. *Journal of Personality and Social Psychology, 3,* 54–62.

BANDURA, A., & WALTERS, R. H. (1959). *Adolescent aggression*. New York: Ronald Press.

BANDURA, A., & WALTERS, R. H. (1963). *Social learning and personality development*. New York: Holt, Rinehart & Winston.

BANNISTER, D. (Ed.). (1984). *Further perspectives in personal construct theory*. New York: Academic Press.

BANNISTER, D., & FRANSELLA, F. (1971). *Inquiring man: The theory of personal constructs*. New York: Penguin.

BANNISTER, D., & MAIR, J. M. M. (1968). *The evaluation of personal constructs*. New York: Academic Press.

BARASH, D. P. (1979). *The whisperings within: Evolution and the origin of human nature*. New York: Penguin.

BARASH, D. P. (1982). *Sociobiology and behavior* (2nd ed.). New York: Elsevier.

BARASH, D. P. (1986). *The hare and the tortoise: Culture, biology, and human nature*. New York: Penguin.

BARASH, D. P. (1987). *The arms race and nuclear war*. Belmont, CA: Wadsworth Publishing.

BARASH, D. P., & LIPTON, J. E. (1982). *Stop nuclear war! A handbook*. New York: Grove Press.

BARASH, D. P., & LIPTON, J. E. (1985). *The caveman and the bomb: Human nature, evolution, and nuclear war*. New York: McGraw-Hill.

BECKER, W., MADSEN, C., ARNOLD, C., & THOMAS, D. (1967). The contingent use of teacher attention and praising in reducing classroom behavior problems. *Journal of Special Education, 1,* 287–307.

BELMONT, L., & MAROLLA, F. A. (1973). Birth order, family size, and intelligence. *Science, 182,* 1096–1101.

BEM, D. J., & ALLEN, A. (1974). On predicting some of the people some of the time: The search for cross-situational consistencies in behavior. *Psychological Review, 81,* 506–520.

BIERI, J. (1955). Cognitive complexity-simplicity and predictive behavior. *Journal of Abnormal and Social Psychology, 51,* 61–66.

BLECHMAN, E. A., TAYLOR, C. J., & SCHRADER, S. M. (1981). Family problem solving versus home notes as early intervention with high-risk children. *Journal of Consulting and Clinical Psychology, 49,* 919–926.

BLUM, G. (1962). The Blacky test—sections II, IV, and VII. In R. Birney & R. Teevan (Eds.), *Measuring human motivation* (pp. 119–144). New York: Van Nostrand.

BOSLOUGH, J. (1972, December 24). Reformatory's incentive plan works. *Rocky Mountain News*, 13.

BOTTOME, P. (1957). *Alfred Adler: A portrait from life*. New York: Vanguard.

BOUCHARD, T. J., JR. (1984). Twins reared together and apart: What they tell us about human diversity. In S. W. Fox (Ed.), *Individuality and determinism* (pp. 147–184). New York: Plenum Press.

BOUDIN, H. M. (1972). Contingency contracting as a therapeutic tool in the deceleration of amphetamine use. *Behavior Therapy*, 3, 604–608.

BOURNE, E. (1978). The state of research on ego identity: A review and appraisal: I. *Journal of Youth and Adolescence*, 7, 223–251.

BOWERS, K. S. (1973). Situationism in psychology: An analysis and a critique. *Psychological Review*, 80, 307–336.

BRELAND, H. M. (1974). Birth order, family constellation, and verbal achievement. *Child Development*, 45, 1011–1019.

BREUER, J., & FREUD, S. (1955). Studies on hysteria. In *The standard edition* (Vol. 2). London: Hogarth Press. (Original work published 1895)

BUSS, D. M. (1987). Sex differences in human mate selection criteria: An evolutionary perspective. In C. Crawford, M. Smith, & D. Krebs (Eds.), *Sociobiology and psychology: Ideas, issues, and applications* (pp. 335–351). Hillsdale, NJ: Lawrence Erlbaum Associates.

BUTLER, J. M., & HAIGH, G. V. (1954). Changes in the relation between self-concepts and ideal concepts consequent upon client-centered counseling. In C. R. Rogers & R. F. Dymond (Eds.), *Psychotherapy and personality change: Co-ordinated studies in the client-centered approach*. Chicago: University of Chicago Press.

CAPLAN, P. J. (1979). Erikson's concept of inner space: A data-based reevaluation. *American Journal of Orthopsychiatry*, 49, 100–108.

CARLSON, R. (1980). Studies of Jungian typology: II. Representations of the personal world. *Journal of Personality and Social Psychology*, 38, 801–810.

CARLSON, R., & LEVY, N. (1973). Studies of Jungian typology: I. Memory, social perception, and social action. *Journal of Personality*, 41, 559–576.

CARTWRIGHT, D. S. (1956). Self-consistency as a factor affecting immediate recall. *Journal of Abnormal and Social Psychology*, 52, 212–218.

CATTELL, R. B. (1950). *Personality: A systematic, theoretical and factual study*. New York: McGraw-Hill.

CATTELL, R. B. (1957). *Personality and motivation structure and measurement*. Yonkers, NY: World Book Company.

CATTELL, R. B. (1965). *The scientific analysis of personality*. Baltimore: Penguin.

CATTELL, R. B. (1973). *Personality and mood by questionnaire*. San Francisco: Jossey-Bass.

CATTELL, R. B. (1974). Autobiography. In G. Lindzey (Ed.), *A History of Psychology in Autobiography* (Vol. 6). Englewood Cliffs, NJ: Prentice-Hall.

CATTELL, R. B. (1975). Clinical analysis questionnaire (CAQ). Champaign, IL: Institute for Personality and Ability Testing.

CATTELL, R. B. (1979, 1980). *Personality and learning theory* (Vols. 1 & 2). New York: Springer.

CATTELL, R. B. (1982). *The inheritance of personality and ability*. New York: Academic Press.

CATTELL, R. B., BREUL, H., & HARTMAN, H. P. (1952). An attempt at a more refined definition of the cultural dimensions of syntality in modern nations. *American Sociological Review*, 17, 408–421.

CATTELL, R. B., EBER, H. W., & TATSUOKA, M. M. (1970). *Handbook for the 16 PF questionnaire*. Champaign, IL: Institute for Personality and Ability Testing.

CATTELL, R. B., & NESSELROADE, J. R. (1967). Likeness and completeness theories examined by sixteen personality factors measured by stably and unstably married couples. *Journal of Personality and Social Psychology*, 7, 351–361.

CATTELL, R. B., SAUNDERS, D. R., & STICE, G. F. (1950). *The 16 personality factor questionnaire*. Champaign, IL: Institute for Personality and Ability Testing.

CATTELL, R. B., SCHUERGER, J. M., & KLEIN, T. W. (1982). Heritabilities of ego strength (factor C), superego strength (factor G), and self-sentiment (factor Q_3) by multiple abstract variance analysis. *Journal of Clinical Psychology*, 38, 769–779.

CATTELL, R. B., & WARBURTON, F. W. (1967). *Objective personality and motivation tests: A theoretical and practical compendium*. Urbana: University of Illinois Press.

CHIANG, H., & MASLOW, A. H. (Eds.). (1977). *The healthy personality* (2nd ed.). New York: Van Nostrand.

CHODORKOFF, B. (1954). Self-perception, perceptual defense, and adjustment. *Journal of Abnormal and Social Psychology*, 49, 508–512.

CHOMSKY, N. A. (1959). A review of verbal behavior by B. F. Skinner. *Language*, 35, 26–58.

CIACCIO, N. (1971). A test of Erikson's theory of ego epigenesis. *Developmental Psychology*, 4, 306–311.

COAN, R. W. (1977). *Hero, artist, sage, or saint? A survey of views on what is variously called mental health, normality, maturity, self-actualization, and human fulfillment*. New York: Columbia University Press.

COLES, R. (1970). *Erik Erikson: The growth of his work*. Boston: Little, Brown.

CORDES, C. (1984). Easing toward perfection at Twin Oaks. *APA Monitor* (Vol. 15, No. 11), pp. 1, 30–31.

CORSINI, R. J. (Ed.). (1977). *Current personality theories.* Itasca, IL: Peacock Publishers.

COTE, J. E., & LEVINE, C. (1983). Marcia and Erikson: The relationships among ego identity status, neuroticism, dogmatism, and purpose in life. *Journal of Youth and Adolescence, 12,* 43–53.

CRAIGHEAD, W. E., KAZDIN, A. E., & MAHONEY, M. J. (1976). *Behavior modification: Principles, issues, and applications.* Boston, MA: Houghton Mifflin.

CRANDALL, J. E. (1980). Adler's concept of social interest: Theory, measurement, and implications for adjustment. *Journal of Personality and Social Psychology, 39,* 481–495.

CRANDALL, J. E. (1981). *Theory and measurement of social interest: Empirical tests of Alfred Adler's concept.* New York: Columbia University Press.

CRANDALL, J. E. (1982). Social interest, extreme response style, and implications for adjustment. *Journal of Research in Personality, 16,* 82–89.

CRAWFORD, C. (1987). Sociobiology: Of what value to psychology? In C. Crawford, M. Smith, & D. Krebs (Eds.), *Sociobiology and psychology: Ideas, issues, and applications* (pp. 3–30). Hillsdale, NJ: Lawrence Erlbaum Associates.

CRAWFORD. C., SMITH, M., & KREBS, D. (Eds.). (1987). *Sociobiology and psychology: Ideas, issues, and applications.* Hillsdale, NJ: Lawrence Erlbaum Associates.

CROSS, H. J., & ALLEN, J. G. (1970). Ego identity status, adjustment, and academic achievement. *Journal of Consulting and Clinical Psychology, 34,* 288.

CRUMBAUGH, J. C. (1968). Cross-validation of Purpose-in-Life Test based on Frankl's concept. *Journal of Individual Psychology, 24,* 74–81.

DANDES, M. (1966). Psychological health and teaching effectiveness. *Journal of Teaching Education, 17,* 301–306.

DARWIN, C. (1859). *The origin of species: By means of natural selection or the preservation of favoured races in the struggle for life.* New York: New American Library.

DAVIS, A., & DOLLARD, J. (1940). *Children of bondage.* Washington, DC: American Council on Education.

DAVIS, S., THOMAS, R., & WEAVER, M. (1982). Psychology's contemporary and all-time notables: Student, faculty, and chairperson viewpoints. *Bulletin of the Psychonomic Society, 20,* 3–6.

DAWES, A. (1985). Drug dependence. In E. Button (Ed.), *Personal construct theory and mental health: Theory, research, and practice.* Beckenham, England: Croom Helm.

DE CATANZARO, D. (1987). Evolutionary pressures and limitations to self-preservation. In C. Crawford, M. Smith, & D. Krebs (Eds.), Sociobiology and psychology: Ideas, issues, and applications (pp. 311–333). Hillsdale, NJ: Lawrence Erlbaum Associates.

DIAMOND, M. J., & SHAPIRO, J. L. (1973). Changes in locus of control as a function of encounter group experiences: A study and replication. *Journal of Abnormal Psychology, 82,* 514–518.

DIGMAN, J., & TAKEMOTO-CHOCK, N. (1981). Factors in the natural language of personality: Reanalysis, comparison, and interpretation of six major studies. *Multivariate Behavioral Research, 16,* 149–170.

DOBSON, K. S., & BREITER, H. J. (1983). Cognitive assessment of depression: Reliability and validity of three measures. *Journal of Abnormal Psychology, 92,* 107–109.

DOLLARD, J. (1937). *Caste and class in a southern town.* New Haven: Yale University Press.

DOLLARD, J. (1942). *Victory over fear.* New York: Reynal and Hitchcock.

DOLLARD, J. (1943). *Fear in battle.* New Haven: Yale University Press.

DOLLARD, J., DOOB, L. W., MILLER, N. E., MOWRER, O. H., & SEARS, R. R. (1939). *Frustration and Aggression.* New Haven: Yale University Press.

DOLLARD, J., & MILLER, N. E. (1950). *Personality and psychotherapy: An analysis in terms of learning, thinking and culture.* New York: McGraw-Hill.

DOSAMANTES-ALPERSON, E., & MERRILL, N. (1980). Growth effects of experiential movement psychotherapy. *Psychotherapy: Theory, research, and practice, 17,* 63–68.

DREGER, R. M. (1972). (Ed.) *Multivariate personality research: Contributions to the understanding of personality in honor of Raymond B. Cattell.* Baton Rouge: Claitor.

DREIKURS, R. (1957). *Psychology in the classroom.* New York: Harper & Row.

DREIKURS, R. (WITH VICKI SOLTZ). (1964). *Children: The challenge.* New York: Duell, Sloan and Pearce.

DREIKURS, R., & GREY, L. (1968). *A new approach to discipline: Logical consequences.* New York: Hawthorne.

DUNNETTE, M. D. (1969). People feeling: Joy, more joy, and the "slough of despond." *Journal of Applied Behavioral Science, 5,* 25–44.

EIDELSON, R. J., & EPSTEIN, N. (1982). Cognition and relationship maladjustment: Development of a measure of dysfunctional relationship beliefs. *Journal of Consulting and Clinical Psychology, 50,* 715–720.

ELLENBERGER, H. (1970). *The discovery of the unconscious.* New York: Basic Books.

ELLENBERGER, H. (1972). The story of "Anna O.": A critical review with new data. *Journal of the Behavioral Sciences, 8,* 267–279.

ELLIS, A. (1970). Tribute to Alfred Adler. *Journal of Individual Psychology, 26,* 11–12.

ELLIS, A., & GREIGER, R. (1977). *Handbook of rational emotive therapy.* New York: Julian Press.

ELMS, A. C. (1972). Allport, Freud, and the clean little boy. *The Psychoanalytic Review, 59,* 627–632.

ERIKSON, E. H. (1959). *Identity and the life cycle. Selected papers.* New York: International Universities Press.

ERIKSON, E. H. (1963). *Childhood and society.* New York: Norton. (Original work published 1950)

ERIKSON, E. H. (1964). *Insight and responsibility.* New York: Norton.

ERIKSON, E. H. (1968a). *Identity, youth, and crisis.* New York: Norton.

ERIKSON, E. H. (1968b). Identity and identity diffusion. In C. Gordon & K. J. Gergen (Eds.), *The self in social interaction.* New York: Wiley.

ERIKSON, E. H. (1969). *Gandhi's truth: On the origins of militant nonviolence.* New York: Norton.

ERIKSON, E. H. (1975a). Once more the inner space. In E. H. Erikson (Ed.), *Life history and the historical moment.* New York: Norton.

ERIKSON, E. H. (1975b). *Life history and the historical moment.* New York: Norton.

ERIKSON, E. H. (1977). *Toys and reasons: Stages in the ritualization of experience.* New York: Norton.

ERNST, C., & ANGST, J. (1983). *Birth order: Its influence on personality.* New York: Springer-Verlag.

EVANS, R. I. (1968). *B. F. Skinner: The man and his ideas.* New York: Dutton.

EVANS, R. I. (1976). *The making of psychology: Discussions with creative contributors.* New York: Knopf.

EVANS, R. I. (1978, July). Donald Bannister: On clinical psychology in Britain. *APA Monitor* (Vol. 9, No. 7), pp. 6–7.

EYSENCK, H. J., & EYSENCK, M. W. (1985). *Personality and individual differences.* New York: Plenum Press.

FABER, M. D. (1970). Allport's visit with Freud. *The Psychoanalytic Review, 57,* 60–64.

FALBO, T. (1981). Relationships between birth category, achievement, and interpersonal orientation. *Journal of Personality and Social Psychology, 41,* 121–131.

FERSTER, C. B., & SKINNER, B. F. (1957). *Schedules of reinforcement.* Englewood Cliffs, NJ: Prentice-Hall.

FISHER, K. (1988). Preschool delay tactics predict teen competence. *APA Monitor* (Vol. 19, No. 8), pp. 12–13.

FISHER, S., & GREENBERG, R. P. (1977). *The scientific credibility of Freud's theories and therapy.* New York: Basic Books.

FOULDS, M. L. (1969). Self-actualization and the communication of facilitative conditions under counseling. *Journal of Counseling Psychology, 16,* 132–136.

FRANKL, V. E. (1970). Tribute to Alfred Adler. *Journal of Individual Psychology, 26,* 11–12.

FREDERIKSEN, L. W., JENKINS, J. O., & CARR, C. R. (1976). Indirect modification of adolescent drug abuse using contingency contracting. *Journal of Behavior Therapy and Experimental Psychiatry, 7,* 377–378.

FREUD, A. (1936). *The ego and the mechanisms of defense.* New York: International Universities Press.

FREUD, S. (1953). *The interpretation of dreams.* In *The standard edition of the complete psychological works of Sigmund Freud* (Vols. 4 & 5). London: Hogarth Press. (Original work published 1900)

FREUD, S. (1955). *Beyond the pleasure principle.* In *The standard edition of the complete psychological works of Sigmund Freud* (Vol. 18). London: Hogarth Press. (Original work published 1920a)

FREUD, S. (1955). *A difficulty in the path of psychoanalysis.* In J. Strachey (Ed. and Trans.), *The standard edition of the complete psychological works of Sigmund Freud* (Vol. 17, pp. 136–144). London: Hogarth Press. (Original work published 1917)

FREUD, S. (1955). *A note on the prehistory of the technique of analysis.* In *The standard edition of the complete psychological works of Sigmund Freud* (Vol. 18). London: Hogarth Press. (Original work published 1920b).

FREUD, S. (1957). *On the history of psychoanalytic movement.* In *The standard edition of the complete psychological works of Sigmund Freud* (Vol. 14). London: Hogarth Press. (Original work published 1914)

FREUD, S. (1958). *On beginning the treatment.* In *The standard edition of the complete psychological works of Sigmund Freud* (Vol. 12). London: Hogarth Press. (Original work published 1913)

FREUD, S. (1958). *Totem and taboo.* In *The standard edition of the complete psychological works of Sigmund Freud* (Vol. 13). London: Hogarth Press. (Original work published 1913)

FREUD, S. (1960). *Jokes and their relation to the unconscious.* In *The standard edition of the complete psychological works of Sigmund Freud* (Vol. 8). London: Hogarth Press. (Original work published 1905)

FREUD, S. (1960). *The psychopathology of everyday life.* In *The standard edition of the complete psychological works of Sigmund Freud* (Vol. 6). London: Hogarth Press. (Original work published 1901)

FREUD, S. (1961). *Civilization and its discontents.* In *The standard edition of the complete psychological works of Sigmund Freud* (Vol. 21). London: Hogarth Press. (Original work published 1930)

FREUD, S. (1961). *The ego and the id.* In J. Strachey (Ed. and Trans.), *The standard edition of the complete psychological works of Sigmund Freud* (Vol. 19, pp. 3–59). London: Hogarth Press. (Original work published 1923)

FREUD, S. (1961). *The future of an illusion.* In *The standard edition of the complete psychological works of Sigmund Freud* (Vol. 22). London: Hogarth Press. (Original work published 1927)

FREUD, S. (1964). *Moses and monotheism.* In J. Strachey (Ed. and Trans.), *The standard edition of the complete psychological works of Sigmund Freud* (Vol. 23, pp. 3–137). London: Hogarth Press. (Original work published 1939)

FREUD, S. (1964). *New introductory lectures on psychoanalysis.* In J. Strachey (Ed. and Trans.), *The standard edition of the complete psychological works of Sigmund Freud* (Vol. 22, pp. 3–182). London: Hogarth Press. (Original work published 1933)

FREUD, S. (1966). *Introductory lectures on psychoanalysis.* New York: Norton. (Original work published 1917)

GAGNON, J. H., & DAVISON, G. C. (1976). Asylums, the token economy and the merits of mental life. *Behavior Therapy, 7,* 528–534.

GAY, P. (1988). *Freud: A life for our time.* New York: Norton.

GENDLIN, E. T. (1988). Carl Rogers (1902–1987). *American Psychologist, 43,* 127–128.

GENDLIN, E. T., BEEBE, J., III, CASSENS, J., KLEIN, M., & OBERLANDER, M. (1968). Focusing ability in psychotherapy, personality, and creativity. In J. M. Schlien (Ed.), *Research in psychotherapy* (Vol. 3). Washington, DC: American Psychological Association.

GENDLIN, E. T., & TOMLINSON, T. M. (1967). The process conception and its measurement. In C. R. Rogers, E. T. Gendlin, D. J. Kiesler, & C. B. Truax (Eds.), *The psychotherapeutic relationship and its impact: A study of psychotherapy with schizophrenics.* Madison: University of Wisconsin Press.

GEWIRTZ, J. L. (1971). Conditional responding as a paradigm for observational, imitative learning and vicarious imitative learning and vicarious reinforcement. In H. W. Reese (Ed.), *Advances in child development and behavior* (pp. 274–304). New York: Academic Press.

GILMAN, S. L. (Ed.). (1982). *Introducing psychoanalytic theory.* New York: Brunner/Mazel.

GOLDBERG, L. R. (1981). Language and individual differences: The search for universals in personality lexicons. In L. Wheeler (Ed.), *Review of Personality and Social Psychology* (pp. 141–165). Beverly Hills, CA: Sage.

GOLDSTEIN, A. P., & MICHAELS, G. Y. (1985). *Empathy: Development training and consequences.* Hillsdale, NJ: Lawrence Erlbaum Associates.

GOULD, S. J. (1978). Sociobiology: The art of story telling. *New Scientist, 80,* 530–533.

GOULD, S. J., & LEWONTIN, R. C. (1979). The spandrels of San Marco and the Panglossian paradigm: A critique of the adaptationist programme. *Proceedings of the Royal Society of London, 205,* 581–598.

GRAHAM, W., & BALLOUN, J. (1973). An empirical test of Maslow's need hierarchy theory. *Journal of Humanistic Psychology, 13,* 97–108.

GREENSPOON, J. (1955). The reinforcing effect of two spoken sounds on the frequency of two responses. *American Journal of Psychology, 68,* 409–416.

GURMAN, A. S. (1977). The patient's perception of therapeutic relationships. In A. S. Gurman & A. M. Razin (Eds.), *Effective psychotherapy: A handbook of research.* Oxford: Pergammon Press.

HAFNER, J. F., FAKOURI, M. E., & LABRENTZ, H. L. (1982). First memories of "normal" and alcoholic individuals. *Individual Psychology, 38,* 238–244.

HALL, C. S. (1954). *A primer of Freudian psychology.* Cleveland: World Publishing.

HALL, C. S., & LINDZEY, G. (1978). *Theories of personality* (3rd ed.). New York: Wiley.

HALL, C. S., & NORDLY, J. (1973). *A primer of Jungian psychology.* New York: New American Library.

HALL, C. S., & VAN DE CASTLE, R. L. (1965). An empirical investigation of the castration complex in dreams. *Journal of Personality, 33,* 20–29.

HALL, M. H. (1968, July). A conversation with Abraham Maslow. *Psychology Today,* pp. 35–37, 54–57.

HAMILTON, W. D. (1964). The genetical evolution of social behavior I & II. *Journal of Theoretical Biology, 7,* 1–52.

HANNAH, B. (1976). *Jung: His life and his work.* New York: Putnam.

HARPER, R. G., WIENS, A. N., & MATARAZZO, J. D. (1978). *Nonverbal communication: The state of the art.* New York: Wiley.

HAWTON, H. (1948). *Philosophy for pleasure.* London: Watts.

HAYDEN, B., & NASBY, W. (1977). Interpersonal conceptual structures, predictive accuracy, and social adjustment of emotionally disturbed boys. *Journal of Abnormal Psychology, 86,* 315–320.

HERGENHAHN, B. R. (1972). *Shaping your child's personality.* Englewood Cliffs, NJ: Prentice-Hall.

HERGENHAHN, B. R. (1974). *A self-directing introduction to psychological experimentation* (2nd ed.). Monterey, CA: Brooks/Cole Publishing.

HERGENHAHN, B. R. (1986). *An introduction to the history of psychology.* Belmont, CA: Wadsworth.

HERGENHAHN, B. R. (1988). *An introduction to theories of learning* (3rd ed.). Englewood Cliffs, NJ: Prentice-Hall.

HOFFMAN, E. (1988). *The right to be human: A biography of Abraham Maslow.* Los Angeles, CA: Jeremy P. Tarcher.

HOLDEN, C. (1987, August). The genetics of personality. *Science, 237,* 598–601.

HOLDSTOCK, T. L., & ROGERS, C. R. (1977). Person-centered theory. In R. J. Corsini (Ed.), *Current personality theories*. Itasca, IL: Peacock Publishers.

HOMME, L. E., CSANYI, A., GONZALES, M., & RECHS, J. (1969). *How to use contingency contracting in the classroom*. Champaign, IL: Research Press.

HORNEY, K. (1937). *The neurotic personality of our time*. New York: Norton.

HORNEY, K. (1939). *New ways in psychoanalysis*. New York: Norton.

HORNEY, K. (1942). *Self-analysis*. New York: Norton.

HORNEY, K. (1945). *Our inner conflicts*. New York: Norton.

HORNEY, K. (1950). *Neurosis and human growth: The struggle toward self-realization*. New York: Norton.

HORNEY, K. (1967). *Feminine psychology*. New York: Norton. (Original work published 1923–1937)

HORNEY, K. (1980). *The adolescent diaries of Karen Horney*. New York: Basic Books.

HULL, C. L. (1943). *Principles of behavior*. New York: Appleton-Century-Crofts.

HUNDLEBY, J. D., PAWLIK, K., & CATTELL, R. B. (1965). *Personality factors in objective test devices: A critical integration of a quarter of a century's research*. San Diego, CA: Knapp.

HUNT, J. M. (1979). Psychological development: Early experience. *Annual Review of Psychology, 30*, 103–143.

HUNTLEY, C. W., & DAVIS, F. (1983). Undergraduate study of values scores as predictors of occupation twenty-five years later. *Journal of Personality and Social Psychology, 45*, 1148–1155.

ILARDI, R., & MAY, W. (1968). A reliability study of Shostrom's personal orientation inventory. *Journal of Humanistic Psychology, 8*, 68–72.

INGRAM, D. H. (Ed.). (1987). *Karen Horney: Final lectures*. New York: Norton.

JACOBSON, N. S. (1978). Specific and nonspecific factors in the effectiveness of a behavioral approach to the treatment of marital discord. *Journal of Consulting and Clinical Psychology, 46*, 442–452.

JANKOWICZ, A. D. (1987). Whatever became of George Kelly? Applications and implications. *American Psychologist, 42*, 481–487.

JONES, E. (1953, 1955, 1957). *The life and work of Sigmund Freud*. (Vols. 1–3). New York: Basic Books.

JOURARD, S. M. (1974). *Healthy personality: An approach from the viewpoint of humanistic psychology*. New York: Macmillan.

JUNG, C. G. (1928). *Contributions to analytical psychology*. New York: Harcourt Brace Jovanovich.

JUNG, C. G. (1953). The psychology of the unconscious. In *The collected works of C. G. Jung* (Vol. 7). Princeton: Princeton University Press. (Original work published 1912)

JUNG, C. G. (1956). *Two essays on analytical psychology*. New York: Meridian Books.

JUNG, C. G. (1960). The psychology of dementia praecox. In *The collected works of C. G. Jung* (Vol. 3). Princeton: Princeton University Press. (Original work published 1907)

JUNG, C. G. (1961). *Memories, dreams, reflections*. New York: Random House.

JUNG, C. G. (1961). The theory of psychoanalysis. In *The collected works of C. G. Jung* (Vol. 4). Princeton: Princeton University Press. (Original work published 1913a)

JUNG, C. G. (1964). *Man and his symbols*. New York: Doubleday.

JUNG, C. G. (1966). Two essays on analytical psychology. In *The collected works of C. G. Jung* (Vol. 7). Princeton: Princeton University Press. (Original work published 1917)

JUNG, C. G. (1968). *Analytical psychology: Its theory and practice*. (The Tavistock Lectures.) New York: Pantheon.

JUNG, C. G. (1969). The structure of the psyche. In *The collected works of C. G. Jung* (Vol. 8). Princeton, NJ: Princeton University Press. (Original work published 1931)

JUNG, C. G. (1971). Psychological types. In *The collected works of C. G. Jung* (Vol. 6). Princeton: Princeton University Press. (Original work published 1921)

JUNG, C. G. (1973). On the doctrine of complexes. In *The collected works of C. G. Jung* (Vol. 2). Princeton: Princeton University Press. (Original work published 1913b)

JUNG, C. G. (1973). The psychological diagnosis of evidence. In *The collected works of C. G. Jung* (Vol. 2). Princeton: Princeton University Press. (Original work published 1909)

KAHN, S., ZIMMERMAN, G., CSIKSZENTMIHALYI, M., & GETZELS, J. W. (1985). Relations between identity in young adulthood and intimacy at midlife. *Journal of Personality and Social Psychology, 49*, 1316–1322.

KAZDIN, A. E. (1977). *The token economy: A review and evaluation*. New York: Plenum Press.

KAZDIN, A. E. (1980). *Behavior modification in applied settings*. Homewood, IL: Dorsey.

KAZDIN, A. E., & BOOTZIN, R. R. (1972). The token economy: An evaluative review. *Journal of Applied Behavior Analysis, 5*, 343–372.

KELLEY, M. L., & STOKES, T. F. (1982). Contingency contracting with disadvantaged youths: Improving classroom performance. *Journal of Applied Behavior Analysis, 15*, 447–454.

KELLY, G. A. (1955). *The psychology of personal constructs: A theory of personality* (2 vols.). New York: Norton.

KELLY, G. A. (1958). Man's construction of his alternatives. In

G. Lindzey (Ed.), *Assessment of human motives.* New York: Holt, Rinehart & Winston.

KELLY, G. A. (1963). *A theory of personality: The psychology of personal constructs.* New York: Norton.

KELLY, G. A. (1964). The language of hypotheses: Man's psychological instrument. *Journal of Individual Psychology, 20,* 137–152.

KELLY, G. A. (1969). The autobiography of a theory. In B. Maher (Ed.), *Clinical psychology and personality: Selected papers of George Kelly* (pp. 40–65). New York: Wiley.

KELLY, G. A. (1970). A brief introduction to personal construct theory. In D. Bannister (Ed.), *Perspectives in personal construct theory.* New York: Academic Press.

KIERKEGAARD, S. (1944). *The concept of dread* (W. Lowrie, Trans.). Princeton: Princeton University Press. (Original work published 1844 as *The concept of anxiety.*)

KILMANN, R. H., & TAYLOR, V. A. (1974). A contingency approach to laboratory learning: Psychological types versus experimental norms. *Human Relations, 27,* 891–909.

KINKADE, K. (1973). *A Walden Two experiment.* New York: Morrow.

KIRSCHENBAUM, H. (1979). *On becoming Carl Rogers.* New York: Dell Publishing.

KLAVETTER, R., & MOGAR, R. (1967). Stability and internal consistency of a measure of self-actualization. *Psychological Reports, 21,* 422–424.

KLINE, P. (1972). *Fact and fantasy in Freudian theory.* London: Methuen.

KLUCKHOHN, C., & MURRAY, H. A. (1953). Personality formation: The determinants. In C. Kluckhohn, H. A. Murray, & D. M. Schneider (Eds.), *Personality in nature, society, and culture* (2nd ed.) (pp. 53–67). New York: Knopf.

KRASNER, L. (1970). Token economy as an illustration of operant conditioning procedures with the aged, with youth, and with society. In D. J. Levis (Ed.), *Learning approaches to therapeutic behavior change* (pp. 74–101). Chicago: Aldine.

KUHN, T. S. (1973). *The structure of scientific revolutions* (2nd ed.). Chicago: University of Chicago Press.

LANDFIELD, A. W., & LEITNER, L. M. (Eds.). (1980). *Personal construct psychology: Psychotherapy and personality.* New York: Wiley.

LEAK, G. K., & CHRISTOPHER, S. B. (1982). Freudian psychoanalysis and sociobiology: A synthesis. *American Psychologist, 37,* 313–322.

LEITNER, L. (1984). The terrors of cognition. In D. Bannister (Ed.), *Further perspectives in personal construct theory.* New York: Academic Press.

LEMAY, M., & DAMM, V. (1968). The personal orientation inventory as a measure of self-actualization of underachievers. *Measurement and Evaluation in Guidance,* 110–114.

LESTER, D., HVEZDA, J., SULLIVAN, S., & PLOURDE, R. (1983). Maslow's hierarchy of needs and psychological health. *Journal of General Psychology, 109,* 83–85.

LEVANT, R. F., & SCHLIEN, J. M. (Eds.). (1984). *Client-centered therapy and the person-centered approach: New directions in theory, research, and practice.* New York: Praeger.

LEWIN, K. (1935). *A dynamic theory of personality.* New York: McGraw-Hill.

LEWONTIN, R. C., ROSE, S., & KAMIN, L. J. (1984). *Not in our genes.* New York: Pantheon.

LOWRY, R. J. (1979). *The journals of A. H. Maslow* (Vols. 1 & 2). Monterey, CA: Brooks/Cole.

LUMSDEN, C. J., & WILSON, E. O. (1981). *Genes, mind, and culture: The coevolutionary process.* Cambridge, MA: Harvard University Press.

LUMSDEN, C. J., & WILSON, E. O. (1985). The relation between biological and cultural evolution. *Journal of Social and Biological Structures, 8,* 343–359.

MADDI, S. R. (1972). *Personality theories: A comparative analysis.* Homewood, IL: Dorsey.

MAHER, B. (Ed.). (1969). *Clinical psychology and personality: The selected papers of George Kelly.* New York: Wiley.

MAHONEY, J., & HARNETT, J. (1973). Self-actualization and self-ideal discrepancy. *Journal of Psychology, 85,* 37–42.

MALOTT, R. W., RITTERBY, K., & WOLF, E. L. C. (1973). *An introduction to behavior modification.* Kalamazoo, MI: Behaviordelia.

MANCUSO, J. C., & ADAMS-WEBBER, J. R. (Eds.). (1982). *The construing person.* New York: Praeger.

MANN, R. A. (1972). The behavior-therapeutic use of contingency contracting to control an adult behavior problem: Weight control. *Journal of Applied Behavior Analysis, 5,* 99–109.

MARCIA, J. (1966). Development and validation of ego identity status. *Journal of Personality and Social Psychology, 3,* 551–558.

MARCIA, J., & FRIEDMAN, M. L. (1970). Ego identity status in college women. *Journal of Personality, 38,* 249–263.

MARROW, A. J., BOWERS, D. G., & SEASHORE, S. E. (1967). *Management by participation.* New York: Harper & Row.

MASLING, J. (Ed.). (1983). *Empirical studies of psychoanalytic theories.* Hillsdale, NJ: Analytic Press.

MASLOW, A. H. (1942). Self-esteem (dominance-feeling) and sexuality in women. *Journal of Social Psychology, 16,* 259–294.

MASLOW, A. H. (1964). *Religions, values and peak experiences.* Columbus, OH: Ohio State University Press.

MASLOW, A. H. (1965). *Eupsychian management: A journal.* Homewood, IL: Irwin-Dorsey.

MASLOW, A. H. (1966). *The psychology of science: A reconnaissance.* New York: Harper & Row.

MASLOW, A. H. (1968). *Toward a psychology of being* (2nd ed.). New York: Van Nostrand.

MASLOW, A. H. (1970). *Motivation and personality* (2nd ed.). New York: Harper & Row.

MASLOW, A. H. (1971). *The farther reaches of human nature.* New York: Viking.

MASLOW, A. H. (1987). *Motivation and personality* (3rd ed.). (Revised by Frager, R., Fadiman, J., McReynolds, C., & Cox, R.). New York: Harper & Row.

MASSERMAN, J. H. (1961). *Principles of dynamic psychiatry* (2nd ed.). Philadelphia: Saunders.

MASSEY, R. F. (1981). *Personality theories: Comparisons and syntheses.* New York: Van Nostrand.

MASSON, J. M. (1984). *The assault on truth: Freud's suppression of the seduction theory.* New York: Farrar, Straus, and Giroux.

MASSON, J. M. (1984, February). Freud and the seduction theory. *The Atlantic Monthly,* pp. 33–60.

MASTERS, J. C., BURISH, T. G., HOLLON, S. D., & RIMM, D. C. (1987). *Behavior therapy: Techniques and empirical findings* (3rd ed.). Orlando, FL: Harcourt Brace Jovanovich.

MATHES, E. W., ZEVON, M. A., ROTER, P. M., & JOERGER, S. M. (1982). Peak experience tendencies: Scale development and theory testing. *Journal of Humanistic Psychology, 22,* 92–108.

MAY, R. (1939). *The art of counseling: How to give and gain mental health.* Nashville: Abingdon-Cokesbury.

MAY, R. (1940). *The springs of creative living: A study of human nature and God.* New York: Abingdon-Cokesbury.

MAY, R. (1950). *The meaning of anxiety.* New York: Ronald Press.

MAY, R. (1953). *Man's search for himself.* New York: Norton.

MAY, R. (Ed.). (1961). *Existential psychology.* New York: Random House.

MAY, R. (1967). *Psychology and the human dilemma.* New York: Van Nostrand.

MAY, R. (1969). *Love and will.* New York: Norton.

MAY, R. (1972). *Power and innocence: A search for the sources of violence.* New York: Norton.

MAY, R. (1973). *Paulus: Reminiscences of a friendship.* New York: Harper & Row.

MAY, R. (1975). *The courage to create.* New York: Norton.

MAY, R. (1981). *Freedom and destiny.* New York: Norton.

MAY, R. (1983). *The discovery of being: Writings in existential psychology.* New York: Norton.

MAY, R., ANGEL, E., & ELLENBERGER, H. F. (Eds.). (1958). *Existence: A new dimension in psychiatry and psychology.* New York: Basic Books.

McGAW, W. H., RICE, C. P., & ROGERS, C. R. (1973). *The steel shutter.* LaJolla, CA: Film Center for Studies of the Person.

McGUIRE, W. (Ed.). (1974). *The Freud/Jung letters.* Princeton: Princeton University Press.

MILLER, G. A. (1965). Some preliminaries to psycholinguistics. *American Psychologist, 20,* 15–20.

MILLER, N. E. (1944). Experimental studies of conflict. In J. M. Hunt (Ed.). *Personality and the behavior disorders* (Vol. 1). New York: Ronald Press.

MILLER, N. E. (1948a). Studies of fear as an acquirable drive: I. Fear as motivation and fear reduction as reinforcement in the learning of new responses. *Journal of Experimental Psychology, 38,* 89–101.

MILLER, N. E. (1948b). Theory and experiment relating psychoanalytic displacement to stimulus response generalization. *Journal of Abnormal and Social Psychology, 43,* 155–178.

MILLER, N. E. (1959). Liberalization of basic S-R concepts: Extensions to conflict behavior, motivation and social learning. In S. Koch (Ed.), *Psychology: A study of a science* (Vol. 2). New York: McGraw-Hill.

MILLER, N. E. (1964). Some implications of modern behavior theory for personality change and psychotherapy. In P. Worchel & D. Bryne (Eds.), *Personality change.* New York: Wiley.

MILLER, N. E. (1982). Obituary: John Dollard (1900–1980). *American Psychologist, 37,* 587–588.

MILLER, N. E. (1983). Behavioral medicine: Symbiosis between laboratory and clinic. In M. R. Rosenzweig & L. W. Porter (Eds.), *Annual Review of Psychology, 34,* 1–31.

MILLER, N. E. (1984). *Bridges between laboratory and clinic.* New York: Praeger.

MILLER, N. E., & DOLLARD, J. (1941). *Social learning and imitation.* New Haven: Yale University Press.

MILLER, P. M. (1972). The use of behavioral contracting in the treatment of alcoholism: A case report. *Behavior Therapy, 3,* 593–596.

MISCHEL, W. (1968). *Personality and assessment.* New York: Wiley.

MISCHEL, W. (1969). Continuity and change in personality. *American Psychologist, 24,* 1012–1018.

MISCHEL, W. (1977). The interaction of person and situation. In D. Magnusson & N. S. Endler (Eds.), *Personality at the crossroads: Current issues in interactional psychology.* Hillsdale, NJ: Lawrence Erlbaum Associates.

MISCHEL, W. (1981). *Introduction to personality* (3rd ed.). New York: Holt, Rinehart & Winston.

MISCHEL, W. (1984). Convergences and challenges in the search for consistency. *American Psychologist, 39,* 351–364.

Mischel, W. (1986). *Introduction to personality* (4th ed.). New York: Holt, Rinehart & Winston.

Mischel, W., & Peake, P. K. (1982). Beyond déjà vu in the search for cross-situational consistency. *Psychological Review, 89,* 730–755.

Mitchell, C., & Stuart, R. B. (1984). Effect of self-efficacy on dropout from obesity treatment. *Journal of Consulting and Clinical Psychology, 52,* 1100–1101.

Monte, C. F. (1987). *Beneath the mask: An introduction to theories of personality* (3rd ed.). New York: Praeger.

Morris, R. (1983). *Evolution and human nature.* New York: Seaview/Putnam.

Mosak, H. (1973). (Ed.). *Alfred Adler: His Influence on Psychology Today.* Park Ridge, IL: Noyes Press.

Murray, E. J. & Berkun, M. M. (1955). Displacement as a function of conflict. *Journal of Abnormal and Social Psychology, 51,* 47–56.

Myers, I. B. (1962). *The Myers-Briggs type indicator manual.* Palo Alto, CA: Consulting Psychologists Press.

Neimeyer, G. J., & Hudson, J. E. (1984). Couples' constructs: Personal systems in marital satisfaction. In D. Bannister (Ed.), *Further perspectives in personal construct theory.* New York: Academic Press.

Neimeyer, R. A. (1984). Toward a personal construct conceptualization of depression and suicide. In F. R. Epting and R. A. Neimeyer (Eds.), *Personal meanings of death: Applications of personal construct theory to clinical practice* (pp. 127–173). New York: Hemisphere/McGraw-Hill.

Neimeyer, R. A. (1985a). Personal constructs in clinical practice. In P. C. Kendall (Ed.), *Advances in cognitive-behavioral research and therapy* (Vol. 4, pp. 275–339). New York: Academic Press.

Neimeyer, R. A. (1985b). *The development of personal construct psychology.* Lincoln: University of Nebraska Press.

Neimeyer, R. A., & Neimeyer, G. J. (1985). Disturbed relationships: A personal construct view. In E. Button (Ed.), *Personal construct theory and mental health: Theory, research, and practice.* Beckenham, England: Croom Helm.

Olson, H. A. (Ed.). (1979). *Early recollections: Their use in diagnosis and psychotherapy.* Springfield, IL: Charles C Thomas.

Orgler, H. (1963). *Alfred Adler: The man and his work.* New York: Liveright.

Paige, J. M. (1966). Letters from Jenny: An approach to the clinical analysis of personality structure by computer. In P. J. Stone (Ed.), *The general inquirer: A computer approach to content analysis.* Cambridge, Mass.: M.I.T. Press.

Panzarella, R. (1980). The phenomenology of aesthetic peak experiences. *Journal of Humanistic Psychology, 20*(1), 69–85.

Parker, A. (1981). The meaning of attempted suicide to young parasuicides: A repertory grid study. *British Journal of Psychiatry, 139,* 306–312.

Paxton, R. (1980). The effects of a deposit contract as a component in a behavioral programme for stopping smoking. *Behaviour Research and Therapy, 18,* 45–50.

Paxton, R. (1981). Deposit contracts with smokers: Varying frequency and amount of repayments. *Behavior Research and Therapy, 19,* 117–123.

Pervin, L. A. (1980). *Personality: Theory, assessment, and research* (3rd ed.). New York: Wiley.

Pervin, L. A. (1984). *Current controversies and issues in personality* (2nd ed.). New York: Wiley.

Pervin, L. A. (1989). *Personality: Theory and research* (5th ed.). New York: Wiley.

Popper, K. (1963). *Conjectures and refutations.* New York: Basic Books.

Progoff, I. (1973). *Jung, synchronicity, and human destiny: Noncausal dimensions of human experience.* New York: Dell.

Ravizza, K. (1977). Peak experiences in sport. *Journal of Humanistic Psychology, 17*(4), 35–40.

Reeves, C. (1977) *The psychology of Rollo May.* San Francisco: Jossey-Bass.

Rigdon, M. A., & Epting, F. R. (1983). A personal construct perspective on an obsessive client. In J. Adams-Webber & J. C. Mancuso (Eds.), *Applications of personal construct theory.* New York: Academic Press.

Rivers, P., & Landfield, A. W. (1985). Alcohol abuse. In E. Button (Ed.), *Personal construct theory and mental health: Theory, research, and practice.* Beckenham, England. Croom Helm.

Roazen, P. (1976). *Erik H. Erikson: The power and limits of a vision.* New York: Free Press.

Roazen, P. (1980). Erik H. Erikson's America: The political implications of ego psychology. *Journal of the History of the Behavioral Sciences, 16,* 333–341.

Robinson, P. J., & Wood, K. (1984). Fear of death and physical illness: A personal construct approach. In F. R. Epting & R. A. Neimeyer (Eds.), *Personal meanings of death: Applications of personal construct theory to clinical practice.* Washington, DC: Hemisphere.

Rogers, C. R. (1939). *The clinical treatment of the problem child.* Boston: Houghton Mifflin.

Rogers, C. R. (1942). *Counseling and psychotherapy: Newer concepts in practice.* Boston: Houghton Mifflin.

Rogers, C. R. (1951). *Client-centered therapy: Its current practice, implications, and theory.* Boston: Houghton Mifflin.

Rogers, C. R. (1954). The case of Mrs. Oak: A research analysis. In C. R. Rogers & R. F. Dymond (Eds.), *Psychotherapy and personality change.* Chicago: University of Chicago Press.

Rogers, C. R. (1955). Persons or science? A philosophical question. *American Psychologist, 10,* 267–278.

Rogers, C. R. (1956a). Intellectualized psychotherapy. *Contemporary Psychology, 1,* 357–358.

Rogers, C. R. (1956b). Some issues concerning the control of human behavior (Symposium with B. F. Skinner). *Science, 124,* 1057–1066.

Rogers, C. R. (1956c, February). Implications of recent advances in prediction and control of behavior. *Teachers College Record, 57,* 316–322.

Rogers, C. R. (1957). Implications of recent advances in prediction and control of behavior. In E. L. Hartley & R. E. Hartley (Eds.), *Outside readings in psychology* (2nd ed.). New York: T. Y. Crowell.

Rogers, C. R. (1959). A theory of therapy, personality, and interpersonal relationships, as developed in the client-centered framework. In S. Koch (Ed.). *Psychology: A study of a science* (Vol. 3). New York: McGraw-Hill.

Rogers, C. R. (1961). *On becoming a person: A therapist's view of psychotherapy.* Boston: Houghton Mifflin.

Rogers, C. R. (1963). Actualizing tendency in relation to motives and to consciousness. In M. R. Jones (Ed.), *Nebraska Symposium on Motivation, 1963.* Lincoln: University of Nebraska Press.

Rogers, C. R. (1966). Client-centered therapy. In S. Arieti (Ed.), *American handbook of psychiatry.* New York: Basic Books.

Rogers, C. R. (1967). Autobiography. In E. G. Boring & G. Lindzey (Eds.), *A history of psychology in autobiography* (Vol. 5). New York: Appleton.

Rogers, C. R. (1969). *Freedom to learn.* Columbus, OH: Charles E. Merrill.

Rogers, C. R. (1970). *Carl Rogers on encounter groups.* New York: Harper & Row.

Rogers, C. R. (1972a). My personal growth. In A. Burton (Ed.), *Twelve therapists.* San Francisco: Jossey-Bass.

Rogers, C. R. (1972b). *Becoming partners: Marriage and its alternatives.* New York: Delacorte.

Rogers, C. R. (1973). My philosophy of interpersonal relationships and how it grew. *Journal of Humanistic Psychology, 13,* 3–15.

Rogers, C. R. (1974). In Retrospect: Forty-six years. *American Psychologist, 29,* 115–123.

Rogers, C. R. (1977). *Carl Rogers on personal power.* New York: Delacorte.

Rogers, C. R. (1980). *A way of being.* Boston, MA: Houghton Mifflin.

Rogers, C. R. (1983). *Freedom to learn for the 80s.* Columbus, OH: Charles E. Merrill.

Rogers, C. R., & Ryback, D. (1984). One alternative to nuclear planetary suicide. In R. F. Levant and J. M. Shlien (Eds.), *Client-centered therapy and the person-centered approach: New directions in theory, research, and practice.* New York: Praeger.

Rosenbaum, M., & Muroff, M. (Eds.). (1984). *Anna O.: Fourteen contemporary reinterpretations.* New York: The Free Press.

Rosenberg, L. A. (1962). Idealization of self and social adjustment. *Journal of Consulting Psychology, 26,* 487.

Rosenthal, D. A., Gurney, R. M., & Moore, S. M. (1981). From trust to intimacy: A new inventory for examining Erikson's stages of psychosocial development. *Journal of Youth and Adolescence, 10,* 525–537.

Rowe, I., & Marcia, J. E. (1980). Ego identity status, formal operations, and moral development. *Journal of Youth and Adolescence, 9,* 87–99.

Rubins, J. L. (1978). *Karen Horney: Gentle rebel of psychoanalysis.* New York: Dial.

Rubinstein, J., & Slife, B. (1988). *Taking sides: Clashing views on controversial psychological issues* (5th ed.). Guilford, CT: Dushkin Publishing Group.

Rule, W. R. (1972). The relationship between early recollections and selected counselor and life style characteristics (Doctoral Dissertation, University of South Carolina). *Dissertation Abstracts International, 33,* 1448A–1449A. (University Microfilms No. 72–25, 921).

Rule, W. R., & Traver, M. D. (1982). Early recollections and expected leisure activities. *Psychological Reports, 51,* 295–301.

Santogrossi, D., O'Leary, K., Romanczyk, R., & Kaufman, K. (1973). Self-evaluation by adolescents in a psychiatric hospital school token program. *Journal of Applied Behavior Analysis, 6,* 277–287.

Sartre, J.-P. (1956). Existentialism. In W. Kaufmann (Ed.), *Existentialism from Dostoevsky to Sartre.* New York: Meridian Books.

Scarf, M. (1971, February 28). The man who gave us "inferiority complex," "compensation," "aggressive drive" and "style of life." *New York Times Magazine,* pp. 10ff.

Schaefer, H. H., & Martin, P. L. (1969). *Behavioral therapy.* New York: McGraw-Hill.

Schiedel, D. G., & Marcia, J. E. (1985). Ego identity, intimacy, sex role orientation, and gender. *Journal of Personality and Social Psychology, 21,* 149–160.

Schill, T., Monroe, S., Evans, R., & Ramanaiah, N. (1978). The effects of self-verbalizations on performance: A test of the rational-emotive position. *Psychotherapy: Theory, research, and practice, 15,* 2–7.

Schur, M. (1972). *Freud: Living and dying.* New York: International Universities Press.

SHEPHER, J. (1971). Mate selection among second generation kibbutz adolescents and adults: Incest avoidance and negative imprinting. *Archives of Sexual Behavior, 1,* 293–307.

SHEPHER, J. (1983). *Incest: A biosocial view.* Orlando, FL: Academic Press.

SHOSTROM, E. L. (1963). *Personal orientation inventory.* San Diego: Educational and Industrial Testing Service.

SHOSTROM, E. L. (1964). An inventory for the measurement of self-actualization. *Educational and Psychological Measurement, 24,* 207–218.

SHOSTROM, E. L. (1966). Manual for the personal orientation inventory (POI): An inventory for the measurement of self-actualization. San Diego: Educational and Industrial Testing Service.

SHOSTROM, E. L. (1974). *Manual for the personal orientation inventory.* San Diego: Educational and Industrial Testing Service.

SHOSTROM, E. L., KNAPP, L. F., & KNAPP, R. R. (1976). *Actualizing therapy: Foundations for a scientific ethic.* San Diego: Educational and Industrial Testing Service.

SILVERMAN, I. (1987). Race, race differences, and race relations: Perspectives from psychology and sociobiology. In C. Crawford, M. Smith, & D. Krebs (Eds.), *Sociobiology and psychology: Ideas, issues, and applications* (pp. 205–221). Hillsdale, NJ: Lawrence Erlbaum Associates.

SILVERMAN, L. (1976). Psychoanalytic theory: "The reports of my death are greatly exaggerated." *American Psychologist,* 31, 621–637.

SINGER, P. (1981). *The expanding circle: Ethics and sociobiology.* New York: Farrar, Straus and Giroux.

SKINNER, B. F. (1938). *The behavior of organisms: An experimental analysis.* Englewood Cliffs, NJ: Prentice-Hall.

SKINNER, B. F. (1948). *Walden Two.* New York: Macmillan.

SKINNER, B. F. (1951). How to teach animals. *Scientific American, 185,* 26–29.

SKINNER, B. F. (1953). *Science and human behavior.* New York: Macmillan.

SKINNER, B. F. (1957). *Verbal behavior.* Englewood Cliffs, NJ: Prentice-Hall.

SKINNER, B. F. (1958). Distinguished scientific contribution award. *American Psychology, 13,* 735.

SKINNER, B. F. (1959). A case history in scientific method. In S. Koch (Ed.), *Psychology: A study of a science* (Vol. 2). New York: McGraw-Hill.

SKINNER, B. F. (1967). Autobiography. In E. G. Boring & G. Lindzey (Eds.), *A history of psychology in autobiography* (Vol. 5) (pp. 387–413). New York: Appleton-Century-Crofts.

SKINNER, B. F. (1968). *The technology of teaching.* New York: Appleton-Century-Crofts.

SKINNER, B. F. (1971). *Beyond freedom and dignity.* New York: Knopf.

SKINNER, B. F. (1972). Gold medal award. *American Psychology, 27,* 72.

SKINNER, B. F. (1974). *About behaviorism.* New York: Knopf.

SKINNER, B. F. (1976). *Particulars of my life.* New York: Knopf.

SKINNER, B. F. (1978). *Reflections on behaviorism and society.* Englewood Cliffs, NJ: Prentice-Hall.

SKINNER, B. F. (1987). *Upon further reflection.* Englewood Cliffs, NJ: Prentice-Hall.

SKINNER, B. F., & VAUGHAN, M. E. (1983). *Enjoy old age.* New York: Norton.

SMITH, M. S. (1987). Evolution and developmental psychology: Toward a sociobiology of human development. In C. Crawford, M. Smith, & D. Krebs, (Eds.), *Sociobiology and Psychology: Ideas, issues, and applications* (pp. 225–252). Hillsdale, NJ: Lawrence Erlbaum Associates.

SMITH, T. W. (1983). Changes in irrational beliefs and the outcome of rational-emotive psychotherapy. *Journal of Consulting and Clinical Psychologists, 51,* 156–157.

SPELTZ, M. L., SHIMAMURA, J. W., & McREYNOLDS, W. T. (1982). Procedural variations in group contingencies. *Journal of Applied Behavior Analysis, 15,* 533–544.

STANOVICH, K. E. (1986). *How to think straight about psychology.* Glenview, IL: Scott, Foresman.

STERN, P. J. (1976). *C. G. Jung: The haunted prophet.* New York: Dell.

STEVENS, S. S. (1951). Psychology and the science of science. In M. H. Marx (Ed.), *Psychological theory: Contemporary readings.* New York: Macmillan.

STEVENSON, L. (1987). *Seven theories of human nature* (2nd ed.). New York: Oxford University Press.

STEWART, R. A. C. (1968). Academic performance and components of self-actualization. *Perceptual and Motor Skills, 26,* 918.

STEWART, V., & STEWART, A. (1982). *Business applications of repertory grid.* New York: McGraw-Hill.

STOLOROW, R. D., & ATWOOD, G. E. (1979). *Faces in a cloud: Subjectivity in personality theory.* New York: Aronson.

STUART, R. B., & LOTT, L. A. (1972). Behavioral contracting with delinquents: A cautionary note. *Journal Therapy and Experimental Psychiatry, 3,* 161–169.

STUMPHAUZER, J. S. (1972). Increased delay of gratification in young prison inmates through imitation of high delay peer models. *Journal of Personality and Social Psychology, 21,* 10–17.

SUINN, R. M., OSBORNE, D., & WINFREE, P. (1962). The self concept and accuracy of recall of inconsistent self-related information. *Journal of Clinical Psychology, 18,* 473–474.

SULLOWAY, F. J. (1979). *Freud: Biologist of the mind.* New York: Basic Books.

Sutich, A. (1976). The emergence of the transpersonal orientation: A personal account. *Journal of Transpersonal Psychology, 1,* 5–19.

Symons, D. (1987). If we're all Darwinians, what's the fuss about? In C. Crawford, M. Smith, & D. Krebs (Eds.), *Sociobiology and psychology: Ideas, issues, and applications* (pp. 121–146). Hillsdale, NJ: Lawrence Erlbaum Associates.

Tesch, S. A., & Whitbourne, S. K. (1982). Intimacy status and identity status in young adults. *Journal of Personality and Social Psychology, 43,* 1041–1051.

Thompson, G. C. (1968). George Alexander Kelly (1905–1967). *Journal of General Psychology, 79,* 19–24.

Thompson, T., & Grabowski, J. (1972). *Reinforcement schedules and multi-operant analysis.* Englewood Cliffs, NJ: Prentice-Hall.

Thompson, T., & Grabowski, J. (Eds.). (1977). *Behavior modification of the mentally retarded.* New York: Oxford University Press.

Thorne, F. C. (1975). The life style analysis. *Journal of Clinical Psychology, 31,* 236–240.

Thorne, F. C., & Pishkin, V. (1973). The existential study. *Journal of Clinical Psychology, 29,* 387–410.

Thornhill, N. W., & Thornhill, R. (1987a). Evolutionary theory and rules of mating and marriage pertaining to relatives. In C. Crawford, M. Smith, & D. Krebs (Eds.), *Sociobiology and psychology: Ideas, issues, and applications* (pp. 373–400). Hillsdale, NJ: Lawrence Erlbaum Associates.

Thornhill, R., & Thornhill, N. W. (1983). Human rape: An evolutionary analysis. *Ethology and sociobiology, 4,* 137–173.

Thornhill, R., & Thornhill, N. W. (1987b). Human rape: The strengths of the evolutionary perspective. In C. Crawford, M. Smith, & D. Krebs (Eds.), *Sociobiology and psychology: Ideas, issues, and applications* (pp. 269–291). Hillsdale, NJ: Lawrence Erlbaum Associates.

Tillich, P. (1952). *The courage to be.* New Haven: Yale University Press.

Trigg, R. (1982). *The shaping of man: Philosophical aspects of sociobiology.* New York: Schocken Books.

Trivers, R. L. (1971). The evolution of reciprocal altruism. *Quarterly Review of Biology, 46,* 35–57.

Truax, C. B., & Mitchell, K. M. (1971). Research on certain therapist interpersonal skills in relation to process and outcome. In A. E. Bergin & S. L. Garfield (Eds.), *Handbook of psychotherapy and behavior change.* New York: Wiley.

Turner, R. H., & Vanderlippe, R. H. (1958). Self-ideal congruence as an index of adjustment. *Journal of Abnormal and Social Psychology, 57,* 202–206.

Vaihinger, H. (1925). *The philosophy of "as if."* New York: Harcourt Brace Jovanovich. (Original work published 1911)

van den Berghe, P. L. (1987). Incest taboos and avoidance: Some African applications. In C. Crawford, M. Smith, & D. Krebs (Eds.), *Sociobiology and psychology: Ideas, issues, and applications* (pp. 353–371). Hillsdale, NJ: Lawrence Erlbaum Associates.

Van der Post, L. (1975). *Jung and the story of our time.* New York: Pantheon.

Van Kaam, A. (1966). *Existential foundations of psychology.* Pittsburgh, PA: Duquesne University Press.

Verplanck, W. S. (1955). The operant, from rat to man: An introduction to some recent experiments on human behavior. *Transactions of the New York Academy of Science, 17,* 594–601.

Viney, L. L. (1983). *Images of illness.* Miami, FL: Krieger.

Viney, L. L. (1984). Concerns about death among severely ill people. In F. R. Epting & R. A. Neimeyer (Eds.), *Personal meanings of death.* Washington, DC: Hemisphere.

Wachtel, P. L. (1977). *Psychoanalysis and behavior therapy: Toward an integration.* New York: Basic Books.

Wagner, M. E., & Schubert, H. J. P. (1977). Sibship variables and United States Presidents. *Journal of Individual Psychology, 33,* 78–85.

Wallace, R. A. (1979). *The genesis factor.* New York: William Morrow.

Waterman, A. S. (1982). Identity development from adolescence to adulthood: An extension of theory and a review of research. *Developmental Psychology, 18,* 341–358.

Waterman, A. S., Geary, P. S., & Waterman, C. K. (1974). Longitudinal study of changes in ego identity status from the freshman to the senior year at college. *Developmental Psychology, 10,* 387–392.

Waterman, C. K., Buebel, M. E., & Waterman, A. S. (1970). Relationship between resolution of the identity crisis and outcomes of previous psychosocial crises. *Proceedings of the 78th Annual Convention of the American Psychological Convention, 5,* 467–468.

Watson, J. B. (1926). Experimental studies on the growth of the emotions. In C. Murchison (Ed.), *Psychologies of 1925.* Worcester, MA: Clark University Press.

Weiss, R. L., Birchler, G. R., & Vincent, J. P. (1974). Contractual models for negotiation training in marital dyads. *Journal of Marriage and the Family, 36,* 321–330.

Weisstein, N. (1975). Psychology constructs the female, or the fantasy life of the male psychologist (with some attention to the fantasies of his friends, the male biologist and the male anthropologist). In I. Cohen (Ed.), *Perspectives on psychology.* New York: Praeger.

Westermarck, E. A. (1891). *The history of human marriage.* London: Macmillan.

Wiggins, J. S. (1968). Personality structure. In *Annual review of psychology* (Vol. 19). Palo Alto, CA: Annual Reviews.

Wiggins, J. S. (1984). Cattell's system from the perspective of mainstream personality theory. *Multivariate Behavioral Research, 19,* 176–190.

Wilson, C. (1972) *New Pathways in psychology.* New York: Taplinger Publishing.

Wilson, E. O. (1971). *The insect societies.* Cambridge, MA: Harvard University Press.

Wilson, E. O. (1975). *Sociobiology: The new synthesis.* Cambridge, MA: Harvard University Press.

Wilson, E. O. (1978). *On human nature.* New York: Bantam Books.

Wilson, E. O. (1980). Comparative social theory. *The Tanner lectures on human values.* Presented at the University of Michigan, Ann Arbor, MI.

Wilson, E. O. (1985). In the queendom of the ants: A brief autobiography. In Donald A. Dewsbury (Ed.), *Leaders in the study of animal behavior: Autobiographical perspectives* (pp. 464–484). Cranbury, NJ: Bucknell University Press.

Wolf, A. P., & Huang, C. S. (1980). *Marriage and adoption in China, 1845–1945.* Stanford, CA: Stanford University Press.

Wrightman, L. S. (1981). Personal documents as data in conceptualizing adult personality development. *Personality and Social Psychology Bulletin, 7,* 367–385.

Zajonc, R. B., & Markus, G. B. (1975). Birth order and intellectual development. *Psychological Review, 82,* 74–88.

Zimbardo, P., & Ruch, F. (1977). *Psychology and life* (9th ed.). Glenview, IL: Scott, Foresman.

NOTES

CHAPTER 3

Memories, Dreams, Reflections, by C. G. Jung, recorded and edited by Aniela Jaffe, translated by Richard and Clara Winston. Copyright © 1961, 1962, 1963 by Random House, Inc. Reprinted by permission of Pantheon Books, a division of Random House, Inc.

C. G. Jung, Essays on Analytical Psychology. In *The Collected Works of C. G. Jung* (Vol. 7). Princeton University Press, 1966. (Originally published 1917.)

CHAPTER 4

A. Adler. Individual Psychology. In C. Murchison (ed.), *Psychologies of 1930.* Worcester, Mass.: Clark University Press, 1930.

H. L. Ansbacher and R. R. Ansbacher (eds.). *The Individual Psychology of Alfred Adler.* New York: Basic Books, 1956.

CHAPTER 5

K. Horney. *Our Inner Conflicts.* New York: Norton, 1945.

CHAPTER 6

E. H. Erikson (1963). *Childhood and Society* (2nd ed.). New York: Norton.

CHAPTER 7

G. W. Allport. *Becoming: Basic Considerations for a Psychology of Personality.* New Haven, CT: Yale University Press, 1955.

G. W. Allport. *Pattern and Growth in Personality.* New York: Holt, Rinehart & Winston, 1961.

CHAPTER 8

R. B. Cattell. *The Scientific Analysis of Personality.* Baltimore: Penguin, 1965.

R. B. Cattell. *Personality: A Systematic, Theoretical and Factual Study.* New York: McGraw-Hill, 1950.

CHAPTER 9

Reprinted with permission of Macmillan Publishing Company from *Science and Human Behavior* by B. F. Skinner. Copyright 1953 by Macmillan Publishing Company; copyright renewed 1981 by B. F. Skinner.

Beyond Freedom and Dignity by B. F. Skinner. Copyright © 1971 by B. F. Skinner. Reprinted by permission of Alfred A. Knopf, Inc.

B. R. Hergenhahn. (1988). *An Introduction to Theories of Learning* (3rd ed.). Englewood Cliffs, N.J.: Prentice Hall.

CHAPTER 10

N. E. Miller and J. Dollard. *Social Learning and Imitation.* New Haven, CT: Yale University Press, 1941.

J. Dollard and N. E. Miller. *Personality and Psychotherapy: An Analysis in Terms of Learning, Thinking and Culture.* New York: McGraw-Hill, 1950.

CHAPTER 11

B. R. Hergenhahn. (1988). *An Introduction to Theories of Learning* (3rd ed.). Englewood Cliffs, N.J.: Prentice Hall.

W. Mischel (1986). *Introduction to Personality* (4th ed.). New York: Holt, Rinehart & Winston.

CHAPTER 12

C. Crawford, M. Smith, and D. Krebs (eds.) (1987). *Sociobiology and Psychology: Ideas, Issues, and Applications.* Hillsdale, N.J.: Lawrence Erlbaum Associates.

D. Symons (1987). If We're All Darwinians, What's the Fuss About? In C. Crawford, M. Smith, and D. Krebs (eds.), *Sociobiology and Psychology: Ideas, Issues, and Applications* (pp. 121–146). Hillsdale, N.J.: Lawrence Erlbaum Associates.

R. Thornhill and N. W. Thornhill (1987). Human Rape: The Strengths of the Evolutionary Perspective (pp. 269–291); and N. W. Thornhill and R. Thornhill (1987). Evolutionary Theory and Rules of Mating and Marriage Pertaining to Relatives. Both appearing in C. Crawford, M. Smith, and D. Krebs (eds.), *Sociobiology and Psychology: Ideas, Issues, and Applications.* Hillsdale, N.J.: Lawrence Erlbaum Associates.

D. de Catanzano (1987). Evolutionary Pressures and Limitations to Self Preservation. In C. Crawford, M. Smith, and D. Krebs (eds.), *Sociobiology and Psychology: Ideas, Issues, and Applications* (pp. 311–333). Hillsdale, N.J.: Lawrence Erlbaum Associates.

M. S. Smith (1987). Evolution and Developmental Psychology: Toward a Sociobiology of Human Development. In C. Crawford, M. Smith, and D. Krebs (eds.), *Sociobiology and Psychology: Ideas, Issues, and Applications* (pp. 225–252). Hillsdale, N.J.: Lawrence Erlbaum Associates.

P. L. van den Berghe (1987). Incest Taboos and Avoidance: Some African Applications. In C. Crawford, M. Smith, and D. Krebs (eds.), *Sociobiology and Psychology: Ideas, Issues, and Applications* (pp. 353–371). Hillsdale, N.J.: Lawrence Erlbaum Associates.

D. M. Buss (1987). Sex Differences in Human Mate Selection Criteria: An Evolutionary Perspective. In C. Crawford, M. Smith, and D. Krebs (eds.), *Sociobiology and Psychology: Ideas, Issues, and Applications* (pp. 335–351). Hillsdale, N.J.: Lawrence Erlbaum Associates.

The Hare and the Tortoise by David Barash. Copyright © David Barash, 1986. All rights reserved. Reprinted by permission of Viking Penguin, a division of Penguin Books USA, Inc.

E. O. Wilson (1978). *On Human Nature.* New York: Bantam Books.

Excerpts from *The Whisperings Within* by David Barash. Copyright © 1979 by David Barash. Reprinted by permission of Harper & Row, Publishers, Inc.

I. Silverman (1987). Race, Race Differences, and Race Relations: Perspectives from Psychology and Sociobiology. In C. Crawford, M. Smith, and D. Krebs (eds.), *Sociobiology and Psychology: Ideas, Issues, and Applications* (pp. 205–221). Hillsdale, NJ: Lawrence Erlbaum Associates.

CHAPTER 13

D. Bannister and F. Fransella. *Inquiring Man: The Theory of Personal Constructs.* New York: Penguin, 1971.

G. A. Kelly. *The Psychology of Personal Constructs: A Theory of Personality* (2 vols.). New York: Norton, 1955.

CHAPTER 14

C. R. Rogers. *On Becoming a Person.* Copyright © 1961 by Houghton Mifflin Company. Used with permission.

C. R. Rogers. A Theory of Therapy, Personality, and Interpersonal Relationships, as Developed in the Client-Centered Framework. In S. Koch (ed.). *Psychology: A Study of a Science* (Vol. I). New York: McGraw-Hill, 1959.

CHAPTER 15

Excerpts from *Motivation and Personality* by Abraham H. Maslow. Copyright 1954 by Harper & Row, Publishers, Inc. Copyright © 1970 by Abraham H. Maslow. Reprinted by permission of the publisher.

A. H. Maslow. *Toward a Psychology of Being* (2nd ed.). New York: D. Van Nostrand Co., 1968.

A. H. Maslow. *The Farther Reaches of Human Nature*. New York: Viking, 1971.

CHAPTER 16

R. May. *Love and Will*. New York: Norton, 1969.

R. May. *Psychology and the Human Dilemma*. New York: D. Van Nostrand Co., Inc., 1967.

PHOTO CREDITS

Name Index

Subject Index